Languages of
Labor and Gender

Social History, Popular Culture, and Politics in Germany
Geoff Eley, Series Editor

Cities, Sin, and Social Reform in Imperial Germany, Andrew Lees

Languages of Labor and Gender: Female Factory Work in Germany, 1850–1914, Kathleen Canning

The Challenge of Modernity: German Social and Cultural Studies, 1890–1960, Adelheid von Saldern

That Was the Wild East: Film Culture, Unification and the "New" Germany, Leonie Naughton

Anna Seghers: The Mythic Dimension, Helen Fehervary

Staging Philanthropy: Patriotic Women and the National Imagination in Dynastic Germany, 1813–1916, Jean H. Quataert

Truth to Tell: German Women's Autobiographies and Turn-of-the-Century Culture, Katharina Gerstenberger

The "Goldhagen Effect": History, Memory, Nazism—Facing the German Past, Geoff Eley, editor

Shifting Memories: The Nazi Past in the New Germany, Klaus Neumann

Saxony in German History: Culture, Society, and Politics, 1830–1933, James Retallack, editor

Little Tools of Knowledge: Historical Essays on Academic and Bureaucratic Practices, Peter Becker and William Clark, editors

Public Spheres, Public Mores, and Democracy: Hamburg and Stockholm, 1870–1914, Madeleine Hurd

Making Security Social: Disability, Insurance, and the Birth of the Social Entitlement State in Germany, Greg Eghigian

The German Problem Transformed: Institutions, Politics, and Foreign Policy, 1945–1995, Thomas Banchoff

Building the East German Myth: Historical Mythology and Youth Propaganda in the German Democratic Republic, 1945–1989, Alan L. Nothnagle

Mobility and Modernity: Migration in Germany, 1820–1989, Steve Hochstadt

Triumph of the Fatherland: German Unification and the Marginalization of Women, Brigitte Young

Framed Visions: Popular Culture, Americanization, and the Contemporary German and Austrian Imagination, Gerd Gemünden

(continued on last page)

Languages of Labor and Gender

Female Factory Work in Germany, 1850–1914

KATHLEEN CANNING

With a Foreword by Konrad H. Jarausch

Ann Arbor
THE UNIVERSITY OF MICHIGAN PRESS

This edition for the Social History, Popular Culture, and Politics in Germany series is published by arrangement with Cornell University Press.

Paperback edition copyright © by the University of Michigan 2002
Original edition copyright © 1996 by Cornell University
All rights reserved
Published in the United States of America by
The University of Michigan Press
Manufactured in the United States of America
♾ Printed on acid-free paper

2005   2004   2003   2002   4 3 2 1

No part of this publication may be reproduced, stored in a retrieval system, or transmitted in any form or by any means, electronic, mechanical, or otherwise, without the written permission of the publisher.

A CIP catalog record for this book is available from the British Library.

Library of Congress Cataloging-in-Publication Data applied for
ISBN 0-472-08766-5

*To the memory of Peggy Brennan Canning (1931–68)
and Edna Wollensak Brennan (1907–95)*

Contents

Foreword to the Paperback Edition ix
Preface to the Paperback Edition xv
Preface xix

Introduction: German Labor History and the Meanings of Women's Work   1

1 Gender and Sexual Politics in the Transition from Home to Factory Industry   16

2 "The Man Transformed into a Maiden"? Feminization in the Textile Industries of the Rhineland and Westphalia   38

3 Sexual Difference and the Social Question in the Transition to the "Industrial State," 1844–1889   85

4 State, Social Body, and Public Sphere: Regulating Female Factory Labor during the 1890s   126

5 Social Policy, Body Politics: Factory Labor, Maternity, and *Volkskörper*, 1900–1914   170

6 Work Experiences, Work Identities: Dissolving the Dichotomy between Home and Work   218

7 Behind the Mill Gate: Gender and the Culture of Work   283

Conclusion   324

Index   333

Foreword to the Paperback Edition
Konrad H. Jarausch

At its original publication *Languages of Labor and Gender* created quite a stir, because the book appeared at a moment when labor history was under considerable pressure. Since the late nineteenth century progressive intellectuals had studied the history of Marxist ideas, the development of socialist parties and trade unions, or the formation of the working class in order to voice their criticism of bourgeois society. But by the mid-1990s the inglorious collapse of communism had tarnished this project, while the transition to postindustrial society had undercut its socioeconomic basis of high industrialism. Just as critical scholars started to shift their interests to other issues such as the environment, this innovative work reaffirmed the vitality of labor history as a field by suggesting some of its continuing potential.

A chief reason for its strong impact was the provocative nature of the contribution, which self-consciously sought to challenge the reigning conventions of labor history. Prefigured in a series of programmatic articles titled "Gender and the Politics of Class Formation" (*American Historical Review* 98 [1992]: 736–68), the book presented itself not just as another sound empirical study, but rather as an effort to reorient an entire research area by striking out in a new methodological and substantive direction. As a result the work was widely reviewed on both sides of the Atlantic and uniformly praised as a "theoretically ambitious, empirically rich, and highly original study," in short, called a brilliant success (M. Nolan, *German Politics and Society* 16 [1998]: 153). Its reception as "a very important book" (E. Weitz, *Central European History* 30 [1997]: 446ff.) demonstrates that its agenda-setting intent was indeed welcomed.

Although the Conference Group for Central European History's book prize underlined this text's significance, it is nonetheless a challenging one to approach. Successive cohorts of graduate students have muttered about its mixture of theoretical reflections, statistical tables, and discursive deconstructions. The author's vocabulary is demanding and her style favors complexity, sometimes echoing the less fortunate characteristics of her Teutonic subject. Accessible passages with graphic descriptions and pointed polemics are intermingled with more difficult sections, replete with references to arcane debates among historians. What is it about this work that nevertheless demands its reissue as paperback and continues to excite its readers?

A close rereading of the text, scholarly commentary, and additional essays of the author reveals that the importance of the book is based on its methodological ingenuity, substantive findings, and suggestive agenda. The very development of the project from a quantitative dissertation at Johns Hopkins to a postmodernist book is emblematic of a broader historiographical transition from structure to language, signaling the cultural turn of an entire generation of labor historians. One of the inspirations of this change, partly overlooked by reviewers, is its emphasis on the everyday, promoted by *Alltagsgeschichte,* as an effort to break down large structural generalizations and recover specificity. Instead of just staying on the national level, the book presents four regional microstudies, based on company records, which provide a high level of empirical concreteness. Only by looking at individual factories with distinctive production lines can the diversity of female experiences in mill society be recovered and, following the suggestion of Alf Lüdtke, elements of self-assertion (*Eigensinn*) be detected. This aspect of the work helps transport a new German approach to an American labor history audience.

Another perspective permeating the book is suggested by the first word of its title—the linguistic turn. In effect, *Languages of Labor and Gender* follows a methodological shift developed by labor historians like William H. Sewell who sought to reconstruct working-class aspirations by taking a closer look at the language used by workers. Pioneered by E. P. Thompson several decades earlier, this attention to the rhetoric of the labor movement took workers seriously as thinking beings who combined artisan and radical democratic traditions in a new synthesis, suited to voicing their aspirations for equality. Going beyond earlier studies of working-class culture, Canning develops her own form of Foucauldian discourse analysis in order to look at the extensive debate regarding women's work in Imperial Germany and deconstruct the meaning of various contending arguments. Thereby she projects American culturalist approaches into the previously structural and organizational arena of labor history in Germany.

Finally, and most importantly, the book also employs a gender approach, developed among feminist historians on both sides of the Atlantic during the last two decades. This methodology transcends the older interest in women's work, which had investigated the various forms of female labor as a separate subject. Instead, *Languages of Labor and Gender* sees the development of women's factory labor as a relational subject, always conditioned by competition with and regulation from males in the form of fellow workers, company owners, or government inspectors. However, the book does not just treat gender as a mere cultural construct (like some writings inspired by Joan Scott) but continues instead to ground discourses in the structural constraints of different work situations or material interests. By dramatizing the heuristic utility of such an interactive conception of gender for labor history, this work strengthens feminist efforts to escape their institutional and intellectual marginalization among societal historians in Germany.

A second set of reasons for the continuing relevance of *Languages of Labor and Gender* has to do with the richness of its substantive information on a new subject area. The initial structural part begins with a pithy summary of the problematic transition from home production to factory industry in the textile sector that drew in women at a high rate, leading to charges of *Verweiblichung* by male workers. In four detailed case studies of the production of cotton in München-Gladbach, woolens in Aachen, linen in Bielefeld, and silk in Krefeld, the book presents a finely shaded picture of diverse gender relations in the workplace, ranging from grudging acceptance to outright hostility. Where men had attractive alternatives or could rise into supervisory positions, they apparently accommodated themselves to the influx of females without too many complaints; but where artisan traditions were strong and mechanization lagged (as in silk production) a fierce displacement conflict ensued in which men resorted to a revival of guild restrictions to defend their territory. The details need not be repeated here, but the local approach suggests the importance of a differentiated and contextualized reading.

Similarly the discursive analysis of the debate about women's work in the middle part sheds much new light on the gendered origins of the modern welfare state. The author discerns successive stages in the intensive debate among clergymen, social reformers, government inspectors, union advocates, and the like, who commented on the dangerous consequences of female factory work. From the 1870s on, moral concerns about "sexual licentiousness" in the mills as a result of unsupervised encounters between young males and females led to the passage of special protective legislation for women. During the 1890s feminists succeeded in blocking conservative demands for redomestication and helped make married women's work a matter of scientific interest as well as public policy. In the last prewar decade the imperialist rhetoric shifted to a eugenic concern for the natalist consequences that made the female body a site for state regulation. This nuanced reconstruction of the evolution of public debate helps explain the origins of gendered welfare provisions that created two different kinds of citizenship.

The last chapters of the book also address the elusive issues of female self-conceptions and collective identities in factory work. The quantitative evidence derived from employers' personnel records suggests more labor stability and balance between the demands of the factory and the home than had previously been recognized. Canning reaffirms prior findings of gendered skill hierarchies, which consigned women to the lower rungs, but she also shows a paternalist concern evident in the establishment of special housing and child-care provisions for women by employers. There are a few suggestive pages on female forms of contestation of factory discipline and some hints at efforts of collective rebellion against excessive exploitation, which imply a mixture of accommodation and resistance. But this section remains tantalizingly tentative, since written sources expressing the subjectivity of female laborers are exceedingly scarce. The overall impression is, nonetheless, of a solidly researched and carefully argued case study with wider interpretative implications.

The final aspect, which makes grappling with *Languages of Labor and Gender* so worthwhile, derives, ironically, from the fresh questions posed by its limitations. By moving women from the margins of labor history to the center, the book rescues them from academic condescension and restores their dignity as subject as well as their agency. No doubt, the break with the competitive or paternalist perspective of male contemporaries is liberating for historians, but it in turn creates an interest in women's voices, in hearing a different set of stories that articulate female viewpoints and desires. Unfortunately the bureaucratic and discursive sources used are still predominantly male, and the occasional polemics of feminists or female union members cannot replace authentic statements by the presumed subjects of this study. Due to the muteness of the principals, perhaps the only method that might be able to provide some such testimony would be oral history, albeit for a later period than the Empire.

The challenge for future scholars consists of going further, without romanticizing the subject, in the exploration of female factory experience—a paradoxical blend of the repressive and liberating. Circumstantial evidence suggests less authority and lower pay on the basis of gender, a discrimination and exploitation that must have aroused considerable resentment. But leaving home and going to work also could provide a sense of limited financial independence, a possibility for camaraderie with fellow workers, and a basis for pride in skilled production. Similarly, the relative delay of union organization and the paucity of female strikes imply acquiescence, but they underplay the degree of daily subversion of work routines through slowdowns, sassing of superiors, and lack of discipline. Therefore the sense of self, the *Eigensinn* of working women, still remains to be explored further in order to get a feel for the special character of their life perspectives, conditioned by but also cutting across social class.

A last issue, raised by the conclusion, is the role of women in the emergence of German civil society within an authoritarian state. The protective rhetoric of social reform revolves around a conception of maternalism that seems to be especially strong in Germany, reinforcing the conception of the *Sonderweg* in the realm of women's history. But the book also demonstrates a diversity of female work situations and elements of self-assertion that subvert the stereotype of nationalist patriarchy, associated with a frequent misreading of the term *Vaterland* that ignores its classical origins in the Latin *patria*. While an emphasis on female difference was often used to buttress male efforts at control, feminists could also employ references to *Eigenart* so as to create a legitimate space for women's aspirations. Does a gendered perspective therefore support or qualify the thesis of German deviance from Western norms? If it is the mark of good scholarship that it suggests the exploration of further questions, then this book has been quite successful in this regard.

Five years after its publication, *Languages of Labor and Gender* continues to be rewarding to read—a testimony to its own contribution to shifting the historiographical agenda. The book's strong impact on labor history is evident in the softening of the entrenched opposition between proponents of structure and advocates of language, leading gradually to a more interactive approach toward material conditions and cultural reflections. The progression from Jürgen Kocka's original socioeconomic conception of class formation through Klaus Tenfelde's in-depth regional studies of the Ruhr toward Thomas Welskopp's examination of masculine attitudes indicates how far German labor historians have come in the last decade. By opening up the discursive dimension without replacing the old social with a new cultural determinism, Kathleen Canning's work has helped to pave the way for this encouraging trend of restoring attention to experience in German labor history.

This work is also an excellent example of the productivity of gender methodology in approaching problems of social and cultural history. While its focus on women's work remains primarily female-centered, the analysis is nonetheless developed in a relational way, seen as conditioned by and responding to male power. The dissolution of the private and public binary helps restore a sense of wholeness to women's lives, the attention to the gender division of workplaces pulls no punches in denouncing inequality, and the investigation of female responses offers fascinating suggestions about identity. One of the most important contributions of this book is its rewriting of the origins of the welfare state, which pays more attention to the protective provisions for women and children that created gendered notions of citizenship. This perspective therefore opens up a whole new area of research that revolves around the material conditions, symbolic meanings, and legal controls of the body, but in fact concerns restrictions of female behavior in the guise of promoting national reproduction.

Finally, Kathleen Canning's book also raises important questions about the shape of a progressive history after the dissolution of master narratives. Due to the discrediting of hypernationalism after the atrocities of the Third Reich, radical intellectuals in the East adopted Marxist-Leninist perspectives, while Western liberals embraced modernization theory in order to explain the German catastrophe and recover from it. The collapse of communism and the solvent effect of postmodernism have, in the last several decades, undercut these rescue efforts, calling into question their large-scale developmental schemata. Where are alternatives for these metanarratives to be found—or are they necessary at all? Instead of substituting feminism as new norm, Canning treats gender methodology as a heuristic tool, thereby breaking through the constraints of the class struggle as well as of modernization perspectives and initiating a fundamental rewriting of labor history. By seeking to reconcile structure with discourse, eclectically blending theories with empirical evidence, and balancing emphatic advocacy with analytical distance, this book provides an inspiring example of how to turn the new uncertainties into a compelling history.

Preface to the Paperback Edition

This book was written while gender history and the conceptual shifts that guided it were being vigorously debated, as historians of labor and of women/gender took up the challenges of the "linguistic turn" with particular vigor. In the meantime the field of contention that framed this book has dispersed or dissolved for the most part, but the keywords of experience, agency, and discourse have remained at the heart of methodological reflection and empirical research. Historians still struggle to define these terms, to uncover, identify, and analyze their workings in specific historical times and places. Thus, I was very pleased when the University of Michigan Press decided to publish a paperback edition of this book. I thank my colleague and friend Geoff Eley, editor of the series Social History, Popular Culture, and Politics in Germany, and Liz Suhay, editor at the University of Michigan Press, for their efforts in this regard. I also would like to thank Konrad Jarausch, who generously agreed to write a foreword for this edition that situates this book in new ways.

When I set out as a young dissertator to conduct research in German archives, the first eminent German historian I encountered cautioned me about the virtual impossibility of the project of understanding the meanings of class for women, of uncovering more than the barest shreds of information about their work cultures or consciousness. As much as the research for this book was driven by the impulse to uncover and discover these very things, it also involved the search for the historical lens that would make visible the workings of gender in the world behind the mill gate. The shift toward a history of meaning, perhaps the most lasting effect of the linguistic turn, helped provide that lens, rendering gender more meaningful even where female actors remained elusive, and opening labor history to arenas beyond the workplace in which the meanings of gender and work were created and contested.

In this sense this book has many friends, for it took shape within the field of gender-labor studies that both propelled and helped define the linguistic turn during the late 1980s and early 1990s. The flourishing of scholarship in the gender-labor field during that time reinvigorated and redefined labor history in a fundamental sense, although this fact seems to have gone unnoticed by those who continued to bemoan the death of labor history. As a result, the history of labor became a less bounded inquiry, which (as I have argued elsewhere) had the potential to reach far beyond the factory workshop to offer new interpretations of state, public sphere, and the emergence of the "social." The historical meanings of work expanded, spilling over into the histories of state and social reform and prompting new understandings of citizenship and consumption, of empires and diasporas, of bodies and subjectivities, in which labor had not previously been central.[1]

Disparate methodologies propelled the process by which the study of gendered labor histories spilled over into areas of inquiry well beyond shop floors or union halls. Indeed, reviewers of this book have noted a certain methodological eclecticism in my attempt to distinguish structural from rhetorical transformation, to interpret one in terms of the other, to view these processes as different productions of distinct meanings. Yet different interpretive strategies are necessary if histories of gender are conceived as encompassing the ways in which gender was both imagined and lived, as both ideology and practice. In this book, for example, I read local against national histories, statistical against textual evidence, comparing employment statistics with the passionate pamphlets of male weavers who decried their own transformation into "maidens." My interpretation of "feminization" as a layered process of structural and rhetorical change makes visible the frequent dissonance between these two kinds of source material, allowing neither to speak merely for itself. Furthermore, my attempt to write a history of the meanings of work led me to analyze not only how discourses "constructed" divisions of labor or notions of wages and skill, but also to explore the way discourses were themselves sites of agency, in which the representational strategies of their participants, the ways in which they read, wrote, spoke, or visually depicted the social question of female factory labor propelled changes in ideologies and practices, significantly transforming the field of contest surrounding it during the last two decades of the nineteenth century.

1. Kathleen Canning, "Gender and the Languages of Labor History: An Overview," *Traverse: Zeitschrift für Geschichte* 2000/2 (June 2000): 33–46.

In this book I have also understood experience as a process of assigning and making meanings of events and structures, of forming subjectivities in relation to (but not determined by) discourses and institutions of power. Here and there reviewers have pointed out that this book has mustered scant evidence of women workers' experiences in everyday factory life. Indeed, the existence of only fleeting testimony from women workers forced me to rely, problematically, on sources that record the views of those who observed and interpreted the actions and visions of workers who spoke so rarely for themselves. A case in point is the social scientist Marie Bernays, student of Alfred Weber, who spent several months disguised as a "mill girl" in the weaving and spinning mills of the Lower Rhine. The evidence she gathered for Weber's far-reaching project on the "psychophysics of work" offers invaluable insights into the camaraderie and conflicts on the shop floor, and the meanings female workers assigned to their labor. Testimony of an observer like Bernays, the occasional petition or letter to the editor, the factory inspector's report on rape or sexual coercion, offer only small snapshots of women's experience in which the photographer must be at least as carefully considered as the subject of the snapshot. This is an incomplete story, written on the basis of archival fragments, of disjunctures in records, so that factory *Stammrollen* (employment records), devotedly preserved by a family firm, can seldom be matched against trade union sources or local demographic data, destroyed by bombs or Nazi terror. The very unevenness of these sources is part of the gender story this book aims to tell. It is both a German particularity and at the same time exemplary of the silences of countless histories of those whose subjectivities did not allow their own stories, if they wrote them at all, to become a matter of public record or the object of public preservation.

While this book set out to critique some of the keywords in the history of German labor and to dissolve the oft-postulated deterministic relationship between discourse and experience, it also left some of the very terms that helped dissolve this dichotomy only implicitly examined. Nothing about the title or framing of this book reveals that this study is also concerned with the history of laboring bodies, which were centrally implicated in the making of the social, as the "female organism" became a key site of intervention for both the regulatory and tutelary regimes of state social policy and social reform. Female bodies figure here as markers of the very hybrid character of women's work, of the melding of paid and unpaid (domestic) labor. In this sense they defy the legendary separation of home and work, often in quite graphic terms (miscarrying or birthing at their machines in the mills). While this notion of hybridity might offer an intriguing site at which discourses and experiences converge, it has been much more difficult to trace histories of bodily experiences or of bodies as locations of subjectivity/memory, a preoccupation of my current study of embodied citizenships in Weimar Germany. The suggestive concept of citizenship skitters across these pages as well, as protective labor legislation expanded to lay the groundwork for subordinate female citizenship within a growing welfare state. Yet the meanings of citizenship for a history of the changing arenas of gender and industrial labor have not been traced here, not least because of the prevalent claims of class in which social identities of citizenship were encoded during the prewar years.

These reflections on contexts and methods that shaped this book should make clear that I wrote it not as a new history of labor, written from the "perspective of gender," as some reviewers might benevolently describe it, but as history of gender, as a discursive force and experiential terrain at the heart of the defining processes of German modernity—industrial transformation, welfare-state formation, medicalization and "scientification" of the social, working-class formation and self-articulation of the German *Bürgertum*. In fact, it is exceedingly difficult to discern the threads linking these processes—the dichotomies of home/work, production/reproduction, public/private that had a defining place in each of these processes—without gender as an analytical lens. Even as I assert this, I am not sure that it is any easier for those whose work is not crucially concerned with gender to see this now than five years ago, when this book first appeared, or ten years ago, when the furor surrounding the "linguistic turn" was at its high point. Some have contended, in fact, that gender history can only become a vital, indispensable part of the story of these grand processes when, no longer subversive, it can be mainstreamed, that is, when a sufficient accumulation of knowledge permits the gender part of the story to be woven somewhat seamlessly into the narratives and periodizations of historical analysis. This book still seeks to interrogate the terms of the story first, before seeking to rewrite it. In that sense it represents an important step along a path Lynn Hunt has recently outlined of actively engaging the "premises of history"—the concepts, tropes, and temporalities underpinning histories of class and citizenship, social reform and welfare state in this case—before embarking upon the writing of new metanarratives, which will be the challenge of the next wave of gender history.[2]

KATHLEEN CANNING

2. Lynn Hunt, "The Challenge of Gender, Deconstruction of Categories and Reconstruction of Narratives in Gender History," in Hans Medick and Anne-Charlott Trepp, *Geschlechtergeschichte und Allgemeine Geschichte: Herausforderungen und Perspektiven* (Göttingen: Wallstein Verlag, 1998), p. 81.

Preface

This inquiry into the languages of labor and gender in Imperial Germany began over a decade ago during a dismal winter in the Prussian State Library in (then) West Berlin. The long days I spent perusing the Social Democratic and Communist women's papers from the Weimar period left me with a set of unanswered questions: about the implicit audience for these papers—the female workers who seemed to figure as objects rather than subjects of the so-called *Frauenzeitungen*—and about the particularly German genealogies of the identities and rhetorics of class that had come to dominate working-class politics by the turn of the twentieth century. As I worked, focusing on the textile industry as a site of particular gender conflict encompassing the arenas of shop floor and union politics, I confronted the problematic disjunctures between ideological prescriptions and everyday practices, between the discourses about female factory labor and the experiences of women workers. Having skirted the "outer face" of both workplace and unions, I sought to understand the complex moments of accommodation and resistance on the "inner face" of both (to appropriate a term from Alf Lüdtke). In the meantime the theoretical and historiographical contexts in which this inquiry was launched—women's history and labor history—were recast and replenished by the "new cultural history," by the shift to gender history and the critical rethinking by scholars in both fields of the key words "experience," "agency," "discourse," and "identity." My own work of rewriting began amid this sea of change, as I set out to analyze the implications of my empirical findings for the tenacious category of "class," to understand the origins of the ideologies of women's work that permeated each aspect of my inquiry, and to probe the complex ways in which both structural and rhetorical transformations shaped female factory work in Germany.

I pursued this quest in many academic and geographic milieus over the years, incurring many intellectual and personal debts. My list of thanks begins with my teachers at Johns Hopkins University: Vernon Lidtke, whose probing and critical questions helped give this project coherence, grounding, and life and whose counsel and support have since been invaluable; Mack Walker, from whom I learned more than is evident on the surface of this book; and Toby Ditz for her indispensable insights into European and American family and women's history and her incisive comments on an earlier version of this manuscript. This book also profited from the advice of many friends and colleagues: Jean Quataert, who prompted me to rethink my analysis of the transition from home to factory industry; Jane Caplan, Roger Chickering, David Crew, Elisabeth Domansky, Laura Frader, Atina Grossmann, Michael Hanagan, Young-Sun Hong, Isabel Hull, Patrick Joyce, Molly Nolan, James Retallack, Mary Louise Roberts, Eve Rosenhaft, Bill Sewell, and Louise Tilly, with whom I discussed my work or who commented on chapter drafts or conference papers. Robert Moeller and Alf Lüdtke deserve special thanks for their generous reading of my work at several stages of revision. I also express my appreciation to my German colleagues: to Doris Kaufman for helpful advice and good company, and to Karin Hausen, Carola Sachse, Karin Zachmann, and Christiane Eifert.

I am perhaps most indebted to my colleagues and friends at the University of Michigan, where this book took shape, who inspired many of my attempts to rethink my work and whose companionship and collegiality made doing so less arduous. Geoff Eley's astute comments at a very early stage of this work spurred me on to tackle many of its unanswered questions: both my book and I have benefited enormously from his candid advice and incisive readings as well as from our shared experiences as teachers, mentors, and friends. Bill Rosenberg, Maris Vinovskis, and Terry McDonald offered wise advice on various aspects of this book. Robert Picard and Francine Lafontaine provided invaluable help with the analysis and presentation of my empirical data. For camaraderie, good food, and an abundance of intellectual stimulation I thank Jane Burbank, Fred Cooper, Laura Lee Downs, Eleanor and Geoff Eley, Carol Karlsen, Sonya Rose, Peggy Somers, Michael MacDonald and Carol Dickerman, Lora Wildenthal and Carl Caldwell, Sally Silk and Tom Wolfe, and Sharon Gold-Steinberg. I am certain I learned more from my graduate students at the University of Michigan than I could possibly have taught them. In particular I thank those who helped with my research, including Lora Wildenthal, Teresa Sanislo, Kathy Pence, Todd Ettelson, Maureen Stewart, and Andy Donson.

Archivists, scholars, and friends who aided my research in Germany and who generously welcomed me back during several subsequent summers also deserve my sincere thanks: the kind and efficient staff at the Nordrhein-Westfälisches Hauptstaatsarchiv Düsseldorf, and at the Kreisarchiv Viersen; Dr. Reinhard Vogelsang at the Stadtarchiv Bielefeld, who kindly allowed me access to the personnel records of the Mechanische Weberei Bielefeld; the helpful staff at both the Archiv des Deutschen Gewerkschaftsbundes and the Gewerkschaft Textil-Bekleidung in Düsseldorf; the firm archivist and personnel director at Johann Wülfing und Sohn in Lennep and the personnel director at the Frowein company in Wuppertal, who allowed me access to their firms' invaluable personnel records. I extend special thanks to Johannes Lipp of the Heimatverein in Oedt near Krefeld, who shared his knowledge of the local textile industry and introduced me to the rich findings of the Kreisarchiv Viersen in Kempen and to the personnel records of the Girmes company. I also learned a great deal from Dr. Jochem Ulrich, who shared his expertise on the textile workers of the Lower Rhine, guided me through partially uncatalogued materials at the Stadtarchiv Viersen, and provided me access to the personnel records of the Crous company. He and his wife, Rosemarie, were generous hosts during many visits in the Rhineland. Special thanks are also due to Dr. Jürgen Weise of the Rheinisch-Westfälisches Wirtschaftsarchiv in Cologne, whose archival skill as well as friendship, empathy, and curiosity enriched my study and enlivened my stay in the Rhineland.

My life in Düsseldorf was made both bearable and interesting by my friends Usch and Wolfgang Schloeder-Weck and their daughter Anne, who shared their home with me and much more. I also express my heartfelt thanks to Gerda Bullacher, Margot Schloeder, and Jochem Bullacher, who helped make my research possible in more respects than I can name here. The Bielefeld segment of my research was enriched by various members of the Fakultät für Geschichtswissenschaft at the Universität Bielefeld, in particular Professors Jürgen Kocka and Hans-Ulrich Wehler, who invited me to present my initial findings to their Doktorandencolloquium, and by Ute Frevert, Claudia Huerkamp, Ute Daniel, Heidrun Homburg, Josef Mooser, Michael Prinz, Rudolf Boch, and Reinhard Schüren, who offered advice and hospitality. I also thank Karl Ditt, who provided many valuable tips on the history of Bielefeld's textile industry.

Several institutions and foundations made this book possible: the Stanford Humanities Center, where I was an Andrew W. Mellon Fellow during 1991–92; the American Council of Learned Societies, which awarded me a fellowship for 1992; the German Academic Exchange Service (DAAD), which supported my research trip to Germany in the summer of 1991; the Office of the Vice-President for Research and the Rackham

Graduate School at the University of Michigan for faculty grants and fellowships to support research and writing; and the Department of History at the University of Michigan for release time from teaching and administrative duties during my "duty-off-campus" semester.

Many parts of this book have been presented at seminars or conferences over the years, including the Department of History Faculty Colloquium and the interdisciplinary Program for the Comparative Study of Social Transformation (CSST) at the University of Michigan; the annual meetings of the Social Science History Association in 1989, 1991, and 1993; the conference "The *Kaiserreich* in the 1990s: New Research, New Directions, New Agendas," held in February 1990 at the University of Pennsylvania; the annual meetings of the German Studies Association in 1989 and 1991 and of the American Historical Association in 1994; and the conference "Gender and Modernity in the Era of Rationalization," held at Columbia University in September 1994. I am grateful to those who invited me to present my work in seminars and forums at the German Historical Institute, Washington, D.C.; Georgetown University Center for German and European Studies; the Departments of History at the University of Wisconsin, the University of Washington, Pitzer College, and the Technische Universität Berlin; and the Department of German Studies, Stanford University.

Parts of the Introduction and Conclusion appeared in my article "Gender and the Politics of Class Formation: Rethinking German Labor History," *American Historical Review* 97 (June 1992): 736–68; I thank the American Historical Association for permission to use this material. Other portions of those two chapters first appeared in "Feminist History after the 'Linguistic Turn,'" *Signs* 19:2 (Winter 1994): 368–404, © 1994 by the University of Chicago, all rights reserved; that material is used here by permission of the University of Chicago Press. Parts of chapters 6 and 7 were published as "Gender and the Culture of Work: Ideology and Identity in the World behind the Mill Gate, 1890–1914," in *Elections, Mass Politics, and Social Change in Modern Germany: New Perspectives*, ed. James Retallack and Larry Eugene Jones (New York: Cambridge University Press, 1992), pp. 175–99; those sections are reprinted by permission of the publisher.

I am also indebted to my editor at Cornell University Press, Peter Agree, whose enthusiasm and support for this project sustained me during the more arduous moments of writing and revision. His advice, both intellectual and practical, helped my manuscript become the book I had envisioned.

Finally, I thank those who have kept closest company with this book over the years and helped bring it to fruition: Hubert Rast, whose own gifts as a reader and writer inspired me to write and rewrite countless times, and Samuel Rast, who reminded me daily of all I was missing as I did so.

KATHLEEN CANNING

Ann Arbor, Michigan

Introduction

German Labor History and the Meanings of Women's Work

The history of the transformation of the nineteenth-century German industrial landscape is usually written in terms of socioeconomic structures in transition: workshop to factory, community to society, estate to class. A principal aim of this book is to explore the ideologies and politics of gender as elements of these transformations from the textile mills and towns of the Rhineland and Westphalia to the national arenas of social reform and state social policy between 1850 and 1914. Gender was at the heart of these transitions, from the founding of the first mechanized mills at midcentury to the emergence of textiles as the largest industrial employer of women by the First World War. In contrast to the "men's industries" of mining, machine building, and steel, which employed negligible numbers of women before 1914, here conflicts about gender formed a crucial part of the changing meanings and structures of work during the transition from home to factory textile production, as revealed in the dramatic campaigns of weavers in the Rhineland against "feminization" (*Verweiblichung*) of the industry and "displacement" of male workers (*Verdrängung*) during the 1880s and 1890s. Gender remained a point of contention as the textile industry became the only industrial sector with a sizable female *Stammarbeiterschaft* (core workforce) during the prewar period. Within the newly mechanized mills, gender shaped the politics of work, defining and dividing the world behind the mill gate, governing how workers perceived and organized work experiences, shop-floor cultures and protests, the work identities they formed, and the meanings they assigned to the social identity of class.

Underpinning this story are a number of German particularities, beginning with the protracted transition from handicraft production to mechanized mills in the northwest German textile belt and the congealing of gender-specific labor markets and divisions of labor. As industrial growth speeded up during the late 1880s and 1890s, factory employers confronted a continuous labor shortage in nearly all sectors, prompting a segmentation of the labor market into male and female spheres and a steady expansion of the female workforce in the "women's industries" of textiles, garments, and cigar making. Germany's rapid industrial growth and recurrent labor shortages in industrial regions, like the Rhineland and Westphalia after 1890 in particular, meant that single and married women there were drawn into the workforce in unprecedented numbers, whereas in England, for example, the percentage of married women working outside the home had already begun to decline.[1] Female factory labor came to represent an urgent social problem in Germany, a profound rupture in the relations between the sexes, between social order and sexual order. Similar crises over women's wage labor had occurred across Europe—such as in England during the 1830s and 1840s, culminating in the passage of the Ten Hours Bill in 1847—as expanding industrial labor markets drew more women into factories and sweatshops.[2] The French crisis coincided with the emergence of female factory employment as a new social question in Germany and, in particular, with the vigorous campaign for a legal ban on married women's factory employment during the 1890s. Unlike the German debates, in which the separation of home and work figured prominently, with the purported *severing* of the two spheres in working women's daily lives and the perceived intrusion of the (public) factory into the (private) home as key concerns, the French discourses on women's work focused on sweatshops and home industry, in which the privacy, integrity, and order of the working-class family was endangered by the *proximity* of production and reproduction, by the absence of boundaries between them.[3]

---

1. The numbers of married women working outside the home nearly doubled in Germany between the census surveys of 1882 and 1907. In the four years between 1895 and 1899, the proportion of married women among adult female factory workers rose sharply from 21 to 29 percent. See chapter 1 for a more detailed discussion of the female labor market in imperial Germany. See, for example, Stefan Bajohr, *Die Hälfte der Fabrik, Geschichte der Frauenarbeit in Deutschland* (Marburg: Verlag Arbeiterbewegung und Gesellschaftswissenschaft, 1979), p. 25, and Hanns Dorn, "Die Frauenerwerbsarbeit und ihre Aufgaben für die Gesetzgebung," *Archiv für Rechts- und Wirtschaftsphilosophie* 5 (1911–12): 86–87.

2. See, for example, Sonya O. Rose, "Factory Reform in Nineteenth Century Britain: Gender, Class and the Liberal State," in *Gender and Class in Modern Europe*, ed. Laura L. Frader and Sonya O. Rose (Ithaca: Cornell University Press, 1996), and Robert Gray, "The Language of Factory Reform in Britain, c. 1830–1860," in *The Historical Meanings of Work*, ed. Patrick Joyce (Cambridge: Cambridge University Press, 1989), pp. 143–79.

3. Judith Coffin, "Social Science Meets Sweated Labor: Reinterpreting Women's Work in Late Nineteenth-Century France," *Journal of Modern History* 63, no. 2 (1991): 230–70.

In the most advanced industrial regions of Germany the dislocation and disorder associated with the transition from home industry to factory, and with the rapid and visible expansion of female factory labor, lingered well into the late 1890s, not only shaping the emergent labor movement but also sparking the interest of social reformers and social scientists like Alfons Thun, Heinrich Herkner, Robert Wilbrandt, and Heinrich Brauns, who investigated, interpreted, and transmitted to the national public this sense of crisis in the textile towns of the Rhineland and Westphalia.[4] It formed the backdrop for the parliamentary debates and controversies in the expanding public sphere about the regulation and restriction of female factory labor and thus left its imprint on the interventionist welfare state that emerged in Germany during the 1890s.

The Textile Industry as a Site of Inquiry

As a *Frauenindustrie* (women's industry), the textile industry has not figured as a central site of inquiry for German labor historians, whose abundant studies of social conditions and organized movements have relegated textile workers to the lowest echelon of skill, wage, social status, and political consciousness, precisely because they were largely female. Textile workers and textile mills are central to this inquiry, which in its broadest guise explores the significance of women's work in Germany's much-debated transformation from agrarian to industrial state, in contemporaries' perceptions of "die Schrecken des überwiegenden Industriestaats" (the horrors of the industrial state).[5] As the first German industry to move production from household to factory, textiles became an emblem of modernization, of the transformation of technologies and tools, families, communities, and divisions of labor. The industry also came to signify the social and sexual dangers associated with the expanding employment of women: the licentiousness of factory culture, the physical and moral ruin of the "female organism," and the social dissolution of the working-class family. The textile industry posed unique dangers to masculine identity as well, for in the narratives of social reform and weavers' protest, the mechanized textile mills symbolized "the problem of female competition in cap-

---

4. Alfons Thun, *Die Industrie am Niederrhein und ihre Arbeiter: Staats- und sozialwissenschaftliche Forschungen*, vols. 1 and 2 (Leipzig: Duncker und Humblot, 1879); Robert Wilbrandt, *Die Weber in der Gegenwart* (Jena: Gustav Fischer, 1906), and idem, *Die Frauenarbeit: Ein Problem des Kapitalismus* (Leipzig: B. G. Teubner, 1906); Heinrich Brauns, *Der Übergang von der Handweberei zum Fabrikbetrieb in der niederrheinischen Samt- und Seidenindustrie und die Lage der Arbeiter in dieser Periode* (Leipzig: Duncker und Humblot, 1906); Heinrich Herkner, *Die Arbeiterfrage. Eine Einführung*, 4th ed. (Berlin: de Gruyter, 1905), first published in 1894.

5. Lujo Brentano, *Die Schrecken des überwiegenden Industriestaats* (Berlin: Leonhard Simion, 1901).

italism": they were the first factories to make male workers superfluous, to "cast the *Familienväter* [fathers of families] into the streets."[6]

Textile mills, with their large contingents of female and teenage workers, captured both the experts' gaze and the public imagination as the long-term effects of women's factory employment on the working-class family came to constitute a new social question. The industry set the stage for social reform and state social policy initiatives toward women workers, in particular for the formulation of protective labor legislation and the renovation of social policy that took place during the "new course" of the 1890s.[7] The mills came to constitute a complex laboratory, a site of investigation and intervention for state bureaucrats and academic social reformers who sought to alleviate the abuses of factory labor for women and youths and to resolve the crisis of the family that accompanied the transition from home to factory industry. Indeed, their scholarly inquests, parliamentary motions, and polemical tracts had a formative part in the expansion of the German welfare state during the 1890s. After the turn of the century, as concern about the declining German birthrate deepened and social reform became ever more interwoven with social hygiene and eugenics, the high rates of illegitimacy, illness, and infant and maternal mortality among textile workers and their children figured importantly in the public perception of a "state of emergency" surrounding working-class motherhood. They also inspired and underpinned the efforts of social reformers to enact maternity insurance, pregnancy leave, and other protective measures for mothers and children.

The Boundaries of German Labor History

Although the textile industry is neither typical nor representative of the German patterns of industrial transformation, welfare-state formation, or the emergence of class cultures or conflicts, I argue here that it forms a singular site of linkage among these processes from the mid-nineteenth century through the eve of the First World War. In its emphasis on such linkage, this book seeks to "push at the boundaries" of German labor history, to transcend its narrative strictures and structures, its embeddedness in an *Entwicklungs- und Verlaufsmodell* of class formation—a model that outlines the progressive advancement of the various levels of class formation as shaped less by human actors than by structures and processes (for

---

6. Wilbrandt, *Die Weber*, pp. 1, 124.
7. On the "new course" in social policy, see Hans Jörg von Berlepsch, *"Neuer Kurs" im Kaiserreich? Die Arbeiterpolitik des Freiherrn von Berlepsch 1890 bis 1896* (Bonn: Neue Gesellschaft, 1987).

example, by changing market relations and the expansion of wage labor).[8] The pervasiveness of the divisions between economic, social, cultural, and political class formation, of the dichotomies between the class and "nonclass" lines of differentiation—ethnicity, nationality, religion, and gender—that run "next to, over, under or across class divisions," led its proponents to implicitly or explicitly exclude female textile workers, servants, and agricultural and home industrial employees from the decisive domain of German labor history—class—based on their low wages and status, lack of *Berufsidentität* (identification with their jobs), or dispersed and disparate sites of employment.[9] Underpinning both the more and the less teleological versions of this approach to the history of class are the gendered narratives of the labor movement itself and the social identity of class they constructed.[10] Despite its universalist claims, the dominant social identity and rhetoric of class of the late nineteenth and early twentieth centuries was cast in terms of a certain idealized relationship to production, a rigid demarcation between work and "nonwork," production and reproduction, that by definition excluded most female workers. A closer scrutiny of the relationships between the various levels of class formation makes it clear that women workers cannot be made to fit into the progression from one level to another, for the attempt to find a place for gender and women in this model disarranges teleologies, blurs boundaries between levels, or breaks the model apart altogether.

Far from a new interrogation of established concepts and categories, Germany's preeminent labor historians have recently undertaken a massive

8. For a call to "push at the boundaries" of labor history, see Gay Gullickson, "Commentary: New Labor History from the Perspective of a Women's Historian," in *Rethinking Labor History: Essays on Discourse and Class Analysis*, ed. Lenard Berlanstein (Urbana: University of Illinois Press, 1993), p. 207.

9. Jürgen Kocka, *Lohnarbeit und Klassenbildung: Arbeiter und Arbeiterbewegung in Deutschland, 1800–1875* (Bonn: J. H. W. Dietz, 1983), p. 29. Also see his *Weder Stand noch Klasse: Unterschichten um 1800* (Bonn: J. H. W. Dietz, 1990), pp. 38–39, and *Arbeitsverhältnisse und Arbeiterexistenzen: Grundlagen der Klassenbildung im 19. Jahrhundert* (Bonn: J. H. W. Dietz, 1990) (vols. 1 and 2 of the series Geschichte der Arbeiter und der Arbeiterbewegung in Deutschland seit dem Ende des 18. Jahrhunderts, edited by Gerhard A. Ritter). I am using the term "nonclass" for Kocka's "nicht klassenmäßige Trennungslinien."

10. Two somewhat different explications of the levels model can be found in Hartmut Zwahr, *Zur Konstituierung des Proletariats als Klasse: Strukturuntersuchung über das Leipziger Proletariat während der Industriellen Revolution* (Berlin: Akademie, 1978), and Jürgen Kocka, "Problems of Working-Class Formation: The Early Years, 1800–1875," in *Working-Class Formation: Nineteenth-Century Patterns in Western Europe and the United States*, ed. Ira Katznelson and Aristide Zolberg (Princeton: Princeton University Press, 1986), pp. 279–351. Kocka's models are generally regarded as far less teleological (in the sense of explicit political outcomes at the final, fourth level of class formation) than Zwahr's. For a critical discussion of both versions of the levels model, see Kathleen Canning, "Gender and the Politics of Class Formation: Rethinking German Labor History," *American Historical Review* 97 (June 1992): 736–68.

project of synthesizing and summarizing the findings and accomplishments of this expansive field in a new and definitive series on the history of workers and the workers' movement in Germany since the end of the eighteenth century, which, despite its occasional concession to the history of experience and *Alltag* (history of everyday life), remains encapsulated in the levels model of class formation.[11] Indeed, the furor in the American and British academies over the "linguistic turn" in the social sciences, the burgeoning interest of French, British, and American labor historians in language as constitutive, not merely reflective, of historical events and human consciousness, appears to have provoked little controversy in Germany.[12] Labor history within the German academy has remained largely impervious to the "crisis of labor history," the overturning and rethinking of key concepts like class, exploring their cultural dimensions and analyzing them in relation to gender, race, and ethnicity, that characterize recent British, French, and American labor historiography.[13] Closer to home, the

11. I refer here to the series edited by Gerhard A. Ritter, Geschichte der Arbeiter und der Arbeiterbewegung in Deutschland seit dem Ende des 18. Jahrhunderts (Bonn: J. H. W. Dietz). The volumes that have appeared thus far include the previously cited vols. 1 and 2 by Kocka (*Weder Stand noch Klasse* and *Arbeitsverhältnisse*) and vols. 9, 10, and 11 by Heinrich August Winkler, *Von der Revolution zur Stabilisierung: Arbeiter und Arbeiterbewegung in der Weimarer Republik, 1918 bis 1924* (1984); *Der Schein der Normalität: Arbeiter und Arbeiterbewegung in der Weimarer Republik, 1924 bis 1930* (1988); and *Der Weg in die Katastrophe: Arbeiter und Arbeiterbewegung in der Weimarer Republik, 1930 bis 1933* (1987). Additional volumes by Ritter and Klaus Tenfelde are due to appear over the next several years.

12. For excellent discussions of the "linguistic turn," see Lenard Berlanstein, "Working with Language: The Linguistic Turn in French Labor History, a Review Article," *Comparative Studies of Society and History* 33 (April 1991): 426–40; Geoff Eley, "Is All the World a Text? From Social History to the History of Society Two Decades Later," in *The Historic Turn in the Human Sciences*, ed. Terence J. McDonald (Ann Arbor: University of Michigan Press, 1996); John Toews, "Intellectual History after the Linguistic Turn: The Autonomy of Meaning and the Irreducibility of Experience," *American Historical Review* 92 (October 1987): 879–907. See also the special issue of *Central European History* titled *German Histories: Challenges in Theory, Practice, Technique*, vol. 22 (September–December 1989), in particular the essays by Michael Geyer and Konrad Jarausch, "The Future of the German Past: Transatlantic Reflections for the 1990s," pp. 229–59; Jane Caplan, "Postmodernism, Poststructuralism, and Deconstruction: Notes for Historians," pp. 260–78; and Isabel V. Hull, "Feminist and Gender History through the Literary Looking Glass: German Historiography in Postmodern Times," pp. 279–300. Also see Kathleen Canning, "Feminist History after the 'Linguistic Turn': Historicizing Discourse and Experience," *Signs* 19 (winter 1994): 368–404. Examples of pathbreaking studies that helped effect the "linguistic turn" in European labor history include William H. Sewell Jr., *Work and Revolution in France: The Language of Labor from the Old Regime to 1848* (Cambridge: Cambridge University Press, 1980), and Gareth Stedman Jones, *Languages of Class: Studies in English Working Class History, 1832–1982* (Cambridge: Cambridge University Press, 1983).

13. Some examples include Ava Baron, "Gender and Labor History: Learning from the Past, Looking to the Future," in *Work Engendered: Toward a New History of American Labor*, ed. Ava Baron (Ithaca: Cornell University Press, 1991); Berlanstein, *Rethinking Labor History*; Joyce, *Historical Meanings of Work*, and Patrick Joyce, *Visions of the People: Industrial England and the Question of Class, 1848–1914* (Cambridge: Cambridge University Press,

anthropologically oriented *Alltagsgeschichte*, a history of everyday life that dissolves the boundaries between workplace, household, and community in its exploration of experience and identity formation, has posed radical and inventive challenges to the teleological narratives of class that have gone largely unheeded by their advocates.[14] Like *Alltagsgeschichte*, feminist history persists in a kind of *Außenseiterdasein* (outsider status) in Germany, marked by a relationship of "mutual distancing" with German historical social science.[15] Thus many of the fine historical monographs on women's work, everyday lives, and political movements have been produced in relative isolation from the mainstream of historical social science, while most German social and labor historians continue to relegate women and gender to the margins of their histories of work, working-class formation, or *Gesellschaftsgeschichte* (history of society). The recent shift to *Geschlechtergeschichte* (gender history), which obviously seeks to engage "mainstream" history in its disavowal of the "separatist" pursuit of women's history, its incorporation of men and masculinity and emphasis on the relation between the two sexes, has changed little in this regard.[16]

1991); William Reddy, *Money and Liberty in Europe: A Critique of Historical Understanding* (Cambridge: Cambridge University Press, 1990); William H. Sewell, "How Classes Are Made: Critical Reflections on E. P. Thompson's Theory of Working-Class Formation," in *E. P. Thompson: Critical Perspectives*, ed. Harvey J. Kaye and Keith McClelland (Philadelphia: Temple University Press, 1990), pp. 50–70; Joan W. Scott, "Gender: A Useful Category of Historical Analysis," *American Historical Review* 91 (December 1986): 1053–75.

14. Classic texts in *Alltagsgeschichte* include Alf Lüdtke, "Organizational Order or *Eigensinn*? Workers' Privacy and Workers' Politics in Imperial Germany," in *Rites of Power, Symbolism, Ritual and Politics since the Middle Ages*, ed. Sean Wilentz (Philadelphia: Temple University Press, 1985), pp. 303–33; Alf Lüdtke, ed., *Alltagsgeschichte: Zur Rekonstruktion historischer Erfahrungen und Lebensweisen* (Frankfurt: Campus, 1989); Dorothee Wierling, "Alltagsgeschichte und Geschichte der Geschlechterbeziehungen," in Lüdtke, *Alltagsgeschichte*, pp. 169–90; and Alf Lüdtke, *Eigen-Sinn: Fabrikalltag, Arbeitererfahrungen und Politik vom Kaiserreich bis in den Faschismus* (Hamburg: Ergebnisse, 1993). For discussions of the place of *Alltagsgeschichte* in German history, see David Crew, "*Alltagsgeschichte*: A New Social History from Below?" *Central European History* 22 (September–December 1989): 394–407, and Geoff Eley, "Labor History, Social History, *Alltagsgeschichte*: Experience, Culture, and the Politics of the Everyday—a New Direction for German Social History?" *Journal of Modern History* 61 (June 1989): 297–343.

15. Ute Frevert, "Klasse und Geschlecht—ein deutscher Sonderweg?" in *Nichts als Unterdrückung? Geschlecht und Klasse in der englischen Sozialgeschichte*, ed. Logie Barrow, Dorothea Schmidt, and Jutta Schwarzkopf (Münster: Westfälisches Dampfboot, 1991), p. 262. Also see Eve Rosenhaft, "Women, Gender, and the Limits of Political History in the Age of 'Mass' Politics," in *Elections, Mass Politics, and Social Change in Modern Germany: New Perspectives*, ed. Larry E. Jones and James Retallack (Cambridge: Cambridge University Press, 1992), p. 150, and "Geschichten und ihre Geschichte: Ein Nachwort," in Frevert, *Nichts als Unterdrückung*, pp. 248–50.

16. Frevert, "Klasse und Geschlecht," pp. 261–62, 266, and her essay "Männergeschichte oder die Suche nach dem 'ersten' Geschlecht," in *Was ist Gesellschaftsgeschichte? Positionen, Themen, Analysen*, ed. Manfred Hettling, Claudia Huerkamp, Paul Nolte, and Hans-Walter Schmuhl (Munich: Beck, 1991), p. 34; Hull, "Feminist and Gender History," p. 279;

8　Introduction

Although the social science paradigms of modernization, urbanization, and class and state formation remain securely in place in Germany despite the vital challenges of *Alltagsgeschichte* and *Geschlechtergeschichte*, this book matured during a marked change in social, labor, and women's history on this side of the "Atlantic divide" in German history.[17] Historical practice during the past decade in the United States and Britain has been marked by a fruitful fracturing of disciplinary boundaries, by the questioning, disassembly, and recasting of these paradigms in light of new histories of women and gender, race, ethnicity, and sexuality. Feminist historians, for example, leveled criticism at labor history for elaborating rather than replacing "a whole series of conceptual dualisms—capitalism/patriarchy, public/private, production/reproduction, men's work/women's work—which assume that class issues are integral to the first term of each pair and gender is important only to the second."[18] At the same time, poststructuralist theory posed challenges to both labor history and women's history/gender history as its practitioners declared obsolete many of the familiar tools, concepts, and epistemologies in both fields, including the keywords of social-historical analysis—experience, agency, and identity.[19]

The Changing Meanings and Structures of Work

These challenges, as well as the impossibility of fitting my historical subjects into an established conceptual framework, have necessitated an ap-

---

Rosenhaft, "Geschichten und ihre Geschichte," p. 248; Hanna Schissler, "Einleitung: Soziale Ungleichheit und historisches Wissen. Der Beitrag der Geschlechtergeschichte," in *Geschlechterverhältnisse im historischen Wandel*, ed. Hanna Schissler (Frankfurt am Main: Campus, 1993), pp. 26–27. In Hans-Ulrich Wehler's otherwise comprehensive *Deutsche Gesellschaftsgeschichte*, vols. 1 and 2 (Munich: Beck, 1987), women and gender appear only in disparate footnotes.

17. On the Atlantic divide in German history, see Geyer and Jarausch, "Future of the German Past." The term refers to the striking divergence in the ways German history is conceptualized and practiced on either side of the Atlantic.

18. Baron, "Gender and Labor History," p. 17.

19. See, for example, Denise Riley, *"Am I That Name?" Feminism and the Category of "Women" in History* (Minneapolis: University of Minnesota Press, 1988); Joan W. Scott, *Gender and the Politics of History* (New York: Columbia University Press, 1988); Mary Poovey, "Feminism and Deconstruction," *Feminist Studies* 14 (spring 1988): 51–65; Leslie Wahl Rabine, "A Feminist Politics of Non-identity," *Feminist Studies* 14 (1988): 11–31; Linda Nicholson, ed., *Feminism/Postmodernism* (New York: Routledge, 1990); Joan W. Scott, "The Evidence of Experience," *Critical Inquiry* 17, no. 3 (1991): 773–97; Judith Butler and Joan W. Scott, *Feminists Theorize the Political* (New York: Routledge, 1992); Michèle Barrett and Anne Phillips, eds., *Destabilizing Theory: Contemporary Feminist Debates* (Stanford: Stanford University Press, 1992); Leora Auslander, "Feminist Theory and Social History: Explorations in the Politics of Identity," *Radical History Review* 54 (1992): 158–76; Laura Lee Downs, "If 'Woman' Is Just an Empty Category, Then Why Am I Afraid to Walk Alone at Night? Identity Politics Meets the Postmodern Subject," *Comparative Studies in Society and History* 35, no. 2 (1993): 414–37.

proach that expands the boundaries of German labor history, exploring both the discourses and the experiences of women's work in imperial Germany. In examining the transition from handicraft production to mechanized mills in the Rhineland and Westphalia, the first part of this book (chapters 1 and 2) seeks to distinguish the structural transformations from the changing meanings that contemporaries ascribed to women's work. These chapters attend to the expansion and gendered demarcation of labor markets, the ruptures and continuities in the divisions of labor, the reinvention of craft traditions by the male weavers' *Innungen* (guilds) and their impassioned campaigns against women's work at the looms. The second part (chapters 3, 4, and 5) analyzes the place of female factory labor in the national arenas of social reform and labor legislation where the social question was cast and recast between 1850 and 1914. Female textile workers figured centrally in the debates about women's work that engaged social reformers across the political spectrum and prompted the state to regulate, restrict, and protect their labor in 1878, 1891, and 1908. Chapters 6 and 7, which compose the third part, seek to uncover the meanings women workers themselves made of their labor as they encountered and sometimes contested the dominant discourses about it. The analysis in these chapters of career patterns, work identities, and work cultures also aims to debunk a key myth of German labor history: that the nature of female factory employment—as purportedly temporary, supplemental, unskilled, and poorly paid—prevented women workers from identifying with or finding meaning in their jobs. Furthermore, this section seeks to trace how the discourses of women's work shaped the structures and relations of work, the hierarchies of skill and wage, regimes of factory discipline and punishment, and employers' institutions of charity and tutelage.

In its pursuit of changing meanings as well as structures, this book draws on both textual and quantitative evidence, including the reports of factory inspectors, social reformers' scholarly studies, polemical texts, and parliamentary motions, police reports, insurance records, and local and company histories as well as personnel records from several textile firms in the Rhineland and Westphalia. It relies on necessarily disparate research strategies, from the detailed data analysis of male and female workers' career patterns to the decoding of images, rhetorics, and tropes in the textual sources that lent coherence to the discourses of social reform. Furthermore, my inquiry spans both region and nation, establishing a framework in which the textile towns of the Rhineland and Westphalia serve as a lens through which to examine processes and settings—the transition from home to factory industry, career patterns, and the cultures of work in the new mills—that are most meaningful when specified rather than examined in terms of national, generalized patterns. The regional focus of this book not only has allowed for more concrete exploration of the origins and outcomes of important shifts in the discourses of women's work but has also uncovered intriguing links between the debates about women's work at the levels of high and low politics, between the strikes of male silk weavers in the Rhineland and the representations of feminization in social reformers' texts.

Methodological Reflections on Discourse, Experience, and Agency

Cast as a study of both the discourses and experiences of work, this book seeks to resolve the opposition between these terms, to untangle their relationship, and to resist a fixed notion by which one of the pair (discourse) always seems to determine or "construct" the other (experience). Despite the uneasiness of many historians with the term "discourse," as with any other historical method, the specific uses and effectiveness of discursive analysis are determined by the nature of the historical inquiry. In the case of the history of *gender*—as a symbolic system or as a signifier of relations of power in which men and women are positioned differently—discursive analysis is a significant, even essential, conceptual tool.[20] Indeed, where the voices of historical actors (female textile workers, for example) resound only rarely in archival sources and are generally difficult to "retrieve," the painstaking work of reconstructing discursive domains, of appraising the power of rhetoric and imagery to construct gender, becomes a necessary prerequisite for the analysis of "lived experience," especially when the history of experience is defined as a process of making, assigning, or contesting meanings.[21]

Discourse is understood here as a convergence of statements, texts,

20. This definition of gender is derived from Donna Haraway, "'Gender' for a Marxist Dictionary: The Sexual Politics of a Word," in *Simians, Cyborgs, and Women: The Reinvention of Nature*, ed. Donna Haraway (New York: Routledge, 1991), p. 143, and Scott, "Gender: A Useful Category," p. 1067.

21. My own working definition of discourse and discursive domains has been shaped by Michel Foucault, *History of Sexuality*, vol. 1, *An Introduction* (New York: Vintage, 1980); Richard Terdiman, *Discourse/Counter-discourse: The Theory and Practice of Symbolic Resistance in Nineteenth-Century France* (Ithaca: Cornell University Press, 1985); Peter Stallybrass and Allon White, *The Politics and Poetics of Transgression* (Ithaca: Cornell University Press, 1986); Judith Walkowitz, *City of Dreadful Delight: Narratives of Sexual Danger in Late-Victorian London* (Chicago: University of Chicago Press, 1992); Mary Poovey, *Uneven Developments: The Ideological Work of Gender in Mid-Victorian England* (Chicago: University of Chicago Press, 1988); Sonya O. Rose, "Text and Context: A 'Double Vision' as Historical Method," unpublished paper presented at Social Science History Association annual meeting, 1991; Dorothy Smith, *Texts, Facts, and Femininity: Exploring the Relations of Ruling* (New York: Routledge, 1990); and Chris Weedon, *Feminist Practice and Poststructuralist Theory* (Oxford: Basil Blackwell, 1987).

signs, and practices that are formulated or enacted across different, even dispersed sites (from courtrooms to street corners, parliamentary papers to feminist or union journals, for example).²² As both a textual and a social relation, it was constituted by agents whose positions within discursive domains differed according to their authority and expertise, according to their discrepant abilities and (social, economic, cultural) power to constitute, contest, or transform discourses. As a historically specific formation, discourse required the existence of a public sphere that transcended local settings; furthermore, as Richard Terdiman has pointed out, it relied on "the techniques for assuring discursive penetration" as well as those of "symbolic subversion" such as newspapers, associational networks, and new disciplines and bodies of knowledge like statistics and management.²³

While attending to the internal workings of the discourses of women's work, to the languages that structured them and the rhetorical strategies they implemented, this book analyzes them as embedded in the broader context of nineteenth- and early twentieth-century German history, as both shaped by and in turn constitutive of a nexus of specific social relations and historical transformations, from the rise of factory industry to the emergence of the public sphere and the expansion of the German welfare state. It seeks to render concrete the abstract and intangible in discourse(s) by investigating the historical origins, material, and ideological outcomes of specific discourses, tracing the conflicts within and between discursive domains and the forces that ultimately disordered or transformed them.²⁴ It posits a fluid and vital relationship between discourses and historical, material context in which material reality exists "as a certain pressure, a destabilizing force on cultural production, forcing representations to be reworked, shored up, reconstructed."²⁵

In my case study, for example, the transformation of the labor market—the steady and perceptible expansion of the female factory workforce examined in chapters 1 and 2—precipitated the discursive shift from the "worker question" to the new social question of female factory labor dur-

22. On the dispersed sites of discourse, see Walkowitz, *City of Dreadful Delight*, p. 6, and Stallybrass and White, *Politics and Poetics*, p. 194; Terdiman, *Discourse/Counter-discourse*, pp. 44–46; and Smith, *Texts, Facts, and Femininity*, pp. 161–67.
23. Terdiman, *Discourse/Counter-discourse*, pp. 12, 44, 54, 66, 74.
24. See, for example, Weedon, *Feminist Practice*, p. 127.
25. See the roundtable discussion including Judith Walkowitz, Myra Jehlen, and Bell Chevigny titled "Patrolling the Borders: Feminist Historiography and the New Historicism," *Radical History Review* 43 (1989): 31. Walkowitz points to the ways representations derived their power "in good part from the material context in which they appear[ed], from the social spaces where they [were] enunciated, and from the social and political networks that [were] organized around them." Also see Rose, "Text and Context," pp. 7–8; Walkowitz, *City of Dreadful Delight*, pp. 9–11, 233–41; and Gabrielle Spiegel, "History, Historicism, and the Social Logic of the Text in the Middle Ages," *Speculum* 65 (1990): 71.

ing the 1880s and 1890s. Chapters 3, 4, and 5 trace the emergence of overlapping, often competing discourses: Social Democratic, liberal social reformist, Social Catholic, industrialist-capitalist, bourgeois feminist, medical-biological, nationalist-eugenicist, and the paternalist-interventionist practices of the welfare state, which during the last two decades of the nineteenth century formed a new discursive domain of women's work. Indeed, each sought to resolve the discrepancy between the continued expansion of the female workforce and its own dominant notions about the biological, moral, and social character of the sexes. At the same time, these chapters also elucidate the complex moralizing as well as regulative outcomes of the changing discourses about women's work, as agitation at diverse sites (parliaments, pubs, strike lines) formed a groundswell of social pressure that ultimately prompted the state to mediate, intervene, and sanction an official resolution of the new social question through the expansion of protective labor legislation.[26]

Finally, chapters 6 and 7 explore both the subjects and the objects of the discourses of social reform. Resisting a one-sided view of women and workers as objects of discursive construction, I seek not only to recover the voices of political economists holding forth on the perils of the industrial world, but also to render as subjects those whose labor was inscribed with ideologies of gender. In aspiring to break the silence of women workers (however difficult this may be), wherever possible I analyze the reception, the contestation, the multiple meanings of texts, resisting the tendency of discourse analysis to displace the subject or to reduce her "to a mere bearer of systemic processes."[27] I explore work cultures and work identities in terms of the meanings women derived from their wage work, the ways they interpreted, subverted, or internalized discourses of labor or ideologies of work. Examination of the expressive cultural practices—the everyday struggles over pride and honor, gossip and respectability, bodies and sexuality—through which workers adapted to and subverted ordained locations within the factory regime reveals not only complicity and resistance but also the multiple subject positions female factory workers inhabited in their daily lives, as workers, mothers, and wives.[28]

A keyword in this exploration of the politics of work, in particular of

26. On moralizing and regulative outcomes of discourses of social reform, see Mary Poovey, "Domesticity and Class Formation: Chadwick's *Sanitary Report*," in *Subject to History*, ed. David Simpson (Ithaca: Cornell University Press, 1991), p. 65, and Mary Jacobus, Evelyn Fox Keller, and Sally Shuttleworth, eds., *Body/Politics: Women and the Discourses of Science* (New York: Routledge, 1990), pp. 1–10.
27. Smith, *Texts, Facts, and Femininity*, p. 161.
28. See Mary Poovey, "Speaking of the Body: Mid-Victorian Constructions of Female Desire," in Jacobus, Keller, and Shuttleworth, *Body/Politics*, pp. 29, 43, and Walkowitz, Chevigny, and Jehlen, "Patrolling the Borders," pp. 30–31, 43.

the formation of work identities and work cultures and of the contested boundaries of class politics, is "experience." Experience has served as the principal concept in social history since the 1960s, particularly in histories of subjugated or invisible groups. In the narratives of labor history, for example, experience denotes the "vast, multiple, contradictory realm" that lay between the relations of production and the awakening of class consciousness.[29] Labor and feminist historians usually mean by experience more than the mere "living through of events"; the term also encompasses the way "people construed events as they were living through them." William H. Sewell Jr. defines experience as "the linguistically shaped process of weighing and assigning meaning to events as they happen." According to Sewell, experience is embedded in the "cultural understandings and linguistic capacities" of historical subjects.[30] One of the most innovative fields of German social history, *Alltagsgeschichte,* has focused on everyday experience as the site where "abstract structures of domination and exploitation were directly encountered."[31] Alf Lüdtke's notion of *Eigensinn,* a key concept in German historiography of everyday life, signifies a particular way of responding to or making meanings of events as they happen, a "striving for time and space of one's own"; a sense of self-preservation and self-presentation as well as a "self-willed distancing" that aids a "reframing," "reorganizing," or "creative reappropriation of the conditions of daily life."[32] This emphasis on construing, reframing, and reappropriating implies that subjects do have some kind of agency, even if the meanings they make "depend on the ways of interpreting the world, on the discourses available to . . . [them] . . . at any particular moment."[33]

Experience, as the rendering of meaning, is entwined with the notion of agency, with a vision of historical subjects as actors who, in Sewell's terms, "put into practice their necessarily structured knowledge."[34] Indeed, the concept of agency forms the critical link in analyzing how discourses change, how subjects mobilize the experiences and exigencies of their everyday lives to contest power in its discursive form. Without the intervention of agents who render them contingent and permeable, discourses re-

29. Sewell, "How Classes Are Made," pp. 55–56.
30. Ibid., p. 64, and William H. Sewell Jr., "Gender, History, and Deconstruction: Joan Wallach Scott's *Gender and the Politics of History,*" CSST Working Paper 34 (Ann Arbor, Mich.: Program in the Comparative Study of Social Transformation, 1989), p. 19.
31. Eley, "Labor History, Social History," p. 324.
32. Lüdtke, "Organizational Order," pp. 304–5, 312–15, and Lüdtke, *Alltagsgeschichte*; Crew, "*Alltagsgeschichte,*" pp. 394–407.
33. Weedon, *Feminist Practice,* p. 79.
34. William H. Sewell Jr., *Toward a Theory of Structure: Duality, Agency, and Transformation,* CSST Working Paper 29 (Ann Arbor, Mich.: Program in the Comparative Study of Social Transformation, 1989), p. 5.

main fixed hegemonic systems. A notion of agency as a site of mediation between discourses and experiences serves not only to dislodge the deterministic view in which discourse always seems to construct experience, but also to dispel the notion that discourses are, to paraphrase anthropologist Sherry Ortner, shaped by everything but the experiences of "the people the text claims to represent."[35] According to Ortner, uncovering the ways historical subjects mapped, transformed, and "reterritorialized" political locations and discourses requires us to make room for those on the other side of our historical or ethnographic texts, to recognize that as "we attempt to push these people into the molds of our texts, they push back."[36]

In this book the female body constitutes an intriguing point at which discourses and everyday experiences converge. Women workers encountered and often subverted the scrutiny of their bodies, the meanings imparted to them by idealized visions of motherhood, by the prescriptions of social and reproductive hygiene. As women's factory employment and its long-term effects on the working-class family came to constitute a new social question, during the last quarter of the nineteenth century, the female body, as the centerpiece of the working-class family, was marked as a new site of intervention for the moralizing and regulatory regimes of industrial paternalism and social reform—indeed, for the nascent welfare state. For under the gaze of male mill owners, trade unionists, factory inspectors, medical doctors, and parliamentary legislators, female workers were always embodied. Circumscribed by machines and piecework, depleted by the long hours of mill work and the continual cycles of pregnancy, birth, miscarriage, and abortion, women workers' embodied experiences became a formative part of work cultures and work identities, of their encounters with employers' regimes of discipline and tutelage. Women workers' bodily experiences, which defined the legendary separation of home and work, family and factory, shaped women workers' claims on the state, their visions of citizenship, and their particularly gendered encounters with and resistance to the organized politics of class.

Although the textile industry is neither representative nor typical of the history of German labor, this book argues that it is of singular importance to that history: as the largest factory employer of women, as a unique site of gender conflict during industrial transformation, and as a key site of intervention for the expanding German welfare state. The expansion of female factory labor and its definition as a new social question placed gen-

---

35. Sherry Ortner, "Some Theoretical Problems in Anthropological History and Historical Anthropology," in McDonald, *Historic Turn*.
36. Ortner, "Some Theoretical Problems," p. 24. Donna Haraway makes a similar point in "Situated Knowledges: The Science Question in Feminism and the Privilege of Partial Perspective," in Haraway, *Simians, Cyborgs and Women*, p. 198.

der at the center of the debates about the transformation of German society from an agrarian to an industrial state. The protests of male workers and the growing consternation of middle-class, Social Democratic, and Catholic social reformers about the future of the working-class family underpinned the new discourses about women's work and prompted the expansion of the German welfare state. Social policy, in which the family came to figure as the key site of intervention, sought then to fix gender roles, to align sexual divisions of labor with the social order, and to regulate the social body by policing female bodies. The mythology of the separation of home and work, the dichotomies of public/private, work/nonwork, production/reproduction that were recast in the debates about women's work—at the level of state and in the expanding public spheres of both bourgeoisie and workers during the 1880s and 1890s—came to anchor the social identities of estate, class, and citizenship, which I will explore in subsequent work.

1

Gender and Sexual Politics in the Transition from Home to Factory Industry

The "prolonged and tortuous" transition from home industrial hand spinning and handweaving to mechanized, centralized textile production took place in Germany during the second half of the nineteenth century.[1] The particularities of this transformation varied widely among regions and across the myriad branches of textile production, yet a common thread of gender conflict, of competition between the sexes, of male weavers displaced by female hands links the disparate stories and social studies of individual regions and branches. As the first to mechanize and centralize production, the textile industry occupies a unique place not only in the narratives of German economic history, but also in the annals of Germany's first generation of social scientists, for whom it became an emblem of the *Schrecken des Industriestaats*, of the horrors and the dangers inherent to the transformation from an agrarian to an industrial state.[2]

This book approaches the transition from home to factory industry both as a structural change and as a central chapter in the history of the chang-

1. Robert Wilbrandt, *Die Weber in der Gegenwart* (Jena: Gustav Fischer, 1906), p. 1. Throughout the book, translations are my own unless otherwise noted.
2. Lujo Brentano, *Die Schrecken des überwiegenden Industriestaats* (Berlin: Leonhard Simion, 1901). The social reformers whose work made textile production emblematic of this transition include Alfons Thun, *Die Industrie am Niederrhein und ihre Arbeiter: Staats- und sozialwissenschaftliche Forschungen*, vols. 1 and 2 (Leipzig: Duncker und Humblot, 1879); Robert Wilbrandt, *Die Frauenarbeit: Ein Problem des Kapitalismus* (Leipzig: B. G. Teubner, 1906); Heinrich Brauns, *Der Übergang von der Handweberei zum Fabrikbetrieb in der niederrheinischen Samt- und Seidenindustrie und die Lage der Arbeiter in dieser Periode* (Leipzig: Duncker und Humblot, 1906); Heinrich Herkner, *Die oberelsässische Baumwollindustrie* (Strassburg: K. J. Trübner, 1887); and idem, *Die Arbeiterfrage: Eine Einführung*, 4th ed. (Berlin: De Gruyter, 1905).

ing meanings of work. The perceptions of the separation of home and work, of its purported "destruction of all foundations of inherited culture, . . . [its] extirpation of property and marriage," the feminization of the textile workforce—juxtaposed ironically with the "defeminization" of the household as wives and mothers departed for the mills—not only denote shifts in the meanings of work but also constitute markers in the histories of the family, class, and citzenship in "modern" Germany.[3] The disruptions and disordering of craft traditions, family structures, and gender ideologies left indelible traces on the histories of the textile unions, both Social Democratic and Catholic, and in the collective memories and class identities of union leaders. These perceptions, etched in the history of social reform by the scholarly studies of eminent professors of political economy, by their *Studienreisen* through the textile regions of Germany, also influenced the social policy of the emergent German welfare state.

This chapter thus analyzes the historical context of the discursive and legislative constructions of female factory labor, of the experiences and identities of work in the world behind the mill gate, that are explored in subsequent chapters. Rather than taking a one-sided or deterministic view of discourses as reflections of discernible material realities, I am interested here in both their origins and their outcomes, in examining the transition from home to factory as both a structural and a discursive process in which the two workplaces interacted and shaped one another. Glancing ahead to the later chapters of this book, the transition from household to factory production occupies a crucial place in the genealogy of the social question of late industrialization, in the discourses about female factory labor of the late 1880s and 1890s. Furthermore, the discourses of social reform, which were cast within this transition from home to factory, in turn shaped the world behind the mill gate, the sexual division of labor, the hierarchies of wage and skill, and the cultures of work in which men and women formed work identities.[4] This book employs necessarily disparate methods—from analysis of census and employment statistics to exploration of the human dramas behind the profound alterations of craft, community, and family depicted in the vivid reports of mayors, district magistrates, factory

---

3. Quotation from Thun, *Die Industrie am Niederrhein*, p. 178. On the historically contingent meanings of work, see Patrick Joyce, "The Historical Meanings of Work: An Introduction," in *The Historical Meanings of Work*, ed. Patrick Joyce (Cambridge: Cambridge University Press, 1987), pp. 1–31.

4. Rather than seeing the opposition that historian Joan Scott appears to perceive between the discourse about women's work as "being caused by industrial conditions" or as "helping to shape them," I view the two processes as intertwined. See Joan W. Scott, "'L'Ouvrière! Mot Impie, Sordide . . .': Women Workers in the Discourse of French Political Economy, 1840–1860," in *Gender and the Politics of History*, ed. Joan W. Scott (New York: Columbia University Press, 1988), pp. 139–63.

inspectors, and employers—to distinguish between the rhetoric and the *representations* of feminization, on the one hand, and the structural transformations of the industrial labor market on the other.

At the heart of this difficult distinction is the complex question of the origins of the sexual division of labor in the modern textile factories, in particular the attempt to discern continuities and ruptures in the organization of work from protoindustrial rural households to the newly mechanized mills. Jean Quataert's innovative work on textile-working families in the woolen districts of the Oberlausitz in Saxony has emphasized the various ways women's contributions to home industry have escaped the historical record, being intentionally concealed by weavers themselves from representatives of the state or rendered invisible because those same officials were unable to regard the labor of a weaver's wife at the loom as "work" or "employment."[5] Although it would be impossible to condense or summarize the recent proliferation of local, regional, or industry-specific studies of the origins of the sexual division of labor in various European settings, reading them against one another reveals several important shared attributes that originate beyond the so-called sphere of production, in the "broader spheres of ideology and social constructs."[6] Each of the diverse and fluid patterns of dividing labor, by which some tasks were "clearly and exclusively women's work in one factory, town or region" but were "exclusively men's work in another factory, town or region," was "formed within the shifting mutuality and antipathy of gender relations and the relations of production."[7] As Sonya Rose's work on the British

5. Jean H. Quataert, "Social Insurance and the Family Work of Oberlausitz Home Weavers in the Late Nineteenth Century," in *German Women in the Nineteenth Century*, ed. John C. Fout (New York: Holmes and Meier, 1984), pp. 270–89, and idem, "Teamwork in Saxon Homeweaving Families in the Nineteenth Century: A Preliminary Investigation into the Issue of Gender Work Roles," in *German Women in Eighteenth and the Nineteenth Centuries*, ed. Ruth-Ellen Joeres and Mary Jo Maynes (Bloomington: Indiana University Press, 1986), pp. 3–23.

6. Maxine Berg, "Women's Work, Mechanisation and the Early Phases of Industrialization in England," in Joyce, *Historical Meanings of Work*, p. 66. For comparison, see: Hans Medick, "The Proto-industrial Family Economy: The Structural Function of Household and Family during the Transition from Peasant Society to Industrial Capitalism," *Social History* 3 (October 1976): 291–315; Cynthia Cockburn, *Brothers: Male Dominance and Technological Change* (London: Pluto Press, 1983); Jean H. Quataert, "The Shaping of Women's Work in Manufacturing: Guilds, Household, and the State in Central Europe, 1648–1870," *American Historical Review* 90 (December 1985): 1122–48; and Sonya O. Rose, *Limited Livelihoods: Gender and Class in Nineteenth-Century England* (Berkeley: University of California Press, 1992).

7. Joy Parr, "Disaggregating the Sexual Division of Labour: A Transatlantic Case Study," *Comparative Study of Society and History* 30 (1988): 512, 533, compares the hosiery knitting industries in southern Ontario and the English East Midlands. Also see Parr, *The Gender of Breadwinners: Women, Men and Change in Two Industrial Towns, 1880–1950* (Toronto: University of Toronto Press, 1990); Mary Freifeld, "Technological Change and the 'Self-Acting' Mule: A Study of Skill and the Sexual Division of Labor," *Social History* 11

hosiery industry has shown, these patterns represent divergent outcomes of the protests, boycotts, and strikes of male workers that created "gender segregation as they attempted to preserve their own jobs in the face of transformations of the labor process."[8] Qualifying the frequent contention that the sexual division of labor emerged as new technologies were encoded with gender, sociologist Joy Parr emphasizes that "given technologies have been contingent and biddable, the products of 'conflicts between men and women as well as between management and the workforce over machines.'"[9] In pursuit of the continuities and dissonances and the distinct meanings of the separation of home and work for male and female textile workers, this book explores the gender conflict that accompanied women from the protoindustrial household into the newly mechanized and centralized mills. Although this is not strictly a regional study, the expansive region of Rhineland and Westphalia, where mechanization and centralization of textiles began earlier than in other regions, serves here as a lens with which to examine these processes of transition and as a means of grounding and specifying their complexity. Although my focus is the textile industry *after* the demise of home industry, the examination of its protracted transition, of the contests between craft and class, men and women, employers and workers about the meanings of work, helps to explain the origins of the sexual division of labor in the new textile mills, of the discursive and legislative arenas of social reform, and of the new identities and work cultures that prevailed among the factory workforce.

Economic Webs: Textiles and the Patterns of German Industrial Development

The narratives of economic history point to 1830 as the beginning of the first phase of Germany's industrial revolution, in which consumer goods industries—textiles and garments above all—fueled economic development and dominated production. Critical to German industrial growth during the second, more intense phase of industrialization between 1870 and 1900 was the proliferation of capital goods industries like iron, steel, mining, metalworking, and machine building, which expanded rapidly yet did not immediately displace consumer goods from their pri-

---

(October 1986): 319–43, and Gay Gullickson, *Spinners and Weavers of Auffay: Rural Industry and the Sexual Division of Labor in a French Village, 1750–1850* (Cambridge: Cambridge University Press, 1986).

8. Sonya O. Rose, "'Gender at Work': Sex, Class, and Industrial Capitalism," *History Workshop* 21 (spring 1986): 120. Also see Barbara Taylor, *Eve and the New Jerusalem: Socialism and Feminism in the Nineteenth Century* (New York: Pantheon, 1983).

9. Parr, "Disaggregating the Sexual Division of Labour," p. 533.

mary position in the German economy. Although a balance was achieved between the two sectors during the third phase of industrialization, beginning after the turn of the century, the consumer goods branches were not entirely eclipsed by capital goods until the fourth phase, which West Germany reached in the 1950s according to the traditional typology of economic historian Walther G. Hoffmann.[10] From the perspective of the regional variations, however, it is difficult to validate singular patterns or models of industrial transformation or to determine a date by which Germany as a whole had become definitively industrialized.[11]

The transition from home textile production to factory industry was an uneven and protracted process that spanned nearly a century between the introduction of the first cotton spinning machines in the Rhineland in the 1780s and the final "victory march of the machine" through the silk-weaving districts of the Lower Rhine more than a century later.[12] This process, characterized by regional variation and "unequal progress toward technical efficiency and large-scale factory production," first embraced cotton spinning, then cotton weaving, followed successively by the woolen, linen, velvet, and silk branches.[13] The piecemeal progress of mechanization and centralization in textile and garment production stood in contrast to the rapid modernization of the capital goods sectors, which took place within two to three decades. Although the disparate regional patterns of industrialization in textiles make it difficult to assess the industry's role in the "take-off" of the national economy in the 1870s, local and regional studies explicate its significance in sparking the growth of local and regional economies. In Saxony, for example, the introduction of the spinning jenny stimulated the expansion of the machine-building industry; similarly, the proliferation of chemical plants in the Wupper Valley stemmed from the demand of textile producers for chemical dyes and bleach.[14]

---

10. Walther G. Hoffmann, *The Growth of Industrial Economies* (Manchester: Manchester University Press, 1958), pp. 2–5, 47–50.
11. See especially Frank B. Tipton, *Regional Variations in the Economic Development of Germany in the 19th Century* (Middletown: Wesleyan University Press, 1976).
12. Brauns, *Der Übergang der Handweberei*, p. 7.
13. Jochem Ulrich, "Soziale Entwicklungen im industriellen Umbruch: Die Anpassungskrise in der niederrheinischen Textilindustrie, dargestellt am Gebiet der heutigen Stadt Viersen, 1890–1913" (Dissertation, Universität Duisburg, 1984), p. 6.
14. Horst Blumberg, *Die deutsche Textilindustrie in der industriellen Revolution* (Berlin: Akademie, 1965), pp. 23, 25, 28, 32; Friedrich Wilhelm Henning, *Die Industrialisierung in Deutschland, 1800–1914*, 5th ed. (Paderborn: F. Schöningh, 1973), pp. 144–45. For examples of local and regional studies, see, for example, Peter Borscheid, *Textilarbeiterschaft in der Industrialisierung: Soziale Lage und Mobilität in Württemberg* (Stuttgart: Klett Cotta, 1978); Karl Ditt, *Industrialisierung, Arbeiterschaft und Arbeiterbewegung in Bielefeld* (Dortmund: Gesellschaft für Westfälische Wirtschaftsgeschichte e.V., 1982); Wolfgang Köllmann, *Sozialgeschichte der Stadt Barmen im 19. Jahrhundert* (Tübingen: J. C. B. Mohr, 1960); Reinhard

The contribution of the textile industry to Germany's economic growth between 1873 and 1913 was substantial: the productivity of its labor force increased by 115 percent, was second only to the metal industry's phenomenal increase of 270 percent.[15] Although the absolute numbers of those employed in the textile sector increased steadily through 1914, the importance of the industry as an employer declined relative to the booming expansion of the workforce in the capital goods sector (see table 1). While still in the throes of mechanization in several branches of production, in the mid-1880s textiles lost its position as the largest industrial employer, surpassed by the revitalized and expanding domestic—rather than factory—workshops of the garment industry, which experienced "colossal growth" as female appendages to the expanding urban *Männerindustrien* (men's industries) in Germany's industrial cities.[16] As the economic landscape of Germany was altered by the rapid expansion of the metal, machine building, chemical, and paper industries, the competition for industrial workers intensified during the late 1880s and early 1890s: by the end of the 1890s the textile industry had become the fifth largest industrial employer in Germany.[17]

The rhythm of expansion and contraction in the textile labor market corresponded not only to the cyclical upswings and downturns of the national economy after 1871, but also to branch-specific cycles that often proved more erratic than those for industry and crafts overall (see

---

Schüren, *Staat und ländliche Industrialisierung: Sozialer Wandel in zwei Dörfern einer deutsch-niederländischen Textilgewerberegion, 1830–1914* (Dortmund: Gesellschaft für Westfälische Wirtschaftsgeschichte, 1985); Jochem Ulrich, *Industrie und Gesellschaft am Niederrhein: Soziale Entwicklungen im industriellen Umbruch. Die Anpassungskrise in der niederrheinischen Textilindustrie dargestellt am Gebiet der heutigen Stadt Viersen, 1890–1913* (Cologne: Rheinland, 1986).

15. Hermann Aubin and Wolfgang Zorn, *Handbuch der deutschen Wirtschafts- und Sozialgeschichte*, vol. 2 (Stuttgart: Klett Cotta, 1976), p. 539; Henning, *Die Industrialisierung*, pp. 217–19; and Walther G. Hoffman, *Das Wachstum der deutschen Wirtschaft seit der Mitte des 19. Jahrhunderts* (Berlin: Springer, 1965), p. 68. Between 1850 and 1913 textile production grew at the annual rate of 3 percent, a figure that lagged slightly behind that for German industry overall (3.8 percent). Similarly, the number of employees in the textile, garment, and leather industries increased by a mere 32 percent between 1875 and 1913, while the corresponding percentages for metals were 210, construction trades 208, mining 200, chemicals 162, and paper 120.

16. Alfred Weber, "Die Entwicklungsgrundlagen der großstädtischen Frauenhausindustrie," introduction to *Hausindustrie und Heimarbeit in Deutschland und Österreich*, vol. 2, *Die Hausindustrie der Frauen in Berlin* (Leipzig: Duncker und Humblot, 1899), p. xvi. Also see the more recent studies by Barbara Franzoi, *At the Very Least She Pays the Rent: Women and German Industrialization, 1871–1914* (Westport, Conn.: Greenwood Press, 1985); Rosemarie Beier, *Frauenarbeit und Frauenalltag im deutschen Kaiserreich: Heimarbeiterinnen in der Berliner Bekleidungsindustrie, 1880–1914* (Frankfurt: Campus, 1983).

17. Aubin and Zorn, *Handbuch*, p. 534.

Table 1. Development of individual branches of industry according to numbers of employees (millions), 1800–1913

Branch of industry	1800		1835		1850		1875		1893		1913	
	No.	%	No.	%	No.	%	No.	%	No.	%	No.	%
Metals	170	7.6	250	7.7	333	9.4	751	13.9	1,122	14.3	2,330	20.1
Construction	240	10.4	325	10.0	368	10.3	530	9.8	1,055	13.7	1,630	14.0
Masonry	70	3.1	150	4.6	166	4.7	398	7.3	714	9.4	1,042	8.9
Light metals	20	0.9	30	0.9	37	1.0	83	1.5	129	1.7	217	1.9
Textiles, leather goods	1,170	52.5	1,585	48.7	1,638	46.1	2,048	37.7	2,387	30.9	2,705	23.3
Paper and printing	230	10.3	360	11.1	397	11.2	652	12.0	926	12.0	1,430	12.2
Food and beverages	300	13.4	470	14.5	520	14.6	676	12.5	962	12.5	1,427	12.2
Mining	40	1.8	80	2.5	95	2.7	286	5.3	423	5.5	863	7.4
Total	2,240	100	3,250	100	3,554	100	5,424	100	7,718	100	11,644	100

Source: Adapted from Friedrich W. Henning, Die Industrialisierung in Deutschland, 1800–1914, 5th ed. (Paderborn: F. Schöningh, 1973), pp. 136–37.

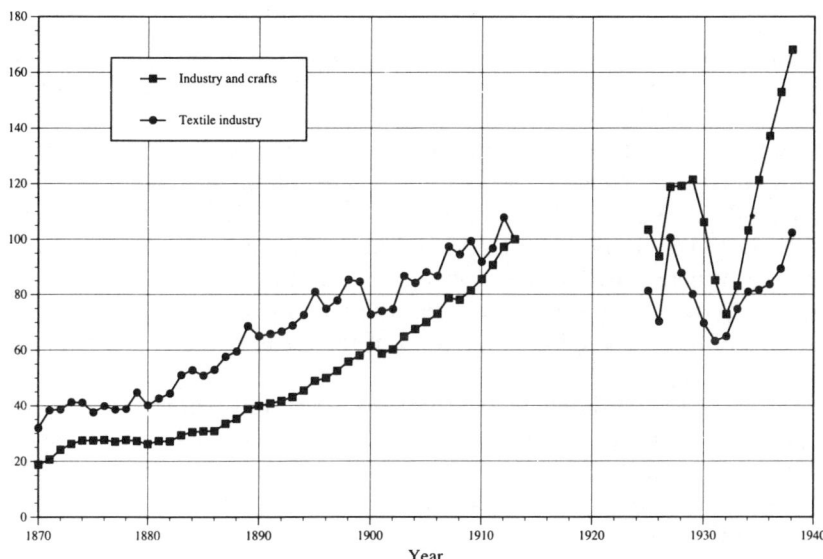

Figure 1. Productivity, 1870–1938 (1913 = 100). Based on tables in Walther G. Hoffmann, *Das Wachstum der deutschen Wirtschaft seit der Mitte des 19. Jahrhunderts* (New York: Springer-Verlag, 1965), pp. 369–70, 391–95.

fig. 1). Although the productivity of all branches of textile production tended to sink during periods of severe national recession, as in the years 1873–78, 1900–1902, and 1907–8, most German textile mills were dependent on a continuous supply of imported raw materials, for example, cotton from the United States and India, silk from southern Europe and Asia, and flax from Russia, Belgium, and Ireland.[18] Furthermore, finished cloth goods were tied into the international market through export, especially to North America. In an industry particularly vulnerable to shifts in the international market, shortages or sudden price hikes of raw materials—often owing to calamitous weather or crop infestation—or the loss or instability of an export market because of recession, war, or new tariff policies often led to overstocked warehouses, abbreviated work hours, or prolonged unemployment for textile workers. Even more capricious, changing tastes in fashion precipitated instant surges in demand for ex-

18. Deutscher Textilarbeiter Verband, *Jahrbuch* 1910 (Berlin: DTAV, 1911), p. 3; Ulrich, "Soziale Entwicklungen," p. 147; Hans Schmidt, *Von Leinen zur Seide: Die Geschichte der Firma Delius und Söhne und das Wirken ihrer Inhaber für die Entwicklung Bielefelds, 1722–1925* (Lemgo: F. L. Wagener, 1926), p. 236; Karl Schürmann, *Die Struktur der deutschen Textilindustrie und ihre Wandlungen in der Nachkriegszeit* (Bonn: Ludwig Röhrscheid, 1933), p. 15. German spinning mills were not able to fulfill the demands of the home market for yarn.

ports or led to longer-term restructuring of an entire branch of textiles to accommodate designers' desire for new fabrics. Complicating industrial patterns of development, cyclical upswings and downturns varied across the branches of textile production even within local economies: for example, whereas the silk weavers of Krefeld in the Rhineland worked overtime during the early 1890s to meet consumer demand for silk cloth, the velvet and plush weavers in the neighboring towns of Viersen, Dülken, and Süchteln faced prolonged idleness because of sluggish demand for their fabrics.[19] Where textile workers were not bound to their communities by ownership of farmland or homesteads, these periodic crises often changed patterns of dispersal and concentration of the textile workforce within local economies.[20]

The expansion of the industrial labor market and its segmentation along gender lines forms an important backdrop for the so-called *Verweiblichung* (feminization) of the textile workforce during the last three decades of the nineteenth century.[21] The pace and pattern of change in the German economy, particularly the changing relation between consumer and capital goods industries between 1870 and 1914, was an important factor in defining male and female sectors of industrial employment and demarcating the boundaries between them.[22] In the course of the accelerated phases of industrial growth between the late 1880s and the First World War, the number of women who worked outside the home increased steadily. Indeed, the female industrial workforce expanded faster than its male counterpart: between 1882 and 1907 the absolute number of full-time female

19. Ulrich, "Soziale Entwicklungen," pp. 303–6.
20. The velvet center of Dülken, for example, experienced an economic downswing during the crisis of the late 1880s and early 1890s, while in the surrounding silk and cotton towns mill owners lamented the shortage of workers and sought to recruit new employees from among the local unemployed.
21. See Hans van der Upwich, *Die Geschichte und die Entwicklung der Rheinischen Samt- und Seidenindustrie* (Krefeld: Kramer und Baum, 1920), p. 172; Brauns, *Der Übergang von der Handweberei*, p. 152; Heinrich Koch, *Die deutsche Hausindustrie* (Mönchen-Gladbach: Verlag des Volksvereins für das Katholische Deutschland, 1905), p. 30; and Barbara Franzoi, "Women and Industrial Work in the German Reich, 1871–1914" (Dissertation, Rutgers University, 1979), pp. 205–6. Men predominated not only in weaving, but also in home textile manufacture overall until about the turn of the century, making up 64 percent of all persons employed in domestic textile production in 1882, 54 percent in 1895, and 41 percent in 1907. See chapter 2 for more specific discussion of gender composition of the home industrial workforce in Rhenish textile villages.
22. Angelika Willms, "Modernisierung durch Frauenarbeit? Zum Zusammenhang von wirtschaftlichem Strukturwandel und weiblicher Arbeitsmarktlage in Deutschland, 1882–1939," in *Historische Arbeitsmarktforschung*, ed. Toni Pierenkämper and Richard Tilly (Göttingen: Vandenhoeck und Ruprecht, 1982), pp. 45, 58; Angelika Willms, "Segregation auf Dauer? Zur Entwicklung des Verhältnisses von Frauenarbeit und Männerarbeit in Deutschland, 1882–1980," in *Strukturwandel der Frauenarbeit, 1880–1980*, ed. Johann Handl, Walter Müller, and Angelika Willms (Frankfurt am Main: Campus, 1983), pp. 107–81.

employees nearly doubled while the male workforce grew by 39 percent.[23] Between 1882 and 1925, the participation of women relative to that of men rose only moderately, from 29 to 36 percent, in the German workforce overall. Although the relative expansion of women's labor by comparison with men's may appear modest—from 17 percent in 1882 to 25.3 percent in 1925—the absolute number of women employed in industry and crafts rose markedly during the same period, from 1.2 million to 2.9 million.[24]

The segmentation of the industrial labor market created a female sector, based largely in the textile and garment industries, encompassing some 75 percent of female wage earners in industries and crafts in the census years 1882 and 1895. In fact over 50 percent of married female factory workers were employed in the textile industry in 1895.[25] Industries like textiles and garments were "feminized" in a two-pronged process by which the size of their female workforce expanded continuously while the demand for labor in the expanding "men's industries" like mining and machine building, drew male workers away from protoindustrial or textile factory employment. As the female labor market widened and became more diverse between 1895 and 1914, an increasing number of women went to work in the food and beverages, paper, electrical, and optical industries, and the concentration of women in textiles and garments began a gradual decline: by 1907, 68 percent of female wage earners worked in textiles and garments. The next occupational census, taken in 1925, reflected the development of an increasingly complex female labor market in the wake of war, rationalization of industry, and expansion of the commercial and white-

---

23. These figures are for full-time employees (*hauptberuflich Beschäftigte*). Wilhelm Böhmert, "Wandlungen der deutschen Volkswirtschaft, 1882–1907: Ein Blick auf die Ergebnisse der Berufs- und Betriebszählungen," *Arbeiterfreund, Centralverein für das Wohl der Arbeiterklasse* 48 (1910): 24–25. Also see Stefan Bajohr, *Die Hälfte der Fabrik, Geschichte der Frauenarbeit in Deutschland 1914 bis 1945* (Marburg: Arbeiterbewegung und Gesellschaftswissenschaft, 1979), p. 17.

24. Hoffmann, *Growth of Industrial Economies*, pp. 205, 210; Bajohr, *Die Hälfte der Fabrik*, p. 18.

25. "Married women" here denotes married and formerly married women (widows and women who were divorced or separated from husbands). The married female workforce grew by 90 percent, the single female workforce by 78 percent between 1882 and 1907. See Bajohr, *Die Hälfte der Fabrik*, p. 25; Hanns Dorn, "Die Frauenerwerbsarbeit und ihre Aufgaben für die Gesetzgebung," *Archiv für Rechts- und Wirtschaftsphilosophie* 5 (1911–12): 86–87; Rose Otto, *Über die Fabrikarbeit verheirateter Frauen*, Münchener Volkswirtschaftliche Studien, vol. 4 (Stuttgart: Cotta, 1910), pp. 10, 93, 99–101; Helene Simon, *Der Anteil der Frau an der deutschen Industrie nach den Ergebnissen der Berufszählung von 1907*, Schriften des ständigen Ausschusses zur Förderung der Arbeiterinneninteressen, no. 2 (Jena: Gustav Fischer, 1910), p. 7; Ludwig Pohle, "Die Erhebungen der Gewerbeaufsichtsbeamten über die Fabrikarbeit verheirateter Frauen," *Jahrbuch für Gesetzgebung, Verwaltung, und Volkswirtschaft* 25 (1901): 158–61.

collar sectors of employment: although 53 percent of female wage earners still worked in textiles and garments, the number of female white-collar workers had increased steadily, and incursions of women into rationalized industrial sectors like metals had become more frequent.[26]

The inscription of whole sectors of industrial employment with attributes of gender was a complex and historically contingent process, as noted above, for which no single argument regarding technologies, physiological abilities or affinities, or capitalist rationalities suffices. Although all these factors had a significant part in shaping the industrial sexual division of labor, its particular markers were drawn and redrawn in the course of conflicts between employers and workers, rural and urban producers, industry and the state, women and men. How contingent and fluid they were was made clear during the First World War when the departure of millions of male workers for the front turned the prevalent sexual division of labor upside down. The intense effort of state, employers, and labor unions to reestablish those boundaries after the war also underscores the importance of human agency in encoding and enforcing them.

Patterns of Transition: The Shift from Household to Factory Textile Production

During the second half of the nineteenth century textile production in the German states was concentrated in four main geographical regions: the eastern region, including Silesia and the kingdom of Saxony east of the Elbe, centers of flax and linen production; the province and kingdom of Saxony in central Germany, which primarily produced wool and cotton and encompassed two-thirds of the German spindles and looms operating in 1840; the southwestern region, including the woolen- and cotton-producing districts in southern Bavaria and Württemberg as well as the silk industry of Baden; and finally, the northwestern German textile belt encompassing the northern Rhine province and northern Westphalia, in particular the Prussian government districts of Düsseldorf, Aachen, and Münster.[27] Approximately one-fifth of the German textile workforce was employed in this region, which included five distinct textile centers of its

---

26. Willms, "Modernisierung," pp. 45, 58. On the history of women's work in the white-collar sector see Carole Elizabeth Adams, *Women Clerks in Wilhelmine Germany: Issues of Class and Gender* (Cambridge: Cambridge University Press, 1988); on the culture of rationalization in Weimar Germany, see Mary Nolan, *Visions of Modernity: American Business and the Modernization of Germany* (New York: Oxford University Press, 1994).

27. On the geographic regions of textile productions, see Blumberg, *Die deutsche Textilindustrie*, pp. 56–59. See also W. O. Henderson, *The Rise of German Industrial Power, 1834–1914* (Berkeley: University of California Press, 1975), p. 61, and Fritz Knoop, "Der Arbeitsmarkt der bergischen Textilindustrie unter besonderer Berücksichtigung seiner Nachkriegskonjunktur" (Dissertation, Universität Münster, 1928), pp. 15–16.

own, three of them west of the Rhine River: Aachen's woolen cloth industry; Krefeld's silk and velvet industry; and the cotton spinning and weaving industries of Mönchen-Gladbach, Rheydt, and surrounding towns.[28] In the Wupper Valley, east of the Rhine, specialty textile production of ribbon, lace, trim, and braided articles predominated, next to clusters of woolen and silk cloth production. Finally, the Westphalian cotton industry, dispersed throughout the small towns around Münster, and the eastern Westphalian linen industry, concentrated in and around the city of Bielefeld in the government district of Minden, formed additional textile centers in the northwestern textile region. Unlike Saxony and Thuringia, where handweaving remained vital, in the Rhineland and Westphalia most branches of textile production had become highly mechanized by 1875.[29] Moreover, nearly all the main branches of the textile industry were represented within this northwestern region, and the manufacture of yarn, ribbon, or cloth continued to occupy a formative place in the changing industrial terrains of these textile cities and towns even as their economies became increasingly diverse and the pace of industrial growth quickened.[30]

In the early nineteenth century the term "textile industry" was nearly synonymous with linen production, in which 55 percent of all textile workers and 70 percent of all looms were employed. At midcentury textile production still represented "the most important economic activity in Germany apart from agriculture" in terms of units of production, number of employees, and share in exports.[31] Most German textile goods were still manufactured in preindustrial or protoindustrial workshops, organized by merchants in the putting-out system and crafted by home weavers, spinners, or shearers. In most textile centers of the Rhineland the economic structure and social organization of preindustrial textile manufacture was shaped by the agricultural economy it emerged from and that it continued to supplement.[32] Flax spinning and linen weaving were the main textile

28. See Max Schlenker, "Die verarbeitenden Industrien," in *Wirtschaftskunde für Rheinland und Westfalen*, ed. Bruno Kuske, Otto Most, and Heinrich Weber (Berlin: Reimar Hobbing, 1931), p. 511. The Rhenish textile industry employed 54 percent of all silk workers in Germany, 53 percent of ribbon, lace, and braid workers, and 23 percent of cotton workers.

29. One-fifth of the spindles and 16.5 percent of the looms operating in Germany in 1875 were in the Rhineland and Westphalia. See Blumberg, *Die deutsche Textilindustrie*, pp. 58, 61.

30. Bernhard Ordemann, "Der westdeutsche Arbeitsmarkt," in Kuske, Most, and Weber, *Wirtschaftskunde*, p. 208; Gerhard Adelmann, "Das ländliche Textilgewerbe des Rheinlandes vor der Industrialisierung," *Rheinische Vierteljahresblätter* 43 (1979): 263–65.

31. Henderson, *Rise of German Industrial Power*, pp. 60, 143. Another 20 percent of textile workers were employed in the woolen industry, 10 percent in the cotton industry, and 5 percent in the silk industry. See Aubin and Zorn, *Handbuch*, p. 378; Hermann Kellenbenz, *Deutsche Wirtschaftsgeschichte*, vol. 2 (Munich: Beck, 1981), p. 88.

32. Protoindustrialization generally refers to rural regions in which a large part of the population has been drawn into industrial mass production for the interregional and interna-

branches in the Rhineland during the eighteenth century, and both were closely tied to flax cultivation in the flatlands of the Lower Rhine. Traditions of craft- and guild-dominated textile production existed in only a few cities, such as Cologne, Aachen, Lennep, and to some extent Elberfeld. Guilds, where they had formally existed, had been disbanded by the French during the Napoleonic occupation of the Rhineland, and thus their influence had eroded significantly by the onset of mechanization.[33] During the late eighteenth century merchants had become crucial in organizing the economy of protoindustrial linen production, the rhythm of supply and demand, the circulation of raw materials to spinners and weavers, and the distribution of their finished products on the rapidly expanding national and international markets. As the demand for textile goods grew, merchants in search of home spinners and weavers stimulated rural textile production across the Rhenish countryside, drawing it ever further into the national and international economies and defining new divisions of labor between urban and rural producers. In Krefeld, for example, handweaving of silk cloth remained a preserve of the city center, while home weavers in the surrounding villages gained a monopoly on the production of velvet ribbons. The frequently simultaneous expansion of urban and rural textiles meant that rural clusters of textile manufacture often formed cohesive zones of textile manufacture surrounding an urban textile center and were bound to one another and to the center through an intricate division of labor.[34]

The disruption of international trade and loss of foreign markets during the Napoleonic Wars caused a severe crisis in German linen production, and by the mid-nineteenth century its golden age as Prussia's most important export industry and source of foreign currency had passed. As technological innovations transformed the British linen and cotton trades, handspun and handwoven German products were unable to compete on the international market with the greater quantities of goods produced on power looms at lower cost. Located within a protoindustrial economy of subsistence rather than profit, linen production in the German states was

---

tional markets through the putting-out system. The implication here is that the *Verlagssystem* was not part of the old social formation of feudal agrarian society but instead had an important role in the genesis of capitalism. See Peter Kriedte, Hans Medick, and Jürgen Schlumbohm, *Industrialization before Industrialization: Rural Industry in the Genesis of Capitalism* (Cambridge: Cambridge University Press, 1981), pp. 6–7, and for more recent discussion, Peter Kriedte, Hans Medick, and Jürgen Schlumbohm, "Proto-industrialization Revisited: Demography, Social Structure, and Modern Domestic Industry," *Continuity and Change* 8, no. 2 (1993): 217–52.

33. Adelmann, "Das ländliche Textilgewerbe," pp. 269–70.

34. Ibid., pp. 268–69, 272, and Peter Kriedte, "Proto-Industrialisierung und grosses Kapital: Das Seidengewerbe in Krefeld und seinem Umland bis zum Ende des Ancien Regime," *Archiv für Sozialgeschichte* 22 (1983): 263–65.

Table 2. Percentage of textile production by individual branches, 1861–1907 (%)

Year	Cotton	Wool	Linen	Silk
1861	29.8	39.4	20.8	10.0
1875	37.8	34.0	18.2	10.0
1882	38.5	35.2	15.0	11.2
1907	46.0	35.1	8.9	10.0

Source: Hermann Aubin and Wolfgang Zorn, eds., *Handbuch der deutschen Wirtschafts- und Sozialgeschichte*, vol. 2 (Stuttgart: Klett Cotta, 1976), p. 553.

slow to mechanize, becoming "the lame duck of the German textile industry in the nineteenth century."[35] By the late 1840s linen production was fraught with chronic underemployment and declining wages for home weavers and flax spinners, whose sufferings received great public attention in the debates about pauperism, the social question of the "hungry 1840s."

In the meantime, however, cotton production came to usurp linen's predominant position within textiles during the 1840s. The first German industry to mechanize on a large scale and to organize production along centralized factory lines, cotton soon employed a larger workforce than linen and quickly garnered greater profits as well. By 1907 cotton goods accounted for nearly half of textile production[36] (see table 2). Whereas the production of cotton nearly doubled between 1895 and 1914, the woolen industry showed more modest growth, representing some 35 to 40 percent of textile production continuously from the early 1860s through the census of 1907. The silk industry, an arena rife with gender conflict during the 1880s and 1890s, also maintained a steady 10 percent share during these years.[37]

Although widely divergent in terms of the prerequisites and the social consequences of industrialization across regions and branches of textile production, the transition from home to factory industry can be usefully analyzed as a series of interrelated developments that occurred in most textile regions of Germany at different times from the 1820s through the 1890s: (1) replacement of individual tools by a mechanical system (as in wool spinning, where both the preparatory tasks and the spinning itself were mechanized concurrently); (2) differentiation of production into a

35. Henderson, *Rise of German Industrial Power*, pp. 63, 146–47.
36. Aubin and Zorn, *Handbuch*, pp. 331, 553. See table 2.
37. Aubin and Zorn, *Handbuch*, pp. 553–54; Walther G. Hoffmann, "Die Textilindustrie im Wachstumsprozess der Volkswirtschaft," in *Textilwirtschaft im Strukturwandel* (Tübingen: J. C. B. Mohr, 1966), p. 10; Kellenbenz, *Deutsche Wirtschaftsgeschichte*, p. 264.

series of separate tasks, or the emergence of a new division of labor that corresponded to this mechanical system; (3) mobilization of a workforce with adequate skills or one that could quickly become familiar with the raw material or technical process; (4) introduction of technology, especially mechanization of the power supply (steam, gas, or electrical power) and eventually an increase in the speed, efficiency, and productive capacity of the mechanical system; (5) removal of textile production from the clusters of home workshops in textile towns and villages across Germany and its relocation to centralized factories.[38] Unable to compete with the vastly more productive mechanical spindles or looms, master weavers and other producers in home industry suffered erosion of wages, undermining of craft skills, and finally marginalization, unemployment, or acquiescence to a new life and work identity in the mill "penitentiary."

In the case of spinning, centralization usually preceded the implementation of mechanized tools, so workers continued to spin yarn by hand or work partially mechanized mules in the first spinning manufactories. The first fully mechanized cotton spinning mills were founded in the Rhineland and Westphalia about 1840, and by 1870 the branches of cotton, flax, and woolen spinning had been fully mechanized.[39] The expanded efficiency and productivity of the spinning operation, including the steady and reliable supply of yarn, provided the key impetus for the mechanization of weaving. Weaving, however, generally followed a more protracted path of modernization than spinning, for home weavers and handlooms often continued to resist the intrusion of the new machines for ten to twenty years after the founding of the first mechanized weaving mills. Domestic textile production had a longer life in small textile towns and villages that were not integrated into railway networks and did not readily attract entrepreneurs to locate new factories there. Once factories were founded, however, home weaving survived only as long as it could complement and supplement factory weaving by producing specialty cloth that could not be woven mechanically, such as Jacquard or other types of patterned fabrics. By contrast with spinning, which in many regions passed through a "manufactory stage" of centralized but nonmechanical production, here the dual processes of mechanization and centralization generally occurred simultaneously. Most weaving factories also modernized preparatory and finishing tasks like reeling, winding, and dyeing, consolidating them into one enterprise along with spinning or weaving. As in spinning, the mechanization of cotton weaving preceded that of linen, woolen, velvet, or silk.

Notable exceptions to this general pattern of industrialization could be

---

38. George Jahn, "Die Entstehung der Fabrik," *Schmollers Jahrbuch für Gesetzgebung, Verwaltung und Volkswirtschaft* 69, no. 1 (1949): 89–116; 69, no. 2 (1949): 65–100; Schürmann, *Die Struktur der deutschen Textilindustrie*, p. 61.

39. Silk yarn is not included here because it was generally imported.

found in the continued reliance of many factories on home industrial workers for certain preparatory or finishing tasks, like the female nappers and darners who worked in their homes for the woolen mills of Lennep and Aachen well into the twentieth century. Domestic production of certain intricate types of fabric and specialty goods like ribbon and silk neckties, an enclave of women's work in Krefeld, flourished until the eve of the First World War, and in some branches domestic manufacture continued to thrive alongside factory production.[40] Similarly, the branches of ribbon, lace, and braid weaving, which were concentrated in the Wupper Valley, remained an outpost of home industry until the war, utilizing the most modern of machines, the small electric motor, to power mechanical ribbon frames and centralizing work not in factories but in *Mietfabriken* (cooperative workshops) where weavers paid rent for space and electricity and set up their own looms.[41] Indeed, the ribbon weavers of the Wupper Valley are an excellent example of Sabel and Zeitlin's "alternatives to mass production," that is, a "system that reverses the principles of mass production," flexibly utilizing both machines and skilled labor "to make an ever-changing assortment of semi-customized products."[42]

Feminization as Structural Transformation

In 1875 some 400,000 German textile mills and shops—including small household workshops—provided a livelihood for approximately 900,000 people, only one-third of them female. In an exemplary case of feminization, women came to compose nearly half of the textile workforce by 1907 and superseded men in many textile-producing regions by 1913, as table 3

---

40. For glimpses into the coexistence of domestic and factory production in the Lower Rhine see, for example, Nordrhein-Westfälisches Hauptstaatsarchiv (HStAD), Regierung Düsseldorf (Reg. Düss.), Handel und Gewerbe (H&G) 24751, "Bericht des Gewerbeinspektors Crefeld (Landkreis und Stadt) vom 11.7.1913 bezüglich des Hausarbeitsgesetz," which indicates that there were 1,748 home workers employed in the manufacture of silk ties in Krefeld in 1913, nearly all female. Also see Kreisarchiv Viersen (KrA Vie), Gemeindeamt (GA) Lobberich, 1820, "Brief von de Ball, Lobberich vom 19.12.1884 an den Bürgermeister," which reports that in 1884 the company employed 161 winders in home industry and 97 factory winders, 57 shearers in home industry, and 30 factory shearers.

41. On the persistence of home industrial production in Krefeld, see HStAD, Reg. Düss., H&G 24751, "Bericht des Gewerbeinspektors des Landkreises und der Stadt Crefeld vom 11.7.1913"; on the particularities of ribbon production in the Wupper Valley, see Horst Heidermann, *Die Hausindustrie in der Bergischen Bandweberei* (Göttingen: Otto Schwartz, 1960), pp. 31–32. According to Heidermann, in 1913 some 8,000 mechanical looms were operating in weavers' households, and there were another 3,000 *Riemengänge* or ribbon looms in centralized shops.

42. Charles Sabel and Jonathan Zeitlin, "Historical Alternatives to Mass Production: Politics, Markets and Technology in Nineteenth-Century Industrialization," *Past and Present* 108 (1985): 133–34.

Table 3. The textile workforce, 1882–1925

	German Reich			Prussia			Rhine Province			Government District Düsseldorf (Prussia)		
	Men	Women	Total	Men	Women	Total	Men	Women	Total	Men	Women	Total
1882												
N	527,079	323,780	850,859									
%	61.9	38.1										
Growth												
1895												
N	517,230	427,961	945,191	125,210	120,492	245,702				50,880	40,846	91,366
%	54.7	45.3		51.0	49.0					55.7	44.3	
Growth	−1.9%	32.2%	11.1%									
1907												
N	529,008	528,235	1,057,243	234,867	210,585	445,452	101,282	73,425	174,707			
%	50.0	50.0		52.7	47.3		58.0	42.0				
Growth	2.3%	23.4%	11.9%	87.6%	74.8%	81.3%						
1913												
N				199,058	205,120	404,178				60,852	62,992	123,844
%				49.3	50.7					49.1	50.9	
Growth				−15.2%	−2.6%	−9.3%				19.6%	55.6%	35.5%
1925												
N	514,858	681,262	1,196,120	229,012	245,471	474,483	88,205	78,915	167,120			
%	43.0	57.0		48.3	51.7		52.8	47.2				
Growth	−2.7%	29.0%	13.1%	15.0%	19.7%	17.4%	−12.9%	7.5%	−4.3%			

Sources: Wilhem Bochmert, "Wandlungen der deutschen Volkswirtschaft, 1888–1907: Ergebnisse der Berufs- und Bertriebszählungen," *Arbeiterfreund* 48 (1910): 24–25, 136; George Neuhaus, "Die berufliche und soziale Gliederung im Zeitalter des Kapitalismus," in *Grundriss der Sozialökonomik* (Tübingen: J. C. B. Mohr, 1914), 9: 399, 424–25.

illustrates. As textile mills grew in size and efficiency between 1882 and 1907, the number of female employees increased by 63 percent while the male workforce stagnated, growing only 0.03 percent during this quarter century. According to the national census figures for 1907 and 1925, the number of female textile workers continued to increase after the First World War, growing by 29 percent during this period while men's employment declined by 2.3 percent. A recurrent shortage of male workers was one important factor in this process of feminization.[43] Other factors that explain the discrepant patterns of male and female employment include the lower wages paid to women and the steadily rising cost of living, which made it impossible for working-class families to subsist on one member's earnings. Finally, the norms and ideologies that led employers to ascribe femine attributes to certain textile jobs underpinned this gender-specific segmentation of the industrial labor market during the rapid expansion of German industry.[44]

The trend toward feminization was pervasive in each of the four textile regions, but its pace and intensity varied depending on the exigencies of local and regional labor markets and the division of labor in each region's largest branches of production. In the Rhineland and Westphalia it went hand in hand with the booming growth of heavy industry, which absorbed an increasing number of male workers.[45] Iron and coal represented the backbone of this region's economy in every sense, including their steadily expanding share in the industrial labor market after 1882. Male textile workers constituted one source of labor for the enlarged mines and for iron, steel, and metal plants, especially in textile towns that bordered on centers of heavy industry, like Langenberg and Neviges on the periphery of Elberfeld and Barmen, or in the small towns outside Aachen. In cities with more diverse industrial landscapes, like Bielefeld, women textile

---

43. See, for example, HStAD, Reg. Düss., H&G Jahresberichte der Königlichen Preussischen Gewerberäthe (hereafter JBdKPG) 1898: Aachen, p. 397; 1907: Münster, pp. 304–5; and Cologne, pp. 449–50; 1912: Aachen, pp. 608–9. Of particular interest are the reports compiled by the inspectors in 1908 on the shortages of male and female labor and the degree of displacement of men by women: JBdKPG 1908: Münster, p. 302; Minden, p. 316; Düsseldorf, pp. 402–3; Cologne, pp. 431–32; Aachen, p. 474. Also see Simon, *Der Anteil der Frau*, pp. 58–60, and Lilly Nielsen, "Die Verdrängung von Männerarbeit durch Frauenarbeit in der Industrie" (Dissertation, Universität Bonn, 1920), p. 37.

44. According to Simon, *Der Anteil*, pp. 58–60, "the particular capacity of the woman for certain tasks" was one of the five crucial factors in the expansion of women's factory employment.

45. Bruno Kuske, "Rheinisch-Westfälische Wirtschaftsgeschichte seit Anfang des 19. Jahrhunderts," in Kuske, Most, and Weber, *Wirtschaftskunde*, p. 102. In 1882, 20.4 percent of industrial workers in the Rhineland were employed in the textile industry; by 1907 this figure had declined to 12.3 percent and by 1925 to 10.1 percent, while the metal industry's share increased from 17.4 percent in 1882 to 33.3 percent in 1925.

workers replaced men as they left for jobs in the metal and machine industries, which offered higher pay and status. Census figures confirm the process of labor market segmentation by gender: female employment in the Rhineland and Westphalia increased considerably faster than the national growth of 39.5 percent between 1907 and 1925. While the overall size of the workforce in the Rhineland grew by 34 percent, the numbers of women working increased by 47 percent. The figures for Westphalia are even more striking: the female workforce expanded by 66 percent, while the numbers of wage earners in industry and crafts grew 43.4 percent between 1907 and 1925.[46]

Feminization as a Language of Protest

As contemporaries deployed the term, "feminization" encompassed several entwined processes. In its simplest sense, it denoted the infiltration of women into previously male arenas of paid employment and was thus usually paired with, or even coterminous with, the subsidiary process of *Verdrängung*, the displacement of men from their jobs by the incursion of women workers. In the rhetoric of those who protested against female factory labor, both terms became signifiers of the horrors of the industrial state, which galvanized public opinion because they evoked dramatic visions of the destruction of household economies and families. Weaving, widely perceived and publicly represented as a male craft, especially in regions like Aachen with urban guild traditions, came to symbolize feminization and its particular outcome, the fierce competition between the sexes for employment.[47] For social reformers Robert Wilbrandt and Heinrich Brauns, who helped publicize the plight of the male weavers in the arenas of left-liberal social reform, the weavers had become an emblem "of the problem of female competition in capitalism, if not for the general situation of the proletariat."[48] The frequent strikes of male weavers against the hiring of women and the tenacious battles of the weavers' *Innungen*—a short-lived and voluntary form of guild that was revived in some Rhenish textile regions during the early 1880s—against women's work in both home weaving and the newly mechanized mills, effaced the lifelong labor of women in weaving households across the Rhineland. As the examination of the velvet and silk regions of the Lower Rhine in chapter 2 illustrates, women had an

46. Otto Most, "Die wirtschaftliche und soziale Gliederung nach den Ergebnissen der Berufs- und Betriebszählungen," in Kuske, Most, and Weber, *Wirtschaftskunde*, p. 160.
47. See, for example, the exemplary texts by Robert Wilbrandt, *Die Weber in der Gegenwart* and *Die Frauenarbeit*.
48. Wilbrandt, *Die Weber in der Gegenwart*, p. 1; also see Brauns, *Der Übergang von der Handweberei*, p. 240.

indispensable place in protoindustrial weaving households, not only in preparatory and finishing tasks, but also as skilled weavers who often worked their own looms and helped train journeymen and apprentices.

To contemporaries, feminization had many faces: to those master weavers whose desperate material circumstances propelled them into the forbidding mills, it came to signify the confrontation with a "heretofore unfamiliar adversary"—the weavers' own wives and daughters, who had been unable to work the broadlooms in home production but whose "dexterity at the mechanical loom, especially for the piecing together of the broken threads, [was] in high demand."[49] The new technologies of production and the redefinition of skill that accompanied the deployment of female labor broke two crucial monopolies of male handweavers—skill and physical strength—which had been essential in the weaving of particularly heavy and wide types of cloth.[50] Feminization therefore signified the confrontation of male weavers with female competition, not only from within their own families, but also, depending on the regional industrial landscape, from the daughters of miners, servants, bakers, or carpenters from the outlying villages and towns. The influx of *Fremde*, strangers to town and craft, was controversial as well, for unlike the weavers' daughters or wives, the new workers were unfamiliar with the traditions, customs, and skills of cloth weaving.[51] Although the new factories could absorb only a fraction of the handweavers left unemployed by the transition to factory industry, those who did find work in the new mills now faced an unprecedented and profound transformation, as captured by Wilbrandt: "For when at last the handweaver, who has long wished, helplessly, to advance to the job of factory weaver, is introduced . . . to its technological wonders, he is transformed from a master into a hired hand [*Handlanger*], from a man into a maiden."[52]

To others feminization meant the loss of a way of life, including the erosion of family and community. Alfons Thun became an eyewitness to this transition on his journeys through the textile districts of the Lower Rhine in the late 1870s. His impressions, recorded in his study on the industry of the Lower Rhine, found wide dissemination in the circles of bourgeois social reformers from the late 1870s through the early 1890s. In his monograph of 1879 he reported that, as a result of the transition from home to factory industry,

49. Thun, *Die Industrie am Niederrhein*, p. 28.
50. Wilbrandt, *Die Weber in der Gegenwart*, p. 24.
51. Thun, *Die Industrie am Niederrhein*, pp. 63, 173; van der Upwich, *Die Geschichte und die Entwicklung*, p. 115.
52. Wilbrandt, *Die Weber in der Gegenwart*, p. 31; also see Brauns, *Der Übergang von der Handweberei*, pp. 88–90.

the old masters, who lived in the country, found themselves expropriated without compensation and had to leave their native soil; the holy bonds of marriage have been loosened; young girls have been taken from their homes, children from their parents; the health of the population has been attacked in a most deadly fashion, and the spiritual development of the people has been thoroughly thwarted. The girls who were to become mothers of German men, the children we once thought would grow up to thrive, have been made into cripples, have become dull and untamed.[53]

Indeed, as both Thun and Wilbrandt pointed out, the *Verweiblichung* of the textile factory workforce was often accompanied by a parallel process, *Entweiblichung* (defeminization), in handweavers' communities across the Rhineland as the newly mechanized mills drew the young girls out of the households while the men remained home at the handlooms.[54]

In the weavers' campaigns against feminization the wage was the key mechanism of displacement as the family or household wage, paid to home industrial producers for the products of the family's collective labor, was gradually replaced by the gender-encoded wages of the *Familienväter* (family fathers or male breadwinners) and the *Frauenlohn* (women's wage). Although a pronounced discrepancy of 30 to 40 percent existed between men's and women's wages from the outset of factory textile production, contemporaries, contending with the fact that female workers now earned an independent wage, asserted polemically that young girls earned as much as or even more than the "family fathers" in the mechanized mills. Certainly the lower wages paid to the first generation of textile mill workers, comprising large numbers of women and children, helped both to fuel the industry's growth and to preempt the absorption of many skilled male handweavers into the mills. As Wilbrandt noted, "The textile industry was the first factory industry in the world to throw the male workers, who became superfluous time and time again, into the streets," not only because mechanical looms broke their monopolies on skill and physical strength, but also because their labor had become too costly by comparison with that of women, youths, and children.[55]

Thus feminization represents both a set of rhetorical strategies and a structural transformation of the technologies and relations of production. This view of feminization helps to distinguish the moments of change

53. Thun, *Die Industrie am Niederrhein*, p. 178.
54. Wilbrandt, *Die Weber in der Gegenwart*, p. 39. Wilbrandt also charts the opposite development: in villages without factories nearby, he found that the young girls remained at the handlooms in their parents' household, whereas their brothers left home to take factory jobs in faraway towns.
55. Wilbrandt, *Die Weber in der Gegenwart*, p. 124.

from those of continuity in the history of the transition from home to factory textile production. The outcry against feminization by labor leaders, social reformers, and state officials both obscured the long traditions of women's work in protoindustrial textile households and effaced the distinctions between regional labor markets, thereby generalizing the discrepant origins and consequences of the expansion of female factory labor in each. Although it provided labor leaders and social reformers with powerful rhetorical tools to critique the transition from agrarian to industrial state, the feminization of production was not a uniform process even within one region or one branch of textile production. The next chapter explores four distinct settings in which feminization occurred during the second half of the nineteenth century in the Rhineland and Westphalia, producing disparate, even discordant, images from the stories of the transition from home to factory.

2

"The Man Transformed into a Maiden"? Feminization in the Textile Industries of the Rhineland and Westphalia

One of the most visible and controversial features of the transition from home to factory textile production was the steady stream of female workers, single and married, into the newly mechanized mills. The case studies presented here include four branches of textiles in the Lower Rhine and Westphalia in which feminization figured centrally. These abbreviated case studies analyze the divergent ways gender figured as what Sonya Rose calls a "determining factor in the structuring of employment opportunities from the very start of the transformation to modern industrial organization." They also underscore the importance of "noneconomic" factors, of ideological conceptions of gender and proper work for men and women, in shaping the structure of textile production, especially as its female workforce expanded between 1870 and 1914.[1] The juxtaposition of the four cases makes clear the difficulty of discerning a pattern of feminization in the German textile industry that can be generalized across regions, branches, and historical periods. Rather than being seen as comprehensive histories or representative paradigms, these case studies of the role of gender in the transition from household to factory weaving in the cotton towns of Mönchen-Gladbach, the wool-producing region of Aachen, the linen mills of the Westphalian city of Bielefeld, and the silk and velvet regions of Krefeld and Kempen should be viewed as a series of historical snapshots, each capturing distinct images of gender, of the terrains of conflict between men and women in the course of this transition. The array of images from the Rhineland—the sexual dangers associated with the spinning girls of

1. Sonya O. Rose, "'Gender at Work': Sex, Class, and Industrial Capitalism," *History Workshop* 21 (spring 1986): 119.

the cotton towns, the citizen-workers displaced from their looms in the woolen districts, the men transformed into maidens as married women went to work in the silk and velvet villages of the Lower Rhine—contrast with the feminization of linen production in Bielefeld, where the adaptability and vitality of the local labor market made textile labor undesirable, "unfit" for men.

These case studies, based on close readings and comparisons of archival documents, secondary histories, and local and company histories, also reveal how historical legends are constructed and reproduced, weaving a thread of continuity and concordance from monographs and local histories of the nineteenth and early twentieth centuries through more recent historical studies of regional and local industrialization. The separation of home and work, for example, a central myth as well as a criterion for the onset of modernization in many German histories of industrialization and class formation, has seldom been studied from the perspective of those who negotiated the boundaries between these spheres in their daily lives. Parallel to this myth is the standard depiction of the transition from home to factory industry as a profound disruption not only of the industrial order, but also of the sexual order, a view that rests on the generally unexamined assumption that domestic weaving was a male sphere of production and that women had at best a subsidiary role within protoindustrial household production. These historical narratives, in which feminization of the factory and defeminization of the household figure as two aspects of the same process, are enormously difficult to dissect or refute because of the paucity of archival evidence (in all but one case study here). Thus the examination of these disparate images serves as a kind of archaeological dig—a search for the origins of the myths surrounding women's work, for the "realities" behind the rhetorics of transition, for the structural transformations that underpinned and gave rise to the discourses about female factory labor during the late nineteenth century. In that sense this inquiry is also a genealogy of these discourses, an exploration of the origins of the images and oppositions—between male *Weberstamm* (core workforce of weavers) and single spinning girls, male breadwinners and female "wage cutters"—that both underpinned and lent coherence to the discourses of state and social reformers about female factory labor.

Weberstamm and Spinning Girls: The Cotton Industry of Mönchen-Gladbach

The transition to factory industry began in the cotton branch with the founding in 1784 of the first spinning mill on the continent, J. G. Brügelmann's Cromford mill, in Ratingen near Düsseldorf.[2] Inspired by Cromford's success and by the availability of the partially mechanical water mule, a series of new cotton mills were founded across the Rhineland in the following two decades, most in the Wupper Valley. The locus of cotton production shifted permanently from its place of origin, the Wupper Valley, to the left banks of the Rhine (also known as the Lower Rhine) during the Napoleonic occupation of the Rhineland. Cotton production on the left banks of the Rhine expanded rapidly in the *Treibhausatmosphäre* (hothouse atmosphere) of the French-dominated zones of free trade, soon supplanting not only the local linen industry, but also cotton production in the Wupper Valley, which was hindered in its growth by the newly imposed French customs borders at the Rhine.[3] Between 1800 and 1812 the number of spinning manufactories in the Lower Rhine (in which production was centralized but not fully mechanized) increased fourfold (from nine to thirty-seven), while seven of the fifteen spinning mills in the Wupper Valley closed their gates.[4] The wide-scale mechanization of cotton spinning took place in the Rhineland between 1835 and the mid-1860s, when the self-acting mule had come to replace nearly all hand mules, marking the definitive triumph of the fully mechanized spinning mill.[5] In contrast to the weaving sector, where thousands of handweavers were displaced by mechanical looms, cotton spinning had been primarily a manufactory industry rather than a vital sphere of domestic production. Because few hand spinners were displaced by the new machines in the Rhineland, this transition appears to have provoked little resistance from cotton spinners or their assistants.[6]

The increasing productivity of the cotton spinning branch soon unleashed a parallel process in weaving as Rhenish cotton entrepreneurs in-

2. See Stadtmuseum Ratingen, *Die Macht der Maschine: 200 Jahre Cromford-Ratingen: Eine Ausstellung zur Frühzeit des Fabrikwesens* (Ratingen, 1984), p. 181; Franz Josef Gemmert, *Die Entwicklung der ältesten kontinentalen Spinnerei: Eine betriebswirtschaftlich-historische Untersuchung* (Leipzig: Dr. Jänecke Verlagsbuchhandlung, 1927).

3. Karl Emsbach, *Die soziale Betriebsverfassung der rheinischen Baumwollindustrie im 19. Jahrhundert* (Bonn: Ludwig Röhrscheid, 1982), pp. 28, 30, 75.

4. Emsbach, *Die soziale Betriebsverfassung*, p. 43. The only cotton spinning mill that survived in the Wupper Valley after 1860 was J. G. Brügelmann in Ratingen.

5. The self-acting mule predominated in German cotton mills even after the invention in the 1830s of the more advanced ring-spinning machine, which was not widely used in Germany until the end of the nineteenth century. Stadtmuseum Ratingen, *Die Macht der Maschine*, p. 181; Emsbach, *Die soziale Betriebsverfassung*, pp. 286–87; Walter English, *The Textile Industry: An Account of the Early Inventions of Spinning, Weaving, and Knitting Machines* (London: Longmans, 1969), pp. 173–78.

6. Horst Blumberg, *Die deutsche Textilindustrie in der industriellen Revolution* (Berlin: Akademie, 1965), p. 20; Peter Borscheid, *Textilarbeiterschaft in der Industrialisierung: Soziale Lage und Mobilität in Württemberg* (Stuttgart: Klett Cotta, 1978), pp. 53, 69.

troduced large numbers of mechanical looms in centralized factories between 1860 and 1880.[7] Cotton weaving, like spinning, was highly concentrated in the government districts of Düsseldorf in the Rhineland: the cities of Mönchen-Gladbach and Rheydt, Kempen, and Grevenbroich in the Lower Rhine, and the fifteen kilometers of rural cotton outposts that connected them constituted the largest concentration of cotton production in Prussia.[8] Indeed, the industrialization of cotton weaving, more than that of spinning, transformed the architectural and social topography of these cities and towns not only through the construction of new industrial buildings, but also through the migration of thousands of unemployed local home weavers, as well as recruits from other regions, to fill the demand for labor in the cotton towns.[9]

In contrast to hand spinning, preindustrial cotton weaving had been a flourishing home industry in the Lower Rhine.[10] Cotton home weaving was organized as a *Verlagssystem* (putting-out system) by which merchants usually delivered yarn spools and often supplied tools to weavers who worked on one or two looms in their homes.[11] Lacking a guild tradition, cotton weavers in the Rhineland were apparently not steeped in the rich and complex customs of *Handwerk* (craft), nor did a system of formal craft training or apprenticeship prevail. Skill was transmitted informally, passed on from father to son—and in the absence of sons, presumably to daughters—within the household economies. Indeed, cotton home weavers appear to have employed or trained few journeymen or assistants and relied instead on members of family or nearby relatives as a source of labor.[12] An industrial survey of 1841 for the city of Rheydt shows that both women and children formed part of a vital labor force in the domestic cotton workshops: of the 5,694 total employed persons, 1,661 (29 percent) were adult women, and children likely composed another third.[13]

Social and economic dislocation did not follow immediately upon the introduction of mechanical looms into Rhenish cotton production. Rather, the handweavers experienced a gradual decline of their trade. Dur-

7. Emsbach, *Die soziale Betriebsverfassung*, p. 67. Spinning mill owners, who now had a larger supply of yarn to sell, were first to experiment with mechanical looms in the 1840s.

8. Friedrich O. Dilthey, *Die Geschichte der niederrheinischen Baumwollindustrie* (Jena: Gustav Fischer, 1908), pp. 1–3; Emsbach, *Die soziale Betriebsverfassung*, pp. 379, 384. Of the 119 cotton weaving mills in the Rhine province in 1909, only 6 were outside this district.

9. Emsbach, *Die soziale Betriebsverfassung*, p. 390.

10. See ibid., pp. 103–7, for charts of home weavers' residences across the Lower Rhine.

11. Ibid., pp. 77, 213. Emsbach points out that weavers in rural areas, for whom weaving was supplementary to farming, usually had one loom in their households, whereas urban cotton weavers usually had two looms.

12. Ibid., p. 219.

13. Ibid., p. 258. Emsbach estimates that children consistently made up approximately one-third of the cotton home industrial workforce during the 1840s.

ing the two decades between 1860 and 1880, domestic handweaving saw a brief upswing, as the increasing productivity of cotton spinning and the ready availability of cotton yarn briefly injected it with new life. In 1861 there were 5,250 cotton handlooms and 1,200 mechanical looms in operation in the textile district of Mönchen-Gladbach, but by 1880 the relation between the two types of production had been reversed: the remaining 1,000 handlooms could scarcely compete against the 7,000 highly productive mechanical looms.[14] By 1894 a government inquiry found no cotton home weavers in the city of Mönchen-Gladbach, and the chamber of commerce of Wesel reported a similar transition in the cotton town of Bocholt:

> Handweaving, which once flourished in our district, has been fully displaced by mechanical weaving. Only in a few rural districts where life is insufficiently productive does one still meet the rare . . . old people, who take up the handloom only in the winter when no farmwork can be carried out and who use it only to produce coarse cotton. Full-time handweavers who are employed year-round in that capacity no longer exist, for their earnings [on the cloth] have been almost wholly supplanted by the mechanically produced cloth. Most of the younger workers have found work in the nearby factory.[15]

By the turn of the century there were some 16,000 mechanical looms operating in cotton factories in the Gladbach district, denoting a transition more rapid and more final than similar processes in the cotton regions of Saxony and Thuringia.[16] A series of crises—the acute shortage of raw cotton during the middle decade caused by the American Civil War, the economic crises of 1861–65, followed a decade later by the depression of the

---

14. The mechanical looms were purportedly five times as efficient as handlooms. See Emsbach, *Die soziale Betriebsverfassung*, p. 385; Dilthey, *Die Geschichte*, p. 31; Kreisarchiv Viersen (KrA Vie), Gemeindeamt (GA) Lobberich 1820: "Nachweisung betr. die Handweberei am Niederrhein unter Angabe der Bevölkerungszahl, des Flacheninhaltes und der Hauptnahrungszweige der einzelner Bürgermeisterei im Kreise 1880/81."

15. Nordrhein-Westfälisches Hauptstaatsarchiv Düsseldorf (HStAD), Regierung Düsseldorf (Reg. Düss.), Handel und Gewerbe (H&G) 13758, "Schreiben des Mönchen-Gladbacher Oberbürgermeisteramts vom 17.11.1894" and "Schreiben der Handelskammer Wesel an die Königliche Regierung vom 23.5.1894."

16. Emsbach, *Die soziale Betriebsverfassung*, pp. 383–85; Blumberg, *Die deutsche Textilindustrie*, p. 61, and Willy Fränken, *Die Entwicklung des Gewerbes in den Städten Mönchen-Gladbach und Rheydt im 19. Jahrhundert*, Schriften zur Rheinisch-Westfälischen Wirtschaftsgeschichte, vol. 19 (Cologne: Rheinisch-Westfälisches Wirtschaftsarchiv, 1969), p. 79. In 1882, 41.5 percent (52,152) of all persons employed in cotton weaving in Germany worked in home industry. By 1895 this figure had declined to 22.6 percent (33,208). In 1907 only 13.4 percent (21,358) of employees in the cotton weaving branch worked in home industry. See Hans Michel, *Die hausindustrielle Weberei Deutschlands: Entwicklung, Lage, Zukunft* (Jena: Gustav Fischer, 1921), p. 46.

mid-1870s, propelled this transition forward as new technologies were implemented and wages periodically reduced. In most Rhenish districts the foundations of cotton handweaving had been shattered by the mid-1870s, leaving only a few home weavers in control of the production of special patterned cloth that could not yet be manufactured on mechanical looms.[17]

The transition from home to factory production of cotton yarn and cotton cloth also relied on a sizable female workforce, recruited largely but not exclusively from the ranks of home industry. In 1846 women composed 43 percent of the workforce in the Rhineland's first mechanical spinning mills, a figure that by 1858 had increased to 48 percent.[18] Although few strikes or protests by male spinners or weavers against female factory labor are recorded in archival documents, the employment of women in the new spinning mills became controversial in at least one respect. The arrival of significant numbers of young women—as many as five hundred at a time from nearby villages and distant towns, even foreign countries—to fill the demand for labor in the new spinning mills of the Lower Rhine represented a novel phenomenon, a shocking consequence of the new factory system.[19] Mills like the Aktienspinnerei in Mönchen-Gladbach, which employed over 1,000 workers by 1859, or the flax spinning mill in Viersen, founded in 1864, were apparently unable to hire enough workers from the nearby textile communities. Moreover, in the first year or two of operation, the owners of the spinning mills, in need of workers familiar with the mechanical spinning mules, were often compelled to recruit skilled female spinners from England or Ireland to train local workers in mechanized flax or cotton spinning.[20] Thus by 1875 the spinning mills constituted a highly feminized sector of textile employment, with a female workforce some 32 percent larger than its male counterpart. Furthermore, many more female workers—some one-fifth—had come to the Lower Rhenish textile towns from outlying towns and villages in search of employment, in contrast to one-tenth of male workers.[21]

Although this disparate array of female spinning mill employees did not

---

17. Emsbach, *Die soziale Betriebsverfassung*, pp. 384–87, and Alphons Thun, *Die Industrie am Niederrhein und ihre Arbeiter*, Staats- und sozialwissenschaftliche Forschungen, vols. 1 and 2 (Leipzig: Duncker und Humblot, 1879), p. 161.

18. Emsbach, *Die soziale Betriebsverfassung*, p. 326. These figures are for the cotton spinning industry in the government district of Düsseldorf. The increase in female employment likely stemmed less from the displacement of male workers than from the decline in children's employment resulting from the passage of the new child labor law in 1853.

19. Thun, *Die Industrie am Niederrhein*, p. 173.

20. Stadtarchiv Viersen (StA Vie) 7 (018), Dr. P. Norrenberg, "Erster Jahresbericht des katholischen Arbeiterinnen-Vereins in Viersen" (Viersen, 1877), pp. 17–21, 34–35; Emsbach, *Die soziale Betriebsverfassung*, pp. 322, 323.

21. Emsbach, *Die soziale Betriebsverfassung*, p. 521. These figures are for the five textile towns of the Mönchen-Gladbach textile district in 1875.

displace male craftsmen from their jobs, they represented a different danger to local communities and customs, a peril that the newly founded Catholic associations for women workers sought to deflect through moral tutelage and domestic training.[22] For from the specter of "this mass of girls, detached from their families and homes and thrust from rural isolation into the midst of strangers in the city" came the reformers' visions of *Sumpf und Trunk* (gutter and drink), of "complete social and economic decay," of "sexual excesses, of earnings squandered on fashion, dance, games, and alcohol."[23] Thus the young, single female spinners of the Rhenish textile towns became the signifiers of one kind of "horror" of the industrial state, particularly when contrasted with their opposite, the old *Weberstamm* who were deeply embedded in family and local community, "the sober and frugal heads of household who planned ahead for hard times and had acquired a house, a garden, a field."[24] The large and often unruly communities of young female spinners, representing an amalgam of dialects and hometowns including some quite foreign to the Rhineland, figured in the narratives of this transition alternatively as victims and as perpetrators of the transition to the industrial state. Herded into the new dormitories and company housing complexes to be inculcated with moral and domestic values, they became the main object of employers' paternalism and reformers' moralistic zeal. It became imperative, both for the efficient functioning of the mills and for the health and harmony of the social body, that they be tutored and policed by employers and local welfare or charity associations, in which the Catholic and Protestant churches had a significant role.[25] Unable to defend themselves against sexual enticement or the everyday abuses in the mills, from low wages to chronic illness and overwork, the young female spinners came to embody the prototypical single woman worker whose labor and whose organism required the urgent protection of the state. As such, the single mill girls presented a distinctly different threat to the social and sexual order than did married women workers, whose factory employment had allegedly led to neglect of their families' moral and physical well-being. The mill girls, in their purported sexual licentiousness, their fascination with finery and luxury, their entry en masse into public sites of production and reproduction, repre-

22. StA Vie 7 (018), Dr. P. Norrenberg, "Erster Jahresbericht des katholischen Arbeiterinnen-Vereins in Viersen" (Viersen, 1877), pp. 17–21, 34–35. See subsequent reports through 1890.
23. Thun, *Die Industrie am Niederrhein*, pp. 123, 151, 173–74.
24. Ibid., p. 124.
25. Excellent examples of this kind of narrative can be found in Heinrich Brauns, *Der Übergang von der Handweberei zum Fabrikbetrieb in der niederrheinischen Samt- und Seidenindustrie und die Lage der Arbeiter in dieser Periode* (Leipzig: Duncker und Humblot, 1906), pp. 216–18.

sented all that had seemingly become ungovernable in the capitalist culture of urban factories.

Although most female cotton workers were employed in the spinning mills, both in the preparatory tasks and at the self-acting mules, significant numbers of women worked in weaving factories as reelers, nappers, or darners, preparatory and finishing jobs that were "truly female in nature."[26] During the last two decades of the nineteenth century, however, women made significant incursions into the weaving mills as well: in the Cromford weaving mill, for example, in 1880 three-quarters of the weavers were male; by 1890 men represented only half of the weaving workforce.[27] Yet the employment of women in mechanized weaving mills does not appear to have been the burning social question here that it became in other textile-producing regions. Karl Emsbach, whose comprehensive history of the social relations in the Rhenish cotton industry remains the authoritative work on the topic, argues that both employers and male weavers regarded women's work in the early cotton mills as something "so self-evident . . . that no one even thought of discussing or studying it. Even less did they think of demanding special protection for women workers."[28] Many home weavers sought to resist the new factories by refusing factory jobs and clinging tenaciously to the craft of handweaving. Those who accepted factory jobs often sought to resist all aspects of work the weaver could not control, in particular the imposition of factory ordinances and the erosion of a division of labor based in the family, which had become incompatible with the factory organization of work.[29]

Thus, even when they voiced discontent with the new weaving mills the cotton weavers of the Rhineland did not seem to use the same language of craft as the woolen, silk, or velvet weavers or to aim their protest at female weavers or the gradual but steady feminization of their trade. In contrast to the reactions of the silk weavers of Krefeld and the woolen weavers of Aachen and Lennep, who resorted to machine smashing when protesting against the new mills, the transition to factory cotton production occurred without provoking similar resistance from the cotton weavers of the Rhineland, according to Emsbach. Cotton weavers appeared to have accommodated themselves to the transformed conditions of production, as some turned to the still thriving trade of handweaving silk, while others demonstrated remarkable flexibility by "traveling a double track," weaving

26. Hermann Hölters, "Die Arbeiterverhältnisse in der niederrheinischen Baumwollindustrie mit besonderer Berücksichtigung der männlichen Arbeiter" (Dissertation, Universität Heidelberg, 1912), pp. 13–14.
27. Emsbach, *Die soziale Betriebsverfassung*, p. 530.
28. Ibid., p. 325.
29. Ibid., p. 390.

silk at home during boom times in the silk trades and returning to the cotton factory when the demand for silk declined.[30] Dispersed across the rural landscapes of the Lower Rhine in disparate clusters, many cotton handweavers owned their own homes and remained immersed in local agrarian economies rather than being trapped in wholesale dependence on handweaving.[31] Moreover, it is also possible that the male cotton weavers—in contrast to the silk and velvet weavers in neighboring communities, who reinvented guilds and revitalized the language of craft when faced with female competition—were better able to find work in the newly mechanized mills than their compatriots in those branches. After 1880, however, the ranks of the home weavers slowly ceased to be replenished by their children, and cotton home weaving disappeared as its practitioners died out.[32]

The *Bürgerarbeiter* of Aachen and the Transition from Home to Factory Weaving

The woolen industry had two main centers in the Rhineland, one in Aachen, close to the Belgian border, and the other in Lennep in the heart of the Bergisches Land, the hilly towns and villages that bordered the Wupper Valley. In contrast to the cotton industry, the nineteenth-century trades of woolen weaving and shearing were shaped by the legacy of the powerful guilds of weavers and shearers that had formed the cornerstone of the urban economy in the towns of Aachen and Lennep since the late Middle Ages. The rise of nonguild protoindustrial woolen workshops in the small towns that lined the Dutch and Belgian borders near Aachen, founded by Protestants who fled Aachen during the mid-seventeenth century, soon began to undermine the monopoly of the urban woolen guilds. After a series of journeymen's revolts during the French occupation of the Rhineland, the weavers' and shearers' guilds in the city of Aachen were disbanded by decree of the French in 1798.[33] Thus the modern woolen industry was shaped by dual traditions: the dormant but still influential

30. Emsbach, *Die soziale Betriebsverfassung*, p. 390.
31. Ibid., pp. 76, 204, 234–36, 390. According to Emsbach, whose lengthy book is based on vast archival sources, the handweavers "showed no craftsmenlike actions or reactions" to the transition from home to factory industry.
32. Ibid., pp. 30, 386–87.
33. Gertrud Startz, "Die Arbeiterschaft der Aachener Textilindustrie: Eine Untersuchung der geschichtlichen und örtlichen Besonderheiten der Aachener Textilarbeiterschaft und ihre Arbeitsbedingungen in der kapitalistischen Wirtschaftsordnung" (Dissertation, Universität Giessen, 1929), and Franz Decker, *Die betriebliche Sozialordnung der Dürener Industrie im 19. Jahrhundert*, Schriften zur Rheinisch-Westfälischen Wirtschaftsgeschichte, vol. 12 (Cologne: Rheinisch-Westfälisches Wirtschaftsarchiv, 1965).

customs of urban craft and guild production and the family organization of work in the protoindustrial households in nearby towns and rural areas.

Wool merchants, unable to compete with high-quality British yarn or finished cloth, particularly after the dissolution of the Continental System (1806–15), provided the impetus for the mechanization of wool spinning.[34] Although steam engines were operating in Aachen as early as 1817–18, the first mechanical woolen spinning mules were introduced in the woolen districts of the Rhineland and Württemberg during the 1840s.[35] Unlike cotton spinning mills, which were sizable from the outset, the first woolen yarn manufactories were small to middle-sized shops employing ten to fifty workers. Woolen yarn was also spun in *Lohnspinnereien*, a type of centralized putting-out shop; these were not founded and directed by sole entrepreneurs but were run jointly by several woolen merchants or master weavers.[36] The workforce of the rural manufactories included mainly women and children who worked part time and seasonally, organizing their wage labor according to the rhythm of agricultural production. The size and location of the manufactories favored a gradual integration of former hand spinners rather than the abrupt disruptions that characterized this transition in the cotton industry.[37]

At the same time, the tendency toward centralization of all aspects of fabrication into one woolen mill proceeded apace. Rather than singular processes by which branches of production, such as spinning or weaving, were modernized separately, the new woolen workshops assembled all the pre- or semimechanical operations of cloth production—spinning, weaving, shearing, and other preparatory and finishing tasks—under one roof. Thus the transition to centralized (even if not yet fully mechanized) woolen production was swift by comparison with that for cotton. By 1829, for example, the five largest cloth factories in Düren near Aachen encompassed shops for spinning, shearing, cleaning, weaving, fulling, dyeing, and fluffing the wool.[38]

Woolen cloth weaving, in which the practices and consciousness of craft proved most tenacious, was the last branch of woolen production to be incorporated into the new factories.[39] Although mechanization of weaving

---

34. See Clemens Bruckner, *Zur Wirtschaftsgeschichte des Regierungsbezirks Aachens*, Schriften zur Rheinisch-Westfälischen Wirtschaftsgeschichte, vol. 16 (Cologne: Rheinisch-Westfälisches Wirtschaftsarchiv, 1967), p. 200; Borscheid, *Textilarbeiterschaft*, pp. 75–76. The hand-spun German yarn produced fabric that was coarse, irregular, and heavier than English cloth.
35. Decker, *Die betriebliche Sozialordnung*, p. 22; Thun, *Die Industrie am Niederrhein*, p. 23.
36. Borscheid, *Textilarbeiterschaft*, p. 78; Decker, *Die betriebliche Sozialordnung*, p. 22.
37. Borscheid, *Textilarbeiterschaft*, p. 78.
38. Decker, *Die betriebliche Sozialordnung*, pp. 20–21.
39. Startz, "Die Arbeiterschaft," p. 7; Thun, *Die Industrie am Niederrhein*, p. 23.

itself began during the second decade of the nineteenth century, the first mechanical looms were only slightly more efficient than handlooms and did not find broad acceptance. In fact the technical improvement of handlooms for woolen weaving enabled them to keep pace with mechanical looms until well after the mid-nineteenth century.[40] Thus, between 1840 and the 1870s three coexistent systems of woolen cloth weaving functioned side by side: protoindustrial household production in rural areas and small towns; workshops of craftsmen-weavers in the wool centers of Aachen and Lennep; and the centralized manufactories in which spinning was usually mechanized but weaving was still done by hand.

The transition from preindustrial and protoindustrial weaving to mechanized weaving in centralized factories took place in the Aachen district earlier than in other woolen-producing regions of the German empire. Although household production of woolen cloth had more or less disappeared in Düren by 1876, a year later the chamber of commerce and trade in neighboring Aachen reported that 2,000 workers were employed in domestic woolen production, while mechanized woolen mills employed some 10,000.[41] The transition in Lennep appears to have been more gradual: the government office in Düsseldorf reported 851 handlooms and 1,042 mechanical looms in its woolen industry in 1883.[42] After 1880 both the number of cloth factories and their average size increased rapidly: between 1887 and 1889, for example, the number of cloth factories in Aachen-Burtscheid grew from 115 to 151 and the number of workers from 10,700 to 13,700.[43] The ever unpredictable whims of fashion, together with the expansion of the garment industry, were important in the emergence of large-scale woolen factories during the late 1870s, as shifting consumer taste came to favor the finer combed or worsted cloth while the popularity of carded woolens declined.[44] Because the machines that manu-

40. Borscheid, *Textilarbeiterschaft*, pp. 89–90.
41. By 1882, only 22 percent (23,603) of employees in woolen weaving in the German empire worked in home industry. Although this figure declined to 18.2 percent by 1895, the absolute number of home workers in woolens increased to 27,790 by 1895 during an upswing in the woolen branch, which temporarily revived home industry. By 1907, however, only 10.4 percent (13,724) of the remaining woolen weavers worked in home industry. See Robert Wilbrandt, *Die Weber in der Gegenwart* (Jena: Gustav Fischer, 1906), p. 35.
42. HStAD, Reg. Düss., H&G 24752, "Statistik der am 16. Mai 1883 vorhandenen Webstühle, Wirkstühle und Riemengänge in den rechtsrheinischen Kreisen des Regierungsbezirks Düsseldorf"; Decker, *Die betriebliche Sozialordnung*, p. 27; Startz, "Die Arbeiterschaft," p. 8.
43. Startz, "Die Arbeiterschaft," p. 9. A further reason for favoring locations outside town was the space available for future expansion of the factory. Decker, *Die betriebliche Sozialordnung*, pp. 42–44.
44. Bruckner, *Zur Wirtschaftsgeschichte*, p. 201; Thun, *Die Industrie am Niederrhein*, p. 44.

factured worsted yarn were more complicated and required a more substantial capital investment than those producing carded yarn, the new worsted mills usually originated as large-scale factories employing several hundred workers. The new worsted branch proved to be one of the most dynamic sectors of textile production during the last decades of the nineteenth century, and its upswing regenerated the woolen industry during the crisis of the 1870s.[45]

The new factories built during the 1880s in Aachen and Düren were fully modern in their use of steam engines and electricity, in their organization of work, and in their attempts to conform to existing health and safety standards enforced by factory inspectors. Many entrepreneurs built their new mills outside the city limits not only to utilize waterways as a source of power, but because of the abundance of "reserve labor" in the communities of rural home weavers. Indeed, during this period of rapid expansion of woolen factory production, a continuous shortage of qualified factory workers encouraged the assimilation of many home weavers into the new mills. As cloth factories multiplied in size and number, they were not "penetrated by outsiders or especially by foreign unskilled workers" like the nearby coal and iron industries.[46] Instead, the proliferation of new railroad networks enabled entrepreneurs to recruit a workforce of *Stammarbeiter* (core workers) from a wide radius around the textile towns, who were rooted in local textile workers' communities and highly valued by employers for their "inherited" or assimilated skills.[47]

Unique to the woolen weavers and shearers of Aachen was a social identity, harking back to the heyday of flourishing urban guilds, as "*bürgerlich*, not proletarian," as *Bürgerarbeiter* (citizen-workers), distinct from the unskilled masses of mill hands who streamed into the Rhenish cotton factories.[48] Local historical narratives constructed the male woolen weaver as a "highly skilled, elite worker" who was "bound to traditions and shaped

---

45. Borscheid, *Textilarbeiterschaft*, p. 85; Thun, *Die Industrie am Niederrhein*, p. 23; Blumberg, *Die deutsche Textilindustrie*, p. 39.

46. Startz, "Die Arbeiterschaft", pp. 1, 14; Decker, *Die betriebliche Sozialordnung*, p. 27.

47. Decker points out that employers usually recruited workers from within a twenty-kilometer radius of Düren, most of whom lived in factory housing during the week and returned to their families on the weekends. Decker, *Die betriebliche Sozialordnung*, pp. 140–43; Startz, "Die Arbeiterschaft," p. 16; and Dieter Dowe, "Legale Interessenvertretung und Streik: Der Arbeitskampf in den Tuchfabriken des Kreises Lennep (Bergisches Land) 1850," in *Streik: Zur Geschichte des Arbeitskampfes während der Industrialisierung*, ed. Klaus Tenfelde and Heinrich Volkmann (Munich: Beck, 1981), pp. 35–38.

48. Startz, "Die Arbeiterschaft," pp. 1, 14, 16. Startz was a social worker for the city of Aachen's *Gesundheitsamt* (public health department) during the early 1920s. Decker's study of Düren conveys the same image of wool factory workers. See his *Die betriebliche Sozialordnung*, p. 140.

above all by his history," who incarnated not merely individual skills but the training of generations.⁴⁹ *Bodenständig* (of long-established standing), highly qualified and well paid, the woolen weavers of Aachen had not, according to these narratives, sunk to the level of the proletariat in the course of the transition to mechanized mills. Instead the "citizen-worker" occupied a social space bounded by family and the Catholic religion, was "fully imbued with a sense of home [*Heimat*] and had a dignified relation to work."⁵⁰ The representation of male home weavers as citizen-workers constituted a complex rhetorical strategy that aimed to deflect the narratives of proletarianization, one that revitalized the younger generations of woolen weavers and sought to instill in them a pronounced sense of regional and trade-specific male identity amid a morass of changing industrial structures, relations, and identities. A strike of woolen weavers in 1850 in the Lennep cloth factories points to the ways weavers mobilized this identity in confrontation with employers. Although the striking workers—both male and female—were factory weavers and not home industrial producers, their demands were still expressed in the terminology of craftsmen that underpinned the identity of citizen-worker. Capturing their generation's collective experience of the transition from home to factory industry, the striking weavers lamented in a petition that "the machine is not the tool of the worker, but the worker a tool of the machine, a slave of the most imposing mechanical system. The machine renders all skill superfluous and demands only a routine mechanical supervision."⁵¹

The embrace of the ideal of the citizen-worker and of the revived language of craft illustrates how woolen weavers in the Rhineland reworked the past, utilizing the "mythology of the handloom weaver to manage the changes consequent upon factory mechanization."⁵² It also signified and reproduced male working-class visions of respectability, skill, and honor that came to underpin both the Social Democratic notion of the class-conscious worker and the campaigns of the Catholic weavers' association to protect *Stand* (estate) and family from the destructive effects of industrial transformation. At the same time, however, the image of *Bürgerarbeiter*, just like that of the young, single mill girl in the cotton towns, was defined explicitly or implicitly in terms of its opposite. Despite the impor-

49. Indeed, it was even customary for the mill owners to address them as *Bürgerarbeiter* (citizen-workers). See Startz, "Die Arbeiterschaft," pp. 1, 14, 16.
50. Startz, "Die Arbeiterschaft," pp. 14, 16.
51. Dowe, "Legale Interessenvertretung," pp. 31–35. On the traditions of resistance among woolen weavers, see Blumberg, *Die deutsche Textilindustrie*, pp. 90–91, and Borscheid, *Textilarbeiterschaft*, p. 90.
52. Patrick Joyce, "The Historical Meanings of Work: An Introduction," in *The Historical Meanings of Work*, ed. Patrick Joyce (Cambridge: Cambridge University Press, 1987), p. 21. In this passage Joyce refers to the textile workers of Lancashire and Yorkshire.

tance of women's labor to the protoindustrial household economy, their exclusion from the "mysteries of craft" and the "economy of honor," from the embryonic rights of citizenship male guild members enjoyed, was integral to the notion of citizen-worker.[53]

Juxtaposing employment statistics with the ideal of *Bürgerarbeiter* reveals, however, that women as well as men must have belonged to this community of elite, stable, and skilled workers that was bounded by family and religion. Between the two census surveys of 1882 and 1895, the number of female weavers in the mechanized woolen mills of Germany increased at a much higher rate than the number of men, for "the advance of the woman workers [faced] no technological obstacles" in this branch.[54] Thus, although the legacies and skills of male cloth makers and craftsmen left indelible traces in local histories, in the narratives of the first socialist and Catholic weavers' unions, the newly mechanized woolen factories depended as well on an equally experienced female workforce of skilled domestic workers, whose labor was indispensable to the manufacture of woolen cloth. Indeed, the mechanized cloth factories in the Aachen district employed more women than men: in 1914, 7,059 women and 5,420 men worked in Aachen's textile mills.[55] As in other textile branches, there were gender-specific spheres of employment; the spinners and their assistants were largely female, while men worked almost exclusively in supervisory positions. Those finishing operations that utilized chemicals, like cloth dyeing, remained male spheres of production, whereas the tasks of napping and darning, crucial in determining the appearance of the finished cloth, constituted a domain of skilled female labor, performed outside the mills in the homes of individual female subcontractors.

In the branch of woolen weaving, however, the contests between male and female weavers were frequent and virulent as increasing numbers of single and married women found jobs at the new mechanical looms. By the eve of the First World War women composed nearly 40 percent of the weaving workforce in Aachen's cloth factories.[56] Although little is known

---

53. On the "mysteries of craft," see Maxine Berg, "Women's Work, Mechanisation and the Early Phases of Industrialization in England," in Joyce, *Historical Meanings of Work*, p. 74. On the "economy of honor" in Krefeld's silk weaving industry, see Peter Kriedte, *Eine Stadt am seidenen Faden: Haushalt, Hausindustrie und soziale Bewegung in Krefeld in der Mitte des 19. Jahrhunderts* (Göttingen: Vandenhoeck und Ruprecht, 1991), p. 130.

54. Alexander Wachs, *Die volkswirtschaftliche Bedeutung der technischen Entwicklung der deutschen Wollindustrie* (Leipzig: Klinkhardt, 1909), pp. 92–93, 116. Between 1882 and 1895 the number of male weavers in the German wool industry increased by 8 percent (from 74,794 to 80,642), while the number of women increased by 71 percent (from 33,644 to 57,527).

55. Startz, "Die Arbeiterschaft," p. 19.

56. Ibid., p. 29. Startz indicates that the proportion of women weavers in Aachen cloth

about the organization of work in the protoindustrial weavers' households, it is likely that the high percentage of female weavers and the significant presence of married women among woolen weavers in factories reflect continuities rather than departures from these traditions.[57] As in home woolen weaving, both men and women had a vital role in the *Stammarbeiterschaft* of Aachen's woolen industry. Moreover, in wool centers with long traditions of woolen cloth weaving like Aachen, Düren, and Lennep, the core workforce comprised largely textile-working *families*. Indeed, the mill owners of Düren contended in the 1870s that the factory labor of married women was essential not only to the vitality of industry, but also to the stability of the working-class family. Married women's employment was necessary, they argued, "not for their own sake, but rather in order to ensure that respectable workers' families, living in orderly circumstances, do not lose a vital part of their incomes."[58]

Despite the likely continuities between the organization of work in protoindustrial woolen weaving and the division of labor in the new woolen mills, male weavers launched spirited protests against the perceived feminization of their craft and against the wage reductions that aided the advance of female workers at the expense of unemployed handweavers. Demands of male weavers that women be banned from the new mechanical woolen looms were raised frequently, for example, at the 1873 congress of Christian workers of the Rhineland and Westphalia held in Aachen.[59] Weavers went on strike at the Mezer firm in Burtscheid near Aachen in 1895 when they interpreted the announcement of pending wage cuts as a signal that the firm intended to hire women to run the mechanical looms. Similarly, the next year in Montjoie, near the border with Belgium, the entire weaving workforce walked off the job when the firm announced its intention to hire female weavers. The town's mayor intervened as mediator, and the weavers successfully forced the firm to abandon its plans.[60]

Even if the men's protests could not preserve weaving as a male enclave, they did succeed in demarcating gender-specific tasks and spheres of labor

---

factories declined from 40 to 27 percent after introduction of the double loom. Employers appear to have regarded supervising of two looms as men's work. On the protests of male weavers against female factory work in a national rather than regional arena, see Karin Zachmann, "Männer arbeiten, Frauen helfen: Geschlechtsspezifische Arbeitsteilung und Maschinisierung in der Textilindustrie des 19. Jahrhunderts," in *Geschlechterhierarchie und Arbeitsteilung: Zur Geschichte ungleicher Erwerbschancen von Männern und Frauen*, ed. Karin Hausen (Göttingen: Vandenhoeck und Ruprecht, 1993), p. 83.

57. Startz, "Die Arbeiterschaft," p. 30.
58. Decker, *Die deutsche Textilindustrie*, p. 155.
59. Startz, "Die Arbeiterschaft," p. 8.
60. HStAD, Reg. Aachen, H&G 1633, "Bericht des Bürgermeisters Burtscheids vom 24.1.1895"; H&G 1634, "Bericht des Bürgermeisters Montjoies vom 8.10.1896."

within the weaving sector, whereby the size and number of looms and the quality of the fabric determined who would work them. Women weavers therefore worked at smaller looms fabricating lesser-quality cloth and were usually assigned only a single loom, as opposed to the double looms that male weavers frequently supervised. Thus, despite apparent feminization, male weavers were able to enforce new gender hierarchies, embedded in the technologies of work and in the machinery and raw materials of production, and to retain in the factory the supervisory authority they likely had held over the work of the family unit in the protoindustrial household.[61]

The Linen Industry of Bielefeld: Gender and the Making of a Local Labor Market

German linen production was concentrated in Silesia, Minden-Ravensberg, and Württemberg during the early to middle nineteenth century. Despite the national decline of the industry after the linen crisis of the 1840s, the city of Bielefeld in Minden-Ravensberg remained an important linen center. As elsewhere in Germany, many flax spinners and linen weavers in the region around Bielefeld were flax farmers who spun and wove to supplement their agricultural incomes and to supply their own households with linen cloth. Approximately 20,000 people were employed in protoindustrial linen production in and around the market center of Bielefeld during the 1840s.[62] Local particularities, such as the high quality and favorable reputation of its specialty linen products, as well as the growing demand for linen among local garment producers, help explain its continued vitality.[63] A grave crisis in linen production occurred during the 1840s, as cheaper cotton products began to flood the traditional export markets for Ravensberg's flax and linen products and as the British producers expanded their exports of high-quality linen goods, based in mechanized yarn and cloth production during the 1830s and 1840s.[64] The necessity of competing with British goods and the mass pauperization of the handspinners and handweavers of Ravensberg provided the impetus for modernization of linen production.

The linen merchants of Bielefeld established the first mechanized flax-

61. Zachmann, "Männer arbeiten," pp. 81–85.
62. Karl Ditt, *Industrialisierung, Arbeiterschaft und Arbeiterbewegung in Bielefeld* (Dortmund: Gesellschaft für Westfälische Wirtschaftsgeschichte e.V., 1982), p. 21. The linen industry was highly concentrated in the city of Bielefeld, which had five-sixths of all weaving looms in the government district of Minden.
63. Ibid., p. 166.
64. Ibid., p. 25.

spinning mills in the 1850s just outside the gates of the city, where a traditional hand-spinning population was now in desperate search of work.[65] The modernization of flax spinning encompassed not only a shift from one site of production, the household, to another, the factory, but also the relocation of a rural protoindustry to urban locations.[66] The founding of the Spinnerei Vorwärts in 1852 and the Ravensberger Spinnerei in 1853 marked the beginning of the first wave of Bielefeld's industrial transformation: the Ravensberger Spinnerei, for example, became the largest spinning mill in Prussia, employing over 1,000 workers and operating some 20,000 spindles a few years after its founding.[67] Despite their high technical capacity and enormous plants, the new linen mills were plagued by labor shortages soon after their founding and throughout the rest of the century. According to one local historian, early on "the unemployed workers in hand spinning communities could not be moved—with money or good promises—to go to work in the factories, which appeared to them to be barracks or prisons."[68] As a result, from the outset the mills were forced to enlist local workers inexperienced in flax spinning and to recruit hundreds of workers from distant parts of Germany and eastern Europe.

Far from supplanting domestic linen weaving with one swift blow, the increased availability and improved quality of linen yarn first stimulated an expansion of protoindustrial home weaving. It continued to flourish in the countryside surrounding Bielefeld, coexistent with the urban mechanized mills, until the turn of the century when linen handweaving in the region began its irreversible decline.[69] The increased productivity of local flax-spinning mills soon prompted Bielefeld's leading linen merchants, cogni-

65. Gerhard Adelmann, "Die Stadt Bielefeld als Zentrum fabrikindustrieller Gründungen nach 1850," in *Festschrift für Edith Ennen: Die Stadt in der europäischen Geschichte*, ed. Werner Besch et al. (Bonn: L. Röhrscheid, 1972), pp. 884–95.
66. Ibid., pp. 888–90; Karl Ditt, "Technologischer Wandel und Strukturveränderung der Fabrikarbeiterschaft in Bielefeld, 1860–1914," in *Arbeiter im Industrialisierungsprozeß: Herkunft, Lage und Verhalten*, ed. Werner Conze and Ulrich Engelhardt (Stuttgart: Klett Cotta, 1979), pp. 237–38.
67. Ditt, "Technologischer Wandel," pp. 237–38; Karl Ditt, "Arbeitsverhältnisse und Betriebsverfassung in der deutschen Textilindustrie des 19. Jahrhunderts unter besonderer Berücksichtigung der Bielefelder Leinenindustrie," *Archiv für Sozialgeschichte* 21 (1981): 63; Stadtbibliothek Bielefeld, Otto Sartorius, *75 Jahre Bielefelder AG* (Bielefeld: Bielefelder AG, 1935), p. 30.
68. Stadtbibliothek Bielefeld, Gustav Engel, *Bielefelder Webereien AG, Festschrift zur 100 Jahre Feier* (Bielefeld: Bielefelder AG, 1964), p. 62.
69. Adelmann, "Die Stadt Bielefeld," p. 890; Hans Schmidt, *Vom Leinen zur Seide: Die Geschichte der Firma Delius and Söhne und ihre Vorgängerinnen und das Wirken ihrer Inhaber für die Entwicklung Bielefelds, 1722–1925* (Lemgo: F. L. Wagener, 1926), pp. 235, 368–69; Engel, *Bielefelder Webereien*, pp. 57–59; Sartorius, *75 Jahre Bielefelder AG*, pp. 44–47, 53–54.

zant of the downswing in cotton production caused by the American Civil War, to mechanize and centralize production. Bielefeld's first mechanized weaving mill, the Mechanische Weberei, was founded in 1863 by the owners of the Ravensberger Spinnerei; thus the mechanization of weaving followed close on the heels of the mechanized flax spinning. Advertising in 1863 for one *Webermeister* (master weaver, male), one *Schlichtmeister* (master sizer, male) and thirty *Webermädchen* (weaving girls), the founders clearly envisioned a mainly female workforce supervised by male *Textilhandwerker* (textile craftsmen). Discovering, however, that local weavers lacked the technical understanding of the mechanized looms, the mill's founders were compelled to "import" a master weaver and thirty women weavers from Ireland to instruct local handweavers in the use of the mechanized looms. By the end of the first year, 140 mechanical looms were in operation, and the 100 local weavers had proved so readily teachable that the workers from Ireland could be sent home in the summer of 1865.[70]

According to accounts of local and company historians, the introduction of mechanized linen weaving did not initially meet with a hostile response among handweavers, for local weavers had already become accustomed to wage labor through the putting-out system. Furthermore, because home weaving remained a vital craft in the outlying areas surrounding Bielefeld, weavers still had the chance "to work as independent weavers or for a merchant in the putting-out system, to stay bound to their familiar soil, and to earn supplementary income through farming."[71] For despite the decline of the national and international markets for linen cloth, the local manufacture of underclothing required a steady supply and thus nurtured production both in the local linen weaving mills and in rural domestic industry. Those weavers who did go to work in the newly founded linen weaving factories apparently fashioned a narrative of progression in which the mechanical looms were viewed as continuous with the traditions of handweaving, for "each mechanical loom needed an individual weaver to run it, just like a handloom."[72] The importance of this sense of continuity is confirmed by the strike reports of the mid-1860s: soon after the Mechanische Weberei began operation, the weavers went on strike against the firm's mandate that each weaver work two looms: "The work at two looms was apparently perceived as a violation of craft and home industrial customs and thus as an unacceptable burden. For when the handweaver had more than one loom, according to craft traditions, he employed a journeyman weaver or a member of his family."[73]

70. Sartorius, *75 Jahre Bielefelder AG*, p. 48.
71. Schmidt, *Vom Leinen zur Seide*, pp. 368–69.
72. Ibid., p. 247.
73. Ditt, *Industrialisierung*, p. 125.

A crucial spark to industrialization in Bielefeld, the linen industry was soon overshadowed by the swift diversification of the city's industrial landscape, by the rapid development of metal production and the marked expansion, rather than contraction, of home industrial garment production. Indeed, the vitality of both garment and textile fabrication spurred the production of metal goods and machines, in particular sewing machines and mechanical spindles and looms for the local garment workshops and textile mills.[74] Between 1881 and 1900, for example, the employees in Bielefeld's metal factories more than tripled (from 1,708 to 5,547) while the workforce in the local garment industry (which produced mostly underclothing) nearly quadrupled (from 744 to 2,921). The textile workforce expanded only modestly by comparison, from 2,279 to 3,238 employees between 1881 and 1900. This trend accelerated between 1900 and 1913, when the garment industry employed over 6,000 and the metal workforce expanded to nearly 13,000, while at the same time the number of textile workers shrank slightly to 3,106.[75]

This transformation of Bielefeld's industrial profile also altered the local labor market, forcing linen mill owners into fierce competition for workers with the metal and garment industries and ultimately forming highly segmented spheres of female labor in textiles and garments and male labor in the metal industry. Thus the sexual division of labor that is most pertinent here is between the various industrial sectors rather than within them. Because of the particularities of the city's labor market, especially the metal sector as a site of well-paid and high-status employment for men, the workforce in the local textile mills—from flax spinners to linen weavers and later to silk weavers—was highly feminized from the outset. The workforce in the Mechanische Weberei, for example, was 57 percent female shortly after the company's founding in the mid-1860s: by 1890 women composed 70 percent and by 1900, 76 percent of its workers. Most of the men who made up the remaining 20 to 25 percent of employees in the Mechanische Weberei were supervisors, skilled mechanics, or office workers. Similarly, in 1864 women composed 55 percent of the workforce in the Spinnerei Vorwärts and 58 percent of that in the Ravensberger Spinnerei.[76]

Although the percentage of male textile workers contracted over the

74. Ditt, "Technologischer Wandel," pp. 238–39; Schmidt, *Vom Leinen zur Seide*, p. 262.
75. Adelmann, "Die Stadt Bielefeld," pp. 891–92; Ditt, "Technologischer Wandel," p. 240.
76. Ditt, "Technologischer Wandel," p. 249; Engel, *Bielefelder Webereien AG*, p. 58; Stadtarchiv Bielefeld (StA Bi), Mechanische Weberei Bielefeld 28/1; Personalbuch I, 1863–1925; Mechanische Weberei Bielefeld 29/1, Namen der Arbeiter bis 1907; Mechanische Weberei Bielefeld 51, Personalbuch 1925–34. My own study of these personnel records from the Mechanische Weberei demonstrates this point; see relevant data in chapter 6.

years of rapid industrialization, the steady growth in the number of female textile workers did not occur at their expense. Rather, rapid growth in the metal sector and chronic labor shortages in nearly all of the mills meant that male workers in particular enjoyed a certain mobility between industrial sectors as they sought to improve their wages and working conditions.[77] Young men who began working in the textile mills as teenagers might have moved on to metal production, while the textile industry's core female workforce migrated from spinning to weaving to garment sewing or later from linen to silk weaving. Indeed, the segmentation of the labor market in this fashion helped inscribe each sector with highly gendered notions of status. Historian Karl Ditt argues, in fact, that by the late nineteenth century the association of textile production with women made mill jobs unappealing to men: "The increasing tendency of women's work to leave its imprint on the textile industry only enhanced the already negative image of textile work and workers. Considering the alternatives for employment elsewhere, working in a branch of industry that was dominated by women, with its poor wages and working conditions, meant a loss of esteem in a work world shaped by men."[78] Yet however accurate Ditt's rendition of the gendered meanings of factory work in the various industries might be, the world of work in Bielefeld was not defined only by men. Because one of the key industrial sectors in Bielefeld's local economy was dependent on female labor for some 80 percent of its workforce, it offers a unique case of a highly complex local female labor market in which women constituted far more than a mere "reserve army."

With the emergence of the segmented local labor market came a hierarchy of more and less desirable jobs in Bielefeld's factories. Although in 1870 the owners of the Mechanische Weberei already lamented the difficulty of retaining workers in the face of competition from other local industries, the flax-spinning mills fared far worse, facing actual constriction of production as experienced spinners abandoned the mechanized mills of Bielefeld in favor of the weaving mills or garment industries.[79] The low wages, high temperatures, and working conditions that many workers considered dirty and demeaning meant that the local flax-spinning mills occupied the lowest place in the employment hierarchy. In response to the chronic dearth of workers, their owners intensified their efforts to enlist workers from the rural regions close to Bielefeld, rewarding recruiters with "head premiums" of one taler per worker hired from the region.[80] The owners of the Ravensberger Spinnerei, for example, sought to make em-

77. Ditt, "Technologischer Wandel," pp. 248, 258–59.
78. Ibid., p. 249.
79. Schmidt, *Vom Leinen zur Seide*, pp. 247, 368–69.
80. Engel, *Bielefelder Webereien*, p. 69; Ditt, "Technologischer Wandel," p. 54.

ployment more attractive by constructing modern apartment housing for employees. Regardless of these efforts, the Ravensberger and other local spinning mills were forced to recruit large numbers of young women from Silesia, Bohemia, East Prussia and even Ireland to fill their demand for labor. By 1895 some 70 percent of the workers in the Ravensberger Spinnerei were *Fremde* (immigrants).[81] The constant shortage of workers in Bielefeld resulted in *Stadtflucht* (escape from the city) by several entrepreneurs who opened weaving mills in small towns or villages near Bielefeld. One case is the branch mill of the Mechanische Weberei, which was founded in 1907 in Spenge, a small town adjoining the regions of domestic tobacco production, where unemployment was relatively high. The mill's owners hoped thereby "to circumvent the constant disruptions in Bielefeld as well as the steadily increasing dearth of qualified workers."[82] Although the linen market began to contract across Germany in the face of competition from cotton and cotton-woolen blends, Bielefeld's weaving mills continued to specialize in fine linen, and the city retained its position as one of the leading linen centers in Germany throughout the nineteenth century.[83]

Although the linen weaving mills offered higher wages and status and reputedly more "respectable" working conditions than spinning, garment sewing also occupied a relatively high place in the job hierarchy for married women who sought to combine paid labor with housework and child rearing. Local weaving mill owners bemoaned the loss of many of their most experienced female weavers to the garment industry during the 1880s and 1890s so that, like their counterparts in spinning, they could no longer fill their demand for labor with urban workers and were also compelled to draw on marginally or seasonally employed workers from nearby rural communities. Between 1890 and 1910 the number of city residents employed in the Mechanische Weberei declined from 63 to 42 percent, while those of rural origins increased from 37 to 58 percent of the total workforce.[84] Despite the recurrent shortages of qualified workers, the Mechanische Weberei became the largest linen weaving mill in Germany during the 1890s, with a workforce of nearly 1,000 at its peak, including hundreds of female *Stammarbeiter*.[85] Furthermore, for many of the workers recruited to the urban mills from the rural clusters of former domestic

81. Engel, *Bielefelder Webereien*, p. 69; Adelmann, "Die Stadt Bielefeld," p. 890; Ditt, "Technologischer Wandel," pp. 254–55; Schmidt, *Vom Leinen zur Seide*, p. 365.
82. Adelmann, "Die Stadt Bielefeld," p. 894; Sartorius, *75 Jahre Bielefelder AG*, pp. 58–60; Ditt, *Industrialisierung*, pp. 165–66.
83. Ditt, *Industrialisierung*, p. 166.
84. Ditt, "Technologischer Wandel," p. 253.
85. Ibid., p. 244. On the presence of female "core workers," see my data analysis in chapter 6.

linen producers, textile work remained hereditary even if the site of production had shifted to Bielefeld's factories. As Ditt has argued, the existence of virtual dynasties of textile-working families among the workers of Bielefeld's largest mills also attests to the likelihood that informal family networks influenced hiring and firing.[86]

The new factory production of silk, plush, and damask, which began in Bielefeld in the 1880s, caused further constriction of the city's labor market. While some 1,000 hand weavers had been producing silk on handlooms in protoindustrial households in Ravensberg since the early 1860s, silk became an increasingly attractive alternative for many linen merchants.[87] Inspired by the Krefeld traditions of silk weaving, a number of mechanical silk mills were established in and around Bielefeld, the first with the assistance of experienced silk weavers from Krefeld. By the turn of the century there were some 1,500 mechanical silk looms in Bielefeld's factories, and another 600 handlooms continued to produce silk specialty cloth in surrounding rural towns and villages.[88] Because of the exigencies of the local labor market, the development of a vital branch of mechanical silk cloth manufacture necessarily intensified the competition for workers among the city's textile mills. The workers who found jobs in the new silk mills were usually the most experienced and skilled weavers from the local linen mills, most of them female. Silk weaving, which was commonly regarded as cleaner and less physically taxing than flax spinning or linen weaving and also paid significantly higher wages, became the most desirable textile employment for women during the late 1890s.[89]

Since the segmentation of Bielefeld's labor market was even more rigidly defined by late in the century than at the founding of the city's first mechanical flax spinning and linen weaving mills, the development of the silk weaving sector depended on a female labor force even more than the linen sector. The decision of the Delius family, long-established textile entrepreneurs, to found a silk factory in 1913 in the village of Augustdorf in Lippe was influenced by a number of factors that made this outpost a particularly

---

86. Ditt, "Arbeitsverhältnisse," p. 74. Tamara Hareven's classic study of the family networks in the textile mills of New England offers a useful comparison here: *Family Time and Industrial Time: The Relationship between the Family and Work in a New England Industrial Community* (Cambridge: Cambridge University Press, 1982).

87. Heinz Potthoff, "Die Ravensberger Leinenindustrie und ihre Töchtergewerbe," *Schmollers Jahrbuch für Gesetzgebung, Verwaltung und Volkswirtschaft im Deutschen Reich* 34 (1910): 279–92. According to Potthoff, there were three silk merchants who put out to 180 handlooms in 1851; in 1856, six merchants and 600 handlooms; and in 1860, eleven merchants and 1,000 handlooms.

88. Schmidt, *Vom Leinen zur Seide*, pp. 188, 299–300; Ditt, *Industrialisierung*, p. 168. The first fully mechanized silk weaving mill opened in Bielefeld during the 1880s.

89. Schmidt, *Vom Leinen zur Seide*, pp. 187–88, 264–65, 331.

favorable location, not least the contests among local employers for qualified female workers. For one, the absence of a railroad line near Augustdorf meant its workers would have few employment alternatives. Moreover, since male workers, "even after repeated hirings . . . could not be harnessed to the mill for longer than a few weeks" and instead sought "seasonal employment in the brickworks," their wives became the *Stammarbeiter*, even if employed only part time or seasonally in the new mills.[90]

Thus the diverse and complex industrial landscape of Bielefeld spawned a relatively uncontested sphere of female employment within the local labor market, and women came to predominate in all of its textile mills, from flax spinning to silk weaving, while the elite supervisory positions were preserved for the relatively few male textile craftsmen. In a remarkable contrast to the Rhenish towns, which were bound to more homogeneous local economies, the massive expansion of the married and single female factory workforce in Bielefeld did not become an urgent social question among either its local elite or its organized workers and thus did not resonate in the national arenas of social reform or social policy.

The Weaver's Lament: Women's Work and the Revival of Craft in the Silk and Velvet Regions of Krefeld and Kempen

Silk and velvet weaving were the branches of textile manufacture in which home industry proved most tenacious and the transition to factory industry occurred last. Although the 1880s represented the "decade of struggle" for velvet weavers in the Rhineland, the life-and-death battle of silk weavers lasted from the mid-1880s through most of the 1890s.[91] Indeed, about 1870 "scarcely a factory smokestack protruded" above the villages and scattered homesteads of rural weavers across the plains of the Lower Rhine, or above the thriving city of Krefeld, hub of the region's silk industry.[92] The destruction of the handweavers' way of life in urban and rural Krefeld and Kempen, in which feminization figured alternatively as the cause and the outcome, became a parable of the dangers of "the industrial state." Unlike parallel transitions in cotton, woolen, and linen weaving, it drew attention in the national arenas of parliamentary politics and social reform, far beyond the terrains of conflict in the Lower Rhine.

---

90. Ibid., pp. 328–31.
91. Brauns, *Der Übergang von der Handweberei*, p. 7; HStAD Reg. Düss., H&G 24741, "Schreiben von Schiller, Crous & Cie., Crefeld vom 9.2.1881," p. 179.
92. Hans van der Upwich, *Die Geschichte und die Entwicklung der rheinischen Samt- und Seidenindustrie* (Krefeld: Kramer und Baum, 1920), p. 116.

The unusual visibility of the weavers' despair can be explained in part by their own attempts to publicize their plight, their petitions to the Reichstag, their efforts to dispatch a delegation to the Ministry of Trade in Berlin, and finally their request for an audience with the kaiser. Their solicitations, however futile, attest to the changing face of the German state during the last two decades of the nineteenth century, to the hopes sparked among the weavers of the Rhineland that the state's new interest in the "worker question" and the flurry of activity in the realm of social policy might prompt it to intervene in their struggle for survival.[93] Specifically, the weavers' resolute resistance to feminization of silk and velvet weaving reverberated in the legislative and discursive arenas, which pronounced female factory labor an urgent social question and a primary matter of state social policy. Alfons Thun's inventive social investigation of the industry in the Lower Rhine and its workers, which appeared in Gustav Schmoller's prestigious series *Staats- und sozialwissenschaftliche Forschungen*, had alerted social reformers to the dangers of female factory labor as early as 1879. The later studies of reformers Robert Wilbrandt and Heinrich Brauns made the struggles of the silk and velvet weavers of Krefeld and Kempen emblematic of the problem of women's work in capitalism—of the feminization of factory production and the displacement of male workers.[94]

The narratives of these texts, as well as of some of the weavers' own documents of protest against a world turned on its head, represent the massive incursions of women into the factories as a definitive rupture with the customs and practices of family labor in protoindustrial silk manufacture. Yet the critical moment of fracture remains obscure in these texts, not least because the division of labor between husbands and wives, parents and children remained largely impervious to the gaze of state and social commentators and subsequently to historians. Did it occur when women were hired as weavers, which most accounts depict as more or less an exclusively male domain? Or did the relocation of female weavers' work from the enigmatic household economy to the new and highly visible public space of the factory constitute the crucial fissure? These questions frame this analysis of the changing meanings of women's work during the transition from home to factory industry in the silk and velvet producing regions of the Lower Rhine.

93. The labor code was revised in 1878. The social insurance laws include health insurance, instituted in 1883, accident insurance in 1884, and old age–disability insurance in 1889.
94. Thun, *Die Industrie am Niederrhein*; Robert Wilbrandt, *Die Frauenarbeit: Ein Problem des Kapitalismus* (Leipzig: B. G. Teubner, 1906), idem, and *Die Weber*; Brauns, *Der Übergang von der Handweberei*.

Industrial Topography

During the seventeenth century Mennonite settlers transformed the "insignificant little town" of Krefeld into a bustling capital of the linen trade. Just fifteen years after the von der Leyen family founded the first silk enterprise in 1720, silk production began to outpace linen manufacture, encompassing twice as many handlooms as linen by 1735. By the end of the eighteenth century, Krefeld had become a thriving center of silk production, and linen weaving had vanished as a viable trade in the city and surrounding countryside. Although the von der Leyens had secured a monopoly over silk manufacture within the city limits, their competitors fostered the growth of silk production on the outskirts of town and in the rural district of the town of Kempen.[95] By the time the family's heirs dissolved their companies at midcentury, 93 percent of silk looms operating in the Rhine province were in the government district of Düsseldorf, and a further geographic division of labor had developed within the Krefeld silk region.[96] The fabrication of velvet cloth and ribbons was concentrated in the rural towns of the Kempen district—Hüls, Anrath, Grefrath, Lobberich, Oedt, Süchteln—where weavers often worked only part time or seasonally as their crops allowed, while the production of more specialized patterned and fashionable silk fabric and ribbon remained under the merchants' direct control in Krefeld itself. By midcentury the silk and velvet trades had come to dominate the labor market of the Rhineland, encompassing 40 percent of all textile workers in the province in 1849.[97]

The putting-out system survived in silk and velvet weaving until the late 1880s and early 1890s, when silk merchants established the first mechanized mills, with velvet as the forerunner. During the early 1870s, mechanical looms became available for velvet ribbon production, inspiring the velvet merchant (and later factory owner) Niedieck, from Lobberich near Kempen, to commission the design of a mechanical loom for velvet cloth production and to introduce the first successful version to his workshop in 1877.[98] Velvet merchants continued to refine and improve the

---

95. Peter Kriedte, "Proto-Industrialisierung und großes Kapital: Das Seidengewerbe in Krefeld und seinem Umland bis zum Ende des Ancien Regime," *Archiv für Sozialgeschichte* 23 (1983): 222–23, 250.

96. See van der Upwich, *Die Geschichte und die Entwicklung*, pp. 101–2; Gerhard Adelmann, "Das ländliche Textilgewerbe des Rheinlandes vor der Industrialisierung," *Rheinische Vierteljahresblätter* 43 (1979): 263.

97. Adelmann, "Das ländliche Textilgewerbe," pp. 263, 286; van der Upwich, *Die Geschichte und die Entwicklung*, pp. 102, 122; Fränken, *Die Entwicklung*, pp. 88, 98–99. By 1875 the small cities of Viersen and Rheydt, both within ten miles of Krefeld, had also become centers of the silk and velvet industries.

98. Jochem Ulrich, "Soziale Entwicklungen im industriellen Umbruch: Die Anpassungskrise in der niederrheinischen Textilindustrie, dargestellt am Gebiet der heutigen

Table 4. Number of mechanical and handlooms in the Krefeld silk and velvet districts, 1870–1913

	1870	1880	1885	1890	1895	1900	1905	1910
Velvet cloth								
Handloom	14,774	17,464	15,785	6,902	1,758	846	360	141
Mechanical loom	—	—	1,149	2,907	2,420	2,076	1,619	1,664
Velvet ribbon								
Handloom	2,472	242	673	964	243	221	51	25
Mechanical loom	—	—	44	197	151	276	140	229
Silk cloth								
Handloom	6,498	15,196	11,062	14,263	10,839	5,834	2,826	2,163
Mechanical loom	—	—	1,044	2,484	4,488	7,151	7,378	8,176

Source: Jahresberichte der Krefelder Handelskammer, as compiled by Franz Wischer, "Organisationsbestrebungen der Arbeiter in der Krefelder Seiden- und Samtindustrie" (Dissertation Universität Köln, 1921), appendix B.

loom's efficiency and productivity, so by the early 1880s, fully mechanized velvet factories had begun operating in the villages around Kempen. By 1884, Lobberich's velvet factories and shops employed over 1,000 mechanical velvet looms, while 250 handlooms remained in the households of handweavers. As Table 4 illustrates, the number of velvet handlooms declined markedly from 17,464 in 1880 to 6,902 in 1890, and by 1895 only 1,758 continued to operate in the Krefeld district. A comparison of this drastic reduction of handlooms with the only moderate increase of mechanical looms not only suggests that the factory looms were significantly more productive than the handlooms but also makes it clear why the mechanized mills were unable to absorb more than a small segment of the displaced handweavers. The employment statistics for the region verify the heavy casualities of the battle between handweaving and mechanical weaving: of the 51,000 workers producing velvet cloth in 1880 (including weavers, shearers, winders, and others in both the preparatory and finishing sectors), fewer than 9,000 were still employed in 1906. And because a single weaver on a mechanical velvet loom could do the work of eight to twelve handweavers, the 9,000 velvet workers produced significantly more than the 51,000 workers had in 1880, as Heinrich Brauns laconically pointed out in his study of this transition.[99]

Although the mechanization of velvet production proceeded swiftly, silk

---

Stadt Viersen, 1890–1913" (Dissertation, Universität Duisburg, 1984), p. 84. See also Johannes Lipp, *Hundert Jahre Girmes Oedt, 1879–1979* (Oedt bei Krefeld: Heimatverein Oedt, 1982). The Girmes company installed the first 100 mechanical looms in the new factory in 1886. By 1891, Girmes employed 450 workers and 200 looms; by 1904, 1,000 workers and 500 looms.

99. Brauns, *Der Übergang von der Handweberei*, pp. 44, 89, 176; van der Upwich, *Die Geschichte und die Entwicklung*, p. 123; Ulrich, "Soziale Entwicklungen," p. 99. Also see KrA Vie, GA Lobberich 1820, "Erhebung über die Lage der Sammtindustrie vom 20.12.1884."

merchants remained skeptical about the productive capacity of the first mechanical looms. Indeed, the lag in the mechanization of silk weaving was mainly due to the technical properties of silk yarn, for it proved extremely difficult to construct a mechanical loom that could weave the fine yarn into cloth of uniform quality and consistency faster than handlooms. Moreover, as long as the silk entrepreneurs of Krefeld retained a monopoly on an array of fabrics, they were well able to afford the luxury of home-industrial production.[100] It was precisely the threat of losing that privileged market position to cheaper, mechanically produced goods, which arose during the early 1880s when French silk began to flood the European markets, that sparked the first wave of mechanization among silk producers in the Rhineland. Indeed, the representatives of one silk company, Schiller-Crous of Krefeld, called on fellow merchants and weavers to understand that "the expansion of mechanical silk weaving is a life-and-death question for our entire industry" as "each season, handweaving loses more of its ground in our most important markets in England and America . . . to the French or the Swiss, who surpass us because of the superiority of their mechanized mills and their cheaper labor costs."[101]

Despite this apparent urgency, the mechanization of silk weaving proved more gradual than the parallel transformation of velvet production, displacing silk weavers over some fifteen years, whereas the decline of hand velvet weaving was more rapid (see table 4). Correspondingly, the the two sites of production—household and factory—coexisted longer in silk: in 1882, when mechanization of silk was in the early stages, only 460 of the 16,855 silk looms in operation in the Lower Rhine were mechanical. By 1890 mechanical looms had increased only to some 2,500, while home weavers continued to employ some 14,260 handlooms.[102] The fierce contest between hand and factory silk weaving intensified as mechanization accelerated during the 1890s. By the end of that decade the number of silk handlooms had dwindled to 5,834, while mechanical looms had grown to 7,151. At the same time, the workforce in silk production dwindled by two-thirds, from 33,000 in 1880 to 11,000 in 1906.[103] The handweavers who continued to manufacture silk cloth between the turn of the century and the First World War were usually specialized producers

---

100. Brauns, *Der Übergang von der Handweberei*, p. 118; van der Upwich, *Die Geschichte und die Entwicklung*, p. 117.
101. HStAD, Reg. Düss., H&G 24741, "Schreiben von Schiller, Crous & Cie, Crefeld vom 9.2.1881," p. 179.
102. Brauns, *Der Übergang von der Handweberei*, pp. 89, 176–77; van der Upwich, *Die Geschichte und die Entwicklung*, p. 133.
103. Brauns, *Der Übergang von der Handweberei*, pp. 176–77.

for certain patterns or weights of fabric. Contemporaries noted that the silk merchants continued to depend on handweavers for certain specialty cloth that the mechanized factories could not produce as well or as cheaply. In 1913 there were still 1,722 silk handlooms in operation in the Krefeld region, of which only 99 remained after the war.[104]

Gender and the Organization of Work in Silk and Velvet Weavers' Households

An important aspect of the legacy of silk and velvet weaving, founded and organized by merchants as a *Verlagssystem* (putting-out system) from the outset, is the absence of craft guild traditions. Unlike the organization of work in the guild masters' shops, which was shaped by the highly codified process of skill transmission between master and nonfamily journeymen and apprentices, the productive unit in the handweaving household consisted mainly, often exclusively, of the male weaver, head of the household, his wife (who was often a skilled weaver in her own right), and their children, parents, or other close relatives, "integrating and training the labor of all family members" including both boys and girls.[105] Handweaving parents passed their skills on to their children informally; most learned to spool or creel at age five or six and began to assist at the looms at twelve or thirteen. In his travels through the textile centers of the Lower Rhine, Alfons Thun lingered in Krefeld long enough to reflect on the implications of the (male and female) handweavers' lifelong work at the looms, beginning in early childhood:

> The premature marriages of parents, the very early labor of children [who work] in a hunched-over position in crowded rooms, the young men's consumption of whiskey, have created a hereditary weavers' estate [*Weberstand*], with its many characteristic traits, in all of the weavers' communities. A weaver who has been working since earliest childhood is easily recognized: his visage is waxen, pallid, and languid, his eyes lively, legs thin, arms scrawny like those of children, hands delicate and white; his whole body exudes more agility than strength; the man is a weakling, worn out and consumptive at age fifty. No wonder that in 1872 only 15 percent of the weavers of Kempen were eligible for the military at the first examination!

104. Ibid., p. 157; Franz Wischer, "Organisationsbestrebungen der Arbeiter in der Krefelder Seiden- und Samtindustrie" (Dissertation, Universität Köln, 1921), appendix B.
105. HStAD, Reg. Düss., H&G 24742, "Bericht der Firma Christian Mengen vom 12.5.1883"; van der Upwich, *Die Geschichte und die Entwicklung*, pp. 110–12; Brauns, *Der Übergang von der Handweberei*, pp. 28, 58, 153. This observation was part of Mengen's comments on the organization of work in domestic silk weavers' households.

Crooked legs and a tendency toward tuberculosis were the most common reasons [for rejection]. And that is only the adult weavers! Not even the child in its mother's womb is spared, for thrusts of the loom's carriage deliver hard blows to the baby."[106]

Peter Kriedte, noted scholar of protoindustrialization in the Krefeld region, considers the labor of family members a key point of demarcation between *Handwerk* (craft) and *Hausindustrie* (household production). According to this schema, women and children remained peripheral to productive labor in craft production or were barred from it, whereas the functioning of a protoindustrial weaver's household depended on the active participation of women and children.[107] If the silk weavers' household had only one loom, it was usually attended by the male head of household; where second or third looms operated, they were tended by his wife or daughters, most likely under his direction. Small children or elderly grandparents often spooled or wound the yarn in addition to weaving; the wife and mother was responsible for cleaning the warp. Kriedte's discovery of a high degree of intermarriage among silk weavers' daughters and master silk weavers suggests not only that a young woman's experience and skill in silk production were critical criteria in a male weaver's decision to marry, but also that the work of married women weavers was something both men and women took for granted in the formation of new silk weaving households.[108] In the absence of a son or on the death of the husband or father, female weavers, many with lifetime experience at the looms, became managers of household production, although few obtained the status of independent master weaver or the right to train or supervise nonfamily employees.[109]

The archival documents on handweaving in the Kempen district offer an incomplete picture of handweaving households at midcentury in which female labor remains virtually undetectable. Government surveys of the 1880s and 1890s, by contrast, indicate that 10 to 30 percent or more of the master weavers who were officially counted by local authorities or health insurance boards were female. The lists of silk and velvet weavers in the mayoralty of Grefrath near Kempen for 1848, 1850, and 1852–53

---

106. Thun, *Die Industrie am Niederrhein*, p. 151.
107. Kriedte, *Eine Stadt am seidenen Faden*, p. 162.
108. Ibid., p. 210; Brauns, *Der Übergang von der Handweberei*, p. 154. Kriedte's data analysis of the occupations of brides and bridegrooms shows that in 1838–40 some 80 percent of female silk weavers married male silk weavers. Two-thirds of male silk weavers, in turn, married daughters of silk weavers.
109. Kriedte, *Eine Stadt am seidenen Faden*, pp. 114–16, 129, 144. Kriedte estimates that one-tenth of female weavers were heads of households.

include no women, a fact Kriedte attributes to the common practice among officials of listing silk workers' wives "as a matter of principle . . . as wives and not as silk workers, even though they assisted their husbands with the work at the loom or worked a loom themselves."[110] Yet in 1854 a thirteen-year-old girl, Johanna Meyers, from Straelen, signed an official apprenticeship contract with a master velvet weaver in Lobberich, who was to instruct her in the art of velvet weaving for three years (see plate 1).[111] Although Hans van der Upwich's local study of 1920 asserts that "formal apprenticeship training was, like all craft traditions, of little significance" among the silk and velvet weavers of the Lower Rhine, the language of the contract, its elaboration of *Dienstverhältnis* (terms of service), *Lehrgeld* (remuneration), and other aspects of the relations between apprentice and *Lehrherr* (master in the guild sense), and its official registration with the mayor's office shed light on the ways skilled weavers were able to reappropriate and reinvent the traditions of guild production, which in this mid-nineteenth century guise now included women.[112] Particularly because velvet handweaving was reputed to be mainly a male domain, this contract suggests that women's presence, even formal training, in velvet weaving may have been more common than implied in the legends and narratives of the transition from home to factory industry.[113]

Indeed, a local survey of velvet and silk home weavers in the Kempen district indicates that in 1892, 20 (11 percent) of the 170 master weavers were female and two-thirds of the 66 *Gesellen* (journeymen/women) and 14 (44 percent) of the apprentices were female.[114] Although Kriedte points to an advance of women in the region's handweaving industry in the

110. Ibid., p. 131. For a parallel story in a different part of Germany, see Jean H. Quataert, "Social Insurance and the Family Work of Oberlausitz Home Weavers in the Late Nineteenth Century," in *German Women in the Nineteenth Century*, ed. John C. Fout (New York: Holmes and Meier, 1984), p. 275.
111. KrA Vie, GA Lobberich 1797: *Lehrvertrag* Johanna Meyers.
112. The contract, which apparently conformed to paragraph 158 of the Prussian trade regulations, was signed by the master weaver, the young girl, and her father. That it appears to revive a formal apprenticeship system can be explained in terms of the emergence in 1848 of weavers' guilds, *Innungen*, that pursued these goals.
113. On this distinction between silk and velvet production, see Brauns, *Der Übergang von der Handweberei*, p. 28; van der Upwich, *Die Geschichte und die Entwicklung*, p. 141. On training and apprenticeship in silk and velvet weaving, see Kriedte, *Die Stadt am seidenen Faden*, p. 135.
114. KrA Vie, Stadtarchiv Kempen (StA Kemp) 1058, "Zahl der Hausweber und Gehilfen im Kreis Kempen 1881–1892," and "Übersicht der Handwebstuhl-Verhältnisse in der Stadtbürgermeisterei Kempen und der Landbürgermeisterei Schmalbroich 1887" indicate a similarly high percentage of women in the categories of journeymen and apprentices. Of the 221 masters, 12 percent (27) were female; of the 75 *Gesellen*, 64 percent (48) were female; of the 39 apprentices, 38 percent (15) were female.

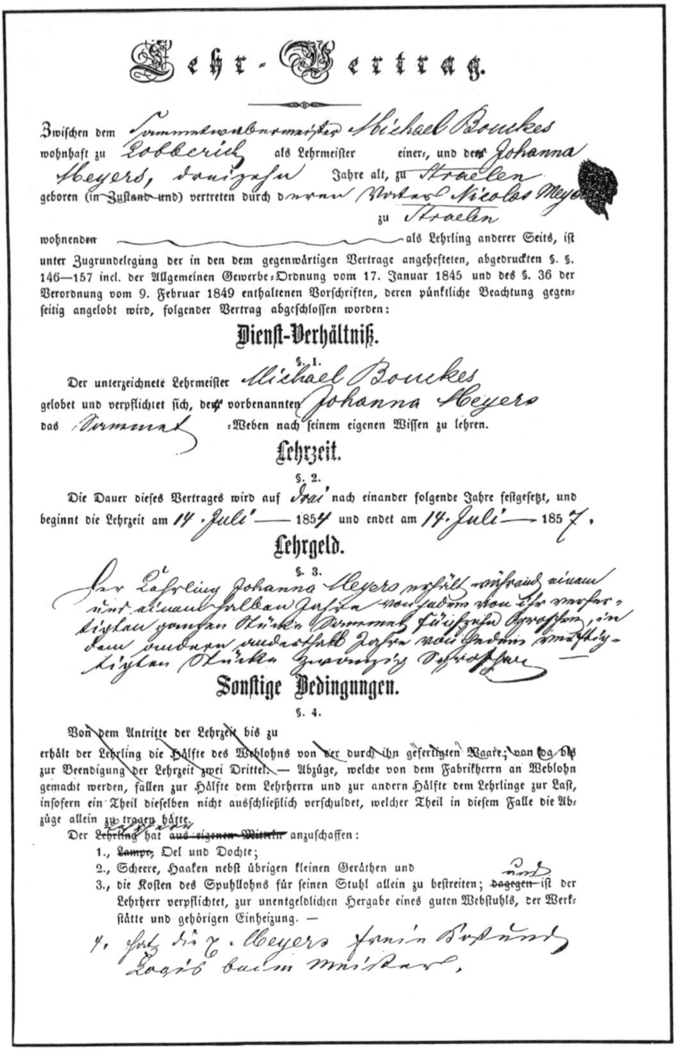

Plate 1. Apprenticeship contract of Johanna Meyers (age thirteen) with the master weaver Michael Bouckes, covering 14 July 1854 through 14 July 1857. Reproduced courtesy of the Kreisarchiv Viersen from the file Gemeindeamt Lobberich no. 1797.

course of the nineteenth century, it is unclear whether the increased visibility of women was due to an actual increase in their number or to the growing interest of the authorities in their presence in home industry.[115] Close study of the survey confirms van der Upwich's contention that many

---

115. Kriedte, *Eine Stadt am seidenen Faden*, p. 130.

journeymen and journeywomen and apprentices within the largely informal system of skill transmission in both silk and velvet weaving were the wives, sons, and daughters of master weavers: 13 of the female *Gesellen* served as assistants to their husbands, brothers, or fathers (who are listed as masters). Of the female masters, 7 also had husbands listed as masters; 11 (including 2 widows) worked independently without assistance, and 2 more worked as masters next to a brother and a father.[116] Another inquiry of 1884 reveals that of the 219 *Gesellen* and apprentices in silk weaving households of Kempen and nearby Schmalbroich, just over half were female (112); 107 (49 percent) of the 219 male and female assistants worked with family members in their own households, while the remaining 51 percent worked for nonfamily employers.[117]

The membership figures of the *Ortskrankenkasse* (local health insurance board), which insured weavers who worked independently in their homes and thus were not on the payroll of local textile mills, also attest to the significant presence of women among the region's silk and velvet handweavers. The list reveals a marked decline in the number of independent home weavers from 215 members in 1892 to 118 in 1899 and 65 in 1907. During the same period, however, the proportional representation of women increased from 21 percent (45) in 1892 to 29 percent (34) in 1899 and 63 percent in 1907 (41), suggesting that handweaving became an increasingly female domain in the course of its decline as male weavers either retired or sought employment in a local factory.[118] Finally, the brief accounts of elderly female weavers' working lives, summarized in their applications to local charities for financial assistance for old age and in their requests for coverage under the national old age and disability insurance law, offer poignant testimony of the lifelong full-time work of women in home weaving. One female weaver's son recounts in 1900, "My mother, Catharina Agnes Jores, widow of Johnann H. Joosten, was born on 20 November 1830 and has worked since she was twelve years old, that is, since 1842, at the weaving loom in order to earn her daily bread. She worked [in her home] for the firms Diergardt, Scheibler and Ebeling. . . . My mother has been completely unable to work since 1894, and thus I apply for assistance on her behalf."[119] Indicating the tendency of handweavers to work for more than one silk merchant, particularly during the

---

116. KrA Vie, StA Kemp 1058, "Zahl der Hausweber und Gehilfen im Kreis Kempen 1881–1892."

117. KrA Vie, StA Kemp 1058, "Übersicht über die Seidenweber, Kempen und Schmalbroich, nach der Zählung vom 13. Mai 1884."

118. KrA Vie, GA Grefrath 1302, "Statut der Ortskrankenkasse für Weber und Wirker der Bürgermeisterei Grefrath," 1892–1902, 1902–7.

119. Ibid.

crisis years of the 1880s and 1890s, another application reported that "Maria Louisa Herschels, now the wife of Lambert Diederichs, resident of Lobberich, born in Viersen in 1829 . . . was steadily employed as a handweaver since completion of her schooling. According to her attached documents, she worked from early 1863 until the end of 1873, from February 1874 through June of 1885 for the Niedieck company here in Lobberich, and from June 1885 through February 1891 for the de Ball company here, at which time she gave up handweaving and has been taking care of the household since that time."[120]

By 1913, when only remnants of handweaving remained in the silk and velvet regions of Krefeld and Kempen, "nearly the entire house industrial production [was] carried out by women," who represented 90.5 percent of the 4,442 home workers in the region in 1913, including some 1,400 silk and velvet workers, among them weavers, shearers, and winders; 1,750 producers of silk ties, an item of Krefeld's specialty silk trade; and 634 seamstresses in the garment industry.[121] Although women's work was long established in all of these domestic workshops, the factory inspector who wrote the report nonetheless noted: "Most of them, with the exception of the seamstresses who produce the silk neckties, are women, who work to supplement the earnings of their husbands."[122] By 1913 home weaving had become a preserve not only of women, but of the elderly, as the younger women, both married and single, abandoned it in favor of the "higher wages and easier work on the mechanically powered machines." Home industry, the inspector predicted, "is bound to disappear completely after the deaths of the old handweavers."[123] Indeed, the feminization of home industry could not deter its continuing decline and eventual demise during the First World War.

Gender in the Crisis of Transition from Home to Factory Industry

The first acute crisis in the transition from home to factory velvet weaving occurred in 1880–81 when the introduction of mechanical velvet looms in the Lower Rhine coincided with a shift in fashion trends that paralyzed the velvet ribbon branch and sent its weavers to the cloth weavers' workshops in a desperate search for work. As a result of these

120. Ibid.
121. HStAD, Reg. Düss., H&G 24751, "Bericht des Gewerbeinspektors, Stadt und Landkreis Krefeld vom 11.7.1913." The urban/rural distribution of the home industrial workers was as follows: 2,868 of the 4,442 were employed within the city limits of Krefeld; 318 in the rural district of Krefeld, and 1,256 in the Kempen district.
122. Ibid.
123. Ibid.

converging processes—mechanization and the contraction of velvet ribbon weaving—all but 400 of 13,000 velvet handlooms in the villages around Kempen were idled in 1881.[124] As analyzed by Heinrich Brauns in 1906, the atmosphere of crisis and conflict during the early 1880s represented "the revenge for the sins" of the previous decade, a period of upswing in both the silk and velvet trades, of booming trade and shortage of qualified weavers. The merchants and masters had sought to alleviate the shortage "in those days . . . by travel[ing] the countryside on behalf of entrepreneurs and train[ing] farmhands and servant girls in the skills of weaving." Indeed, "soon after they had woven a piece of cloth or two, these 'apprentices' were regarded as independent master weavers."[125]

Weavers, entrepreneurs, and town officials alike perceived this initial crisis of 1881 as the opening battle in a longer contest between home weavers and their employers, both merchants and mill owners, a conflict that was particularly bitter in the small towns and villages outside Krefeld, where the weavers had few employment alternatives. Levin Indenklef, an unmarried thirty-three-year-old velvet weaver who worked with his mother and three siblings in their household in Oedt, a small village near Kempen, took the bold and highly public step in 1881 of drafting a letter to Kaiser Wilhelm I about the misfortunes of the velvet weavers of the Lower Rhine.

> Your Majesty! Thousands of silk weavers in the Krefeld and Kempen districts are at present out of work and without bread, suffering the most bitter deprivations, and are actually starving! For years the wages of the poor weavers were bargained down and arbitrarily reduced. The shrewdest speculators reduced wages a few pennies. And the others? With a few exceptions, they followed suit. What do we get today for a meter of the same quality of velvet, which brought in 3–3.60 marks in 1870–74? The most humane of companies . . . pays 2 to 2.20 marks and the others only 1.50 marks. By now the starving weavers are so beaten down that they will even accept 1 mark for the same length of cloth. . . . But it is self-evident that he who gives the worker employment is obliged to pay him a wage he can live on. The wages have been reduced to such a low level that even the weaver who has work cannot sustain himself.[126]

124. HStAD, Reg. Düss., H&G 24742, "Brief der Handelskammer Mönchen-Gladbach an das Regierungspräsidium bezüglich der Lage der Sammt- und Seidenweberei im Crefelder-Gladbacher Bezirk"; KrA Vie, GA Lobberich 1820, "Bericht des Regierungspräsidenten vom 9.3.1885"; Brauns, *Der Übergang von der Handweberei*, p. 53.
125. Brauns, *Der Übergang von der Handweberei*, p. 54.
126. KrA Vie, GA Lobberich 1820, "Notruf der Weber des Niederrheins, besonders der Kreise Kempen und Crefeld, an ihren erhobenen Kaiser und König von Levin Indenklef"

Indenklef's highly public lament sparked a flurry of letters among mayors and provincial authorities, entrepreneurs, and government officials about the accuracy of his depiction. Although opinions were divided as to his character and his *Tüchtigkeit* (proficiency) as a weaver (one official attributed his outspokenness to Social Democratic sympathies and another disqualified him as an indolent worker), the mayor of Oedt confirmed Indenklef's claims regarding rampant unemployment and periodic wage reductions.[127] The mayor of Dülken, another participant in the debates among local government bureaucrats about Indenklef's protest, elaborated on his own town's grave plight: "The wages of the weavers have been in decline in the last several years and have now reached the point where it is scarcely possible for a married weaver to earn the minimal living to support his (usually) very large family," a fact the mayor confirmed in his interviews with four "respectable weavers," who were earning between 1.50 and 1.60 marks a day.[128] Entrepreneurs, mayors, *Landräte* (district officials), and provincial authorities sought to alleviate these hardships by opening soup kitchens, finding work for weavers in other textile branches in the vicinity, and instituting funds to support unemployed and elderly weavers. Furthermore, local officials sought to give entrepreneurs incentives to build new factories in communities plagued by high unemployment.[129]

The mass unemployment in the velvet regions lasted only a few months in 1881, but by the middle of the decade it became chronic and prolonged, as the number of velvet handlooms in the Krefeld district continued its steady decline and only a fraction of the former handweavers were able to find work in the newly mechanized mills. A similar crisis beset both the velvet and silk industries in 1884 when more than one-fourth of the nearly 33,000 silk and velvet handlooms in the Lower Rhine were idled because of a downturn in the international markets for silk and velvet cloth.[130] By the mid-1880s the mayor of Lobberich reported to the provin-

---

(1881). See also KrA Vie, *Heimatbuch des Kreises Kempen-Krefeld* (Kempen, 1970), in particular the essay by Walter Tillmann, "Die Soziale Lage der Handweber am Niederrhein, 1848–1898," pp. 105–21.

127. KrA Vie, GA Lobberich 1820, and HStAD, Reg. Düss., H&G 24741, pp. 94–186, contain the series of letters to and from town officials, silk and velvet entrepreneurs, and the government authorities in Düsseldorf about the validity of Indenklef's claims. Also see "Bericht des Landrats Kempen von 12.2.1881," p. 141 of the latter file.

128. HStAD, Reg. Düss., H&G 24741, "Bericht des Bürgermeisters Dülken vom 7.2.1881; Bericht des Bürgermeisters Oedt vom 7.2.1881," pp. 169, 190.

129. Van der Upwich, *Die Geschichte und die Entwicklung*, p. 126.

130. The late mechanization of silk and velvet production in the Rhineland had given the edge to French and Swiss competitors in the international markets. HStAD, Reg. Düss., H&G 24742, "Brief der Handelskammer Mönchen-Gladbach an das Regierungspräsidium bezüglich der Lage der Sammt- und Seidenweberei im Crefelder-Gladbacher Bezirk"; KrA Vie, GA Lobberich 1820, "Bericht des Regierungspräsidenten vom 9.3.1885"; Brauns, *Der Übergang von der Handweberei*, p. 53.

cial authorities that "the battle of the handloom with the mechanical loom is becoming ever more hopeless for many important goods. Already now we can say with confidence that a large segment of the handweavers have become permanently superfluous, that is, that the smooth and light silk and plush fabrics are lost to the handloom and that handweaving will be sustained only in the patterned, heavy, and synthetic wool velvets and silk fabrics."[131] Following this crisis silk handweaving was briefly reinvigorated as handlooms increased from 11,062 in 1885 to 14,263 in 1890, but then it began a steady downward spiral after 1890. By the century's end the victory march of the mechanical silkloom was complete. Among the handweavers who remained, the tradition of skill transmission within the household gradually eroded. Recognizing the dissolution of their craft, handweavers now sent their children off to the mechanized mills, where wages were higher and the work was cleaner and less physically burdensome than at the handloom.[132]

Although both silk and velvet manufacture were "feminized" by the end of the nineteenth century, the implications and outcomes of this process differed in the two sectors. Most of the uprooted velvet handweavers, for example, lost their jobs to mechanized looms, not to female competitors. The new velvet factories employed relatively few women as weavers, whereas velvet shearers and winders were predominantly female, a division that was usually explained in terms of the heavy velvet looms and the use of the double winder in velvet production.[133] In the sizable Girmes velvet mill in Oedt, for example, there was almost no overlap between male and female spheres of employment: whereas the 412 male workers (63.5 percent of the workforce) were weavers, machinists, dyers, and foremen, the 237 women worked as piecers, shearers, winders, bobbin setters, nappers, darners, and seamstresses.[134] In silk weaving, by contrast, women made up one-third to one-half of factory silk weavers by the end of the 1890s. In 1901 the 110 silk factories of the government district of Düsseldorf, including both ribbon and cloth production, employed some 10,926 work-

131. KrA Vie, GA Lobberich 1820, "Bericht des Bürgermeisters Lobberichs über die Lage der Industrie vom 1.10.1885."
132. Brauns, *Der Übergang von der Handweberei*, pp. 37–40.
133. According to the strike records for this region, some 6 percent of velvet weavers in the Kempen district were female in 1899, during the mass strike in the velvet industry. See HStAD, Reg. Düss., H&G 24691, "Bericht der Polizeiverwaltung Crefeld vom 14.1.1899" (including a list of the factories affected by the strike and the numbers of their male and female weavers). The report lists a total of 924 striking weavers, including 56 women. The number of female shearers, winders, and so on was considerably larger.
134. Johann Girmes AG, Oedt bei Krefeld, *Arbeiterstammrollen*, 1885–1917 (private holdings of Johannes Lipp, director of the Heimatverein Oedt). These figures seem congruous with those for the Düsseldorf district in 1901, whereby 3,494 women worked in the fifty-two velvet factories of the Düsseldorf district, composing 35 percent of the workforce of 10,053. Also see Brauns, *Der Übergang von der Handweberei*, pp. 175–79.

ers, 53 percent (5,800) of them women. Moreover, among the female workers in the new silk and velvet factories were growing numbers of married women: in 1899, 19 percent of the female workers in Krefeld's silk mills were married, a figure that increased to 21.4 percent in 1904.[135]

As the factory became "a concentrated metaphor for hopes and fears about the direction and pace of industrial change" among the weavers of the Rhineland, the return of women workers to the home—more than the removal of women from paid labor per se—became the rallying cry of both employed and unemployed weavers.[136] Silk and velvet weavers across the Rhineland organized to thwart the advance of the factory and the feminization of the factory workforce during the 1880s. The weavers' voluntary *Innungen* (guilds), revived during the crisis of 1881, relied on reinvented structures and narratives of craft guild traditions both in form and in content. The *Innungsbewegung* (guild movement) of the 1880s harked back to the short-lived guild movement of 1848, which had dissolved by the mid-1860s. Master silk weavers had founded the first short-lived *Innungen* in Krefeld during the late 1840s in order to negotiate a *Lohnliste* (a comprehensive wage list for various articles of cloth and ribbon) with the local silk merchants. The *Lohnliste*, which aimed to regulate not only the piece rates for various kinds of cloth but also the more fundamental complex of relations between merchants and weavers, also envisioned imposing guildlike restrictions on the labor of female weavers. A key point in the mediation of the agreement, which ultimately was approved by the burgomaster of Krefeld, the city council, the chamber of commerce, and the trade courts, was the weavers' demand that "a merchant may employ only male workers as master weavers in his workshop," except for daughters of deceased master weavers "who worked the looms themselves." Furthermore, the weavers stipulated, "once she [the daughter] has married, however, she may no longer continue her occupation as master weaver."[137] The successful negotiation of the agreement was celebrated by a parade of "several thousand masters, journeymen, and citizens" through the streets of Krefeld, signifying the attempts of the first guildsmen to anchor the recognition of craft in the city's civic culture.

The revival of the guild movement during the crisis of the early 1880s quickly encompassed 4,500 silk and velvet weavers—some one-fourth of the region's weavers—in forty local guilds throughout the Lower Rhine,

---

135. Jochem Ulrich, *Die soziale und wirtschaftliche Entwicklung in der Stadt Krefeld, 1870–1918* (Krefeld: Stadtarchiv Krefeld, forthcoming 1996). 145; Brauns, *Der Übergang von der Handweberei*, p. 180.

136. Robert Gray, "The Language of Factory Reform in Britain, c. 1830–1860," in Joyce, *Historical Meanings of Work*, pp. 143, 171.

137. Wischer, *Die Organisationsbestrebungen*, pp. 22–23.

and in 1883 the local guilds consolidated their forces to form the Niederrheinischer Weberbund (Weavers' Union of the Lower Rhine).[138] The rekindled movement not only emerged from the acute distress of the weavers during the early 1880s but also coincided with the passage of a new *Innungsgesetz* (guild law) in 1881, which permitted and even encouraged independent craftsmen to organize guilds to protect their skill and status, a solution that both provincial and imperial authorities also recommended to Levin Indenklef in response to his public letter. The goals of the *Innungen* as envisioned by government officials were "to prevent the exploitation of distress through united interventions against employers' excesses; to attain favorable working conditions and adequate and, wherever possible, stable wages that fluctuate as little as possible; and to improve the training of apprentices and journeymen by mandating fixed training periods, imposing new stipulations for the master's examination, and setting a minimum age for the achievement of master status." Finally, the revived guilds were to institute self-help measures such as sickness and burial funds and consumer cooperatives.[139] Members sought to remake themselves as craftsmen, and under authority of the guild law, membership in the Innungen was restricted to "all male persons who have come of age and who practice silk [or velvet] weaving independently and possess the civic rights of citizenship [*bürgerliche Ehrenrechte*]." The wife of a guild member was permitted, if her husband died and she took over the workshop, "to inherit the prerogatives and obligations of the deceased [within the *Innung*], with the exception of the right to vote."[140] With respect to the factory weaver, "who had begun his employment before he had completed his three years' work at the [hand]loom," the guild statutes decreed that "if he wishes to establish himself as an independent master, he must make up that part of the three years' training that is missing before he can be admitted for the master's examination or permitted to join the *Innung*."[141]

The primary goals of the *Innungsbewegung*, as formulated by the Weavers' Union of the Lower Rhine, were to halt the degradation of independent master weavers to factory workers; to reinvigorate a vital sector of handweaving; and to reach agreements with local employers regarding

138. Brauns, *Der Übergang von der Handweberei*, pp. 97, 101, 106; van der Upwich, *Die Geschichte und die Entwicklung*, p. 183.
139. Brauns, *Der Übergang von der Handweberei*, pp. 98–101. These guidelines for the *Innungen* were elaborated to the chamber of commerce of Krefeld by the imperial district government in Düsseldorf in a letter of 22 August 1881, which Brauns cites.
140. KrA Vie, GA Lobberich 1756, "Statuten der Seiden- und Wirkerinnung zu Boisheim und Lobberich, genehmigt 1887." Membership criteria can also be found in KrA Vie, StA Kemp 1058, "Statuten der Seidenweber- und Wirkerinnungen zu Kempen-Schmalbroich, gegrundet 1881."
141. Brauns, *Der Übergang von der Handweberei*, p. 100.

hours and earnings for independent master weavers.[142] Key to the realization of each of these goals was the prohibition of *unabhängige Frauenarbeit* (independent work of women) in home weaving for all women but master weavers' widows. Furthermore, to prevent the transmission of skill to future competitors, women were to be barred from the official *Lehrzeit* (training) required of male journeymen and apprentices and prevented from training their own journeymen or assistants.[143] Battling on two fronts against the displacement of male weavers by women, the weavers' guilds also raised frequent demands for the eradication of women's work at the factory looms.[144]

Athough the voluntary guilds could not stem the tide of mechanization or feminization, they successfully mobilized local public opinion on behalf of their struggle to limit the domains of female employment, in both domestic and factory industry. One mayor reported in 1883, for example, that local merchants, under pressure from the guilds, had continued to commission work from adult female weavers but had restricted their dealings to those who had completed three years of training; and as a further concession to the guilds, no journeymen or apprentices employed by female master weavers were given work.[145] Public deliberations of the statutes of one *Innung* suggest, however, that the stringent demands of the guilds regarding women's work necessitated negotiation not only with employers but also occasionally with the handweavers themselves. For example, at one assembly the speaker pleaded on behalf of the independent female weavers for an amendment to the guild statutes that would permit them to employ their children, siblings, and other close relatives, for "otherwise many widows will no longer be able to earn their living." In reply, the privy councillor of the Düsseldorf district, Gustav Königs, emphasized

---

142. Wischer, *Die Organisationsbestrebungen*, p. 26.
143. KrA Vie, GA Lobberich 1820, "Bericht des Regierungspräsidenten vom 27.1.1883." Similar measures regarding a minimum age for master status were included to prevent young men's premature accession to master status.
144. KrA Vie, StA Kemp 1058, "Bericht über die Weberversammlung der Seidenweber- und Wirkerinnungen zu Kempen und Schmalbroich vom 26.6.1882"; HStAD, Reg. Düss., H&G 24742, pp. 170–76, excerpts from the *Crefelder Zeitung, Niederrheinische Volkszeitung, Gladbacher Zeitung* of February and March 1883, pp. 218–22, "Bericht von der Firma Christian Mengen über die Innungsbewegung unter den Webern in der Hausindustrie." Also see Wischer, *Die Organisationsbestrebungen*, pp. 35–36.
145. KrA Vie, GA Lobberich 1820, "Bericht des Regierungspräsidenten vom 27.1.1883," which contains his "Vorschlag zur Besserung der Lage." Also see HStAD, Reg. Düss., H&G 24741, pp. 186–90, "Schreiben des Bürgermeisters von Oedt vom 7.2.1881." In this report the mayor of the velvet mill village of Oedt suggested that women should not be working at the looms, but rather should remedy the *Dienstmädchenmangel* (shortage of servants) in the vicinity.

that this amendment must represent "the outermost concession to the female weavers, for they really must not employ other young people, besides their children and close relatives, as apprentices or journeymen. The weavers regard this restriction as crucial, for even if we cannot wholly abolish women's work, we should do that to the best of our ability: the woman belongs in the home more than she does at the loom."[146] Similarly, when 450 male velvet weavers went on strike at the Niedieck company of Lobberich in 1885, their demands included grievances regarding women's work in the mill. In response, the owners underscored the fluid, rather than rigid, boundaries between the "oldest, best, and most steadfast workers"—as the weavers represented themselves—and the expanding female workforce in the firm's factory and home-industrial workshops. While acknowledging that the mill employed three hundred young women, the owners pointed out that "most of them belong to the weavers' families," as did "a number of women who [worked] as shearers for the mechanical mill or as velvet handweavers in home industry."[147]

The revived rhetoric of craft and guild, both legal and popular, defined new boundaries and assigned new meanings to women's work in the silk and velvet weavers' communities, effacing the legacy and customs of women's work in protoindustrial family economies and contesting their right to continue weaving in the new setting of the factory. In the winter of 1886 the Weavers' Union of the Lower Rhine dispatched a delegation from Krefeld to Berlin, carrying a petition from silk and velvet weavers describing the calamitous conditions of home industry there and calling for ameliorative measures, which they sought to present to the "appropriate authorities." The petition, signed by some 9,000 weavers, echoed the guilds' demands for state-imposed restrictions on the mechanical production of silk and velvet; for a ban on the work of women or minors either in the mechanical mills or as independent weavers in home industry; and for state-sanctioned wage agreements between weavers and employers.[148] The weavers' delegation was first received by Hans Freiherr von Berlepsch, governor of the Düsseldorf district, who accompanied "his dear weavers

---

146. HStAD, Reg. Düss., H&G 24742, Auszug aus der *Gladbacher Volkszeitung* no. 54 (5.5.1883), which discusses the public deliberation of the guild statutes.

147. KrA Vie, GA Lobberich, "Brief der Arbeiter von Niedieck an den Bürgermeister von Lobberich vom 22.5.1885"; "Bericht über eine Arbeitseinstellung bei DeBall wegen Lohnherabsetzung vom 21.5.1885"; "Bericht der *Niederrheinischen Volkszeitung* vom 26.5.1885"; "Bericht des Bürgermeisters Lobberich vom 1.10.1885." The weavers represented themselves to authorities and the public as "precisely the oldest, best, and most steadfast workers," not "frivolous or full of bravado."

148. HStAD, Reg. Düss., H&G 24752, pp. 103–11, "Bericht über eine allgemeine große Weberversammlung für Elberfeld und Umgegend am Sonntag, den 1. August 1886."

from the Lower Rhine" to their meeting with then minister of commerce Bötticher. In subsequent days the weavers' delegation also was granted an audience with both Kaiser Wilhelm I and the crown prince, in which they elaborated their demands.[149] The journey of the Krefeld delegation was the topic of discussion and debate in guild circles in subsequent months: at one weavers' assembly later that year, a discussion ensued about the guild's demand for a *Verbot* (ban) on the employment of women and minors in the mechanized mills. Underscoring the importance of adequate wages for male workers "so they can support their families," the speakers also affirmed the principle that "the woman belongs not in the factory, but in the household." In the search for consensus on this issue, however, one speaker sought to clarify that the key issue was "not to ban women from working altogether, but to restrict their work to care of the household [*Haushaltung*]," a measure that would contribute significantly to solving the social question.[150]

As the "victory march" of the mechanical loom proceeded relentlessly through the Lower Rhine during the late 1880s and early 1890s, the basis of the guild movement began to deteriorate. By 1892 mayors in the small towns surrounding Kempen began dissolving their local *Innungen*, which in the meantime had come to exist in name only.[151] Although the struggle for craft had been irretrievably lost, the battle to define gender-specific spheres of factory labor had just begun. For even once the *Innungen* had collapsed, the mentalities of craft and guild lived on in the labor struggles of the late 1890s and after the turn of the century. During the massive velvet weavers' strike of 1899 in the Kempen area, for example, the mainly male strikers portrayed their struggle as one "for a more humane and worthy way of life," central to which was the restriction of women's work: "We no longer want to see our wives, our mothers being forced to enter the factories with us and to have to endure this struggle to support their families."[152] The 2,000 strikers also protested the firm's attempts to retrain female assistants as weavers during the strike. Male strikers angrily confronted twelve female weavers after their first day of work, demanding that they relinquish their jobs and intimidating several so they did not return

---

149. HStAD, Reg. Düss., H&G 24752, pp. 103–11. Berlepsch, it should be noted, became Prussian minister of commerce in 1890, just before Bismarck left office, and pioneered "the new course" in state social policy during the 1890s, in particular the advance of protective labor legislation. (See chapter 4.)

150. HStAD, Reg. Düss., H&G 24752, p. 111.

151. KrA Vie, StA Kemp 1058, "Seidenweber- u. Wirkerinnungen zu Kempen und Schmalbroich."

152. HStAD, Reg. Düss., Polizeiberichte 24691, "Bericht der Krefelder Zeitung no. 205 (24.4.1899)." The assembly at which these demands were raised was attended by some 1,000 persons.

the next day.[153] Ironically, the Social Democratic textile union, which had many supporters among the striking weavers, played a key role in this conflict, first excluding women workers from strike support, citing severe dearth of funds. Then, realizing that the firm intended to retrain many female assistants as weavers, the union quickly reversed itself and agreed to offer financial support to female workers, if only to prevent them from being trained or hired as weavers.[154]

The visions and struggles of the disintegrating weavers' guild movement left an imprint not only on the strike movements of the 1880s and 1890s, but also on the local notables and social reformers whose new moral and civic duties included ameliorating the weavers' distress. In the fall of 1896 the "social commission" of the city of Krefeld, comprising mainly members of the city council, took up the social problem of the handweavers' communities, which were plagued by high unemployment, destitution, and misery.[155] In the course of its deliberations the commission concluded that the main cause of the crisis was

> to be found in the current progression of the transition from hand production to factory production and that the repetition of such calamities will not cease until those displaced by the transition to mechanical production either find work in those factories or are given jobs in other types of production. . . . The possibilities that those jobless handweavers will find work are encumbered by the fact that so many women, including married women, are employed in the local mechanized weaving mills, especially those that manufacture silk cloth. Although the social commission recognizes that our main industry cannot do without the female hand for certain tasks (winding, shearing, bobbin setting), we do not refrain from observing that it seems inadvisable to employ girls as weavers and that, moreover, married women should generally be barred from employment in mechanized factories. If this were to be realized, not only would we fulfill the social imperative of returning the woman to her home, of saving her for her family, but above all—and that appears to be most urgent and desirable at the moment—the idle handweavers could be given work at those looms that have been vacated.[156]

153. The Deussen firm argued that the young women, already employed before the strike, were in danger of losing their jobs because of reduced production during the strike and were retrained as weavers so as not to be laid off.
154. HStAD, Reg. Düss., Polizeiberichte 24691, "Berichte der Polizeiverwaltung Krefeld" vom 12.1.1899, 16.1.1899, 8.2.1899, and 9.2.1899; "Bericht der Krefelder Zeitung no. 205 (24.4.1899)."
155. StA Krefeld 4/1209–GT, "Schreiben der sozialen Kommission der Stadt Krefeld." I thank Jochem Ulrich for alerting me to this document.
156. Ibid.

Furthermore, the social commission drafted a memorandum calling on the owners of the region's silk and velvet mills to alleviate the dire conditions among the handweavers by refusing employment to women weavers in favor of the master weavers who remained chronically out of work.[157]

However futile the battle of the guilds against the factory and women's work, the weavers' "rhetorical self-creation" as craftsmen changed the mental landscape of citizenship, estate, and class across the plains of the Lower Rhine.[158] The "moral communities of artisans jealously defending their independence and their rights" against the incursions of female workers would form the kernel of both the Social Democratic textile union, which had a significant presence in the Rhineland after the mid-1890s, and the Christian union, which emerged from the webs of the small local Catholic weavers' unions in the Rhineland in 1901.[159] At the founding assembly of the Social Democratic Textile Workers' Union (DTAV) in Kettwig in 1895, the speakers referred, for example, to the expansion of female labor in the textile mills as an aggravation (*ein Mißstand*), for women "belonged in the home," but the "miserable wages of their husbands [forced] them into the mills."[160] Similarly, an unusual conference of silk workers, which the DTAV and the Christian union sponsored jointly in 1902, passed a unanimous resolution endorsing the impassioned call of Christian textile union leader Jakob Pesch for "the absolute abolition of industrial employment for married women" and demanding reforms that were to benefit "the family, community, state, and human society in general," such as instruction for young women "in their future callings as housewives and mothers."[161]

The revived guilds had imbued the silk and velvet weavers of the Rhineland with a language and an identity that endured far beyond the years of crisis and transition from which they had emerged. They upheld ideals of honorable masculine labor embedded in notions of independence, respect-

---

157. HStAD, JBdKPG 1896, Düsseldorf, p. 389. See also Brauns, *Der Übergang von der Handweberei*, p. 181.

158. The term "rhetorical self-creation" is Patrick Joyce's, elaborated in "Historical Meanings of Work," p. 21.

159. On the "moral communities of artisans," see Maxine Berg, *The Age of Manufactures: Industry, Innovation and Work in Britain, 1700–1820* (Oxford: Oxford University Press, 1985), and her "Women's Work," as well as John Rule, "The Property of Skill in the Period of Manufacture," in Joyce, *Historical Meanings of Work*, p. 107.

160. HStAD, Reg. Düss., H&G 24752, "Bericht über die Versammlung des DTAV in Kettwig a.d. Ruhr vom 17.11.1895."

161. DTAV, *Der Textilarbeiter* 14 (14 June 1902); Zentralverband christlicher Textilarbeiter, *Der Christliche Textilarbeiter* 4 (14 June 1902). Both newspapers reported the unanimous approval of Pesch's resolutions. On the shared views of the two unions toward female factory labor, see "Sozialdemokratie und Fabrikarbeit verheirateter Frauen," *Textilarbeiterzeitung* 11 (17 April 1909): 58.

ability, and skill. Reworking and revitalizing the rhetoric as well as the structure of craft guilds helped displaced weavers come to terms with the separation of household and factory production and the changing meanings of both men's and women's work during a time of rapid structural transformation. At this crucial historical moment, the guildsmen rewrote the history of women's work as they sought to expunge it from both household and factory, rendering it transient and temporary, stripping it of generations of accumulated skill and tradition.

The first workers to endure the transition from home to factory industry, the first men to be "thrown into the streets" by the advance of women workers—the silk and velvet weavers of the Lower Rhine, whose demands were heard at the highest echelons of the state in 1886—became a national emblem of "feminization" and "displacement," of the dissolution of sexual and social order that accompanied the transition to the industrial state. In this respect their plight left its imprint on the debates about female factory labor that preoccupied the social policy arena between 1890 and the First World War, leading social reformers like Brauns and Wilbrandt to conclude that the expansion of women's work was the most detrimental aspect of the new factory system.[162]

Conclusion

This study of the transition to the factory system in the Rhineland explicates how and why female factory labor became a new social question in many textile-producing regions in late nineteenth-century Germany. Although the origins and outcomes of feminization were distinct in each of the four instances examined here, the individual cases show that the sexual division of labor in the newly mechanized mills was shaped by more than the exigencies of production. Rather, the structures of production and divisions of labor represented outcomes of political contests among historical agents, of conflicts between state and industry, mill owners and workers, women and men. Employers sought out women workers, organized work according to their specific qualities, and encouraged the growth of a long-term female *Stammarbeiterschaft* despite the vigorous protests of male workers in some regions and the prevalent social sanctions against the factory employment of married women. Similarly, the first generation of male mill workers fought vigorously to define a place for themselves in the first textile factories in the Rhineland, challenging both employers and female workers and appealing to the state to stem the tide of feminization

162. Brauns, *Der Übergang von der Handweberei*, p. 245.

of the new industrial workforce.[163] Although little is known about the response of female weavers to male workers' protests, women also shaped the world behind the mill gate as they stepped into the contested domain of the factory and sought to render compatible the two spheres of labor they now inhabited.

However distinct the patterns of feminization in each branch of textile production, *Verdrängung* and *Verweiblichung* were issues of debate and contest in regions where textiles remained the dominant industry throughout the course of industrialization. But within those regions it is important to distinguish between cases like velvet production, in which male handweavers were displaced by the augmented productivity of the mechanical looms—in other words, in which the demand for labor declined with the transition to mechanized weaving—and those like silk in which the growing demand for female labor engendered a new kind of competition between women and men, even if the actual *displacement* of men by women is difficult to document. It is also important to differentiate between the regions and branches in which feminization occurred without inflaming contention and those in which the legacy of once powerful craft-guild traditions, as in Aachen, for example, or their reinvention and adaptation by the silk and velvet weavers' *Innungen* in Krefeld and Kempen, helped to fuel the opposition to women's work, to inscribe the vocabulary of feminization in the transition to factory weaving. In cases like the velvet and silk trades in Krefeld and Kempen or the woolen industry of Aachen, the terminology of feminization and displacement obscures more than it illuminates, for these terms imply that men had predominated in handweaving and then were dislodged by the influx of female workers. This scenario was highly unlikely in silk weaving, however, for detailed local studies like Kriedte's offer convincing evidence that both men and women were a vital presence in handweaving households.

The relative absence of controversy surrounding feminization in and around Mönchen-Gladbach can be explained not only in terms of a more fluid labor market, which expanded rapidly rather than contracted during the transition from home to factory cotton production. The chronic labor shortages of the early years of the transition, during the 1860s and 1870s, suggest that the new cotton mills were able to absorb most of the former handweavers. Furthermore, the presence of a vital core of "worker-peasants" among the cotton handweavers of the region meant that some unemployed handweavers might have returned to full-time farming rather than

---

163. On the role guild traditions played in the formation of this attitude among the first generation of male workers, see Jean H. Quataert, "The Shaping of Women's Work in Manufacturing: Guilds, Household, and the State in Central Europe, 1648–1870," *American Historical Review* 90 (December 1985): 1134, 1146–48.

accepting the strictures of work in the new mills.¹⁶⁴ Similarly, in the case study of Bielefeld, the gendered segmentation of the city's complex industrial landscape forms the key site of investigation, rather than the division of labor within the textile sector itself. The contest within the city for male and female labor, the rise of the metal industry, which more or less coincided with the mechanization of linen weaving, spurred the feminization of flax spinning and linen weaving as the metal factories drew more and more men away from the textile mills. The sharply bifurcated division of labor within the linen weaving mills, between female weavers, winders, spoolers, nappers, and darners and the exclusively male textile craftsmen—foremen, machinists, dyers, and supervisors—meant that the feminization of linen weaving remained uncontested in Bielefeld, as did the founding of the first silk weaving mills, which were an almost exclusively female domain from the outset.

The silk and velvet weaving regions around Krefeld and Kempen occupy a special place in this analysis, not only because of the rich archival evidence on the place of gender in the struggle between home and factory weaving, but also because the traumas of this transition, the last in the textile branches, coincided with the growing interest of social reformers and state social policy experts in the social problem of female factory labor, which they helped kindle with their widely publicized appeals to the imperial state. The revived artisanal communities of the guilds, their struggles to demarcate the boundaries of gender in the new factory workplace, represented an upheaval in the meanings of work more than in the actual practices of labor.

The formation of the new factory workforce of silk and velvet weavers from the communities of local handweavers signified both continuity and disjunction with the customs and practices of home industry. Although women's work in silk weaving was not in itself anything new to either male or female weavers, the relocation of work from the household to the factory, the recurrent unemployment and permanent displacement of thousands of handweavers from their craft, the fragmentation of the family wage into individual, gender-specific wages, and the final and permanent usurpation of the domestic workshop by the factory represented critical and lasting ruptures in the weavers' way of life. Female factory labor became a key part of the cultural matrix through which male weavers decoded the new world of work, an interpretive grid through which they read employers' wage reductions, the implementation of the double looms, or the chronic periods of unemployment and shortened work hours that

---

164. On the "worker-peasant," see Jean Quataert, "The Politics of Rural Industrialization: Class, Gender, and Collective Protest in the Saxon Oberlausitz of the Late Nineteenth Century," *Central European History* 20 (June 1987): 91–124.

became the constant companion of the new factory workforce.[165] As an immediate consequence of the break between household and mechanized weaving, the factory came to figure as a public and visible site at which men and women, married and single, merged and mingled in new and unpredictable ways; and its emergence also necessitated the renegotiation of the boundaries between household and market, family and state, sexual and social order.

165. Ulrich, "Soziale Entwicklungen im industriellen Umbruch," p. 95.

3

Sexual Difference and the Social Question in the Transition to the "Industrial State," 1844–1889

As an emergent Germany confronted the ills of "modernization" during the second half of the nineteenth century, the social question came to constitute a discursive nexus where the relationships between state and citizenry, factory and family, production and reproduction, public and private, were defined, contested, and periodically reimagined. This chapter examines the history of the social question from the crisis of pauperism during the "hungry 1840s" to the formulation of the "worker question" of the 1870s and 1880s. In particular, it explores the growing importance of gender in the perceptions of social order and disorder as more and more women went to work in factories after midcentury. The textile industry, first to mechanize and the largest factory employer of women, figured prominently in social reform debates as reformers marked textile mills as key sites of state regulation and intervention. As Germany's first generation of social scientists investigated and publicized conditions in the textile towns and textile factories during the 1870s, the powerful representations of a morally dissolute and physically declining workers' estate, of families torn apart by the expansion of the female factory workforce—children left to fend for themselves, men driven into the pubs by dirty, inhospitable living quarters in the absence of wife and mother—gave the textile mills a pivotal place in the national arena of social reform.[1] From the founding of the first middle-class association for workers' welfare in 1844, the family had been a symbol of the social and political dislocation accompanying

1. See, for example, Alphons Thun, *Die Industrie am Niederrhein und ihre Arbeiter: Staats- und sozialwissenschaftliche Forschungen*, vols. 1 and 2 (Leipzig: Duncker und Humblot, 1879).

urbanization and industrialization. Its meanings changed, however, as the number of women working outside the home expanded steadily during the last quarter of the century: the family became a more frequent object of scholarly study and state intervention, a more familiar trope in the rhetoric of social reform. Amid the growing anxieties about Social Democracy, social discord, and imperial expansion, reformers sought to preserve the working-class family as an anchor in a rapidly changing world, a bulwark against poverty, disorder, and decay, by "regulating" and "protecting" the labor of all "weak hands," in particular women and youths. The definition of the social question as a *sittliche Kulturfrage* during the 1860s and 1870s sought to remake family and state and imparted to both a decisive role in ameliorating social ills.[2]

While the discourses of social reform and their legislative outcomes shaped the structures and relations of production in "women's industries" like textiles, they also had important implications for the world beyond the mill gate. The dichotomy between the "weak hands" and the independent male citizen that underwrote reformers' campaigns for labor protection shaped the formation of "the social" as "an arena of conflicts over the reproduction of labor," situated between the state and the "realm of markets and property relations."[3] Reformers' explicit concern with the "female organism" during the 1870s marked the female body as a new object of intervention for both the regulatory and the tutelary regimes of state social policy and industrial paternalism.[4] As carriers of the next generation, working women's bodies were at the center of the parliamentary debates about the revision of the labor code during the mid-1870s and of the revised code of 1878, which extended legal protection, including maternity leave, to working women for the first time. The "female organism" was the object of both moral and hygienic concern as some reformers utilized statistics or medical diagnostics while others recounted sensational stories of seduction and sexual abandon in the carnal underworld of the

2. On the "weak hands," see Alfred Weber, "Die Entwickelung der deutschen Arbeiterschutzgesetzgebung," *Schmollers Jahrbuch* 21 (1897): 1149. For an explication of the social question as a *sittliche Kulturfrage*, see Gustav Schmoller, "Die Arbeiterfrage," *Preussische Jahrbücher* 14 (1864): 393–424, 523–47; 15 (1865): 32–63; Bishop Wilhelm Emmanuel von Ketteler, *Die Arbeiterfrage und das Christentum* (Mainz: F. Kirchheim, 1864).
3. George Steinmetz, "Workers and the Welfare State in Imperial Germany," *International Labor and Working-Class History* 40 (fall 1991): 20–21. Also see his *Regulating the Social: The Welfare State and Local Politics in Imperial Germany* (Princeton: Princeton University Press, 1993), pp. 55–70.
4. On moralizing and regulative outcomes of discourses of social reform, see Mary Poovey, "Domesticity and Class Formation: Chadwick's *Sanitary Report*," in *Subject to History*, ed. David Simpson (Ithaca: Cornell University Press, 1991), p. 65, and her "Introduction," in *Body/Politics: Women and the Discourses of Science*, ed. Mary Jacobus, Evelyn Fox Keller, and Sally Shuttleworth (New York: Routledge, 1990), pp. 9–10.

factory.⁵ These narratives fixed women's place in production and anchored both class and citizenship in a particular vision of the female body, which itself became centrally implicated in and representative of the ills of the social body. By the 1880s "the social" had become a key site for the articulation of sexual difference, for the formulation of claims and identities of citizenship.

The debates about women's work and endangered families, and the labor codes they engendered, also had an important role in the expansion of the German welfare state, specifically in widening the scope of state intervention not only to regulate the "pathogenic" conditions of work but also to prescribe, implicitly at least, standards of health, hygiene, and morality for working-class households. In the newly founded German nation-state of the 1870s the social question was formulated and deliberated in the realm of high politics, in government ministries and the Reichstag, in which the bourgeois social reform association, the Verein für Sozialpolitik, had a highly influential role. Its members played a crucial part, for example, in framing the official state inquiry into the dangers of factory labor for women and youths, conducted by the factory inspectorate in 1875, and the revision of the labor code in 1878. When the Verein relinquished its role as the "combat patrol of social reform" in the early 1880s, seeking to influence social policy only indirectly through scholarship and scientific inquiry, the Reichstag became the terrain of deliberation and negotiation about female factory labor and its effects on the working-class family. Throughout the decade, parliamentarians from the Catholic Center, Social Democratic, and Conservative Parties persistently proposed, compromised, and rewrote motions to extend the scope of labor protection beyond the code of 1878, engaging in heated debates about the compatibility of factory work with women's "nature" and its detrimental effects on the health and morality of women workers, their families, and future generations. These parliamentary debates, which often drew factory inspectors, employers, medical doctors, and bourgeois social reformers into the

---

5. The vocabulary of "female organism" typified the discussion of women's factory labor across the political spectrum. See, for example, Ludwig Hirt, *Die gewerbliche Thätigkeit der Frauen vom hygienischen Standpunkt aus* (Breslau: F. Hirt, 1873), pp. 5–6; Heinrich Herkner, "Zur Kritik und Reform der deutschen Arbeiterschutzgesetzgebung," *Archiv für Soziale Gesetzgebung und Statistik* 3 (1890): 226–27; Johannes Wenzel, *Arbeiterschutz und Centrum mit Berücksichtigung der übrigen Parteien* (Berlin: Verlag der Germania A.G., 1893), p. 86; August Bebel, *Woman under Socialism*, translated from the German of the 33d edition by Daniel De Leon (New York: Schocken, 1971), pp. 89–90; 123–24; Clara Zetkin's (untitled) article in *Die Gleichheit* 7 (1897): 128, 137–38. On the Verein für Sozialpolitik's attention to the female organism at its founding meeting, see Else Conrad, *Der Verein für Sozialpolitik und seine Wirksamkeit auf dem Gebiet der gewerblichen Arbeiterfrage* (Jena: Gustav Fischer, 1906), p. 96.

fray, created a realm of oppositional social policy within the Reichstag, posing a direct challenge to the policies of Chancellor Otto von Bismarck. Bismarck, widely heralded for the innovative social insurance laws of the 1880s, waged a determined battle against extension of the protective labor laws, which he regarded as detrimental to the position of German industry in an increasingly competitive world market. By the end of the 1880s a legislative consensus had been formed in favor of protecting female and teenage workers, including the provision of maternity leave, reduced working hours, and the removal of women and youths from night work and employment in mines. This consensus and Bismarck's intractability on the issue of expanded labor protection led to a deep rift within high politics between the Reichstag and the chancellor, who was backed by the Prussian ministries of state. This rift would erupt into crisis in 1889–90, prompting the shift in social policy known as the "new course"; ultimately it would pave the way toward Bismarck's resignation.[6]

This chapter begins the task of uncovering the central and heretofore largely neglected place that factory legislation occupies in the history of the German welfare state.[7] Indeed, protective labor laws have remained a *Schattenseite* (shadow side) in most European, including German, historiography of the welfare state, submerged between its dominant strands or streams: the "male strand" of social insurance and the "maternal and child welfare strand" of poor relief and public assistance. As a social policy aimed almost exclusively at protecting female and teenage workers, mothers and children *at work*, labor legislation disrupts the dichotomy between the two streams, for it implicitly erases the boundary between them. Unlike the social insurance laws of the 1880s, which Bismarck initiated in the absence of genuine popular demand and in collaboration with employers' associations, protective labor legislation represented the outcome of intense discursive and social mobilization around the social question of female factory labor.[8]

6. See Hans-Jörg von Berlepsch, *"Neuer Kurs" im Kaiserreich? Die Arbeiterpolitik des Freiherrn von Berlepsch 1890 bis 1896* (Bonn: Neue Gesellschaft, 1987); Karl-Erich Born, *Staat und Sozialpolitik seit Bismarcks Sturz: Ein Beitrag zur Geschichte der innenpolitischen Entwicklung des deutschen Reiches, 1890–1914* (Wiesbaden: Franz Steiner, 1957); Otto Pflanze, *Bismarck and the Development of Germany*, vol. 3, *The Period of Fortification, 1880–1898* (Princeton: Princeton University Press, 1990), pp. 327–70.

7. The work of Jean H. Quataert is an important exception here. She established the importance of factory legislation for the history of German women workers in her article "A Source Analysis in German Women's History: Factory Inspectors' Reports and the Shaping of Working-Class Lives, 1878–1914," *Central European History* 16 (June 1983): 100–120.

8. Jean Quataert, "Woman's Work and the Early Welfare State in Germany: Legislators, Bureaucrats, and Clients before the First World War," in *Mothers of a New World: Maternalist Politics and the Origins of Welfare States*, ed. Seth Koven and Sonya Michel (New York: Routledge, 1993), p. 161; Rüdiger Baron, "Weder Zuckerbrot noch Peitsche: Historische Konstitutionsbedingungen des Sozialstaats in Deutschland," *Gesellschaft: Beiträge zur Marx-*

This chapter traces the history of the social question in Germany from the founding of the first social policy organization in 1844 to the formation of the legislative consensus around the issue of women's factory work in the late 1880s. It establishes the rhetorical and legislative framework for the turning point of 1889–90, when the social question of female factory employment exploded into a public controversy for the first time, when the expanding public sphere, shaped by both *Bildungsbürgertum* (academic and professional bourgeoisie) and working class, began to play a decisive role in shaping protective labor legislation. This chapter seeks to unravel the many threads of social reform—the work of scholars and "socialists of the chair," Catholics, Social Democrats (also known as Socialists), and factory inspectors—that formed the complex tapestry of narratives about family and female factory labor from midcentury until the end of the 1880s, narratives that would frame discussions of women's work well into the twentieth century. It reveals the central role of the textile industry in setting the stage for social reform in Germany, in representing the dramas and dangers associated with the employment of women in factories and the decline of the working-class family. Finally, it explicates the intricate ways the welfare state and social reform constructed gender and established the discursive and legislative frameworks within which German workers formed identities of citizenship and class.

Women's Work and the Social Question, 1844–1880

The history of the social question forms a crucial part of German historiography of the labor movement, of liberalism and the formation of the *Bürgertum*, and of the making of the modern nation-state.[9] The convergence in the revolutions of 1848–49 of the national question, the consti-

---

schen Theorie 12 (1979): 15–16; Rüdiger vom Bruch, "Bürgerliche Sozialreform im deutschen Kaiserreich," in *Weder Kommunismus noch Kapitalismus: Bürgerliche Sozialreform in Deutschland vom Vormärz bis zur Ära Adenauer*, ed. Rüdiger vom Bruch (Munich: C. H. Beck, 1985), pp. 9–10; Florian Tennstedt, *Sozialgeschichte der Sozialpolitik in Deutschland vom 18. Jahrhundert bis zum Ersten Weltkrieg* (Göttingen: Vandenhoeck und Ruprecht, 1981), p. 190; Berlepsch, *"Neuer Kurs,"* pp. 11–13.

9. See, for example, Berlepsch, *"Neuer Kurs"*; Gerhard A. Ritter, *Staat, Arbeiterschaft und Arbeiterbewegung in Deutschland: Vom Vormärz bis zum Ende der Weimarer Republik* (Berlin: Dietz, 1980), and idem, *Vom Wohlfahrtsausschuss zum Wohlfahrtsstaat: Der Staat in der modernen Industriegesellschaft* (Cologne: Markus, 1973); Werner Conze, *Die Arbeiterbewegung in der nationalen Bewegung: Die deutsche Sozialdemokratie vor, während und nach der Reichsgründung* (Stuttgart: E. Klett, 1966); Günther Brakelmann, *Die soziale Frage des 19. Jahrhunderts* (Bielefeld: Luther, 1981); Albert Müssiggang, *Die soziale Frage in der historischen Schule der deutschen Nationalökonomie* (Tübingen: J. C. B. Mohr, 1968); Gustav Schmoller, *Die soziale Frage: Klassenbildung, Arbeiterfrage, Klassenkampf* (Munich: Duncker und Humblot, 1918).

tutional question, and the social question, as opposed to their successive rise in the history of France or England, marks one of the most intriguing "peculiarities" of modern German history.[10] From the founding in 1844 of the first social policy organization, the Centralverein für das Wohl der Arbeitenden Klassen (Central Association for the Welfare of the Working Classes), reformers directed their attention to the family as they sought to prevent the "impending dissolution of society into two opposing and hostile classes."[11] Wilhelm Heinrich Riehl's ethnographic foray of the 1850s, in *Die Naturgeschichte des Volkes als Grundlage einer deutschen Social-Politik* (The natural history of the people as the foundation of German social policy), lamented the loss of "family consciousness" and family bonds.[12] While reformers of the pathbreaking Centralverein mustered statistical and scientific methods to determine the moral and physical condition of urban families, Riehl called for investigation of families and households that transcended the limits of census and church registers and encompassed the gaze of the "statesman," who, he contended, should "be allowed into the house itself."[13] Thus, even before capitalism had become predominant or factories had begun to transform urban and rural landscapes on a wide scale and before the formation of the German nation-state, bourgeois reformers had mapped out the founding principles and methods of social policy, including the focus on the family that would continue to shape social policy associations and debates in Germany during the next several decades.

During the 1850s and 1860s pauperism, the social question of the "hungry 1840s," was gradually supplanted by the *Arbeiterfrage* (worker

10. Jürgen Kocka, *Lohnarbeit und Klassenbildung: Arbeiter und Arbeiterbewegung in Deutschland, 1800–1875* (Bonn: Dietz, 1983); idem, "Problems of Working-Class Formation: The Early Years, 1800–1875," in *Working-Class Formation: Nineteenth-Century Patterns in Western Europe and the United States*, ed. Ira Katznelson and Aristide R. Zolberg (Princeton: Princeton University Press, 1986), pp. 279–351.

11. Vom Bruch, "Bürgerliche Sozialreform," p. 3; Jürgen Reulecke, "Die Anfänge der organisierten Sozialreform in Deutschland," in vom Bruch, *Weder Kommunismus*, pp. 21–59. The Centralverein, founded mainly by industrialists and bureaucrats from state ministries, became a marginal social reform organization after the founding of the Verein für Sozialpolitik in 1873 (which absorbed many of its members), but the Centralverein was not disbanded until 1914.

12. Wilhelm Heinrich Riehl's four-volume study *Die Naturgeschichte des Volkes als Grundlage einer deutschen Social-Politik* (Stuttgart: J. G. Cotta, 1897) was first published between 1853 and 1869. Volume 3 is on the "natural history of the family."

13. Anthony Oberschall, *Empirical Social Research in Germany, 1848–1914* (New York: Basic Books, 1965), p. 65. Also see Jürgen Reulecke, "Stadtbürgertum und bürgerliche Sozialreform im 19. Jahrhundert in Preussen," in *Stadt und Bürgertum im 19. Jahrhundert*, ed. Lothar Gall (Munich: R. Oldenbourg, 1990), p. 187; Gerhard A. Ritter, *Social Welfare in Germany and Britain: Origins and Development*, trans. Kim Traynor (Leamington Spa: Berg, 1986), p. 19; and Berlepsch, *"Neuer Kurs,"*, p. 200.

question) as workers unleashed the first waves of protest against factory regimes and political repression.¹⁴ Reformers of the 1860s like Gustav Schmoller, founding member of the Verein für Sozialpolitik (Association for Social Policy) and renowned professor of politics and government, and Wilhelm Emmanuel von Ketteler, bishop of Mainz, framed the "worker question" as a *sittliche Kulturfrage*, a social problem embedded in issues of morality, culture, and family rather than one defined mainly in terms of wage inequities or working conditions.¹⁵ The mid-1860s saw not only a sharp rise in the number of workers' strikes, but also the coalescence of a discursive arena around the "worker question" as eminent liberals and Catholics released a spate of publications on the topic, including Hermann Schulze-Delitzsch's *Kapitel zu einem deutschen Arbeiterkatechismus* (1863), Schmoller's "Die Arbeiterfrage" (1864), and Ketteler's *Die Arbeiterfrage und das Christentum* (1864).¹⁶ These founders of German social policy sought not merely to achieve a more equitable distribution of goods and services, but also to mend the moral and cultural fabric of family and community that industrial and urban growth had torn apart. For even more troubling than the material gulf between *Bürgertum* and workers were the profound disparities in education and cultural understanding, in morals, values, and ideals.

Thus new visions of both citizenship and state had a crucial place in social reform campaigns across the political boundaries dividing Catholic, bourgeois, and Social Democratic reformers. Despite the fundamental differences in their worldviews, Social Catholics, Lassalleans, and most of the academic social reformers around Schmoller shared the emphatic renunciation of liberal "Manchesterite" visions of a free market economy and of the state as a "night watchman."¹⁷ Ferdinand Lassalle's rising popularity and the founding of his Allgemeiner Deutscher Arbeiterverein (General German Workers' Association, or ADAV) in 1863 prompted both liberals and Catholics to amend their own views of social policy. Bishop Ketteler, who at first emphasized the importance of religion, morality, and ethics in solv-

14. Heinrich Volkmann, *Die Arbeiterfrage im preußischen Abgeordnetenhaus, 1848–1869* (Berlin: Duncker und Humblot, 1968), pp. 186–87.
15. On the meanings of *sittliche Kulturfrage*, see vom Bruch, "Bürgerliche Sozialreform," p. 67; Hans Gehrig, *Die Begründung des Prinzips der Sozialreform: Eine literarisch-historische Untersuchung über Manchestertum und Kathedersozialismus* (Jena: Gustav Fischer, 1914), pp. 140–41; Müssiggang, *Die soziale Frage*, pp. 133–34; Tennstedt, *Sozialgeschichte der Sozialpolitik*, pp. 148–49; Paul Grebe, *Die Arbeiterfrage bei Lange, Ketteler, Jörg, Schäffle (aufgezeigt an ihrer Auseinandersetzung mit Lassalle)* (Berlin: Emil Ebering, 1935), pp. 39–79.
16. Hermann Schulze-Delitzsch, *Kapitel zu einem deutschen Arbeiterkatechismus* (Leipzig: E. Keil, 1863); Schmoller, "Die Arbeiterfrage"; von Ketteler, *Die Arbeiterfrage und das Christentum*.
17. Grebe, *Die Arbeiterfrage*, p. 76; vom Bruch, "Einleitung" and "Bürgerliche Sozialreform," in *Weder Kommunismus*, pp. 11, 77–78.

ing the social question, turned to the state in response to Lassallean agitation, shifting the emphasis of Catholic social reform from spiritual healing and the revival of estate society to a dual vision of social reform in which both state and church would seek concrete solutions to the problems of poverty, unemployment, and social unrest. In Ketteler's view, Lassallean social policy—Lassalle's own advocacy of self-help through productive associations and the ADAV's campaigns for material improvements of proletarian living and working conditions—constituted "a Christian endeavor," wholly compatible with "the duties of a devout Catholic." Catholic social reform was also to encompass Ketteler's model of the "Christian factory," in which owners and workers were bound to one another not only by economic ties, but also by moral and religious ones.[18]

Reformers of the 1860s summoned German *Bürger* (citizens) to *Pflichterfüllung*, fulfillment of ethical duty through the creation of an economic order based on ethics and moral principles. At the same time they also sought to reinvent the state, to transform the German *Rechtsstaat*, embedded in positivist understandings of law, into a *Kulturstaat*, which was to fulfill humanitarian and ethical imperatives and forge ethical and cultural bonds among its citizens. They aimed to banish "hatred, mistrust, and irreconciliability" from the workers' hearts, "to repair the broken bridges" between workers and the state, workers and their fellow (bourgeois) citizens.[19] Those who cast the social question as a *sittliche Kulturfrage* envisioned the "ethical training" of the lower classes through the upper classes, the awakening of virtue, responsibility, and the capacity for self-help, in which the family had a key role. For the family, as Katherine Lynch has pointed out for France, "assumed a powerful hold over the minds of social commentators and policymakers," not least "because it served such a central function in the bourgeoisie's own definition of itself."[20]

18. Grebe, *Die Arbeiterfrage*, pp. 43–59, 71–76; Franz Josef Stegmann, "Geschichte der sozialen Ideen im deutschen Katholizismus," in *Geschichte der sozialen Ideen in Deutschland: Deutsches Handbuch der Politik*, vol. 3, ed. Helga Grebing (Munich: G. Olzog, 1969), pp. 354–57, 395–99; Wenzel, *Arbeiterschutz*, p. 16. According to Stegmann, the state began to figure prominently in Catholic social reform programs after the *Katholikentag* at Bamberg in 1868.
19. Ritter, *Staat, Arbeiterschaft und Arbeiterbewegung*, pp. 57, 70–71. Ritter cites social reformer Baron Hans-Jörg von Berlepsch's essay "Soziale Entwicklungen im ersten Jahrzehnt nach Aufhebung des Sozialistengesetzes," in *Die Verhandlungen des 12. Evangelisch-sozialen Kongresses* (held in Braunschweig 28–30 May 1901), p. 114. Also see Müssiggang, *Die soziale Frage*, pp. 127–28; 133, 175; Ritter, *Social Welfare*, p. 17; vom Bruch, "Bürgerliche Sozialreform," p. 67.
20. Katherine A. Lynch, *Family, Class, and Ideology in Early Industrial France: Social Policy and the Working-Class Family, 1825–1848* (Madison: University of Wisconsin Press, 1988), p. 226. Lynch's study makes it clear that there was nothing particularly German about the role of the family as an object of social reform discourse or state social policy. On the importance of the family in the identity of the German *Bürgertum*, see David Blackbourn, "The German Bourgeoisie: An Introduction," in *The German Bourgeoisie: Essays on the Social History of the*

German social reformers of the midcentury, as a key part of the emergent *Bildungsbürgertum*, viewed the family as underpinning and reinforcing the "bonds of social solidarity"; it thus figured both as a signifier of social dissolution and as a site of social policy intervention from the 1840s on.[21]

By the mid-1860s social policy had become a "preferred weapon" in the political battles between the opposing factions of the emergent Social Democratic labor movement, the Lassalleans and the Eisenacher. Wilhelm Liebknecht and August Bebel, leaders of the radical Eisenacher Social Democratic faction, who viewed the state as an opponent and an obstacle to genuine social reform, enlivened their bid for leadership of the incipient labor movement after Lassalle's death with visions of impending social revolution. In response, Lassalle's heir, Johann Schweitzer, vowed to fend off revolution through social reform and "peaceful emancipation" through protective labor codes and workers' self-help organizations. Social policy also figured centrally in the contests among Catholics, Social Democrats, and liberal reformers associated with Schulze-Delitzsch "to win over the masses" during the early to mid-1860s.[22] The growing labor militancy during that decade and the widespread perception that a destructive process of "proletarianization" was under way meant that social policy, from its inception, had the dual function of preserving and policing, of protecting the bodily and moral integrity of workers in order to prevent a dangerous spiral of social discontent and conflict.

The *Kulturstaat*, in partnership with reform-minded and responsible *Bürger*, was to ensure "a normal family life among the lower classes," a task that became more complex as factories supplanted protoindustrial cottage production, especially in textiles, and as the female factory workforce steadily expanded. Female factory labor was only one aspect of the worker question, albeit one that was present from the inception of bourgeois social reform in the mid-1860s. Yet it soon came to represent a crucial disruption of "normal family life," which reformers defined in terms of cleanliness, frugality, and *häuslicher Sinn* (a sense of domesticity).[23]

Since 1848 social policy had been spurred on by the "fear of revolution," and between 1848 and the end of the 1860s social reformers' views

---

German Middle Class from the Late 18th to the Early 20th Century, ed. David Blackbourn and Richard J. Evans (London: Routledge, 1991), p. 10.

21. Lynch, *Family, Class and Ideology*, p. 226; Blackbourn, "German Bourgeoisie," p. 10; Müssiggang, *Die soziale Frage*, pp. 133–36; Gehrig, *Die Begründung*, pp. 172–73.

22. Volkmann, *Die Arbeiterfrage im preußischen Abgeordnetenhaus*, pp. 141–42, 190. The attempts of Schweitzer and other Lassalleans, as well as of social conservatives, to expand the scope of the Prussian labor code of 1853, which mandated the restriction of child and youth labor, were thwarted by the parliamentary opposition of liberals and industrialists during the 1860s. Also see Franz Hitze, *Die Arbeiterfrage und die Bestrebungen zu ihrer Lösung* (Berlin: Commissionsverlag der Germania, 1900), pp. 10–12, 27; Grebe, *Die Arbeiterfrage*, p. 76.

23. Gehrig, *Die Begründung des Prinzips*, pp. 197–98.

of the family had increasingly been cast in terms of social dissolution and the necessity of state regulation.[24] The rise of Social Democracy during the early 1870s served as the impetus to link the two, to explain the sense of impending revolution through the decline of the family, to view the policing of families as the solution to the social question and the threat of social revolution. In fact, the founding of the the Catholic Center Party in 1870, of the Verein für Sozialpolitik in 1872, and of the Socialist Workers' Party of Germany (SAPD) in 1875 heralded the end of the "social-political vacuum" of the period of national unification.[25] With the question of national unification formally resolved and German industrial growth continuing apace, the social question gained in importance and visibility as the new state sought to stabilize its power, to ground itself in what Max Weber later termed "the social unification of the nation."[26] As political economist Gustav Schönberg explained in 1871, "since the national question has found its resolution, the so-called social question has perhaps become the most important question of the future."[27]

Analogous to their common repudiation of liberal views of economy and state, Catholics, Lassalleans, and the first generation of academic social reformers shared the same fears about female factory labor and its effects on male workers' wages and the well-being of their families. Moreover, similar tropes and rhetorical strategies were deployed by the disparate reformers to give expression to those fears and hostilities.[28] Before the founding of the Socialist Workers' Party in 1875, the Lassallean wing of the movement regarded female factory labor as "one of the most outrageous abuses of our age," one that destroyed the family and thus worsened rather than enhanced the material well-being of the workers.[29] Claiming that the situation of women was best ameliorated "when men receive their full due for their labor," Lassalleans called on working men to wage strikes for the expulsion of women from all jobs "outside the female sphere," a strategy they believed would diminish male unemployment and lead to

24. Volkmann, *Die Arbeiterfrage im preußischen Abgeordnetenhaus*, p. 190.
25. Ibid., p. 198.
26. Wolfgang J. Mommsen, *Max Weber and German Politics, 1890–1920*, (trans. Michael S. Steinberg (Chicago: University of Chicago Press, 1984), p. 101.
27. Gustav Schönberg, "Arbeitsämter, eine Aufgabe des Deutschen Reiches: Akademische Antrittsrede" (1871), p. 31, as cited by vom Bruch, "Bürgerliche Sozialreform," p. 70.
28. As noted by Müssiggang, *Die soziale Frage*, p. 133, and Wenzel, *Arbeiterschutz und Centrum*, p. 15, Schmoller's *Arbeiterfrage* called for the restriction of female and child labor, while Bishop Ketteler underscored the damaging effects of factory employment of women and young girls on family life and morality.
29. This demand constituted point 4 in the "Resolution der 6. Generalversammlung des Allgemeinen Deutschen Arbeitervereins," which took place in 1867, as cited in Werner Thönnessen, *Frauenemanzipation: Politik und Literatur der deutschen Sozialdemokratie zum Frauenbewegung, 1863–1933* (Frankfurt a.M.: Europäische Verlagsanstalt, 1976), p. 13.

higher wages for men.³⁰ When the General German Social Democratic Workers' Congress of 1869 brought the opposing factions of Eisenacher and Lassalleans together to discuss a common political program, female factory labor remained a divisive issue in their deliberations. The Lassallean front clamored for a resolution to prohibit women's wage labor in factories, whereas the radical Eisenacher underscored the urgent economic needs of working women, evoking visions of female workers banned from the factories and then forced into a sordid struggle for survival as prostitutes. The Eisenacher prevailed, and the SAPD's program of 1869 foresaw the abolition of child factory labor and restriction of women's labor in occupations deemed dangerous. Importantly, it also called on Social Democrats to confront female competition not with the weapon of exclusionary strategies, but by recruiting women to join trade associations.³¹ When the two factions convened at the Gotha Party Congress of 1875 to put aside their differences and establish a unified Socialist Workers' Party, dissension once again arose around the question of female factory labor. The Lassalleans, dissatisfied with the proposed party program, rejected the call for the mere "restriction" of women's factory work, demanding instead a categorical and legal *Verbot* (ban). But the majority voted in favor of a compromise resolution to eliminate children's factory labor as well as women's employment in industries that endangered their bodily or moral health. Yet workers' trade associations and unions held tenaciously to their negative view of women's work at the same time: the Erfurt trade union congress of 1872, for example, called on its members "to agitate against and to abolish all types of women's work in factories."³²

As Social Democrats debated their differences over women's factory employment, Bishop Ketteler espoused a similar rhetoric on behalf of Catholic social reformers. His speech of 25 July 1869 in Offenbach demanded that mothers and young girls be barred from factory work, which damaged morality and destroyed family life. The "Draft of a Catholic Political Program of 1873" embraced economistic arguments about how family earnings, instead of showing a marked increase when women and children

30. Hilde Lion, *Zur Soziologie der Frauenbewegung: Die sozialistische und katholische Frauenbewegung* (Berlin: F. A. Herbig, 1926), p. 26; Gisela Losseff-Tillmanns, *Frauenemanzipation und Gewerkschaften* (Wuppertal: Peter Hammer, 1979), pp. 36–37, 103.
31. Thönnessen, *Frauenemanzipation*, pp. 28–29. See also the account in Franz Mehring, *Geschichte der deutschen Sozialdemokratie*, vol. 2, *Von Lassalles "Offenes Antwortsschreiben" bis zum Erfurter Programm 1863 bis 1891* (Berlin: Dietz, 1976), pp. 330–48.
32. Lion, *Zur Soziologie*, p. 30; Thönnessen, *Frauenemanzipation*, pp. 31, 33–37; Mehring, *Geschichte der deutschen Sozialdemokratie*, 2:447–62. Thönnessen points to a gulf between incipient party and trade unions on the issue of women's work. Because of their focus on the concrete improvement of material living and working conditions, he argues, the early unions were "strict opponents" of female factory labor.

went to work, appeared to decrease in the long run because of the displacement of male breadwinners by cheaper female and child labor.[33] The first major social policy initiative in the national parliamentary arena was launched by the Catholic Center Party with Graf Friedrich von Galen's motion to the German Reichstag in 1877. Still encased in corporatist notions of trade, craft, and family, the motion sought to protect the institution of marriage and the "sanctity of the family," the "seed of the organic formation of society," from the free market forces that had begun to dismantle the last of the protective walls around the family organism, endangering the "root of the entire Christian social order."[34] Contending that the families of factory workers were particularly vulnerable, the motion's primary goal was to remove married women from factories. For "where the mother is absent, there is no sense of domesticity [*Häuslichkeit*], no family; but where the mother, the woman, is home, the children have their sustenance and nurturing and the man his domestic bliss."[35] The motion, often cited years later by Center politicians as proof of the party's role as harbinger of protective labor legislation, represented the inauguration of the Center Party's long-term and tenacious campaign to regulate the labor of women and youths.

Similar to their compatriots in the social reform milieu of the 1860s, the bourgeois social reformers who founded the Verein für Sozialpolitik in 1873 brought to bear on the "worker question" both *sittliches Pathos* (moral-ethical ardor) and the belief in statistical, scientific investigation. In doing so, they also defined female factory labor as a particular object of social scientific inquiry.[36] The first generation of Verein members included

---

33. Emil Ritter, *Die katholisch-soziale Bewegung und der Volksverein* (Cologne: Bachem, 1954), pp. 103–6; Stegmann, "Geschichte der sozialen Ideen," p. 400; Wenzel, *Arbeiterschutz*, pp. 15–17. Wenzel offers an interesting comparison of the Social Democratic Eisenach program of 1869 and the "Draft of a Catholic Political Program" written by Bishop Ketteler and published as *Die Katholiken im Deutschen Reiche: Entwurf zu einem politischen Programm* in 1873.

34. Wenzel, *Arbeiterschutz*, pp. 24–25. Wenzel cites the text of Galen's motion (*Antrag Galen*).

35. Wenzel, *Arbeiterschutz*, p. 27.

36. On the founding and the history of the Verein für Sozialpolitik, see Gehrig, *Die Begründung des Prinzips*, pp. 169–70; Berlepsch, "Neuer Kurs," pp. 131–32; Conrad, *Der Verein für Sozialpolitik*; Dieter Lindenlaub, *Richtungskämpfe im Verein für Sozialpolitik: Wissenschaft und Politik im Kaiserreich vornehmlich vom Beginn des "Neuen Kurses" bis zum Ausbruch des Ersten Weltkrieges (1890–1914)*, 2 vols. (Wiesbaden: Franz Steiner, 1967); Marie-Louise Plessen, *Die Wirksamkeit des Vereins für Sozialpolitik von 1872–1890: Studien zum Katheder- und Staatssozialismus* (Berlin: Duncker und Humblot, 1975). The Verein für Öffentliche Gesundheitspflege was also founded in 1873 and quickly acquired a leading role in formulating the norms for "public health" in Germany. See Florian Tennstedt, *Vom Proleten zum Industriearbeiter: Arbeiterbewegung und Sozialpolitik in Deutschland 1800 bis 1914* (Cologne: Bund, 1983), pp. 371–74.

men of diverse professional training—professors and civil servants, local politicians and industrialists, lawyers and medical doctors—who shared the passionate renunciation of *Manchestertum*, free-trade views of economic and social policies, best represented by the school of Berlin economists around Ludwig Bamberger. Although their rejection of Manchesterism coincided with that of the Social Democrats, Verein members also repudiated the socialist notion that natural laws, as opposed to moral-ethical principles, governed economic life. This two-pronged delineation of boundaries—against liberal economists on the one side and Social Democrats on the other—would continue to shape the Verein's efforts to infuse ethics into both the theory and the practice of political economy until the First World War.[37]

Female factory labor, and its effects on the working-class family, came to occupy a key place in that ethical understanding; it also figured prominently in reformers' efforts to improve workers' material circumstances.[38] In October 1872, a year before the Verein was founded, 159 of its future members met in Eisenach for a special session on the social question. While Schmoller spoke on the topic of workers' organizations and strikes and Ernst Engel, director of the Royal Prussian Statistical Bureau, examined the "housing question," Lujo Brentano outlined the history and goals of German factory legislation as a crucial aspect of the social question. He also appealed for enhanced legal protection for female and teenage workers.[39] The Prussian labor code of 1853, which prohibited work in factories for children under age twelve, mandated a maximum six-hour day for children twelve to fourteen years old, and authorized regular inspection of factories by the state, was widely viewed as "as a paradigm of liberal capitalist economic legislation." It had been adopted by the North German Confederation in 1867 and revised only slightly in 1869.[40] Pointing to the minimal protection of labor afforded by existing legislation and claiming that "the Reich is obliged at last to tell the German people about the

37. Lindenlaub, *Richtungskämpfe*, pp. 1–6. According to Lindenlaub, p. 6, although professors represented only one-sixth of the members of the Verein, they were highly influential in founding and guiding the organization, composing two-third of the board of directors.
38. Müssiggang, *Die soziale Frage*, p. 133.
39. Vom Bruch, "Bürgerliche Sozialreform," p. 76; Lindenlaub, *Richtungskämpfe*, p. 7; Conrad, *Der Verein für Sozialpolitik*, pp. 83–88; James J. Sheehan, *The Career of Lujo Brentano: A Study of Liberalism and Social Reform in Imperial Germany* (Chicago: University of Chicago Press, 1966), p. 70.
40. Lothar Machtan, "Workers' Insurance versus Protection of the Workers: State Social Policy in Imperial Germany," in *The Social History of Occupational Health*, ed. Paul Weindling (London: Croom Helm, 1985), p. 209. The revision of the labor code of the North German Confederation in 1869 contained no new protective measures and in fact represented "the triumph of strictly liberal economic principles," according to Berlepsch, *"Neuer Kurs,"* pp. 129–30.

conditions of its workers," the Verein's founders summoned its members to explore the *Innenleben* (interior life) of the factories, to expand the basis of statistical information on working and living conditions, and to investigate the need in particular for legal protection of female and teenage workers.[41]

The founding of the Verein and the articulation of social policy programs by the Catholic Center and Socialist Workers' Parties marks a formative moment in the history of "the social." If the social is understood as "an arena of conflicts over the reproduction of labor,"[42] and if the family was at the heart of the social and the woman "the heart of the family," then it is important to consider the ways gender inscribed the social: the ways women were aligned with the social, came under "the public gaze" that constituted the social, and were assigned certain tasks within it from its inception.[43] The social, then, became a key site for the articulation of sexual difference, for the formulation of ideologies of gender that would eventually recast state social policy. Brentano's address of 1872 on German factory legislation offers a glimpse into this articulation of sexual difference within the formation of the social. First, Brentano sought to distinguish between "those who genuinely [required] protection"—women and children, who lacked the political rights to assert and defend their own needs—and male breadwinners, who were able to assert and defend their own interests through political association.[44] By contrast to his laudatory view of male workers' associations, Brentano contended that women had little "capability for building coalitions." Elaborating his "ethical" objections to female unions or clubs, Brentano argued that a woman could wage a successful struggle against employers only at the price of a "hardened character." This transformation of her character, however, would "sacrifice the very qualities that make women a significant force in society, that foster women's moralizing influence on male workers." Ultimately, he concluded, "it would mean poisoning family and society at their very source."[45]

---

41. Berlepsch, *"Neuer Kurs,"* pp. 131–32. Berlepsch cites transcripts from an 1873 meeting of the Verein's founders. As Berlepsch points out, the demand for statistical investigations was made in a petition to the Reichstag of 30 April 1873.

42. Steinmetz, "Workers and the Welfare State," pp. 20–21.

43. Denise Riley, *"Am I That Name?" Feminism and the Category of "Women" in History* (Minneapolis: University of Minnesota Press, 1988), pp. 50–51.

44. Brentano's speech is cited by Conrad, *Der Verein für Sozialpolitik*, p. 86. For French and British versions of the same argument, see Mary Lynn Stewart, *Women, Work, and the French State: Labour Protection and Social Patriarchy, 1879–1919* (Kingston: McGill-Queen's University Press, 1989), p. 47; Sonya O. Rose, "Factory Reform in Nineteenth Century Britain: Gender, Class and the Liberal State," in *Gender and Class in Modern Europe*, ed. Laura L. Frader and Sonya O. Rose (Ithaca: Cornell University Press, 1996), MS pp. 5–6.

45. Lindenlaub, *Richtungskämpfe*, p. 6; Sheehan, *Career of Lujo Brentano*, pp. 35–44; Conrad, *Der Verein für Sozialpolitik*, p. 88. For Brentano's views on guilds, see Lujo Brentano, *Die Arbeitergilden der Gegenwart* (Leipzig: Duncker und Humblot, 1871–72).

Underpinning this distinction between the independent male citizen-worker on the one hand and women and children on the other were particular perceptions of the female body. Responding to Brentano, for example, Max Hirsch, leader of the Hirsch-Duncker trade unions, pointed to the "eminent import of considering the health of the woman" when deliberating protective measures, "for a woman can hardly endure a longer working day [than ten hours] without harming herself or her offspring."[46] Similarly, Ludwig Hirt's 1873 investigation of women's work "from a hygienic standpoint," a founding text of *Arbeitsmedizin* (industrial medicine), explored the ways the reproductive work of the female body absorbed most of the body's strength, so that the combined effects of menstruation, childbirth, nursing, and menopause rendered women workers "pathological" some twenty-five of every hundred working days over their lifetimes.[47] Hirt intended his analysis of the reproductive burdens of women workers' bodies to identify those most in need of urgent and expansive protection—pregnant women or nursing mothers, for example. Thus the female body figured as a powerful marker of the dichotomy between the independent citizen-workers and those who required the protection of the state. As a primary locus of intervention within the social, the female body inscribed social reform and the state social policy that was shaped by it.

Indeed, as early as the mid-nineteenth century, the social question represented a confluence of moral and medical concerns, both designating families and female bodies as sites of intervention. Although the "moral condemnation of poverty" was a key feature of the "social consciousness of the bourgeois public" at midcentury, reform-minded medical doctors regarded poverty as a social disease, one best treated with medical and hygienic measures.[48] The liberal doctor Rudolf Virchow, for example, emphasized the social over the moral in his diagnosis of illness, insisting that an epidemic like typhus, which swept through Upper Silesia in the mid-1840s, stemmed from "social misery." Virchow approached medicine as a "social science" and defined politics as "nothing more than medicine by and large."[49]

Although the "sanitary idea" had many proponents by the late 1850s, it still lacked the institutional foothold it would gain with the enactment of

---

46. *Verhandlungen der Eisenacher Versammlung*, 7 October 1872, pp. 18, 36–37, 42, 60–66, as cited in Conrad, *Der Verein für Sozialpolitik*, p. 88.

47. Hirt, *Die gewerbliche Thätigkeit der Frauen*, pp. 11–12.

48. Ute Frevert, *Krankheit als politisches Problem, 1770–1880: Soziale Unterschichten in Preußen zwischen medizinischer Polizei und staatlicher Sozialversicherung* (Göttingen: Vandenhoeck und Ruprecht, 1984), p. 138. For an interesting contrast with England, see Robert Gray, "Medical Men, Industrial Labour and the State in Britain, 1830–1850," *Social History* 16 (January 1991): 19–43.

49. Oberschall, *Empirical Social Research*, p. 39; Alfons Labisch, *Homo hygienicus: Gesundheit und Medizin in der Neuzeit* (Frankfurt: Campus, 1992), pp. 133–34, 253–54.

health insurance legislation in 1883.⁵⁰ Morality, rather than health and hygiene, served as the principal instrument of social discipline from the mid-1840s through the late 1880s. Indeed, morality—*Sittlichkeit*— was a code word for a complex tangle of dangers and desires involving both the moral character and the physical health of workers and the poor. Like the word "morality" in English, *Sittlichkeit* "condensed a plethora of meanings all jostling for attention," which "served as synonym for culture, or cultural lack" and subsumed such disparate transgressions as alcoholism, prostitution, venereal disease, infant mortality, unwed motherhood, and the general deterioration of family life, each replete with both moral and medical meanings.⁵¹ Moreover, *Sittlichkeit* could and often did encompass *Sauberkeit* (cleanliness), as well as diligence, orderliness, frugality, respect for family bonds, and fulfillment of family duties. Conversely, *Sauberkeit* or *Gesundheit* (health) was often encoded with presumptions regarding morality and virtue as prerequisites of good health.⁵²

The "imaginative trigger" of social reform discourses in the 1870s was the sexual licentiousness of factory workers, in particular in the textile mills, where men and women mingled with one another and with "half-grown boys and girls."⁵³ To the extent that *Sittlichkeit* represented a repertoire of bourgeois concerns about morals and workers' alleged transgressions, it also mapped out a domain of sexuality around the poles of pollution and cleanliness, depravity and industriousness. In fact many bourgeois reformers viewed the widespread poverty of the "hungry 1840s" as the outcome of a complex Malthusian chain that linked unbridled sexuality to unrestrained drives and desires, and those in turn to premature family formation, which led finally to pauperism among the lower classes. Pauperism, in turn, fostered further *Entsittlichung* (moral degeneracy), *Verwilderung* (running wild), and *sexuelle Zügellosigkeit* (sexual abandon) among the lower classes.⁵⁴ Enmeshed in the social question, then, were not

50. Poovey, "Domesticity and Class Formation," p. 65.
51. Frank Mort, *Dangerous Sexualities: Medico-moral Politics in England since 1830* (London: Routledge, 1987), pp. 26–27, 37. Mort points out that the loose and expansive use of the term "moral" makes it difficult to deconstruct its fields of reference. Also see Alfons Labisch, "Doctors, Workers and the Scientific Cosmology of the Industrial World: The Social Construction of 'Health' and the 'Homo Hygienicus,'" *Journal of Contemporary History* 20 (1985): 600.
52. Alfons Labisch, "'Hygiene ist Moral—Moral ist Hygiene': Soziale Disziplinierung durch Ärzte und Medizin," in *Soziale Sicherheit und soziale Disziplinierung: Beiträge zu einer historischen Theorie der Sozialpolitik*, ed. Christoph Sachße and Florian Tennstedt (Frankfurt a.M.: Suhrkamp, 1986), pp. 276–79.
53. Thun, *Die Industrie am Niederrhein*, 1:174–75. On the "imaginative trigger" of social reform, see Ludmilla Jordanova, *Sexual Visions: Images of Gender in Science and Medicine between the 18th and 20th Centuries* (Madison: University of Wisconsin Press, 1989), p. 80.
54. Mort, *Dangerous Sexualities*, pp. 26, 38; Frevert, *Krankheit als politisches Problem*, pp.

only moral-ethical visions of national economies, factories, urban spaces, and families, but also the delineation of boundaries between classes, between sexes, and between bodies.

Although the health of industrial workers and urban dwellers remained a primary concern of social reformers, it evoked far less passion and public interest than the "moral outrages" of factories, cities, and deteriorating family life that social reformers of all political persuasions documented and publicized. The discourses about *Sittlichkeit* and *Entsittlichung* formed "a mental landscape" within which bourgeois social reformers, Catholics, and skilled male Social Democrats deployed similar tropes of respectability and depravity to define distinct and often opposing social identities.[55]

When Alphons Thun set out in the 1870s to explore "the industry of the Rhineland and its workers," he traversed the streets of textile towns, visiting not only woolen factories but also pubs, dance halls, and over one hundred workers' households. Thun was a student of the statistician Ernst Engel and protégé of Gustav Schmoller, and his 1877 study quickly found an audience among members of the Verein für Sozialpolitik as well as among Catholic social reformers, many of whom had initiated social reform campaigns in their own hometowns in the Rhenish textile region (for example, Franz Hitze, priest and reformer; textile mill owner Franz Brandts; and Freiherr Georg von Hertling, Catholic Center delegate to the Reichstag).[56] Although Thun returned to his native Livland (Baltics) shortly after the publication of his book, his text took on a life of its own, resounding in social reformers' narratives for the next quarter century. His study became a model because of its innovative mix of statistics and sensation, both grounded in a social scientific method of firsthand observation and investigation.[57]

136–38. Mort has aptly argued that "there were no positive representations of sexuality in this discourse." For an interesting parallel with France, see Joan Scott's essay, "'L'Ouvrière! Mot Impie, Sordide . . .': Women Workers in the Discourse of French Political Economy, 1840–1860," in *Gender and the Politics of History* by Joan W. Scott (New York: Columbia University Press, 1988), pp. 139–63.

55. Gareth Stedman Jones, *Outcast London: A Study in the Relationship between Classes in Victorian Society* (Harmondsworth: Penguin Books, 1976), p. 151. Also see Rose, "Factory Reform," MS p. 12 and Tennstedt, *Sozialgeschichte der Sozialpolitik*, pp. 373–76.

56. Thun, *Die Industrie am Niederrhein*. Hitze was the author of several key texts of Catholic social reform, including *Die Arbeiterfrage und die Bestrebungen*; *Die sociale Frage und die Bestrebungen zu ihrer Lösung, mit besonderer Berücksichtigung der verschiedenen socialen Parteien in Deutschland* (Paderborn: Bonifacius/J. W. Schröder, 1877); and *Kapital und Arbeit und die Reorganisation der Gesellschaft* (Paderborn: J. W. Schröder, 1880).

57. On the place of Thun's investigation in German social science, see Oberschall, *Empirical Social Research*, pp. 70–72. Oberschall points out that Thun's study was based on little firsthand observation, instead relying on contact with factory owners, chambers of commerce members, policemen, mayors, and such, and that Thun apparently did not recognize the

The tropes of danger in Thun's text were both moral and physical, ranging from the declining health of undernourished workers to the disorderly and grimy households, the absent mothers, and the "astonishing fertility of the working-class population."[58] Thun distinguished the respectable old *Weberstamm* (core workforce of weavers), the sober and frugal family fathers who had provided for the future, from those weavers who had succumbed to *Sumpf und Trunk* (gutter and drink) and those who spent all their money on dances, games, or elaborate clothing. Concurring with many of his contemporaries that the hot, steamy air of the cotton spinning mills aroused sexual desire, he described how "in the early factory system and to some extent even today, children, half-grown boys and girls, men and women work together without distinction in overheated shops," sweaty and scantily clad, so that "during the day the basis was laid for the excesses of the night." Thun concluded: "Thus all modesty necessarily disappeared. The tone, like the dress, was crude and unrestrained. So at dusk . . . and also during the night, when they worked back to back or side by side, vulgar words became vulgar deeds."[59] In particular, Thun singled out young female workers as the cause of the *sittliche Verpestung des Volkes* (the moral infestation of the people). Drawing on the report of one of his local contacts, Dr. P. Norrenberg, head of the Katholischer Arbeiterinnenverein (Catholic Women Workers' Association) in the textile town of Viersen, Thun evoked images of cornfields "shockingly ravaged" by female mill workers and their lovers, who indulged their passions on the way home from the factories. Similarly, those who lived too far away to walk home fell not into a peaceful sleep when the lights were out, but into "the most dreadful orgies of wild lust amid the leftover scraps and spools in the dusty and dirty shops, with curious children looking on."[60]

The Catholic parish of Viersen had entrusted Dr. Norrenberg with establishing the Women Workers' Association in 1876 in response to precisely this kind of "moral infestation." In 1875 "several trainloads" of

---

irony of grounding an investigation in "contacts with people of all estates and social classes" while generally accompanied by policemen or government officials. See Thun, *Die Industrie am Niederrhein*, preface, p. 1.

58. Thun, *Die Industrie am Niederrhein*, 1:66–67, 123–24.

59. Ibid., p. 174; Nordrhein-Westfälisches Hauptstaatsarchiv Düsseldorf (HStAD), Reg. Düss. 24652, p. 11, "Bericht des Gewerbeinspektors für den Regierungsbezirk Düsseldorf von 24.10.1878 über die Zustände in den Spinnereien." The report of the Düsseldorf district factory inspector from 1878 alleges that among workers in the cotton spinning mills, "their clothing and their positions are such that sexual stimulation is inevitable. Now and then, of course, the supervision is so strict that abuses do not seem to occur." Note that abuses are constructed here as the norm, which only now and then do *not* occur. On the trope of heat in social reformers' texts and its sexual meanings, see Gray, "Medical Men," pp. 39–40, and Rose, "Factory Reform," MS p. 11.

60. Thun, *Die Industrie am Niederrhein*, 1:173–75.

young female spinners from Dundee had arrived in Viersen to train "their German sisters" in flax spinning. Instead the "Scottish girls" quickly "became the moral scourge of the community." As they were independent of home and family, unconstrained by religious strictures, the young women's "passionate enjoyment of spirits" had led them "to succumb to every type of seduction and abandon," unleashing a sexual bedlam in Viersen when the "otherwise virtuous" German girls followed suit.[61] The Women Workers' Association was founded to "confront the danger" of factory work and female independence, to insulate the local girls from similar depravity and dissolution, to combat the "generally immoral consequences" of factory work on the female population of Viersen. Within months the association articulated a program of local reform, centered on the establishment of *Arbeiterinnenhospize*, dormitories for single women workers, especially for those from far away (Holland, East Prussia, the Eifel, and the Oberrhein). While young women would find both shelter and spiritual guidance in the dormitories, usually run by religious orders, the association itself offered them instruction in the fine arts of homemaking—sewing, cooking, embroidery—as well as in virtuous comportment, manners, respectability, and the creation of a comfortable home. Attending to both the moral and the bodily, the Women Workers' Association instructed its members on diet and nutrition, planted its own garden, and arranged spring and summer expeditions complete with "vigorous exercise," all aimed at shielding young women workers and future mothers from the many illnesses associated with industrial life.[62]

Reformer and ventriloquist, Alphons Thun catapulted not only the female spinners of Viersen, but also Dr. Norrenberg and his solutions to the moral and sexual dangers of Viersen, onto the national stage of social reform and into the halls of the Verein für Sozialpolitik and the texts of eminent political economists. When Thun's study appeared in 1877, the issue of female factory labor still constituted a subtext in reformers' debates about the worker question. But his study would resonate in new and powerful ways when women's work came to preoccupy the social reform milieu during the late 1880s and early 1890s. The moral outrages that Thun uncovered as he toured the streets of the Rhenish textile towns sent shock waves through the social reform milieu. The fears of bourgeois reformers in Germany were likely similar to those Robert Gray describes for England during the 1830s, stemming on the one hand from "the discovery of a working-class population resistant to middle-class social discipline and remote from the standards of domestic propriety which the middle class

61. Ibid. Thun cites the following report rather freely: Stadtarchiv Viersen 7 (StA Vie) 7 (018), Dr. P. Norrenberg, "Erster Jahresbericht des katholischen Arbeiterinnen-Vereins in Viersen, 1877," pp. 17–21, 34–35.
62. StA Vie 7 (018): Norrenberg, "Erster Jahresbericht," pp. 26–27.

was defining for itself" and on the other from the patriarchal fear and fantasy about both "the 'animal propensities'" and "the economic and social independence of factory women."⁶³ Thus, in the course of their local and national initiatives to improve the conditions of factory work, reformers also constructed a domain of sexuality in direct relation to themes of danger, disease, filth, and depravity and to the social problems of illegitimate births, venereal disease, and *Gelegenheitsprostitution* (occasional prostitution) that were thought to prevail among young, single female workers.⁶⁴

The classic text of the socialist articulation of the woman question, August Bebel's best-selling *Woman under Socialism*, first published in 1878, also made textile mills and their female employees emblematic of the transformations of industry, family, and the relations between the sexes. Bebel's central claim that economic development was the cause of women's oppression was embedded in a rich and highly ambiguous text that ranged from detailed analysis of prostitution and marriage to depictions of "morally objectionable" factory and household conditions that reflected the bourgeois preoccupation with *Sittlichkeit* and *Entsittlichung*.⁶⁵ Deploying many of the same metaphors and tropes as his contemporary Alphons Thun, Bebel supported protective labor laws to safeguard the woman worker "as a mother and rearer of children," to keep her from occupations "that are especially injurious to the female organism."⁶⁶ "With an eye to its

63. Gray, "Medical Men," p. 39.

64. Although social reformers and factory inspectors occasionally mentioned prostitution among female factory workers, their fears seem to have focused mainly on illegitimate births and on the subversive, transgressive meanings of sexuality within and outside the factory. In her *Studien über die Wuppertaler Textilindustrie und ihre Arbeiter in den letzten zwanzig Jahren* (Leipzig: Duncker und Humblot, 1903), Elisabeth Gottheiner claimed that the female textile workers of the Wupper Valley formed a sizable contingent among the local prostitutes. Also see Regina Schulte, *Sperrbezirke: Tugendhaftigkeit und Prostitution in der bürgerlichen Welt* (Frankfurt a.M.: Syndikat, 1984), pp. 68–70, 79–98, 217–18.

65. August Bebel's *Die Frau und der Sozialismus* (1883) was first published in 1878 under the purposely deceptive title *Woman in the Past, Present, and Future* (owing to the repressive Socialist Law that was in effect from 1878 through 1890). It went through fifty editions between 1879 and 1909 and was translated into many other languages. A best-seller, reputed to be the most widely read book among Social Democrats, *Die Frau* was also read by academics, scientists, and bourgeois politicians. On German Socialist views of the family, see Richard J. Evans, "Politics and the Family: Social Democracy and the Working-Class Family in Theory and Practice before 1914," in *The German Family: Essays on the Social History of the Family in Nineteenth- and Twentieth-Century Germany*, ed. Richard J. Evans and W. R. Lee (Totowa, N.J.: Croom Helm, 1981), pp. 273–74.

66. Citations are from the English version *Woman under Socialism*, cited in note 5, pp. 89–90. I checked these citations against the 1883 edition of Bebel's *Die Frau* (Hottingen-Zürich: Schweizerische Volksbuchhandlung, 1883), p. 62, to be certain they accurately represent Bebel's thinking of the 1880s rather than his later views. The term "organism" appears throughout the 1883 edition, although this specific reference to the female organism does not appear in that edition.

sexual mission," he argued, "the female organism requires particular care, —good food, and at certain periods, the requisite rest." Echoing Dr. Hirt's medical text, he pointed to the consequences of factory labor: "disease of the organs connected with the sexual purpose."[67] Although Bebel rebuffed the demands of male workers for the prohibition of female labor, he shared their concern—and that of bourgeois social reformers—that "with the extension of female labor, the family life of the working class goes ever more to pieces, the dissolution of marriage and the family is a natural result, and immorality, demoralization, degeneration, diseases of all natures and child mortality increase at a shocking pace."[68] Bebel's study is rich in metaphors of sexual danger, and as in Thun's, the cultural distance between the author and the workers he observed is an integral part of the text. At times virtually indistinguishable from a social scientist like Thun or a local pastor like Norrenberg, Bebel also marked the workplace as a locus of both desire and depravity:

> Among the poor, it is certain exhausting occupations, especially of a sedentary nature, that promotes [sic] congestion of blood in the abdominal organs, and promotes [sic] sexual excitation. One of the most dangerous occupations in this direction is connected with the, at present, widely spread sewing machine. This occupation works such havoc that, with ten or twelve hours' daily work, the strongest organism is ruined within a few years. Excessive sexual excitement is also promoted by long hours of work in a steady high temperature, for instance, sugar refineries, bleacheries, cloth-pressing establishments, night work by gaslight in overcrowded rooms, especially when both sexes work together.[69]

At the same time, the Socialist Workers' Party was scarcely able to mask the divisions among its parliamentary representatives on the issue of female factory labor. In 1878, SPD representative Julius Motteler, for example, claimed on behalf of his party: "We are totally opposed to all industrial employment of women ... in particular in factory industry or [in any area] outside that sphere that is naturally suitable for women. We want to return the woman to her proper destiny, and that is why we demand her liberation from the moral and physical yoke of factory work."[70] The powerful concordance among disparate, even opposing, political and social reform groups is a cardinal feature of the social reform milieu of the 1870s.

67. Bebel, *Woman under Socialism*, pp. 122–23; *Die Frau* (1883), p. 63.
68. Bebel, *Woman under Socialism*, pp. 180–81; *Die Frau* (1883), p. 93.
69. Bebel, *Woman under Socialism*, pp. 139–40; *Die Frau* (1883), pp. 73–74.
70. As quoted in Rose Otto, *Über die Fabrikarbeit verheirateter Frauen*, Münchener Volkswirtschaftliche Studien, ed. Lujo Brentano und Walther Lotz (Stuttgart: Cotta, 1910), vol. 104, p. 135.

Even the industrialists whose hiring policies seemed to be transforming "men into maidens" embraced the trope of the family when responding to male workers' protests about female factory labor. During the 1870s mill owners in the textile town of Düren, for example, deliberated the detriments and dangers of hiring married women and mothers, determining in the end that married women should be hired "not for their own sake, rather in order to ensure that *respectable* workers' families, living in orderly circumstances, do not lose a vital part of their incomes."[71] In the view of contemporary Johannes Wenzel, curate and Center Party delegate to the Reichstag, the consensus among reformers, employers, and unionists about family and social order offered "proof of how deeply and ineradicably the God-granted social order is engraved in the bosom of every person, so that even those who want to destroy this order and replace it with one of their own invention . . . always revert to the familiar vision of what this new social order should comprise."[72]

Indeed, by the 1870s this consensus shaped the minimum common legislative program that had formed around the Verein für Sozialpolitik, the Center Party, and the Social Democrats. The agitation of each of these groups at the level of "high politics" in the Reichstag, within the informal channels of contact between the Verein and highly placed government bureaucrats, had moved protective labor legislation from the periphery, the "taboo zone" to which it had been relegated by economic liberals, to the center of state social policy.[73] The so-called *Gründerkrach* of the 1870s, the economic crisis and depression that followed national unification, was particularly acute between 1873 and 1878. The crisis, which Friedrich Engels called "an earthquake that shook bourgeois society to its core," roused "the German social conscience regarding the social conditions of the workers" and sparked legislative interest in the factory question.[74] It left particularly fertile ground for the "combat patrol of social reform," the Verein für Sozialpolitik, to influence the government's response. So when officials in the Ministry of Trade began to prepare an official government inquiry into women's and children's factory labor in 1873, they drew on the expertise of Verein members regarding the scope and the content of the inquest. Both formally, in its recommendations to the Chancellery re-

71. Franz Decker, *Die betriebliche Sozialordnung der Dürener Industrie im 19. Jahrhundert*, Schriften zur Rheinisch-Westfälischen Wirtschaftsgeschichte, vol. 12 (Cologne: Rheinisch-Westfälisches Wirtschaftsarchiv, 1965), p. 155.
72. Wenzel, *Arbeiterschutz*, p. 74.
73. Berlepsch, *"Neuer Kurs,"* p. 132.
74. Engels, as cited in Tennstedt, *Sozialgeschichte der Sozialpolitik*, pp. 139–40. On the slow awakening of the German social conscience, see Hans von Berlepsch, "Die Anfänge des gesetzlichen Arbeiterschutzes," in *Soziale Arbeit im neuen Deutschland, Festschrift zum 70. Geburtstage von Franz Hitze*, ed. August Pieper (Mönchen-Gladbach: Volksvereins, 1921), p. 88.

garding the inquiry, as well as informally, through its close ties to legislators on national and provincial levels, to leading government officials, and to the factory inspectors who would implement the survey, the Verein "exerted a fundamental influence on the formulation of the questionnaire."[75] The role of the Verein in helping to constitute the inquest fulfilled its scholarly as well as its political goals. In contrast to its pronounced political neutrality during the 1880s, the Verein not only sought to frame scholarly investigation and provide the "scientific" foundation for a state policy of social reform during the 1870s, but also aspired to influence the state bureaucracy, the parliamentary arena, and public opinion.[76] Indeed, in Schmoller's own estimation, the deliberations regarding the inquest of 1874–75 and the Reichstag debates about protective labor legislation of 1877 represent the peak of the Verein's influence on parliament and bureaucracy.[77] Although the social reform milieu and the government, in particular Bismarck, would draw different, even opposing conclusions from the survey, the two forces concurred in 1873 that only the state could definitively solve the social question, which they viewed as a vital part of the "internal founding" of the Reich.[78]

Thus, as a culmination of previous reform efforts, in 1875 the Bundesrat (upper house of the legislature) requested that the factory inspectors conduct a study of the dangers factory work posed to female and teenage workers. Appointed by the individual states and endowed with the authority of a police agency, the factory inspectors were *Beamte* (civil servants) who were well-educated professionals. Inspectors crossed a wide social gulf when they set out to investigate the perils female factory labor posed to morality and health and to the structure and stability of working-class families, as well as its effects on age of marriage, births (legitimate and illegitimate), and the social problems of drunkenness and debauchery in the workers' milieu.[79] Although it was not yet an issue of public debate,

---

75. Machtan, "Workers' Insurance," p. 212. Also see Dieter Krüger, "Max Weber and the Younger Generation in the Verein für Sozialpolitik," in *Max Weber and His Contemporaries*, ed. Wolfgang J. Mommsen and Jürgen Osterhammel (London: Allen Unwin/GHI London, 1987), p. 71. These ties are what constituted the Verein für Sozialpolitik as a "research hub in the larger welfare nexus," according to Quataert, "Woman's Work," pp. 165–66.

76. Ritter, *Social Welfare*, p. 27. See also Lindenlaub, *Richtungskämpfe*; Rüdiger vom Bruch, *Wissenschaft, Politik und öffentliche Meinung: Gelehrtenpolitik im Wilhelminischen Deutschland (1890–1914)* (Husum: Matthiesen, 1980), pp. 64–65; Harry Liebersohn, *Fate and Utopia in German Sociology, 1870–1923* (Cambridge: MIT Press, 1987), pp. 110–11.

77. As noted in Tennstedt, *Vom Proleten zum Industriearbeiter*, p. 371.

78. Tennstedt, *Sozialgeschichte der Sozialpolitik*, pp. 142–45.

79. For further discussion of the legal position and social background of the factory inspectors, see Quataert, "Source Analysis," pp. 102–3; Berlepsch, *"Neuer Kurs,"* pp. 269–90; and Wolfgang Bocks, *Die badische Fabrikinspektion: Arbeiterschutz, Arbeitsverhältnisse und Arbeiterbewegung in Baden 1879 bis 1914* (Freiburg: Alber, 1978).

the inspectors were to gather viewpoints from various publics—employers, local chambers of commerce, doctors, and workers themselves—regarding the feasibility and desirability of restricting women's factory employment.[80] Informed by the social scientists of the Verein für Sozialpolitik and the political activists from both the Social Catholic and the Social Democratic milieus, the inquest marked the first official state inquiry into the conditions and consequences of female factory labor.

While the results of the survey were still being compiled and analyzed, the Prussian minister of trade presented a bill to the Chancellery and to the Ministry of State recommending a number of strict protective measures for women and children and a significant expansion of the factory inspectorate. The bill, described by Lothar Machtan as the "first state political negation of the liberal axiom of a factory as a non-public, and more or less secret realm beyond the reach of the law," had been developed under the supervision of Theodor Lohmann, minister of trade, a leading force in the development of German social policy during the 1870s.[81] A year later, in March 1877, the Center Party, followed in April by the Socialist Workers' Party, brought before the Reichstag the first motions for the protection of labor. Graf von Galen's motion on behalf of the Center Party called on the state to protect the "sanctity of the family" through restrictions on women's work in factories, a ban on the employment of youths under age fourteen, and the elimination of Sunday work. Furthermore, the enactment of obligatory *Arbeitsordnungen* (factory ordinances) was to define the terms of the relationship between employers and workers.[82] The Social Democratic motion, the first piece of comprehensive legislation introduced by the newly formed party, tacitly endorsed the Center's call to safeguard the family, framing its demands in terms of health and hygiene, with the family more an implicit than an explicit presence.[83] The SAPD's motion of 1877 made even more extensive demands on the state than that of the Catholic Center, including the call for a mandatory eight-hour maximum workday for women and youths; a general ban on night work for women and youths; special protection for pregnant women; the institution of the ten-hour maximum workday for adult men; the eradication of all remnants of the truck system; the reorganization of work through local *Arbeitskammer* (employment bureaus); and the even-

80. Reichskanzler-Amt, *Ergebnisse der über die Frauen- und Kinderarbeit in den Fabriken auf Beschluss des Bundesraths angestellten Erhebungen, zusammengestellt im Reichskanzler-Amt* (Berlin: Heymanns, 1878).
81. Machtan, "Workers' Insurance," p. 214. On Theodor Lohmann, see Berlepsch, *"Neuer Kurs,"* pp. 51–52, 161, 182, 200–202.
82. Berlepsch, *"Neuer Kurs,"* p. 133, and Wenzel, *Arbeiterschutz*, pp. 23–39.
83. Vernon L. Lidtke, *The Outlawed Party: Social Democracy in Germany, 1878–1890* (Princeton: Princeton University Press, 1966), pp. 56–57.

tual establishment of national ministries of health and labor.[84] Alfons Labisch views the SAPD's motion of 1877, particularly the restrictions it proposed on the factory employment of women and teenagers, as an integral part of the party's *Gesundheitspolitik* (policies on health), and Vernon Lidtke's authoritative study, *The Outlawed Party*, views the motion of 1877 as emblematic of the "ambivalent parliamentarism" that marks the history of the Social Democratic movement from its founding through 1933.[85] Protective labor legislation is an excellent example of this ambivalence: on the one hand, the SAPD voiced an uncompromising rejection of the capitalist order as the origin of all misery, while on the other the party sought to utilize parliament as an arena for social reforms that, in the words of August Bebel, would "improve the conditions for all immediately."[86]

The parliamentary initiatives of the two parties, launched separately yet coalescing to form a powerful legislative campaign, met with resounding defeat in 1877. Citing evidence compiled by factory inspectors in their survey of 1875, government and Reichstag opponents claimed that the restrictive measures would have a calamitous effect on certain branches of German industry and pointed out that the survey had uncovered insufficient evidence of detrimental conditions and abuses in German factories to warrant such comprehensive legislative intervention.[87] The final report of the inspectors' findings, published in 1878, offers striking evidence of the ways inspectors mediated among the many distinct and contrary voices of those they interviewed, privileging some over others, as they explicated their conclusion that women's work outside the home was not *necessarily* detrimental to the health and welfare of working-class families. While faulting mill owners here and there for poorly ventilated, dusty, and overheated shops, inspectors determined that workers and their families were healthier overall in the late 1870s than during the era of domestic textile production. The report conveyed the impression of a broad consensus that the harmful effects of women's factory work could best be remedied by renovating factory buildings and making other technical improvements, not by imposing legal limits on women's labor.[88] Inspectors also empha-

---

84. Berlepsch, "*Neuer Kurs,*" p. 133; Wenzel, *Arbeiterschutz*, pp. 41–45, 70–72. Also see Thönnessen, *Frauenemanzipation*, p. 35, and Emmanuel Wurm, "'Ehret die Frauen!' Das Scheitern des Zehnstundengesetzes für Arbeiterinnen," *Neue Zeit* 23, no. 2 (1905) 158.
85. Alfons Labisch, "Die gesundheitspolitischen Vorstellungen der deutschen Sozialdemokratie von ihrer Gründung bis zur Parteispaltung (1863–1917)," *Archiv für Sozialgeschichte* 16 (1976): 335–37; Lidtke, *Outlawed Party*, pp. 56–57; Wenzel, *Arbeiterschutz*, p. 79.
86. As cited by Wenzel, *Arbeiterschutz*, p. 79.
87. Wenzel, *Arbeiterschutz*, pp. 36, 57; Berlepsch, "*Neuer Kurs,*" pp. 134–35.
88. Reichskanzler-Amt, *Ergebnisse*, p. 67.

sized that the earnings of wives and teenagers augmented the family income, providing workers with better nourishment, housing, and clothing that, in the words of the Düsseldorf inspector, "compensated to some extent for the negative effects of factory work." At the same time, however, they recounted the exhortation of one cotton weaver that frugality and more efficient housekeeping skills could render women's wage labor unnecessary.[89] Echoing the views of middle-class social reformers, the inspectors attributed the poor living conditions of some families to the deficient household skills of working women, implicitly proposing a domestic solution for a social problem. A ban on female factory labor would not be necessary, they argued, if young women could receive regular, obligatory training in "female handiwork" and if work hours for married women were arranged to allow them "time to take care of their homes or . . . to obtain practical training as good housewives."[90] In fact, the inspectors found that many employers already enacted flexible policies with this goal in mind:

> Wherever the operation of the factory allows it, married women are given piecework. At their request, they are allowed to leave work one hour before the noon break . . . and to organize [their working day] entirely around the needs of their households. . . . In nearly all the factories [in the Iserlohn and Arnsberg districts] work begins for married women at 9:00 in the morning; they may leave work from 11:00 A.M. until 2:00 P.M. and are allowed to leave work earlier in the evening. Furthermore, they are permitted to arrange their work on Mondays, as well as in the spring and fall, according to their own wishes, to interrupt it for any number of days in order to take care of their gardens and fields.[91]

Finally, the inspectors lent the imprint of state authority to the sexual domain that the discourses of social reform had begun to define. They focused on the mingling of the sexes at work, specifically on the failure of mill owners to establish sexually segregated restrooms, washrooms, changing rooms, dining halls, exits, and entry halls or to prohibit women from going to or from work in the dark.[92] While ostensibly prescribing moral codes for the workplace alone, their concern with the workers' passage to and from work makes it clear that the inspectors aimed, as historian Jean Quataert has previously argued, to set moral standards at work, at home,

89. Ibid., pp. 42, 74.
90. Ibid., pp. 70–72.
91. Ibid., p. 32.
92. Ibid., pp. 67–69, 72.

and at play—that is, in the taverns and dance halls.[93] Similar to the tropes in Thun's account of the Rhenish textile towns, the inspectors took careful note of the consequences of absent or inadequate moral codes, pointing to the frequent *geschlechtliche Ausschreitungen* (sexual excesses), especially among the young single workers from distant towns or provinces. At the same time, however, their declaration that most premarital pregnancies resulted in hastily arranged marriages rather than desertion of the young mother served to articulate and uphold a specifically working-class practice of middle-class morality.[94]

Finally, mediating between those, like the Social Democratic *Arbeiterbildungsverein* (workers' educational club) of Stuttgart, that called for an absolute ban on women's work in factories and factory owners and local chambers of commerce, which categorically rejected the idea, the inspectors ascertained no compelling need for the state to intervene or stem the growth of the female factory workforce.[95] Their report not only made it clear that in the 1870s most factory inspectors and state bureaucrats "still accepted the notion that lower-class women had to work, even if this meant outside the home in factories," but also regarded banning women from work "that they had performed for decades, even centuries, outside the factories" as something "harmful to natural relations."[96] The failure of the inquest to deliver compelling statistical proof of the need for protective legislation confirmed Bismarck's own marked disinclination toward state interference in industrial relations. Thus the chancellor concluded in 1877 that the social question could best be remedied, and the economy reinvigorated, through "rigorous measures against the socialists and support of the employers' interests."[97]

Despite the defeat of the Center and SPD initiatives, the debates and legislative contests in the Reichstag about the inspectors' report and workers' protection resulted in the revision of the protective labor code in 1878. The new code, which remedied only the most egregious abuses of industrial employment, failed to realize the goals of either Center or Social Democratic politicians or to fulfill the visions of its instigator of the early 1870s, Theodor Lohmann. Lohmann had foreseen restricted work hours for both male and female workers under age sixteen and had also sought to prohibit women and teenagers from working at night and on Sundays. The code prohibited female labor in mines, and in response to intensified pressure by both Center and Social Democratic delegates in the Reichstag,

93. Ibid., pp. 45–46; Quataert, "Source Analysis," p. 109.
94. Reichskanzler-Amt, *Ergebnisse*, pp. 44–46.
95. Ibid., p. 91.
96. Quataert, "Source Analysis," p. 108; Reichskanzler-Amt, *Ergebnisse*, p. 77.
97. Ritter, *Social Welfare*, p. 31.

on the second reading of the motion legislators also agreed to bar women from the workplace for the first three weeks after giving birth, thus extending protective legislation to women for the first time, albeit without reimbursement for lost pay.[98] The revised code laid the foundation for the regulation of women's work hours and the definition of female spheres of factory employment, marking both health and morality as realms of intervention while failing to specify standards for either.[99] Perhaps the most significant measure was the reorganization of the factory inspectorate and the widening of its surveillance to all factories with more than ten employees, which occurred mainly in response to the growing government interest in female factory workers, as Quataert's examination of the factory inspectorate demonstrates.[100] The Center delegates, undaunted and convinced that the results of the government inquiry had been prejudiced by the inspectors' failure to interview enough workers, proposed an amendment during the second reading of the bill to increase maternity protection from three to six weeks and to restrict night work and the length of the workday for both adult women and young girls.[101] Although these measures again met with resounding defeat, in the course of the deliberations about them the Center delegates introduced a new kind of statistical evidence into the debates about female factory labor, namely, investigations of workers' household budgets that revealed the rather meager contribution women's wages made to family income. While continuing to pursue a moral-ethical vision of social reform, with the family at its center, social reformers were now able to deploy a complex of rhetorical strategies, including economistic arguments about the profitability of female factory labor.[102]

The revision of the labor code in 1878 marks the end of the first phase

98. Rosika Schwimmer, "Historische Zusammenstellung über wichtige Momente in der Entwicklung des Mutterschutzes," in *Mutterschaft: Ein Sammelwerk für die Probleme des Weibes als Mutter*, ed. Adele Schreiber (Munich: Albert Langen, 1912); "Die Frauenarbeit als Gegenstand der Fabrikgesetzgebung, von einem Sachverständigen," *Jahrbuch für Gesetzgebung, Verwaltung und Volkswirtschaft im Deutschen Reich (Schmollers Jahrbuch)* 9, no. 2 (1885): 95; Wenzel, *Arbeiterschutz*, pp. 70–74; Franz Hitze, "Zur Vorgeschichte der deutschen Arbeiterschutzgesetzgebung," *Schmollers Jahrbuch* 22, no. 2 (1898): 725–34.

99. Quataert, "Source Analysis," pp. 102, 107.

100. Ibid., pp. 101–5, and "Von der Geschichte der Fabrikinspektion," *Die Christliche Arbeiterin* 10 (1905–6): 78–79. After the revision of the labor code, the numbers of factory inspectors increased steadily from 46 in 1880 (inspectors and assistants for the Reich) to 71 in 1887, 97 in 1890, 260 in 1895, and 388 in 1903 (of which 237 were employed in Prussia). See both of the works above for an account of the agitation among women workers and middle-class feminists for the appointment of female inspectors, which began in 1884. Hessen appointed the first female inspector's assistant in 1898 followed by Bavaria, Württemberg, and in 1900, Baden. By 1906 there were 25 women employed by the factory inspectorate, most of them salaried assistants rather than tenured inspectors.

101. Wenzel, *Arbeiterschutz*, pp. 57, 70–74; Hitze, "Zur Vorgeschichte," p. 733.

102. Wenzel, *Arbeiterschutz*, pp. 70–73.

of labor legislation in imperial Germany. Framed within the discursive domain of the "worker question" yet extending protection mainly to female and teenage workers, the new provisions of the code attest to the growing concern at the level of high politics—among parliamentarians in the Reichstag, factory inspectors, and academic social policy experts—about women's factory employment and its consequences for both the health and the moral well-being of female workers and their families. Yet in many respects the labor code of 1878 also marks the inception of reformers' long-term campaign to compel the state to regulate industrial working conditions, to curb the *Krebsschäden* (cancerous growths) of industrial work, the abuses and excesses of factory work that threatened to eat away at the "moral glue" of society—the family.[103] The social investigations, scholarly debates, and legislative initiatives that produced the labor code of 1878 also shaped the social knowledge and the mental landscape of the social reform milieu, furnishing it with rhetorical and legislative strategies that it would continue to deploy in the reform campaigns of the 1880s. The textile industry, with the largest contingent of female factory employees, formed the main stage on which the dramas of the "worker question" were played out during this first phase in the history of state social policy.

At the same time, the coalescence of this milieu during the 1870s represents a formative moment in the history of the *Bildungsbürgertum* as associations like the Verein für Sozialpolitik sought to strengthen the bond between citizens and state by transforming the *Beamtenstaat* (bureaucratic state) or *Rechtsstaat* into both *Kulturstaat* and *Wohlfahrtsstaat* (welfare state). In defining the social as a realm of state intervention and as a key part of the emergent public sphere, reform-minded academics, bureaucrats, and parliamentarians articulated key aspects of the social identity of the German *Bildungsbürgertum*: its embrace of civic responsibility and moral pathos with regard to the "worker question," its pursuit of both moral and scientific solutions to this question, and its espousal of a vibrant German liberalism that vehemently opposed "Manchesterite" views of the relation between state and industry. Bound together by educational training and a shared view of the family as the critical agent of social cohesion across the class divide, the social scientists of the *Bildungsbürgertum* calmed bourgeois fears of moral and physical decrepitude, of pollution, contagion, and class conflict, through their espousal of social-scientific epistemologies and promotion of their own social norms regarding health and hygiene.[104] In social reform rhetoric of the 1870s the moral and hy-

103. Berlepsch, "Die Anfänge des gesetzlichen Arbeiterschutzes," p. 87.
104. Blackbourn, "German Bourgeoise," pp. 1–45; Alfons Labisch, "Gesundheitskonzepte und Medizin im Prozeß der Zivilisation," in *Medizinische Deutungsmacht im sozialen Wandel des 19. und frühen 20. Jahrhunderts*, ed. Alfons Labisch and Reinhard Spree (Bonn:

gienic family became, as Robert Gray has aptly pointed out for England, "a metaphor for the proper relations between classes."[105] This vision of the family had a key role in defining and shaping the social as a terrain of contest over the reproduction of labor, contests that were inscribed with gender from their inception. As a crucial site for the demarcation of sexual difference, the social also became a key context in which identities of class and of citizenship formed among both workers and *Bildungsbürger*.

The Social Question of Married Women's Factory Employment during the 1880s

Intrinsic to but not yet distinct from the broader worker question, during the 1870s female factory labor was defined as a social problem at the level of high politics. Social policy activists in the parliament and policymakers in the interior ministry and factory inspectorate deliberated the regulation of women's work in the arenas of government, while the Verein für Sozialpolitik served as a link between the bureaucracy of state and bourgeois public opinion and as an essential source of academic expertise for reform initiatives.[106] Although the labor code of 1878 had laid the foundation for a comprehensive policy of preventive labor protection, social insurance formed the linchpin of Bismarckian social policy. Contrary to the counsel of some of his own policy experts, the chancellor waged an energetic battle against further revision or expansion of the code or its enforcing agency, the factory inspectorate, during the 1880s.[107] Chancellor Bismarck's intransigence on this issue meant that agitation and debate about female factory labor continued unabated throughout the 1880s, as both the Catholic Center and the Social Democrats bombarded the Reichstag with one legislative motion after another for increased protection of female and teenage workers. A source of constant friction between chan-

---

Psychiatrie, 1989), pp. 15–36; Labisch, *Homo hygienicus*, especially chapter 4, "'Sauberkeit und Sittlichkeit' als Lebensstil der Industrialisierung," pp. 105–41.

105. Robert Gray, "The Language of Factory Reform in Britain, c. 1830–1860," in *The Historical Meanings of Work*, ed. Patrick Joyce (Cambridge: Cambridge University Press, 1989), p. 158.

106. See vom Bruch, "Bürgerliche Sozialreform," pp. 125–28, as well as his monograph *Wissenschaft, Politik und öffentliche Meinung*, pp. 64–65. Also see Müssiggang, *Die soziale Frage*, pp. 154–55; Tennstedt, *Vom Proleten zum Industriearbeiter*, pp. 370–71; Born, *Staat und Sozialpolitik*, pp. 33–34.

107. Ritter, *Social Welfare*, pp. 65–67; Berlepsch, "*Neuer Kurs*," pp. 51–52; Lothar Machtan and Hans-Jörg von Berlepsch, "Vorsorge oder Ausgleich—oder beides? Prinzipienfragen staatlicher Sozialpolitik im deutschen Kaiserreich," *Zeitschrift für Sozialreform* 32 (May 1986): 266–72.

cellor and Reichstag, the parliamentary contests over labor protection reached their pinnacle between 1884 and 1890 as a majority in the Reichstag came to favor state regulation of female factory labor while Bismarck remained stubbornly impervious to the shifting groundswell of parliamentary and public opinion on the issue.[108]

The emergence of female factory labor as a new social question is best understood in the context of the shifting terrain of social reform and social policy. The Reichstag, rather than the state ministries or the network of bourgeois social reform associations, became the primary social policy arena during the 1880s. The Verein für Sozialpolitik abdicated its role as the "combat patrol of social reform" after a bitter and divisive battle over protective tariffs in 1879–80 prompted its leaders in 1881 to terminate the practice of voting on specific policy proposals or political initiatives. Forfeiting its goals of mobilizing public opinion and shaping social legislation, the Verein now shifted its attention to scientific research and scholarly study of the most urgent socioeconomic problems.[109] At the same time, the passage of the social insurance laws of 1883, 1884, and 1889 captured the social policy arena and appeared to wrest the social reform agenda from the Verein and other social policy advocates, only to place it firmly under the control of the state. The instigators of the new laws sought to recast the social question, mapping out new realms of state responsibility for health, accident, old age, and disability insurance among skilled, full-time, permanently employed—and thus by definition mainly male—wage workers. Female workers who qualified for disability and old age insurance paid two-thirds of the rate designated for men and thus received lower benefits, based on the assumption that skilled workers had "different needs compared with so-called day laborers."[110] Seeking to appease both industry and labor, state social insurance recognized the need of male breadwinners for minimal economic security amid the volatile expansions and contractions of the industrial labor market. An integral part of Bismarck's "carrot and stick" policy toward organized labor, the insur-

---

108. According to Berlepsch, "Neuer Kurs," pp. 134–37, 272–77, Bismarckian social policy remained tailored to the needs of industry. Also see Machtan and Berlepsch, "Vorsorge oder Ausgleich?" p. 266.

109. Lindenlaub, *Richtungskämpfe*, p. 33. Also see Sheehan, *Career of Lujo Brentano*, pp. 86–88; Conrad, *Der Verein*, pp. 69–70; vom Bruch, "Einleitung," in *Weder Kommunismus*, p. 13; Oberschall, *Empirical Social Research*, p. 21; and Tennstedt, *Vom Proleten zum Industriearbeiter*, pp. 370–71.

110. Ritter, *Social Welfare*, p. 45. Also see Sheehan, *Career of Lujo Brentano*, p. 96. Sickness insurance was instituted in 1883, accident insurance in 1884, and old age/disability insurance in 1889. On the history of social insurance in Germany and its role in shaping the welfare state, see Steinmetz, "Workers and the Welfare State," pp. 24–26; Tennstedt, *Sozialgeschichte der Sozialpolitik*, pp. 139–92; and Ritter, *Social Welfare*, pp. 1–128.

ance laws formed an essential counterpart of the repressive Socialist Law of 1878 that banned the political activities of the Socialist Workers' Party and its affiliated unions.[111] Although social insurance legislation was to solve one aspect of the social question—economic security for skilled male workers, who posed the greatest political challenge to the Bismarckian state—it also demarcated a male stream of welfare, one that extended a new kind of social citizenship to skilled male workers while inscribing with dependency the position of women within the expanding realms of welfare state and citizenship. The notion of sexual difference that was articulated within the emergent sphere of the social during the 1870s was now anchored in the bifurcation between social insurance and labor protection, between independent male and dependent female and youthful workers, and codified in law.

Mapping out a place for women, youths, and children within the welfare state, Social Democratic and Catholic Center parliamentarians fought vigorously to append protective measures to the insurance bills and resolutely voted against them when the measures failed.[112] The bills of the late 1880s aimed to extend the scope of "protection" significantly beyond that of 1878, calling for the exclusion of women from night work, an eleven-hour day for women workers, expanded maternity leave, and more stringent guidelines on the separation of the sexes at work. With the Center Party's reform activity increasingly focused on the social consequences of *married* women's factory employment, the 1881 motion of its representative Georg von Hertling identified "the complete banishment of married women from factories" as the foremost goal of protective legislation, while proposing piecemeal measures that were to pave the way toward this goal.[113] Although by the 1880s the Social Catholic reform program ap-

111. On employer demand as a key impetus of social insurance legislation of the 1880s, see Frevert, *Krankheit als politisches Problem*, p. 181; Baron, "Weder Zuckerbrot," pp. 15–18, and Monika Breger, *Die Haltung der industriellen Unternehmer zur staatlichen Sozialpolitik in den Jahren 1878–1891* (Frankfurt a.M.: Haag und Herchen, 1982), pp. 37, 124, 156, 212. Steinmetz argues that another of Bismarck's goals for social insurance was to break up the influence of the SPD within the various private workers' and company insurance funds. See Steinmetz, "Workers and the Welfare State," p. 24.

112. The Center Party remained divided over the issue of social insurance: while some of its Reichstag delegates (Ludwig Windthorst and Georg von Hertling) regarded it as an undesirable expansion of state power and an expression of "state socialism," others (such as Franz Hitze and Karl Reichensperger) voted in favor of the insurance laws. A similar ambivalence also prevailed in the SPD as some members supported social insurance legislation but remained reluctant to voice their views openly for fear of undermining their party's oppositional stance toward Bismarck. See Lidkte, *Outlawed Party*, pp. 159–68; Heide Gerstenberger, "The Poor and the Respectable Worker: On the Introduction of Social Insurance in Germany," *Labour History* 48 (May 1985): 69–70; Ritter, *Social Welfare*, pp. 68–70; Baron, "Weder Zuckerbrot," pp. 40–41.

113. Hertling's motion to the Reichstag, as cited in Wenzel, *Arbeiterschutz*, p. 85.

peared less imbued with its earlier vision of a return to a "Christian-Social world order in which economic life was no longer run by egoistic powers, but was constructed in an organic fashion,"[114] Hertling argued on behalf of his motion that "even in the most highly developed states, . . . the family is still the "cornerstone and foundation of the social order, the requisite source of all true human morality, because it is the primary and most sacred site of tutelage and training." Even the most vibrant growth of industry," he pointed out, "would offer no advancement if, as a result of this development, family life among the German people should continuously decline or even completely disintegrate."[115] The Center's motions of 1884 and 1885 mandated a six-hour day and a certificate of employment eligibility for married women, an extension of maternity leave from three to eight weeks, elimination of work on Sundays and holidays, and institution of a universal *Maximalarbeitstag*, restricting the length of the workday for all workers. Faced with the certain failure of the bill, Center delegate Franz Hitze urged passage of a motion limiting women's work in textile factories as a first and crucial step toward the comprehensive regulation of all industrial sectors.[116] Fueled by the marked gains of the SPD in the Reichstag election of 1884, the Conservative and Free Conservative Parties joined the Center in demanding improved labor protection for women and minors, while the National Liberals, previously inclined to endorse only comprehensive surveys of factory conditions, now proclaimed their support for those measures as well.[117]

The Socialist Workers' Party, by contrast, remained enmeshed in the dilemmas of ambivalent parliamentarism, navigating carefully between its status as an "outlawed party" and its role in the Reichstag as a leading advocate—with the Catholic Center Party—for legislative reform of industrial working conditions.[118] Social Democratic activists charted a difficult course between the party's official stance on women's emancipation and the prevalent "proletarian antifeminism" of its rank and file. Although SPD leaders proclaimed that women should be led "out of the narrow sphere of strictly domestic life to a full participation in the public life of the people," many of its members shared the sense that family life was

114. This is how Alfred Weber described the worldview of Social Catholic reformers of the 1860s and 1870s. See the debate between Weber and Franz Hitze in *Schmollers Jahrbuch* 1897 and 1898, in particular Weber, "Erwiderung," *Schmollers Jahrbuch* 22, no. 2 (1898): 383–84, a response to Hitze's "Zur Vorgeschichte," pp. 371–80, in the same issue.
115. Hertling, as cited in Wenzel, *Arbeiterschutz*, p. 85.
116. Wenzel, *Arbeiterschutz*, p. 85; Hitze, "Zur Vorgeschichte," p. 377; Berlepsch, "*Neuer Kurs*," p. 140.
117. On the positions of the various political parties on social insurance and labor protection, see Born, *Staat und Sozialpolitik*, pp. 64–74, and Berlepsch, "*Neuer Kurs*," pp. 137–38.
118. Lidtke, *Outlawed Party*, p. 193.

"going to pieces" because of the "the extension of female labor."[119] Disdaining the "twaddle" of the "domestic life fanatics" about the natural calling of woman, August Bebel deemed the decline of the family "a mark of progress in spite of everything, just like the beginning of free trade."[120] In the legislative arena, the Social Democrats consistently rejected Center proposals to restrict married women's factory employment and to enforce the separation of the sexes at work. Invoking health and hygiene rather than the Center's visions of morality and immorality, the SPD motion of 1885 endorsed the Center's demands for elimination of Sunday and holiday work, universal limits on daily working hours, and health and safety restrictions on the labor of adult women and youths. Widely perceived among nonsocialists as a serious and innovative set of legislative proposals and debated at length, the Social Democratic bill, introduced by Bebel and Karl Grillenberger, also foresaw the establishment of a network of imperial agencies to oversee industrial labor.[121] As a key site of legislative "deliberations, battles, and compromises" during the mid-1880s, the Center's 1885 motion was debated over nineteen Reichstag sessions, and one of its subcommittees spent nine contentious meetings on the SPD's bill of the same year.[122]

Although both bills were defeated in 1884–85, the protracted Reichstag debates gradually undermined the liberal parliamentary opposition to state intervention on behalf of female and teenage factory workers. As a broad consensus formed across the political spectrum, the Reichstag assembled a large majority to pass one bill in 1887 expanding protection for female and teenage workers and another in 1888 that deemed Sundays and holidays days of rest for all industrial workers.[123] Despite the over-

119. Bebel, *Woman under Socialism*, pp. 180–81, 187; *Die Frau* (1883), p. 93. As the juxtaposition of these citations makes clear, the contradictions existed not only within the party, but also within the thought of leading parliamentarians and theorists like Bebel. On proletarian antifeminism, see Thönnessen, *Frauenemanzipation*, pp. 6, 8, 12, and Mary Nolan, "Proletarischer Anti-Feminismus, dargestellt am Beispiel der SPD-Ortsgruppe Düsseldorf, 1890–1914," in *Frauen und Wissenschaft, Beiträge zur Berliner Sommeruniversität* (Berlin: Courage, 1976): 356–77.
120. Bebel, *Woman under Socialism*, pp. 182, 186; Bebel's address to the Reichstag, as cited in Wenzel, *Arbeiterschutz*, pp. 167–68.
121. Lidtke, *Outlawed Party*, pp. 214–17; Wenzel, *Arbeiterschutz*, pp. 70–71, 162–68; Labisch, "Die gesundheitspolitischen Vorstellungen," pp. 326–70.
122. Born, *Staat und Sozialpolitik*, p. 1.
123. Berlepsch, *"Neuer Kurs,"* pp. 51–52, 143, 152, 161, 182–84; Born, *Staat und Sozialpolitik*, pp. 71–98. On the shifting stance of Left Liberals on protective labor legislation after the elections of 1887, see Weber, "Die Entwickelung der deutschen Arbeiterschutzgesetzgebung," pp. 1145–46. On the relevant electoral shifts between 1884 and 1887, see James J. Sheehan, *German Liberalism in the 19th Century* (Chicago: University of Chicago Press, 1978), pp. 214–16.

whelming consensus in the Reichstag, the Bundesrat rejected both bills, and its leading authority, Chancellor Otto von Bismarck, asserted that expanded protection would negatively affect both the living conditions of the workers and the profitablity of German industry. Speaker Karl Heinrich von Boetticher explained on behalf of the Bundesrat that "all limitations on the factory employment of adult women are unnecessary and harmful, for they would prevent the woman worker from earning the extra pennies she needs, only for the sake of principle or benevolence."[124] Bismarck and his allies thus insistently viewed labor protection as primarily a question of economics, whereas social reformers of all political persuasions framed it as a *Kulturfrage* encompassing the cultural, moral, and physical health of the nation. The government and the Reichstag would remain at odds on factory legislation until the momentous events of 1890—the appointment of eminent reformer Baron Hans von Berlepsch to the Prussian Ministry of Commerce, the announcement of Kaiser Wilhelm's February edicts on workers' protection, and the resignation of Bismarck from office—which signaled the beginning of the "new course" in state social policy.[125]

Interestingly, Social Democrats, Social Catholics, and the so-called *Kathedersozialisten* (socialists of the chair) of the Verein für Sozialpolitik each claimed credit for having inspired the "surge of voices in the German Reichstag" and effecting the marked shift in viewpoints toward protective legislation during the late 1880s.[126] Despite the retreat of the Verein from legislative and government arenas during that decade, it continued to shape state social policy: several of its members occupied distinguished university chairs in political economy and government and thus served at the provincial and imperial levels as "advisers of the ruling powers and educators of bureaucrats."[127] In a retrospective analysis of labor legislation from 1897, Alfred Weber emphasized the long-term influence of the "so-

124. As cited in Berlepsch, *"Neuer Kurs,"* pp. 256, 431, and Wenzel, *Arbeiterschutz*, pp. 90, 179.
125. On the gulf between Bismarck and the social reformers, between the notion of labor protection as an *Einkommensfrage* versus that of a *Kulturfrage*, see Otto, *Über die Fabrikarbeit*, p. 171. The authoritative works on the "new course" are Berlepsch, *"Neuer Kurs,"* and Born, *Staat und Sozialpolitik*.
126. Weber, "Erwiderung," pp. 383–84.
127. Vom Bruch, *Wissenschaft, Politik und öffentliche Meinung*, pp. 48, 64–65; Born, *Staat und Sozialpolitik*, pp. 43–45. As Born demonstrates, the Kathedersozialisten had a predominant presence in scholarly journals like the *Preußische Jahrbücher, Schmollers Jahrbuch* (also known as the *Jahrbuch für Gesetzgebung und Volkswirtschaft im Deutschen Reiche*), Bücher's *Jahrbücher für Nationalökonomie und Statistik*, as well as the *Zeitschrift für die gesamte Staatswissenschaft*, which were frequently read by bureaucrats. Schmoller apparently enjoyed particular personal esteem and authority among state bureaucrats until his death in 1917.

cialists of the chair," not only among high-ranking officials of state, but also in the wider arenas of Reichstag and bourgeois public sphere, in which they had framed both the social question and its solutions. Reformers like Lujo Brentano and Friedrich Neumann, he argued, had cast the social problems of female and child labor in scholarly and scientific terms, while Social Catholics' views had been shaped by religious fervor and those of the labor movement by male workers' fears of feminization and displacement. At the same time Franz Hitze, member of both the Verein für Sozialpolitik and the Center Party's Reichstag delegation, underscored the views common to both on female factory labor. Those who participated in the legislative compromise of the late 1880s, Hitze claimed, did so out of the "same reasons of humanity and justice, out of consideration for the moral and physical well-being of the people, the preservation of the national army and laboring classes and therewith also of economic progress."[128] On behalf of the Socialist Workers' Party, August Bebel proclaimed: "If there had been no Social Democrats and if so many had not been so afraid of them, the moderate progress we have made thus far in the realm of social reform would not have taken place."[129]

At issue here were not only the emergent social question of female factory labor, but also more fundamental differences among reformers and parliamentarians about Germany's ongoing transition from a predominantly agrarian to a primarily industrial society in which "modernity" became a site of contest. Whereas the "socialists of the chair" viewed Catholic social reform as infused by antimodern desires for an organic society of estates, the Verein für Sozialpolitik, Weber claimed, aimed to eradicate only the excessive and defective aspects of modern social and economic development.[130] Although Weber later conceded that Social Catholicism had largely shed its antimodernist approach by the end of the 1880s, he viewed the Center Party's continued efforts to ban married women from factories as evidence of its residual hostility to a process that had become an integral part of modernity—the steady expansion of female factory employment. Rather than pursuing the illusory goal of eradicating married women's wage labor, the Verein's "socialists of the chair" asserted the right of all "weak hands," those unable to defend themselves in the struggle for better working conditions, to be protected by the state. Because the

128. Weber, "Erwiderung," pp. 383–84; Hitze, "Zur Vorgeschichte," pp. 375, 377. Weber refers here specifically to Brentano's address to the Verein's founding meeting in 1872 and to Friedrich Julius Neumann's oration on factory legislation at the first annual meeting in 1873.
129. August Bebel, "Die Gewerbeordnungsnovelle," *Neue Zeit* 9, no. 37 (1890–91): 326–27; Wenzel, *Arbeiterschutz*, introduction, pp. 1–6.
130. Lujo Brentano, *Die Schrecken des überwiegenden Industriestaats* (Berlin: Leonhard Simion, 1901), p. 49.

vitality of the nation depended significantly on women's physical and moral well-being, they occupied a particular place in this vision.[131]

Despite the differences among social reformers of these three political traditions, Catholics and Social Democrats shared with one another and with bourgeois social reformers this understanding of sexual difference, similarly delineating independent (male) workers from dependent women and children and distinguishing women's contribution to state and nation from that of men. Whereas Catholics sought restriction of women's wage work as a means to protect families, Social Democrats located the problem of female factory labor within the rapid growth of capitalism. Yet by the end of the 1880s the reform efforts of the three groups coalesced around a shared vision of working-class domesticity, one that also came to underpin a common notion of citizenship. Thus, whether the impetus of social reform was the vigor of family, nation, estate, or class, an ideal of domesticity, rather than the various legal measures to restrict or regulate women's work, formed the core of the consensus that was forged among Reichstag politicians at the end of the 1880s.

Within this mental landscape, married and single working women posed different dangers to the social body. On the one hand, the shocking visions of slovenly households and sickly children prompted calls to restrict married women's work and to construct a system of tutelage in which female workers would acquire the skills of proper housekeeping and hygiene, nutrition, and child rearing. On the other hand, the rhetoric about single women's work was often highly sexualized and the factory rendered as a kind of carnal underworld in which young girls succumbed to seduction or unbridled desire. For married women, fulfillment of the ideal of domesticity meant factory work should no longer negatively influence health or moral character, marriage or family life. Factory legislation, then, was "to regulate women's work so as to not detach them from their true calling as housewives or, where this has already occurred, to return them to it." Young single women, for their part, were to be prevented from working under conditions that damaged the formation of the "bodily, economic, or moral qualities" required of future housewives and mothers.[132]

Thus, training in domestic skills along the model of Dr. Norrenberg's *Arbeiterinnenverein* of Viersen, unusual for the 1870s, became a more widely acclaimed amelioration for these dangers during the 1880s. Learn-

131. Weber, "Die Entwickelung," p. 1149; Born, *Staat und Sozialpolitik*, p. 43.
132. "Die Frauenarbeit als Gegenstand der Fabrikgesetzgebung," pp. 90–93. Also see Karl Baumbach, *Frauenarbeit und Frauenschutz* (Berlin: Leonhard Simion, 1889), pp. 7–8; Kuno Frankenstein, "Die Lage der Arbeiterinnen in den deutschen Großstädten," *Schmollers Jahrbuch* 12 (1888): 204–9. On the simultaneous condemnation and eroticizing of working women in England, see Mort, *Dangerous Sexualities*, p. 47.

ing to cook, sew, and maintain households properly was to become a significant leisure-time activity, an alternative to both frivolous and subversive time away from work for single women. Privately sponsored by employers, local charities, and religious or bourgeois women's groups, courses of this nature set new standards of hygiene and efficiency, and often of moral virtue, to which working-class women were to aspire. For example, the Verband Arbeiterwohl (Association for Workers' Welfare), founded in 1880 by Catholic employers in the Rhineland, published an extensive handbook titled *Das häusliche Glück* (Domestic happiness).[133] Beginning with the "virtues the housewife needs in order to establish domestic happiness" and based on the undocumented assumption that female factory workers had little or no training in housekeeping skills, the lengthy brochure aimed to provide complete domestic instruction for women of the workers' estate, including detailed advice on furnishing and maintaining the household in an efficient and orderly fashion.[134] The section on nutrition and cooking, for example, offered an array of recipes, weekly meal plans, and sample food budgets, as well as helpful hints on sewing and mending clothing or linens. The textile firm of David Peters in Neviges in the Wupper Valley became a model of national repute for its innovative kindergarten and for its courses in cooking, ironing, and housekeeping for female mill workers and employees' daughters, which the owner's wife personally organized and taught.[135] Furthermore, the Association for Workers' Welfare promoted its vision of the *christliche Fabrik* (Christian factory), in which a kind of domesticity underpinned factory relations, binding employers and workers' committees together within factory com-

133. Verband Arbeiterwohl, *Das häusliche Glück: Vollständiger Haushaltungsunterricht nebst Anleitung zum Kochen für Arbeiterinnen* (Mönchen-Gladbach: A. Riffarth, 1882). Some 150,000 copies of the brochure were printed during the early 1880s. All citations are from a reprint of same title edited by Richard Blank (Munich: Rogner und Bernhard, 1975). On the significance of this text, see Ute Frevert, "'Fürsorgliche Belagerung': Hygienebewegung und Arbeiterfrauen im 19. und frühen 20. Jahrhundert," *Geschichte und Gesellschaft* 11 (1985): 429. The goals of the Verband Arbeiterwohl were to improve factory welfare, to advise the Center Party on social policy issues, and to educate workers in "self-help" through organization along the lines of estate rather than class. On the history of the Verband, see Ritter, *Die katholisch-soziale Bewegung*, pp. 131–36; Stegmann, "Geschichte der sozialen Ideen," pp. 392–94, 418–22.
134. Jean Quataert points out that factory inspectors offered no evidence in their reports for their claims that female factory workers lacked domestic skills. She argues that the few extant "autobiographical statements on working-class home life show clearly that girls learned to cook, sew, shop, and generally to help mothers run the home." See Quataert, "Source Analysis," p. 11.
135. Baumbach, *Frauenarbeit und Frauenschutz*, p. 40; see also Karl Baumbach, "Die Mitteilungen der Fabrikinspektoren über die industrielle Frauenarbeit," *Die Nation* 5, no. 7 (1887), reprinted in Margrit Twellman, *Die deutsche Frauenbewegung im Spiegel repräsentativer Frauenzeitschriften* (Meisenheim a.G.: Anton Hain, 1972), 2:518.

munities through a "family ethic of harmony." The weaving mill of Catholic reformer and entrepreneur Franz Brandts of Mönchen-Gladbach in the Rhineland served as the exemplary "Christian factory," thus placing the social relations of textile production at the center of the reform debates in Social Catholicism.[136]

At the same time, social reformers began to explore the quality of workers' domestic lives from another angle, analyzing household budgets and weighing women's earnings against the savings acquired through resourceful and frugal housekeeping. As early as the late 1870s Catholic Center delegates had presented arguments to this effect to the Reichstag, but the idea found wider dissemination and legitimation in the milieu of social reform when *Schmollers Jahrbuch* published an article by H. Mehner on workers' budgets in 1886, asserting that married women contributed more to the family income through efficient household management than through factory earnings.[137] Mehner's approach was innovative not only because he was one of the first German social scientists who directly observed workers' everyday lives to garner empirical evidence, but also because he lauded "women's domestic activity" as "a significant part of national production" and argued that "the return of the housewife to her true calling" would significantly increase family wages.[138] Mehner's depiction of married women's factory work as "unnatural" and "the root source of economic deprivation" signaled a transition in public opinion about their factory employment, for as historian Jean Quataert has argued, it laid poverty "firmly at the doorsteps of working-class wives."[139]

The new emphasis on domestic skills had "a strong moralizing and ideally regulative component," rendering the sanitary household the locus of

136. Vom Bruch, "Bürgerliche Sozialreform im deutschen Kaiserreich," pp. 88–89. Brandts was also the first general secretary of the Verband Arbeiterwohl.

137. In 1877, for example, in the course of a Reichstag debate on female factory employment, a Center delegate disputed the prevalent view that married women worked out of economic necessity, contending that their earnings usually composed 8 to 10 percent of family income at best. Recounted in Otto, *Über die Fabrikarbeit*, pp. 160–63. See also Reichskanzler-Amt, *Ergebnisse*, p. 74, and Wenzel, *Arbeiterschutz*, pp. 85–86.

138. H. Mehner, "Der Haushalt und die Lebenshaltung einer Leipziger Arbeiterfamilie," *Schmollers Jahrbuch* (1886), reprinted in *Seminar: Familie und Gesellschaftsstruktur*, ed. Heidi Rosenbaum (Frankfurt a.M.: Suhrkamp, 1982), pp. 329–32. For other studies of family budgets, see Gottlieb Schnapper-Arndt's study of 1883 on villages in the Taunus, "Fünf Dorfgemeinden auf dem Hohen Taunus," *Staats- und Sozialwissenschaftliche Forschungen* 4, no. 2 (1883); Margarete Freudenthal, "Gestaltwandel der städtischen bürgerlichen und proletarischen Hauswirtschaft unter besonderer Berücksichtigung des Typenwandels von Frau und Familie, 1760–1910," part I (Dissertation, Universität Frankfurt am Main, 1933). On the use of evidence from workers' lives in reformers' studies, see Oberschall, *Empirical Social Research*, pp. 70–73.

139. Quataert, "Source Analysis," pp. 112–13; "Frauenfrage: Erwerbs- oder Hausarbeit der Arbeiterfrau," *Soziale Praxis* 6, no. 22 (1896–97): 533–36.

social discipline through the prescription of "new standards of behavior, which pervaded many spheres of social life, including relations between members of the family, diet, housing, clothing, leisure, and sexuality."[140] The attention to domesticity during the late 1880s might also be viewed as part of the incipient process of medicalization, which was fostered by the health insurance law of 1883.[141] Although the moral and the sanitary were clearly intertwined in reformers' rhetoric on domesticity, the household became a new locus of hygienic reform efforts. The Bergischer Verein für Gemeinwohl, founded in 1885 by a coalition of textile employers and government officials, for example, sought to improve "the hygienic and housing conditions of the workers" as a crucial part of its campaign to "enhance the well-being of the working classes in economic, moral and religious terms."[142] In the course of the 1880s health and hygiene became "multivalent terms," "scientific, neutral concepts," buttressed by the new reliance on statistics and significantly less controversial across political and class lines than attempts to prescribe and enforce standards of morality.[143]

As the rhetoric and politics of social reform were transformed during the 1880s, domesticity became an integral part of the social in a dual sense: while the household increasingly became a site of intervention for private and public welfare initiatives, for medical prescription and policing, domesticity also figured more centrally as a cultural matrix, as an ideology at the heart of the social. At the end of the 1880s, therefore, the social question of female factory labor constituted a discursive field, by

140. Citations are respectively from Poovey, "Domesticity and Class Formation," pp. 70–71, and Paul Weindling, "Bourgeois Values, Doctors and the State: The Professionalization of Medicine in Germany, 1848–1933," in Blackbourn and Evans, *German Bourgeoisie*, p. 215. For further discussion of social policy and social discipline, see Frevert, "'Fürsorgliche Belagerung,'" pp. 420–46; Labisch, *Homo hygienicus*; and Christoph Sachße and Florian Tennstedt, "Sicherheit und Disziplin: Eine Skizze zur Einführung," in Sachße and Tennstedt, *Soziale Sicherheit und soziale Disziplinierung*, pp. 11–43.

141. For excellent discussions of medicalization, see Frevert, *Krankheit als politisches Problem*, pp. 15–16, and Claudia Honegger, "Überlegungen zur Medikalisierung des weiblichen Körpers," in *Leib und Leben in der Geschichte der Neuzeit* (Vorträge eines internationalen Colloquiums 1981), ed. Arthur E. Imhof (Berlin: Duncker und Humblot, 1983), pp. 203–13.

142. Berlepsch, *"Neuer Kurs,"* pp. 43–45. The founders of the Bergischer Verein termed it an "employers' self-help organization" mobilized for "struggle against Social Democracy." For an interesting contrast with the social intervention into French workers' households, see Judith Coffin, "Social Science Meets Sweated Labor: Reinterpreting Women's Work in Late Nineteenth-Century France," *Journal of Modern History* 63, no. 2 (1991): 230–70. Coffin argues that social investigators were encouraged to imagine themselves as doctors visiting diseased patients and examines the ways their (social) diagnoses blended medical and economic "pathologies."

143. Alfons Labisch argues that during the 1880s health provided a scientific, neutral concept by which "to assist the colonization or assimilation of peripheral social classes." See his "'Hygiene ist Moral,'" pp. 276–79, and Tennstedt, *Sozialgeschichte der Sozialpolitik*, p. 150.

now distinct from the broader worker question yet still diffuse in all that it merged and mingled: rhetorics of morality and hygiene, polarities of family and factory, domesticity and promiscuity, and fears about social hierarchies and social bodies, all shaped by the competing visions of class, *Stand* (estate), and citizenship.

4

State, Social Body, and Public Sphere: Regulating Female Factory Labor during the 1890s

Female factory labor emerged as a social question in its own right during the 1890s, as a wide spectrum of participants and an array of competing discourses converged to reshape the domain of social reform. The mass strike of coal miners in the Rhine and the Ruhr in spring 1889 revealed the fissures in Bismarckian social policy, above all the failure of social insurance to forge lasting bonds of loyalty between workers and state. It also brought to a head the brewing conflicts between kaiser and chancellor, chancellor and Reichstag, over social policy and the Socialist Law. The strike galvanized public opinion around social reform, drawing attention to the poor conditions of work in the mines as well as to the unruliness of youth and the militancy of adult men, which many linked to the alleged erosion of working women's skills as housewives and mothers. Entangled in the public readings of the strike, then, were deeper concerns that it signaled the decline of the working-class family, that it was a symptom of the rapid and disruptive transformation of Germany from an agrarian to an industrial nation-state. Even though the strike participants were overwhelmingly male, the Reichstag debates and the legislative consensus of the late 1880s about the regulation and restriction of female and youth labor framed the response of the state and of social reformers to the climate of crisis surrounding the strike.

Convinced now of the urgent need to bridge the gulf between workers and state, to break Bismarck's stranglehold on social policy and chart a path of his own, Kaiser Wilhelm stunned the German public with the announcement of his "February edicts" on 4 February 1890, which validated that consensus. Outlining a far-reaching program of labor protection and calling for an international congress on labor protection to be convened in Berlin in March 1890, the edicts marked the beginning of the "new course" in social policy. Extending the purview of the German welfare state to encompass labor protection, the edicts laid the groundwork for the revision of the labor code in 1891 and for its further expansion in 1908.[1] From the restoration of the German family envisioned by the kaiser's February edicts to the consensus underpinning the programmatic demands of the international congress of March 1890, the protection of female and youth labor was the principal aim of the reforms of the new course. As in previous decades, the conditions and relations of textile production had a central place in reformers' texts, both scholarly and sensational. The steady increase in the number of women working in textile factories during the 1880s, made highly visible by reformers' inquiries and agitation, lent urgency to the regulation of female labor. With the revision of the labor code in 1891, specifically its extension of maternity leave, the eleven-hour limit it placed on women's workday, and its designation of *Haushaltsschulen* (housekeeping schools) as a form of recognized skill training, the state acknowledged and certified the improvement of working women's domestic skills as a long-term solution for the new social question of female factory labor.

The debates about the regulation and restriction of female labor analyzed in this chapter offer interesting insights into the complex ways in which the history of the welfare state can be linked to the expansion of the public sphere, the history of the body and the process of medicalization, and the formation of identities of citizenship and class, both working class and middle class. While reproducing middle-class visions of morality and hygiene, labor legislation demarcated the boundaries of the working class, shaping class and citizenship as social concepts and political identities.[2] The reforms of the early 1890s sanctioned and inscribed in law the notion of social citizenship that distinguished adult male workers, whose independence and ability to defend their own interests rendered state protection superfluous, from women, youths, and children, who lacked the rights of political citizenship and whom the state was therefore compelled to pro-

---

1. See, for example, Hans-Jörg von Berlepsch, *"Neuer Kurs" im Kaiserreich? Die Arbeiterpolitik des Freiherrn von Berlepsch 1890 bis 1896* (Bonn: Neue Gesellschaft, 1987), and Karl-Erich Born, *Staat und Sozialpolitik seit Bismarcks Sturz: Ein Beitrag zur Geschichte der innenpolitischen Entwicklung des deutschen Reiches, 1890–1914* (Wiesbaden: Franz Steiner, 1957).

2. On the relation between the state and class formation in Germany, see Mary Nolan, "Economic Crisis, State Policy, and Working-Class Formation in Germany, 1870–1900," in *Working-Class Formation: Nineteenth-Century Patterns in Western Europe and the United States*, ed. Ira Katznelson and Aristide R. Zolberg (Princeton: Princeton University Press, 1986), pp. 354, 361, and George Steinmetz, "Workers and the Welfare State in Imperial Germany," *International Labor and Working-Class History* 40 (fall 1991): 18–46.

tect from exploitation. This is particularly true of the 1890s, when the transformation of the public sphere—the emergence of the Social Democrats as a mass party, the popular mobilization of Catholics, feminists, liberal social reformers, and right-wing nationalists—changed the meaning of both class and citizenship.[3]

Also a marker of the new course, the expanding public sphere had an important role in shaping state social policy during the 1890s. Reformist ministers of state, like Hans von Berlepsch, articulated a new sense of duty and accountability to public opinion in seeking to fulfill the lofty visions of the kaiser's February edicts. And opponents of female factory labor, inspired by the restrictive and protective measures of 1891 and by the public's newly awakened interest in this issue, launched a renewed and more vigorous campaign for a legal ban on married women's factory employment during the early 1890s. Previously confined to the arenas of high politics and academic social reform, the impassioned calls for such a legal ban drew the public, both *bürgerlich* and working-class, into the debates of the early 1890s. These debates are significant not because the attempt to define proper spheres for the sexes was new, but because the visible and controversial expansion of the female factory workforce had begun to challenge the definitions of *Geschlechtscharakter*—the dichotomies of male and female spheres—in new and persistent ways.[4]

Some participants in these debates spoke with a purported scientific expertise, others spoke as *Betroffene* (those directly affected or victims), who decried the *Verweiblichung* (feminization) of the factory workforce and the *Verdrängung* (displacement) of male workers by women. However disparate their social contexts and political languages, the discourses of social reform were linked by webs of cross-references and by a common appeal to the German state as mediator of social and industrial relations.[5] Amid

---

3. On the transformation of the public sphere during the 1890s see Geoff Eley, "Notable Politics, the Crisis of German Liberalism and the Electoral Transition of the 1890s," in *In Search of a Liberal Germany: Studies in the History of German Liberalism from 1789 to the Present*, ed. Konrad Jarausch and Larry Eugene Jones (New York: Berg, 1990), pp. 187–216; also see Geoff Eley, "Nations, Publics, and Political Cultures: Placing Habermas in the Nineteenth Century," in *Habermas and the Public Sphere*, ed. Craig Calhoun (Cambrdige: MIT Press, 1992), pp. 289–339.

4. Karin Hausen, "Family and Role-Division: The Polarisation of Sexual Stereotypes in the Nineteenth Century—an Aspect of the Dissociation of Work and Family Life," in *The German Family: Essays on the Social History of the Family in Nineteenth- and Twentieth-Century Germany*, ed. Richard J. Evans and W. R. Lee (Totowa, N.J.: Croom Helm, 1981), pp. 57–58; Claudia Honegger, *Die Ordnung der Geschlechter: Die Wissenschaften vom Menschen und das Weib* (Frankfurt a.M.: Campus, 1991); and Ute Frevert, ed., *Bürgerinnen und Bürger: Geschlechterverhältnisse im 19. Jahrhundert* (Göttingen: Vandenhoeck und Ruprecht, 1988), especially the essay by Isabel V. Hull, "'Sexualität' und bürgerliche Gesellschaft," pp. 49–66.

5. The term "webs of cross-references" is Denise Riley's, as cited by Joan Scott, *Gender and the Politics of History* (New York: Columbia University Press, 1988), p. 141.

the din of voices were not only prominent politicians and officials of state but also some of Germany's leading intellectuals and social scientists: Gustav Schmoller, Lujo Brentano, and the subsequent generation of reformers including Ferdinand Tönnies, Heinrich Herkner, and Max and Alfred Weber. First under the auspices of the Verein für Sozialpolitik and after the turn of the century through the Gesellschaft für Soziale Reform (Society for Social Reform), they not only sought to collect and analyze empirical evidence of social transformation but also, abrogating the Verein's explicitly apolitical stance during the 1880s, aspired again to leave their imprint on state social policy during the politically charged years of the late 1890s.[6] A new constituency—middle-class feminists—also stepped forward to defend the right of women to work outside the home. Banned by the Prussian Law of Association from official participation in most of the social reform associations, educated women, many of whom were students or protégées of the eminent political economists and reformers, perceived many parallels between their own lack of political, social, and economic rights and the plight of working-class wives and mothers. Forging links between the middle-class *Frauenfrage* (woman question) and the *Arbeiterfrage* (worker question), they challenged the images of working women that filled the texts of social reformers.

The sites of discussion and debate about the new social question spanned high and low politics, encompassing both the realm of governing—the Reichstag or the Prussian Ministry of Commerce and Trade, for example—and the arena of public opinion. The narratives of danger about female factory labor were constituted across a range of statements, texts, signs, and practices: from academic lectures and scientific surveys, state inquiries and parliamentary resolutions to union brochures and feminist tracts, employers' sanctions, and even calls to strike against the hiring of women workers.[7] They encompassed scholarly treatises on nature and gender, on male and female sexual characteristics, as well as scandalous revelations about the effects of women's work—bodies ravaged by machines and long hours of labor, infant mortality, filth and squalor in workers' living quarters—that stimulated popular interest in the problem. These narratives evoked dramatic visions of social dissolution replete with analogues

---

6. See Rüdiger vom Bruch, ed., *Weder Kommunismus noch Kapitalismus: Bürgerliche Sozialreform in Deutschland vom Vormärz bis zur Ära Adenauer* (Munich: C. H. Beck, 1985), pp. 13–15, 66–71; idem, *Wissenschaft, Politik und öffentliche Meinung: Gelehrtenpolitik im Wilhelminischen Deutschland, 1890–1914* (Husum: Matthiesen, 1980), pp. 16–31; and Woodruff C. Smith, *Politics and the Sciences of Culture in Germany, 1840–1920* (Oxford: Oxford University Press, 1991), pp. 193–94.

7. On the dispersed sites of discourse, see Judith R. Walkowitz, *City of Dreadful Delight: Narratives of Sexual Danger in Late Victorian London* (Chicago: University of Chicago Press, 1992), p. 6; Peter Stallybrass and Allon White, *The Politics and Poetics of Transgression* (Ithaca: Cornell University Press, 1986), p. 194.

between the destruction of the social body, the body of the family, and the physical bodies of women workers and the children they bore. Embracing the rhetoric of hygiene and health that permeated the social reform milieu during the 1880s, the "moralization" of motherhood and domestic skills became a key part of the solution to the social question, mapping out a new realm of *moral* reform for the 1890s. At the same time, reformers staked out the opposing domain of sexual danger, constructing it in direct relation to themes of danger, disease, filth, and depravity and thus laying the groundwork for an even more explicit medicalized intervention in women's bodies from the late 1890s until the First World War.

The intense scholarly and public debates about married women's factory work continued unabated throughout the 1890s, even beyond the stagnation and termination of the new course at middecade, exerting mounting pressure on the government and finally, in 1898–99, prompting an official state inquiry into married women's factory employment. Deploying the police powers of the state to investigate the influence of women's wage work on the family as a social and biological unit, the factory inspectors traversed the parishes and pubs of industrial towns, interviewing owners and workers, foremen and union leaders, mayors, medical doctors, and midwives. Their final report, published by the Ministry of the Interior in 1901, reflected both the intervention of the public and the attempts of the state to mediate and sanction an official solution to the social question of female factory labor.

State, Public Sphere and the Social Question of Female Factory Labor during the New Course, 1889–1896

Heretofore a matter of social reform expertise, debates about the worker question spilled over into the domain of public opinion in 1889–90. In spring 1889 some 150,000 coal miners in the Rhine and Ruhr regions walked off their jobs after a dispute with mine owners over wages, work time, health, and safety. As the strike quickly spread to the Saar, Saxony, and Silesia, it fueled the tensions brewing over social policy between Reichstag and government, between Bismarck and the young Kaiser Wilhelm II, prompting the shift in state social policy known as the "new course" of the early 1890s.[8] The strike revealed the shortcomings of Bis-

---

8. On the strike see Florian Tennstedt, *Sozialgeschichte der Sozialpolitik in Deutschland vom 18. Jahrhundert bis zum Ersten Weltkrieg* (Göttingen: Vandenhoeck und Ruprecht, 1981), p. 194; Jürgen Reulecke, "Stadtbürgertum und bürgerliche Sozialreform im 19. Jahrhundert in Preussen," in *Stadt und Bürgertum im 19. Jahrhundert*, ed. Lothar Gall (Munich: R. Olden-

marckian social policy, widely admired across Europe at the time for its unparalleled social insurance legislation, and dramatized its failure to regulate or ameliorate the "pathogenic" aspects of the industrial workplace or to form a genuine bond between workers and the state.[9] The largest mass walkout in the history of the Kaiserreich thus far, the strike engaged both working-class and bourgeois opinion and left a deep impression on the young emperor, who was horrified that the beginning of his reign might be stained "with the blood of [his] subjects."[10]

Under pressure of the impending Reichstag elections in February 1890, kaiser and chancellor, as well as the leaders of the major political parties, discussed and debated the implications of the strike for state social policy. Even after the miners returned to work in late May, public pressure in favor of state intervention continued to mount. By the time a new strike wave began in the coal mines in December 1889, spreading soon thereafter to other industrial branches, the urgency of the social question had captured the public imagination, sparking agitation in arenas from the political parties to "the universities, the press, even the theater."[11] The strike of mainly male coal miners not only created a profound sense of social crisis and a groundswell of parliamentary and public pressure but also unleashed a wave of public and government initiatives aimed, ironically, not at adult men but at women, youths, and the working-class family.[12] Although the large number of Catholics on the strike lines had made it clear that something other than a Social Democratic conspiracy was at work, the youth and unruliness of many of the strikers had seemed to reflect a dangerous decline of the working-class family, at the heart of which was the problem of working mothers and wives.[13]

---

bourg, 1990), p. 194; Otto Pflanze, *Bismarck and the Development of Germany*, vol. 3, *The Period of Fortification, 1880–1898* (Princeton: Princeton University Press, 1990), pp. 327–45; Vernon L. Lidtke, *The Outlawed Party: Social Democracy in Germany, 1878–1890* (Princeton: Princeton University Press), pp. 294–95.

9. Berlepsch, *"Neuer Kurs,"* pp. 13, 432–33. See also Rüdiger vom Bruch, "Streiks und Konfliktregelung im Urteil bürgerlicher Sozialreformer, 1872–1914," in *Streik: Zur Geschichte des Arbeitskampfes in Deutschland während der Industrialisierung*, ed. Klaus Tenfelde and Heinrich Volkmann (Munich: C. H. Beck, 1981), p. 257.

10. Kaiser Wilhelm II, as cited in Berlepsch, *"Neuer Kurs,"* p. 25; Pflanze, *Bismarck*, 3:358; Lidtke, *Outlawed Party*, pp. 294–95.

11. According to the memoirs of journalist Gustav Mayer as cited in James J. Sheehan, *The Career of Lujo Brentano: A Study of Liberalism and Social Reform in Imperial Germany* (Chicago: University of Chicago Press, 1966), pp. 114–15. On the second wave of strikes see Pflanze, *Bismarck*, 3:353.

12. Tennstedt, *Sozialgeschichte der Sozialpolitik*, p. 194; Pflanze, *Bismarck*, 3:327; vom Bruch, *Weder Kommunismus*, pp. 8–10; Berlepsch, *"Neuer Kurs,"* p. 393.

13. August Bebel, "Die Gewerbeordnungsnovelle," *Neue Zeit* 9, no. 37 (1890–91): 331, and Berlepsch, *"Neuer Kurs,"* pp. 321–22.

Deliberation of social policy soon became more complicated as it became entangled in parliamentary and public debates about the Socialist Law, due to lapse at the end of September 1890. Social policy became an integral part of a complex web of negotiations about the rights of workers as citizens and the dominion of civil society vis-à-vis the state. Whereas Bismarck took the stance that the strikes should "burn themselves out" without state intervention, Kaiser Wilhelm sought to mediate the strife through direct negotiations with separate delegations of miners and mine owners.[14] Convinced by his encounter with the miners that social conditions, not Social Democracy, constituted the greatest threat to social peace, Wilhelm was now prepared to abandon the repressive Socialist Law. Bismarck, however, lobbied furiously for its renewal, proclaiming the advance of Social Democracy a "question of war and peace" in "the highest degree."[15] While Bismarck continued to insist that social policy should discipline the active, articulate, and hence politically dangerous wage workers, Wilhelm, in consultation with his social policy advisers, contemplated new channels for workers' self-representation, like *Arbeiterkammer* and *Arbeiterausschüsse* (workers' chambers and workers' factory committees). Facing the growing opposition of both kaiser and Reichstag to his stance on Social Democracy and social policy, Bismarck resigned his post as Prussian minister of commerce and trade two days after the Reichstag voted to suspend the Socialist Law.[16] The kaiser appointed as his successor the eminent social reformer and governor-general of the Rhine province, Baron Hans von Berlepsch, who would become the helmsman of the new course in state social policy.

Thus in early 1890 both the Reichstag and the kaiser had critical roles in charting the path toward expanded state intervention into factory working conditions. In late January a large majority of the Reichstag approved a resolution in favor of new protective measures for female and teenage workers and the elimination of Sunday employment. During the same week Kaiser Wilhelm, proclaiming that "the people must know that their king is concerned about their welfare," convened the Crown Council to outline a revision of the labor code.[17] The next day, 25 January 1890, the Reichstag voted overwhelmingly against renewing the Socialist Law, restoring full legal status to the Social Democratic Party (SPD) as of Sep-

14. Pflanze, *Bismarck*, 3:331–34, 353; Lidtke, *Outlawed Party*, pp. 294–95.
15. Otto von Bismarck as cited in Pflanze, *Bismarck*, 3:354; see also pp. 342–43.
16. Vom Bruch, *Weder Kommunismus*, pp. 8–10; Tennstedt, *Sozialgeschichte der Sozialpolitik*, p. 146; Pflanze, *Bismarck*, 3:344, 361; Berlepsch, "Neuer Kurs," pp. 24–25; Born, *Staat und Sozialpolitik*, pp. 8–9.
17. Kaiser Wilhelm II, as cited in Pflanze, *Bismarck*, 3:354–57. On the Kaiser's draft edits and the Reichstag resolution, see Berlepsch, "Neuer Kurs," pp. 146, 255–56.

tember of that year.[18] With the stigma of outcast, outlawed party soon to be erased, the repeal of the Socialist Law would transform the symbolic order that underpinned social policy debates. As reformers increasingly linked social distress and social conflict to the defects of working-class families rather than to the exploitative structures of mill and mine, the focus of state social policy shifted from the specter of dangerous, politicized workers to the endangered family.[19]

February 1890 marked the high point of the new course. The kaiser took his reform program, debated thus far only behind the closed doors of the Crown Council, to the public when the official government paper, the *Reichsanzeiger*, published his two edicts on 4 February 1890.[20] Wilhelm's original draft of the edicts had outlined a minimum program of protective measures that, in close agreement with the Reichstag resolution of the previous month, aimed to alleviate the most deplorable working conditions for women and minors and affirmed the right of industrial workers to form associations. The version that reached the public, however, was markedly more ambitious, asserting the fundamental principle that "it is one of the duties of the state to regulate the hours, the length, and the type of employment so that the workers' health, standards of morality, and economic needs may be preserved and their claims to equality before the law sustained."[21]

The first of the kaiser's edicts sought to establish a Europeanwide context for German labor legislation, calling for an international conference on labor protection to be held in Berlin in March 1890. Underlying the vision of the conference was the belief that "in view of international competition in the world market, an improvement in workers' conditions is possible only based on an international accord among the leading industrial states."[22] The second edict, directed to the Prussian ministers for public works and commerce and trade, proposed to expand state protection for female and teenage industrial workers through "immediately practicable measures," limiting the workday to eleven hours, banning women and youths from employment in mines, on Sundays, or at night, providing maternity leave to women for three weeks before and three weeks after

18. Pflanze, *Bismarck*, 3:358; Born, *Staat und Sozialpolitik*, p. 13.
19. See Jacques Donzelot's interesting exploration of "how the family came to constitute an effective way of warding off the dangers that hung over a liberal definition of the state when the poor revolted" in Jacques Donzelot, *The Policing of Families* (New York: Pantheon, 1979), p. 53.
20. Pflanze, *Bismarck*, 3:361; Berlepsch, "Neuer Kurs," p. 31.
21. Kaiser Wilhelm's February edicts, as cited in Born, *Staat und Sozialpolitik*, pp. 8–9. Wilhelm based his program on detailed studies of social conditions he had ordered prepared by his advisers.
22. Born, *Staat und Sozialpolitik*, pp. 8–9.

childbirth, and endorsing an additional half-hour break for women who wanted to prepare a midday meal for their families at home. Measures that were to be negotiated between employers and workers included the obligatory institution of workers' committees, elected at the factory level, and the issuance of factory ordinances, no longer under the sole purview of employers, but now requiring the consent of the workers' factory committees as well.[23]

As a crucial marker of the new course, the February edicts became a point of conflict and subversion between kaiser and chancellor, chancellor and public opinion when Bismarck, whom Wilhelm had directed to edit the original draft, instead substantially altered the kaiser's text. In a perplexing turn of events, Bismarck helped to draft the innovative document that would frame the new course for both bureaucracy and public—one he abhorred. He intended the revised version to signal a drastic shift in social policy, to send shock waves through government and reform circles, and to awaken hopes and spark demands from the workers that it could not fulfill, thus forcing the kaiser and his advisers to concede that the social question could not "be solved with rosewater; for that you need blood and iron."[24] When the edicts were announced to the public, the break with previous imperial policy was evident to all, including some among the ranks of industry and aristocracy who protested that they came dangerously close to endorsing Social Democratic principles, particularly with respect to the duties of the state. At the same time, however, the edicts prompted a wave of public acclaim that could not be contained. Social Democrats, Catholic Center leaders, and "socialists of the chair" each hailed the edicts as a consummation of their own principles. As the SPD sought to "affirm above everything else . . . the moral victory which Social Democracy has gained in the shift of government policy," its members read the kaiser's decrees as signaling the end of their political isolation, celebrating them on placards carried through the streets.[25] Similarly, the Catholic Center Party saluted the kaiser's decision to align himself with the

---

23. Berlepsch, "*Neuer Kurs,*" pp. 24–25; Born, *Staat und Sozialpolitik*, pp. 8–12; "Zur Erinnerung: Die beiden Erlässe Kaiser Wilhelms II. vom 4. Februar 1890," *Soziale Praxis* 7 (7 October 1897): 7.

24. Bismarck, as cited in Pflanze, *Bismarck*, 3:359–60. On Bismarck's editing of the kaiser's February edicts, also see Berlepsch, "*Neuer Kurs,*" pp. 27–28; Born, *Staat und Sozialpolitik*, pp. 11–17.

25. Lidtke, *Outlawed Party*, pp. 296–97; Berlepsch, "*Neuer Kurs,*" pp. 30–33; Born, *Staat und Sozialpolitik*, pp. 9–10. August Bebel even asserted that the February edicts and the call to the international conference on labor protection were inspired by the resolutions of the international (socialist) workers' congress held in Paris in 1889. See Bebel, "Die Gewerbeordnungsnovelle," p. 326.

Reichstag majority, "which under the leadership of the Center, had demanded labor protection for years."[26]

Bismarck's deception thus foundered on his thorough misreading of wider public opinion.[27] Because the public took the edicts as an expression of the kaiser's forthright intentions, Minister Berlepsch now viewed his ministry as accountable to the surging swell of sentiment regarding social policy. Apparently unaware of any discrepancy between the two versions of the decrees, Berlepsch sought to put them into practice as quickly as possible, as he undertook arrangements for the international conference and prepared draft legislation revising the labor code.[28] The Reichstag election, held at the end of February amid the swirl of public debate about social reform, reflected the ongoing shift in political climate as the advances of the Catholic Center, left liberals, and Social Democrats dislodged the "cartel" parties of the Bismarckian era (National Liberals and Conservatives) from their electoral dominance, further eroding Bismarck's status with respect to both kaiser and public.[29] However genuine Wilhelm's interest in social reform had been thus far, by this time social policy had also become a lever with which "to toss Bismarck out of the saddle." By mid-March Bismarck's positions on both social policy and Social Democracy had become increasingly untenable, and on 18 March he resigned at the kaiser's request. His departure was widely perceived as removing the final impediment to the anticipated reform legislation.[30]

26. Franz Josef Stegmann, "Geschichte der sozialen Ideen im deutschen Katholizismus," in *Geschichte der sozialen Ideen in Deutschland: Deutsches Handbuch der Politik*, vol. 3, ed. Helga Grebing (Munich: G. Olzog, 1969), pp. 410–11. Berlepsch points out in *"Neuer Kurs,"* p. 33, that both the left liberals (Freisinn) and the Conservative Party also interpreted the edicts as fulfilling their own social reform programs.

27. Berlepsch, *"Neuer Kurs,"* pp. 27–28, 34. Berlepsch refers to the reaction among industrialists as "much head shaking and long faces."

28. Born, *Staat und Sozialpolitik*, pp. 20, 96, 120. Although Bismarck wrote the edicts, they were signed only by the kaiser, rather than by both kaiser and chancellor. This fact was noticed and remarked on in governing and social reform circles, leading to speculation about Bismarck's eroding position vis-à-vis the kaiser. Born claims that on presenting Wilhelm with the final version of the edicts, Bismarck pleaded with him to hurl them into the fire rather than publish them. Whether Wilhelm noticed the revision of the edicts remains unclear; it appears, though, that he signed the final version without reading it.

29. On the popular mood on the eve of the election, see vom Bruch, *Wissenschaft, Politik und öffentliche Meinung*, p. 20; Pflanze, *Bismarck*, 3:350; Johannes Wenzel, *Arbeiterschutz und Centrum mit Berücksichtigung der übrigen Parteien* (Berlin: Verlag der Germania AG, 1893), p. 10. On the transition that took place in 1890 between "two distinct electoral systems—the Bismarckian and the Wilhelminian," see Eley, "Notable Politics," pp. 192–93. On the election results see James J. Sheehan, *German Liberalism in the Nineteenth Century* (Chicago: University of Chicago Press, 1978), p. 216, and Stanley Suval, *Electoral Politics in Wilhelmine Germany* (Chapel Hill: University of North Carolina Press, 1985).

30. Born, *Staat und Sozialpolitik*, pp. 30–31.

Two days before Bismarck's departure, the international conference on workers' protection convened in Berlin under the leadership of Baron von Berlepsch. Restrictions on the labor of women and minors formed the core points of debate among the fourteen European nations represented at the conference. Their delegates easily reached unanimous agreement on the abolition of night work for minors and of women's work in mines and on the extension of maternity leave to the first four weeks after giving birth.[31] Although this international forum produced few tangible results and none of the participating states was obligated to enact any of the recommended reforms, the conference galvanized public opinion as the delegates worked to establish common goals and guidelines for future legislative change. Although England, where the ten-hour day had been in effect since the 1840s, was widely recognized as the forerunner of labor reform on the Continent, most of the delegates endorsed Sunday rest (except Belgium and France), agreed with a minimum working age of twelve (with Spain, Portugal, and Italy dissenting), and voted against night work and in favor of an eleven-hour day for women workers (except Belgium and France).[32] Both the edicts and the international conference singled out female factory workers as the primary objects of state protection. No longer submerged within the broader worker question, the social problem of female factory work had attained new legitimacy and visibility as it was incorporated into national and international programs of social reform.

As the second significant outcome of the new course, in late 1890 the Reichstag began discussion of a revised industrial labor code that was to give the kaiser's edicts the force of law. This time the deliberation and negotiation of the protective bills not only took place within the state bureaucracy and the legislature but also encompassed the public sphere, as workers, Social Democrats, and other citizens gathered signatures and petitioned the Reichstag on specific aspects of labor protection.[33] The expanding public arena gained new importance in deciding the social question as the bureaucratic languages of social reform came to permeate the popular languages that shaped the social.[34] The bill passed the Reichstag in

31. Alfred Weber, "Die Entwickelung der deutschen Arbeiterschutzgesetzgebung seit 1890," *Schmollers Jahrbuch* 21 (1897): 1152–55; Born, *Staat und Sozialpolitik*, pp. 84–88. In attendance were representatives from Germany, Great Britain, France, Austria-Hungary, Italy, Belgium, Switzerland, Denmark, Sweden, Norway, the Netherlands, Spain, Portugal, and Luxembourg.

32. Born, *Staat und Sozialpolitik*, pp. 87–88; Berlepsch, "Neuer Kurs," pp. 57–63.

33. Berlepsch, "Neuer Kurs," p. 159, points out that of the 11,512 petitions to the Reichstag on labor protection, some 10,400 demanded the incorporation of the resolutions of the Congress of the Socialist International held in Paris in 1889.

34. On the overlap between the language of state reform and popular languages in communities and workplaces, see Robert Gray, "The Language of Factory Reform in Britain, c.

May with the support of all parties but the Social Democrats, who opposed the code's coupling of *Arbeiterschutz* and *Arbeitertrutz*, protective and repressive measures, which offered workers improved health and safety protection but curtailed their right to organize and to strike. On 1 June the Bundesrat also endorsed the revised code, declaring it law and rendering it effective as of 1 April 1892.[35]

An essential marker of the new course in social policy, the revised labor code of 1891 mapped out a new role for the German state as mediator of labor relations, a task Bismarck had resolutely resisted throughout the 1880s as harmful to the competitive vitality of German industry in an increasingly complex world market. The intervention of the protective laws in the realms of work and family required a significant extension of the prerogatives and power of the German state as the factory inspectorate was centralized and enlarged and inspectors' districts were reduced to permit more frequent and regular inspections.[36] Competing voices and visions sought to refashion the inspectorate: some imagined it as a neutral site of mediation and peacemaking, whereas others regarded the inspectors as combat troops for workers' protection. Still others sought to transform the inspectorate by infusing it with more women and medical doctors and by setting new standards for professional training.[37] At the same time a new institution, the Commission for Statistics on Workers, was to conduct inquiries and compile statistics in order to enforce the code more efficiently and discern the need for further protective measures.[38] Finally, the revised code attests to the profoundly disparate ways the various parts of the welfare state were made. Whereas popular agitation and imagination had been absent from the deliberations over the social insurance laws during the 1880s, debates about the protective laws delineated a new place for the public in shaping the welfare state.

Concerns about hygiene and morality converged in the revised labor

---

1830–1860," in *The Historical Meanings of Work*, ed. Patrick Joyce (Cambridge: Cambridge University Press, 1989), p. 177.

35. On the repressive aspects of the new code, see Bebel, "Die Gewerbeordnungsnovelle," p. 332, and Heinrich Herkner, "Der Entwurf eines Gesetzes betr. die Abänderung der Gewerbeordnung," *Archiv für Soziale Gesetzgebung und Statistik* 3 (1890): 567–68; also see Wenzel, *Arbeiterschutz*, p. 203; Born, *Staat und Sozialpolitik*, p. 105; Berlepsch, "Neuer Kurs," p. 159.

36. Born, *Staat und Sozialpolitik*, p. 105; Berlepsch, "Neuer Kurs," pp. 276–77, 282–83; Tennstedt, *Sozialgeschichte der Sozialpolitik*, pp. 193–94. According to the new protective laws, all shops employing more than five workers were to be inspected every two years. The laws applied to all shops that regularly used steam power, as well as to mines, docks, and the construction industry, thus excluding home industry.

37. Berlepsch, "Neuer Kurs," pp. 282–83.

38. Born, *Staat und Sozialpolitik*, p. 105.

code of 1891 as stricter measures regarding "dangers to life and health" were imposed on employers, who were now obliged to provide sufficient light and ventilation, to eliminate dust, gases, moisture, and waste before they accumulated in the plant, and to equip all machines with adequate safety mechanisms. In response to the prevalent perception that the factory had become the source of moral ruin for female and teenage workers, paragraph 120 proclaimed the separation of the sexes in all spheres of the workplace: on the shop floor, and in cafeterias, courtyards, and washrooms.[39] Bourgeois reformers and delegates from the Conservative and Catholic Center Parties hailed the measure, but the Social Democrats vowed to vote it down, repudiating the rhetoric of "moral pollution" with the bold claim that the mingling of the sexes at work in fact represented "the best available schooling in morality."[40] Although the object of the revised code of 1891 was the regulation of factory working conditions, many of its individual measures pertaining to women and youth blurred the boundaries between factory and family. Youth labor had become a particular concern of the state since the miners' strike of 1889, which drew attention to alleged unruliness and insolence among the young workers who had formed a vanguard on the strike lines.[41] Taking aim at two of the frequently cited causes of their insurgence—teenagers' independent earnings and the subsequent loss of parental authority—the revised code restricted the right of youths to choose their place of residence, required parental approval of apprenticeship or employment contracts, and sanctioned the payment of young workers' wages to parents or guardians. Furthermore, paragraph 134b entrusted employers to include in their *factory* ordinances measures prescribing appropriate moral comportment within as well as outside the factory, with the aim of curtailing young workers' pursuit of pleasure through frequent visits to pubs, dance halls, and public assemblies. The Social Democrats denounced these measures with particular vehemence, noting that their aim of deploying the police powers of the

---

39. On health and safety measures, see Born, *Staat und Sozialpolitik*, pp. 98–99. On the perception of the factory as a site of "moral decline," see Nordrhein-Westfälisches Hauptstaatsarchiv (HStAD), Landratsamt Mönchen-Gladbach 710, p. 108, "Bericht des Gewerbeaufsichtsbeamten Mönchen-Gladbach vom 14.12.1874," and HStAD, Jahresberichte der Königlich Preußischen Gewerberäte (JBdKPG) 1891, p. 290.

40. On paragraph 120 and the separation of the sexes, see Heinrich Herkner, "Die Reform der deutschen Arbeiterschutzgesetzgebung," *Archiv für Soziale Gesetzgebung und Statistik* 5 (1892): 231; Karl Baumbach, "Die Mitteilungen der Fabrikinspektoren über die industrielle Frauenarbeit," *Die Nation* 5, no. 7 (1887): 85–87, reprinted in Margrit Twellmann, *Die deutsche Frauenbewegung im Spiegel repräsentativer Frauenzeitschriften: Ihre Anfänge und erste Entwicklung, 1843–1889* (Meisenheim a.G.: Anton Hain, 1972), 2:518; Berlepsch, "Neuer Kurs," p. 188. On the SPD's view of these measures, see Wenzel, *Arbeiterschutz*, pp. 247–48, and Bebel, "Die Gewerbeordnungsnovelle," pp. 330–35.

41. Berlepsch, "Neuer Kurs," pp. 332–33.

state to educate the family would only bring *Zank und Unfrieden* (strife and dissension) into households.[42]

Although women and youth were susceptible to the moral and physical dangers of factory work in somewhat different ways, social reformers and state social policy experts cast the protection of both in terms of the vulnerability of their bodies—in the case of adult women because of the burdensome effects of pregnancy, childbirth, and motherhood on the "female organism," and in the case of youth because "their bodies were still in the process of maturation."[43] Adhering closely to the kaiser's February edicts on female and youth labor, the code enacted a ban on work at night and in mines for women and youths and decreed an eleven-hour maximum workday for adult women and a ten-hour day for youths. Maternity leave was extended from three to six weeks with the provision that women could return to work after four weeks with a doctor's permission.[44] Despite the long-term campaign of the Catholic Center to ban married women from factory work, the code differentiated married women and mothers from single women workers only with respect to the extra half-hour midday break "for those with households to tend to." As in the case of youth, the revised code sought to determine more than the mere conditions of work in the mills, drawing the household into the regulatory complex and mapping out the paths women traversed between the two. By extending the daily lunch break and curtailing working hours on Saturdays so women could shop and clean, the new legislation aimed not to banish women from factories but, as Jean Quataert has argued, "to give the gainfully employed woman more time in the day to learn and perform her crucial household tasks."[45] The miners' strike had left a deep impression of the destructive consequences of poor housekeeping and mothers' neglect on both the bureaucratic and the public imagination, inspiring a new reformist impetus with respect to domestic skills. Although training in household tasks had been left primarily to private initiatives of employers and charita-

---

42. Bebel, "Die Gewerbeordnungsnovelle," pp. 331–33; Herkner, "Der Entwurf," pp. 573–74; Wenzel, *Arbeiterschutz*, pp. 212–14; Berlepsch, "*Neuer Kurs*," pp. 322–23. On the perceived social crisis of youth, see Derek Linton, *"Who Has the Youth, Has the Future": The Campaign to Save Young Workers in Imperial Germany* (Cambridge: Cambridge University Press, 1991).

43. Heinrich Herkner, "Zur Kritik und Reform der deutschen Arbeiterschutzgesetzgebung," *Archiv für Soziale Gesetzgebung und Statistik* 3 (1890): 226–27.

44. JBdKPG, Regierung Düsseldorf (Reg. Düss.) 1892, pp. 324–29; Rosika Schwimmer, "Wichtige Momente in der Entwicklung des Mutterschutzes und der Mutterschaftsversicherung," in *Mutterschaft: Ein Sammelwerk für die Probleme des Weibes als Mutter*, ed. Adele Schreiber (Munich: Albert Langen, 1912), pp. 373–74.

45. Jean H. Quataert, "A Source Analysis in German Women's History: Factory Inspectors' Reports and the Shaping of Working-Class Lives, 1878–1914," *Central European History* 16 (June 1983): 111–12, and HStAD, JBdKPG, Reg. Düss. 1892, pp. 328–30.

ble or welfare associations during previous decades, the revised labor code of 1891 sought to extend the opportunities for young women to gain domestic skills.[46] The new laws widened the offical denotation of *Fortbildungsschulen* (continuation schools for young male workers)—and hence notions of female skill—to include *Haushaltsschulen* (housekeeping schools), thereby fulfilling a key demand of bourgeois reform campaigns, which the empress Augusta had personally endorsed in 1888. Training in the continuation schools was to instill in young workers the qualities of "order, discipline, and mental stimulation," which had quite different meanings for the two sexes. Whereas young women were to complete courses in "female handiwork and housework," young men were to receive instruction in reading, writing, arithmetic, drawing, and trade-specific subjects like textile fabrics or mechanics.[47]

In all these respects the revised code represented a negotiated compromise between the alarmist visions of social decay, abundant in the rhetoric of social reform, and the growing demand of mill owners, particularly in textiles, for female workers during the late 1880s and 1890s. Although the Centralverband Deutscher Industriellen (Central Association of German Industrialists, or CVDI) had emphatically rejected the proposed legislation of 1887–88, it accepted most of the protective laws of 1891 pertaining to the "weaker hands," that is, women and children. Its leaders objected to one measure or another—to abbreviated working hours on Saturday and in some cases to the Sunday holiday—and protested vehemently against the enhancement of workers' right to self-representation.[48] Despite the occasional protests of employers, the fact that the protective laws did not represent "one-sided measures designed for the exclusive benefit of women" was revealed in the broad range of exceptions available at em-

---

46. According to Berlepsch, "*Neuer Kurs,*" p. 244, in the wake of the strike an Oberregierungsrat Gamp (presumably of the strike region) even contended that training future wives and mothers in domestic skills was an important strike prevention measure.

47. Kreisarchiv Viersen (KrA Vie), Gemeindeamt (GA) Grefrath 1154, "Gewerbliche Fortbildungsschule, 1864–1912"; HStAD, Reg. Düss. 1889, p. 268. Also see Marie Elisabeth Lüders, *Die Fortbildung und Ausbildung der im Gewerbe tätigen weiblichen Personen und deren rechtliche Grundlage* (Leipzig: Duncker und Humblot, 1912), pp. 22–23; Berlepsch, "*Neuer Kurs,*" pp. 243–47; Herkner, "Der Entwurf," p. 575. Attendance at the *Fortbildungsschulen,* operated by district or city governments, was voluntary until 1891, when it became mandatory for men in several German states and for both sexes in Baden, Württemberg, and Bavaria.

48. The CVDI was founded in 1876. See Monika Breger, *Die Haltung der industriellen Unternehmer zur staatlichen Sozialpolitik in den Jahren 1878–1891* (Frankfurt a.M.: Haag und Herchen, 1982), pp. 161–65, 179–82; Born, *Staat und Sozialpolitik,* p. 80; Dieter Lindenlaub, *Richtungskämpfe im Verein für Sozialpolitik: Wissenschaft und Sozialpolitik im Kaiserreich vornehmlich vom Beginn des "Neuen Kurses" bis zum Ausbruch des Ersten Weltkrieges, 1890–1914* (Wiesbaden: Franz Steiner, 1967), pp. 49–51.

ployers' behest.[49] A generous allowance of overtime was built into the limits on working hours for women and youths, permitting women to work eighty hours of overtime a year, an option that textile employers appear to have utilized frequently during the 1890s. Workers had to request the extra half-hour lunch break, a matter of often complicated negotiation between individual female workers and their supervisors. Moreover, maternity leave was accessible only to the relatively few women covered by the sickness insurance law of 1883, which compensated them for only half of their lost wages for the four weeks of mandatory maternity leave.[50]

Although the revised code of 1891 was widely touted as reform "in the interests of the community, [that is,] for the health and the well-being of the *whole nation*," in fact it defined the social identities of class and citizen in highly gendered terms.[51] The new laws delimited the political rights of adult men at work, restricting some (right to quit, right to strike), augmenting others (elected workers' committees in each factory) and generally excluding men from protective measures such as restricted working hours. The code's cumulative effect, then, was to transform the male worker from "object to subject," indeed, into a "contracting partner," while enhancing the dependent status of women and youths.[52] Thus, from the social policy debates of the late 1880s, the mass strikes of 1889–90, and the legislative innovation of 1891 had emerged two distinct social questions and two categories of citizenship: on the one hand, the state expanded protection of women, adolescents, and children at work, thereby undertaking a thorough reform of family life by intervening on their behalf in the workplace.

49. Alice Salomon, *Labour Laws for Women in Germany* (London: Women's Industrial Council, 1907), p. 11. On the revised code in practice, also see H. Lux, "Die sozialpolitische Wirkungen des neuen deutschen Arbeiterschutzgesetzes," *Sozialpolitisches Centralblatt* 3, no. 6 (1893–94): 67–70. On overtime and adherence to hours legislation, see Berlepsch, *"Neuer Kurs,"* pp. 258–60, 263–64; HStAD, JBdKPG, Reg. Düss. 1892, pp. 327, 330–31; 1893, pp. 383–84; 1894, pp. 478–79; and Marlene Ellerkamp, *Industriearbeit, Krankheit und Geschlecht* (Göttingen: Vandenhoeck und Ruprecht, 1991), pp. 181–88.

50. On maternity leave and insurance, see Schwimmer, "Wichtige Momente," pp. 373–75; Irene Stoehr, "Housework and Motherhood: Debates and Policies in the Women's Movement in Imperial Germany and the Weimar Republic," in *Maternity and Gender Policies: Women and the Rise of the European Welfare States, 1880s–1950s*, ed. Gisela Bock and Pat Thane (London: Routledge, 1991), p. 223; Seth Koven and Sonya Michel, "Introduction: 'Mother Worlds,'" in *Mothers of a New World: Maternalist Politics and the Origins of Welfare States*, ed. Seth Koven and Sonya Michel (London: Routledge, 1993), p. 27.

51. Salomon, *Labour Laws for Women*, p. 11. Similarly, Alfred Weber underscored that "it is the interest of the *nation* to protect the health and morality of women in particular"; see his essay "Die Entwickelung," p. 1149; Herkner, "Zur Kritik und zur Reform," p. 229, and *Handwörterbuch der Staatswissenschaften* (Jena: Gustav Fischer, 1890–94), entries under *Arbeiter, Arbeiterfrage*, p. 389.

52. Born, *Staat und Sozialpolitik*, p. 61. The core question of social policy according to Friedrich Naumann, whom Born discusses here, was how to ease shift in workers' status from object to subject.

On the other hand, it established new organs of representation through which adult male workers could assert their claims to economic and civic equality, their rights of representation, association, and expression. Labor legislation demarcated the boundaries of the working class, dividing it by gender and age and fixing the place of women in the work process, but also within family, class, and civil society.[53] And each of these social identities was embedded in particular notions of female bodies as integral to the body of the family and to the social body. Finally, while shaping the external boundaries and internal differentiations of the working class, the protective labor laws also marked a significant moment in the making of the German *Bürgertum*, which had come to define itself through the encounters with both working class and state within the milieu of social reform.

This milieu, which now encompassed popular, bourgeois, and bureaucratic agencies of reform, was itself fundamentally altered by the rapid expansion of the public sphere in the early 1890s as the electoral shift of 1890 and the revocation of the Socialist Law reinvigorated the parliamentary arena. Furthermore, the advent of popular mass movements of Catholics and Socialists, and of right-wing pressure groups of nationalists and colonialists, began to change the face of the political parties during the early 1890s. This was a process that would radically alter the relation between parties and their popular constituencies by the end of the decade, as the work of David Blackbourn and Geoff Eley has shown.[54] Along with the rapid growth of the Social Democratic Party, in 1890 its affiliated free unions formed a confederation across industries and trades, the Allgemeiner Deutscher Gewerkschaftsbund (General German Trade Union Confederation), or ADGB. From the Catholic social movement emerged at the same time the Volksverein für das Katholische Deutschland (People's Association for Catholic Germany), founded in the textile town of Mönchen-Gladbach in the Rhineland in 1890. Its leaders—social reformers August Pieper and Franz Hitze and textile entrepreneur Franz Brandts—conceived of the Volksverein as a mass organization with the explicit goal of challenging and contesting "Social Democratic errors," not least on the issues of women and family. The Volksverein aimed to establish a network of people's bureaus throughout Germany and to effect a broad mobilization of German Catholics to pursue religious, civic, and

53. On the role of the state in shaping the identities of class and citizenship, see Nolan, "Economic Crisis," pp. 360–61; Steinmetz, "Workers and the Welfare State," p. 23; Gerhard A. Ritter, *Staat, Arbeiterschaft und Arbeiterbewegung in Deutschland: Vom Vormärz bis zum Ende der Weimarer Republik* (Berlin: Dietz, 1980), p. 68.

54. David Blackbourn, *Class, Religion and Local Politics in Wilhelmine Germany: The Centre Party in Württemberg before 1914* (New Haven: Yale University Press, 1979), and Geoff Eley, *Reshaping the German Right: Radical Nationalism and Political Change after Bismarck* (New Haven: Yale University Press, 1981).

social-political goals.⁵⁵ Despite its own ambivalence about "the modern," the founding of the Volksverein marked the transformation of Social Catholicism into a movement that embraced modern modes of political mobilization and "sparked a broad range of diverse political activities" during the 1890s.⁵⁶ Its efforts were spurred on by Pope Leo XIII's encyclical of May 1891, *Rerum novarum*, in which the church acknowledged the widespread impoverishment that accompanied industrial and urban growth and sought to confront the deepening social divide between workers and owners, proletarians and *Bürger*. Affirming the Social Catholic vision of social reform, the encyclical emphasized the importance of the state, in conjunction with the church and workers' self-help organizations, in ameliorating these conditions and in restoring harmony to the social body. The encyclical is generally viewed as signaling a departure of Social Catholicism from prevalent notions of *Standesgesellschaft* (estate society) toward a reluctant recognition of the power of class identities and class antagonisms in industrial society.⁵⁷

The year 1890 also marked the birth of a distinctly Protestant social reform movement, the Evangelisch-Sozialer Kongress (Evangelical-Social Congress, or ESK), which united theologians like Adolf Stöcker, reformist officials like Berlepsch, and eminent university professors and "socialists of the chair" like Schmoller and Adolf Wagner to undertake the "unprejudiced investigation of social conditions among the people" and to evaluate "those conditions against the touchstone of the moral and religious commandments of the Gospels."⁵⁸ Inspired by the reorientation of state social

55. Emil Ritter, *Die katholisch-soziale Bewegung und der Volksverein* (Cologne: Bachem, 1954), p. 143; Wilfried Loth, "Katholizismus und Moderne: Überlegungen zu einem dialektischen Verhältnis," in *Zivilisation und Barberei: Die widersprüchlichen Potentiale der Moderne. Detlev Peukert zum Gedenken*, ed. Frank Bajohr (Hamburg: Christians, 1991), pp. 90–93; Stegmann, "Geschichte der sozialen Ideen," pp. 417–19. According to Stegmann, the Volksverein had 108,000 members in its second year (1891); by 1901 it had 184,000 members and 200,000 subscribers to its newspaper. By 1914 the Volksverein had 805,000 members.

56. Loth, "Katholizismus und Moderne," pp. 85–86. For an excellent survey of recent literature on German Catholicism, see Margaret L. Anderson, "Piety and Politics: Recent Work on German Catholicism," *Journal of Modern History* 63 (December 1991): 681–716.

57. As cited in Stegmann, "Geschichte der sozialen Ideen," pp. 411–13, the encyclical stated: "If the employer should burden the workers with an excessive load or present them with inhuman working conditions, should their health suffer through overwork or a certain kind of work, which is not appropriate for their age or sex, the power and the authority of the law, within its limits, must be applied." It also recognized the importance of workers' self-help institutions, including unions.

58. Quotation from Rita Aldenhoff, "Max Weber and the Evangelical-Social Congress," in *Max Weber and His Contemporaries*, ed. Wolfgang J. Mommsen and Jürgen Osterhammel (London: Allen and Unwin, 1987), p. 194; vom Bruch, *Wissenschaft, Politik, und öffentliche Meinung*, pp. 343–44. Other members of the ESK over the years included Max Weber, Ernst Troeltsch, Hans Delbrück, Robert Wilbrandt, and female reformers Marie Baum, Elisabeth Gnauck-Kühne, Gertrud Dyhrenfurth, and Anna von Gierke.

policy at the outset of the new course, the Evangelical-Social Congress placed the freedom and independence of industrial workers in the forefront of its goals, while also raising demands for expanded maternity leave and health insurance coverage for pregnant women and mothers. The ESK was unusual within the milieu of social reform for its bold stance on women's rights, calling on women "from a Christian standpoint to become whole persons" and granting them equal rights as active participants within the organization.[59] Its view of female factory labor thus differed significantly from that of Social Catholics, who sought to ban married women from factories, or that of Social Democrats, who, officially at least, viewed wage labor as the source of women's emancipation. Recognizing the *Zwiespalt* (schism) between wage work and motherhood in working women's lives, the ESK emphasized not family over factory but harmony and balance between the two.[60]

Somewhat ironically, however, both the power of the interventionist state and the vitality of civil society were enhanced by the reforms of the new course: the state enjoyed new prestige "as a harbinger of progress 'from above,'" while mass organizations like the Catholic Volksverein and the Social Democratic Party, bourgeois associations like the Verein für Sozialpolitik, and the newly founded ESK drew on and deployed "new structures of public communication" in pursuit of social reform goals of the 1890s.[61] Dense discursive networks were formed through political journals like the *Preußische Jahrbücher*, *Schmollers Jahrbuch*, *Jahrbücher für Nationalökonomie und Statistik*, *Zeitschrift für die gesamte Staatswissenschaft*, and *Grenzboten*, in which bourgeois reformers read, cited, and debated one another's viewpoints, on occasion prompting lively, often polemical re-

---

59. Quotation from Manfred Schick, *Kulturprotestantismus und soziale Frage: Versuche zur Begründung der Sozialethik, vornehmlich in der Zeit von der Gründung des Evangelischen-Sozialen Kongresses bis zum Ausbruch des 1. Weltkrieges (1890–1914)* (Tübingen: J. C. B. Mohr, 1970), p. 79. See also the excellent study by Ursula Baumann, *Protestantismus und Frauenemanzipation in Deutschland, 1850–1920* (Frankfurt a.M.: Campus, 1993), pp. 79–98 and Gottfried Kretschmar, *Der Evangelisch-Sozialer Kongreß: Der deutsche Protestantismus und die soziale Frage* (Stuttgart: Evangelisches Verlagswerk, 1972), pp. 118–19. Among the topics addressed at its annual meetings during the 1890s were protective labor legislation (1890); training of teenage female workers (1891); the educative effects of the protective labor code (1892); and the social conditions of women (1895).

60. Kretschmar, *Der Evangelisch-Sozialer Kongreß*, pp. 9–10, 23, 88–89. Kretschmar points out that the membership of the ESK and the Verein für Sozialpolitik overlapped significantly.

61. Quotations from David Blackbourn, "The German Bourgeoisie: An Introduction," in *The German Bourgeoisie: Essays on the Social History of the German Middle Class from the Late 18th to the Early 20th Century*, ed. David Blackbourn and Richard J. Evans (London: Routledge, 1991), p. 24 and Geoff Eley, "Introduction I: Is There a History of the Kaiserreich?" in *Society, Culture and the State in Germany, 1870–1930*, ed. Geoff Eley (Ann Arbor: University of Michigan Press, 1996), p. 11.

sponses in the pages of Social Democratic monthlies like *Neue Zeit* or *Sozialistische Monatshefte*.⁶² The 1890s even witnessed the resurgent influence of the bourgeois "socialists of the chair" on both public opinion and parliament. During the second reading of the *Umsturzvorlage* (Subversion Bill) in 1894, for example, some 22,000 people, most of them German academics and intellectuals, signed petitions to the Reichstag against the bill.⁶³

The legislative innovations of 1890–91 and the expansion and enrichment of the public sphere through the proliferation of new assocations like the ESK and the Volksverein, as well as the revitalization of the established Verein für Sozialpolitik and the Social Democratic Party, represent significant outcomes of the new course in social policy. The new course came to an effective end soon after the revised code became law in 1892, however. The interest of kaiser and chancellor in protective labor legislation began to wane as early as 1893, and by 1894 the emphasis of social policy shifted away from benevolent paternalism toward authoritarian repression of politicized workers as the kaiser began to consider ways to correct the "mistake" of lifting the Socialist Law. Berlepsch, who had already become disheartened about the prospects for further social policy innovation, resigned in 1896, marking the official end of the new course.⁶⁴ The subsequent "Stumm era," named after the industrialist Baron Carl Ferdinand von Stumm, denoted a reversal of the innovations of the new course—even a backlash. The shift in social policy found its most virulent expression in the Subversion Bill of 1894 and the *Zuchthausvorlage* (Penitentiary Bill) of 1898, which aimed to curb workers' rights to unionize, to strike, and to advocate revolution. Although both bills were voted down in the Reichstag (in 1896 and 1899, respectively), the debates surrounding them represented a profound crisis of citizenship, a deep fissure in the relationship between workers and the German state in which bourgeois social reformers became deeply implicated.⁶⁵

In the expanded public sphere of the 1890s, the policy innovations of

62. Vom Bruch, *Wissenschaft*, pp. 22, 32, 27–38, 48, 55. Social Democrats Karl Kautsky and Franz Mehring apparently followed the debates among bourgeois social reformers very closely in the pages of the *Neue Zeit*, first published by the SPD in 1883. The SPD party congress of 1903 banned publication of articles by bourgeois authors in the Social Democratic press and also prohibited Social Democrats from publishing in bourgeois journals.

63. Vom Bruch, *Wissenschaft*, p. 62.

64. Born, *Staat und Sozialpolitik*, pp. 92–98, 106, 118–19; Berlepsch, "*Neuer Kurs*," pp. 151–52, 268. The labor code was revised and expanded again in 1908, but it contained no policy shifts or fundamental innovations.

65. On the meanings of the term *Ära Stumm*, see Born, *Staat und Sozialpolitik*, pp. 112–18. Born argues that the term is used because the industrialist Baron von Stumm most clearly and explicitly articulated the reactionary views of labor and social policy during the mid-1890s, not because he had a concrete role in shaping government policies.

1890 and 1891 figured as the starting point of a new discourse about the social question of female factory labor rather than embodying its definitive solution. For even after the revised code became law, Social Democrats, Catholics, and left liberals continued to debate many of the social policy goals the legislation of 1891 had left unfulfilled. The Catholic Center Party, for example, renewed its call for expanded maternity leave and a ten-hour day for women workers, demanding the urgent enactment of a six-hour maximum workday for married women and once again invoking the specter of children abandoned and husbands driven into pubs by the collapse of the core of the working-class family.[66] The Social Democrats, whose women's movement, by contrast with the party's Reichstag delegation, had campaigned ardently against special protective measures for women during the late 1880s, also resumed their struggle to expand the protective scope of the 1891 laws. By 1892 *Die Gleichheit*, the Social Democratic women's journal, edited by Clara Zetkin, had shifted its views on protective measures for women, endorsing them as "a hygienic necessity" and thus consolidating the party's efforts on behalf of labor legislation.[67] Interestingly, despite the parallel expansion of married women's work in home industrial production during these years, the convergence of work and family at this site did not appear to endanger the family in the same way as the sharp division between the two that seemed to occur when women went to work in factories.[68] Moreover, the widespread perception of the inexorable decline of this sector in the face of the rapid growth of factory industry led both legislation and reform discourses to focus on the factory as a public site of particular danger. Home industry and urban sweatshops remained largely shielded from public view and hence from state regulation until 1911, when social insurance became available to workers in these sectors.[69]

---

66. Franz Hitze, *Die Arbeiterfrage und die Bestrebungen zu ihrer Lösung* (Berlin: Commissionsverlag der Germania, 1900), pp. 30, 76–80. Hitze recommended that married women be required to obtain a *Zulassungsschein* (certificate of eligibility) from local authorities before taking employment, which would be issued for short periods and thus would require frequent renewal.

67. "Der gesetzliche Arbeiterinnenschutz, eine hygienische Notwendigkeit," *Die Gleichheit* 2 (1892): 137, as cited in Karin Bauer, *Clara Zetkin und die proletarische Frauenbewegung* (Berlin: Oberbaum, 1978), p. 126.

68. On the disparate perceptions of danger to the working-class family, see Richard J. Evans, "Politics and the Family: Social Democracy and the Working-Class Family in Theory and Practice before 1914," in Evans and Lee, *German Family*, pp. 258–60.

69. On home industry, see Alfred Weber, "Die Entwicklungsgrundlagen der großstädtischen Frauenhausindustrie," in *Die Hausindustrie der Frauen in Berlin*, vol. 2 of *Hausindustrie und Heimarbeit in Deutschland und Österreich*, ed. Alfred Weber (Leipzig: Duncker und Humblot, 1899), pp. xiv–xix and xl–xli. Also see Barbara Franzoi, *At the Very Least She Pays the Rent: Women and German Industrialization, 1871–1914* (Westport, Conn.: Green-

The ways the labor laws of 1891 were applied, circumvented, and contested by inspectors, employers, and workers not only shaped the structure and experience of work but also helped frame the debates about social policy and women's work that engaged the social reform associations and the public through the end of the decade. During the 1890s the issues of working-class domesticity and motherhood served as imaginative triggers for deeper and more complex discussions of the permanence or mutability of the character of the sexes, which in turn were shaped by and entwined with concerns about the rapid transformation from agrarian to industrial society, the rise of a militant mass movement of socialist workers, and the perception of an acute crisis of the family. Although this purported crisis appears to have preoccupied reformers across industrialized Europe during the 1890s, this particular confluence of concerns in the context of expanding bourgeois and working-class public spheres marks one of the more intriguing "peculiarities of German history."[70]

Another peculiarity—and the immediate cause of the heightened concern with the female factory worker—was the steady and perceptible expansion of the female industrial labor market, which occurred as the pace of industrial growth quickened and industrial employers confronted recurrent labor shortages in nearly all sectors, including the "women's industries" of textiles, garments, and cigar making, during the late 1880s and 1890s. By contrast with the protracted process of industrialization in England, for example, Germany's rapid industrial growth meant that the number of married female factory workers continued to expand a decade or more after beginning to decline in England. In Germany the number of married women working outside the home nearly doubled between the census surveys of 1882 and 1907, and in the four-year period between 1895 and 1899 the percentage of married women among adult female factory workers rose sharply, from 21 to 29 percent.[71] In fact, in 1895 over

---

wood Press, 1985) and Robert Wilbrandt, "Hausindustrielle Frauenarbeit," *Die Frau* 8 (1900–1901): 539.

70. David Blackbourn and Geoff Eley, *The Peculiarities of German History: Bourgeois Society and Politics in 19th Century Germany* (New York: Oxford University Press, 1984). On the crisis of the family during the 1890s, see Eve Rosenhaft and W. R. Lee, "State and Society in Modern Germany: Beamtenstaat, Klassenstaat, Wohlfahrtsstaat," in *The State and Social Change in Germany, 1880–1980*, ed. Eve Rosenhaft and W. R. Lee (New York: Oxford University Press, 1990), pp. 27–29.

71. "Married women" here denotes married and formerly married women (widows and women who were divorced or separated from their husbands). The married female workforce grew by 90 percent and the single female workforce by 78 percent between 1882 and 1907. The absolute number of married female employees in German factories increased from 140,000 in 1895 to 230,000 in 1899. Figures cited here are based on Stefan Bajohr, *Die Hälfte der Fabrik, Geschichte der Frauenarbeit in Deutschland*, (Marburg: Verlag Arbeiterbewegung und Gesellschaftswissenschaft, 1979), p. 25; Hanns Dorn, "Die Frauenerwerbsarbeit

50 percent of married female factory workers were employed in the textile industry. Accompanying the steady influx of female workers into factories was the rhetoric of feminization and the specter of *Lohndrückerei* (wage cutting), of men displaced from their jobs by women whose labor was allegedly cheaper and whose disposition was more docile.[72] The prominence of female factory labor in the social policy debates and interventions of the early 1890s rendered this increase highly visible. Thus the decade was marked not only by a tangible transformation of the female labor market, but also by a change in the "social prism" through which women's factory work was viewed.[73]

The norms and principles of the revised labor code were reproduced and disseminated as factory inspectors undertook to visit restrooms, cafeterias, and changing rooms, enforcing the separation of the sexes wherever possible and supporting the efforts of mill owners and local authorities to fulfill the vision of domesticity outlined in the code by instituting cooking and sewing classes, founding homes for single and pregnant women workers, and in a few exceptional cases, mandating the dismissal of female workers upon marriage.[74] In general, married women appeared much more frequently in the factory inspectors' reports after 1891 than during the 1880s, thus emerging as a new object of state attention and intervention.[75] In the more dispersed arena of the public sphere, however, debates about the transformation of the female labor market took place within the discursive framework of the late 1880s and early 1890s in which the family rather than the individual had emerged as the "primary element of the economic side of human life, . . . as the most fundamental economic unit that, based on the natural order, joins production, consumption, and re-

---

und ihre Aufgaben für die Gesetzgebung," *Archiv für Rechts- und Wirtschaftsphilosophie* 5 (1911–12): 86–87; Rose Otto, *Über die Fabrikarbeit verheirateter Frauen*, Münchener Volkswirtschaftliche Studien, vol. 4 (Stuttgart: Cotta, 1910), pp. 10, 99–101; Helene Simon, *Der Anteil der Frau an der deutschen Industrie nach den Ergebnissen der Berufszählung von 1907*, Schriften des ständigen Ausschusses zur Förderung der Arbeiterinneninteressen, no. 2 (Jena: Gustav Fischer, 1910), p. 7; Ludwig Pohle, "Die Erhebungen der Gewerbeaufsichtsbeamten über die Fabrikarbeit verheirateter Frauen," *Jahrbuch für Gesetzgebung, Verwaltung, und Volkswirtschaft* 25 (1901): 158–61.

72. Otto, *Über die Fabrikarbeit*, p. 93.

73. On casual labor and the changing social prism through which it was viewed in mid-nineteenth-century Britain, see Gareth Stedman Jones, *Outcast London: A Study in the Relationship between Classes in Victorian Society* (Harmondsworth: Penguin Books, 1976) p. 327.

74. HStAD, JBdKPG, Reg. Düss. 1891, pp. 290, 308; 1892, pp. 353–54; 1893, pp. 387–88; 1894, pp. 482–83. These factory inspectors' reports chart the transformation of the workplace according to the labor code of 1891.

75. Otto, *Über die Fabrikarbeit*, pp. 88–89, and Quataert, "Source Analysis," p. 111. Quataert observes that the description of knitting, sewing, and cooking courses took up ever greater space in the inspectors' reports after 1891 and that the inspectors "saluted unequivocally the role of *middle-class* business wives and ladies in these reform efforts."

production."⁷⁶ Within this schema the increasing number of female factory workers figured as a serious distortion of the social and sexual order, for "the man is accorded work in production, the woman has her particular calling in consumption, and the common vocation of both is reproduction." The specific goal of subsequent labor legislation was therefore to regulate factory work "so that the woman is not deprived of her proper calling as housewife, or so that she may be returned to it."⁷⁷ Underpinning the code's explicit attention to domesticity and motherhood was the perceived "difference in body formation" that ascribed to women a "distinctive task in the reproduction of the human race."⁷⁸ Thus, as reformers attempted to resolve the growing discrepancy between prevalent notions about the (embodied) character of the sexes and the continued increase of the female workforce during the 1890s, they also sought to recast the relationship between family and state, between sexual and social order.⁷⁹

Narratives of Danger: Married Women's Factory Work and the Social Body, 1896–1900

Indeed, not long after the revision of the labor code, the issue of a legal ban on married women's factory employment erupted into virulent debates in which the scholarly and the sensational entwined to convey a powerful impression of the social body endangered and sexual hierarchies disarranged. Social reform experts launched new empirical studies of household budgets, nutrition, illness, and infant mortality in order to determine the tangible impact of female factory labor on working-class family life, thus furnishing opponents of women's factory employment with "scientific" evidence to back up their heretofore idealistic appeals.⁸⁰ Opponents of married women's factory work could now utilize a range of schol-

---

76. "Die Frauenarbeit als Gegenstand der Fabrikgesetzgebung von einem Sachverständigen," *Jahrbuch für Gesetzgebung, Verwaltung und Volkswirtschaft im Deutschen Reich (Schmollers Jahrbuch)* 9, no. 2 (1885): 89–90.

77. Ibid.

78. Baumbach, *Frauenarbeit*, p. 6.

79. A good example of how "the character of the sexes" was defined in terms of the female body is Hermann Ploss's text *Das Weib in der Natur- und Volkskunde* (Leipzig: T. Grieben, 1885). It was published first in serial form, then as a book, and appealed to a wider lay audience than most medical texts. Ploss, an important medical and political figure in Leipzig, established the first midwifery clinic in Leipzig and also was a member of the city countil between 1875 and 1881; he was widely regarded as the founder of what was then termed "ethnographic gynecology."

80. See, for example, H. Mehner, "Der Haushalt und die Lebenshaltung einer Leipziger Arbeiterfamilie," *Schmollers Jahrbuch* (1886), reprinted in *Seminar: Familie und Gesellschaftsstruktur*, ed. Heidi Rosenbaum (Frankfurt a.M.: Suhrkamp, 1982), pp. 329–32. Mehner's article was cited frequently by reformers in the early 1890s. On Mehner's article as a "transition piece," see Quataert, "Source Analysis," p. 112.

arly studies, published in reputable academic journals, to lend plausibility to their often polemical assertions. So, for example, infant mortality studies of the 1880s and 1890s could be used to substantiate the controversial claim of the Catholic reform movement from the 1870s that "women's employment, where infant mortality is high, borders on infanticide."[81] Yet the narratives of danger and scandalous revelations about both work and family also left a deep impression on the public, for the tropes and images they invoked conveyed a sense of fundamental disintegration of social, cultural, and moral order, a theme that recurred across a wide range of reformers' texts throughout the 1890s. For example, the entry under *Arbeiter* in the scholarly *Handwörterbuch der Staatswissenschaft* (Pocket dictionary of government science), compiled between 1890 and 1894, cataloged a series of "economic and moral abuses" in working-class families. Despite the apparently impartial encyclopedic format, the list of abuses evokes a barrage of impressions of social decay, beginning with the moral abuses, including

> above all, poor housekeeping skills and a wretched family life among the workers, caused by the frivolous, premature, and immoral entry into marriage, by the crudeness and immorality of the marriage partners and parents, by the miserable conditions in their homes, the improvidence and poor training of housewives, and not infrequently by the regular employment of housewives and mothers outside the home, and also the immoderate and immoral bearing of children and their pathetic upbringing.[82]

Prescribing a similar moral economy for both factory and family, the handbook also noted the destructive effects of other abuses, namely the "lack of diligence and frugality, excessive extravagance, alcoholism, impiety, mistrust of the employers, . . . and loathing of the owning classes." The task of social reform outlined in the text was the improvement not only of working conditions and earnings, but also of "family life, child rearing, housekeeping, and housing," all prerequisites for the elevation "of the workers' estate into a class of higher moral and spiritual standing."[83] The eradication of female factory labor thus emerged as an essential part of this transformation, as a solution to the complex of moral and social ills that constituted the new social question of the 1890s.

Whereas a ban on married women's factory employment had emerged as the negative, punitive answer to the social question, during the 1890s the moralizing of motherhood became a positive solution and a powerful sym-

81. As cited in Otto, *Über die Fabrikarbeit*, p. 144.
82. *Handwörterbuch der Staatswissenschaften*, pp. 390–91.
83. Ibid., p. 389.

bol of class reconciliation, of reordering the social.[84] Even the Social Democratic organ of women's emancipation, *Die Gleichheit*, idealized motherhood, not framing its demands for special protection of female workers in the familiar rhetoric of women as "weaker hands," but recognizing women's particular contribution to society as mothers, as "producers of the future producers."[85] Similarly, the Social Democratic women's movement, led by Zetkin, tacitly accepted the notion of traditional female duties within the household, proclaiming in 1896, for example: "It is not the task of our agitation among women to alienate women from these duties, rather our agitation should make them more able to fulfill them successfully." Historian Anna Freier points out that the paper's supplement, "For Our Mothers," which addressed mainly housewives rather than working women, presented idealized pictures of motherhood and suggested that they could be realized even under the conditions of capitalism.[86] At the same time, the bourgeois women's movement, which consolidated its manifold associations into the Bund Deutscher Frauenvereine (Federation of German Women's Associations, or BDF) in 1894, and which had an increasingly important role in shaping private and municipal welfare policies, placed motherhood in the forefront of the *Frauenfrage* (woman question) of the 1890s.[87] On the rhetorical level, bourgeois feminists sought to extend the influence of "social motherhood" throughout German society, signifying a moral, not a political, vision of reform that frequently involved disseminating bourgeois values pertaining to family,

84. On motherhood as a solution to the social question in England, see Anna Davin, "Imperialism and Motherhood," *History Workshop* 5 (1978): 12, 53; in Sweden and the United States, see Barbara Hobson, "Feminist Strategies and Gendered Discourses in Welfare States: Married Women's Right to Work in the United States and Sweden," in Koven and Michel, *Mothers of a New World*, pp. 396–429. On the moralizing of motherhood in Germany, see Claudia Honegger, "Frauen und medizinische Deutungsmacht im 19. Jahrhundert," in *Medizinische Deutungsmacht im sozialen Wandel des 19. und frühen 20. Jahrhunderts*, ed. Alfons Labisch and Reinhard Spree (Bonn: Psychiatrie Verlag, 1989), p. 182.

85. *Die Gleichheit* 3 (1893): 150, as cited in Bauer, *Clara Zetkin*, p. 130. See the interesting exchange between Johanna Loewenherz and Clara Zetkin in *Die Gleichheit* 3 (1893): 124–60 on protective measures for women. Also see Evans, "Politics and the Family," pp. 256–88.

86. Quotation from *Die Gleichheit* 6 (1896): 171, as cited in Anna E. Freier, *"Dem Reich der Freiheit sollst Du Kinder gebären": Der Antifeminismus der proletarischen Frauenbewegung im Spiegel der "Gleichheit," 1891–1917* (Frankfurt a.M.: Haag und Herchen, 1981), pp. 13–14.

87. On the history of the Bund Deutscher Frauenvereine, see Barbara Greven-Aschoff, *Die bürgerliche Frauenbewegung in Deutschland, 1894–1933* (Göttingen: Vandenhoeck und Ruprecht, 1981), pp. 78–124, and Richard J. Evans, *The Feminist Movement in Germany, 1894–1933* (London: Sage, 1976), pp. 37–53. According to Evans, p. 37, on its founding in 1894 the Bund united 34 women's associations of various types. One year later there were 65 member associations with some 50,000 members; by 1901 it encompassed 137 organizations with approximately 70,000 members.

health, hygiene, and education among the working class. On a practical level, however, middle-class women established networks of municipal health clinics to combat infant mortality, organized courses in domestic skills, and sponsored social work training courses for their own members in order to professionalize and systematize their efforts at social assistance, thereby defining the sphere of feminist social intervention as family and motherhood.[88]

From the early 1890s through the first decade of the new century, those social reformers who wished to curtail female factory labor beyond the minimal restrictions of 1891 dispersed "a flood of books and brochures" that sought to reclaim the working wife and mother for family and household. In 1894 Heinrich Herkner, a highly respected economist and member of the Verein für Sozialpolitik, explored the widespread sense of social disorder in a popular book, *Die Arbeiterfrage: Eine Einführung* (The worker question: An introduction). Herkner, who had completed his doctoral dissertation on the cotton workers of Upper Alsace in 1887, combined sensationalist voyeurism with scholarly expertise on an industrial setting where the worst abuses purportedly prevailed.[89] First summoning visions of moral decay inside the factory itself, Herkner excerpted from Alfons Thun's classic study of the textile industry in the Lower Rhine the titillating passages describing the sexual underworld of the textile mills, in which men and women huddled together overnight in piles of rags and shreds of cloth in the corners of the mill, where "it is warmer and softer than in their hard beds at home." When the lights had been extinguished it was not "the serenity of slumber" that filled the room, but "the most

---

88. On "social motherhood," see Christoph Sachße, "Social Mothers: The Bourgeois Women's Movement and German Welfare-State Formation," in Koven and Michel, *Mothers of a New World*, pp. 136–58, and his *Mütterlichkeit als Beruf: Sozialarbeit, Sozialreform und Frauenbewegung, 1871–1929* (Frankfurt a.M.: Suhrkamp, 1986); also see Dietlinde Peters, *Mütterlichkeit im Kaiserreich: Die bürgerliche Frauenbewegung und der soziale Beruf der Frau* (Bielefeld: B. Kleine, 1984), and Else Wex, *Staatsbürgerliche Arbeit deutscher Frauen, 1865 bis 1928* (Berlin: F. A. Herbig, 1929), pp. 46–47. The BDF established its first Committee on the Protection of Women Workers in 1898.

89. All citations here are from Heinrich Herkner, *Die Arbeiterfrage: Eine Einführung*, 4th ed. (Berlin: J. Guttentag, 1905). The first edition appeared in 1894 (Berlin: J. Guttentag). Herkner, son of a Bohemian textile entrepreneur, completed his dissertation, published as *Die oberelsässische Baumwollindustrie und ihre Arbeiter* (Strassburg: Karl J. Trübner, 1887), under the supervision of Lujo Brentano and G. F. Knapp. On Herkner's professional life as a university professor and scholar at the Universities of Freiburg, Karlsruhe, Zurich (1898–1907), and Berlin (Technische Hochschule, 1907–12), see Lindenlaub, *Richtungskämpfe*, pp. 65, 165–67, and Heinrich Herkner, "Der Lebenslauf eines 'Kathedersozialisten,'" in *Die Volkswirtschaftslehre der Gegenwart in Selbstdarstellungen*, ed. Felix Meiner (Leipzig: Felix Meiner, 1924), pp. 77–116. In 1912 Herkner was appointed to succeed Gustav Schmoller at the University of Berlin. He also served as chairman of the Verein für Sozialpolitik and later of the Gesellschaft für Soziale Reform.

frightful of orgies."⁹⁰ Then Herkner addressed the implications of women's factory work for family and community, pointing to the example of England, where rising income among male workers had enabled many married women to return to the household. He aimed to show that the era of married women's factory work had left an indelible mark on English working-class family life. Here he cited an eyewitness report titled *Wie der englische Arbeiter lebt?* (translated as *How the English Workman Lives*), by a German miner who had worked for several years in England. Implicitly warning his readers about the consequences of the expansion of married women's factory employment in Germany, Herkner evoked a vision of domesticity turned upside down:

> English workers' wives are often not capable of preparing an ordinary meal. What they do understand however, is how to drink whiskey. . . . It is certain that more women than men are addicted to drink. The factory workers' wives are usually drunkards. As far as morality goes, one can only imagine. Married women offer themselves for sale when they are drunk. . . . Most workers' wives are too lazy to sew, even though every young girl must learn how to sew at school. An outsider, who is not familiar with the conditions and who wanders through a working-class quarter at nine or ten A.M., would be astonished to see that two-thirds of the women have fastened their clothes together with pins, are unwashed and uncombed.⁹¹

In his other writings Herkner drew on the factory inspectors' reports for images of young children playing on the dusty floor under the machines in the woolen spinning and weaving mills, of women working at their looms with their infants in their arms.⁹² Replete with shocking revelations like these, yet firmly rooted in scholarly methods and discourse, social reformers' accounts of working-class life stimulated popular interest in the problem of female factory labor.

Others elevated the new social question to the more abstract level of women's "true nature," portraying factory work as destructive of the feminine character and ultimately of the social order. In 1892 Rudolf Martin, barrister at the district court in Crimmitschau, Saxony, investigated the

90. Alfons Thun, *Die Industrie am Niederrhein und ihre Arbeiter: Staats- und sozialwissenschaftliche Forschungen* (Leipzig, 1879), 1:174, here as cited in Herkner, *Die Arbeiterfrage*, p. 27. Herkner notes in his autobiographical reflections that he was highly influenced by Thun's "descriptive approach" to political economy. See Herkner, "Lebenslauf," p. 88.
91. Ernst Dückershoff, *How the English Workman Lives, by a German Coal Miner*, trans. C. H. d'E. Leppington (London: P. S. King, 1899), as cited in Herkner, *Die Arbeiterfrage*, pp. 38–40. Dückershoff's text was published in German in 1898 under the title *Wie der englische Arbeiter lebt?*
92. Herkner, "Zur Kritik und Reform," p. 229.

relation between factory and family life among married female textile workers in his vicinity, to explore the possibility of a legal ban on married women's factory employment. The article, titled "Die Ausschliessung der verheirateten Frauen aus der Fabrik: Eine Studie an der Textilindustrie" (The exclusion of married women from the factory: A case study of the textile industry), was published in the 1896 edition of the distinguished and influential *Zeitschrift für die gesamte Staatswissenschaft*. Martin was evidently the first social reformer to link empirical evidence from factories and working-class neighborhoods with theoretical ideals about women's nature.[93] The textile industry served in his text, as in many previous studies of women's work, as the field of contest over female factory employment.

Martin's article represents a critical juncture in the history of the discourse on women's work, for it shifted the emphasis from protective measures toward consideration of a legal ban on married women's factory employment. In exploring the relation between "sexual character" and social order, Martin drew on the classic work by Ferdinand Tönnies, *Gemeinschaft und Gesellschaft*, first published in 1887. Tönnies, a sociologist and member of the Verein für Sozialpolitik, gave female factory labor a leading part in his analysis of the dissolution of the *Gemeinschaft* (community) and the formation of modern *Gesellschaft* (society).[94] In the "second book" of *Gemeinschaft und Gesellschaft*, Tönnies argued that "the home and not the market, their own or friend's dwelling, and not the street, is the natural seat of [women's] activity." Factory work was inherently incompatible with women's nature:

> As woman enters into the struggle of earning a living, it is evident that trading and the freedom and independence of the female factory worker as contracting party and possessor of money will develop her rational will, enabling her to think in a calculating way, even though, in the case of factory work, the tasks themselves may not lead in this direction. The woman becomes enlightened, cold-hearted, and conscious. Nothing is more foreign and terrible to her original inborn nature, in spite of all later modifications. Possibly nothing is more characteristic and important in the process of formation of the Gesellschaft and the destruction of Gemeinschaft. Through

---

93. Rudolf Martin, "Die Ausschliessung der verheirateten Frauen aus der Fabrik: Eine Studie an der Textilindustrie," *Zeitschrift für die gesamte Staatswissenschaft* 52 (1896): 104–46, 383–418. Martin was born in 1867, worked for some time as a barrister at the Crimmitschau court, and later became a *Regierungsrat* (privy councillor).

94. See Harry Liebersohn, *Fate and Utopia in German Sociology, 1870–1923* (Cambridge: MIT Press, 1987), especially chapter 2, "Ferdinand Tönnies: In Search of Community," pp. 11–35. Also see Richard Terdiman's interesting reflections on Tönnies in his *Present Past: Modernity and the Memory Crisis* (Ithaca: Cornell University Press, 1993), pp. 5–6, 38–44, 235–36.

this development, the "individualism" that is the prerequisite of Gesellschaft comes to its own.⁹⁵

Following Tönnies, Martin asserted that in the course of their "abduction" from the home and domestic workshop, women had become emancipated. But he rendered even more dramatic images of social dissolution than Tönnies when he claimed that women's work would ultimately destroy (*zerrütten*) the social body (*Gesellschaftskörper*).⁹⁶ Martin drew a parallel between the "deterioration of the social body," the body of the family, and the physical bodies of women workers and the children they bore. He argued that women who worked in factories harmed the social body in a twofold manner: first through what they failed to do—that is, provide adequate care for their homes, husbands, and children—and secondly through the mechanical work they performed in the mills. In his view women's neglect was "one main cause of the mortality rates among children, especially among infants . . . it spoils the human material and damages the labor power of the nation."⁹⁷ Here Martin held working women responsible not only for poverty, but also for the moral degeneration of the workers' estate and the physical decline of the human "[raw] material." In posing the fundamental question of *why* women went to work in factories, Rudolf Martin broke with previous assumptions—like those that permeated the inspectors' report of 1878—that women had always worked, whether in home industry or factories, and that their employment was compatible with housework and child rearing.⁹⁸ Concretely, Martin drew on a study conducted by Arthur Geissler, a medical doctor and *Oberregierungsrat* (high privy councilor) in Saxony, who examined the relation between illness and mortality rates among children of female textile workers during the mid-1880s. His study contended that infant mortality in textile towns, where a large percentage of married women worked in factories, exceeded that in all other districts of Saxony.⁹⁹ Geissler's findings, as well as subsequent research on other textile regions, apparently contributed to a growing sense of urgency among opponents of female factory labor that women workers must be enlightened as to the grave consequences of their double burden.

95. Ferdinand Tönnies, *Community and Society* (London: Transaction, 1974), pp. 162, 166.
96. Martin, "Die Ausschliessung," pp. 399–400.
97. Ibid., pp. 399–400, 417–18.
98. According to Jean Quataert, "Source Analysis," p. 115, "To ask . . . why married women worked in factories implied that ideally married women ought not to work, a new assumption, as seen, that accompanied the industrial age."
99. Geissler's apparently unpublished study is cited by Martin, "Die Ausschliessung," p. 404. On Geissler's career as medical doctor and medical statistician, see *Deutsches Biographisches Archiv*, no. 376 (Munich: K. G. Sauer, 1986), pp. 409–10.

While Martin mustered scholarly empirical and philosophical arguments to analyze the social consequences of female factory labor, he also appealed to male workers, whether skilled, well-paid "aristocrats of labor" or unskilled factory hands, who stood to benefit from restrictions on women's factory employment. His investigation established a correlation between lack of skill and low pay among married male workers and their wives' propensity to work in factories. In Crimmitschau, for example, he discovered that 55 percent of married female textile workers had husbands who also worked in the textile mills, most in positions of low skill and status. Martin found that a mere 10 percent of the well-paid self-actor spinners "allowed their wives to work," whereas the wives of one-third of the lesser-paid weavers worked in the mills.[100] Martin could not deny that most of these women worked because their husbands' earnings could not support a family. But he viewed the men who were forced to send their wives to work as themselves indirect victims of women's labor. In his view the competition of cheap female hands, particularly in textile regions, had led to a noticeable reduction of male wages. Thus, for this group of male workers the expulsion of married women should inspire hopes of higher wages. In a similar vein, Heinrich Herkner envisioned limitations on the factory employment of young mothers as not only resulting in higher wages for the workers who remained but also providing jobs for between 200,000 and 300,000 men.[101]

Furthermore, Martin articulated and embraced an ideal of the male breadwinner in his intriguing differentiation between the "false" and the "true aristocracy of labor." Challenging the prevalent view that women commonly sought factory jobs to satisfy their families' basic needs, he argued that skilled workers' wives who worked in factories did so only to satisfy "their own or their family's desire for respectability or luxury." Castigating their husbands as "false aristocrats" who strove to elevate themselves above the mass of common workers by accumulating income and material goods, Martin claimed that they failed to "respect the higher, ideal purity of the family" when they sent their wives into the mills, "even though the family has enough to live on." "Real aristocrats," he asserted, valued the family and the "highest duties" of their wives more than material welfare and insisted on keeping them at home.[102] In Martin's view, banishing skilled workers' wives from factories would have a positive rather than a detrimental influence on their family lives, for it would help to curb their extravagant spending.

"Luxury" or excessive consumption, explicitly attributed to women,

100. Martin, "Die Ausschliessung," p. 386.
101. Herkner, "Zur Kritik und Reform," p. 229.
102. Martin, "Die Ausschliessung," pp. 384–85.

served to demarcate the true and false aristocrats of labor in Martin's text, adhering to the tendency in reformist social thought of the late nineteenth and early twentieth centuries to view consumption and production as opposing realms of social life—to "subordinate consumption to production," as historian Warren Breckman has argued, "to bridle the impulse to consume with the injunction to produce."[103] The tropes of *Putzsucht* (attachment to finery) and *Pflichtvergessenheit* (neglect of duty) helped to construct images of women transformed, estranged from their natural roles and responsibilities by the entry into the public spheres of production and consumption. Social reformers' rhetoric about luxury added a new dimension to the debates about female factory labor: they reproached women workers not only for purportedly earning more than they needed to subsist, but also for their "excessive" consumption of those "superfluous" goods utilized to represent or to remake the self, such as clothing, furnishings, and trinkets, which reformers viewed as incongruous with the social and economic location women workers were to inhabit. The concern with consumption thus opened another front in a contest over morals, for the trappings of luxury and the display of the self suggested sexual desire and seduction. In Heinrich Herkner's terms, "The young [male] factory workers squander their wages on alcohol, whores, and tobacco, while the better-paid segment of the unmarried female workforce finds its gratification in finery," in hats and dresses that "are dreadfully elegant and splendidly colorful."[104] These tropes established an irresolvable opposition between the gender order of the family and its destabilization in the spheres of both production and consumption, an opposition that shaped and supported the social identities of class and citizenship.

The widely read studies by Herkner and Martin furnished the framework for the debate on women's work—the key questions and the controversial solutions—that engaged social reformers during the next decade, as the new course in social policy was dismantled during the mid- and late 1890s. Martin's work in particular inspired numerous subsequent studies and commentaries by social reformers of diverse political persuasions, including members of the Verein für Sozialpolitik like Ludwig Pohle and Robert Wilbrandt and feminist social reformers Henriette Fürth and Elisabeth Gnauck-Kühne.[105] Looking back in 1902, Fürth noted that since

---

103. Warren G. Breckman, "Disciplining Consumption: The Debate about Luxury in Wilhelmine Germany, 1890–1914," *Journal of Social History* 24 (spring 1991): 490.

104. Herkner, *Die Arbeiterfrage*, p. 49. See also Herkner's essay "Über Sparsamkeit und Luxus vom Standpunkte der nationalen Kultur- und Socialpolitik," *Schmollers Jahrbuch* 20 (1896): 1–22.

105. See Herkner, *Die Arbeiterfrage*, pp. 36–40; Ludwig Pohle, *Frauenfabrikarbeit und Frauenfrage: Eine prinzipielle Antwort auf die Frage der Ausschliessung der verheirateten Frauen*

the publication of Martin's article "this question [of married women's factory employment], the critical importance of which is recognized by all sides, has not ceased to engage the world of social policy."[106]

Responding to the gravity of the proposed ban, middle-class feminists and the Social Democratic women's movement rose to defend women's right to work outside the home and to resist the imagery of woman worker as *Schmutzkonkurrentin* (unfair competitors) and *Streikbrecherin* (strikebreakers), objecting vigorously to the construction of married women's factory employment as an "illness of the social body" akin to the endemic economic crises of capitalism.[107] Henriette Fürth, writing in the bourgeois women's journal *Die Frau*, forged links between the plight of middle-class and of working-class women, between the so-called *Ehefrage* (marriage question) for middle-class women and the great outcry against the employment of working-class women in factories. Declaring these protests "ridiculous or at least short-sighted," Fürth pointed out that "marriage does not solve the question of providing for women [*Versorgungsfrage*] once and for all." For women of both classes, she argued, "marriage is the possible, while employment is the necessity." "Why, therefore," she asked, "do they demand the impossible with their clamoring for the expulsion [of women] from their jobs?"[108] Similarly, Elisabeth Gnauck-Kühne, one of the first female social scientists, who founded the women's group of the Evangelical-Social Congress and led it from 1894 until 1899, employed rhetorical strategies that differed markedly from the lamentations and admonitions of her male middle-class counterparts regarding the moral and

---

aus der Fabrik (Leipzig: Von Veit, 1900), pp. 47–48, 113; Robert Wilbrandt, *Die Frauenarbeit: Ein Problem des Kapitalismus* (Leipzig: B. G. Teubner, 1906), pp. 146–47; Henriette Fürth, *Die Fabrikarbeit verheirateter Frauen* (Frankfurt a.M.: Schnappen, 1902), pp. 9–11, 16; Elisabeth Gnauck-Kühne, *Die soziale Lage der Frau* (Berlin: Otto Liebmann, 1895), and idem, *Die deutsche Frau um die Jahrhundertwende: Statistische Studie zur Frauenfrage* (Berlin: Otto Liebmann, 1907).

106. Fürth, *Die Fabrikarbeit*, pp. 9–10. Also see the following articles in *Die Frau: Monatsschrift für das gesamte Frauenleben unserer Zeit*: Henriette Fürth, "Die Ehefrage und der Beruf: Sozialistische Betrachtungen," 4 (1897): 710–18; Alice Salomon, "Frauen-Fabrikarbeit und Frauenfrage," 8 (1901): 193–99; and "Fabrikarbeit und Mutterschaft," 13 (1905–6): 365–69.

107. See, for example, "Das Prinzip der Gleichberechtigung der Frau und der gesetzliche Arbeiterinnenschutz," *Die Gleichheit* 3/19 (1893), and "Eine dringende Aufgabe," *Die Gleichheit* 5/6 (1895).

108. Fürth, "Die Ehefrage," 4 (1897): 717–18. Fürth and Lily Braun were leaders of a minority group within the Social Democratic women's movement that urged solidarity between bourgeois and socialist women. Henriette (Katzenstein) Fürth was born in Giessen in 1861, the daughter of a successful businessman. On Fürth, see Ann Taylor Allen, *Feminism and Motherhood in Germany, 1800–1914* (New Brunswick, N.J.: Rutgers University Press, 1991), pp. 149–50, 156.

spiritual consequences of female factory labor. Concurring with most middle-class reformers that "the destruction of family life among the workers' estate is the darkest moment in our industrial development," Gnauck-Kühne nonetheless emphatically insisted that working mothers and wives should not bear the blame for this destruction. In her hallmark address to the annual meeting of the Evangelical-Social Congress in 1895, she asserted boldly that compared with the women of the "owning classes" who employ servants and maids, "women of the proletarian class manage to fulfill their natural duties in home and family to a greater extent . . . although many of them work for wages in industry or in other sectors' or seasonal employment at the same time and thus must endure an overabundance of work and responsibilities all at once."[109] Mustering a wide range of evidence to buttress her claim that "the theory of the wholesale exclusion of women [from factories] is untenable," she challenged the frequently cited studies of workers' household budgets, arguing that the families of female factory workers were dependent on their wages regardless of how meager their contribution to family income, and pointed out that the suggested alternatives to factory work—home industry or domestic service—were not viable replacements.[110] Both Gnauck-Kühne and journalist Minna Wettstein-Adelt drew on their own ethnographic forays into the "other world" of the factory to repudiate the manifold negative visions of women workers, abundant in reformers' texts. Arguing that women workers' bodies were far from the fragile or delicate organisms reformers imagined, Wettstein-Adelt underscored their tenacity and physical strength in toiling long hours in hot, damp, and dusty shops on meager sleep, poorly nourished and often afflicted with chronic respiratory illness.[111] Gnauck-Kühne energetically contradicted the clichés of women workers as im-

---

109. Elisabeth Gnauck-Kühne's address to the sixth congress of the Evangelischer-Sozialer Kongress in Erfurt on 6 June 1895 was published as *Die soziale Lage der Frau*, pp. 1, 27–28, 31 (cited in note 105). See Baumann, *Protestantismus und Frauenemanzipation*, pp. 89–90, who recounts the extraordinary impression Gnauck-Kühne's speech left on the members of the ESK, mainly because it was the first time a woman publicly addressed a gathering of theologians and social reformers. Also see Kretschmar, *Der Evangelisch-Sozialer Kongreß*, pp. 88–89.

110. Elisabeth Gnauck-Kühne, *Ursachen und Ziele der Frauenbewegung* (Berlin: Lesser, 1893), pp. 14, 52, and idem, *Die soziale Lage der Frau*, pp. 27–28.

111. The term "other world" is from Gnauck-Kühne's speech, *Die soziale Lage der Frau*, p. 25. "It is only one step," she said, "from the woman question of the socially privileged classes to the woman question of the working class, but this one step brings us into another world." Minna Wettstein-Adelt, a journalist and writer who apparently sympathized with the Social Democratic Party, spent several months working incognita in various factories across Germany and analyzed her experiences in her *Drei-ein-halb Monate Fabrikarbeiterin* (Berlin: J. Leiser, 1893). See here pp. 20–21.

moral, promiscuous, and consumed by the quest for luxury and pleasure, calling on the "owning classes" to scrutinize their own "lax morals and pursuit of pleasures, both fine and crude."[112]

Like Henriette Fürth, many of the middle-class feminists who emerged as a crucial force in the milieu of social reform during the 1890s perceived a common cause between middle-class and working-class women, a coalescence of the increasingly controversial woman question of the bourgeois women's movement—the right to employment, education, and the privileges of citizenship—with the social question of female factory labor.[113] Indeed, during the late 1890s the discourses about female factory labor coincided with the "storm of indignation" that swept through the bourgeois feminist movement about the revision of the German civil code and the status it accorded women, in particular with respect to marriage and divorce. At issue in the bitter debates, mass meetings, and circulation of petitions of 1896 and 1897 was the "system of tyrannical and arbitrary domination of women by men"—the legal privileges of men over their wives with respect to divorce, marital property, and parental rights and duties.[114] The 1896 draft of the code decreed, for example, that the "career, employment, and social position of the man forms the foundation for family life," while according to paragraph 1356 it was "a man's duty to provide for his wife" just as "the woman is [both] entitled and obliged to run the common household."[115] More fundamentally, feminists contested the code's conception of the family "as a private realm separate from civil soci-

---

112. Baumann, *Protestantismus und Frauenemanzipation*, p. 92. According to Baumann, Gnauck-Kühne spent the summer of 1894 working in a carton factory in Berlin while completing her study "Die Lage der Arbeiterinnen in der Berliner Papierwaren-Industrie: Eine sociale Studie," *Jahrbuch für Gesetzgebung, Verwaltung und Volkswirtschaft im Deutschen Reiche (Schmollers Jahrbuch)*, n.s., 20 (1896): 25–79, which she conducted under the supervision of Gustav Schmoller.

113. Allen, *Feminism and Motherhood*, p. 145; Wex, *Staatsbürgerliche Arbeit*, pp. 46–47.

114. Gottlieb Planck, *Die rechtliche Stellung der Frau nach dem bürgerlichen Gesetzbuch* (Göttingen: Vandenhoeck und Ruprecht, 1899), p. 1. On the mobilization of bourgeois women against the draft code of 1896, see Allen, *Feminism and Motherhood*, pp. 137–48, and Eve Rosenhaft, "Women, Gender, and the Limits of Political History in the Age of 'Mass' Politics," in *Elections, Mass Politics, and Social Change in Modern Germany: New Perspectives*, ed. Larry Eugene Jones and James Retallack (Cambridge: Cambridge University Press, 1992), p. 152. According to Allen, pp. 137–38, "The Legal Committee [of the Bund Deutscher Frauenvereine] drafted a petition for revision of the Civil Code, which was sent to the Reichstag in 1896 with 25,000 signatures." The petition was rejected, leading to "the most massive protest movement ever organized by a feminist organization." Also see Anna Schulz (Dr. jur.), "Frauenforderungen an die Gesetzgebung," in Schreiber, *Mutterschaft: Ein Sammelwerk*, pp. 672–87.

115. Hermann Jastrow, *Das Recht der Frauen nach dem bürgerlichen Gesetzbuch, dargestellt für die Frauen* (Berlin: Otto Liebmann, 1897), pp. 18–25. On the history of the civil code, see Michael John, *Politics and the Law in Late Nineteenth-Century Germany: The Origins of the Civil Code* (Oxford: Oxford University Press, 1989).

ety," demanding "that the rights of citizenship existing in the public realm be applied also in the home."[116] The mobilization of thousands of middle-class women in opposition to the draft civil code during the late 1890s fueled the feminist opposition on another terrain of law, as many of those who contested the civil code simultaneously sought to shift social reformers' attention from a legal prohibition to enhanced protective labor laws and to deflect the negative images of women workers reproduced in the debates about the legal ban.

Although the texts by Herkner and Martin framed the discourses about female factory labor, middle-class feminists and Social Democratic labor leaders sought to dissect and contest these discourses at several sites during the 1890s. The International Congress for Protective Labor Legislation, which convened in Zurich less than a year after the publication of Martin's study, revealed how divisive this issue had become within the European labor movement. The congress assembled representatives of European workers' associations, "irrespective of political and religious views," who favored "the intervention of the state on behalf of the working class."[117] The German delegation included numerous union leaders and members of Catholic and Social Democratic workers' associations, a few representatives from the Protestant workers' movement, and several members of the Reichstag. Also present as guests (without voting rights) were eminent German social reformers from the left-liberal and Catholic reform spectrum, including Heinrich Herkner, Ferdinand Tönnies, Werner Sombart, Heinrich Brauns, and Paul Göhre, and from the bourgeois feminist ranks, Elisabeth Gnauck-Kühne, Helene Simon, Alice Salomon, and Minna Cauer. Consensus was reached at the congress on many aspects of labor protection such as the Sunday holiday, expanded maternity leave, the eight-hour day for women, and the extension of protective legislation to other sectors of female employment like domestic service and home industry. The otherwise harmonious deliberations were disrupted by the "sharp disonnance" surrounding the debates about married women's work outside the home.[118] Although most delegates agreed that "the factory employment of married women, under current conditions, [posed] an acute

---

116. Allen, *Feminism and Motherhood*, p. 140.

117. See *Amtlicher Bericht des Organisationskomitees, Internationaler Kongress für Arbeiterschutz Zürich* (23–28 August 1897) (Zurich: Kommissionsverlag, 1898), pp. 199–200; the English version is *Circulars of the Organising-Committee, International Congress for Protective Labour-Legislation at Zurich* (23–28 August 1897) (Zurich: Dépot en Commission: Librairie de la Société Suisse du Grutli, 1897), p. 3. For a further report on the conference, see the newspaper of the Deutscher Textilarbeiterverband (DTAV), *Der Textilarbeiter*, 13 (17 May 1901).

118. Pohle, *Frauenfabrikarbeit*, pp. 3–4; *Amtlicher Bericht*, pp. 198–99; for a list of participants at the conference, see pp. 131–49.

danger for the family," their attempts to define and agree upon common remedies for this social problem caused a clash between "two irreconcilable worldviews."[119] The textile industry again was the impetus toward reform as delegates invoked the steady growth of its married female workforce, the high rates of illness and infant mortality in textile workers' families, and the process of "feminization," perceived as particularly acute in weaving during the 1890s, by which the growth of the female workforce caused a steady decline in men's wages or displaced men from their jobs altogether. Margarete Greulich, speaker from the municipal *Arbeitskammer* in Zurich, invoked Rudolf Martin's case study of the textile industry, only to voice emphatic disagreement with the notion of a legal ban. Instead, she suggested, protective measures like the eight-hour day and the establishment of higher pay rates for male workers would serve far more effectively than a legal ban to halt the decline of the working-class family.[120] The dissension over married women workers erupted when Henri Carton de Wiart, delegate of the Belgian Christian Workers' League, proposed a resolution calling for their total exclusion from factories, declaring somewhat dramatically that "women's work, as capitalism has organized it, is an assault [*ein Attentat*] against the laws of physiology, against nature and against the tendency of historical progress. For even those tasks that appear to be the least strenuous for the woman, such as spinning, nonetheless prevent her from fulfilling her natural calling, her social mission."[121] The debate that ensued, one of the few "live"—as opposed to textual—debates about the ban on married women's factory employment, continued for nearly three days. In response to the Christian motion, German Social Democrats Clara Zetkin and Lily Braun staunchly defended women's inviolable right to employment, contending that measures of this nature would only force them back into marginal and more exploitative work in domestic industry or agriculture.[122] Emphasizing the need for expanded protection of women workers, especially in industries where their bodies could be harmed, Zetkin and Braun vigorously rejected the notion of a general ban on married women's factory employment. In a clever inversion of Christian reformers' rhetoric, Braun demanded "in the name of the highest morality" that women be permitted to work in factories, underscoring the social dangers a legal ban would engender—inhibited marriages and rampant concubinage, rising illegitimacy rates, and the certain enlargement of "that tumor of the social body," prostitution.[123] Here

119. Fürth, *Die Fabrikarbeit*, p. 10; *Amtlicher Bericht*, pp. 199–200.
120. *Amtlicher Bericht*, pp. 202–3.
121. Ibid., p. 207.
122. Ibid. The speaker on this occasion was Lily Braun. Also see p. 210, with remarks by Clara Zetkin; pp. 217–19, with remarks by August Bebel.
123. Ibid., pp. 207–8, 210.

Braun utilized the same tropes of morality and sexual danger to argue *against* the ban that Christian reformers had deployed to press *for* the urgent restriction of female factory labor. After long hours of acrimonious debate on the moral and ethical, social and economic implications of Carton de Wiart's motion, the participants rejected it in a vote of 165 to 98, thus concluding the congress on a note of discord that would divide the European labor movement for years to come.[124] For by the late 1890s the Christian unions across Europe had become the most energetic and consistent advocates of a ban on female factory labor, while the leaders of the socialist labor movement assumed the role of guardians of women's right to work, despite the active agitation of many of their own rank-and-file members for curtailment of female factory employment.

As the social question of female factory labor was debated fervently within the labor movement and the milieu of bourgeois social reform—and increasingly across the boundaries between them as well—it also continued to engage the Reichstag during the 1890s. The Center Party, encouraged by the concessions of 1891 regarding the protection of women and minors and propelled by the growing popularity of the SPD with working-class voters, intensified its campaign for restriction of married women's employment soon after the new code became law. Asserting that state social policy had thus far been grounded in a deficient grasp of the workers' conditions, and presuming that social investigation would advance and expand protective legislation, the Center introduced a motion to the Reichstag in 1894 requesting a formal state inquiry, complete with statistical compilations, into the effects of married women's factory work on their families' physical and moral well-being.[125] Although the measure failed in 1894, by the late 1890s the debate and agitation around the issue formed a groundswell of social pressure upon the German state to mediate, intervene, and sanction an official resolution of the new social question. Thus in 1898 the chancellor authorized an official state inquiry into this social problem.

The next year, in each government district of Germany factory inspectors set out to determine precisely how many married women worked outside the home and why they sought wage work, thereby reiterating the question Rudolf Martin had raised a few years earlier. Based on a study far more extensive than the inspectors' report of 1877, including interviews with workers, unions, and employers' associations, with local chambers of commerce, health insurance boards, priests, teachers, doctors, midwives, married women, and male workers, the inspectors were to determine the

---

124. Ibid., p. 220.
125. Otto, *Über die Fabrikarbeit*, p. 177; Ludwig Pohle, "Die Erhebungen," p. 149; Berlepsch, "Neuer Kurs," pp. 431–32; Herkner, "Die Reform der deutschen Arbeiterschutzgesetzgebung," pp. 243–44.

feasibility of a general or industry-specific ban on the employment of married women; of a system of mandatory certificates of eligibility, requiring permission for employment from medical doctors and other authorities; and finally, of the viability of segregating pregnant women and nursing mothers from male workers on the shop floor.[126] Compiling information about the gender, age, and marital status of industrial workers, in addition to data on their place of residence, earnings, number of dependent children, and career patterns (when employment began, was interrupted, or terminated), the state aimed to explore the consequences of eventual restrictions and to determine, for example, whether the loss of a woman's income would significantly affect the family's standard of living and how it would influence male workers, specifically their propensity to marry. Further, they investigated the potential effects of restrictions on German industry and sought to discern whether employers would be able to replace married women with single women or male workers.[127]

The decision of Reichstag and chancellor to investigate the viability of a legal ban on married women's factory employment marked the peak of the campaign for their exclusion from factories and attested to its success in capturing the attention of the state.[128] In signaling its intention to resolve the controversy about this social question, the German state prompted a new surge of discursive interventions from the public sphere, as reformers across the political spectrum sought to mobilize public opinion and to influence the outcome of the inspectors' survey. As it was publicized and debated in the press, "the broadest circles" of the population awaited the results of the inquiry "with great interest."[129] Although many feared it would prepare the groundwork for the expulsion of married women from factory work, others doubted its merits from the outset, pointing to the

126. It is clear from a comparison of the factory inspectorate's two inquiries into female factory employment—the first in 1875 and the second in 1898–99, that in the latter case the inspectors undertook a wider sampling of opinion among the various constituencies, in particular workers and their associations. Because the inspectors' methods of investigation in 1898–99 varied so widely, their reports on the conditions and causes of married women's factory employment are not necessarily comparable across districts and regions. Whereas some inspectors interviewed women workers directly, others asked them to complete questionnaires or relied on secondhand information. See Pohle, "Die Erhebungen," p. 150, for an elaboration of his methodological criticism of the inspectors' survey.

127. Reichsamt des Innern, *Die Beschäftigung verheirateter Frauen in Fabriken, nach den Jahresberichten der Gewerbeaufsichtsbeamten für das Jahr 1899, bearbeitet im Reichsamt des Innern* (Berlin: R. v. Decker, 1901), pp. 1–2. For a sample questionnaire from this survey, distributed in the government district of Aachen, see HStAD, Reg. Aachen, 7862, Formular "Statistik betr. die Beschäftigung verheirateter Arbeiterinnen in Fabriken."

128. Salomon, "Frauen-Fabrikarbeit," pp. 193–99. On Salomon's influential role among feminist social reformers, see Dora Peyser, *Alice Salomon, die Begründerin des sozialen Frauenberufes in Deutschland: Ihr Leben und ihr Werk* (Cologne: Heymanns, 1958).

129. Alice Salomon, "Der Schutz der Frau und des Hauses," *Centralblatt des Bundes Deutscher Frauenvereine* 1 (1 December 1899): 133–34.

haphazard manner of investigation by which inspectors in each district drafted their own questionnaires and themselves determined whom to interview. That some inspectors polled male and female factory workers, workers' associations, and clubs while others relied more upon the views of employers, mayors, and local chambers of commerce generated skepticism about the comparability of the results and prompted reflection on the methods of social investigation.[130]

Attesting to the profound transformation of civil society during the 1890s, the German public formed a new and critical audience for the social investigation of the state, not only intruding on the process of information gathering, but also intervening in the interpretation of the results as they became public.[131] While the inquiry was under way in Württemberg, for example, the Social Democratic union stewards invited the six district factory inspectors to their regional conference, engaging them in lively debate on the "causes and consequences of married women's factory employment." Through this exchange of views and the distribution of a questionnaire on female factory employment to union members in the previous months, the Württemberg inspectors conveyed the impression of conducting "a much less biased and more objective assessment of the views of the workers' organizations than their colleagues in many other states" and gave the organized workers a stake in shaping social policy.[132] Similarly, the inspectors in Aachen assimilated the "experiences and viewpoints" of the Christian-Social Female Textile Workers' League of Aachen into their final report, including the women's own views of how their work harmed their bodies and affected their households and children.[133]

Beyond the organized labor movement, the Social Democratic women's

130. On social-science methods of investigation among German social reformers, see Anthony Oberschall, *Empirical Social Research in Germany, 1848–1914* (New York: Basic Books, 1965), pp. 4–6, 21–23. On the methodology of this particular inquiry, see Salomon, "Der Schutz der Frau," p. 133; Alice Salomon, "Die Reichsenquete über die Fabrikarbeit verheirateter Frauen," *Centralblatt des Bundes Deutscher Frauenvereine* 2 (1 December 1900): 129; "Kann das Verbot der Fabrikarbeit verheiratheter Frauen die Proletarierin dem Heim und den Kindern zurückgeben?" *Die Gleichheit* 9 (1 February 1899): 17–18. On the conduct of the survey in various districts, see the series in *Die Gleichheit:* "Die württembergischen Gewerkschaften und die Frage einer Beschränkung der Fabrikarbeit verheiratheter Frauen, bzw. des gesetzlichen Arbeiterinnenschutzes," 9 (20 December 1899): 203–4; "Die Fabrikarbeit verheiratheter Frauen in Baden," 10 (9 May 1900): 73–76; "Die Berichte der hessischen Fabrikinspektoren zur Frage des Ausschlusses der verheiratheten Frauen aus der Fabrik," 10 (7 November 1900): 178–80; "Die Fabrikarbeit verheiratheter Arbeiterinnen in Preußen," 11 (13 March 1901): 43–46, and 11 (27 March 1901): 50–52.

131. Salomon, "Der Schutz der Frau," pp. 133–34.

132. "Die württembergischen Gewerkschaften," *Die Gleichheit* 9 (20 December 1899): 203. The conference was held on 26 November 1899 in Stuttgart and was attended by twenty-eight male and four female union stewards in addition to the six inspectors.

133. HStAD, Reg. Aachen 7862, pp. 31–32, "Befragung des Christlich-sozialen Textilarbeiterinnenvereins für Aachen und Umgegend."

movement also seized the opportunity of the inspectors' inquiry to undermine and challenge the rhetoric of the opponents of female factory labor as they organized rallies, drafted resolutions, and circulated thousands of leaflets. Castigating Rudolf Martin's study and the Catholic Center Party, which in their view took a similar stance on this issue, the Social Democratic organ for women workers, *Die Gleichheit*, explicated the complex social and economic developments that propelled women into factories, including the erosion of many facets of housework through the growth of the modern consumer economy and the eradication of differences of gender and skill through new textile technology. Challenging Martin's notion that women went to work in factories to satisfy their compulsion toward consumption, the editors of *Die Gleichheit* demanded that reformers draw a precise boundary between dire need and the "humble luxuries" now deemed necessities in a modern consumer society.[134] At the same time, the paper lauded those inspectors who had drawn working wives and mothers themselves into the survey, through either oral interviews or written questionnaires, and whose conclusions were certain to help clarify this boundary.

The journals of the bourgeois women's movement, like the bimonthly *Centralblatt des Bundes Deutscher Frauenvereine*, organ of the Federation of German Women's Associations (BDF), also sought to intervene in the making of public opinion during the inquiry. In one issue of December 1899 Alice Salomon admonished the inspectors and the public to recognize that "driving the woman out of the factory does not mean driving her into the home, for it cannot eliminate the factors that force the woman to leave her home and children behind."[135] That same month the BDF submitted a petition to the Reichstag on behalf of its 50,000 members calling for the extension of protective legislation to home industry, not least to dispel the fantasy of many reformers that female factory workers, once displaced from their jobs, could replace their lost earnings in domestic service or in home industry. On the other side of the issue, political economist Ludwig Pohle, university lecturer and member of the Verein für Sozialpolitik, saluted the proposed ban on married women's factory work as a "genuinely desirable" and "entirely feasible" measure that could be enacted without detriment to any of those affected by it. Based on a detailed analysis of the gender composition of the textile workforce and quoting liberally from Martin's text, Pohle disputed the inspectors' preliminary conclusions that "dire need" drove most wives and mothers into factories. Contending that "dire need is indeed a relative concept," he sug-

---

134. "Das Verbot der Fabrikarbeit," pp. 17–18; "Keine soziale Gleichstellung ohne wirtschaftliche Selbständigkeit," *Die Gleichheit* 9 (15 March 1899): 202; Bauer, *Clara Zetkin*, p. 132.

135. Salomon, "Der Schutz der Frau," p. 134.

gested that most women, whose labor was generally unskilled, could satisfy that need just as well in the agricultural, home industrial, or commercial sectors.[136] Pohle, who would soon break with the "armchair socialism" he had been trained in at the university and in the Verein für Sozialpolitik, warned that female factory workers' children could only constitute "inferior material for human society" given the social and economic circumstances of most workers' families.[137] Emphasizing that even "with the restriction of the woman to the home, our task will not be complete," Pohle proposed obligatory housekeeping courses or a mandatory *hauswirtschaftliches Dienstjahr* (a year's service in housekeeping) that girls would be required to complete before reaching adulthood or receiving permission to marry.[138] At the same time employers' federations, in which textile mill owners were especially vocal on labor protection for women workers, also appealed to the state to consider their interests. In a directive of December 1899 to the Imperial Chancellery, the Federation of Textile Employers from Chemnitz and Vicinity recounted the "alarm that swept through the employers in the textile industry" on receipt of the inspectors' questionnaires with their mention of the proposed prohibition of married women's factory employment.[139]

With this inquiry, initiated in the Reichstag, commissioned by the imperial chancellor, and conducted by factory inspectors, the German state officially recognized the new social question of female factory labor and lent its authority to its resolution. At the same time, the state entered into the discourses that both constituted and attempted to resolve that question. Through the revised labor code of 1891 and the inspectors' inquiry of 1898–99, the expanding welfare state involved itself directly in the task of delineating male and female spheres of work and codifying a sexual division of labor. Indeed, the efforts of the German state to respond to public agitation concerning female factory labor reveal it to be a "permeable arena in which contending social and political forces [interacted],"[140]

136. Pohle, *Frauenfabrikarbeit*, pp. 10, 22–25, 43–48.
137. Born in 1869 and member of the Verein für Sozialpolitik for several years, sometime after the turn of the century Pohle became a vigorous opponent of "socialism of the chair" represented by many of the eminent members of the Verein. On his academic career at the Akademie für Sozial- und Handelswissenschaft in Frankfurt am Main, the University of Frankfurt, and the University of Leipzig and his role as editor of the *Zeitschrift für Sozialwissenschaft*, see Hans Strodel and Gerhard Lüdtke, ed., *Kürschners deutscher Gelehrten-Kalender* (Berlin: De Gruyter, 1925), pp. 779–80; vom Bruch, *Wissenschaft*, pp. 300–304, 307–9, 312–15; Lindenlaub, *Richtungskämpfe*, pp. 12–13, 439–40.
138. Pohle, *Frauenfabrikarbeit*, pp. 107–10.
139. Rheinisch-Westfälisches Wirtschaftsarchiv, Handelskammer Duisburg 20: 43, no. 6 (Gewerbe und Industrie, vol. 1), Verband der Textilindustriellen von Chemnitz und Umgebung, "Schreiben an das Hohe Reichskanzleramt zu Berlin vom 9. Dezember 1899."
140. Geoff Eley, "German History and the Contradictions of Modernity: The Bour-

"a space for struggle and negotiation, rather than an incorporative machine."¹⁴¹ Read in this light, the mobilization for social reform, in particular protective labor legislation, becomes an integral part of what Geoff Eley and David Blackbourn have termed the reshaping of the political nation that occurred during the Wilhelmine period as new structures of public communication changed "the very terms in which political life took place."¹⁴² Labor legislation marks a prime site for analyzing the ways "opposing publics maneuvered for space" within an expanding public sphere, especially during the 1890s when the social reform nexus, a cross section of liberal academics, Catholics, Social Democrats, feminists, and intellectuals, succeeded in dislodging the social question from the sphere of high politics and locating it in the widening arena of public opinion.¹⁴³ Their debates about female factory labor, about the changing relation between women and family, family and state, were critical parts of the discursive and social mobilizations that transformed the relationship between civil society and the state, challenging and ultimately widening the scope of the German welfare state and reconstituting the "social."¹⁴⁴ Thus the case of labor legislation affirms not only the porosity of the German welfare state, but also the importance of discursive struggle as a particular means of recasting it. The debates about women's work during the 1890s took place at a critical historical juncture, which Richard Terdiman, in a laudable attempt to historicize the concept of discourse, has termed the "classic [historical] moment" of the nineteenth century, when "the techniques for assuring discursive penetration," as well as those of symbolic subversion—newspapers, new disciplines and bodies of knowledge such as statistics and management—"solidified themselves." As social discourses became the locus of "increasingly conscious struggle," Terdiman argues, they also brought into existence a newly influential category of citizens able to uti-

---

geoisie, the State, and the Mastery of Reform," in Eley, *Society, Culture and the State in Germany*, p. 94.

141. Robert Gray, "Medical Men, Industrial Labour and the State in Britain, 1830–1850," *Social History* 16 (January 1991): 21, and idem, "The Language of Factory Reform," p. 172.

142. Eley, "Is There a History of the Kaiserreich?" p. 11. Recent scholarship by Eley, Rüdiger vom Bruch, and Young-sun Hong has taken the existence of a vital welfare state as a basis for critique of the authoritarian model of political rule in German social-science history. See, for example, Blackbourn and Eley, *Peculiarities of German History*; vom Bruch, *Weder Kommunismus*; and Young-sun Hong's work in progress, "The Ambiguities of Modernity and the Contradictions of the Welfare State: Poor Relief, Charity and Welfare Reform in Germany, 1830–1933."

143. Geoff Eley, "Nations, Publics, and Political Cultures," p. 325; Eley, "German History and the Contradictions of Modernity," p. 89.

144. On the significance of the 1890s in German history, see Eley, *Reshaping the German Right*, and idem, "Is There a History of the Kaiserreich?" pp. 11–15.

lize and administer the new mechanisms.¹⁴⁵ Finally, this history of the discursive terrain of labor legislation also complicates the functionalist view of the German welfare state, which explains its origins and outcomes in terms of its ability to legitimate and secure the conditions of capitalist reproduction by uncovering the diverse coalitions, the claims of professionalism and expertise, the assertion of scientific knowledge, and the contests about gender that shaped state social policy during the 1890s.¹⁴⁶

---

145. Richard Terdiman, *Discourse/Counter-discourse: The Theory and Practice of Symbolic Resistance in Nineteenth-Century France* (Ithaca: Cornell University Press, 1985), pp. 44, 66, 74.

146. Here I am responding to contentions regarding the welfare state's legitimation of capitalism by Geoff Eley, "Social Imperialism in Germany: Reformist Synthesis or Reactionary Sleight of Hand?" in *From Unification to Nazism: Reinterpreting the German Past*, ed. Geoff Eley (Boston: G. Allen and Unwin, 1986), p. 161, and Rosenhaft and Lee, "State and Society in Modern Germany," p. 24. Formative for my thinking on this issue, in addition to the interesting reflections in Rosenhaft and Lee, pp. 29–30, were Mary Lynn Stewart, *Women, Work, and the French State: Labour Protection and Social Patriarchy, 1879–1919* (Kingston: McGill-Queen's University Press, 1989); Michael Hanagan's review of Stewart's book, *International Labor and Working-Class History* 39 (spring 1991): 98–100, and Frank Mort, *Dangerous Sexualities: Medico-moral Politics in England since 1830* (London: Routledge, 1987), p. 6.

5

Social Policy, Body Politics: Factory Labor, Maternity, and *Volkskörper*, 1900–1914

The turn of the century marks a watershed in the history of the social question as the German state set out to mediate the controversy over female factory labor. The final report of the factory inspectors' findings, compiled and published by the Ministry of the Interior in 1901, subdued the campaign for a ban on married women's factory work while setting the legislative agenda and framing the discursive contests about the issue until the eve of the First World War. Rather than breaking new legislative ground, the amended and expanded labor code of 1908 remained bounded by the 1891 protective law, only partial fulfilling the factory inspectors' recommendations of 1901. Yet in the discursive arenas of social reform, female factory labor was cast in terms of a new and more explicit polarization between working mothers and male breadwinners, sometimes referred to as *Familienväter* (family fathers), who now were to be protected from the effects of female competition in the labor market: "wage cutting," erosion of skill hierarchies, or even job displacement. The competition between the sexes was to be defused and the boundaries between the spheres of male and female labor were to be fixed through a two-pronged strategy of restricting female factory labor and improving its conditions. Key to both tasks was melding factory work and domesticity, limiting the hours women worked so they could fulfill their duties as mothers and wives, and ameliorating conditions that endangered the health as well as the morality of female workers and their children. Outside the workplace reformers sought to promote the refinement of working women's domestic skills, which were widely regarded as crucial to the preservation of the working-class family. Domesticity acquired new meanings, however, as motherhood and the vitality of the *Volkskörper* (people's body) became essential elements of the German quest for empire, in which the public—bourgeois social reformers as well as popular nationalist associations—became increasingly invested.

The German state had sought definitive resolution of the social question of female factory labor when it commissioned the factory inspectors' inquiry in 1898–99. Yet Germany's imperial desires opened up new terrains of contest about women's work outside the home as reformers became increasingly preoccupied with national fertility and infant health during the late 1890s and after the turn of the century. Widening the scope of the social question from the factory to the (imperial) nation, reformers explored the links between the conditions of work and the conditions of (national) reproduction, between female factory labor and the declining national birthrate.[1] The milieu of social reform was transformed as nationalism and racial hygiene displaced ethics and religion as its motivating force and as conflicts between national cultures, empires, and races supplanted the divisions of class that had cast the social question as a *sittliche Kulturfrage* since the middle of the nineteenth century.[2] Social policy as an expanded set of citizenship rights, as a key link between the nation-state and its citizens, had given German workers a stake in the state, and reformers hoped it would now help to negotiate their consent to the politics of empire and the militarization of politics. Eminent social reformers helped kindle the national fervor for naval expansion during the late 1890s, even while many remained aloof from the right-wing populism of the Navy League and similar patriotic assocations.[3] Many of those who regarded the naval policies as both a reflection and a logical consequence of Germany's accelerated development from agrarian to industrial state

---

1. On the declining birthrate see John E. Knodel, *The Decline of Fertility in Germany, 1871–1939* (Princeton: Princeton University Press, 1974), and James Woycke, *Birth Control in Germany, 1871–1933* (London: Routledge, 1988). On its perception as a national crisis see Paul Weindling, *Health, Race and German Politics between National Unification and Nazism, 1870–1945* (Cambridge: Cambridge University Press, 1989), pp. 10, 90, 189, 203, 242, and Anna Bergmann, "Die rationalisierten Triebe: Rassenhygiene, Eugenik und Geburtenkontrolle im deutschen Kaiserreich" (Dissertation, Free University of Berlin, 1988).
2. This shift was observed by Werner Sombart in his essay, "Ideale der Sozialpolitik," *Archiv für Soziale Gesetzgebung und Statistik* 10 (1897): 15. Sombart deplored the fact that some reformers had redefined the goals of social policy as "preserving and advancing the fitness of our race."
3. On the "naval professors," see Geoff Eley, *Reshaping the German Right: Radical Nationalism and Political Change after Bismarck* (Ann Arbor: University of Michigan Press, 1991), pp. 85–98; Rüdiger vom Bruch, *Wissenschaft, Politik und öffentliche Meinung: Gelehrtenpolitik im Wilhelminischen Deutschland (1890–1914)* (Husum: Matthiesen, 1980), pp. 66–68. Vom Bruch refers to 270 actively engaged "naval professors," many of whom were also prominent social reformers.

held out hope that naval prowess and the acquisition of empire might complete the task of forming a cohesive and unified nation, a task social reform had yet to achieve.[4] As social reform associations became increasingly enmeshed in the webs of nationalist naval, army, and colonial leagues and as the popular associations that aimed to combat tuberculosis, venereal disease, and infant mortality attracted and united feminists, left-liberal reformers, and revisionist Social Democrats, a broad hygienicist consensus emerged about the health and vigor of the nation, its mothers, and its children. Uniting science and social politics, after the turn of the century the rhetoric of social reform resounded with biological analogies and metaphors.[5]

The growing alarm regarding declining fertility rates placed working women's bodies at the center of a hygienicist, natalist enterprise of identifying and eradicating social pathologies, all of which could be attributed directly or indirectly to the moral or bodily deficiencies of women who worked outside the home. As popular eugenicist and hygienicist associations mobilized on behalf of nation and empire, family and race within the expanded civic sphere, the female body became a more explicit focus of the social question, subject to both renewed moral vigilance and new standards of social and reproductive hygiene. The official and popular attention to female factory labor as pathology and to the female body as a productive and reproductive organ extended the purview of the state into new realms of empire as well into private domains that had heretofore been impervious to state power and changed the material and discursive contexts in which female factory labor was debated, in which the social was reconstituted.[6]

The proliferation and popularity of hygienicist and eugenicist organizations, which attained levels of popular mobilization that were nearly as high as those of the right-wing nationalist pressure groups (the Navy League, Army League, Pan-German League, and German Colonial Association), attest to the continued expansion of the public sphere as a site where opposing publics vied for space, while also forging a rhetorical consensus between Left and Right around national health and social hygiene.[7]

---

4. On this stance among social reformers, see vom Bruch, *Wissenschaft*, pp. 66–68, and Eley, *Reshaping the German Right*, p. 89.

5. Weindling, *Health, Race and German Politics*, p. 39; vom Bruch, *Wissenschaft*, pp. 66–80. On the connections between social reform and German militarization, see Geoff Eley, "Social Imperialism in Germany: Reformist Synthesis or Reactionary Sleight of Hand?" in *From Unification to Nazism: Reinterpreting the German Past*, ed. Geoff Eley (London: G. Allen and Unwin, 1986), pp. 154–67, and Karl-Erich Born, *Staat und Sozialpolitik seit Bismarcks Sturz: Ein Beitrag zur Geschichte der innenpolitischen Entwicklung des deutschen Reiches, 1890–1914* (Wiesbaden: Franz Steiner, 1957), p. 51.

6. Weindling, *Health, Race and German Politics*, pp. 175, 184.

7. Ibid., p. 25. On the conflicts between opposing publics within German civil society,

Indeed, "the great furor that seized the people of the German empire" at the start of the new century, when the issues of naval rearmament, population policy, and women's emancipation formed a dense web of overlapping social-political questions, resulted in "agitated gatherings" that, in the words of Lujo Brentano, attracted "not only those we recognize as regular speakers and participants at such meetings, but also those citizens who seldom look beyond their immediate circle of interests, who now leave behind their familiar pubs" to debate questions about the "future of the fatherland" that "are usually left to the experts to decide."[8] Of growing importance among the ranks of both citizens and experts at these assemblies were members of the bourgeois feminist movement, who launched what British reformer Havelock Ellis termed "a new phase of the woman movement . . . based on the demands of woman as mother" after the turn of the century.[9] The political education of its female intelligentsia had included the debates about protective labor legislation and the revision of the civil code during the late 1890s, in which the social and national significance of motherhood, the links between women's rights as mothers and as workers, had been crucial.[10] As social policy discussions about female factory labor became increasingly embedded in social hygienicist and eugenicist campaigns to improve motherhood, feminist intellectuals propagated their own visions of how factory work might be made compatible with motherhood. Amid the growing anxieties about the physical and moral degeneration of *Volkskörper*, nation, and race, the female intelligentsia assumed a vital role in both assigning and contesting the new symbolic and social importance of motherhood and the female body. At the same time, they raised new claims to citizenship, to the enjoyment of full *Bürgerrechte* (rights of citizens) based on women's contribution to the state as mothers.[11]

---

see Geoff Eley, "German History and the Contradictions of Modernity," in *Society, Culture and the State in Germany, 1870–1930*, ed. Geoff Eley (Ann Arbor: University of Michigan Press, 1995), p. 89.

8. Lujo Brentano, *Die Schrecken des überwiegenden Industriestaats* (Berlin: Leonhard Simion, 1901), p. 5.

9. As cited in Ann Taylor Allen, *Feminism and Motherhood in Germany, 1800–1914* (New Brunswick, N.J.: Rutgers University Press, 1991), p. 173.

10. Ibid., pp. 147, 173, and Richard J. Evans, *The Feminist Movement in Germany, 1894–1933* (London: Sage, 1976), p. 36. Evans argues that this female intelligentsia occupied a position somewhere between the left wing of the liberals and the right wing of the Social Democrats.

11. Maria von Stach, "Mutterschaft und Bevölkerungsfrage," and Adele Schreiber, "Mißbrauchte und unwillkommene Mutterschaft," both in *Mutterschaft: Ein Sammelwerk. Für die Probleme des Weibes als Mutter*, ed. Adele Schreiber (Munich: Albert Langen, 1912), pp. 194, 200–202.

Languages of Mediation: The Inspectors' Final Report

The factory inspectors' final report undermined the campaign for a legal ban, discounting many of its main tenets and dampening its often inflammatory overtones. The bureaucratic language of mediation, its purported impartiality, and the inspectors' careful juxtaposition of testimony from the myriad subjects of the survey contrasted with the visions of social disorder and disintegration in the texts by social reformers like Heinrich Herkner, Rudolf Martin, and Ludwig Pohle. The first task of their social investigation was evidently to document and substantiate the perceived expansion of the married female factory workforce, nearly half textile workers. The inspectors' final report made evident for the German public the expansion of the female labor market during the recent rapid periods of industrial growth.[12] Despite their disparate, even incomparable, methods of investigation across the various government districts, the inspectors reached remarkably similar conclusions. Overall, they analyzed the expansion of married women's factory employment as an "irreversible consequence of the material reality among the workers," notably the failure of wages to keep pace with the rising cost of living. In reply to the central question of why married women worked, nearly all the inspectors concurred that most did so out of economic need, despite the distinct conditions in their individual districts.[13] Probing the multivalent meanings of "economic need" as described by employers, mayors, doctors, or the workers themselves, the inspectors understood it as an ambiguous and relative term that in some cases denoted dire poverty and in others signified workers' yearnings for respectability and a standard of living beyond bare subsistence. In marked contrast to the work of reformers like Herkner, Martin, and Pohle, the inspectors' report of 1901 implicitly endorsed this striving as legitimate and reasonable.[14]

12. Ludwig Pohle, "Die Erhebungen der Gewerbeaufsichtsbeamten über die Fabrikarbeit verheirateter Frauen," *Jahrbuch für Gesetzgebung, Verwaltung und Volkswirtschaft* 25 (1901): 156. In many textile towns most of the married female factory workers were employed in textile mills. Of the married female factory workforce in the Münster district 93 percent were textile workers; in the Aachen and Düsseldorf districts, 60 percent. Hauptstaatsarchiv Düsseldorf (HStAD), Jahresberichte der Königlichen Preußischen Gewerbeaufsichtsbeamten (JBdKPG) 1899: Aachen, pp. 600–602; Düsseldorf, pp. 510–11; Münster, p. 370.

13. HStAD, JBdKPG 1899: Düsseldorf, pp. 510–11, 521; Münster, p. 370; Minden, pp. 390–91; Cologne, p. 567; Aachen, pp. 600–602, 610; Reichsamt des Innern, *Die Beschäftigung verheirateter Frauen in Fabriken, nach den Jahresberichten der Gewerbeaufsichtsbeamten für das Jahr 1899 bearbeitet im Reichsamt des Innern* (Berlin: R. von Decker, 1901), pp. 149–52, 217–19. The inspector from Alsace was the only one to advocate the legal exclusion of married women from factories.

14. The inspector from Münster, for example, pointed out that the woman's factory job

Attending to company hiring policies as another important factor in the steady increase of married women in the factory workforce, the inspectors discovered that factory owners attempted to surmount critical labor shortages during economic upswings by "utilizing all means at their disposal to entice the workers' wives to accept employment in their factories," including hiring men only if they agreed to allow their wives to work in the same mill.[15] Beyond the urgent need to fill jobs, the inspectors found that many employers sought to recruit married women as *Stammarbeiter* (long-term, stable "core workers") because they were mature, reliable, proficient, and consistent compared with younger single workers.[16] The Association of Wool Manufacturers of Aachen, for example, justified the high rate of employment of married women in its districts by explaining that they helped create and preserve order and a positive moral climate in the mills, offering "inexperienced young girls reliable support against the various temptations manifest [in the factories]."[17] Thus textile employers in particular responded with indignation and dismay to the prospect of a legal ban on married women's work, declaring that it would render an "utterly devastating blow [to industry], depriving it of the element that was most reliable and earnest and of the highest moral and intellectual standing."[18] Contending that the wide replacement of married women with men or single women was impossible, factory owners pointed out that men would be unsuitable for the many jobs that required women's dexterity: "Women

---

gave her family the "opportunity to live better, to enjoy a few extras, or to save money" or to care for elderly parents. HStAD, JBdKPG 1899: Münster, pp. 370–71. Also see Alice Salomon, "Frauen-Fabrikarbeit und Frauenfrage," *Die Frau* 8 (January 1901): 196, who recounts similar views on the part of the factory inspector from Baden, Dr. Wörrishofer, a recognized authority on women's working conditions.

15. Pohle, "Die Erhebungen," pp. 166, 177. Pohle cites the inspectors from the districts of Meissen and Plauen, who reported that this practice was common among textile employers in their districts. This practice also became the target of a strike in 1910 in Krefeld's Baumwollspinnerei AG, as indicated in HStAD, Reg. Düss. 24706, p. 151.

16. Reichsamt des Innern, *Die Beschäftigung*, p. 246. The inspector from Barmen described married women as indispensable to local industry because they had greater experience and diligence than younger single female workers. Although the favorable view of married women workers appears to have been prevalent among most employers, the Düsseldorf inspector noted that some 10 percent of textile mill owners in his district, most of whom belonged to the Association of Catholic Industrialists, refused to hire married women as a matter of principle. See HStAD, JBdKPG 1899: Düsseldorf, p. 514.

17. Reichsamt des Innern, *Die Beschäftigung*, p. 115. See also HStAD, JBdKPG 1899: Aachen, p. 605; Düsseldorf, p. 514.

18. Reichsamt des Innern, *Die Beschäftigung*, pp. 247–48; see also HStAD, JBdKPG 1899: Aachen, p. 615. According to one employer's view, "If the imperial government should decide to prohibit the work of married women in factories, it would be shorter and simpler to prohibit factories altogether and to maintain both workers and employers at the expense of the state."

workers are more suited than men for many jobs. Indeed, in the textile industry numerous tasks cannot be carried out by men . . . because they do not possess and will not acquire the deftness and dexterity or other qualities these jobs demand. This is *women's work*, which men regard, as such, as beneath their dignity."[19] Concurring with this view, the inspectors also pointed out that neither was "the single woman . . . able to replace the married woman fully, for [the latter] has acquired the unique ability to perform complicated tasks through years of practice and experience," whereas many of the young single women left their jobs before they reached their highest level of dexterity and productivity.[20] Furthermore, based on interviews with female workers, the inspectors concluded that work in the mills represented a continuous rather than an aberrant part of their lives, for most had worked since their late teens and had grown accustomed, even attached, to their jobs and their coworkers.

Although conceding that factory work was harmful to the health of women workers and their young children, the inspectors' accounts failed to evoke the dramatic images of dissolution of family and society that permeated the studies by Martin and Herkner. Although the inspectors confirmed relatively high infant mortality rates in textile towns where large numbers of married women worked in factories, their findings served at the same time to assuage fears about the neglect or abandonment of children of working mothers, confirming that 55 to 65 percent of them stayed with relatives, 25 to 30 percent were in the care of baby-sitters or in nurseries, and 10 to 20 percent stayed at home without supervision.[21] Similarly, based on their interviews with doctors, health insurance boards, and factory owners, the inspectors determined that working conditions presented no greater danger to married women than to single women or to men. Rather, they attributed the higher rate and longer duration of illness among married women to the combined burdens of factory work, housework, and mothering, and in particular to the physical strain of pregnancy

---

19. Rheinisch-Westfälisches Wirtschaftsarchiv (RWWA), Handelskammer Duisburg (HK Duisburg) 20: 43/6, Verband der Textilindustriellen von Chemnitz und Umgebung, "Schreiben an das Hohe Reichskanzleramt zu Berlin von 9. Dezember 1899."

20. Reichsamt des Innern, *Die Beschäftigung*, pp. 246–47. See also RWWA, HK Duisburg, Verband der Textilindustriellen von Chemnitz und Umgebung, "Schreiben an das Hohe Reichskanzleramt zu Berlin von 9. Dezember 1899."

21. HStAD, JBdKPG 1899: Düsseldorf, p. 518; Aachen, p. 606; Pohle, "Die Erhebungen," pp. 200–203; and Ludwig Pohle, *Frauenfabrikarbeit und Frauenfrage: Eine prinzipielle Antwort auf die Frage der Ausschliessung der verheirateten Frauen aus der Fabrik* (Leipzig: von Veit, 1900), p. 104. Pohle cites the inspector for the Breslau district, who reported higher infant mortality among infants of female textile workers, generally absent from home all day, than among female employees of other industries in which women were allowed to interrupt their working day to care for their infants.

and childbirth.²² Although several inspectors observed that pregnant factory workers experienced many more complications in childbirth—above all, miscarriage or premature birth—than housewives or unemployed women, a doctor whose clients were mainly female textile workers listed varicose veins, constipation, maladies of the uterus, and irregular bleeding as frequent consequences of overwork before or after childbirth. The inspectors confirmed that many health insurance companies failed to pay women for lost wages during maternity leave and thus "compel[led] them to return to work as soon as possible after childbirth."²³ In sum, the inspectors agreed that in the environment of the factory the exigencies of the "female organism," specifically its "sexual conditions"—menstruation, pregnancy, and nursing—were seldom taken into account in allocating or regulating work.²⁴ Thus the final report of the Ministry of the Interior echoed the nearly unanimous view of doctors, health insurance boards, and workers' associations that female factory workers were in urgent need of expanded leave both before and after childbirth.

From their singular vantage point as mediators, at the center of a complex web of conflicting concerns—between employers and workers, social reformers and state bureaucracies, workers and *Bildungsbürger*, women and men—all but one inspector concluded that the proposed exclusion of married women from factory work was impractical in several respects.²⁵ However desirable from the "humane standpoint" or in the interest of "family life, child rearing, and domesticity," the inspectors' firsthand experience among those the ban would affect most profoundly convinced them of its potential human costs. Declaring in near unanimity that in the event of a legal ban a married woman "would be unable to find alternative employment with comparable remuneration" without incurring similar harm to "her household, her health, or her moral well-being," the inspectors maintained that the measure would cause "profound economic distress" among the workers.²⁶ Many families, they feared, would be forced to turn

22. HStAD, JBdKPG 1899: Düsseldorf, pp. 518–20; Münster, p. 372. The Barmen inspector reported that the rate of illness was 15 percent higher and the average illness 70 percent longer among married women than among unmarried women. See also Reichsamt des Innern, *Die Beschäftigung*, p. 96.

23. HStAD, JBdKPG 1899: Aachen, pp. 608–9; Reichsamt des Innern, *Die Beschäftigung*, pp. 96–99, 210. A key demand of the Christian Union of Female Textile Workers (Christlicher Textilarbeiterinnenverband) in Aachen was for the expansion of pregnancy protection to ten weeks total: four weeks before birth and six weeks after.

24. Reichsamt des Innern, *Die Beschäftigung*, pp. 98–99.

25. Rose Otto, *Über die Fabrikarbeit verheirateter Frauen*, Münchener Volkswirtschaftliche Studien, vol. 104 (Stuttgart: Cotta, 1910), p. 125. HStAD, JBdKPG 1899: Aachen, pp. 610–14; Reichsamt des Innern, *Die Beschäftigung*, p. 150.

26. Reichsamt des Innern, *Die Beschäftigung*, p. 226.

to the public relief system, for male workers often earned too little to support their families. Furthermore, interviews with male workers suggested that many would be reluctant to marry or to start a family if they could not count on their future wives' earnings as a reliable part of the family budget, leading the inspectors to warn that a legal ban was likely to have deleterious effects on workers' morality, compelling couples to live together in "concubinage" and dramatically increasing illegitimate births.[27] They also considered the potential ban equally detrimental to German industry, which would hardly find enough adult male or single female workers to replace the married women.

In explicating the complex factors that drew married women into factories—economic need, endemic labor shortages, rising cost of living, employers' hiring policies, and the workers' own desire for respectability and comfort—the inspectors shifted the blame for the ills of female factory labor away from working women and toward a complex process of social transformation. Their explorations of the consequences of female factory labor for working-class families—infant mortality, neglect of children, and the bodily afflictions of pregnant women and working mothers—cast a vision of women workers doing their best in desperate circumstances. It deflected the sensationalist evocations of delinquent or spendthrift mothers and wives that abounded in social reformers' texts, thus relaying powerful testimony on behalf of enhanced protective legislation and shifting the burden of remedial action to the state.[28] In the view of feminist Alice Salomon, the factory inspectors' investigation banished "the threatening phantom" that had "persecuted women struggling for economic independence and social equality," namely, "the reactionary demand to ban women from factory work" that was "born in Center Party circles, supported by well-meaning social reformers," and that "gained significance and became increasingly dangerous for women" in the course of the 1890s. With the intervention of the state and the launching of the inspectors' inquiry, however, "the ship had found safe harbor." For in Salomon's view, "women were certain to find greater understanding for their economic needs and difficulties among these men of the practical world" than in the realm of high politics that remained remote from what it sought to protect: the woman worker and her family life.[29]

27. HStAD, JBdKPG 1899: Aachen, p. 614; Cologne, p. 567. Reichsamt des Innern, *Die Beschäftigung*, pp. 231–33.
28. Salomon, "Frauen-Fabrikarbeit," p. 194, refers to the dominant image of the "putzsüchtige, pflichtvergessene Fabrikarbeiterin" in the flood of texts by opponents of female factory labor. Factory inspectors themselves often used these terms to describe single female workers. See, for example, Reichskanzler-Amt, *Ergebnisse der über die Frauen- und Kinderarbeit* (Berlin: Heymanns, 1878), p. 45.
29. Salomon, "Frauen-Fabrikarbeit," pp. 193–94. Constituting the "threatening phantom" were the writings of Rudolf Martin, Clara Elizabeth Collet (whose English works on

As a student of political economists Schmoller, Wagner, and Alfred Weber, a pioneer social worker, and founder of the *soziale Frauenschulen*, whose reform activities consistently centered on working-class women, it is perhaps not surprising that Salomon's prophecy was accurate in several respects.[30] In defining spheres of male and female labor, the inspectors tacitly sought to legitimate married women's factory employment in the eyes of its opponents, while also proposing a practical alternative to prohibition. Observing that a legal ban would be of little benefit to the many families whose female members could not keep house properly, the inspectors adopted at least one of the recommendations of reformers like Martin and Pohle, calling on the individual German states—as opposed to private charity groups, employers, or local and city governments—to institute obligatory housekeeping schools for female factory workers, where young women fourteen to sixteen would learn to cook, sew, and care for infants. "This would be of greater benefit to the welfare of the entire population of workers," its authors claimed, "than the disputable proposal to banish married women from factories altogether." One inspector even suggested that fewer women would seek factory jobs if they were given the opportunity to acquire domestic skills and to discover the "joy and love of their true calling as housewives and mothers."[31] In the promotion of *Häuslichkeit* (domesticity), the inspectors located the solution of the social problem of women's wage labor in both the factory and the home, demarcating specifically female spheres within both arenas, inscribing both with domestic qualities, and thus attempting to render them compatible.

Although some of these conclusions echo the factory inspectors' findings of some twenty years earlier, by the turn of the century the social and political contexts of state social investigation had undergone profound transformation. The inquiry of 1898–99, by contrast with that of 1877, was shaped, debated, and contested in the public sphere; that the final report bears its imprint attests to the attention the inspectors accorded to that public. A more comprehensive investigation than the inquiry of 1877,

---

female factory labor were translated into German), and Ludwig Pohle; Salomon termed the last "Tendenzschriften gegen die Sozialdemokratie." See Pohle, *Frauenfabrikarbeit*; Rudolf Martin, "Die Ausschließung der verheirateten Frauen aus der Fabrik: Eine Studie an der Textilindustrie," *Zeitschrift für die gesamte Staatswissenschaft* 52 (1896): 104–46, 383–418, and Clara E. Collet, *Report by Miss Collet on Changes in the Employment of Women and Girls in Industrial Centres* (London: Eyre and Spottiswode, 1898).

30. Dora Peyser, *Alice Salomon, die Begründerin des sozialen Frauenberufes in Deutschland: Ihr Leben und ihr Werk* (Cologne: Heymanns, 1958), pp. 23, 38–39, 65. Salomon, along with other members of the Verein zur Errichtung von Arbeiterinnenheimen, also founded a residence for working women in Berlin in 1898.

31. HStAD, JBdKPG 1899: Aachen, p. 607; Reichsamt des Innern, *Die Beschäftigung*, pp. 251–52; and Pohle, *Frauenfabrikarbeit*, p. 110.

it sought to distill, even if unsystematically, the views of those most directly affected by protective and restrictive measures—women workers. Although the 1901 report also identified female workers' domestic skills as a crucial means of improving conditions in both family and factory, domesticity had acquired new meanings as it became bound up with "quality motherhood," which emerged as a solution for the social question of female factory labor during the first decade of the twentieth century.[32] Although *Sittlichkeit* and *Unsittlichkeit* (morality and immorality) and working-class sexuality were prevalent themes in the 1877 inquiry as well as in Reichstag debates and reformers' texts of the 1870s and 1880s, the inspectors' final report concluded that the employment of women "gives no occasion to moral misgivings," a finding some reformers found remarkable in light of the declining birthrate in Germany.[33] Instead, morality remained a subtext in the report, underwriting the inspectors' concern with health and hygiene, specifically with the effects of factory work on pregnancy, motherhood, and the care of children.

The factory inspectors' report marked a decisive defeat for the supporters of a legal ban on married women's factory employment, imparting closure to the debates about a legal ban that had inflamed the working-class and bourgeois publics during the 1890s. Confirming reformers' fears and perceptions that the industrial landscape of Germany had been irreversibly altered and the labor market permanently transformed, the report assigned a new legitimacy to married women's employment in factories. In particular, it sanctioned their work in "women's industries" like textiles, which were highly dependent on female labor, thus reaffirming the sexual division of labor within and between industries. While establishing the discursive framework for continued debate about female factory labor, the inspectors opted to defuse rather than deepen the sense of crisis surrounding family, gender, and labor relations.

Codifying Women's Work in the "Age of the Machine"

The factory inspectors' final report opened new terrains of contest about female factory labor, both legislative and discursive, as reformers drew on their findings to revive campaigns for expanded labor protection, and as

32. Anna Davin, "Imperialism and Motherhood," *History Workshop* 5 (1978): 53.
33. Heinrich Brauns, *Der Übergang von der Handweberei zum Fabrikbetrieb in der niederrheinischen Samt- und Seidenindustrie und die Lage der Arbeiter in dieser Periode*, Staats- und sozialwissenschaftliche Forschungen, 25, no. 4 (Leipzig: Duncker und Humblot, 1906), pp. 218–19.

they contended with the inspectors' visions of a more harmonious relation between factory work and motherhood. With the emergence of a public audience for official state inquiries and deliberations of social policy, reformers had acquired new significance as mediators and experts. Following publication of the inspectors' final report, social reformers and feminist activists embraced this role and, in a new series of essays, aspired to explicate its implications for a wider public.[34] The resolution outlined in the report, its delineation of explicitly gendered spheres of work, and its attempt to reconcile factory employment with female nature prompted polemical debates among reformers about its meanings in the everyday world of workplace and union struggle, about its implications for the "micropolitics" of the shop floor as well as the political identities of class and citizenship. With the banishment of married women to the home now a remote prospect, many reform advocates strove to import the home into the workplace, to instill domestic skills in female factory workers and to supplant the imagery of disorder, the specter of feminization and disintegration of gender roles, with a new order founded on a firm division between the male breadwinner and the female "secondary" earner. Underpinning this new order was a consensus among male reformers—Social Democratic, Catholic, conservative, and left-liberal—among inspectors, industrialists, and male trade union leaders about the natural basis of this division and about the rightful claim of male breadwinners to higher earnings, skill, and status. Thus, between the turn of the century and the First World War the social question of female factory labor was recast and rewritten as the emphasis shifted to the male breadwinner wage, which emerged as both an object of and a solution to the social question. As long as the female factory workforce continued to expand and to undercut men's wages, the argument went, men's incomes would remain below subsistence level in many industries. Yet if male workers were able to earn a living wage, their wives would not be forced to seek employment in the mills. The polarization between the *Familienväter* and the "secondary earners," which was codified in the handbooks, encyclopedias, and texts of influential reformers during the first decade of the century, laid the blame for social misery at the feet of working women, even if in different rhetori-

34. Feminist reformer Helene Simon, for example, criticized the inspectors' yearly reports for their small editions, inaccessibility, and abbreviated content. In several of her articles she sought to make their results available to a broader audience. See, for example, Helene Simon, "Jahresberichte der preußischen Gewerberäte," *Neue Zeit* 20 (1901–2): 472; "Jahresberichte der badischen Fabrikinspektoren" and "Der Jahresbericht der hessischen Gewerbeinspektoren für das Jahr 1900," both in *Neue Zeit* 19 (1900–1901): 596–99, as cited in Sabine Klöhn, *Helene Simon (1862–1947): Deutsche und britische Sozialreform und Sozialgesetzgebung im Spiegel ihrer Schriften und ihr Wirken als Sozialpolitikerin im Kaiserreich und in der Weimarer Republik* (Frankfurt a.M.: Peter Lang, 1982), pp. 203–4. See also Pohle, "Die Erhebungen."

cal terms than had the budget studies of the 1880s. It also led reformers to draw sweeping conclusions about women workers' political inclinations and identities. The 1911 edition of the *Handwörterbuch der Staatswissenschaften*, for example, defined "female labor and the woman question," in the following terms:

> Even when women devote themselves completely to working for a living, the main occupation for most women, by contrast to men, is and remains marriage and the family.... The promise of future marriage dampens their interest in occupation and earnings [*Beruf und Erwerb*]. Because women take a completely different view of their work than men, they are more inclined to those jobs that do not require skill or training.... The woman usually has to satisfy only her own individual needs with her earnings, whereas men's wages and earnings must normally cover the needs of an entire family.... That women's view of their employment differs completely from that of men means that the female sex inherently demonstrates much less interest in union activities than male workers.[35]

Robert Wilbrandt, a self-defined "socialist among the social reformers" of the Verein für Sozialpolitik, gave a series of popular lectures in Berlin in the spring of 1905 on the topic "Women's Work in the German Economy." Wilbrandt did not approach this social problem in the "statistical-descriptive terms" typical of academic social reformers; rather, he cast it as a still "urgent problem that has been bestowed on us by capitalism," through which "the woman has been drawn into work of all kinds, even into those that ravage her body, her soul, her morality, and her modesty— in the underground mines, in the sultriness of the spinning mills . . . by day and by night, [she is] drawn into all the places where a woman does not belong, into all kinds of excessive burdens and agonies."[36] Seeking to explicate the ideal ameliorative goal, Wilbrandt exhorted reformers and the public to work toward "a diminished and restricted pursuit of employment

---

35. This entry, "Weibliche Arbeit und Frauenfrage," was composed by Julius Pierstorff, political economist and member of the Verein für Sozialpolitik. See *Handwörterbuch der Staatswissenschaften*, 3d ed. (Jena: Gustav Fischer, 1911), 8:700.

36. Wilbrandt's lectures were compiled and published as a study titled *Die Frauenarbeit: Ein Problem des Kapitalismus* (Leipzig: B. G. Teubner, 1906). Here see foreword and p. 8. On Wilbrandt in the Verein für Sozialpolitik, see Dieter Lindenlaub, *Richtungskämpfe im Verein für Sozialpolitik: Wissenschaft und Sozialpolitik im Kaiserreich vornehmlich vom Beginn des "Neuen Kurses" bis zum Ausbruch des 1. Weltkrieges (1890–1914)* (Wiesbaden: Franz Steiner, 1967), pp. 366–69. Wilbrandt was born in 1876 and received his doctoral at Tübingen in political economy. One of the founders of the Deutsche Gesellschaft für Soziologie, he served at the University of Berlin as a lecturer during the completion of these works and accepted an appointment as a professor at the University of Tübingen in 1908. The term "socialist among the social reformers" is Wilbrandt's own self-description, as recounted by Lindenlaub, p. 367.

that accommodates the calling of motherhood" rather than a legal ban. Indeed, female employment was to conform to the notion that women intrinsically were *bedürfnisloser* (had fewer needs) than male workers and hence aspired only to earn a wage that sufficed for a single individual, whereas most men strove to procure a "family wage."[37] Wilbrandt even suggested an affinity of interests between employers and married women, who "do not have the same interest in a job or profession [*Berufsinteresse*] as the man" and are therefore "extremely difficult to organize." Indeed, in his view married women were "born strikebreakers": "Because they are no longer in that young and vibrant age, rather are more established and because of their children, are more submissive, they are willing to perform every difficult and dirty job that most young girls would refuse. Because they need only to supplement their husbands' wages, it is easy to hire them at lower wage levels."[38] From his vantage point as a Social Democrat, Edmund Fischer, Reichstag deputy and member of the reformist faction of the party, raised somewhat different objections to female factory labor. In an article of 1905 that sparked intense controversy in socialist circles, he repudiated the "emancipation" of women through factory labor—a cornerstone of socialist theory—as a notion fundamentally "opposed to the female nature and human nature in general" and suggested that female factory employment was a "socially unhealthful, harmful," even if transient occurrence, "an ill of capitalism that will disappear when capitalism is abolished."[39]

Also scrutinizing female factory labor through the lens of male workers' needs and status, in 1908 the factory inspectors decided to append to their yearly reports a supplementary inquest into the extent and gravity of *Verdrängung* (displacement of male workers by female workers) in each district, seeking to determine whether the female factory workforce, again mainly in the textile industry, had expanded at the expense of men. Much in the vein of their 1901 report, the inspectors again registered the anxieties of male workers and reformers about the growth of the female factory workforce and sought to assuage them by deploying the tools of social investigation. Although they determined that the percentage of

37. Wilbrandt, *Die Frauenarbeit*, pp. 43–44, 61–62; see also his *Die Weber in der Gegenwart* (Jena: Gustav Fischer, 1906), which was published concurrently with *Die Frauenarbeit*.
38. Wilbrandt, *Die Frauenarbeit*, pp. 58, 84–85.
39. Edmund Fischer, "Die Frauenfrage," *Sozialistische Monatshefte* 9, no. 1 (1905), reprinted in *Sozialismus und Frauenfrage*, ed. Wally Zepler (Berlin: P. Cassirer, 1919), pp. 19, 24. Despite Fischer's aberration from the SPD's official stance on the woman question, one of his critics later observed that he was widely perceived as speaking for many Social Democratic workers: "We have known all along that many party comrades think like Fischer and most of them also share his feelings." See Oda Olberg, "Polemisches über die Frauenfrage und Sozialismus," in Zepler, *Sozialismus*, pp. 44–45.

women had risen in some branches of textile production and in the cigar industry, the inspectors in the Rhineland also pointed to the significant numbers of men who had abandoned their jobs in these branches for better-paying positions in the expanding iron and metal sectors.[40]

The attempts of reformers to codify female factory workers as *bedürfnislos* and to depict the purported "feminization" and "displacement" of male workers as "temporary pathological symptoms of the social body" established a circular mode of explanation by which "female nature" became both the cause and the outcome of women workers' low wages and skill levels. They also prompted spirited and incisive responses from prominent feminists—liberal, socialist, and Christian. Social Democrat Emma Ihrer, for example, issued a scathing attack on Fischer's argumentive article, contesting the primary definition of women workers in terms of motherhood and marriage and disparaging his notion of feminine nature: "Motherhood," she asserted, "is just as little a life goal as fatherhood is."[41] In her view the prerequisite for the stable family life that Fischer idealized was not "the woman's renunciation of her job and the devotion of her mental and physical energy to the household alone . . . but rather the cooperation of all elements, including above all the man, especially in raising the children." Transposing Fischer's arguments, Ihrer asked why women should value wifely and motherly duties so highly when most men regarded them with contempt:

> Today no one imparts to housework in the single household the same value as to even the simplest and lowest-paid employment. That is definitely one of the factors that increasingly encourage women to look for employment in addition to their housework. Men of all social strata view this one-dimensional, repetitive housework as useless and even somewhat contemptible: "What work do you women have to do anyway?" [they ask]. . . . It is not only the lowliest elements among the proletarian women who are discontent, in the long run, with being good little domestic pets who aim only to attend to the comfort of other family members without taking part themselves in higher, larger tasks involving the progress of the human race.[42]

Admonishing male reformers to recognize that female factory labor was far from a temporary or aberrant outgrowth of industrial development,

40. HStAD, JBdKPG 1899: Reg. Düss., pp. 403–5; Reg. Münster, pp. 299–301; Reg. Minden, pp. 316–17; Reg. Arnsberg, pp. 332–33; Reg. Cologne, pp. 432–33; Reg. Aachen, pp. 471–73.
41. Emma Ihrer, "Die proletarische Frau und die Berufstätigkeit," *Sozialistische Monatshefte* 9, no. 1 (1905): 448. Also see, for example, Marie Lischnewska, "Die handwerksmässige und fachgewerbliche Ausbildung der Frau," *Kultur und Fortschritt* no. 315/316 (1910): 6.
42. Ihrer, "Die proletarische Frau," p. 444.

feminist Marie Lischnewska pointed out that women's work is "a necessary part of national production that is steadily expanding." Nor was marriage a "lifetime calling" that could guarantee long-term provision, she argued, again drawing parallels between the circumstances of bourgeois and working-class women and pointing to the fact that half of the working women over age fifty were widowed or single.[43] Middle-class feminists, many of whom belonged to the circles of academic social reformers around Brentano, Schmoller, and Max and Alfred Weber, affirmed the right of married women to work without obscuring the tedious and exploitative nature of most factory jobs or concealing the fact that most women, given the choice, would prefer not to spend their lives in the mills.[44] Marianne Weber, for example, defended the employment of those married women who "derived greater benefit from their jobs, in a mental and moral sense, than they lose by relinquishing or curtailing their duties within the domestic domain." Social Democrat Henriette Fürth claimed that many women valued the economic independence they had gained through their factory jobs, and Wally Zepler outlined a type of female work identity: "The years of working at a job before marriage left their mark on the female soul, awakened forces in her that family life cannot satisfy, that spur her on to uninhibited further development."[45]

In a moment of dissent from the chorus of male social reformers, the eminent left-liberal Friedrich Naumann challenged his peers in 1903 to contemplate the ways the woman question had been redefined in "the age of the machine," claiming that "nothing would be more mistaken than to believe that the woman is, based on her nature, either cheap or only in

43. Lischnewska, "Die handwerksmässige- und fachgewerbliche Ausbildung," pp. 5–6. Elisabeth Gnauck-Kühne makes a similar point in her *Die deutsche Frau um die Jahrhundertwende: Statistische Studie zur Frauenfrage*, 3d ed. (Berlin: Otto Liebmann, 1914), p. 103. This text was first published in 1904.
44. Alice Salomon, "Fabrikarbeit und Mutterschaft," *Die Frau* 13 (1905–6): 365; Henriette Fürth, *Die Fabrikarbeit verheirateter Frauen* (Frankfurt a.M.: Schnappen, 1902), p. 49; Helene Simon, *Der Anteil der Frau an der deutschen Industrie nach den Ergebnissen der Berufszählung von 1907*, Schriften des ständigen Ausschusses zur Förderung der Arbeiterinneninteressen 2 (Jena: Gustav Fischer, 1910), pp. 56–60. In addition to Fürth, Salomon, and Simon, this group of female social reformers included Marie Bernays, Elisabeth Gnauck-Kühne, Rosa Kempf, Marie Lischnewska, and Rose Otto. On the role of female intellectuals within the German *Bildungsbürgertum*, see Claudia Huerkamp, "Frauen, Universitäten und Bildungsbürgertum: Zur Lage studierender Frauen, 1900–1930," in *Bürgerliche Berufe: Zur Sozialgeschichte der freien und akademischen Berufe im internationalen Vergleich*, ed. Hannes Siegrist (Göttingen: Vandenhoeck und Ruprecht, 1988), pp. 200–222.
45. Quotations are from Marianne Weber, lecture, "Beruf und Ehe," as cited in Salomon, "Fabrikarbeit und Mutterschaft," p. 365; and Wally Zepler, "Vorrede," in Zepler, *Sozialismus und Frauenfrage*, p. 15. Also see Fürth, *Die Fabrikarbeit*, p. 49; Lischnewska, "Die handwerksmässige- und fachgewerbliche Ausbildung," p. 6; and Simon, *Der Anteil der Frau*, pp. 56–60.

need of modest income [*bedürfnislos*]."⁴⁶ Maintaining that historically specific circumstances had once justified relegating women to the home, Naumann asserted that current historical conditions—the development of technology and the declining significance of housewifely labor to the national economy—had now propelled them into the labor market. He also chastised male workers for viewing the woman question through the deceptive lens of "female competition," which obscured recognition of the fact that during the economic upswing of the 1890s, when female factory labor had expanded most rapidly, the supply of male workers had been thoroughly depleted and German employers had been forced to hire foreigners to relieve the endemic labor shortages.⁴⁷

Propelled into the debates about the legal ban at the turn of the century, the female intelligentsia now stepped forward to demand job training for women workers instead of housekeeping schools, as well as equal pay for equal work.⁴⁸ Mobilizing against the discrepancy between the *Fortbildungsschulen* for young men and those for young women, middle-class feminists seized the revision of the labor code as the occasion to launch an energetic campaign on behalf of skill training for young female workers, seeking to extend the rights of local and city governments to impose the *Fortbildungszwang* (compulsory attendance at continuation schools), on young women as well as young men. Since most of the continuation schools for girls, they said, "almost wholly disregard specialized job training for women and concentrate instead on educating women workers for their future '*Frauenberuf*,'" the reformers aimed to provide female workers with instruction in subjects relevant to their occupations, along with general subjects like German, geography, and mathematics, which young men routinely studied.⁴⁹ Marie Baum, feminist and factory inspector in Baden,

46. Friedrich Naumann, "Die Frau im Maschinenzeitalter," lecture given 21 November 1903 in Munich, reprinted in Gerritsen Women's History Microfilm Collection, Stanford University Library, pp. 7–8. Naumann (1860–1919), an eminent liberal, was the founder of the National Social Union (1895), through which he sought to create a combined working-class and middle-class political party based on a synthesis of nationalism, social reform, and Protestantism. On Naumann, see Harry Liebersohn, *Fate and Utopia in German Sociology, 1870–1923* (Cambridge: MIT Press, 1987), pp. 89–90; Joan Campbell, *Joy in Work, German Work: The National Debate, 1800–1945* (Princeton: Princeton University Press, 1989), pp. 66–69; and Gerhard A. Ritter, *Der Sozialstaat: Entstehung und Einwirkung im internationalen Vergleich* (Munich: R. Oldenbourg, 1989), pp. 73–74.

47. Naumann, "Die Frau im Maschinenzeitalter," pp. 14–15. Otto, *Über die Fabrikarbeit*, p. 151.

48. Gnauck-Kühne, *Die deutsche Frau*, p. 133. See Klöhn, *Helene Simon*, p. 136, and Evans, *Feminist Movement*, p. 47. Sabine Klöhn refers to the consolidation of a female intelligentsia between 1902 and 1908, promoted by improved educational and professional opportunities for middle-class women.

49. Erna Barschak, *Die Idee der Berufsbildung und ihre Einwirkung auf die Berufserziehung im Gewerbe* (Leipzig: Quelle und Meyer, 1929), pp. 140–41. See also Lischnewska, "Die

used her firsthand experience on the shop floor to explicate the formidable barriers to including women in the *Fortbildungszwang*, including the firm conviction of male workers and mill owners alike that the temporary and secondary nature of female factory employment made skill training superfluous for women workers.[50] Alice Salomon outlined the aspiration of feminist reformers with respect to female skill training: "Women, like men, should be trained and provided with qualifications for jobs, whether or not they practice this occupation continuously or even at all. Women's love for a job, their loyalty and devotion to it, must be nurtured, so that during the time of their employment the entire person is engaged and so that they can lay claim to the earnings of a whole person."[51] Reformers' efforts to open the continuation schools to women, to prevent them from being confined to "the lowest and dullest rung of industrial labor" by widening prevalent definitions of female skill and enhancing their prospects for upward mobility within factory hierarchies, culminated in the founding of the Verband für Handwerksmässige und Fachgewerbliche Ausbildung der Frau (Association for Craft and Specialized Industrial Training of Women) in 1909.[52] Yet even within the Verband the precise boundaries of female skill proved to be a source of intense controversy as Baum and others foresaw a purposeful dual instruction for working women in both homemaking and occupational skills whereas others like Marie Lischnewska vehemently opposed attempts to merge the two or to substitute training in household skills for the acquisition of crucial occupational skills.[53]

Furthermore, in the discursive realm beyond the arena of policy debates, feminist reformers not only considered the needs of the "female soul" but

---

handwerksmässige und fachgewerbliche Ausbildung," p. 27; Zentralverband Christlicher Textilarbeiter Deutschlands, "Gegen die Pflichtfortbildungsschule," *Textilarbeiterzeitung* 16 (7 March 1914): 67.

50. Marie Baum, "Die gewerbliche Ausbildung der Industriearbeiterin," *Kultur und Fortschritt* 107 (1907): 6–9. See also Baum's interesting reflections on her work as a factory inspector in her *Rückblick auf mein Leben* (Heidelberg: F. H. Kerle, 1950), pp. 90–150.

51. Alice Salomon, *Die Ursachen der ungleichen Entlohnung von Männer- und Frauenarbeit* (Leipzig: Duncker und Humblot, 1906), p. 60.

52. Lischnewska, "Die handwerksmässige und fachgewerbliche Ausbildung," p. 14; Anne Schlüter, "Die Entwicklung weiblicher Lehrverhältnisse Anfang des 20. Jahrhunderts aufgezeigt am 'Verband für handwerksmässige und fachgewerbliche Ausbildung der Frau in Deutschland,'" in *Die Ungeschriebene Geschichte: Historische Frauenforschung* (Dokumentation des 5. Historikerinnentreffens in Vienna, April 1984) (Vienna: Wiener Frauenverlag, 1985), pp. 259–67. Members of the Verband included Marie Lischnewska, Josephine Levy-Rathenau, Marie Elisabeth Lüders, Prof. I. Jastrow, Alice Salomon, Marie Baum (factory inspector from Baden), Elisabeth Gottheiner, and Helene Simon.

53. Baum, "Die gewerbliche Ausbildung," pp. 8–9; Lischnewska, "Die handwerksmässige und fachgewerbliche Ausbildung," pp. 14, 29; Rosa Kempf, "Das Interesse der Industrie an der Ausbildung der weiblichen Arbeiterschaft," *Kultur und Fortschritt* 492, no. 4 (1914): 9.

also confronted the power of norms and ideologies about gender to structure relations and divisions of labor and to shape women's experience on the shop floor and within the labor movement. Rosa Kempf, member of the Verein für Sozialpolitik, student of Schmoller, and author of an empirical study on the life of young factory girls in Munich, considered "the opinions of organized workers" to be an especially influential *lohnbildender Faktor* (formative factor of wages) because "the higher the regard for women's work, the greater is the possibility that women workers will advance in a material sense."[54] Similarly, Alice Salomon's study of the origins of the unequal compensation of male and female labor posited a notion of wages that were shaped less by an actual difference in productivity than by the commonly held assumption that men work to support families whereas women's earnings merely supplement family incomes. In her view male labor leaders, who negotiated wage levels based on their own perceived needs, had a decisive role in determining the price of men's labor and in establishing separate wage standards for male and female workers.[55] The crucial issue, according to both Salomon and Kempf, was that women were generally endowed with a lower "social value" than men, a problem that could be solved only by a "transformation of the ideas and viewpoints of the broader society on this entire question of women's work."[56]

In the course of these debates, bourgeois and socialist feminists affirmed that despite occasional futile protests of conservative reformers, the question of the legal ban on married women's factory had long been settled by the very realities that could be observed in everyday life—by the recognition that "no woman is so foolish as to take on the hardship of a factory career if she were not forced to do so by her economic situation."[57] Following the factory inspectors' report, feminist reformers shifted the focus away from how women's factory labor might be eradicated, reformulating the question to ask how such employment might be organized to render it compatible with the "main accomplishment of the woman—motherhood—the production of human beings" and how social policy and social work might be recast to create favorable conditions for that production.[58] Emphasizing that women "had always worked much beyond their accom-

54. Kempf, "Das Interesse der Industrie," p. 5. Also see her monograph *Das Leben der jungen Fabrikmädchen in München*, Schriften des Vereins für Sozialpolitik 35 (Leipzig: Duncker und Humblot, 1911).
55. Salomon, *Die ungleiche Entlohnung*, pp. 18, 41.
56. Ibid., pp. 22, 60.
57. Rosa Kempf, "Die Industriearbeiterin als Mutter," and Adele Schreiber, "Mißbrauchte und unwillkommene Mutterschaft," both in Schreiber, *Mutterschaft: Ein Sammelwerk*, pp. 205, 241.
58. Stach, "Mutterschaft und Bevölkerungsfrage," p. 189; Kempf, "Die Industriearbeiterin als Mutter," p. 241.

plishments as mothers," combining productive and reproductive labor, feminist reformers noted that the dualism between a woman's calling as mother and her paid employment was a fictitious one that originated in the separation of home and workplace, the formative moment of both middle-class and working-class formation that "had consigned mothers to economic dependency and technological backwardness."[59]

In attempting to rewrite the social question of women's factory labor, female reformers deployed and intertwined the rhetorics of both individual rights and maternalism. The ideology of maternalism underwrote many of their texts, exalting "women's capacity to mother and extending to society as a whole the values of care, nurturance, and morality,"[60] thus endowing motherhood with a symbolism so powerful that "often class differences disappeared, along with the realities of working-class life."[61] Motherhood, family, and child welfare, in the view of feminists like Lily Braun, represented the "great unifying concerns" of women across the barriers of class, religion, and party politics. In Braun's view motherhood was "indeed the culmination of womanhood, and no so-called emancipation will put an end to the slavery of women as long as one pregnant woman groans under her burden, as long as one new mother must strain her exhausted body at work, or as long as one neglected baby cries for its mother."[62]

Indeed, a maternalist consensus underpinned the new coalitions of this decade in which bourgeois feminists joined forces with Catholic and liberal workers' advocates and the Association for Social Reform to remedy the impaired *Familienfähigkeit* (family capacity) of working women.[63]

---

59. This argument was made most powerfully by Fürth, *Die Fabrikarbeit*, pp. 5–7; Lily Braun, as cited in Allen, *Feminism and Motherhood*, p. 162; and Gertrud Woker, "Naturwissenschaftliche Streiflichter über das Problem Mutterschaft und Beruf," in Schreiber, *Mutterschaft: Ein Sammelwerk*, p. 221.

60. On the combination of maternalism with individual rights, see Allen, *Feminism and Motherhood*, p. 166, and on maternalism in the making of the welfare state see Seth Koven and Sonya Michel, "Womanly Duties: Maternalist Politics and the Origins of Welfare States in France, Germany, Great Britain and the U.S., 1880–1920," *American Historical Review* 95 (October 1990): 1078–79, 1091–92.

61. Davin, "Imperialism and Motherhood," p. 53.

62. Lily Braun, *Die Frauenfrage: Ihre geschichtliche Entwicklung und wirtschaftliche Seite*, as cited in (and translated by) Allen, *Feminism and Motherhood*, p. 156. Also see pp. 208–13 for discussions of the notion of "social motherhood," as well as Peyser, *Alice Salomon*; Christoph Sachße, *Mütterlichkeit als Beruf: Sozialarbeit, Sozialreform und Frauenbewegung, 1871–1929* (Frankfurt a.M.: Suhrkamp, 1986), pp. 113–14, and idem, "Social Mothers: The Bourgeois Women's Movement and German Welfare-State Formation," in *Mothers of a New World: Maternalist Politics and the Origins of Welfare States*, ed. Seth Koven and Sonya Michel (London: Routledge, 1993), pp. 136–58, 141–42.

63. On *Familienfähigkeit*, see Elisabeth Gnauck-Kühne, *Einführung in die Arbeiterinnenfrage* (Mönchen Gladbach: Volksverein, 1906), pp. 30–31. An example of a coalition of this type is the Ständiger Ausschuß zur Förderung der Arbeiterinnen-Interessen (Standing

Around the turn of the century, for example, the Social Democratic women's newspaper *Die Gleichheit* shifted its coverage away from class struggle and toward amelioration of the specific everyday problems of female workers that could be rectified under capitalism, focusing its efforts on abbreviated working hours to preserve women's *right* to be mothers and housewives while working.[64] As Anna Freier has argued in her study of *Die Gleichheit*, the paper reinforced rather than contradicted or contested the prevalent assumption that a woman's first duty was as a housewife and mother, particularly in its supplement *Für unsere Mütter und Hausfrauen* (For our mothers and housewives), which began publication in 1905.[65] Although the double burden figured in the narratives of *Die Gleichheit* as one main source of "proletarian misery," it effaced all discussion of sexual exploitation or sexual emancipation, questions that would become acute on the eve of the First World War during the virulent debates within the party about the "birth strike."[66]

As both maternalism and social reform became increasingly enmeshed in eugenicist programs and discourses during the first decade of the twentieth century, feminist reformers, thoroughly infused with the languages and paradigms of the wider milieus they belonged to, also began to cast their arguments in new terms, emphasizing women's contributions to *Menschenproduktion* (production of human beings), to the reproduction of the race. This focus on women's biological functions, rights, and duties helped to forge bonds across the boundaries of class and to link the disparate struggles to balance motherhood with paid work, expanding labor protection for female factory workers while seeking to defeat the marriage

---

Committee for the Advancement of Women Workers' Interests), which was founded in 1906 by Margarethe Friedenthal and included members of the Zentralverein für Arbeiterinnen-Interessen, the Bureau for Social Policy, the BDF, the Verband der Erwerbstätigen Katholischen Mädchen und Frauen, and the Verband Deutscher Gewerkvereine (Hirsch-Duncker).

64. Anna E. Freier, *"Dem Reich der Freiheit sollst Du Kinder gebären": Der Antifeminismus der proletarischen Frauenbewegung im Spiegel der "Gleichheit," 1891–1917* (Frankfurt a.M.: Haag und Herchen, 1981), pp. 27–36.

65. Freier, *"Dem Reich der Freiheit,"* pp. 32–41; Richard J. Evans, "Politics and the Family: Social Democracy and the Working-Class Family in Theory and Practice before 1914," in *The German Family: Essays on the Social History of the Family in Nineteenth- and Twentieth Century Germany*, ed. Richard J. Evans and W. R. Lee (Totowa, N.J.: Croom Helm, 1981), pp. 264–65. In seeking to "bind the proletarian woman to her natural calling of housewife," Freier argues, "the supplement could hardly be distinguished from a bourgeois women's paper."

66. On the birth strike debates in the Social Democratic Party, see Anneliese Bergmann, "Frauen, Männer, Sexualität und Geburtenkontrolle: Zur 'Gebärstreikdebatte' der SPD 1913," in *Frauen suchen ihre Geschichte*, ed. Karin Hausen (Munich: Beck, 1983), pp. 81–108.

ban that barred female teachers and civil servants from motherhood while employed.[67]

Maternity and the Ten-Hour Day

Amid the renewed debates kindled by the factory inspectors' report of 1901 and its aftermath, Catholic, Social Democratic, liberal and conservative, feminist, and paternalist reformers founded new organizations and launched new campaigns to expand labor protection for working mothers, widening the scope of both labor protection and social reform. The Catholic Center Party, which still favored a legal ban in principle after publication of the inspectors' report, settled on a quest to extend maternity leave, to shorten the workday for married women to six hours, and to make employment contingent on a series of certificates attesting to married women's medical fitness, economic need, and access to adequate supervision for their children.[68] The Social Democratic parliamentary delegation responded to the inspectors' report by presenting a new bill to the Reichstag in 1901 that foresaw the implementation of the ten-hour day, proposed to bar women from work considered "harmful to the female organism," and to grant pregnant women six to eight weeks of paid maternity leave.[69] In the meantime the German Textile Workers' Union, affiliated with the SPD, debated the implications of the inspectors' final report for its members, male and female, in the pages of the union weekly *Der Textilarbeiter*, mobilizing their findings to issue a rebuttal to Rudolf Martin's arguments of several years earlier. Later that year the weekly of the Christian textile union, *Der Christliche Textilarbeiter*, likewise ran a series of articles on women's work in the textile industry that reiterated many of Martin's sentiments but refrained from endorsing the demand that married women be categorically excluded from factory employment.[70]

The left-liberal social reform spectrum was reinvigorated in January 1901 when liberal reformers, frustrated by the stagnation in state social

67. Allen, *Feminism and Motherhood*, pp. 164, 168–69.
68. Franz Hitze, *Die Arbeiterfrage und die Bestrebungen zu ihrer Lösung* (Berlin: Commissionsverlag der Germania, 1900), p. 80; Pohle, *Frauenfabrikarbeit*, pp. 108–9; Otto, *Über die Fabrikarbeit*, p. 179.
69. The SPD party congress of 1902 also placed maternity insurance on the regular agenda for discussion. Ignaz Zadek, "Arbeiterinnenschutz," *Sozialistische Monatshefte* 5, no. 1 (1901): 163–65, and Henriette Fürth, "Die Lage der Mutter und die Entwicklung des Mutterschutzes in Deutschland," in Schreiber, *Mutterschaft: Ein Sammelwerk*, p. 286.
70. See the series on "Arbeiterinnenschutz" in Deutscher Textilarbeiterverband (DTAV), *Der Textilarbeiter* 13 (17 May 1901) and 13 (7 June 1901), and the series on "Die Organisation der Arbeiterinnen" in *Christlicher Textilarbeiter* 3 (16 November 1901), 3 (30 November 1910), and 3 (7 December 1901).

policy during the Stumm era and aspiring to revive the initiatives of the new course, convened to found a new social reform association, the Gesellschaft für Soziale Reform (Association for Social Reform, or GfSR) under the leadership of Freiherr von Berlepsch, who had guided the new course as Prussian minister of commerce and trade. Although the Association soon shared many eminent members with the still vital Verein für Sozialpolitik—Schmoller, Brentano, Sombart, Hans Delbrück, Franz Hitze, and Max Hirsch, to name a few—the new legion of reformers aimed to extend its influence significantly beyond the ranks of intellectuals and professionals into the organized labor movement, to eschew theoretical debate in favor of practical agitation among the public, and armed with its input, to advise and inspire the legislature and the bureaucracy on matters of social policy.[71] As the Verein für Sozialpolitik shifted its focus toward empirical research after the turn of the century and its members and their students fanned out across Germany's diverse industrial landscapes to study the conditions of home and factory industry, the origins of *Berufsethos* and *Berufswahl* (work ethic and occupational choice) or the "psychophysics of work," the Association and its journal *Soziale Praxis* (Social Practice) took up the Verein's former mantle as the "combat patrol for social reform."[72] Densely intertwined from its founding with both the Evangelical-Social Congress and the leadership of the Catholic Volksverein as well as the Verein für Sozialpolitik, most members and officials of the Association for Social Reform were prominent political and religious leaders, former ministers, state bureaucrats, and academic social reformers.[73]

71. *Soziale Praxis* 10 (28 January 1901): 534; 10/15 (10 January 1902): 357. Ursula Ratz, *Sozialreform und Arbeiterschaft: Die "Gesellschaft für Soziale Reform" und die sozialdemokratische Arbeiterbewegung von der Jahrhundertwende bis zum Ausbruch des Ersten Weltkrieges* (Berlin: Colloquium, 1980), p. 18. Berlepsch's slogan was "everything for the workers and as much as possible through them." On the division of labor between the Verein and the Gesellschaft für Soziale Reform, see vom Bruch, *Wissenschaft, Politik und öffentliche Meinung*, pp. 339–43.
72. Max Weber, "Zur Psychophysik der industriellen Arbeit," *Archiv für Sozialwissenschaft und Sozialpolitik* 28 (1909): 219–77, 719–61; 29 (1909): 513–42; Marie Bernays, *Auslese und Anpassung der Arbeiterschaft der geschlossenen Großindustrie: Dargestellt an den Verhältnissen der Gladbacher Spinnerei und Weberei AG zu Mönchen-Gladbach im Rheinland*, Schriften des Vereins für Socialpolitik 133 (Berlin: Duncker und Humblot, 1910); Alfred Weber, "Das Berufsschicksal der Industriearbeiter: Ein Vortrag," *Archiv für Sozialwissenschaft und Sozialpolitik* 34 (1912): 375–405. Bernays's study was part of a larger project on "Auslese und Anpassung der Arbeiterschaft"; hers is the only one that focuses primarily on female workers.
73. Ratz, *Sozialreform und Arbeiterschaft*, pp. 13–17, 48, 67, 161, 248. The GfSR had some 673 members on its founding in 1901 and by 1906 had reached its highest membership of 1,523. The journal *Soziale Praxis*, founded in 1897, became its organ in 1901. Throughout the first decade of the twentieth century it had between 2,000 and 2,600 subscribers. See also Campbell, *Joy in Work*, pp. 55–59.

Although the Association initially opened its ranks to women, a few weeks after its founding the police in Berlin implemented the Prussian Law of Association that barred women from political assemblies, thus prohibiting feminist reformers Helene Simon, Alice Salomon, and Else Jaffé–von Richthofen from joining the group or even attending its meetings.[74] By the middle of the decade, however, it had forged close ties to the Christian trade union movement, while the Social Democratic trade unions maintained a relationship of cautious distance and limited cooperation with the Association.

Regarded with indignation and animosity by the organized employers, especially the Central Association of German Industrialists (CVDI) for its declared goal of shaping social policy in the legislative and bureaucratic realms, the Association for Social Policy mobilized its broad coalition across boundaries of class and religion to agitate on behalf of expanded labor protection for women and youths and for the preservation of workers' political rights against repressive state policies like the previously proposed penal bill.[75] The issue of the ten-hour day for female workers preoccupied the Association's first conference, held in September 1902, and set the agenda for its reform endeavors throughout the decade. The detailed presentations to the conference on the "necessity and pertinence of the ten-hour day" by August Pieper, general secretary of the Catholic Volksverein, and feminist Helene Simon—prohibited from delivering her speech by the police and forced to listen from a back room as it was read aloud by a male member of the Association—brought the issue into public view.[76] The conference also coincided with an official state inquiry into

---

74. Ratz, *Soziale Reform und Arbeiterschaft*, pp. 43–46; Klöhn, *Helene Simon*, pp. 129–30. The three were then named "German correspondents" of the International Union for Labor Protection, to which the Association belonged. Jaffé-von Richthofen was the first female factory inspector (as opposed to assistant) in the state of Baden. On her life, in particular her relationship with Max Weber, see Martin Green, *The von Richthofen Sisters: The Triumphant and the Tragic Modes of Love. Else and Frieda von Richthofen, Otto Gross, Max Weber and D. H. Lawrence in the Years 1870–1970* (New York: Basic Books, 1974). Simon, born in 1862 and a former student of Gustav Schmoller, was highly respected in the circles of academic social reform despite her reputed socialist sympathies. She was the author of numerous articles on protective labor laws and unionization for female workers and on the German and British factory inspectorate. For an insightful discussion of Simon's place among German social reformers, see Klöhn, *Helene Simon*.

75. Ratz, *Sozialreform und Arbeiterschaft*, pp. 33, 78–80, 162, 167–68, 181–88; Campbell, *Joy in Work*, pp. 56–67.

76. Gesellschaft für Soziale Reform (GfSR), *Die Herabsetzung der Arbeitszeit für Frauen und die Erhöhung des Schutzalters für jugendliche Arbeiter in Fabriken, Schriften der Gesellschaft für Soziale Reform*, nos. 7 and 8 (Jena: Gustav Fischer, 1903), which includes the speeches delivered by August Pieper and Helene Simon to the first general conference of the GfSR, held in Cologne on 22 September 1902. Also see Ratz, *Soziale Reform und Arbeiterschaft*, p. 90.

female workers' regular and overtime hours, conducted by the factory inspectors to determine the need for further restrictions on work time.[77] On the other side of the issue, the inspectors' inquiry prompted a vigorous response from the employers' associations, with textile entrepreneurs in the forefront, who launched a determined campaign against further hours limits or health and safety restrictions on female factory employment, claiming that such measures would cause irreparable harm to German industry in the world market.[78]

The bitter labor struggle of 1903–4 in the mills of Crimmitschau, a small textile town in Saxony, imparted a particular urgency to the issue of hours restrictions for female workers. In late summer 1903, 7,500 workers—nearly half of them women, including some 1,350 married women—walked out of the mills to demand a ten-hour maximum workday. The strike, which quickly escalated into a lockout, became a showdown between labor and capital that polarized public opinion in the national political and social reform arenas. Although the powerful CVDI offered its backing to the mill owners for the duration of the conflict, the strike also prompted employers to band together in new regional and industry-specific associations to defend their interests against the growing number of unionized workers.[79] At the same time, Social Democratic trade unionists and workers from various industrial sectors across Germany circulated petitions and gathered donations for the workers of Crimmitschau, raising one million marks in a few months' time. Eminent academics and intellectuals like Lujo Brentano, Robert Wilbrandt, and Alice Salomon reported on the strike in various scholarly and social reform journals, championing the workers' cause among bourgeois intellectuals. In the pages of *Soziale Praxis*, Salomon, who traversed the streets of Crimmitschau herself inter-

77. The results of the factory inspectors' investigation were compiled by the Ministry of the Interior and published in 1905: Reichsamt des Innern, *Die Arbeitszeit der Fabrikarbeiterinnen* (Berlin: R. von Decker, 1905).

78. RWWA, 20-411-4, *Verhandlungen, Mitteilungen und Berichte des Centralverbandes Deutscher Industrieller*, no. 101 (November 1905) (Berlin: Guttentag, 1905): "Beschluß der Delegiertenversammlung zu Berlin am 5. Mai 1905 betreffend die Verkürzung der Arbeitszeit erwachsener Arbeiterinnen auf 10 Stunden." In this document the CVDI terms the proposed introduction of the ten-hour day for women workers a "serious threat" to the ability of German industry, in particular the textile industry, to compete in the international market. Also see also RWWA, HK Duisburg, 20: 95/8, "Beschluß des Ausschusses vom 3. November 1905 betr. die Arbeitszeit der Arbeiterinnen in Fabriken" "An die königliche Gewerbeinspection," Anlage zum Protokoll der Versammlung von 9. Juli 1902 in Mönchen-Gladbach.

79. On the activities of the employers' associations during the strike, see also Born, *Staat und Sozialpolitik*, pp. 81–82, and Dick Geary, "The Industrial Bourgeoisie and Labour Relations in Germany, 1871–1933," in *The German Bourgeoisie: Essays on the Social History of the German Middle Class from the Late 18th to the Early 20th Century*, ed. David Blackbourn and Richard J. Evans (London: Routledge, 1991), p. 143.

viewing both sides in the conflict, emphasized that far more was at stake in the struggle than the mere reduction of work time, in particular for the many married women on the strike lines: "The workers of Crimmitschau are struggling not for food and shelter, rather on behalf of their family life, their homes, the right to parent their children and to raise them into valuable human beings. They are fighting against the . . . endangerment of women's health and that of the future generation."[80] Brentano also composed an incisive analysis of the strike's implications for social policy, deploring the political persecution of striking workers.[81] The strike ended in thorough defeat for the workers of Crimmitschau and of the national labor movement that had supported their cause. In public opinion, however, it was seen throughout Germany as a bitter "defeat of the working mothers," an image that left its imprint on the struggle for the ten-hour day that would ferment until 1908.

Maternity and *Volkskörper*: Female Factory Labor in the Age of Empire

The textile strike in Crimmitschau, however unsuccessful, placed female textile workers, especially working mothers, and their struggle for the ten-hour day in the foreground of increasingly vigorous debates among social reformers about the "legal, cultural, and ethical implications" of motherhood at middecade.[82] The demands for protective measures—the ten-hour day, longer pregnancy leave, and maternity insurance—acquired new meaning after the turn of the century, when the declining German birthrate became a source of concern and controversy among scientists and social policy experts—conservative, left-liberal, and Social Democratic. As they sought to explain the origins of declining national fertility and contemplate its consequences, reformers came to view Germany as enmeshed in a crisis of "the entire system of reproduction [*Fortpflanzungssystem*]," by which "a socially indispensable contribution—the process of breeding and raising the next generation" had begun to dissolve.[83]

80. Alice Salomon, "Crimmitschau," *Sozialer Praxis* 13 (14 January 1901): 408; Wilbrandt, *Die Weber*, p. 197; Robert Wilbrandt, "Der Hintergrund des Weberstreiks in Crimmitschau," *Der Textilarbeiter* 16 (8 January 1904); DTAV, *Crimmitschau, 1903–1928: Blätter der Erinnerung an Sachsens bedeutsamsten Arbeitskampf* (Berlin: DTAV, 1928); and Michael Schneider, *Streit um Arbeitszeit, Geschichte des Kampfes um Arbeitszeitverkürzung in Deutschland* (Cologne: Bund Verlag, 1984), pp. 72–74.
81. Brentano's article is cited in the brochure compiled by the DTAV, *Crimmitschau*, pp. 234–35, as "an expert opinion on the social-political aspects of the strike" under the rubric "Drei Gutachten über den Klassenkampf in Crimmitschau."
82. Allen, *Feminism and Motherhood*, p. 173.
83. Stach, "Mutterschaft und Bevölkerungsfrage," p. 193.

Although birthrates were on the decline across Europe and dipped even more sharply in several other European countries, the demographic contraction coincided with the rising imperial ambitions of the German nation-state, as expressed in the naval arms race with Britain and the recurrent clashes in the colonial realm with Britain, France, and Russia.[84] The decline of marital fertility, taken together with Germany's high infant mortality and illegitimacy rates, became a metaphor for the "dissolution of the family" and of "'those powers on which the cohesion of our nation rests'" after the turn of the century.[85] At the end of the nineteenth century some 20 percent of babies born to working-class families in Germany died within their first year, while the mortality rates were nearly twice as high among the 10 percent born to unmarried mothers. These statistics were widely read as indicating "a state of emergency" surrounding motherhood in Germany, a crisis in which female factory labor figured centrally.[86]

The national debates about population policy did not reach their peak until about 1910, but during the first decade of the century scientists and social reformers sought a variety of explanations for the waning birthrates, ranging from wealth to impoverishment, from women's emancipation and intellectualization to the "sterility" of urban capitalist society.[87] Amid the

84. Allen, *Feminism and Motherhood*, pp. 176–77. On the German birthrate see H. Silbergleit, "Über Mutterschaftsstatistik," in Schreiber, *Mutterschaft: Ein Sammelwerk*, pp. 576–86; Knodel, *Decline of Fertility*, pp. 63–64. According to Silbergleit, pp. 580–82, the Russian birthrate in 1905 was 44.4 live births per 1,000 people, while the German rate was only 33.0. In 1910 the figures for Germany were 29.8, for Italy 32.9, Hungary 35.6, and Romania 39.8, while the Netherlands, Denmark, and Norway had lower rates of 28.6, 27.5, and 26.1 respectively. In France the birthrate sank to 19.7 in 1910, the lowest among a major Continental power. As statisticians continued to emphasize, Germany's population went on increasing despite the diminished birthrates because lower mortality rates offset them. Only in France, where mortality rates were higher than birthrates, did the size of the population begin to decline.

85. Karl Oldenberg, professor of government from Göttingen, as cited by Bergmann, *Die rationalisierten Triebe*, pp. 6–7.

86. Alice Salomon, "Mutterschutz und Mutterschaftsversicherung," *Concordia* 15 (1908): 458–63, reprinted in Peyser, *Alice Salomon*, pp. 152–63; Silbergleit, "Über Mutterschaftsstatistik," pp. 585–86; Knodel, *Decline of Fertility*, pp. 75–78, 167; Evans, *Feminist Movement in Germany*, p. 168; Allen, *Feminism and Motherhood*, pp. 142–43, 177–78; Ute Frevert, "'Fürsorgliche Belagerung': Hygienebewegung und Arbeiterfrauen im 19. und frühen 20. Jahrhundert," *Geschichte und Gesellschaft* 11 (1985): 436; Marielouise Janssen-Jurreit, "Nationalbiologie, Sexualreform und Geburtenrückgang—über die Zusammenhänge von Bevölkerungspolitik und Frauenbewegung um die Jahrhundertwende," in *Die Überwindung der Sprachlosigkeit, Texte aus der neuen Frauenbewegung*, ed. Gabriele Dietze (Darmstadt u. Neuwied: Luchterhand, 1979), p. 154. According to Allen, the founding manifesto of the League for the Protection of Mothers and Sexual Reform, drafted in 1905, cites infant mortality rates of 34 percent for babies of unmarried mothers. Knodel's figures show a mortality rate for illegitimate babies that was 72 percent higher than that for babies of married mothers.

87. On the "sterility" of capitalist society, see the citations from Friedrich Naumann's *Neue deutsche Wirtschaftspolitik* (Berlin-Schöneberg: Buchverlag der Hilfe, 1906), in Stach,

binary oppositions between normal and pathological that shaped the mental landscape of social reform after the turn of the century, the body became a new site of medicalized social investigation. Social hygienist Alfred Grotjahn, for example, spent ten days in 1902 traversing the streets, factories, slums, and marketplaces of London's East End exploring the extent to which "bodily degeneration went hand in hand with the development of an industrial state," observing "the bodily condition" of the largely working-class population in various poses and at diverse sites, "on the street, while working in public places, on the way to church, at people's assemblies, and on market days." Grotjahn's conclusion that "the undeniable health danger of the urban way of life and industrial occupations is not irreparable" and indeed "perhaps indicates only a temporary atrophy of the affected population" rendered remedial hygienic measures all the more meaningful.[88] In particular, female factory labor came to figure prominently in social hygiene discourses, in the visions they evoked of depleted bodies, consumed by disease and exhaustion, and in their diagnosis of the interlocking pathologies of promiscuity, prostitution, and venereal disease, alcoholism and tuberculosis, sterility and miscarriage, stillbirth and infant death, in which causes could be disentangled from effects only with difficulty.[89]

This proliferation of pathologies stood in stark contrast to the hopeful vision of a compatible relation between factory work and motherhood that underpinned the factory inspectors' report of 1901. Although the inspectors had studiously avoided alarmist cries of moral or physical degeneration, the compelling evidence they had compiled on the dangers of factory work for working mothers and their children—the disproportionately high rates of miscarriage, premature birth, and infant mortality among female textile workers reported by doctors, health insurance officials, and employers in 1898–99—prompted subsequent investigations of these conditions and their significance for the dwindling birthrates in various industrial districts of Germany.[90] Catholic reformer Heinrich Brauns, for

---

"Mutterschaft und Bevölkerungspolitik," p. 190. In Naumann's view, the "rein geldwirtschaftliche System [war] in seinen letzten Konsequenzen ein System der Unfruchtbarkeit."

88. Alfred Grotjahn, *Erlebtes und Erstrebtes: Erinnerungen eines sozialistischen Arztes* (Berlin: Kommissions-Verlag Herbig, 1932), pp. 108–11, 118–21. Also see Weindling, *Health, Race and German Politics*, pp. 126, 184–85, 216–22, 256–58, 345–47, 351–55. Grotjahn (1869–1931), a medical doctor, studied with Gustav Schmoller in Berlin during 1901 and 1902 and was cofounder, with Tönnies, Sombart, Max Weber, and Georg Simmel, of the German Society for Sociology. Grotjahn, who described himself as a *medizinischer Kathedersozialist*, first sought "to apply social science to medicine" in a book on alcoholism and degeneration.

89. Weindling, *Health, Race, and German Politics*, pp. 90, 196, 247, 251–53, 263–66.

90. HStAD, JBdKPG 1899: Düsseldorf, pp. 518–20; Münster, p. 372; Aachen, p. 609.

example, whose 1906 study captured the profound sense of disruption and pathos that accompanied the transition from handweaving to mechanized factories in the Rhenish velvet and silk industries, forged a direct link between two kinds of doom in the age of the machine—the sinking birthrate and the displacement of male weavers—both the result of the influx of women into the new mills. "Once the woman decides to go to work in the factory," he argued, "then the danger is high that she will seek to avoid the encumbrances [of pregnancy and postpartum recovery]." Admonishing the factory inspectors for neglecting to scrutinize this important social and moral consequence of female factory labor in their report of 1901, Brauns concluded (based on his "frequent contact with the workers' circles" and his perusal of family announcements in the local daily papers) that the workers "had contributed their share" to the dwindling birthrates, which were certain, in his view, to spiral further downward in the coming years.[91]

In Robert Wilbrandt's study of "the weavers in the present day," an account of his "social-political journeys" through the weaving districts of Germany in 1903–4, the textile industry also figured as the stage on which the dramas of birthrates and death rates, of feminization and dislocation took place. Observing the effects of mill work on female bodies, Wilbrandt noted that "the damage to the child begins even before its birth" because "the female factory workers, whether married or single, continue working when pregnant, frequently even until the last day." Weaving, he determined, was particularly arduous for pregnant women because of "the constant stretching of the body and movement of the arms that is required to attach the threads." More than the strain and harmful effects of the work itself, the very absence of mothers from their children had grievous consequences: in the mill towns of Saxony Wilbrandt found that nearly 40 percent of babies born to working mothers died before their first birthday, a rate nearly double the national figure and one that had increased steadily with the development of factory industry in the region.[92] Wilbrandt also argued that young girls who began working in the mills in their early teens experienced serious "damage to their organs," which often

---

See also Reichsamt des Innern, *Die Beschäftigung*, pp. 96–99, 210. Social reformers had begun to explore the links between female factory labor and infant mortality as early as the 1880s, well before the decline of the German birthrate had become a national or natalist issue.

91. Brauns, *Der Übergang von der Handweberei*, pp. 218–19. Brauns was a member of the Catholic Center Party and a leading figure in the Christian trade union movement and the Volksverein für das Katholische Deutschland before and after the First World War. He also served as minister of labor during the Weimar Republic (from 1920 to 1928).

92. Wilbrandt, *Die Weber*, pp. 4, 141–42, 157–58. According to Wilbrandt, 32 percent of infants born to female textile workers in Crimmitschau in 1856–67 died before their first birthday; this figure increased to 40 percent during 1881–85.

made them incapable of "healthy motherhood" later. Referring to figures compiled by the factory inspector of Mainz, Wilbrandt pointed out that the mortality rates were significantly lower for babies whose mothers had begun work in factories only after marriage (14 percent) than for those whose mothers had gone to work in the mills in their early teens (31 percent).[93]

Parallel to Wilbrandt's travels, reformer Wilhelm Feld returned to Crimmitschau, the scene of the textile strike of 1903, to explore the problems of child care and child neglect among the female textile workers of the town. Feld determined that nearly half of their children were in the care of relatives or neighbors who lived close to their homes, while one-third of them, 90 percent of whom were under age six, were without supervision while their parents worked.[94] The conditions of mothers and children in Crimmitschau and other textile centers of Saxony, where some 40 percent of married women worked in factories, led Wilbrandt to proclaim dramatically that in towns like these "mothers scarcely exist anymore" ("daß es Mütter kaum noch gibt"), for many were forced "to send their children away" when they went to work in the mills.[95] The high infant and child mortality, as well as the notoriously poor health of the military recruits in industrial regions, formed the basis for the eugenicist view that the employment of women and teenagers in factories had "undermined the capacity of the working classes for physical reproduction," rendered many of them infertile, and produced generations of "frail, sickly, and inviable human beings . . . with poor endurance, who go prematurely to their graves."[96]

The discursive context of the debates about female factory labor widened after the turn of the century to encompass the theories and practices of *Geburtenpolitik* (birth policy), the intervention of medicine and state in the decaying *Volkskörper* (body of the populace), with the goal of enhancing both the quantity and the quality of the German population. On the

93. Wilbrandt, *Die Frauenarbeit*, p. 45.
94. Wilhelm Feld, *Die Kinder der in den Fabriken arbeitenden Frauen und ihre Verpflegung mit besonderer Berücksichtigung der Crimmitschauer Arbeiterinnen*, Probleme der Fürsorge, Abhandlungen der Centrale für private Fürsorge in Frankfurt am Main, vol. 3 (Dresden: Böhmert, 1906), pp. 8, 29, 62–63; Alice Salomon, "Fabrikarbeit von Frauen und Kinderversorgung," *Concordia: Zeitschrift der Centralstelle für Arbeiter und Wohlfahrtseinrichtungen* 13 (15 August 1906): 227–29. Feld relied on the cooperation of the Deutscher Textilarbeiterverband in conducting his inquiry, which encompassed 1,371 of approximately 2,000 female union members in local textile mills, nearly all of whom had participated in the strike of 1903, including 800 single women, 971 married women, and 242 women who were widowed, separated, or divorced.
95. Wilbrandt, *Die Frauenarbeit*, p. 67.
96. Frevert, "'Fürsorgliche Belagerung,'" p. 427; Weindling, *Health, Race and German Politics*, p. 252.

one hand, the neo-Malthusian emphasis of the 1880s on the biological and racial "quality" of the population was revitalized, as medical doctors and feminist-eugenicists advocated contraceptives as an essential means of preventing the "rapacious exploitation" of the female body caused by recurrent pregnancies and births, particularly in combination with factory labor.[97] On the other hand, social and racial-hygienicist fears of depopulation and racial deterioration fueled the growing concern among social reformers and the wider public about the urgent need to stem the dwindling birthrate and enhance population quantity.[98] Eugenicists and population experts decried all at once the "moral degeneration of married life," "the deterioration of the *Volkscharakter* [popular character]," the "moral as well as the national menace to Germanness," and the subversion of the state.[99]

As hygiene became a magic word by which social pathologies could be remedied, "social outsiders integrated, and social relations reformed," doctors and social hygienists, political economists and civil servants joined forces to battle for what Ute Frevert has termed the "hygienic civilizing of the worker-family."[100] In a flood of scholarly and scientific tracts and a surge of popular mobilization, social hygienists crusaded not only against the "growing sterility of families," but also to eradicate the social pathologies of alcoholism, promiscuity, prostitution, infant mortality, and tuberculosis.[101] Following the lead of the popular organizations against alcoholism (1883) and tuberculosis (1895), a coalition of medical doctors, health insurance officials, social scientists (including Brentano and Tönnies), and bourgeois and socialist feminists (such as Marie Stritt and Wally

---

97. Bergmann, "Die rationalisierten Triebe," pp. 75–76. Bergmann points to the gynecologist Dr. Wilhelm Peter Johannes Mensinga of Flensburg (1836–1910) as one of the first and most highly respected German neo-Malthusians. Mensinga's collection, *100 Frauenleben in der Beleuchtung des Paragraphen 1354b des bürgerlichen Gesetzbuches: Eine Studie für Kliniker, auch für praktische Ärzte* (Neuwied: L. Heuser, 1908), offered distressing examples of "mothers' misery" that revealed "the tragedy of motherhood when it is too frequently and too quickly repeated." Also Schreiber, "Mißbrauchte und unwillkommene Mutterschaft," p. 211.

98. See Jacques Donzelot, *The Policing of Families* (New York: Pantheon, 1979), pp. 174–77, who makes it clear that this shift from Malthusian moralizing of the lower classes toward new discourses inveighing against the growing sterility of families took place across Europe between 1890 and the First World War.

99. Bergmann, "Die rationalisierten Triebe," pp. 6–7. According to Bergmann, the Prussian interior minister, Eduard Dietrich, termed the question of reproduction, "die bedeutsamste für die modernen Kulturvölker" in 1911.

100. All citations here from Frevert, "'Fürsorgliche Belagerung,'" pp. 421–22. On the concomitant development of industrial hygiene, see Dietrich Milles, "From Workers' Diseases to Occupational Diseases: The Impact of Experts' Concepts on Workers' Attitudes," in *The Social History of Occupational Health*, ed. Paul Weindling (London: Croom Helm, 1985), pp. 55–77.

101. Donzelot, *The Policing of Families*, p. 175.

Zepler) founded the Society to Combat Venereal Disease in 1902. The Society for Combating Infant Deaths, organized by another broad coalition of "dignitaries, such as aristocrats, bankers and their wives," in 1904, aimed not only at "instructing mothers in domestic hygiene," including breast-feeding, but "at broader targets" like consumerism and luxury.[102] Both this society and the Empress Victoria House for Combating Infant Mortality, founded in 1909, mobilized public support behind conservative views of infant health measures, while the left-liberal and feminist League for the Protection of Mothers and Sexual Reform, founded in 1904, placed the "modern woman," not only the child, at the center of population policy, seeking to remedy the conditions of motherhood for both single and married women while advocating a controversial "new ethic" of sexual freedom and pleasure for women and men.[103]

This proliferation of popular associations, many of which embraced race hygiene and "explicitly included imperialism as a rationale" for their endeavors,[104] attests to the emergence of eugenics as "a relentlessly aggrandizing ideological field . . . [that] . . . convened biomedical knowledge, public health, and racial thought on the ground of social policy" and recast the politics of family and motherhood during the first decade of the twentieth century.[105] Eugenics and race hygiene increasingly permeated social policy debates as the *Volkskörper* came to occupy a central place in the intensified contest for European and imperial hegemony in the years before the outbreak of World War I. As population experts came to view the declining birthrate as synonymous with *Volkstod* or *Rassentod* (the demise of the people or the race), eugenicists stepped up their campaigns to reverse the trend, to enhance the biological quality of the German population by applying the science of heredity, thereby preventing criminals and those afflicted with tuberculosis, alcoholism, venereal disease, or mental illness from reproducing.[106]

---

102. Citations from Paul Weindling, "Hygienepolitik als sozialintegrative Strategie im späten Deutschen Kaiserreich," in *Medizinische Deutungsmacht im sozialen Wandel des 19. und frühen 20. Jahrhunderts*, ed. Alfons Labisch and Reinhard Spree (Bonn: Psychiatrie Verlag, 1989), pp. 45–48. On the various reform groups, see Weindling, *Health, Race and German Politics*, pp. 176–77, 181, 184, 188, 196, 204–5.

103. Allen, *Feminism and Motherhood*, p. 178, points out that the Empress Victoria House was conceived as a conservative alternative to the feminist League for the Protection of Mothers. On the Empress Victoria House, also see Weindling, *Health, Race, and German Politics*, p. 205, and his essay "Bourgeois Values, Doctors and the State: The Professionalization of Medicine in Germany, 1848–1933," in Blackbourn and Evans, *German Bourgeoisie*, p. 218. According to Weindling, the opening of the Empress Victoria House was accompanied "by a massive campaign to mobilize public support for its direction of infant health measures."

104. Weindling, "Bourgeois Values," p. 218.

105. Eley, "German History and the Contradictions of Modernity," p. 102.

106. On the definitions of eugenics, race hygiene, and social hygiene in early twentieth-

Constituting a new field of reformers' intervention, the social problems of youth and the perception that the "nation's young laborers were becoming a palpable threat to the social order" became an intrinsic part of the perceived crisis of motherhood and family after the turn of the century, as the work of Derek Linton has demonstrated.[107] The crusade for youth salvation and the emergent field of *Jugendpflege* (youth welfare) distinguished youth by gender, identifying male youths as a social problem because of their unruliness and uprootedness from their families, whereas social protection of young women had natalist overtones, with reformers emphasizing the tension between their roles as workers and as future mothers. Defining female puberty, the phase "when the woman prepares herself for motherhood," as fraught with particular dangers for the maturing female organism, reformers expressed concern about the steady increase in the size of the teenage female workforce, especially in the textile industry, and its implications for the declining birthrate.[108]

As a growing consensus formed between socialist and bourgeois eugenicist movements regarding the *Verallgemeinerung der hygienischen Kultur* (the generalizing of hygienic culture), the German family—with the wife and mother at its center—became the subject not only of moral propaganda, but also of scientific study.[109] More specifically, the female body became the subject of a new wave of moralizing propaganda, of new tutelary claims to discipline the body and to "rationalize reproduction" as both the state and popular associations launched initiatives to reverse the declining birthrate.[110] Whereas during the 1880s neo-Malthusians had deployed

---

century Germany, see Weindling, *Health, Race and German Politics*, especially chapters 1 and 2. One key difference within the broader field of eugenics was between race hygiene and social hygiene: whereas race hygienists viewed reproduction mainly in terms of biology and heredity, social hygienists generally pointed to the importance of social conditions in favoring or inhibiting healthy reproduction.

107. Derek Linton, *"Who Has the Youth, Has the Future": The Campaign to Save Young Workers in Imperial Germany* (Cambridge: Cambridge University Press, 1991). Also see the important book by Detlev J. K. Peukert, *Grenzen der Sozial-Disziplinierung: Aufstieg und Krise der deutschen Jugendfürsorge, 1878–1932* (Cologne: Bund Verlag, 1986), pp. 52–53.

108. Derek Linton, "Between School and Marriage, Workshop and Household: Young Working Women as a Social Problem in Late Imperial Germany," *European History Quarterly* 18 (1988): 388–89, 399, and Linton, "Who Has the Youth," pp. 23–39, 167–68. Linton points out that male youths were identified as a social problem around the turn of the century, whereas female youths were not included in any youth welfare measures (such as the Youth Cultivation Edict of 1911) until 1913, and then only under pressure from the bourgeois feminist movement.

109. This term was coined by the socialist-eugenicist medical doctor Alfred Grotjahn; see his *Erlebtes und Erstrebtes*, p. 118; Weindling, *Health, Race and German Politics*, p. 141; and Alfons Labisch, *Homo hygienicus: Gesundheit und Medizin in der Neuzeit* (Frankfurt a.M.: Campus, 1992), pp. 146–47.

110. Bergmann, "Die rationalisierten Triebe," pp. 2, 139–40.

both scientific and moralistic arguments on behalf of birth control, after the turn of the century racial hygienists appealed to women in highly moralistic terms to renounce birth control, abortion, and all other "pathological" impediments to childbearing. The disputes and debates over demographic statistics soon became rife with sexual meanings, as conservative social hygienists came to blame the declining birthrate on a voluntary limitation of fertility in marriage or an "obscene" reliance on the criminality of back alleys and neighborhood quacks, abortion potions, and black market contraceptives.[111] As a result the state, in coalition with the medical profession, became more vigilant in policing women's bodies. Determining around the turn of the century that between one-third and one-half of all pregnancies were aborted, the state, relying on medical doctors for most reports of self-induced or illicitly obtained abortions, intensified its efforts to prosecute women and their doctors for violating the criminal statute against abortion, paragraph 218.[112] At the same time, stricter laws were passed in 1900 regulating the display, advertisement, and sale of contraceptives, aiming to inhibit the voluntary restriction of births.[113]

Specifying the significance of the body for social hygiene, the eugenicist medical doctors Alfred Grotjahn and Max Hirsch established *Fortpflanzungshygiene* (reproductive hygiene) as a new branch of both social reform and medicine. Advocates of reproductive hygiene aimed to rationalize reproduction by applying the criteria of origins, heredity, and degeneration to distinguish between inferior and "worthy" life. At the same time, they advocated a system of state support (subventions, pensions, insurance, and protective laws) for the production of healthy human beings.[114] The new science of "social gynecology," a subset of reproductive hygiene, extended the scope of gynecological medicine to encompass the multifarious aspects

111. Ibid., pp. 7–8; Weindling, *Health, Race, and German Politics*, p. 263; Woycke, *Birth Control*, pp. 52–53, 68–81, and chapter 4, "The Abortion Underworld."

112. Weindling, *Health, Race and German Politics*, pp. 266–67; Bergmann, "Die rationalisierten Triebe," pp. 8, 82, 90, 97. Paragraph 218 had been part of the German penal code since 1872. It decreed a punishment of up to five years in prison for women who had illegal or self-induced abortions. According to Weindling, in July 1913 the Prussian Ministry of the Interior requested detailed information from some 12,000 doctors regarding premature births and the incidence of induced abortions. (Only 2,515 replies were received.) Contemporaries estimated in 1912 that there were approximately 100,000 illegal abortions per year and some 10,000 deaths as a result of abortion. The number of prosecutions for abortion increased from 411 in 1900 to 976 in 1910 and 1,755 in 1914.

113. Woycke, *Birth Control*, pp. 138–39; Bergmann, "Frauen, Männer, Sexualität," pp. 84–86, and idem, "Die rationalisierten Triebe," pp. 8–9; Weindling, *Health, Race and German Politics*, p. 268. In 1913 and 1914 additional laws were proposed to tighten the restrictions on abortifacients and contraceptives.

114. Labisch, *Homo hygienicus*, p. 148; Grotjahn, *Erlebtes und Erstrebtes*, p. 118. In his autobiography Grotjahn claimed that "one cannot pursue social hygiene if one does not supplement it with reproductive hygiene or eugenics."

of women's lives as "reproducer[s] of the 'most valuable of all goods.'" For eugenicists like Wilhelm Schallmayer, social gynecology was a "means of awakening the racial conscience of women of superior moral and physical quality to their obligatory duty to the race [*Rassendienstpflicht*]."[115] The new social significance of *Frauenkunde* (gynecology) can be understood in the context of the protracted process of medicalization, by which norms of health and hygiene came to permeate not only institutions and policies of state, but also popular mentalities and public opinion, drawing individuals and families into a net of medical norms, ordinances, and practices through the proliferation of medical institutions and the professionalization of medicine. The concern with the quantity and quality of the population after the turn of the century marked a high point of this process in Germany as medicine—in particular gynecology—became intensely politicized, investing the female body with a new significance that required "constant and detailed policing and regulation."[116] As a result, social gynecologists came to play a key role in the debates and deliberations regarding the birthrate as well as those about the protection of female factory workers.

By the eve of the First World War academic social reformers and state bureaucrats had come to recognize female factory labor as a vital aspect of the birthrate crisis. Delineating clear class-specific causes and meanings of the shrinking birthrates, in 1912 reformer Julius Wolf explained the decline among women of the middle and upper classes in terms of their "compulsion toward luxury consumption." The crucial factor for working-class women, he noted, was the steady expansion of their employment outside the home.[117] In the same year Jean Bornträger, Catholic medical

---

115. Weindling, *Health, Race, and German Politics*, pp. 257–58. Intrinsic to the notion of social gynecology was the recognition of the importance of state social policy in fostering an increase in the birthrate through protective labor laws, social insurance, tax relief, and other forms of state support for motherhood.

116. Martin Hewitt, "Bio-politics and Social Policy: Foucault's Account of Welfare," *Theory, Culture and Society* 2, no. 1 (1983): 71. On medicalization and the politicization of health, see Ute Frevert's *Krankheit als politisches Problem, 1770–1880: Soziale Unterschichten in Preußen zwischen medizinischer Polizei und staatlicher Sozialversicherung* (Göttingen: Vandenhoeck und Ruprecht, 1984); Claudia Honegger, "Überlegungen zur Medikalisierung des weiblichen Körpers," in *Leib und Leben in der Geschichte der Neuzeit* (Vorträge eines internationalen Colloquiums, Berlin 1.–3.12.1981), ed. Arthur E. Imhof (Berlin: Duncker und Humblot, 1983), pp. 203–13; and Claudia Honegger, "Frauen und medizinische Deutungsmacht im 19. Jahrhundert," in Labisch and Spree, *Medizinische Deutungsmacht*, pp. 181–94. On medicalization of the factory inspectorate, including the increasing number of doctors employed as inspectors, see Dietrich Milles, "Industrial Hygiene: A State Obligation? Industrial Pathology as a Problem in German Social Policy," in *The State and Social Change in Germany, 1880–1980*, ed. Eve Rosenhaft and W. R. Lee (New York: Oxford University Press, 1990), pp. 174–75.

117. Julius Wolf, *Der Geburtenrückgang: Die Rationalisierung des Sexuallebens in unserer Zeit* (Jena: Gustav Fischer, 1912), pp. 62–63, as cited in Bergmann, "Die rationalisierten

officer and "government expert" from Düsseldorf, compiled a memorandum on "the birthrate decline in Germany, its evaluation and eradication" for the Prussian Ministry of the Interior, designating Social Democracy and the women's movement—the vocal advocates of women's emancipation—as the main progenitors of the decline.[118] When the Prussian state convened its Medical Advisory Committee in 1911 to investigate the causes of the dwindling birthrate, its members examined not only the "sociology of morals and living patterns" but also "the signs of bodily degeneration" and other physical causes for the decline, including the employment of married women outside the home. As a result of their preliminary findings, in 1912 the Prussian Ministry of the Interior requested that provincial officials conduct an inquiry among mayors and medical officers, factory and school inspectors, regarding the birthrates in their regions. Of the thirty-three reporting authorities who responded to the question about whether women's work was a significant factor in declining fertility, eighteen answered affirmatively.[119]

Thus eugenicist discourses on the declining birthrate and decaying population quality formed the backdrop for the continued debates about the protection of female factory workers, in particular pregnant women and new mothers, during the first decade of the twentieth century. As the norms of social and race hygiene became more pervasive and the emphasis on the reproductive female body more pronounced, the bodies of female factory workers, devoured and depleted by the double burden and bearing the scars not only of factory work but also of successive births, miscarriages, and abortions, seemed to disrupt and defy the consensus that had formed around the ideal of the *Homo hygienicus*—the visions of a hygienic family, community, and civil society.[120] Evoking the surging rates of miscarriage, premature birth, and infant mortality among factory workers and underscoring the high incidence of maternal infection, debilitation, and death, reformers demanded maternity insurance and extended maternity leave to stem the calamitous consequences of recent rapid waves of industrial growth.[121] From the turn of the century on, liberal bourgeois, feminist, Social Democratic, and Catholic reformers waged a concerted battle

---

Triebe," pp. 13–14. On Wolf see Felix Meiner, ed., *Die Volkswirtschaftslehre der Gegenwart in Selbstdarstellungen* (Leipzig: Felix Meiner, 1924), pp. 209–47.

118. Janssen-Jurreit, "Nationalbiologie," pp. 164–65; Bergmann, "Die rationalisierten Triebe," p. 12; and idem, "Frauen, Männer, Sexualität," p. 92.

119. Weindling, *Health, Race and German Politics*, pp. 263–66, 270–80, has compiled and reprinted the results of the committee's inquest, which was sent to some 2,700 various authorities, ranging from governors-general to provincial medical chambers (*Ärztekammer*).

120. Labisch, *Homo hygienicus*, p. 168; Rosa Kempf, "Die Industriearbeiterin als Mutter," in Schreiber, *Mutterschaft: Ein Sammelwerk*, pp. 230–42.

121. Henriette Fürth, "Die Lage der Mutter und die Entwicklung des Mutterschutzes in Deutschland," in Schreiber, *Mutterschaft: Ein Sammelwerk*, pp. 279–80.

to extend the four-week maternity leave and to enact maternity insurance providing full reimbursement of lost earnings so that women would not be forced to work up until the day of delivery or return to work immediately thereafter. In 1909 health insurance officials deemed "the practicable and effective enactment of maternity insurance to be one of the most important and urgent tasks of health insurance reform."[122] A coalescence of initiatives by the Association for Social Reform, the Social Democrats, and the bourgeois feminist movement kept the questions of reduced working hours, pregnancy leave, and maternity insurance in the forefront of public and bureaucratic social policy debates, paving the way toward revision of the labor code in 1908 and the health insurance law in 1903 and 1911.

As early as 1897, Lily Braun had issued a controversial call for state maternity insurance, to be funded by a progressive income tax, but it became a principal demand of both bourgeois and socialist feminist reformers only during the middle of the first decade of the twentieth century. Although in 1901 the female rank and file of the SPD demanded mandatory leave for several weeks before birth and a strict ban on returning to work during the first six weeks after birth, Clara Zetkin refused to endorse Braun's proposal and claimed these measures could be realized only in a socialist society.[123] Nonetheless, most female party and union leaders came to share bourgeois reformers' alarm regarding maternal and child illness and mortality. Emphasizing the particularities of the capitalist economy, Social Democratic feminists concluded that female factory labor, performed under the "conditions of capitalism," constituted a "physical threat" to the reproduction of the working class.[124] At the same time, the radical wing of the bourgeois feminist movement unleashed a flood of articles and brochures between 1901 and 1907 arguing the merits of state maternity insurance.[125] In 1903 the Federation of German Women's Associations petitioned the government to expand maternity leave to six weeks before and six weeks after childbirth. In 1905 the Verband Fortschritt-

122. Fürth, "Die Lage der Mutter," p. 286.
123. Freier, *"Dem Reich der Freiheit,"* pp. 108–9. Braun presented her plan for maternity insurance to the SPD's women's conference, held in 1902 in Munich. In light of Zetkin's objections, the conference voted against Braun's proposal. See *Die Gleichheit* 11 (1901): 67, as cited in Freier, pp. 108–9, for more detailed analysis of this conflict. This issue was the subject of debate within the Social Democratic movement between 1902 and 1906.
124. Freier, *"Dem Reich der Freiheit,"* p. 98.
125. Henriette Fürth advocated a notion of maternity insurance that was similar to Lily Braun's. See Fürth, *Die Fabrikarbeit*, as well as her book *Die Mutterschaftsversicherung* (Jena: Gustav Fischer, 1911), and her article "Die Lage der Mutter," pp. 284–85. Also see Adele Schreiber, "Mutterschutz," *Die Zukunft*, November 1901; Alice Salomon, *Mutterschutz und Mutterschaftsversicherung* (Leipzig: Duncker und Humblot, 1908); and Anna Pappritz, *Die Errichtung von Wöchnerinnenheimen und Säuglingsasylen: Eine soziale Pflicht* (Leipzig: F. Dietrich, 1907).

licher Frauenvereine (Union of Progressive Women's Associations) presented another petition demanding that state maternity insurance, covering the full amount of wages and medical treatment for pregnancy and childbirth, be extended to factory workers as well as those employed in home industry, agriculture, and domestic service.[126]

In the forefront of the struggle for maternity insurance was the Bund für Mutterschutz und Sexualreform (League for the Protection of Mothers and Sexual Reform), in which eugenicist visions of social reform merged with progressive feminist viewpoints.[127] The League united socialist feminists Lily Braun and Henriette Fürth with radical bourgeois feminists Helene Stöcker, Adele Schreiber, and Minna Cauer and also included a notable male contingent of natural and social scientists, medical doctors, and political economists.[128] It soon became a hub of complex and often contradictory social and political initiatives, both feminist and eugenicist, including maternity insurance, maternity homes for single women, and support networks for single mothers, whose plight the League viewed as symptomatic of the shortcomings of the modern family.

Demanding that the emergent "science of population," *Bevölkerungswissenschaft*, and the state *Geburtenpolitik* (birth policies) begin to consider their "most important factor, the modern woman,"[129] the League developed the first "specifically feminist approach to the . . . problems presented by increasing governmental intervention in the previously private sphere of child-rearing and reproduction."[130] Shifting the focus from children to mothers, in particular single mothers, the League's founder, Ruth Bré, pointed out that "the protection of children is and remains piecemeal without the protection of mothers, for the mother is the most vital source of life for the child and is indispensable to its development."[131] The League, led by radical feminist Helene Stöcker after 1905, sought to change the public's predominantly negative view of single mothers not merely out of "compassion," as Henriette Fürth pointed out, but also from the standpoint of "racial hygienic wisdom," for the high mortality of ille-

---

126. Rosika Schwimmer, "Wichtige Momente in der Entwicklung des Mutterschutzes und der Mutterschaftsversicherung," in *Mutterschaft: Ein Sammelwerk*, pp. 377–81.
127. Janssen-Jurreit, "Nationalbiologie," p. 141.
128. The founding members of the Bund für Mutterschutz included Ruth Bré, Helene Stöcker, Adele Schreiber, Lily Braun, and Henriette Fürth. Among the male members of the founding committee were Werner Sombart, Friedrich Naumann, and Alfred Ploetz. Men composed one-third of the League's membership at its peak in 1908, when it had 3,800 members. On its history see Evans, *Feminist Movement*, pp. 120–30; Allen, *Feminism and Motherhood*, pp. 174–90; Janssen-Jurreit, "Nationalbiologie," pp. 156–57.
129. Stach, "Mutterschaft und Bevölkerungsfrage," p. 188.
130. Allen, *Feminism and Motherhood*, p. 176.
131. As cited in Janssen-Jurreit, "Nationalbiologie," p. 154.

gitimate babies represented "a lost source of national strength [*Volkskraft*]."¹³² At the same time, the League emphasized the high maternal mortality, which had been largely ignored by racial hygienists who clamored for one-sided measures to increase the birthrate. Its members pointed out that between 1907 and 1910 nearly 4,000 women died each year in Prussia from the complications of childbirth or puerperal infection, while many others died, became ill, or were debilitated owing to the sheer "excess of motherhood, along with the arduous struggle for existence" that characterized working women's lives.¹³³ Analyzing the declining birthrates not mainly as an outcome of moral degeneration but as the product of structural and social change, feminist eugenicists refuted the spurious dualism between home and work, arguing that "the rationality of the capitalist mode of production [had crossed] over the threshold of the home, drawing 'the production of human beings' into the general process of goods production, into the larger network of supply and demand."¹³⁴ They buttressed their own arguments with Friedrich Naumann's economic analysis of the birthrate decline, citing his contention that *Unfruchtbarkeit* (sterility) was a consequence of the capitalist system:

> Today the producers of human beings are burdened on all sides . . . neither the father nor the mother earns more because of producing children. Every new child constricts the space, increases the needs, and diminishes the independence of the parents. Above all, motherhood means monetary loss. The woman has an easier time as an individual in the capitalist world if she does not become a mother. In that case she does not produce human beings, rather commodities, and sells [her] hands, for no one pays her anything for children.¹³⁵

The League's accentuation of the "tragedy of motherhood," especially "when it is too often and too rapidly repeated," meant that its members demanded "not more births, but better social welfare [*Fürsorge*] of all kinds."¹³⁶ In fact, although most members endorsed the basic principles of eugenics, accepting "the state's interest in the quantity and quality of pop-

---

132. Ibid.
133. Silbergleit, "Über Mutterschaftsstatistik," p. 585; Schreiber, "Mißbrauchte und unwillkommene Mutterschaft," p. 202.
134. Stach, "Mutterschaft und Bevölkerungsfrage," pp. 189–90.
135. Naumann, *Neue deutsche Wirtschaftspolitik*, as cited in Stach, "Mutterschaft und Bevölkerungsfrage," p. 190. The original citation is, "Heute werden die Hersteller von Menschen von allen Seiten belastet. . . . Die Frau geht als Individuum leichter durch die kapitalistische Welt, wenn sie nicht Mutter wird. Sie arbeitet dann nicht Menschen, sondern Ware und verkauft Hände, da ihr niemand für Kinder etwas gibt."
136. Schreiber, "Mißbrauchte und unwillkommene Mutterschaft," pp. 207, 211.

ulation,"[137] and though most understood social hygiene as a "means to a more ordered, progressive, and humane society" rather than as "a means of providing generals with cannon fodder," the League's feminist activists also diverged significantly from the dominant tenets of racial hygiene, often provoking the wrath of male population experts.[138] For one, the League's "new ethic" embraced a notion of sexual emancipation and pleasure that explicitly detached sexuality from motherhood and used the plight of single mothers to criticize the family as a male-dominated institution. Although many of its members embraced the notion of *Keimauslese* or *gesunde Zeugung* (healthy conception), by which the birth of sickly or handicapped children was to be prevented by preemptive sterilization of alcoholics, the mentally ill, handicapped persons, and those with hereditary diseases, most members of the League vigorously resisted the racial hygienicist advocacy of euthanasia for babies born ill or with handicaps.[139] At the same time, League feminists took a bold neo-Malthusian stance on contraception, which countered the view of many racial hygienists that reduced fertility was itself a sign of degeneration. Insisting that racial hygienists consider the social conditions of reproduction and not only its biological aspects, the League disseminated information on birth control among working-class women, and its members organized protests against further legal restrictions on the sale or advertisement of contraceptives.[140]

As in the League's approach to birth control and abortion, complex notions like Adele Schreiber's *mißbrauchte Mutterschaft* (misused motherhood) melded eugenicist views of the population problem with feminist visions of emancipation.[141] In Schreiber's schema motherhood was misused and "bodily and spiritual values were uselessly squandered" when pregnancies or births occurred that "could not fulfill their purpose of providing family and state with a vital member" and therefore represented an economic loss "in private as well as national terms." Warning against the rampant misuse of motherhood among female workers in particular, especially forced childbearing in the absence of available birth control or abortion, Schreiber pointedly asked: "How many children can a woman of the working classes, under the present circumstances, normally give birth to,

137. Allen, *Feminism and Motherhood*, p. 202.
138. Evans, *Feminist Movement*, p. 162. Also see Allen, *Feminism and Motherhood*, p. 158.
139. Evans, *Feminist Movement*, pp. 131, 159; Fürth, "Die Lage der Mutter," pp. 278, 284; Schreiber, "Mißbrauchte und unwillkommene Mutterschaft," pp. 204, 215; Stach, "Mutterschaft und Bevölkerungsfrage," p. 197; Janssen-Jurreit, "Nationalbiologie," p. 163.
140. Janssen-Jurreit, "Nationalbiologie," pp. 146–47; Evans, *Feminist Movement*, p. 131.
141. Schreiber, "Mißbrauchte Mutterschaft," p. 201. Schreiber obviously drew here on the influential thought of Swedish feminist and Darwinian Ellen Key, who coined the term "the misuse of women's energy" in 1895. On Key, see Allen, *Feminism and Motherhood*, pp. 157, 161.

nurse, care for, raise, provide for, without damage to herself or to the quality of her offspring?"[142] Schreiber's associate Maria von Stach argued that the proliferation of small families with one or two children—decried by racial hygienists as hedonistic and egotistical—represented "a thoroughly reasonable compromise solution" given the dire social circumstances most working women faced. Feminists from the League called on women to learn to wield the social contribution of motherhood as a "weapon," to recognize that a woman "holds the keys of life in her hands" and that at her instigation "all wheels stand still," thereby invoking visions of women organized in mothers' unions, engaged in general strikes against compulsory motherhood and demanding expanded state protection of mothers and children. Recasting social citizenship through a new vision of motherhood, League feminists made a woman's consent to motherhood contingent on the awarding of social benefits—state subventions, maternity insurance, and pregnancy leave—as well as on the endowment of women with "the full rights of citizenship."[143]

Thus, between the turn of the century and the First World War the milieu of social reform was transformed and the social question of female factory labor redefined as both feminism and eugenics came to occupy a significant place within the debates about the declining birthrates, the crisis of motherhood, and the protection of women workers. As Paul Weindling has argued, the German state itself did not adopt explicitly eugenicist social policies before the First World War, but the rhetoric of biological fitness and racial degeneration, the emphasis on maternal bodies and *Volkskörper*, permeated the discursive milieu of social reform in which the legislative innovations of this period took shape.[144] So, for example, as the Reichstag was deliberating the revision of the protective labor laws in 1907, the League for the Protection of Mothers joined forces with the Propaganda Society for Maternity Insurance, an organization of medical doctors in Karlsruhe, to present a petition to the Reichstag on behalf of maternity insurance and pregnancy leave.[145] Reflecting its particular blend of feminist eugenics, the petition acknowledged the expansion of married women's employment in all sectors of the economy and asserted resolutely that "this is not a temporary situation, nor is it a symptom of illness in the

142. Schreiber, "Mißbrauchte Mutterschaft," pp. 200–201, 207.
143. Stach, "Mutterschaft und Bevölkerungsfrage," pp. 191, 193, 200; Schreiber, "Mißbrauchte Mutterschaft," p. 206; Allen, *Feminism and Motherhood*, pp. 147, 185–87; Bergmann, "Die rationalisierten Triebe," p. 140.
144. Weindling, *Health, Race and German Politics*, pp. 9, 27.
145. Schwimmer, "Wichtige Momente," p. 380; Allen, *Feminism and Motherhood*, p. 184. The petition is reprinted as "The Manipulation of Motherhood" (Document 39) in Eleanor S. Riemer and John C. Fout, eds., *European Women: A Documentary History, 1789–1945* (New York: Schocken, 1987), pp. 168–71.

social fabric: rather it is the inevitable result of favorable economic conditions." The League called on the state to recognize its "duty . . . to create new means of allowing the mother to work without damage being done to the whole nation," first and foremost by extending maternity protection to "the vast majority of working women," including those in those sectors of agriculture, domestic service, and home and factory industry, "who are completely unprotected." Noting that the infant mortality rates constituted "'a modern infanticide,'" the petition also expressed concern about the "racial deterioration" of the German people. Even those "children who remain alive," its authors argued, "develop weak bodies because of the absence of the mother's milk and are subjected to repeated debilitating illnesses," resulting in a serious "diminution of the number of men fit for military service."[146]

Although the revised labor code of 1908 took shape within this complex discursive field, it nonetheless remained bounded by the framework of the 1891 code: rather than charting new legislative territory, it extended the scope of existing protective measures. At the same time, however, it also partially fulfilled some of the key demands of both feminists and eugenicists, mandating a ten-hour workday for women on weekdays and an eight-hour limit on Saturdays, and barring pregnant women and new mothers from working two weeks before and six weeks after the birth of a child. Furthermore, in a new measure embodying the growing influence of medicine, in particular "reproductive hygiene," in shaping social policy, the code required the new mother to submit a doctor's report evaluating her postpartum recovery and her bodily fitness for work before resuming employment.[147] In addition to protective labor laws, the health insurance code of 1903 deemed female factory workers who had been insured for at least one year eligible for maternity benefits, including partial wage reimbursement and costs of medical treatment, while continuing to exclude from coverage women working in agriculture, domestic service, and home industry. In 1911, however, the provisions of the insurance law were extended to these other categories of employees and members of the free professions. Although the period of coverage was extended to eight weeks, the rate of reimbursement continued to be some half or two-thirds of wages earned.[148]

146. As cited in Riemer and Fout, *European Women*, pp. 169–71.
147. HStAD, JBdKPG 1910, Reg. Düss., pp. 420–22; Schwimmer, "Wichtige Momente," pp. 380–82; Ratz, *Sozialreform und Arbeiterschaft*, p. 162.
148. The provisions of the 1903 law were that women were to receive no less than one-half and no more than two-thirds of their earnings. Wives of workers who had been covered for at least one year were also eligible. Coverage was extended in 1911 to domestic, agricultural, and commercial employees whose incomes did not exceed 3,000 marks. Schwimmer, "Wichtige Momente," pp. 377, 383; Freier, *"Dem Reich der Freiheit,"* pp. 109–11.

Feminist activists thus came to occupy a pivotal place within the expanding public sphere and the increasingly complex fabric of reform associations between the turn of the century and the First World War. From the factory inspectors' attempted resolution of the social question of female factory work in 1901 through the emergent crisis of the decaying *Volkskörper* later in the decade, gender remained in the forefront of social reformers' visions and state social policy during the prewar years. Within each of the respective reform milieus, the female intelligentsia, educated and trained in social science theories and methods, became the requisite experts on the plight of working mothers and their children. In asserting their claims to represent the interests of women workers, these feminist reformers also gained an important role in fostering the expansion of the German welfare state. In a stance reminiscent of Alice Salomon's vision of the ship that had found "safe harbor," middle-class feminists came to regard the welfare state "chiefly as a protective agency for vulnerable women and children." Yet their enthusiastic endorsement of its expansion tended to overlook the ways its widening competence encroached on the individual rights of women and workers as the subjects of social policy.[149]

The analysis offered here of the rich array of feminist contributions to the debates about female factory labor makes it clear that female reformers, both socialist and bourgeois, were able to dissect critically and cleverly the disparaging rhetoric of conservative male reformers regarding female factory labor and to expose the ideologies that underlay them. They fashioned alternative readings of women workers' motivations and consciousness, their reasons for seeking employment, for engaging in militant strikes, or for restricting the number of children they bore. Moreover, they launched effective challenges to the pervasive definitions of skill, wage hierarchies, and divisions of labor. At the same time, however, that most female reformers—bourgeois, Social Democratic, and Catholic—embraced domesticity and motherhood along with dominant notions of health, hygiene, and population quality illustrates how thoroughly embedded these ideas were in the languages and paradigms of their respective milieus. Indeed, it suggests an intriguing ideological and rhetorical proximity between maternalist and paternalist social reformers. So, for example, feminist Social Democrat Lily Braun stunned both socialist and bourgeois feminists with her radical utopian demands for cooperative households, while also chastening unorganized female *Schmutzkonkurrenten* (unfair competitors) for endangering the jobs of male breadwinners and the well-being of the working-class family and thus sharing common rhetorical ground with opponents of female factory labor among the party

---

149. Allen, *Feminism and Motherhood*, p. 237.

rank and file.¹⁵⁰ Similarly, bourgeois feminists of the League for the Protection of Mothers and Sexual Reform defended women's right to abortion and birth control while advocating the enforced sterilization of the biologically unfit, including those with congenital handicaps, chronic diseases, or mental illness as well as alcoholics and criminals. Former female factory inspector Marie Baum, for example, feared that legalizing abortion would "make the State 'an accomplice to the deadening of our racial conscience,'" since only the "laziest and stupidest unmarried pregnant women would fail to get abortions," while the "superior women would no longer be forced to give birth."¹⁵¹ In the forefront of the battle to redefine skill and to create adequate training opportunities for young women, Marie Lischnewska expressed her opposition to abortion in unusually virulent nationalist and racist terms of a German "struggle for world supremacy," against "the vast hordes of our enemies," which required that Germans "populate the colonies we have and the colonies we still have to conquer."¹⁵²

Within their respective social and political milieus, feminist reformers reinforced and reproduced the dominant consensus regarding eugenicist solutions to the increasingly complex tangle of social questions. At the same time, they contested and subverted the social hygienicist claims to "colonize" the female body by calling on women to use motherhood as a weapon and by demanding that the state grant women full citizenship rights in exchange for the services of motherhood.¹⁵³ While prescribing norms of reproductive health and hygiene for women of all classes, feminist reformers also imputed to all women agency, an active voice, in the realm of reproduction. Indeed, the programmatic disciplinary claims of social and reproductive hygiene on the female body and female sexuality

---

150. Braun's "utopian solutions to the conflicts between work and motherhood"—communal kitchens and state maternity insurance—sparked intense controversy among the party's female leaders. Regarding female workers as competitors for men's jobs, she said: "It is only natural that men perceive a danger in this, that they do not simply overlook—with blinded eyes and cold hearts—the destruction of their family life and the neglect of their children." Lily Braun, *Die Frauenfrage: Ihre geschichtliche Entwicklung und ihre wirtschaftliche Seite* (1901; reprint Berlin: Dietz, 1979), pp. 222–23. On Braun, see Jean H. Quataert, *Reluctant Feminists in German Social Democracy, 1885–1917* (Princeton: Princeton University Press, 1979), pp. 76–83; Allen, *Feminism and Motherhood*, pp. 155–56, 167–68; and Freier, *"Dem Reich der Freiheit,"* pp. 53–56, 108–9.

151. As cited in Evans, *Feminist Movement*, pp. 158–59.

152. As cited in Evans, *Feminist Movement*, p. 159. Here Evans cites Lischnewska's contributions of 1905 and 1908 to debates at assemblies of the BDF, or Federation of German Women's Associations.

153. "Colonization" is the Habermasian term Peukert employs in his *Grenzen der Sozialdisziplinierung*. See in particular chapter 20, "Kolonialisierung der Lebenswelten—Widerstand und Marginalisierung."

also had its underside, namely the coalescing of discourses and subcultures that sought to disrupt and contest the rationalization of reproduction and the disciplining of the body.[154] Thus the feminist-eugenicist demand that the contribution of motherhood be respected and rewarded, the declaration that women must have the choice whether to consent to motherhood, suggested in fact that the declining birthrate might be read as "a mass refusal of the socially imposed obligation to bear children."[155]

The crisis of maternity and *Volkskörper*, of dissent and consent to motherhood, reached its culmination in one sector of the reform milieu on the eve of the First World War, as the Social Democratic Party became embroiled in an internal controversy over a proposed "birth strike" that drew thousands of party members and sympathizers into mass assemblies and demonstrations in 1913. The neo-Malthusian socialist doctors Alfred Bernstein and Julius Moses, who as members of the Berlin Association of Family Doctors had actively propagated the use of birth control in working-class clinics, neighborhoods, and women's meetings in Berlin, recognized the steadily dwindling birthrates as an ongoing, if unspoken, birth strike. Similar to the bourgeois feminist view of motherhood as a weapon in the struggle for citizenship rights, the socialist doctors summoned the birth strike as an "unbloody method of class struggle," as a political strategy against workers' chronic impoverishment and their high infant and maternal mortality, and as a means of raising consciousness about the social value of women's contribution to society through childbearing. The campaign struck a raw natalist nerve not only among social policy experts at the level of state, but most acutely perhaps among Social Democratic Party leaders, including the female leaders Clara Zetkin, Rosa Luxemburg, and Luise Zietz.[156] The party convened two turbulent meetings in the Neue Welt in Berlin, which overflowed with some 4,000 participants, including about 2,500 women, marking "the first time in the history of the labor movement that so many women demonstrated such emphatic interest in a party meeting."[157] While the doctors Bernstein and Moses received "roaring, positive applause," Zetkin, Zietz, and Luxemburg either castigated the audience for its backwardness or declared the use of the birth control a "private decision" devoid of all political content. The Social Democratic Party, which had been named by state investigators in 1912 as

154. Detlev Peukert's critique of narrow Foucauldian paradigms of subjection and resistance points to the two-sided nature of youth welfare in Germany, juxtaposing the new social disciplinary institutions aimed at youth welfare to the new youthful subcultures that rose to resist these institutions. See his *Grenzen der Sozialdisziplinierung*, p. 21.
155. Bergmann, "Frauen, Männer, Sexualität," p. 82.
156. Bergmann, "Die rationalisierten Triebe," pp. 144–45; idem, "Frauen, Männer, Sexualität," pp. 94–95.
157. Bergmann, "Frauen, Männer, Sexualität," p. 94.

one of the crucial instigators of the declining birthrate—since the decline was most pronounced in industrial towns and districts—vehemently rejected these claims, asserting its own eugenicist concern with the pattern of slowed population growth.[158] Successfully defeating a motion in favor of the birth strike, party leaders sought to convince their members and sympathizers that "the large mass is of crucial significance in the struggle for its liberation." "A glance at history," argued Clara Zetkin, "shows that rising classes achieve victory not based on their quality, but based on their numbers."[159] Thus, however ineffectual the debate about the birth strike as a strategy of class struggle, its history highlights the claims placed on the female reproductive body not only by the German state, bourgeois experts, and reformers, but also by the leading party of the German working class. Finally, it suggests that the agency of women workers in the realm of reproduction, as much as the specter of a decaying *Volkskörper*, prompted the eugenicist concern with population control during the prewar years.

Conclusion

Between the turn of the century and the outbreak of the First World War the social question of female factory labor, once a vital aspect of the *Arbeiterfrage*, became an intrinsic part of the perceived crisis of motherhood and the German quest for empire. It represented a different sort of *sittliche Kulturfrage* than did the worker question of the mid- and late nineteenth century, yet it relied no less on the dichotomy of moral and immoral in its new emphasis on social and racial health and hygiene. As the protection of female factory labor became entwined with eugenicist and hygienicist solutions to the social pathologies of industrial society, as "medicine [combined] with the state to foster hygiene" and ultimately to surmount these pathologies,[160] the "bodily dimension of individual and collective behavior, in all its facets" became the site of "scholarly decoding," as well as the object of protective labor and health insurance legislation, aimed explicitly at the "female organism."[161] The economy of the body, defined within the increasingly complex and medicalized domain of social reform, transformed the social, placing the female body at the heart of its conflicts over the reproduction of labor. Motherhood, in all its new social, national, and imperial meanings, displaced domesticity as the cul-

158. Ibid., pp. 92–93, 97–98.
159. *Vorwärts* (Social Democratic daily) of 24 August 1913, as cited in ibid., p. 94.
160. Gilles Deleuze, foreword to Donzelot, *Policing of Families*, p. xiv.
161. Labisch, *Homo hygienicus*, p. 169.

tural matrix of the social.¹⁶² The growing fascination with what Michel Foucault termed "biopolitics"—"the proliferation of political technologies" that invested the body and hygiene with new meanings, making the health, welfare, and productivity of bodies "pliable to new technologies of control"—recast the milieu of social reform, if not yet the social policy of the state, in the years prior to the First World War.¹⁶³

At the same time, the emergent "psychophysics of work" and other productivist visions of the body as a human motor began to ascribe to female bodies a new kind of disruptive potential within the *Volkskörper* that required new interventions aimed more explicitly at improved productivity and higher economic utility of bodies at work. Thus the sexual division of labor also became more explicitly embodied.¹⁶⁴ During and after the First World War, the investigations of the body and the science of work would undermine the notion of the female organism as "eternally wounded and needing care every hour of her life" and would emphasize instead that "the woman is the expression of endurance."¹⁶⁵ For, as one scientist, Josefa Ioteyko, argued in 1919, "under the usual physiological conditions, woman is vigorous, full of resistance, and robust." Furthermore, she pointed out, "the sex which pretended to be the weaker, is really the stronger, it has the greater powers of resistance to the forces which destroy life."¹⁶⁶

As the female body became an increasingly explicit presence in both social policy and the sexual division of labor, including the new and more pronounced gulf between male breadwinners and working mothers, it also came to anchor the identities of class and citizenship, both working-class and middle-class. As scientific and social reformers mapped out new disciplinary paradigms for body, health, and family, they widened the arena of social policy, crossing the threshold of the home, extending its influence into the family and the sphere of reproduction and laying the foundation for the expansion of the German welfare state into these realms during the First World War.¹⁶⁷ In dissolving the boundaries between private house-

---

162. On "Körperökonomie," see Frevert, *Krankheit als politisches Problem*, p. 16.
163. Hewitt, "Bio-politics and Social Policy," pp. 67–69.
164. On the psychophysics of work, see Weber, "Zur Psychophysik," and Josefa Ioteyko, *The Science of Labour and Its Organization* (London: Routledge, 1919). Also see Campbell, *Joy in Work*, especially chapter 5, "The Science of Work before the First World War"; Anson Rabinbach, "The European Science of Work: The Economy of the Body at the End of the 19th Century," in *Work in France: Representations, Meaning, Organization, and Practice*, ed. Steven L. Kaplan and Cynthia J. Koepp (Ithaca: Cornell University Press, 1986), pp. 475–513, and his *The Human Motor: Energy, Fatigue, and the Origins of Modernity* (Berkeley: University of California Press, 1992).
165. Ioteyko, *Science of Labour*, p. 111. On Ioteyko, see Rabinbach, "European Science of Work," p. 494.
166. Ioteyko, *Science of Labour*, p. 106.
167. Peukert, *Grenzen der Sozialdisziplinierung*, p. 22. On the role of eugenics as a key

hold and public interest, between individual and social bodies, the scientists and social reformers who shaped social policy demarcated the boundaries between and within classes, in particular between women and men.[168] In establishing the framework for the conflicts, negotiations, and shared understandings between workers and employers, between women and men in the world behind the mill gate, the discursive milieu of social reform, with the legislative interventions it fashioned and enacted, became a formative part of the structures and the experiences of work in concrete ways, as the next chapter illustrates.[169] The protective labor codes of 1878 and 1891 had mapped out a category of female and youth workers requiring special protection and had inscribed their work with secondary and subordinate characteristics. Yet the debates about female factory labor during the early twentieth century, in which the issues of labor protection became entwined with the "pathologies" of the birthrate decline, now anchored women workers' secondary status not merely in skill and wage differentials, but also in the distinct reproductive meanings of male and female bodies.

Although the discursive transformations and legislative innovations with regard to female factory labor did set the parameters for the social relations and identities of class and citizenship, this process too had its underside. For as much as the changing milieu of social reform shaped women workers' subjectivities, the discourses of reform also inspired embodied resistance, as expressed in the voluntary limitation of births, in female workers' attempts to appropriate and contest the meanings of motherhood and factory labor, and in their efforts to organize and defend the intersections between the two spheres of work and sexual politics.

---

ideology in the formation of the middle class, see Weindling, *Health, Race and German Politics*, pp. 6–7.

168. Jean H. Quataert, "Woman's Work and the Early Welfare State in Germany: Legislators, Bureaucrats, and Clients before the First World War," in Koven and Michel, *Mothers of a New World*, p. 161. Quataert argues that the welfare policies of the German state "could reach people in the remotest corners of the realm, at their place of work or home, in the town hall, at the insurance office, or through receipt of a pension check." Also see George Steinmetz on how the welfare state became "deeply implicated in the peculiarities of German working-class formation," in his "Workers and the Welfare State in Imperial Germany," *International Labor and Working-Class History* 40 (fall 1991): 21.

169. Robert Gray, "The Language of Factory Reform in Britain, c. 1830–1860," in *The Historical Meanings of Work*, ed. Patrick Joyce (Cambridge: Cambridge University Press, 1989), p. 177; Woker, "Naturwissenschaftliche Streiflichter," pp. 224–25.

6

Work Experiences, Work Identities: Dissolving the Dichotomy between Home and Work

The making of the textile factory workplace was marked by both structural and discursive transformations. The relocation of cloth manufacture from household to factory, accompanied by new hierarchical wage scales, skill definitions, and systems of factory supervision, as well as the reinvention of male craft identities and the protests of male weavers against women's work that accompanied the transition, shaped work identities and work cultures among the new factory workforce. At the same time, the discursive and legislative interventions into the domain of women's work left a lasting imprint on the policies and programs of state, employers, and labor unions that formed the factory regime. Protective labor legislation, for example, legitimated women's wage work while attempting to contain it within strict boundaries, seeking to regulate the work world in order to preserve the family. The protective labor codes of 1878, 1891, and 1908 recast the division and relations of labor, reducing women's work hours or prescribing architectural changes such as separate entrances, lunchrooms, or restrooms for male and female workers. Moreover, the protective laws established the frameworks within which male and female workers, workers and employers negotiated conflicts and forged understandings—frameworks in which sexual difference was key.[1]

---

1. On the framework within which conflicts and negotiations in the workplace occurred, see Robert Gray, "The Language of Factory Reform in Britain, c. 1830–1860," in *The Historical Meanings of Work*, ed. Patrick Joyce (Cambridge: Cambridge University Press, 1989), p. 177. For examples of the ways labor legislation shaped the workplace, see Jean Quataert, "A Source Analysis in German Women's History: Factory Inspectors' Reports and the Shaping of Working-Class Lives, 1878–1914," *Central European History* 16 (June 1983): 109–10. My examination of factory inspectors' reports for 1888–1918 confirms the inspec-

Textile manufacturers, for their part, challenged prevailing notions of sexual difference by actively recruiting women workers, married and single, and rewarding them for long-term employment. Although mill owners sought to cultivate *Stammarbeiter,* a stable core of female workers, and publicly acknowledged how much they depended on women workers—for example, during the factory inspectors' inquiry of 1899—their policies created a female workforce that remained consistently secondary in terms of wages and skills. Male labor leaders and union members inserted their own visions of domesticity and respectability, their fears as *Familienväter* (fathers of families) about the dissolution of family, into their campaigns for work time reductions and wage increases.[2] The terrain of experience in this "women's industry" was not charted by men alone, however, for many women spurned the dominant images and ideologies that sought to restrict their employment outside the home, even if most were forced to work out of economic necessity. Instead, many female textile workers fought to impose their needs as mothers and wives on the factory regime as they established their own rhythms of work, interrupting employment to give birth or to care for a sick child or relative and returning when their family situation permitted, or transgressing gender boundaries by accepting jobs in "men's shops" or launching wildcat strikes without the support of male colleagues or union leaders.

The term "work identity" signifies the ways male and female textile workers viewed and used their jobs, the multiple meanings they derived from and imparted to their work, the ways it "got under the skin" of their lives.[3] "Work identity" also denotes the ways men and women related to their work sphere, encompassing their machines, the products of their labor, and their ethics of work, the social networks that divided or united the shop floor, and even the physical space of the mill. Work identities admittedly are elusive historical subjects that cannot be reconstructed in any definitive way; instead they are "read" and interpreted by comparing a variety of sources, including company personnel records, factory inspectors' reports, police reports, and social reformers' observations of mill life.[4]

---

tors' regular intervention regarding physical space, the structure of work, and the sexual division of labor.

2. See, for example, Deutscher Textilarbeiterverband (hereafter DTAV), "Wann werden wir den freien Sonnabendnachmittag haben?" *Der Textilarbeiter* 25 (15 August 1913): 266–67.

3. For an interesting discussion of the ways "work got under the skin of everyday life," see Patrick Joyce, *Work, Society, and Politics: The Culture of the Factory in Later Victorian England* (New Brunswick, N.J.: Rutgers University Press, 1984), p. 97.

4. "Work identity" is not a term the nineteenth- or twentieth-century labor movement used. I employ it to denote *Berufsinteresse* or *Berufsidentität*, which figures in union sources as a prerequisite to union membership. The Christian textile union, for example, demanded

In examining work identities I consider the experiences of women as they traversed the borders between family and wage work: the rhythms of their mill careers, the pride they expressed in their work, the bonds that formed and fractured among coworkers, employers, families, and communities, and the needs and desires that propelled women workers into strikes and informal protests. Work identities encompass workers' individual and collective self-definitions as they both resisted and sought accommodation with the factory regime and the dominant ideology of gender underlying it. Pivotal in imagining how women formed work identities is the development of *Berufsethos* (work ethic), a process by which they came to identify with their jobs, feeling pride in the products of their labor and forming bonds or "shared dispositions" with fellow workers based on common fears, aspirations, interests, and loyalties.[5] Integral to the concept of work identity is the potential for agency, revealed in the ways workers sought to position themselves within, and sometimes to distance themselves from, the constraints of the structure of production.[6]

The task of reading and weaving together multiple aspects of women's work experience raises possibilities that conventional labor historiography has ignored or dismissed. Implicit in the rhetoric of the nineteenth-century labor movement, and in the historical studies of German workers, was the assumption of inextricable links between work identities and political (class) consciousness. The worker most likely to become politically active was male and Protestant; his identification with job or craft—a prerequisite for developing class consciousness—was based on skill acquired through formal apprenticeship, relatively well paid employment in an economically vital and highly productive industry, and long-term job stability. The central component of work identity was the relation between the worker and his work and a fundamental comprehension of the work process as a whole, which men were thought to gain through apprenticeship or trade school. Implicit in the construction of this male ideal type was its

---

better job training for women, to solidify the relation between *Arbeiterin und Arbeit*, which would in turn give them the experience and understanding necessary to become trade union leaders. See, for example, Zentralverband Christlicher Textilarbeiter Deutschlands, "Warum braucht die Frau die Erziehung zur Gewerbetätigkeit?" *Textilarbeiterzeitung* 12 (22 January 1910): 10. The term is more implicit than explicit in recent German labor historiography.

5. Jürgen Kocka, "Problems of Working-Class Formation: The Early Years, 1800–1875," in *Working-Class Formation: Nineteenth-Century Patterns in Western Europe and the United States*, ed. Ira Katznelson and Aristide Zolberg (Princeton: Princeton University Press, 1986), p. 282.

6. For interesting discussions of agency, see Joan Scott, "The Evidence of Experience," *Critical Inquiry* 17, no. 3 (1991): 777–78, 792–93; Párveen Adams and Jeff Minson, "The 'Subject' of Feminism," in *The Woman in Question*, ed. Parveen Adams and Elisabeth Cowie (Boston: MIT Press, 1990), pp. 91–93.

opposite, the typical female factory worker: unskilled, *willig und billig* (submissive and cheap), and employed temporarily or irregularly. The crucial differences between male and female industrial labor, according to labor historians, included the sparse opportunities for women to acquire comparable training and the low wages they received. Moreover, the frequent family-related interruptions in women's working lives—as well as their alleged primary identity as mothers and housewives—were thought to hinder formation of work identities and political consciousness.[7]

Thus German labor historiography has defined women's factory labor in terms that echo the organized German labor movement of the late nineteenth and early twentieth centuries—as unskilled, poorly paid, unstable, and offering little opportunity for upward mobility or for the development of *Berufsethos*, a central component of political consciousness. An ethic of work had no place in the popular image of the female worker, an image that had erased the memory of home industry, where women had worked lifelong at looms or spindles and where their double burden had been contained within the walls of a single dwelling. In its place was now the highly modern image of female factory hands who sought only temporary, usually premarital employment, and because of their role as "secondary earners" were generally apathetic toward workplace issues, unions, and strikes. Indeed, German labor historiography is characterized by two underlying contradictory assumptions regarding the relation between production and class formation. First, it assumes that the structure of production was pivotal in shaping how male workers viewed their work and formed work identities. At the heart of this relation between worker and work was the possession of skill—real or mythologized—and the claim to comprehend the labor process as a whole or to assert some control over it. Political or class consciousness originated in the identities workers formed in the workplace, in particular in their struggles at the point of production. The second and contradictory assumption is that women's work identities, unlike men's, were *not* shaped primarily by their experience in and relation to production. Marriage and motherhood, not the ten to twelve hours a day spent on the shop floor, are viewed as constitutive of women's work identities and political behavior.[8]

The concepts of work identity and work culture represent new ways of

---

7. See, for example, Brian Peterson's article "The Politics of Working-Class Women in the Weimar Republic," *Central European History* 10 (June 1977): 95.

8. See Mary Nolan, "Economic Crisis, State Policy, and Working-Class Formation in Germany, 1870–1900," in Katznelson and Zolberg, *Working-Class Formation*, p. 377, and Rosemarie Beier, "'Mechanisch greifen die Hände . . .': Arbeit und Erfahrung von Frauen in der Industrie," in *Die Arbeiter: Lebensformen, Alltag und Kultur*, ed. Wolfgang Ruppert (Munich: C. H. Beck, 1986), pp. 215–23.

thinking about the "politics of production," opening up the terrain of "politics" to encompass everyday work culture as a political "terrain where the abstract structures of domination and exploitation were directly encountered" and contested.[9] The emphasis on *work* in the notion of work identities does not imply a firm boundary between shop-floor experience and family or community. While seeking to underscore the authenticity and significance of women's work experiences in their daily lives and political consciousness, this book contends that the meanings of work were far more complex than awareness of a shared socioeconomic position within the sphere of production.[10] Indeed, the concept of work identities refuses the dichotomy between family and factory that underpins most German labor histories and aims instead to explore how identities were shaped by the continual intersections of family time and industrial time, by the locations of family, neighborhood, and community. In this sense "work identities" emerge in part from the insights of feminist historiography of the past twenty years, which has dissolved the boundary between the private and the public (or political) by uncovering the political fabric of the "private sphere"—of consumption, reproduction, and neighborhood networks.[11] While emphasizing the fluid boundary between family/household and workplace in women's experiences and identities of work, this concept also resists the tendency of some feminist historiography to explain working women's identities and political initiatives primarily in terms of their location in the family, thereby implicitly underplaying the significance of the many hours spent at work.[12] This chapter, like chapters 1 and 2, uses a regional lens to examine the social composition—by age, sex, and geographic and family origin—and career patterns of male and female textile workers in seven textile mills in the Rhineland and Westphalia, analyzing how gender influenced job

---

9. Geoff Eley, "Labor History, Social History, *Alltagsgeschichte*: Experience, Culture, and the Politics of the Everyday—a New Direction for German Social History?" *Journal of Modern History* 61 (June 1989): 324. On the "politics of production," see Michael Burawoy, *The Politics of Production: Factory Regimes under Capitalism and Socialism* (London: Verso, 1985).

10. Kocka, "Problems of Working-Class Formation," p. 282.

11. On the broader theme of the family or the private sphere as a locus of politics, see "Politics and Culture in Women's History: A Symposium," *Feminist Studies* 6 (spring 1980): 26–63. For a more specific examination of this theme for the working-class family, see Temma Kaplan, "Female Consciousness and Collective Action: The Case of Barcelona, 1910–1918," in *Feminist Theory: A Critique of Ideology*, ed. Nannerl O. Keohane, Michelle Z. Rosaldo, and Barbara C. Gelpi (Chicago: University of Chicago Press, 1981), pp. 55–76; Ellen Ross, "Fierce Questions and Taunts: Married Life in Working Class London, 1870–1914," *Feminist Studies* (fall 1982): 575–602, and idem., *Love and Toil: Motherhood in Outcast London, 1870–1918* (New York: Oxford University Press, 1993).

12. Eleanor Gordon refers to the "new orthodoxy" in feminist historiography that points to the "private sphere" of household and family as the most important female political arena. See her article "Women, Work and Collective Action: Dundee Jute Workers, 1870–1906," *Journal of Social History* 20 (1987): 27–28, 44.

stability, the rhythms of family time and industrial time, and the formation of a work ethic among the female *Stammarbeiter*.[13]

Division of Labor and Factory Hierarchies

Despite the continuity between women's work in domestic and factory textile manufacture, the division of labor in the new textile mills represented a fundamentally new organization of work. Modernized textile mills encompassed elements of production that were not present in household workshops: new textile machinery assembled in centralized workshops; entrepreneurs who competed fiercely for the lowest prices and wages; and finally workers, sometimes entire families, who migrated across the plains of the Lower Rhine in search of work when faced with the disintegration of domestic textile production.

An examination of personnel records from seven textile mills in the Rhineland and Westphalia shows that the new factories divided most sectors of production along gender lines (see table 5). Men were still more likely to perform tasks that required formal training, such as warping the looms and repairing, maintaining, and supervising the machinery, while women and teenagers carried out the preparatory and finishing tasks of winding, reeling, bobbin setting, piecing, napping, and darning. The workforce in spinning mills generally included more women than men: men usually worked the self-acting mules, while women performed ring spinning. Weaving became the most intensely contested domain of textile manufacture during the transition from handweaving to mechanized looms, since employers in the branches of silk, cotton, and woolen weaving often favored female weavers over unemployed male handweavers or sought to hire female factory weavers in place of men at crucial points of conflict or upswings in production. Despite the feminization of silk weaving and ongoing contests over women's work in woolen weaving, a sexual division of labor nonetheless prevailed in most shops. Men wove heavy or patterned cloth, ribbons, and velvet and were frequently assigned to double looms, whereas employers allocated the weaving of certain fabrics (usually simpler and plainer) to women. Thus, even where women advanced into spheres of employment that had been constructed as male, male weavers retained a near monopoly on tasks of greater "skill."

The ascription of gendered attributes to technologies and types of fabrics sometimes led to segregation of the sexes in separate weaving shops,

13. See Tamara Hareven, *Family Time and Industrial Time: the Relationship between the Family and Work in a New England Industrial Community* (Cambridge: Cambridge University Press, 1982).

Table 5. Textile mills and sources

Company	Product	Location	Source	Period	Number of observations			Sample
					Men	Women	Total	
Baldus	Wool weaving/knitting	Osberghausen (small town)	*Arbeiterstammrollen* (3)	1865–1915	43% (343)	57% (454)	797	All workers employed 1905–15
Crous	Silk weaving	Viersen (small city)	*Arbeiterstammrolle* (1)	1900–1930	22% (57)	78% (201)	258	All workers employed in 1926
Girmes	Velvet/plush weaving	Oedt (rural town)	*Arbeiterstammrollen* (2)	1885–1917	64% (412)	36% (232)	644	10% of workforce
Wülfing	Worsted wool spinning	Lennep (small city)	*Arbeiterstammrollen* (3)	1892–1935	35% (274)	65% (518)	792	10% of workforce
Mechanische Weberei Bielefeld	Linen weaving	Bielefeld (larger city)	*Arbeiterstammrollen* (4)	1865–1924	18% (117)	82% (534)	651	10% of workforce
Mechanische Weberei Spenge	Linen weaving	Spenge (rural town)	*Arbeiterstammrollen* (2)	1907–1916	61% (92)	39% (58)	150	All workers entering mill 1907–8
Frowein	Silk weaving	Neviges (small town)	List of workers (occupations not listed)	1860–1950	46% (88)	54% (103)	191	5% of workforce

Source: See appendix to this chapter.

Plate 2. Female bobbin setters (spoolers) at the zanella factory of Johann Wilhelm Scheidt, Kettwig/Ruhr (ca. 1913). From a company brochure, "Johann Wilhelm Scheidt, Kettwig/Ruhr" (undated), Rheinisch-Westfälisches Wirtschaftsarchiv, Abt. 60, J. W. Scheidt, Kettwig. Photo reprinted courtesy of the Rheinisch-Westfälisches Wirtschaftsarchiv, Cologne.

and this was encouraged by the revised labor code of 1891, which recommended separating the sexes at work wherever possible.[14] The Scheidt company of Kettwig, for example, operated two weaving mills, one producing woolens and the other zanella cloth, a blend of cotton and woolen threads. The company apparently organized its weaving shops along gender lines according to the different conditions of manufacture for the two types of cloth. Its wage books indicate that 95 percent of the woolen weavers were men, while all 79 zanella weavers were women.[15] Similarly,

14. The Düsseldorf factory inspector's report of 1900 notes that inspectors frequently attempted to enforce this separation. Hauptstaatsarchiv Düsseldorf (HStAD, Regierungspräsidium Düsseldorf (Reg. Düss.), Handel und Gewerbe (H&G), VIII J 18: *Jahresberichte der Königlichen Preussischen Gewerberäthe*, (JBdKPG), 1900: Düsseldorf, p. 308.

15. The wage books (*Lohnbücher*) from the three factories (Kammgarnspinnerei, Zanellafabrik, and Tuchfabrik) for the years 1910–19 are in the Rheinisch-Westfälisches Wirtschaftsarchiv in Cologne, Bestand Scheidt: Abt. 60, Nr. 7 (hereafter RWWA, Scheidt Abt. 60). These personnel records are not included in this chapter's data analysis because of the relatively narrow time frame they cover.

in Scheidt's worsted spinning mill only one of the 105 ring spinners was male, but all 23 self-actor spinners were men.[16]

The transition to factory production underscored the division between exclusively male *Textilhandwerker* (textile craftsmen), the only mill employees who could claim to have acquired "skill" through a craft apprenticeship, and semiskilled workers, both male and female. The master weavers, machinists, mechanics, and foremen who were endowed with the authority to supervise others and who oversaw the operation and repair of the textile machinery were almost exclusively male. For example, the Crous company in Viersen employed four times as many women as men in its silk weaving mill; yet the company's *Arbeiterstammrolle* lists five *Meister* for 1926, the year of my sample, all of them men.[17] Similarly, the nine *Meister* and *Untermeister* who supervised the female zanella weavers in the Scheidt mill were men.[18] Indeed, women performed supervisory tasks in only one of the factories included here. The Scheidt company employed an occasional female *Meister* or *Untermeister* in its worsted spinning mill, but only in shops that were exclusively female, such as combing and sorting. Supervision and technical expertise were the preserve of men, which meant that contests over the exercise of authority were usually infused with gender.

Whereas some employers sought to enforce a sexual and spatial separation of the sexes on the shop floor, others allocated work at looms or spindles by family unit. The Scheidt company wage books reveal that at least two members of one family worked at fourteen of the thirty spinning mules listed. Nine or ten workers were assigned to each pair of mules, usually including one male spinner and several female piecers.[19] In mills where family labor was widespread, employers sought not to segregate the sexes but to separate married workers with families from those who were young and single. A woolen factory in Eupen provided cafeterias for its workers, for example, since many commuted from villages in the Eifel and

16. On the predominance of men in self-actor spinning (despite technological change), see Mary Freifeld, "Technological Change and the 'Self-Acting' Mule: A Study of Skill and the Sexual Division of Labor," *Social History* 11 (October 1986): 319–43.

17. See the appendix to this chapter for full information on the sample from the Crous mill.

18. RWWA, Scheidt, Abt. 60: Lohnbücher der Zanellafabrik, 1910–19. Karl Emsbach, *Die soziale Betriebsverfassung der rheinischen Baumwollindustrie im 19. Jahrhundert* (Bonn: Ludwig Röhrscheid, 1982), p. 504. Emsbach finds considerable upward mobility for both men and women in the spinning sector. Although both could move from piecer to spinner, he notes that for women the step up to *Meister* was "nearly impossible."

19. RWWA, Bestand 60: Scheidt, Lohnbücher der Tuchfabrik (Abt. Kammgarnspinnerei). Spinner Josef Euk, for example, supervised mules twenty-seven and twenty-eight while Frau Euk and Anna Euk, presumably his wife and daughter, worked at his side as piecers. The Strittmacher family worked mules seven and eight, including spinner Victor and his assistants Franz and Josef Strittmacher, who may have been his sons or younger siblings.

Plate 3. Weaving room at the zanella factory of Johann Wilhelm Scheidt, Kettwig/Ruhr (ca. 1913). From a company brochure, "Johann Wilhelm Scheidt, Kettwig/Ruhr" (undated), Rheinisch-Westfälisches Wirtschaftsarchiv, Abt. 60, J. W. Scheidt, Kettwig. Photo reprinted courtesy of the Rheinisch-Westfälisches Wirtschaftsarchiv, Cologne.

could not take their midday meal at home. The mill had separate cafeterias for men and women and "five small dining rooms for workers whose family members brought them their food, so they could take their meals together in peace."[20] The separate cafeterias also reinforced boundaries between indigenous workers, who lived and often worked with their families in the mill, and those from far away, who lived in company dormitories or boarded in town during the work week. The separation of mill space into spheres for men and women, for workers with families and those without, divided the workforce into two groups: the indigenous *Stammarbeiter* or *Bürgerarbeiter* (citizen-workers), as they were known in the woolen mills of Aachen, who were often the children or grandchildren of local handweavers, embedded in local communities and kin networks, and those young, single workers who commuted or had migrated from nearby towns or villages, leaving family and community behind.

20. HStAD, JBdKPG, 1907: Aachen, p. 500. The factory was the Wilhelm Peters company in Eupen.

Social and Geographic Background of the Textile Factory Workforce

Quantitative analysis of personnel records from seven textile companies, juxtaposed with the testimony of factory inspectors and the studies of social reformers, provides insight into the social composition of the factory workforce and permits some reconstruction of employees' working lives. As table 5 illustrates, the conditions of production and the locations of the seven companies vary, ranging from a linen weaving mill in an industrial city to a velvet factory in a rural mill village; yet each of the seven mills was a *Grossbetrieb,* or large factory; most had one hundred or more employees. The personnel records include payroll or wage books and *Arbeiterstammrollen,* record books in which employers registered vital information on each company employee, usually including name, birth date, birthplace, residence, type of employment, and entry and exit dates. Some include the name of the parent or guardian, religious affiliation, and reasons for leaving the job.[21] This source lets us define the contours of only one segment of a working life—the work experience in a single mill—and precludes tracing the movement of individual workers between employers.[22]

Kin Networks

Even where work was not allocated along family lines within individual shops, kin networks were a formative aspect of mill work, especially in the small, one-company towns examined here, like Kettwig, Lennep, Oedt, and Osberghausen. Extensive family clusters were discernible in five of the mills studied.[23] Evidence for probable existence of a family cluster, as defined here, was the presence in one mill of several workers with the same surname, in addition to a shared birthplace, residence, or religious affiliation.[24] It appears that some employers hired families as units, particularly

---

21. See the appendix to this chapter for further discussion of the *Arbeiterstammrollen* I examined. *Lohnbücher,* by contrast to *Arbeiterstammrollen,* were wage books in which method and amount of payment were recorded. The records for the Scheidt mill were *Lohnbücher* rather than *Arbeiterstammrollen.*

22. See the appendix to this chapter for elaboration of available data and method of data compilation and analysis.

23. The records of the other three mills did not provide sufficient information to determine family clusters.

24. For example, where the records list a Josef Schneider, age forty-five, a Frau Josef Schneider, age forty-two, and Maria and Margarete Schneider, ages eighteen and twenty, and all four share either residence, birthplace, or religious affiliation, a family cluster appears to exist. Because it was not possible to corroborate information from personnel records with

those they may have recruited from far away to fill labor shortages. The Scheidt zanella mill, for example, hired four members of the Zuccato family, presumably Italian immigrants, in 1912: Guiseppe, Palmira, and Petronella as weavers in shed II-F and Maria Zuccato as a bobbin setter.[25] The personnel records of the Scheidt spinning mill show that more than one-third of the self-actor spinners and their assistants had other family members who worked not only in the same mill but in the same shop, while 55 percent of workers in the Scheidt zanella mill had relatives working in the same factory.[26] For the Baldus woolen mill the figure was 53 percent; it was 61 percent in the Girmes velvet factory, 64 percent in the Wülfing spinning mill, and 83 percent in the Frowein silk mill in Neviges.[27] Marie Bernays, a student of Alfred Weber, who examined the *Auslese und Anpassung* (selection and adaptation) of the workers in the Gladbacher Spinnerei und Weberei (a cotton spinning and weaving mill in Mönchen-Gladbach) during the first decade of the twentieth century, found that was so for one-quarter of the workers in the mill. Weaving, she discovered, was an occupation with a particularly strong "hereditary" character: 38 percent of male weavers and 37 percent of female weavers in the Gladbach mill were children of weavers.[28] According to her findings, "long-term em-

---

census data, it was difficult to ascertain the precise relationships within apparent family clusters. Although birth dates provide one important clue, the presence of several young workers who have the same family name and are close in age probably indicates a group of siblings or cousins.

25. RWWA, Scheidt, Bestand 60: It appears that some of the largest family clusters in the Scheidt mill were Italian or Spanish families. This conclusion is based on a survey of last names: about 12 percent of the zanella mill workers in my sample appear to have been of foreign origin.

26. RWWA, Bestand 60: Scheidt, Lohnbücher der Tuchfabrik, 1910–19. In the case of the self-actor spinning shop, family members often worked side by side at the same mule.

27. RWWA, Bestand 60: Scheidt, Lohnbücher der Zanellafabrik, 1910–19. For the location of the *Arbeiterstammrollen* from the Baldus company (or mill), Johann Girmes AG, Wülfing und Sohn, and the Frowein company (or mill), see the appendix to this chapter. (The companies above are hereafter listed as Girmes/Lipp, Wülfing, and Frowein.) In some cases I could establish family ties rather than family clusters; that is, family members were employed not simultaneously but subsequent to one another (daughter or son after mother or father). Although this method of analysis might inflate the apparent number of kin networks in the textile workforce, it is at least equally likely that many family clusters, such as those that included relatives by marriage or kin with different surnames, remain invisible and that kin networks were even more widespread than indicated by this calculation.

28. Marie Bernays, *Auslese und Anpassung der Arbeiterschaft der geschlossenen Großindustrie, dargestellt an den Verhältnissen der Gladbacher Spinnerei und Weberei AG zu Mönchen-Gladbach im Rheinland*, Schriften des Vereins für Sozialpolitik, vol. 133 (Leipzig: Duncker und Humblot, 1910), pp. 104–5, 149. On Bernays, see Anthony Oberschall, *Empirical Social Research in Germany, 1848–1914* (New York: Basic Books, 1965), p. 128. Very little is known about Bernays beyond her noted study. She is described by other social reformers as Alfred Weber's protégé and also wrote an occasional article for the bourgeois feminist periodical *Die Frau* or

ployees seek 'good positions' for their children [in the mill] and want to have their children working near their own workplace; siblings or friends want to be near one another, and these wishes are respected as much as possible, because it is also in the interest of the factory [when] . . . workers who work next to one another help each other and put the machines to the best possible use."[29]

Birthplace and Residence

Local community ties also bound textile workers to one another and to the textile mills. Among the three *Arbeiterstammrollen* I examined that contained information on place of birth, a very high percentage of employees were of local origin (born within approximately ten kilometers of their place of employment). Some 92 percent of the 139 employees in my sample of workers in the Mechanische Weberei in the small town of Spenge near Bielefeld were born in Spenge itself or in nearby towns and villages in the Herford district.[30] But the workforce of the Mechanische Weberei's main mill in the sizable industrial city of Bielefeld was also overwhelmingly of local origin: 84.6 percent of the 645 workers in my sample were born in Bielefeld or within a ten-kilometer radius of the city; another 6.4 percent came from towns and villages between ten and fifty kilometers away, and 9 percent had migrated to Bielefeld from distant regions.[31] (See table 6 for analysis of the geographic origins of male and female workers.) The Girmes velvet factory in the mill village of Oedt recruited its workforce largely from Oedt itself or from the neighboring towns of Grefrath, Lobberich, Vorst, and Süchteln, in which velvet production had a long tradition: 68 percent of the 419 workers for whom information on birthplace was available came from Oedt or these neighboring villages. An additional 104 workers (25 percent) came from towns within a radius of ten to fifty kilometers, and only 31 (7 percent) were migrants from other

---

the liberal reform journal *Kultur und Fortschritt*. See, for example, Marie Bernays, "Berufsschicksale moderner Industriearbeiter," *Die Frau* 18 (December 1910): 129–36, 210–15; "Berufswahl und Berufsschicksal des modernen Industriearbeiters," *Archiv für Sozialwissenschaft und Sozialpolitik* 35–36 (1912–13): 123–76, 884–915; "Lehrwerkstätten und Fachschulen in der Textilindustrie," *Kultur und Fortschritt* 492–94 (1914): 20–29. But Bernays does not appear among the public spokeswomen of the "female intelligentsia" discussed in chapter 5. Beyond a note of the study cited above, no further information is available about her in the German biographical lexica.

29. Bernays, "Berufsschicksale," p. 132; Emsbach, *Die soziale Betriebsverfassung*, pp. 522–23. Emsbach also found that textile jobs were hereditary among approximately 40 percent of textile workers, especially spinners and weavers.

30. Stadtarchiv Bielefeld, Bestand Mechanische Weberei (hereafter StA Bi Mech. Web.) 27/1, *Namen der Arbeiter* (Spenge), 1907–32.

31. StA Bi Mech. Web. 28/1, *Personalbuch*, 1863–1925; 29/1, *Namen der Arbeiter bis 1907*; 51, *Personalbuch*, 1925–34.

Table 6. Birthplaces of male and female textile workers (%)

	Distance from factory		
	Within 10 km	10–50 km	Over 50 km
Girmes			
Men (277)	61.4 (170)[a]	28.9 (80)	9.7 (27)
Women (142)	80.3 (114)	16.9 (24)	2.8 (4)
Mechanische Weberei Bielefeld			
Men (117)	76.9 (90)	12.0 (14)	11.1 (13)
Women (528)	86.4 (456)	5.1 (27)	8.5 (45)

Source: See appendix to this chapter.
[a] Number of workers is given in parentheses.

regions.[32] Similarly, most workers in the Gladbacher Spinnerei und Weberei, which Marie Bernays studied, were born in Mönchen-Gladbach or within ten kilometers.[33] According to Bernays's findings, female workers were less likely to leave their hometowns than men.[34] Bernays discovered, for example, that women workers in the Gladbach mill typically practiced one or two occupations and changed employers within the same locality one to five times, whereas men changed employers two to five times in as many different localities.[35] As table 6 suggests, the pattern was similar in Bielefeld's Mechanische Weberei and the Girmes mill in Oedt.

Parallel to my findings regarding birthplace, textile workers in the Rhineland and Westphalia also tended to live near the mills where they worked. Approximately 90 percent of the textile workers included in my samples resided within ten kilometers of their place of employment, including many who lived in company housing.[36] Nearly 40 percent of the

32. Girmes/Lipp, *Arbeiterstammrollen*. Since birthplace was not listed for all Girmes employees, my calculations include only those for whom it was recorded.
33. Bernays, *Auslese und Anpassung*, p. 67; idem, "Berufswahl," p. 145. See also Jochem Ulrich, "Soziale Entwicklungen im industriellen Umbruch: Die Anpassungskrise in der niederrheinischen Textilindustrie, dargestellt am Gebiet der heutigen Stadt Viersen, 1890–1913" (Dissertation, Universität Duisburg, 1984), p. 356. Ulrich investigated the geographic background of workers of silk and metal workers in Viersen and found that nearly all silk workers of both sexes came from Viersen itself or from towns within a radius of twenty-five kilometers, whereas only 61 percent of metal workers were born in the vicinity.
34. Bernays, "Berufswahl," p. 145. Emsbach, *Die soziale Betriebsverfassung*, p. 521, claims, by contrast, that one-fifth of the female workers, but only one-tenth of the Gladbacher Spinnerei und Weberei's employees overall, were born over one hundred kilometers from Mönchen-Gladbach.
35. Bernays, *Auslese und Anpassung*, pp. 149–52, 177.
36. For the Wülfing and Scheidt mills it was possible to discern from personnel records which workers lived in company housing. The place of residence listed in the *Stammrollen* might also have listed the workers' residence during the work week only, however, and thus

Wülfing workers lived in company housing, for example: 27 percent in dormitories and 12 percent in the workers' "colony," most likely a cluster of small homes or apartments for workers with families.[37] The Scheidt company wage books show that 20 percent of zanella workers, 31 percent of spinning mill workers, and 46 percent of woolen cloth weavers paid rent out of their wages for rooms in company-owned *Mädchenheime* (dormitories for girls) or family residences.[38]

Thus textile workers in the traditional textile centers of the Rhineland and Westphalia were largely indigenous, except in flax, cotton, and worsted spinning mills like the Ravensberger Spinnerei in Bielefeld or Scheidt's worsted spinning mill in Kettwig, which, in view of the cyclical labor shortages of the 1890s in particular, were forced to rely on workers recruited from Silesia, Bohemia, Italy, and other European countries.[39] Many textile workers in the Rhineland and Westphalia were born into textile-working families, grew up in textile towns, and worked and lived in them throughout their lives. The vision of textile workers that emerges from this analysis—largely indigenous workers, born and residing close to their place of employment, many of them practitioners of a hereditary craft—contrasts starkly with the historical image of textile workers as highly transient, devoid of ties to the community of work and residence, and unfamiliar with traditions of textile production.

Work Patterns and Job Stability

Long-term job stability, a key component of work identity, is one indication of commitment to job, employer, or the practice of a skill or craft. Although it captures only one segment of a worker's career, this analysis of work patterns and employment stability by gender, occupation, and age provides important insights into the divergent meanings of long-term job commitment for male and female workers. Social reformers like Alfred Weber and Marie Bernays, who studied employment patterns among industrial workers during the early twentieth century, distinguished change that involved a new employer (*Stellenwechsel*) from change of occupation (*Berufswechsel*) and relocation to other cities or towns (*Ortswechsel*). Ber-

---

would not have shown if they had their permanent residence elsewhere and commuted home on the weekends.

37. Wülfing, *Arbeiterstammrollen*.
38. RWWA, Bestand 60: Scheidt, Lohnbücher der Zanellafabrik, Tuchfabrik und Kammgarnspinnerei, 1910–19.
39. RWWA, Bestand 60: Scheidt, Lohnbücher der Zanellafabrik, 1910–19. In my sample from the Scheidt records 31 percent had Polish, Czech, Hungarian, or Italian surnames and likely were immigrants or the children of immigrants.

nays discovered, for example, that workers of higher skill changed *occupations* less frequently than semiskilled or unskilled workers, while skilled workers demonstrated a greater propensity to leave one employer for another. Skilled workers, she argued, quickly became aware of "the monotony of occupational life" because of their "higher intellectual development" and sought to vary their work experience by changing jobs periodically. Alfred Weber also held that *Stellenwechsel* was likely a *positive* indicator that attested to workers' aspirations for higher wages and better working conditions, suggesting to his contemporaries the need to revise the negative interpretation of rapid job turnover as reflecting low levels of *Berufsinteresse* or *Berufsidentität*.[40]

Turnover Rates

That female textile workers have only infrequently been the subject of investigation by German labor historians means that many myths remain unquestioned regarding the nature of their employment as rapidly fluctuating, highly unstable, and inherently temporary—the attributes generally ascribed to all "women's industries." When the Prussian factory inspectors conducted a study of job stability among industrial workers in 1907, they made a remarkable discovery about textile manufacture: textile workers' turnover rates were among the lowest in industry and crafts overall, as shown in table 7. Although turnover was very high in the lead works in the Aachen district—ranging from 110 to 270 percent yearly—and iron and steel workers in the heart of the Ruhr industrial region also left their jobs at the high rate of 135 percent yearly, the average turnover in Aachen's linen industry was markedly lower, at 58 percent.[41] In nearby Düren, a small center of textile and paper production where many workers owned their own homes, the turnover among mill employees was a very

40. Bernays, *Auslese und Anpassung*, p. 180; Alfred Weber, "Das Berufsschicksal der Industriearbeiter: Ein Vortrag," *Archiv für Sozialwissenschaft und Sozialpolitik* 34 (1912): 375–405. Job stability can be measured either in terms of annual turnover rates or by calculating average tenure of employment.

41. HStAD, JBdKPG 1907: Aachen, p. 494. The term "turnover" can be explained as follows: If the turnover rate was 110–270 percent yearly in a factory that employed 500 workers, then the number of workers terminating employment was between 550 and 1,350 yearly. But this does not mean that all 500 workers who were employed at the beginning of the year had left by the end. More likely it indicates high rates of instability or fluctuation among a small percentage of workers while a substantial percentage remained stable. In fact one study of women's work in the spinning mills of Saxony, which had extremely high turnover, estimated that approximately half of the workforce remained stable, while the other half changed jobs frequently. See Johannes Queck, *Die Frauenarbeit in der Spinnereiindustrie Sachsens: Volkswirtschaftliche und wirtschaftsgeschichtliche Abhandlungen* (Leipzig: von Veit, 1915).

Table 7. Monthly turnover rates for individual workers in the government district of Düsseldorf, 1906–1907 (%)

Local district	Mining 1906	Mining 1907	Metal 1906	Metal 1907	Machine 1906	Machine 1907	Chemical 1906	Chemical 1907	Textiles 1906	Textiles 1907
Barmen	—	—	9.1	12.4	5.5	13.1	—	—	5.7	6.5
Düsseldorf (city)	9.3	9.6	6.4	6.9	6.5	7.3	16.5	32.5	10.6	11.2
Düsseldorf (rural)	9.0	8.4	7.1	6.0	4.2	3.3	—	—	4.5	4.5
Duisburg	9.3	8.7	11.3	8.8	8.4	7.2	19.1	19.9	8.2	6.8
Elberfeld	—	—	—	—	—	—	7.1	8.4	2.0	1.3
Essen	6.6	7.1	13.1	14.7	17.6	15.6	18.9	13.5	4.2	5.3
Krefeld	—	—	7.9	7.9	—	—	10.4	10.7	3.9	3.9
Lennep	4.4	3.8	5.1	5.1	7.8	7.1	—	—	2.4	3.8
Mönchen-Gladbach (weaving)	—	—	—	—	—	—	—	—	4.1	4.1
Mönchen-Gladbach (spinning)	—	—	—	—	—	—	—	—	5.2	5.2
Muelheim	6.6	7.4	—	—	7.6	10.0	—	—	4.0	5.0
Neuss	16.6	13.9	5.5	4.7	7.1	5.1	14.5	12.8	4.0	3.4
Solingen	4.5	5.5	3.7	4.3	—	—	—	—	3.2	3.0
Vohwinkel	—	—	6.9	7.6	—	—	—	—	2.6	2.7
Wesel	1.9	1.0	2.4	2.0	—	—	12.8	15.6	2.3	2.4

Source: See appendix to this chapter.

Table 8. Yearly turnover rates for male and female textile workers

Company	Period	Product	Percentage remaining less than 1 year	
			Men	Women
Baldus	1865–1915	Wool weaving/knitting	33.5	22.2
Crous	1900–1930	Silk weaving	45.6	30.3
Frowein	1860–1950	Silk weaving	13.6	18.4
Girmes	1885–1917	Velvet/plush weaving	33.7	26.3
Mechanische Weberei Bielefeld	1865–1924	Linen weaving	19.7	19.5
Mechanische Weberei Spenge	1907–1916	Linen weaving	21.7	22.4
Wülfing	1892–1935	Worsted wool spinning	57.3	50.4

Source: See appendix to this chapter for sources and more statistical detail.

low 16 percent. Analysis of the personnel records from the seven mills in my investigation shows that workers in six of them had considerably lower turnover rates than those cited by factory inspectors in 1907 (see table 8).[42] Marie Bernays determined that workers who had recently entered the Gladbach mill (within one year of her inquiry) had the highest turnover, leaving their jobs at an annual rate of 56 percent in 1908, whereas the rate was significantly lower—35.9 percent—among workers who had worked longer than one year before her inquiry.[43]

The factory inspectors explained variations in turnover in terms of differences in wage levels, health dangers at work, employers' policies toward workers, the structure and flexibility of local labor markets, and the bonds between workers and their communities and neighborhoods. The inspector from Aachen, for example, attributed the negligible turnover in Düren's linen mills to the scarcity of alternative employment there and to the fact that most textile workers lived in rural areas and owned their homes. According to his report, "Here it is not unusual for a man and his children to work in the same factory. Furthermore, the personal relationships that exist between employers and workers are a significant factor [in their job stability]."[44] The Düsseldorf factory inspector rated the local textile work-

42. See also Ulrich, "Soziale Entwicklungen im industriellen Umbruch," pp. 369–71. He determined turnover rates of 24 percent in the Crous silk mill between 1903 and 1913; of 37.3 percent in the Gladbacher Weberei und Spinnerei AG in 1907; and of 46 percent in the Viersener Flachsspinnerei between 1885 and 1887.
43. Bernays, *Auslese und Anpassung*, p. 41.
44. HStAD, JBdKPG 1907: Aachen, p. 494. The Aachen inspector noted that turnover was lower where workers owned their homes.

force as relatively stable because this industry "required the largest core of skilled workers," in contrast to the chemical industry, which employed "a mass of unskilled workers without a specific occupation [*Beruf*]," whose turnover rates were correspondingly higher. The inspector pointed to weavers, who constituted the largest group of textile *Stammarbeiter*, as exemplary for long-term job stability. Indeed, in the inspector's view, young, unmarried workers—those "without a sense of family bonds" were more inclined toward frequent job changes than older, married workers.[45]

My evaluation of personnel records challenges one of the most pervasive assumptions in German labor history regarding the job stability of female workers. I found that male and female textile workers had statistically similar yearly turnover in six of my seven samples, while in the remaining case of the Baldus mill the yearly turnover for men was significantly higher than for women. Also similar to the samples presented here, the factory inspectors found nearly identical turnover for male and female textile workers in the Düsseldorf district (between 52 and 55.6 percent yearly) in 1907.[46] Male textile workers in the cities of Düsseldorf, Duisburg, and Essen had higher turnover than their female colleagues and than male textile workers in smaller textile towns, owing in part to the lure of better-paid jobs in the nearby iron industry, which was itself plagued by rapid fluctuations in its workforce.[47] The Bielefeld inspector reported remarkably low turnover of 40 to 50 percent yearly in the city's two flax spinning mills, considering the availability of employment that was regarded as cleaner and better paid in the garment making and silk industries.[48] Competition from other industries nonetheless caused apparent seasonal oscillation in female employment patterns in Bielefeld, for the inspector reported that turnover in the flax mills increased dramatically every year during the months before Christmas, "when the local cookie and baking powder factories hired women in large numbers for temporary jobs that were well paid and relatively easy to perform." Yet even in view of this periodic instability in the female labor market in Bielefeld, turnover in the male sector of machine building was significantly higher in the local plants, at 83 percent, 85 percent, and 195 percent per year.[49] In sum, my study of personnel records indicates that men were more likely than women to ter-

45. HStAD, JBdKPG 1907: Düsseldorf, p. 422. According to this report, chemical workers had the highest turnover with yearly rates at 150 to 180 percent, followed by the mining, metal, and machine industries with rates of 84 to 96 percent per year. Marie Bernays reported similar distinctions between older, married workers and younger, single employees. Also see Emsbach, *Die soziale Betriebsverfassung*, pp. 506–7, who found that workers under age twenty demonstrated the greatest instability.
46. HStAD, JBdKPG, 1907: Düsseldorf, p. 422.
47. Ibid., p. 423.
48. HStAD, JBdKPG 1907: Bielefeld, p. 324.
49. Ibid.

minate employment within the first five years, while the percentage of men remaining on the job ten years or longer was often twice as high as that of women, as table 9 demonstrates.[50]

Although personnel records offer insights only into fragments of workers' mill careers, they reveal that limited upward mobility within mill hierarchies was possible during the first few years of employment, between age fourteen, when workers generally had acquired informal skills, and the early twenties. The wage books from the Scheidt zanella mill, for example, show that a few women moved up from spooling or bobbin setting to weaving or shifted from one weaving shop to another, which in some cases undoubtedly meant higher pay and improved working conditions.[51] Fluid boundaries of another type also seemed to prevail between weaving and the finishing tasks of napping and darning, often performed in the home, suggesting that female workers sometimes did these jobs while laid off or temporarily absent from the mill. Male teenagers demonstrate mobility from preparatory tasks to spinning or weaving, and older male workers often advanced from master weaver or spinner to supervisor (*Meister* or *Untermeister*). Marie Bernays observed that some upward mobility existed for semiskilled women, for example, in the spinning sector from the position of piecer to that of rover. She found that some skilled male workers demonstrated greater occupational stability than skilled women, which Bernays explained by the higher pay and better working conditions for men and the fact that the average male textile worker was older than the average female.[52] According to Bernays's study, 70 percent of female weavers, 72 percent of female ring spinners, 64 percent of female rovers, and 56 percent of female textile workers overall practiced the same occupation during their entire working lives.[53]

Average Length of Employment

The few recent studies of turnover and fluctuation among industrial workers indicate that the average length of employment for industrial

50. Because of the discrepant nature of data compilation in the *Arbeiterstammrollen*, it is difficult to discern how much the patterns of job longevity changed over time. Figures A1–A6 (appendix to this chapter) analyze these patterns, distinguished by gender, and figures A7–A12 differentiate longevity patterns by job category, pointing to comparable career patterns of male and female weavers. In most of the rolls the longevity is very high for the early years because the sample does not include all workers who entered between 1860 and 1880, in the example of figure A1, Baldus, but rather lists those who entered between 1860 and 1880 and were still present in, say, 1901 when the new *Arbeiterstammrolle* was compiled. This skews the sample toward high longevity for all workers entering during the early years of the sample.
51. RWWA, Bestand 60: Scheidt, Lohnbücher der Zanellafabrik, 1911–19.
52. Bernays, *Auslese und Anpassung*, pp. 40–41, 168.
53. Ibid., p. 162; Bernays, "Berufswahl," p. 895.

Table 9. Length of employment: summary

Percentage employed	Baldus		Crous		Girmes		Wülfing		Mechanische Weberei Bielefeld	
	Men	Women	Men	Women	Men	Women	Men	Women	Men	Women
Less than 1 year	33.5	22.2	45.6	30.3	33.7	26.3	57.3	50.4	19.7	19.5
Less than 5 years[a]	62.0	61.0	72.0	75.0	68.0	63.0	86.5	86.8	51.3	54.7
More than 5 years but less than 10 years	13.0	30.0	5.3	15.0	16.0	26.3	8.2	10.0	14.5	28.8
10 years or more	21.0	7.0	22.7	9.3	16.0	9.7	5.3	2.85	34.2	16.5
Period	1865–1915		1900–1930		1885–1917		1892–1935		1865–1924	
Sample size										
Men	43% (343)		22% (57)		64% (412)		35% (274)		18% (117)	
Women	57% (454)		78% (201)		36% (232)		65% (518)		82% (534)	

Source: See appendix to this chapter.
[a]Figures for those employed less than five years include those employed less than one year.

workers at the end of the 1880s was approximately one year. Historian Hermann Schäfer, for example, defines as *Stammarbeiter*, or core workers, those who remained with one employer for two to three years.[54] In view of these definitions, and considering that the personnel and wage books in my study record only one segment of a worker's employment history, the longevity figures for workers in the seven mills I sampled are striking not for their brevity, but for their length. Male workers in the samples from the Baldus woolen mill, the Crous silk company in Viersen, and the Mechanische Weberei in Bielefeld remained at one job for an average of 6.9 to 10.1 years, while the longest average tenures for women were 6.4 years at the Frowein mill and 5.7 years at Mechanische Weberei in Bielefeld. Female silk weavers in the Crous mill and women workers in the Baldus and Girmes factories worked an average of 4 to 4.5 years.[55] The only mill employees in my samples who tended toward brief—that is, two-year—tenures in one mill were the employees of the Wülfing worsted spinning mill, a sector that both factory inspectors and employers viewed as plagued by rapid turnover.[56] Many spinning mill employees were young single workers who had been recruited from distant regions of Germany or other European countries and who found little incentive to tolerate the low pay and poor working conditions of the mills, particularly during acute labor shortages when better jobs were readily available.

Calculations of average length of employment for the nearly 3,500 mill employees in my samples reveal two distinct patterns: in three of the seven mills listed in table 10, the average tenures of male and female workers diverge significantly, and in the four others they are remarkably similar. In Bielefeld's Mechanische Weberei, the case of sharpest contrast, my sample suggests that male workers stayed at their jobs nearly twice as long as women did (10.3 and 5.7 years).[57] Similarly, the sample of the Baldus woolen factory in Osberghausen shows that men remained on the job an average of 7.2 years, while women stayed only 4.5 years.[58] One important factor in deciphering this disparity between men's and women's job stability is the division of labor in each mill. The Mechanische Weberei, for example, hired relatively few men overall, and most of them belonged to

54. Hermann Schäfer, "Probleme der Arbeiterfluktuation während der Industrialisierung," in *Arbeiter im Industrialisierungsprozeß: Herkunft, Lage und Verhalten*, ed. Werner Conze and Ulrich Engelhardt (Stuttgart: Klett Cotta, 1979), p. 264. Using health insurance records, contemporaries calculated an average tenure of 10.5 months for workers in small and middle-sized factories and of two years for workers in large factories (over fifty employees).
55. StA Bi, Mech. Web. 28/1, 29/1, 51; Crous/Ulrich; Girmes/Lipp, *Arbeiterstammrollen*; RWWA Abt. 63, Nr. 7, F. 3, Baldus, *Belegschaftsbuch*.
56. Wülfing, *Arbeiterstammrollen*.
57. StA Bi, Mech. Web. 28/1, 29/1, 51.
58. RWWA, Bestand 63, Nr. 7, F. 3: Baldus, *Belegschaftsbuch*.

Table 10. Average length of employment for male and female workers

Company	Period	Product	Length of employment (years)	
			Men	Women
Baldus	1865–1915	Wool weaving/knitting	7.2	4.5
Crous	1900–1930	Silk weaving	6.9	4.0
Frowein	1860–1950	Silk weaving	13.4	6.4
Girmes	1885–1917	Velvet/plush weaving	4.7	4.6
Mechanische Weberei Bielefeld	1865–1924	Linen weaving	10.3	5.7
Mechanische Weberei Spenge	1907–1916	Linen weaving	3.1	3.2
Wülfing	1892–1935	Worsted wool spinning	2.3	2.1

Source: See appendix to this chapter for sources and more statistical detail.

the stratum of textile craftsmen, who generally had far longer tenures than the workers they supervised, as table 11 shows. A comparison of work patterns that takes into account the division of labor reveals little or no discrepancy: work patterns of male and female weavers in the Mechanische Weberei Bielefeld, for example, vary considerably less than those of male and female employees overall: male weavers worked on average for 8.4 years, while female weavers remained on the job 6 years.[59] As Table 12 illustrates, women weavers in the Crous silk weaving mill in Viersen had a higher average length of employment (3.9 years) than male weavers (2.7 years),[60] while my calculations for female piecers in my sample of the Baldus mill show that they worked an average of 4.2 years, in contrast with male piecers, who stayed on the job for 2.6 years.[61] (See table 13 for other job categories at Baldus.)

These figures suggest that gender definitions underpinned job categories in the textile mills and exerted a significant influence on employment patterns. According to my findings, women workers displayed greater stability in typically female sectors of production, while men had lower average tenures than women in precisely these sectors. In the case of the Wülfing spinning mill, for example, table 14 shows that male spinners worked

59. StA Bi, Mech. Web. 28/1, 29/1, 51.
60. Crous/Ulrich, *Arbeiterstammrolle*; RWWA, Bestand 63, Nr. 7, F. 3: Baldus, *Belegschaftsbuch*. Although male masters and foremen constituted only 8.8 percent of the Crous workforce, their average tenure (27.3 years) was so long that it obscures the rather low average tenure of male weavers (71.9 percent of male workers.)
61. These calculations are subsumed within the broader category of "preparatory and finishing tasks" in table 13. Taken as a whole, table 13 suggests that men and women had similar lengths of employment in this sector at Baldus.

Table 11. Average length of employment for male and female workers: Mechanische Weberei Bielefeld

Job category	Number of men	Percentage of male workforce	Average length of employment (years)	Number of women	Percentage of female workforce	Average length of employment (years)
Craftsmen/supervisors	41	35.0	12.6	1	0.2	1.8
Weavers	42	35.9	8.4	315	59.0	6.1
Preparatory/finishing tasks	13	11.1	8.1	215	40.3	5.2
Office/warehouse	18	15.4	11.3	3	0.6	2.6
No data	3	2.6	7.8	0		
All categories	117	100.0	10.3	534	100.0	5.7

Source: See appendix to this chapter for sources and more statistical detail.

Table 12. Average length of employment for male and female workers: Crous

Job category	Number of men	Percentage of male workforce	Average length of employment (years)	Number of women	Percentage of female workforce	Average length of employment (years)
Craftsmen/supervisors	13	22.8	17.9	9	4.5	1.8
Weavers	41	71.9	2.7	123	61.2	3.9
Preparatory/finishing tasks	2	3.5	17.2	68	33.8	4.5
Office/warehouse	1	1.8	15.0	1	0.5	6.5
All categories	57	100.0	6.9	201	100.0	4.0

Source: See appendix to this chapter for sources and more statistical detail.

Table 13. Average length of employment for male and female workers: Baldus

Job category	Number of men	Percentage of male workforce	Average length of employment (years)	Number of women	Percentage of female workforce	Average length of employment (years)
Craftsmen/supervisors	22	6.4	13.0	0		
Weavers	62	18.1	9.9	19	4.2	3.7
Spinners	13	3.8	19.0	0		
Preparatory/finishing tasks	246	71.7	5.4	435	95.8	4.5
All categories	343	100.0	7.2	454	100.0	4.5

Source: See appendix to this chapter for sources and more statistical detail.

Table 14. Average length of employment for male and female workers: Wülfing

Job category	Number of men	Percentage of male workforce	Average length of employment (years)	Number of women	Percentage of female workforce	Average length of employment (years)
Craftsmen/supervisors	72	26.3	3.0	0		
Spinners	101	36.9	1.6	243	46.9	2.4
Preparatory/finishing tasks	71	25.9	2.4	245	47.3	1.7
Office/warehouse	13	4.7	4.4	8	1.5	4.8
War production	13	4.7	1.5	17	3.3	2.5
No data	4	1.5	2.0	5	1.0	2.7
All categories	274	100.0	2.3	518	100.0	2.1

Source: See appendix to this chapter for sources and more statistical detail.

only 1.6 years on average, while female spinners and ring spinners worked somewhat longer (2.4 years).[62] From 1883 to 1931, the number of male workers at Wülfing declined continuously while the female workforce steadily expanded: between 1883 and 1890, for example, the new employees hired were 59 percent male and 41 percent female, but over the next ten years this relation was reversed, as women composed 68 percent and men only 32 percent of workers hired by Wülfing between 1891 and 1900, confirming the widespread perception of feminization of textile production during the 1890s.[63] At the Baldus company, employment patterns were gender specific: foremen and masters, who composed only 2 percent of the male workforce, were long-term employees (23 years average tenure), as were spinners (19 years) and weavers (9.9 years). These mill divisions were male spheres at Baldus: as table 13 suggests, nearly all the women employed in the Baldus mill performed preparatory and finishing tasks and remained at their jobs for significantly shorter times (4.5 years) than male spinners, weavers, or foremen.[64]

The records of the Diergardt foundation of Viersen, which rewarded workers for job continuity of twenty-five years or longer, offer compelling evidence for comparable job commitment and stability of male and female textile workers, even where sharp gender divisions prevailed in the workplace. Table 15 reveals that most male recipients were masters, foremen, craftsmen, machinists, or mechanics—that is, workers who had acquired skill through traditional apprenticeships. Female recipients, by contrast, had worked as spinners, winders, bobbin setters, or weavers, jobs that required no formal training and were considered skilled only after years of experience on the shop floor. Despite this pronounced division, women composed nearly half (45 percent) of this elite of the textile *Stammarbeiterschaft*. Their average tenure (27.4 years) overall was only slightly lower than that of men (30.2 years).[65]

In two of the three remaining mills in my sample—Girmes and Wülfing—men and women displayed markedly similar work patterns despite

---

62. Wülfing, *Arbeiterstammrollen*. Indeed, the only long-term male workers at the Wülfing mill were foremen and *Meister*, with average tenures of 10.8 years; machinists and craftsmen at 5.6 years; and combers at 7.1 years. The first two categories have been subsumed in the broader category "craftsmen/supervisors" in table 14, while the third is included in "preparatory/finishing tasks."
63. Wülfing, *Arbeiterstammrollen*. After the First World War and under the Weimar Republic, this tendency was even more unmistakable: the new workforce was less than one-quarter male (24.3 percent) during the early 1920s.
64. RWWA, Bestand 63, Nr. 7, F. 3: Baldus, *Belegschaftsbuch*.
65. Stadtarchiv Viersen (StA Vie), III/056, Diergardt Stiftung, 1904–22. Where men and women performed the same job, however, this slight discrepancy disappeared altogether, for male and female workers demonstrated nearly identical average tenures of employment.

Table 15. Average length of employment among textile workers given awards by the Diergardt Stiftung, Viersen, 1904–1922

	Men		Women	
Job category	Number	Average tenure (years)	Number	Average tenure (years)
Worker	12	25.3	16	26.1
Spinner	0	—	28	27.5
Reeler	0	—	13	28.5
Winder	0	—	13	26.9
Warper	0	—	13	25.0
Weavers	17	26.7	22	26.3
Masters (misc.)	16	28.8	3	25.0
Supervisors/foremen	8	34.4	0	—
Craftsmen (misc.)	17	33.9	0	—
Machinists	6	27.7	0	—
Carpenters/mechanics	8	30.0	0	—
Sorters	10	44.3	0	—
Comber	10	28.0	0	—
Job unknown	93	—	54	—

Source: See appendix to this chapter.

Note: The recipients of Diergardt awards included workers in linen mills (50 percent), silk mills (25 percent), and velvet mills (12 percent).

marked gender segregation between job categories. As table 16 illustrates, the sample from the Girmes mill suggests that skilled male weavers remained on the job for the same average time (5.6 years) as semiskilled female assistants and only slightly longer than the large number of women employed in preparatory and finishing tasks (4.5 years). Despite the marked sexual division of labor between the male domain of self-actor spinning and the female task of ring spinning, the sample from the Wülfing worsted mill in Lennep (table 14) shows that male spinners had shorter average employment (1.6 years) than female spinners (2.4 years).[66] It is unlikely, however, that the sexual division of labor was the sole factor in determining employment stability in these three cases. Rather, that both mills were in rural or one-company towns may be of greater consequence than the sexual division of labor in explaining the similarity between male and female work patterns. The structure of the local labor market or the prevalence of agriculturally based family economies may have had a greater influence on job stability for both sexes than disparities of skill, wages, or job identification between male and female workers.

The pattern and frequency of interruptions among workers in the Girmes mill, for example—which were nearly twice as high as those in the

66. Girmes/Lipp, *Arbeiterstammrollen*; Wülfing, *Arbeiterstammrollen*.

Table 16. Average length of employment for male and female workers: Girmes

Job category	Number of men	Percentage of male workforce	Average length of employment (years)	Number of women	Percentage of female workforce	Average length of employment (years)
Craftsmen/supervisors	68	16.5	4.6	5	2.2	3.9
Weavers	162	39.3	5.6	2	0.9	1.3
Preparatory/finishing tasks	14	3.4	7.5	186	80.2	4.5
Office/warehouse	6	1.5	8.0	16	6.9	5.0
Apprentices	40	9.7	5.5	0		
Assistants: preparatory/finishing tasks	23	5.6	3.8	19	8.2	5.6
No data	99	24.0	2.7	4	1.7	0.6
All categories	412	100.0	4.7	232	100.0	4.6

Source: See appendix to this chapter for sources and more statistical detail.

Table 17. Percentage of workers who interrupted employment

Company	One entry		Two entries		Three or more entries	
	Men	Women	Men	Women	Men	Women
Baldus	94.0	83.0	5.0	12.8	1.0	4.2
Frowein	84.0	85.0	13.0	13.0	3.1	1.8
Girmes	49.5	48.7	23.5	31.8	28.1	18.3
Wülfing	84.7	82.2	9.1	12.8	5.0	3.3
Mechanische Weberei Bielefeld	84.6	79.0	13.7	16.1	1.7	5.0

Source: See appendix to this chapter.

other mills that listed multiple exits and entries for their employees—suggest that factory owner Johann Girmes allowed or even encouraged seasonal employment, by which velvet weavers and their assistants were able to meld their mill employment with part-time farming.[67] As table 17 demonstrates, over half of the workers at Girmes interrupted their employment at least once; more than one-fourth of male workers and nearly one-fifth of female workers suspended and resumed their employment at Girmes at least twice, and many did so three or four times, with some interrupting work as often as eight times. In the other four mills taken together, between 15 and 21 percent of the workforce left and resumed employment in the same factory at least once. Indeed, historians' recent studies of other textile regions in Germany show that seasonal employment patterns were characteristic rather than unusual, particularly in one-company mill villages like Oedt or mill towns that drew significant numbers of workers from surrounding farming communities. Historian Jean Quataert, for example, discovered that female textile workers in the Oberlausitz region of Saxony worked in the mills during the winter while husbands—typically seasonally unemployed construction workers—"would care for children, shop, cook, and clean." In the spring the reverse occurred as "wives would return home and husbands would leave to work for wages."[68]

67. Four of the six companies in my sample listed multiple exits and entries of their employees. On the prevalence of farming among industrial workers in the textile towns of the Lower Rhine, see Derek Linton, "Industrialization and Intergenerational Social Mobility in a Rhenish Textile Town," *Journal of Interdisciplinary History* 18 (summer 1987): 107–26. For the velvet center of Lobberich near Oedt, Linton established that 13 percent of the 2,000 industrial workers were farmers, most of whom cultivated smallholdings of less than five hectares.

68. Jean Quataert, "Teamwork in Saxon Homeweaving Families in the 19th Century: A Preliminary Investigation into the Issue of Gender Work Roles," in *German Women in the Eighteenth and Nineteenth Centuries*, ed. Ruth E. Joeres and Mary Jo Maynes (Bloomington:

The Girmes case points to the existence of a core of textile-working families who, by most standards of measurement, exhibited highly unstable employment patterns. Yet their career cycles of interrupting and resuming employment at Girmes over several decades points to mutual dependence between the mill and local *Stammarbeiter*. Indeed, the case of the Girmes workers illustrates the necessity of defining "job stability" in terms that encompass the rhythms of factory work in mill towns and villages like Oedt, where mill work and family farming continued to coexist long after industrialization. Tamara Hareven's classic study of the Amoskeag mill in Manchester, New Hampshire, suggests that career interruptions were intrinsic to "the organization of work itself" in the mills, even in larger industrial cities where workers were not drawn away from the factories by agricultural cycles. Hareven attributes the multiple hirings and separations that formed the pervasive pattern in the Amoskeag mill to "the intermittent character of textile production, as well as individual workers' personal preferences or handicaps."[69] Her classification of "individuals whose work lives were interrupted either by the . . . [mill's] production schedules or by their own decisions to use the mill as a resource while experimenting with other jobs or rearing children" as "repeaters" redefines the notion of job stability for married women, mothers, and part-time farmers whose mill work may have been lifelong but was never a singular occupation.[70]

Age and Job Stability

Relevant to this study are not only the divisions in the textile workforce along gender lines, but also those of age. Indeed, there is qualitative evidence that the two were often entwined in shaping the hierarchies of labor as well as the conflicts, cultures, and identities of work, in particular where sharp divisions prevailed between older male craftsmen and young, single female workers such as the "spinning girls" of the flax or cotton spinning mills in the Lower Rhine. Table 18 confirms the common observation that women entered the mills at an earlier age and were also generally younger when they terminated employment, for in every mill in my sample the

---

Indiana University Press, 1986), p. 18. Hermann Schäfer's research on Alsatian textile workers and Peter Borscheid's study of textile workers in Württemberg also point to the prevalence of seasonal employment patterns in the textile industry. See Schäfer, "Probleme der Arbeiterfluktuation," p. 268; Peter Borscheid, *Textilarbeiterschaft in der Industrialisierung: Soziale Lage und Mobilität in Württemberg* (Stuttgart: Klett Cotta, 1978).

69. Hareven, *Family Time*, p. 241. More than half of the workers in the sample were employed in the Amoskeag mill more than once, and almost two out of five were employed ten times or more.

70. Ibid., p. 243.

Table 18. Age structure of the workforce in seven textile mills (%)

Age	Baldus		Crous		Frowein		Girmes		Mechanische Weberei Bielefeld		Mechanische Weberei Spenge		Wülfing	
	Men	Women	Men	Women	Men	Women	Men	Women	Men	Women	Men	Women	Men	Women
13 and under	2.9	1.8	0.0	0.0	0.0	0.0	1.0	0.9	0.0	0.0	0.0	0.0	0.0	0.0
14–16	37.9	54.6	8.8	10.9	30.7	48.5	16.0	36.6	29.1	56.0	70.7	55.2	25.9	33.6
17–18	8.5	12.8	8.8	12.9	12.5	12.6	11.4	16.4	5.1	12.2	7.6	15.5	16.8	18.1
19–20	10.8	7.5	7.0	15.4	11.4	5.8	7.3	12.1	8.5	6.9	5.4	1.7	11.7	11.8
21–25	13.1	14.8	14.0	22.9	14.8	16.5	19.2	13.8	17.1	8.8	5.4	13.8	16.1	19.1
26–30	11.1	5.1	14.0	13.9	12.5	6.8	15.0	9.9	15.4	6.0	4.3	5.2	8.4	7.9
31–35	7.9	1.8	7.0	10.0	6.8	5.8	8.7	4.3	11.1	3.7	1.1	5.2	5.1	4.1
36–40	2.0	0.9	1.8	7.0	5.7	2.9	7.0	2.6	6.8	3.4	1.1	1.7	5.5	2.7
41–50	4.4	0.7	17.5	4.5	2.3	1.0	10.0	3.0	4.3	2.2	4.3	1.7	6.9	1.7
51 and over	1.5	0.2	21.1	2.5	3.4	0.0	4.4	0.4	2.6	0.7	0.0	0.0	3.6	1.0
Minimum age of entry	9	10	15	14	14	14	13	13	14	14	14	14	14	14
Maximum age of entry	59	57	71	68	57	41	58	58	55	59	49	41	63	59
Average age of entry	21.6	17.9	35.3	25.5	23.1	19.4	26.9	20.6	24.6	19.2	18.1	19.0	24.1	20.7

average age of men on entry into the mill was higher, and in several cases, notably higher, than that of women.[71] A relatively large percentage of men were hired between ages thirty and forty and worked twenty to thirty years thereafter, suggesting that mill work may have been a "second career" for them. The numbers of women tended to decrease with increasing age, and usually between 10 and 20 percent of female workers were over age thirty. The Crous silk mill, in which nearly one-quarter of the women entering were older than thirty, is one exception. Because silk weaving was one sector of textile production in which the core workforce was female, these numbers probably reflect the presence of numerous "repeaters"—women returning to the mill after a period of interruption. Marie Bernays detected a significant increase in women over thirty in the Gladbach mill for 1891 to 1908, which corresponds to the steady expansion of married women's factory employment in the industry. Her study shows that the percentage of women in the age group seventeen to thirty declined from 72 to 62 percent while the percentage of women over thirty increased from 6.5 to 14.3 percent and that of women over forty rose from 1.2 to 5.9 percent.[72]

An analysis of job stability by age group reveals that among the women workers in my samples of the seven mills, girls who went to work between ages fourteen and eighteen and women who began employment after age forty tended to have the longest tenures. Table 19 shows that women who entered the mills during their childbearing years, above all between twenty-one and thirty, had relatively short—or frequently interrupted—employment. Among male workers in my samples, young men who began working before age twenty demonstrated the lowest longevity, while those who joined the workforce during their early thirties had longer average employment.

In sum, this detailed analysis of fluctuation and longevity among textile workers in the seven mills I examined suggests that job stability in the textile industry was not the preserve of male workers, nor was instability inherently female. Rather, job stability was entwined with and shaped by the division of labor, especially in urban mills, and the shared position of women and men in family agricultural economies may explain their similar patterns of interrupted employment in rural factories or one-company mill villages. Longevity of employment is only one component in this examination of work identities, but the patterns discerned here suggest that job

---

71. Marie Bernays pointed out that the average age of male textile workers was considerably higher than the average age of female textile workers, who were concentrated in the age groups under forty. More than half of female workers and nearly half of male workers were between seventeen and thirty. Bernays, *Auslese und Anpassung*, pp. 24–30.

72. Ibid., p. 31.

Table 19. Average length of employment by age group (years)

Age	Baldus		Crous		Frowein		Girmes		Mechanische Weberei Bielefeld		Mechanische Weberei Spenge		Wülfing	
	Men	Women	Men	Women	Men	Women	Men	Women	Men	Women	Men	Women	Men	Women
13 and under	8.5	9.0	—	—	—	—	6.5	11.4	—	—	—	—	—	—
14–16	6.9	5.1	12.6	3.9	14.9	7.8	6.1	5.3	6.3	6.7	2.9	3.7	3.2	3.0
17–18	4.3	3.6	10.7	3.0	11.4	3.7	3.6	4.7	5.5	5.5	2.8	2.2	0.9	1.7
19–20	5.2	2.8	7.4	2.9	15.6	6.2	3.6	4.1	4.3	3.5	1.3	1.8	0.9	1.4
21–25	6.8	3.0	9.6	3.6	9.4	2.7	3.3	3.5	11.5	3.8	3.2	2.2	2.4	1.5
26–30	12.5	4.7	4.2	4.6	10.5	6.7	4.5	2.1	19.0	2.7	4.6	1.3	2.5	1.7
31–35	10.6	7.5	1.6	3.3	17.1	12.0	5.5	4.1	8.7	3.5	3.9	3.4	1.6	2.0
36–40	8.1	2.7	0.0	5.3	12.3	6.1	7.2	7.0	15.7	6.0	8.2	8.8	3.8	2.3
41–50	2.9	0.6	9.9	9.1	31.5	0.6	5.4	5.9	18.8	5.8	6.5	4.3	3.0	1.0
51 and over	2.8	0.6	2.5	7.2	10.4	—	4.1	7.0	3.1	7.5	—	—	3.7	4.2
All ages	7.2	4.5	6.9	4.0	13.4	6.4	4.7	4.6	10.3	5.7	3.1	3.2	2.3	2.1

stability must be redefined to envision long-term commitment to textile jobs and employers, even given frequent or regular cycles of interrupted employment, mandated by the double burden of women workers or by the demands of the family farm. Furthermore, it suggests that the structures of textile factory employment, in particular the sexual division of labor in the mills as well as the lifelong ties of many workers to the mills, buttressed by kin networks and the networks of local textile workers' communities, formed crucial contexts in which workers assigned meanings to their work, developing work identities and work cultures.

Dissolving the Dichotomy between Home and Work: Reading Women's Work Identities

The career patterns of female textile workers, in particular those of married women, were shaped by the continual conflict and negotiation between family time and industrial time as they interrupted employment to give birth, returned to work for a few months, left again to care for a sick child or other relative, and resumed employment once again when the family situation permitted. As early as 1874, the factory inspector in one textile town noted that "women, who are responsible for a household, come to work later and leave work earlier [than the others]. When someone in the family is ill, they do not come to work at all. There is a general, unspoken agreement by which married women are treated with leniency. Their situation is therefore a relatively favorable one."[73] Although the search for a balance between family and work led many women to give up their jobs upon marriage, national and local employment statistics for the last quarter of the nineteenth century point to a steady increase in the number of women who continued to work in the textile mills after marriage and even after the birth of their children, from 24,165 in 1875 to 70,655 in 1895 and by 1907, to 113,915.[74] Between 1895 and 1907 the number of married female textile workers increased by 61.2 percent, nearly three times the rate of women's employment overall, which grew by 23.4 percent during the same period. Table 20 compares the results of the factory inspectors' surveys of 1899 and 1927 on the employment of married women in factories for the textile districts of the Rhineland and Westphalia, indicating that the trend of expanding female factory employment

73. HStAD, Landratsamt Mönchen-Gladbach 710, "Bericht des Gewerbeaufsichtsbeamten Mönchen-Gladbachs," 14 December 1874, pp. 104–5.
74. Rose Otto, *Über die Fabrikarbeit verheirateter Frauen*, Münchner Volkswirtschaftliche Studien 4 (Stuttgart: Cotta, 1910), pp. 93, 99–105. According to Otto's figures, the percentage of married women in the textile industry in 1907 was Prussia. 18.6; Bavaria, 25.1; Baden, 20.6; Saxony, 19.1; Reuss a.L., 41.3; Reuss j.L., 49.3; Alsace, 24.9.

Table 20. Percentage of married women in the adult female workforce

Government district	1899	1927
Düsseldorf	15.9	29.7
Münster	15.4	16.4
Minden	19.0	27.9
Cologne	17.0	23.4
Aachen	14.9	21.8

Source: See appendix to this chapter.

persisted during and after the First World War. Among the mills in my sample, only three recorded employees' marital status in their *Stammrollen*. The patterns of married women's employment varied according to local cultural and industrial traditions and the particular conditions of production in each branch. Of the women who took up employment at the Mechanische Weberei in Bielefeld between 1870 and 1890, for example, 28 percent were married; this figure rose to 31 percent between 1891 and 1900 and to 40.2 percent for the decade after 1901.[75] By contrast, only 14 percent of female employees in the Girmes velvet factory were married.[76] As the discussion of the Krefeld silk industry in chapter 2 suggests, its silk mills employed a high percentage of married women (21.6 percent) compared with the relatively low participation of married women in factory industry in Düsseldorf (10.2 percent) and in the cotton center of Mönchen-Gladbach (11.5 percent).[77] A highly feminized sector of textile employment, silk weaving offered women higher skill, status, and earnings than most other textile jobs. Marie Bernays established a definite correlation between skill and married women's propensity to remain on the job: according to her findings, over one-half of skilled female textile workers in

75. StA Bi, Mech. Web. 28/1, 29/1, 51. Marital status could be determined from the company's method of recording names. Married women had *Frau* listed in front of their names or the term *geb.* (*geboren*) followed by their maiden names. According to Marie Bernays's study of the Gladbacher Spinnerei und Weberei, 36.8 percent of female workers over age sixteen were married, as were 80.3 percent of male employees over age twenty-one. In the age group thirty to forty, slightly more women (87 percent) than men (85.3 percent) were married. (These figures are for about 1912.) See Bernays, *Auslese und Anpassung*, p. 208.
76. Lipp/Girmes, *Arbeiterstammrollen*.
77. HStAD, JBdKPG 1899: Düsseldorf, p. 512. All figures are for 1899. Compare these figures for Mönchen-Gladbach overall with Bernays's findings for the Gladbach spinning and weaving mill, which are significantly higher. The low rates of married women's employment in Mönchen-Gladbach's cotton mills overall, noted by many contemporary observers and in subsequent secondary studies, might be explained in part by the practice, common among prominent Catholic mill owners like Franz Brandts, of refusing to employ married women. Brandts required his female employees to resign within a few months after getting married.

the Gladbach mill were married, but only one-fifth of their semiskilled counterparts were.[78] Bernays contended in 1910 that "skilled textile work—weaving, ring spinning, and roving—is increasingly becoming the domain of married women," and Ludwig Pohle, a conservative social reformer who conducted an investigation of women's work in the textile industry at the end of the nineteenth century, found a higher percentage of married women among weavers (24 percent on the average) than among spinners (average of 18.7 percent).[79]

The personnel records examined here not only attest to the growing presence of married women among the textile industry's core workforce but also challenge the familiar image of female factory employment as temporary or transient, confined mainly to the years between the middle teens and marriage or the birth of the first child. My analysis of the records from the Mechanische Weberei in Bielefeld suggests that it was customary for women to return to the textile mills after childbirth: of the 426 women who left their jobs because of pregnancy, some one-third returned to work within a few months after giving birth.[80] The profile of Sofia Budde, who undoubtedly belonged to the "core" workforce, offers testimony of one woman's negotiation of family and factory over a lifetime of mill work. Sofia Budde, weaver, worked at the Mechanische Weberei for a total of twenty-nine years between 1890 and 1925, beginning her job in weaving room one at age fourteen and departing for the first time in August 1894 because of pregnancy. Two months later, presumably after the birth of her first child, she returned to work, now listing her name as Sofia Schneider, having apparently married shortly before or after her child's birth. Slightly over two years later she took a seven-month leave, again because of pregnancy, returning to weaving room one in July 1897 at age twenty-one, now the mother of two children. Sofia Schneider stayed on the job until September 1905, when she again interrupted her employment for nine months, this time *auf Wunsch* (at her own request). Yet in view of her lengthy absence following this entry into the *Arbeiterstammrolle*, it is likely that she gave birth to another child. She returned to work in May 1906, to weaving room three, where she remained eleven years without interrup-

78. Bernays, *Auslese und Anpassung*, p. 208.
79. Bernays, "Berufswahl," p. 895; Ludwig Pohle, *Frauenfabrikarbeit und Frauenfrage: Eine prinzipielle Antwort auf die Frage der Ausschliessung der verheirateten Frauen aus der Fabrik* (Leipzig: Von Veit, 1900), p. 22. Pohle based his figures on studies by factory inspectors and other social reformers. He claimed that his figures encompassed nearly one-third (45,721) of all married women in the textile industry.
80. StA Bi, Mech. Web. 28/1, 29/1, 51. This calculation was made for the entire period covered by the *Arbeiterstammrollen*: 1865–1924. It includes only those departures listed as "because of pregnancy." It is likely that many of those listed as *auf Wunsch* could also be attributed to marriage or pregnancy.

tion. Sofia's last leave—between 1917 and 1921—most likely resulted from changes in her family situation during World War I. She returned to her loom in 1921 and left the Mechanische Weberei for the last time in 1925 at age forty-nine.[81]

The long-term cost of the double burden throughout a woman's "best years" is revealed in the story of Anna Klemme's working life. Like most female textile workers she began working at age fourteen, in weaving room three at the Mechanische Weberei. She worked eleven years, left her job "at her own request" in March 1893, married, changed her name to Brockmann, and returned in June, this time to weaving room one. She left again in October 1893 because of pregnancy and returned four months later, shifting at that time to weaving room two. She took three months off in late 1895, gave birth to another child, and was back at the loom in early 1896, where she remained without interruption for the next ten years. In June 1906, now thirty-eight years old, Anna Brockmann left her job to give birth to a third child. Although she now had three children at home, she returned to work a few weeks later and stayed on the job until late 1912, when she gave up her employment because of illness.[82] It is highly likely that when Anna Brockmann, age forty-four, left her weaving loom after twenty-nine years in the mill, the double burden of child rearing and loom tending had taken its permanent toll on her.

Although textile employers were forced to accommodate the rhythms of married women's working lives—the frequent suspensions and resumptions of employment and the special provisions, such as the additional half-hour lunch break for women with families mandated by the revised labor code of 1891, many mill owners nonetheless sought to cultivate a long-term core workforce of married women, a fact the factory inspector from Mönchen-Gladbach explained in the following terms: "[Married women] bring with them a willingness to work, are more attentive, precise, conscientious, and careful than the young girls and are not distracted by a constant search for pleasure. Because they seek more stable and secure employment, they remain with greater tenacity at one job. On the other hand, the single girls like to change [jobs] frequently. Thus the married women workers form the stable core and the reliable portion of the female factory personnel."[83] The records of the Diergardt Stiftung of Mönchen-Gladbach provide further evidence not only of married women's presence

81. StA Bi, Mech. Web. 28/1, 29/1, 51; I reconstructed Sofia Schneider's career pattern based on segments of her working life recorded in the *Arbeiterstammrolle* of the Mechanische Weberei.
82. StA Bi, Mech. Web. 28/1, 29/1, 51; Anna Brockmann's career pattern was also reconstructed from these *Arbeiterstammrollen*.
83. HStAD, JBdKPG, 1899: Düsseldorf, p. 514. A few employers, particularly in the Catholic textile centers of the Lower Rhine, refused to hire married women at all.

Table 21. Textile workers given awards by the Diergardt Foundation of Viersen, 1904–1922

	Men	Women
Total awards (359)	197 (54.9%)	162 (45.1%)
Average length of employment	30.2 years	27.4 years
Average age of entering job	22.6 years	19.8 years
Average age at time of award	54.5 years	47.0 years

Source: See appendix to this chapter.

among the textile *Stammarbeiterschaft*, but also of the rewards factory owners granted them for long-term employment. Freiherr von Diergardt established his foundation in 1904 to honor workers for their loyalty to employers (as expressed in long employment) and to offer financial assistance to ailing or elderly workers.[84] Between 1904 and 1922 some 360 textile workers from Viersen received awards from the foundation—usually certificates, gold pins, and cash. The requirement for nomination was twenty-five years with one employer, and the foundation's records reveal that most of the prizewinners had worked between twenty-five and forty years in the same factory. In a remarkable contrast with my investigation of *Arbeiterstammrollen*, which reveals a relatively low percentage of women who worked longer than ten years, 45 percent of the recipients were female, as table 21 demonstrates. Marital status could be determined only for approximately one-fourth (41) of the female recipients, of whom 21 were married or formerly married. In 1905, for example, G. H. Goeters company, a spinning mill in Viersen, requested an award from the Diergardt foundation for Agnes Schmitz, who was sixty-seven years old and had worked as a reeler for twenty-five years without interruption.

> After the death of her husband, . . . Frau Schmitz supported herself and her children with the "work of her bare hands." That last year her only son also celebrated twenty-five years of employment at the F. H. Meyer company speaks for the sense of cohesion in the family.
> On the morning of 1 April, the workers in the reeling shop presented Frau Schmitz, whose machine had been decorated with flowers, with their gift of an armchair. The company gave her an attractive wardrobe. That evening there was a party in the pub "von Kesselburg" with live music and song presentations in her honor. Because of her outstanding loyalty, hon-

---

84. StA Vie, Diergardt Stiftung III/056, 1904–12: "Ehrungen und Belohnungen für Fabrikarbeiter aus der zu Mönchengladbach bestehenden Diergardt Stiftung, 1904–1912."

esty, and diligence, Frau Schmitz certainly is entitled to such recognition, and it will undoubtedly give her great joy.[85]

The centrality of the machine in these festive ceremonies attests to the identification of women with their work and pride in the products of their labor, confirming Tamara Hareven's contention that "for most women workers, as for men, mastery of a job, no matter how simple, was a source of pride and self-esteem."[86] The journey of one female social reformer, Minna Wettstein-Adelt, through the underworld of the factory also suggests an important place for both the tools of production and the community of the shop floor in the work identities of female *Stammarbeiter*. Wettstein-Adelt, like Bernays, disguised herself as a worker to learn about factory life firsthand, working in several mills over a period of three and a half months. From one weaving mill she reported: "Many of these girls work enthusiastically, especially those who follow the completion of a whole piece, like those who weave smaller rugs or single fitted curtains. They love their machines, as one loves a loyal dog. They clean them until they shine and decorate them with colorful ribbons, holy cards, and other trinkets that their suitors won for them at last summer's fair."[87] Both cases suggest that for female *Stammarbeiter*, just as for male workers, looms, spindles, and bobbins, as well as the relations with coworkers, occupied a central place in rituals of celebration and in the ethics of work. In enlisting women workers, encouraging and promoting their long-term relationship to work, rewarding it with prizes and praise, and allowing female workers to adjust their work rhythms to meet family needs, employers' policies also helped foster the formation of *Berufsethos*, of work ethics, among female *Stammarbeiter*.

In most cases, however, it was not an abstract work ethic or loyalty to the loom that drove women—single, married, or widowed—into the factory. Regardless of the pride they might have taken in the products of their labor, most women worked out of dire economic necessity, as did most men. Indeed, the factory inspectors' inquiry of 1899 into the factory employment of married women refuted the frequent contention of conservative social reformers that most women worked not for their family's bare necessities, but to fulfill their desire for luxury, to attain "extras" such as

85. StA Vie, III/056, Diergardt Stiftung, 1904–22, "Brief von C. H. Goeters an den Bürgermeister Stern von Viersen," 4 April 1905.
86. Hareven, *Family Time*, p. 79. Hareven's interviews with former Amoskeag workers are an invaluable source here. Unfortunately I did not have access to anything comparable. On solidarity among workers and pride in work, see also Bernays, "Berufsschicksale moderner Industriearbeiter," p. 134.
87. Minna Wettstein-Adelt, *Drei-ein-halb Monate Fabrikarbeiterin: Eine Practische Studie* (Berlin: J. Leiser, 1893), p. 20.

finery, tobacco, and alcohol. The inspector from Aachen, for example, reported that only 276 women (12 percent) had the luxury of working "in order to have a better life and save money," while the remaining 88 percent cited economic need as the reason for their employment. Similarly, in the Düsseldorf district 21 percent of women were the main breadwinners for their families, and most others worked because their husbands' wages could not support a family.[88] Some female workers undoubtedly derived a sense of independence from earning their own wages and making vital contributions to the family budget, however, despite the long hours of work at low pay.

At the same time, the mill job also represented a complex site of support and sociability among women workers that extended beyond the monetary value of their wages. The companionship and camaraderie among coworkers on the shop floor, the shared experiences not only of work in all its dimensions, but also of romance and rivalry, pregnancy, birth, illicit abortion, illness, death, and widowhood, the rigors of everyday life, the demands of the double burden on women's time and bodies formed a vital part of their work experiences and work identities. Factory ethnographers like Bernays noted that women were often drawn back to work after marriage or the birth of a child by a longing for the gossip and chatter of the shop floor, for "in her quiet apartment, especially when she has no children, she misses the 'events' in the factory workroom, the company of others, to which she has been accustomed since she was thirteen or fourteen years old."[89] In a parallel case, Tamara Hareven's interviews with former Amoskeag workers indicate that "like men, women developed attachments to their jobs. Women who started working in their teens when they were single were especially likely to continue after marriage because of the ties they had formed and the sociability the job offered."[90] Similarly, Ute Daniel's study of women workers during World War I argues that the solidarity networks among them were so dense that it became almost impossible for employers to transfer female workers from one shop or work team to another without causing widespread protest or a marked decline in morale.[91]

Police reports on textile strikes in the mills of the Lower Rhine also attest to the ways camaraderie and solidarity among female workers under-

---

88. See discussion of the factory inspectors' report in chapters 4 and 5. HStAD, JBdKPG 1899: Aachen, Düsseldorf, pp. 509, 513, 604.
89. Bernays, *Auslese und Anpassung*, p. 200.
90. Hareven, *Family Time*, pp. 245–46.
91. Ute Daniel, "Fiktionen, Friktionen und Fakten: Frauenlohnarbeit im ersten Weltkrieg," in *Arbeiterschaft in Deutschland, 1914–1918*, ed. Günther Mai (Düsseldorf: Droste, 1985), p. 314.

pinned women's work identities and work cultures. In November 1900, for example, 120 workers—mostly women—launched a wildcat strike in the Engländer silk weaving mill in Krefeld when the firm refused to rescind the firing of one woman worker. Although the strike did not have the support of either of the textile unions, the nearly unanimous walkout (120 of the 140 employees of the mill) ended successfully with the reinstatement of the fired woman.[92] In its compilation of "Pictures from the Life of the Women Workers in the Knitting Factories," the Social Democratic textile union reported that when one woman spooler became ill, the others in her shop continued to work her spindles to spare her job until she was well enough to return. This expression of community resulted in conflict with the mill owners when they refused to pay either the sick woman or her colleagues for their labor. In another case a firm declined payment to one woman for fourteen sets of knitted goods because the fabric contained flaws, insisting—in a surprising attempt to revive the truck system—that she keep the blemished goods as payment for her hours worked. In sympathy with the woman's loss of a week's wages, which coincided with the birth of her baby and decreased earnings during her maternity leave, her female coworkers purchased all the knitted items from her, one by one, "so that she would at least have some kind of income during her recovery."[93]

Other work protests in which women predominated offer testimony of the fluid boundaries between factory and family in women's working lives, as they fought to set their own rhythms of work, to preserve the right to come late when dictated by family circumstances, or reported to factory inspectors instances of intimidation by employers, unwilling to grant women the longer lunch breaks mandated by the revised labor code of 1891.[94] In February 1910, for example, 450 of the 491 workers in the largely female Krefelder Baumwollspinnerei (cotton spinning mill in Krefeld) started a wildcat strike when employers rebuffed their vocal demands for the immediate reinstatement of a colleague the company had fired for her chronic, nearly daily, tardiness. First the mill's female workers walked off their jobs, followed a few hours later by the male workers. The mill's

92. HStAD, Reg. Düss. 24693, "Bericht der Polizeiverwaltung vom 26.11.1900"; "Bericht der Polizeiverwaltung vom 29.11.1900."
93. Johann Sassenbach Stiftung, Berlin (formerly Zentralarchiv der Deutschen Gewerkschaften), brochure published by the Deutscher Textilarbeiterverband, *Bilder aus dem Leben der Arbeiterinnen in den Trikotfabriken* (Stuttgart: Rödel/Schober, n.d.), pp. 6–8. The reports from conferences and so on in this text indicate that it was most likely published in 1913.
94. On the factory inspectors' interventions regarding the enforcement of paragraph 137, no. 4 of the revised labor code of 1891, pertaining to the extended lunch break for women workers, see HStAD, JBdKPG 1892: Düsseldorf, p. 327; 1894: Düsseldorf, pp. 482, 504–5.

Arbeiterausschuss (elected workers' committee) mediated a settlement with the firm the next day.[95] Although no reason was listed in the police report for the woman's chronic tardiness, the forceful response of her coworkers suggests they sought to defend her prerogative to balance the demands of work and family according to the exigencies of her personal or family situation. A few months later, however, the same firm was once again the scene of a strike of some 500 workers who protested the firm's new policy, implemented to assuage the chronic shortages of female labor in the mill, of hiring male workers only if their wives also went to work in the mills.[96] The strike was prompted by the firing of a married male worker whose wife had quit her job in the mill because of illness and overwork. Supported by the Social Democratic textile union, the strike became an unusually long and bitter battle, lasting eight weeks and resulting in several instances of violence, including hostile confrontations with strikebreakers and threats of sabotage and vandalism to the mill. The conflict, which eventually also involved wage demands of the female spinners, represents an intriguing instance of mobilization and solidarity across gender boundaries, attesting to the desire and determination of both male and female workers to negotiate their own conflicts and to enforce their own intersections between family time and industrial time wherever possible.

Similarly, the protracted battle for the ten-hour day in the textile industry makes clear the importance of these boundaries between family and factory time in the labor struggles of both unionized and unorganized workers. The legendary Crimmitschau textile strike of 1903, for example, was the culmination of a decade-long movement among the textile workers of Saxony to procure "One more hour for us! One more hour for our families! One more hour for living!"[97] At issue was not only the ten-hour day but also a 10 percent wage increase for pieceworkers to compensate for the shortened work time and the enforcement of the extended lunch

---

95. HStAD, Reg. Düss., 24706, "Bericht der Polizeiverwaltung an den Oberbürgermeister Krefelds vom 25.2.1910"; "Bericht der Polizeiverwaltung an den Oberbürgermeister Krefelds vom 26.2.1910."

96. HStAD, Reg. Düss. H&G 24706, "Bericht der Polizeiverwaltung Krefelds vom 2. Mai 1910"; "Bericht der Polizeiverwaltung Krefelds vom 9. Mai 1910"; "Bericht der Polizeiverwaltung vom 10. Mai 1910"; "Bericht des Gewerbeinspektors vom 26.5.1910"; "Bericht der Polizeiverwaltung vom 5. Juli 1910," pp. 151–59 of the archive file. Also see Stadtarchiv Krefeld: 4/1117, p. 349, "Schreiben der Firma Baumwollspinnerei vom 10. Juni 1910."

97. On the history of the textile workers' movement in Crimmitschau before the strike, see Brigitte Rauer and Volker Ullrich, "Textilarbeiterstreik in Crimmitschau 1903/04," *Geschichtsdidaktik* 2, no. 83 (1983): 127; Alice Salomon, "Crimmitschau," *Soziale Praxis* 13 (14 January 1904): 404; DTAV, *Crimmitschau, 1903–1928: Blätter der Erinnerung an Sachsens bedeutsamsten Arbeitskampf* (Berlin: Textilpraxis, 1928), p. 96. According to the DTAV brochure, the Crimmitschau local was the largest local in the German Reich in 1903.

break for married women, which the mill owners of Crimmitschau refused despite its legal enactment. The strike, which began as a relatively limited walkout of 600 workers in late July 1903, met vehement resistance from the organized textile employers, who quickly responded to the initial demands with a massive lockout of some 7,500 workers.[98] Far from a localized battle between labor and capital, between the local branch of the Social Democratic textile union and the association of Crimmitschau's textile mill owners, the strike soon galvanized national public opinion as unionized workers—both Social Democratic and Christian—and the Social Democratic Party gathered political and monetary support for the workers of Crimmitschau, and as the powerful Central Association of German Industrialists (CVDI) and the local and provincial governments of Crimmitschau and Saxony stepped forward to strengthen the resolve of the employers. Given the high visibility of married women's factory employment in the wake of the factory inspectors' inquiries of 1898–99 and 1902 and the significant numbers of female participants—58 percent—in the strike, the struggle for the ten-hour day in Crimmitschau soon became a national cause célèbre among middle-class social reformers, who had long sought to limit working hours, especially for married women.[99] Furthermore, the fact that the ten-hour day was common practice in the Rhineland and other textile regions of Germany fueled the sympathies of many bourgeois reformers and parliamentarians for the locked-out workers.[100]

During the summer and fall of 1903 the strike's slogan—"One more hour for our families!"—echoed across Germany, as the plight of the 1,350 married female strikers and the 4,500 children of male and female strike participants came to preoccupy public discussions and debates.[101]

---

98. See chapter 5 of this book, pp. 194–95, for a brief discussion of the Crimmitschau strike. On the outbreak and the initial demands of the strike, see Rauer and Ullrich, "Textilarbeiterstreik," p. 130; "Der Zehnstundentag der Textilarbeiter in Crimmitschau," *Die Gleichheit* 13 (16 August 1903): 143–44; "Der Kampf der Textilarbeiter in Crimmitschau," *Die Gleichheit* 13 (9 September 1903): 151–52; and Salomon, "Crimmitschau," pp. 406–7.

99. "Der Kampf der Textilarbeiter in Crimmitschau," *Die Gleichheit* 13, no. 19 (1903): 151–52. Approximately half (3,800) of the striking or locked-out workers were members of the Social Democratic textile union. The factory inspectors' inquiries referred to here include (1) the inquiry into the causes and outcomes of married women's factory employment of 1898–99: Reichsamt des Innern, *Die Beschäftigung verheirateter Frauen in Fabriken, nach den Jahresberichten der Gewerbeaufsichtsbeamten für das Jahr 1899 bearbeitet im Reichsamt des Innern* (Berlin: R.von Decker, 1901); and (2) the inspectors' official inquiry into female workers' regular and overtime hours, conducted in 1902 to determine the necessity of further restrictions on work time: Reichsamt des Innern, *Die Arbeitszeit der Fabrikarbeiterinnen* (Berlin: R.von Decker, 1905).

100. "Der Zehnstundenkampf der Textilarbeiter in Crimmitschau," *Die Gleichheit* 13 (21 October 1903): 175, and "Der Zehnstundenkampf der Textilarbeiter in Crimmitschau," *Die Gleichheit* 13 (18 November 1903): 185–86.

101. Rauer and Ullrich, "Textilarbeiterstreik," p. 128, and DTAV, *Crimmitschau, 1903–1928*, p. 172.

Those images of the working mothers of Crimmitschau fashioned by reformers and labor activists who favored the ten-hour day were remarkably consistent with the findings of the factory inspectors' published report of 1901 on married women's factory employment: the desire for a respectable standard of living, not the urge for luxury goods or the craving for "material pleasures," drove most married women into the mills. For their earnings, however meager at eight or ten marks weekly, made a crucial difference in the living standard of those families whose male breadwinners themselves earned only modest incomes in the local textile mills. As feminist social reformer Alice Salomon argued, the need for additional income rose with the birth of the first child, then again with the second, and married women workers were usually forced to leave their small children with relatives or neighbors while working in the mills.[102] Salomon decried the fact that the female worker of Crimmitschau had "a place to live, but no home; she has children, but cannot be a mother to them; she makes a living, but she has no life." For this reason, she asserted, the struggle in Crimmitschau was not about the interests of a specific class, but on behalf "of the cultural interests of the entire nation."[103] At the same time, middle-class male social reformers like Robert Wilbrandt played on the extraordinary weakness and helplessness of female textile workers, whom he perceived in his journeys through "at least a dozen textile factories" as "deadened, impoverished, downcast, distressed, and hopeless, and if their strength suffices, the loathing glimmers in their eyes."[104]

Whereas Wilbrandt mobilized these images to argue that oppressed and helpless women were in urgent need of the protection of reformers and state, the Social Democratic textile union assembled a quite different portrait. Despite the prolonged workday, which in Crimmitschau generally began at 6:00 A.M. and ended at 6:00 P.M., the union pointed out that working mothers still managed to prepare meals, wash and darn linens and clothes, and "take care of the thousands of other demands of the household." According to this image, the female textile workers of Crimmitschau were hardworking women who were highly efficient and tenacious in their efforts to care for their families, "expending their last drops

---

102. Alice Salomon, "Crimmitschau," *Soziale Praxis* 13 (14 January 1904): 404–6; DTAV, *Crimmitschau, 1903–1928*, p. 173 (excerpts from the reprinted and undated leaflet "An die Arbeiter und Einwohner Crimmitschaus und Umgebung!").

103. As cited in DTAV, *Crimmitschau, 1903–1928*, p. 249. This document is a reprint of a DTAV leaflet "An die kämpfende Arbeiterschaft von Crimmitschau und Umgegend!" of 11 January 1904, which cites Salomon's speech to a conference of bourgeois women's associations in Berlin. Those in attendance drafted a resolution in favor of the demands of the textile workers of Crimmitschau, calling upon the Reichstag to pass a law enacting the ten-hour maximum workday.

104. Robert Wilbrandt, "Der Hintergrund des Weberstreiks in Crimmitschau," in DTAV, *Der Textilarbeiter* 16 (8 January 1904).

of energy . . . to fulfill all of the duties of an 'orderly woman.'" Many of them, weakened not only by work but also by the strain of pregnancy and birth, had become "old, gray, frail, and shriveled" by age thirty and suffered from chronic fatigue.[105]

Yet both union leaders and bourgeois social reformers invoked norms of social and reproductive hygiene to buttress their demand for the enactment of the ten-hour day, reiterating the factory inspectors' admonitions of 1901 regarding the detrimental effects of the double workday on the "female organism" and citing the extraordinarily high infant mortality figures for Crimmitschau: of the 817 babies born there in 1899, 223 (27.3 percent) died before their first birthday.[106] Invoking Rudolf Martin's 1896 study of married women's factory employment, mainly in Crimmitschau, the Social Democratic women's newspaper *Die Gleichheit* pointed out that the pressing need to return to work after childbirth prevented many mothers from breast-feeding their babies, leaving them vulnerable to the infections and inadequate nutrition that were commonly associated with bottle-feeding. Indeed, according to Martin's study, the overwhelming majority of babies who died before their first birthday in Crimmitschau in 1890 had been bottle-fed.[107]

Even more important than the contradictory images of working mothers in the hygienic and political debates about the Crimmitschau strike was perhaps their own highly visible presence, their resolute and enthusiastic participation in the strike itself. Although over half of the female participants in the strike were unorganized, and though women workers received considerably lower strike support payments than men, the female workers of Crimmitschau were acutely aware of the particular meanings of the strike for their own well-being. Indeed, many apparently regarded the strike as the culmination of many previous day-

---

105. DTAV, *Der Crimmitschauer Kampf um den 10-Stunden Tag* (Berlin: Carl Hübsch, 1905), p. 61; "Die Zehnstundenbewegung der Textilarbeiter in Crimmitschau," *Die Gleichheit* 13 (16 August 1903): 143–44.

106. Infant mortality in working-class districts of Germany was estimated to be approximately 20 percent at the end of the nineteenth century. See chapter 5, p. 196. The infant mortality figures in Crimmitschau are listed in "Die Zehnstundenbewegung der Textilarbeiter in Crimmitschau," *Die Gleichheit* 13 (16 August 1903): 143–44. On the hygienic justifications of the strike demands, see Rauer and Ullrich, "Textilarbeiterstreik," p. 134; DTAV, *Crimmitschau, 1903–1928*, pp. 173, 186–87, 237. The DTAV solicited an expert's opinion on the "hygienic justifications of the strike's demands" from Professor Max Gruber, which is reprinted in this brochure.

107. Rudolf Martin's study, "Die Ausschliessung der verheirateten Frauen aus der Fabrik: Eine Studie an der Textilindustrie," *Zeitschrift für die gesamte Staatswissenschaft* 52 (1896): 104–46, 383–418, is cited here in "Preisfechter für die Verkürzung der Arbeitszeit," *Die Gleichheit* 13 (9 September 1903): 146–48. On the debates provoked by his study, see chapter 4 above.

Plate 4. A group of Crimmitschau textile workers on strike, January 1904. From Deutscher Textilarbeiterverband, *Crimmitschau, 1903–1928: Blätter der Erinnerung an Sachsens bedeutsamsten Arbeitskampf* (Berlin: Textilpraxis, 1929), p. 132. Reprinted courtesy of the archive of the Gewerkschaft Textil-Bekleidung, Düsseldorf.

to-day struggles not only for shorter working hours, but also for better provisions in the mills—separate washroooms, toilets, and changing rooms for women workers, for example—which in the past had required the intervention of the factory inspectors or the union.[108] One strike demand that female workers advanced with particular vigor and vehemence was the enactment of married women's legal right to a longer lunch break, which the mill owners of Crimmitschau had thus far managed to circumvent by simply dismissing women who requested it. As the striking female workers insisted, the geographical layout of Crimmitschau was such, however, that most women required an hour or more to walk home and back to the mill, rendering the extra half

108. DTAV, *Crimmitschau, 1903–28*, p. 187. According to Salomon, "Crimmitschau," pp. 406–7, women workers received 6–7 marks per week in strike support, while male workers were paid 9 marks plus 0.75 marks per child up to a maximum of 3 marks for four children. The *Gleichheit* reported that of the approximately 3,500 women participating in the strike, 1,694 were members of the Social Democratic textile union. See "Der Kampf der Textilarbeiter in Crimmitschau," *Die Gleichheit* 13 (9 September 1903): 151–52.

hour "an absolute necessity" if they were to prepare and eat meals at home.[109]

Although the leadership of the strike was clearly in the hands of male functionaries in the Social Democratic textile union, female workers were a vital and controversial presence on the strike lines and in the many meetings convened by the union during the six-month struggle. Six of the twenty-nine members of the organizing committee for the strike were women, and female workers—presumably unionized—addressed each of the large assemblies of locked-out workers, sharing their experiences of the double burden and their problems with managers and foremen. Indeed, according to the union's accounts of the strike, women had been elected to the workers' committees (*Arbeiterausschüsse*) in most of Crimmitschau's factories long before the strike and had thus established the practice of representing their own interests.[110]

Whereas union leaders praised the women workers of Crimmitschau for their calm, determined, and disciplined behavior during the strike, mill owners, city officials, and police expressed shock and dismay about the "impertinent" behavior of the female strikers, whom many apparently regarded as notably "worse than the men."[111] Women paraded under the windows of the mill owners' homes and offices, "shopping basket in arm and knitting in hand . . . bearing the furious looks of the employers," while many mothers took advantage of this chance to take their children for a walk, which they were otherwise seldom able to do. Because of the overwhelming participation of women in the strike, contests about female respectability underlay the constant battles between city authorities and the strike leaders over the legal parameters of strike activities. In one case, for example, police arrested a "housewife" who maintained she was waiting for a friend on the street near one of the mills, claiming that "a woman who loiters in the street from 8:45 A.M. past 10:00 cannot be a respectable housewife." Asserting that "the woman does not belong out on the street, rather in the house," the officers placed the woman in jail for a day. In

---

109. Salomon, "Crimmitschau," pp. 406–7, and "Der Kampf der Textilarbeiter in Crimmitschau," *Die Gleichheit* 13 (9 September 1903): 151–52.

110. DTAV, *Der Crimmitschauer Kampf*, p. 64; Gewerkschaft Textil-Bekleidung, *Dokumente zu 150 Jahren Frauenarbeit in der Textile- und Bekleidungsindustrie* (Düsseldorf: Gewerkschaft Textil-Bekleidung, 1981), p. 26.

111. Rauer and Ullrich, "Textilarbeiterstreik," p. 138, citation from the report of Pastor Schink from Crimmitschau on the strike, which was published in the newspaper *Christliche Welt*. Schink's full report, including his remarks about the comportment of the female strikers, is reprinted in DTAV, *Crimmitschau, 1903–1928*, pp. 247–48. Also see "Der Kampf der Textilarbeiter in Crimmitschau," *Die Gleichheit* 13 (9 September 1903): 151–52, and "Der Zehnstundenkampf der Textilarbeiter in Crimmitschau," *Die Gleichheit* 13 (18 November 1903): 186.

response female workers, accompanied by their children and displaying the various markers of working-class domesticity such as their knitting, darning, or shopping baskets, fashioned their own norms of respectability as the police and city officials of Crimmitschau wielded increasingly repressive measures. In the wake of the arrest of the loitering "housewife," for example, female strikers devised a more creative means of forming strike lines by renting windows in apartments near the mills and watching employers and potential strikebreakers from the window seats of neighboring residences.[112] According to one union report, throughout the strike women workers were showered with fines and tickets for their tactics, and "many mothers were held for hours at the police station."[113] The stakes of the struggle were heightened when the government of Saxony officially declared a "state of siege" in Crimmitschau in early December 1903, drawing striking workers, male and female, unionized and unorganized, into a direct confrontation with the authority of the state. As more and more strikebreakers streamed into Crimmitschau, female workers were forbidden to stroll the streets with their children in buggies, and residents of neighborhoods adjacent to the mills were forced to keep their windows closed to prevent confrontations between striking workers and the newly arriving strikebreakers. By the end of December all meetings and assemblies of the striking workers had been banned, including Christmas celebrations.[114] By 19 January 1904 the mill owners, backed by national employers' associations and city and provincial governments, had succeeded in defeating the wide coalition of striking workers, labor movement activists, and middle-class social reformers. Although the striking workers failed to realize any of their demands, the six-month struggle of the working mothers of Crimmitschau was widely viewed by contemporaries as "ripening the climate" for the revision of the labor code in 1908 and the introduction of the mandatory ten-hour day for female workers.[115]

Although the magnitude and duration of the Crimmitschau strike lent a unique resonance to its cause, the poignant struggles of women workers to balance the burdens of household and wage labor often led to shop-floor protests or strikes in which demands for shorter work hours or longer lunch breaks were raised next to the call for higher wages or more respect-

---

112. "Der Zehnstundenkampf der Textilarbeiter in Crimmitschau," *Die Gleichheit* 13 (7 October 1903): 167. Also see *Die Gleichheit* 13 (18 January 1903): 185–86, for a report on other female strikers who were imprisoned for their strike-related activities.
113. "Der Kampf der Textilarbeiterschaft von Crimmitschau," *Die Gleichheit* 13 (23 September 1903): 159.
114. See the articles titled "Der Zehnstundenkampf der Textilarbeiter in Crimmitschau," in *Die Gleichheit* 13 (2 December 1903): 199; 13 (14 December 1903): 206; and 14 (31 December 1903): 7–8.
115. Rauer und Ullrich, "Textilarbeiterstreik," pp. 135, 145.

ful treatment from foremen or *Meister*. In one silk mill in Krefeld, for example, female silk weavers walked off the job and risked a massive lockout of the silk weavers of the region in 1903 not only to secure the extra half-hour lunch break, which they had thus far been denied, but also to insist on the cleanliness and order in the restrooms and cafeterias, the institution of a changing room for women workers, and a "coffee room" for breaks as well as abolition of the "unjust" factory ordinances and their accompanying penalties and fines.[116] Similarly, nearly a year after the defeat of the Crimmitschau strike, women workers in the yarn factory Feistkorn near Gera requested union backing for their intended strike over the longer lunch break for married women and the establishment of a suitable "cooking room" in the mill for those who could not go home at lunchtime. Furthermore, the women demanded that the mill close its doors by 6 P.M. so they could do their grocery shopping and other errands before the stores closed at 8:00 P.M.[117] Although the intervention of social reformers and politicians in parliament and in the realm of public opinion was indisputably influential in prompting the extension of protective labor legislation in 1891 as well as the establishment of the ten-hour day in 1908, the everyday struggles of women workers themselves also inspired the reformers' campaigns. At the same time, female workers' strikes and shopfloor protests clearly undermined the widely held view that women had little ability to "build coalitions" or to assert and defend their own needs as workers, as citizens, or as wives and mothers.

Conclusion

In its scrutiny and proposed redefinition of notions of job stability and longevity, in its explication of the meanings of the sexual division of labor for the often discrepant career patterns of male and female workers, this chapter has argued that women formed a vital and long-term core workforce in the textile mills of the Rhineland and Westphalia. The fragments of women's working lives, reconstructed from company personnel records, indicate a longevity comparable to or greater than that of the more mobile male workforce in several branches of textile production. Patchwork, like the reassembling of Sofia Budde's working life, not only suggests longevity and membership in the core workforce of the Mechanische Weberei,

116. DTAV, "Eine Riesen-Aussperrung am Niederrhein angekündigt!" *Der Textilarbeiter* 5 (15 April 1903). Although this was the lead story in this issue of the *Textilarbeiter*, the strike was apparently resolved before the employers enacted their plans for a lockout, since no further reports on the conflict appeared.
117. DTAV, *Der Textilarbeiter* 16 (21 October 1904), local report from Gera.

but also offers insight into the ways women themselves viewed and utilized their jobs, the ways work figured as a complex network of support for both single women and those with families to support. The ribbons and bows that decorated the looms and spindles of the core workers in Viersen's textile mills, the celebrations with song and food of twenty-five years in the mill, suggest the meaningful place of work in the lives of female textile workers, including those who at the same time carried the arduous burden of housework, childbirth, and child rearing. Furthermore, the disparate strike reports that bring female actors to the fore make it clear that women workers formed work identities as they balanced their dual burdens, as they traversed and rendered fluid the boundary between family and factory.

Finally, this analysis of women's work identities seeks to expose and dissolve the fictitious separation of home and work that was implicit in the social identities of both class and citizenship and that have confined working women behind the lines of family and household in the narratives of German labor history. The identities and rhetorics of class and citizenship were embedded in the assumed boundary between home and work, in an exclusionary vision of *Berufsethos* as the foundation of "class" consciousness that could only relegate women to the margins of the imagined collectivity of the German working class. Yet the everyday strikes and protests of female workers regarding the length of the workday or the extra half-hour lunch break, as well as their willingness—in the bitter struggle in Crimmitschau, for example—to engage the politics of class and to confront the authority of employers and the state, make it clear that the negotiation of the boundary between home and work was a crucial aspect of their experience of both work and politics. The next chapter explores women's work identities not as situated on the teleological path toward a specific identity of class, but as an integral part of the culture of work, in which confrontations about pride and honor, gossip and respectability, bodies and sexuality, propelled them into intensely political arenas, including the organized politics of class, as increasing numbers of women joined the textile unions between 1908 and 1914. This analysis of female textile workers' identities and cultures of work not only seeks to uncover and analyze the manifold experiences and meanings of work that have been expunged from the narratives of labor history, but also forms an essential genealogy of working-class politics in German history, a foundation for further explorations of working-class formation and the exclusions it was based on. It helps explain why women, once they began to join the textile unions in significant numbers after 1908, would seek to appropriate and transform the vocabulary and ideology of class, to inflect its universal claims, expose its masculine character, and inscribe class with their own meanings.

Appendix: Sources for Tables

Table 5: The data for this analysis of textile workers' career patterns were taken from the *Arbeiterstammrollen* of seven textile mills in the Rhineland and Westphalia. *Arbeiterstammrollen* are company books that list workers chronologically (according to the date they began working at the mill) or alphabetically. These records generally include the following information about individual workers: name, birth date, birthplace, residence, job category, entry and exit dates, and occasionally religious affiliation, reason for departure from the mill, and name of father or guardian. Most companies required workers to enter the information above in the *Stammrolle* on commencing employment, accompanied by their signatures acknowledging receipt of the factory ordinances.

The sources for this table (and for others elaborating workers' career patterns in this chapter) are in the following archives:

Baldus: *Belegschaftsbücher* (similar to *Arbeiterstammrollen*) of the Baldus company are at the Rheinisch-Westfälisches Wirtschaftsarchiv in Cologne, Abt. 63, Nr. 7, F. 3.

Crous: I used the one volume available from Crous while it was in the private possession of Dr. Jochem Ulrich, Schumannstrasse 8, 41747 Viersen-Süchteln. It belonged at that time to the city of Viersen's *Versicherungsamt* (insurance office). The Crous silk weaving mill, formerly at Viktoriastrasse 14, 41747 Viersen, closed its gates at the end of 1979.

Girmes: The *Arbeiterstammrollen* of Johann Girmes AG are in the private archives of Johannes Lipp, Heimatverein Oedt, Oststrasse 15, 47929 Oedt bei Krefeld.

Wülfing: The *Arbeiterstammrollen* are in the company's archive: Johann Wülfing and Sohn, Wülfingstrasse, 42897 Remscheid-Lennep.

Mechanische Weberei AG Bielefeld and Mechanische Weberei AG Spenge: The *Arbeiterstammrollen* of these two factories are at the Stadtarchiv Bielefeld, Bestand Mechanische Weberei 27/1, *Namen der Arbeiter* (Spenge), 1907–32; 28/1, *Personalbuch*, 1863–1925; 29/1, *Namen der Arbeiter bis 1907*; 51, *Personalbuch*, 1925–34.

Frowein: the *Belegschaftsregisterband* of the Frowein company can be found in the firm's archive at Frowein und Companie KG, Friedrich-Ebert-Strasse 125, 42117 Wuppertal 1.

For the larger mills—Girmes, Wülfing, and the Mechanische Weberei Bielefeld—I took random samples of 10 percent. For the Frowein records my sample size was limited to 5 percent because of limited access to the data, as determined by the company. For company records where the number of complete entries was relatively small or only one or two volumes of records exist, or where the period covered by the available records was particularly brief, I recorded all complete entries (100 percent). This was the case for the Baldus mill, whose only surviving records are of workers who were employed between 1905 and 1915 (including, however, some who entered as early as 1865). Similarly, in the case of Crous, the only remaining record is a one-volume *Arbeiterstammrolle* that lists all workers employed at Crous in 1926, as well as those who entered between 1927 and 1930, when the volume ends. (Those present in 1926 include some who began working at Crous as early as 1901.) For the Mechanische Weberei Spenge, which I examined to investigate the similarities and differences between urban and rural career patterns in two mills of the same company, the mill's own life span was relatively short: it was founded in 1907, but the outbreak of the First World War disrupted production, resulting in layoffs and shortened work hours in 1914; the mill closed in 1916 for the rest of the war. My study includes all workers who entered the mill in its first and second years of operation (1907–8). A total of 3,483 workers are included in the seven samples.

The divergent methods of record keeping in these seven mills had a direct bearing on my own methods of data compilation and analysis. For those records that list all workers present within a given period (1905–15 in the case of Baldus, and for Crous, all workers employed in 1926), those workers with high longevity, who began employment as early as 1865 at Baldus or as early as 1901 at Crous, tend to skew the sample toward higher longevity, while no records survive on the work patterns of those who entered and left the Baldus mill, for example, between 1865 and 1905. It is important to note, however, that because most very long-term workers were male, my sample is necessarily biased against my hypothesis that men and women had similar career patterns where they performed the same or similar jobs, thus rendering those cases of similar work patterns for male and female workers even more striking.

In view of the paucity of records of this nature in firm or public archives, the samples included in this table represent the data available, not an ideal population from which to draw the samples. (After extensive inquiries and research, these mills were the only ones in the Rhineland and Westphalia for which I could locate personnel records for the period encompassed by my study.) Nonetheless, many of my findings coincide with or are buttressed by those of contemporaries, such as Marie Bernays's detailed study of the Gladbacher cotton weaving and spinning mill from 1912 or the factory inspectors' statistics, as well as by more recent historical studies, such as Hermann Schäfer's examination of turnover rates. (See notes in this chapter for complete references.) Furthermore, the large sample sizes do permit a high level of confidence in the descriptive statistics for each sample. For example, the .95 confidence intervals for the proportion of women employed in these plants, given in table 5, are Girmes ± 4%; Wülfing ± 3%; Frowein ± 7%; Mechanische Weberei Bielefeld ± 3%. Although the samples for Baldus, Crous, and the Mechanische Weberei Spenge represent 100 percent of those present in a specific year or years, I have also calculated confidence intervals for these samples: Baldus ± 3%; Crous ± 5%; Mechanische Weberei Spenge ± 8%. In all cases but Frowein (in which the percentages of men and women are relatively similar), these figures allow us to make inferences to the population of the individual factories regarding the gender composition of the workforce. Finally, because of the necessary limits on the data available, I have chosen to minimize statistical inference in this chapter, basing my analysis on the descriptive statistics within the individual samples.

Table 6: Sources as listed above for table 5. Readers should note, as indicated in note 32, that birthplace was not listed for all workers in my Girmes sample. Thus my calculations include only those for whom the birthplace was recorded.

Table 7: HStAD, Jahresberichte der Königlichen Preussischen Gewerberäte (JBdKPG), Düsseldorf 1907, pp. 419–22. This table is based on Prussian government statistics, compiled by the factory inspectors of the Düsseldorf district and published in the annual factory inspectors' report for 1907.

Table 8: Sources as for table 5. The calculation of .95 confidence intervals for this table are as follows:

Company	Men	Women
Baldus	± 5	± 3.8
	(28.5–38.5)	(18.4–26.0)
Crous	± 12.9	± 6.4
	(32.7–58.5)	(23.9–36.7)
Frowein	± 3.3	± 5
	(10.3–16.9)	(13.4–23.4)
Girmes	± 4.6	± 5.7
	(29.1–38.3)	(20.6–32.0)
Mechanische Weberei Bielefeld	± 7.2	± 3.4
	(12.5–26.9)	(16.1–22.9)

Company	Men	Women
Mechanische Weberei Spenge	± 8.4 (13.3–30.1)	± 10.7 (11.7–33.1)
Wülfing	± 5.8 (51.5–63.1)	± 4.3 (46.1–54.7)

The calculation of .95 confidence intervals shows that the differences between the departure rates of men and women in six of the seven mills are not statistically significant. Because the confidence intervals around the means for men and women overlap, we cannot be certain the sample means represent the means of the population the samples were drawn from. Although the confidence intervals merely confirm the patterns of departure we can see in the table—namely, the distinct differences between departure rates for men and women at Baldus and relatively similar rates at Frowein, Girmes, Mechanische Weberei Bielefeld, Mechanische Weberei Spenge, and Wülfing—the calculation of confidence intervals suggests greater relative similarity between the departure rates of men and women at Crous than indicated in the table.

Table 9, figures A1–A12: Sources as for table 5. For statistical information about this table, see note above for table 8.

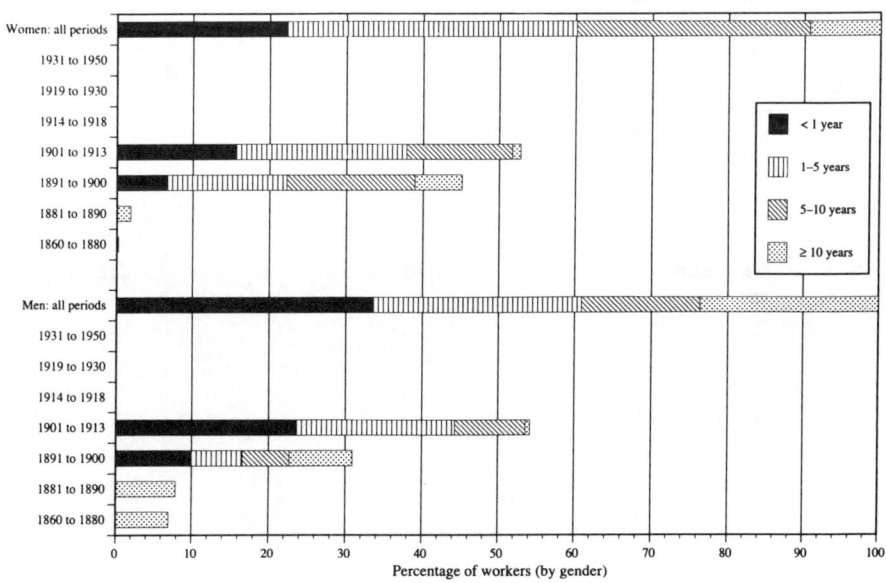

Figure A1. Length of employment by date of entry: Baldus

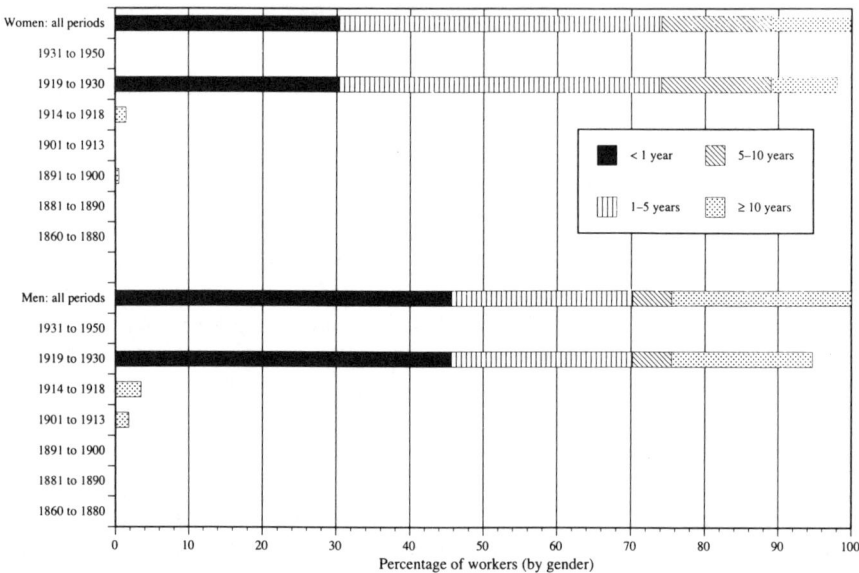

Figure A2. Length of employment by date of entry: Crous

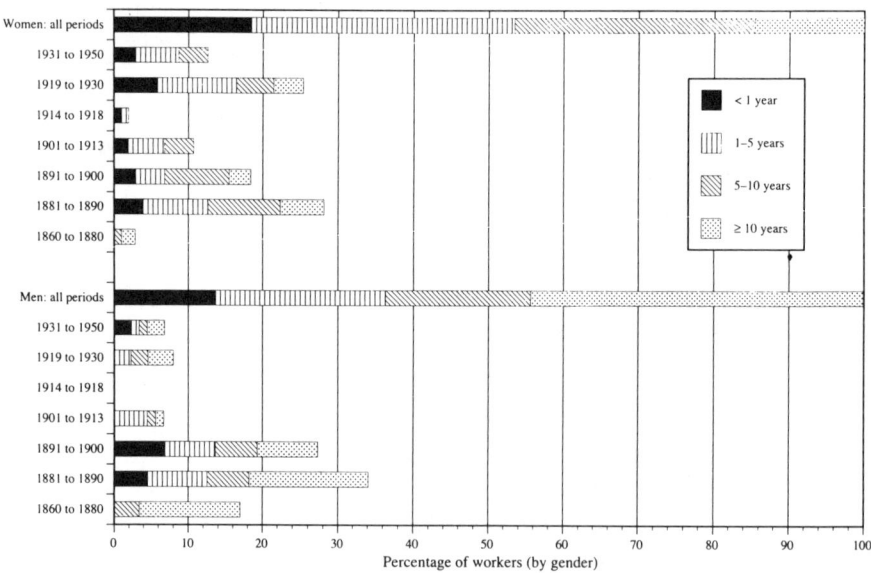

Figure A3. Length of employment by date of entry: Frowein

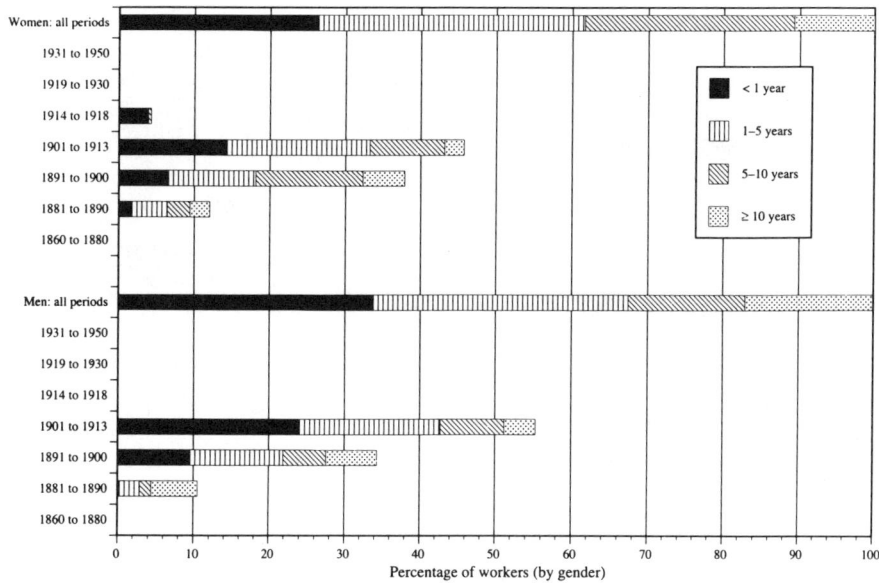

Figure A4. Length of employment by date of entry: Girmes

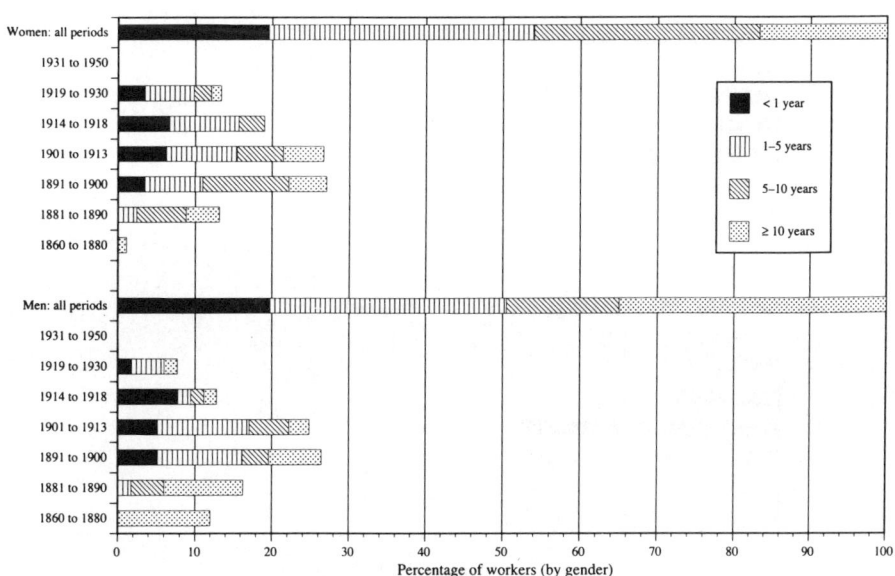

Figure A5. Length of employment by date of entry: Mechanische Weberei Bielefeld

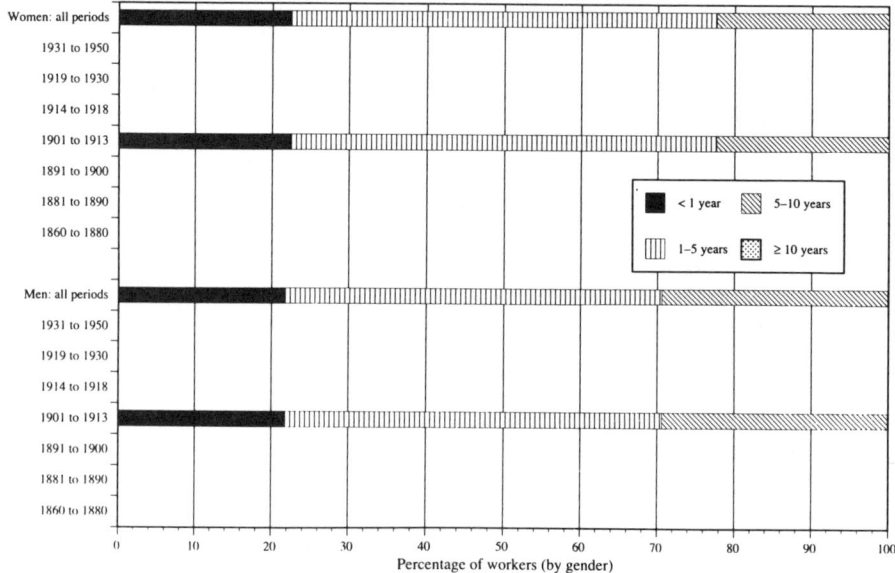

Figure A6. Length of employment by date of entry: Mechanische Weberei Spenge

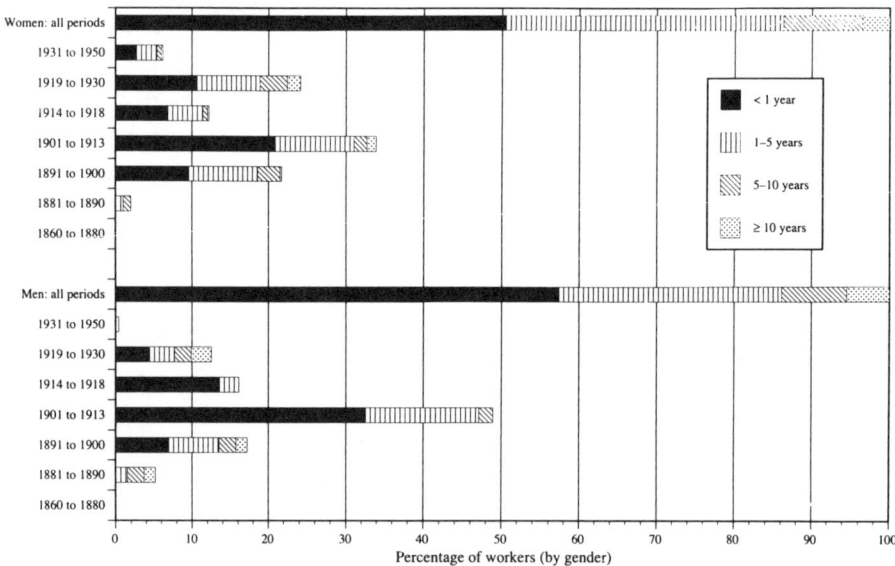

Figure A7. Length of employment by date of entry: Wülfing

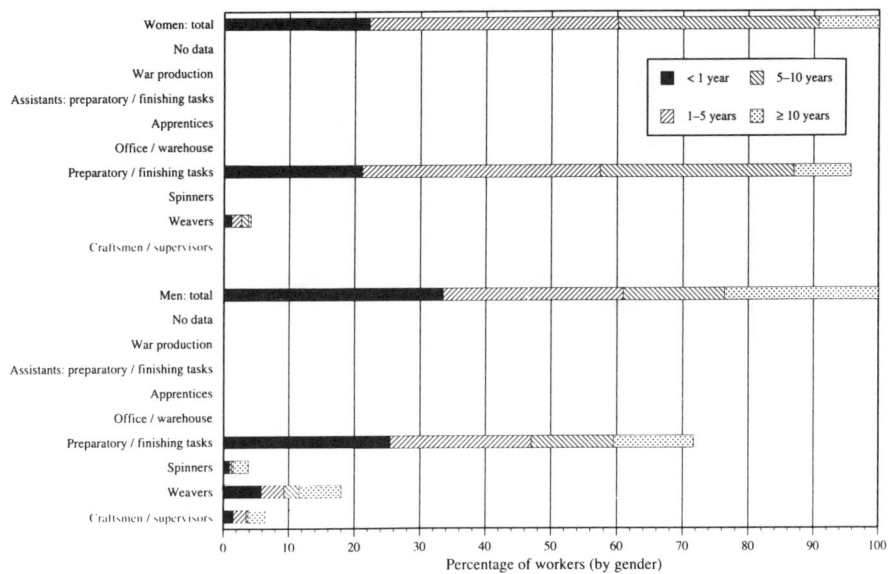

Figure A8. Length of employment by job category: Baldus

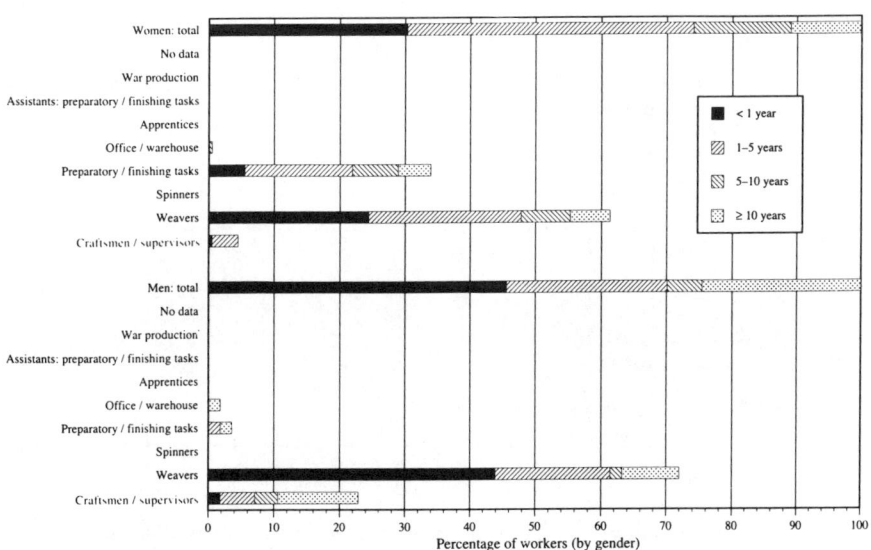

Figure A9. Length of employment by job category: Crous

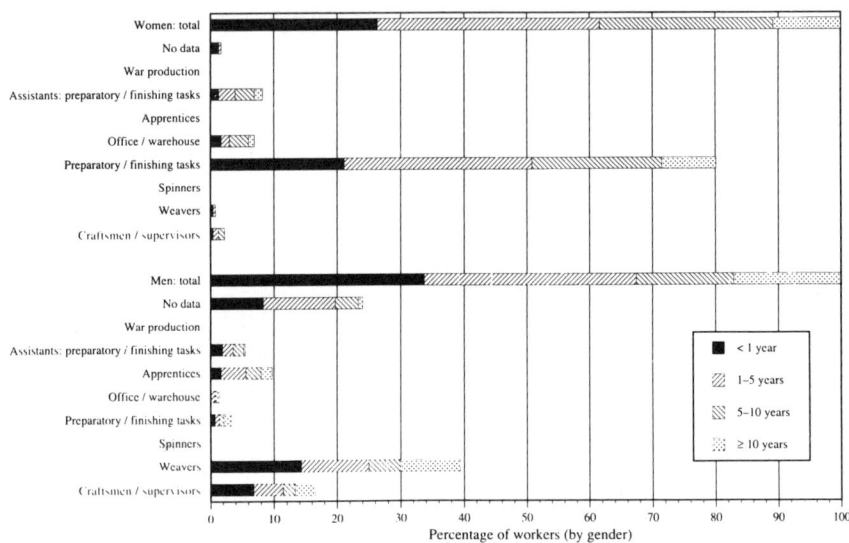

Figure A10. Length of employment by job category: Girmes

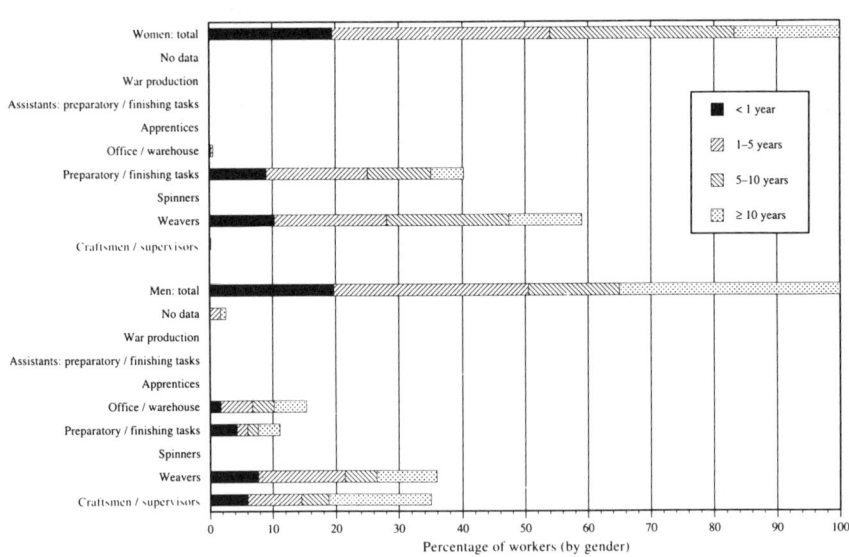

Figure A11. Length of employment by job category: Mechanische Weberei Bielefeld

Work Experiences, Work Identities 279

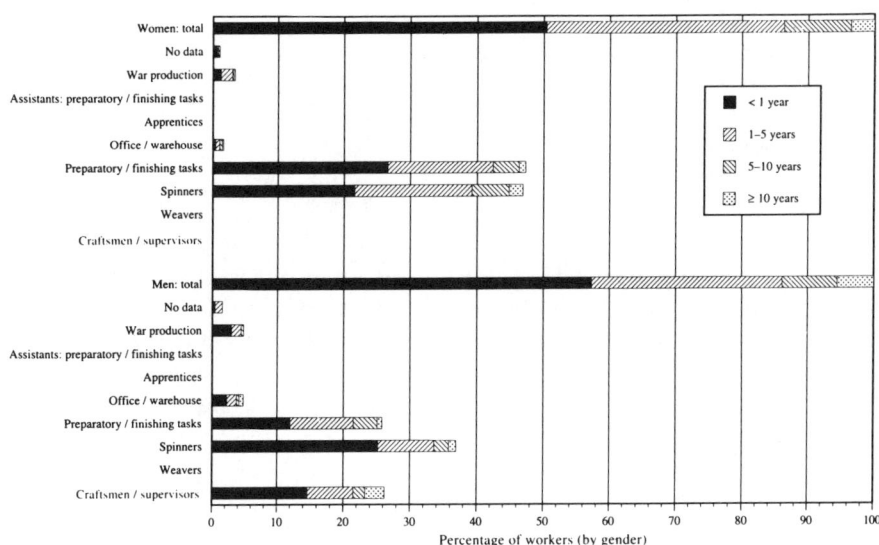

Figure A12. Length of employment by job category: Wülfing

Table 10: Sources as for table 5. I have calculated standard deviations and .95 confidence intervals for the figures in this table (standard deviation = s.d.; confidence interval = c.i.).

Company	Men	Women
Baldus		
s.d	0.5	0.2
c.i.	(6.3–8.3)	(4.1–4.9)
Crous		
s.d.	1.6	0.4
c.i.	(3.7–10.1)	(3.2–4.8)
Frowein		
s.d.	1.4	0.7
c.i.	(10.6–16.2)	(5.0–7.8)
Girmes		
s.d.	0.3	0.3
c.i.	(4.2–5.3)	(3.9–5.2)
Mechanische Weberei Bielefeld		
s.d.	1.1	0.2
c.i.	(8.2–12.4)	(5.2–6.2)

Company	Men	Women
Mechanische Weberei Spenge		
s.d.	0.2	0.3
c.i.	(2.7–3.6)	(2.6–3.8)
Wülfing		
s.d.	0.2	0.1
c.i.	(1.8–2.8)	(1.9–2.4)

Table 11: Sources as for table 5. I have calculated standard deviations and .95 confidence intervals for the larger job categories in the Mechanische Weberei Bielefeld (standard deviation = s.d.; confidence interval = c.i.).

Job category	Men	Women
Craftsmen/supervisors		
s.d.	2.0	n.a.
c.i.	(8.7–16.6)	
Weavers		
s.d.	1.6	0.3
c.i.	(5.2–11.5)	(5.5–6.5)
Preparatory/finishing		
s.d.	2.9	0.4
c.i.	(2.5–13.7)	(4.4–6.1)
Office/warehouse		
s.d.	3.0	1.0
c.i.	(5.5–17.2)	(0.7–4.5)

Table 12: Sources as for table 5. I have calculated standard deviations and .95 confidence intervals for the larger job categories in the Crous mill (standard deviation = s.d.; confidence interval = c.i.).

Job category	Men	Women
Craftsmen/supervisors		
s.d.	5.4	0.3
c.i.	(7.4–28.4)	(1.2–2.3)
Weavers		
s.d.	0.8	0.6
c.i.	(1.2–4.2)	(2.7–5.0)
Preparatory/finishing		
s.d.	n.a.	0.5
c.i.		(3.7–5.4)

Table 13: Sources as for table 5. I have calculated standard deviations and .95 confidence intervals for the larger job categories in the Baldus mill (standard deviation = s.d.; confidence interval c.i.).

Job category	Men	Women
Craftsmen/supervisors		
s.d.	3.0	n.a.
c.i.	(7.0–18.9)	
Weavers		
s.d.	1.5	0.8
c.i.	(6.9–12.9)	(2.2–5.3)
Spinners		
s.d.	4.8	n.a.
c.i.	(9.5–28.5)	
Preparatory/finishing		
s.d.	0.5	0.2
c.i.	(4.5–6.3)	(4.1–4.9)

Table 14: Sources as for table 5. I have calculated standard deviations and .95 confidence intervals for the larger job categories in the Wülfing mill (standard deviation = s.d.; confidence interval = c.i.).

Job category	Men	Women
Craftsmen/supervisors		
s.d.	0.6	n.a.
c.i.	(1.9–4.1)	
Spinners		
s.d.	0.3	0.2
c.i.	(0.9–2.2)	(2.0–2.8)
Preparatory/finishing		
s.d.	0.4	0.2
c.i.	(1.6–3.1)	(1.4–2.0)
Office/warehouse		
s.d.	2.0	1.4
c.i.	(0.6–8.3)	(2.0–7.7)

Table 15: Source: StA Vie, III/056, Diergardt Stiftung, 1904–22.

Table 16: Sources as for table 5. I have calculated standard deviations and .95 confidence intervals for the larger job categories in the Girmes mill (standard deviation = s.d.; confidence interval = c.i.).

Job catagory	Men	Women
Craftsmen/supervisors		
s.d.	0.7	1.4
c.i.	(3.2–5.9)	(1.1–6.7)
Weavers		
s.d.	0.5	1.2
c.i.	(4.6–6.7)	(0.9–3.6)
Preparatory/finishing		
s.d.	1.5	0.4
c.i.	(4.6–10.3)	(3.8–5.3)
Office/warehouse		
s.d.	3.3	0.9
c.i.	(1.5–14.4)	(3.2–6.8)
Apprentices		
s.d.	0.8	n.a.
c.i.	(4.0–7.0)	
Assistants: preparatory/finishing		
s.d.	0.8	1.0
c.i.	(2.2–5.5)	(3.6–7.7)

Table 17: Sources as for table 5.

Table 18: Sources as for table 5.

Table 19: Sources as for table 5.

Table 20: HStAD, JBdKPG, 1899: Düsseldorf, pp. 510–11; 1927: Düsseldorf, p. 523; 1899: Münster, p. 370; 1927: Münster, p. 382; 1899: Minden, pp. 390–91; 1927: Minden, pp. 405–7; 1899: Cologne, p. 567; 1927: Cologne, pp. 562–63; 1899: Aachen, pp. 600–602; 1927: Aachen, p. 595.

Table 21: StA Vie, III/056, Diergardt Stiftung, 1904–22.

7

Behind the Mill Gate: Gender and the Culture of Work

The emergence of female factory labor as a new social question at the end of the nineteenth century established the discursive and legislative frameworks for the formation of work cultures and work identities behind the mill gate. The social reformers, factory inspectors, entrepreneurs, and labor activists who intensively debated the moral and corporal dangers of women's work formulated new policies for the workplace as they sought to resolve the growing discrepancy between the steady expansion of the female workforce and traditional notions about the character of the sexes. Resisting the calls of conservative social reformers to ban married women's employment outside the home during the late 1880s and 1890s, those who drafted and enforced the protective labor codes sought instead to uphold the delicate balance between women's work at home and in the mills, to define and restrict female factory labor in terms of its meanings for the "female organism," the family, and the social body. Thus the legal limits on the workday for women workers—eleven hours in 1891 and ten hours in 1908—and the piecemeal implementation of maternity leave and maternity insurance between 1891 and 1911 aimed to reconcile factory employment with motherhood.[1]

The policies of textile employers enforced a sexual division of labor in the new mills, ascribing to certain technologies or types of fabric inherently masculine or feminine qualities and establishing gendered categories

---

1. See chapters 4 and 5 for discussions of the revision of the labor codes in 1891 and 1908. Also see Hauptstaatsarchiv Düsseldorf, Jahresberichte der Königlichen Preussischen Gewerberäte (Hereafter HStAD, JBdKPG), 1892: Düsseldorf, pp. 328–30, and 1910: Düsseldorf, p. 420.

of wage and skill. In fostering the growth of a female *Stammarbeiterschaft*, however, employers also challenged prevailing notions of sexual difference in a fundamental way, reflected in the resolute opposition of conservative reformers to the employment of married women in factories. Through an array of paternalist *Wohlfahrtseinrichtungen* (welfare or charitable institutions) such as *Haushaltsschulen* (schools that offered training in domestic skills like cooking and sewing), dormitories, and day-care centers, mill owners sought to assuage the growing public anxiety about a profound crisis of working-class motherhood in Germany, to deflect the alarmist visions of physical and moral dissolution among working-class families.[2]

At the same time, male labor leaders and workers fought to demarcate male spheres in an industry that was rapidly becoming a women's domain. Men's embrace of the revived identities of craft in some regions and branches brought new visions of domesticity and a new self-representation as breadwinners, marking a fundamental break with the fluid division of labor in protoindustrial household economies. Indeed, these visions infused and shaped the categories of skill and wage and the campaigns for reduced work time that underpinned the culture of work in the textile mills.[3] The normative and ideological components of gender-based wage scales, specifically the categories of male breadwinners and female supplementary earners, their definition in terms of the distinct *Bedürfnisse* (needs) of each sex rather than their *Leistung* (productivity), represented a key point of consensus between employers and workers, even if the two groups were often at odds about every other aspect of wage negotiation. This concordance across class boundaries regarding the gendered divisions and hierarchies of labor, wages, and skill, the definition of women's work in terms of both domesticity and the female reproductive body, had a principal part in the making of women's work cultures, in the meanings women assigned to work, and in how they negotiated the boundaries between family and factory, between their own individual bodies and the social and sexual order.

Work cultures, as sites of collective and individual experience, were formed as workers assigned and contested the meanings of work. They encompassed "the expressive cultural practices" through which workers adapted to and subverted ordained positions within the factory regime and

---

2. See, for example, Paul Mieck, *Die Arbeiter-Wohlfahrts-Einrichtungen* (Berlin: Heymanns, 1904), p. 194; Minna Wettstein-Adelt, *Drei-ein-halb Monate Fabrikarbeiterin: Eine Practische Studie* (Berlin: J. Leiser, 1893), p. 36.

3. The Social Democratic Textile Workers' Union, for example, formulated its arguments in favor of Saturday restrictions in terms of women's domestic responsibilities. Deutscher Textilarbeiterverband (hereafter DTAV), "Wann werden wir den freien Sonnabendnachmittag haben?" *Der Textilarbeiter* 25 (15 August 1913): 266–67.

asserted their individual needs and desires at work.[4] In this respect they were sites of individual and collective *Eigensinn*—of the defensive preservation of self, the reappropriation of time, space, and bodies that formed what Alf Lüdtke has termed the "inner face" of the shop floor (as well as the arenas of formal politics).[5] The notion of work culture thus implies the possibility of a "relatively autonomous sphere of action on the job" that workers created as they distanced themselves from the structure of production and the authority of employers.[6]

Rooted in discrepant experiences of work, status, and power, work cultures were more likely to be divided by gender, ethnicity, or age than to be welded together by an abstract identity of class. Indeed, a multiplicity of shop-floor cultures emerged as textile workers sought to define their position within the system of production and the ideology of gender that underpinned it. Despite the many experiences male and female workers shared—the physicality of mill work; the confinement behind high walls in mill courtyards and the absence of sunlight; the "unbearable air," high temperatures, and excessive humidity in the spinning shops; the dust, dry air, and noise of the power looms in the weaving shops; the long hours of standing at the machines for both spinners and weavers; and the factory regimes of discipline and punishment—men's work cultures, at least in branches like silk or woolen weaving, were shaped by the strategies and struggles of male workers to protect their privileges of wages, skill, and status against the threat of feminization.[7] Furthermore, the formal political arenas of unions and their affiliated parties were more likely to pervade male work cultures, even to set their tone, at least until the repeal of the

---

4. See Douglas E. Foley, "Does the Working-Class Have a Culture in the Anthropological Sense?" *Cultural Anthropology* 4 (May 1989): 141.

5. Although these needs and desires were expressed in the factory, they might have originated either in the sphere of wage work or in that of the household, family, and neighborhood (or in both). On *Eigensinn*, see Alf Lüdtke, "Organizational Order or *Eigensinn*? Workers' Privacy and Workers' Politics in Imperial Germany," in *Rites of Power, Symbolism, Ritual and Politics since the Middle Ages*, ed. Sean Wilentz (Philadelphia: Temple University Press, 1985), pp. 304, 321. Also see Alf Lüdtke, *Eigen-Sinn: Fabrikalltag, Arbeitererfahrungen und Politik vom Kaiserreich bis in den Faschismus* (Hamburg: Ergebnisse, 1993).

6. Susan Porter Benson, *Counter Cultures: Saleswomen, Managers, and Customers in American Department Stores, 1890–1940* (Urbana: University of Illinois Press, 1986), p. 228. Also see Alf Lüdtke, "The Historiography of Everyday Life: The Personal and the Political," in *Culture, Ideology and Politics: Essays for Eric Hobsbawm*, ed. Raphael Samuel and Gareth Stedman Jones (London: Routledge and Kegan Paul, 1982), p. 46.

7. On the physical space of the textile factory workplace, see Marie Bernays, "Berufsschicksale moderner Industriearbeiter," part 2, *Die Frau* 18 (December 1910): 212–15; Wettstein-Adelt, *Drei-ein-halb Monate*; and the factory inspectors' descriptions in HStAD, Landratsamt Mönchen-Gladbach 710; JBdKPG 1898: Minden, p. 254; 1899: Minden, p. 388; 1902: Düsseldorf, p. 338; 1904: Düsseldorf, p. 445; 1906: Münster, pp. 333–34; 1908: Minden, p. 326; 1912: Minden, pp. 393–94; 1913: Cologne, p. 540.

Prussian Law of Association in 1908, when the number of female union members began to increase rapidly. Although women's work cultures, like men's, were formed in the frequent conflicts about control over the labor process, they might also be viewed as constituting a subculture or an alternative factory culture in which women expressed the demands and desires that male workers and the organized labor movement usually disdained as peripheral. For the structures and ideologies of the sexual division of labor, the discursive framing of women's work, the explicit attention in protective labor codes and employers' policies to female bodies and women's roles as mothers or future mothers meant that female work cultures were also born of struggles about pride and honor, gossip and respectability, bodies and sexuality, charity and tutelage. The following discussion of the hierarchies of skill and wage analyzes how sexual difference became anchored in the structures and relations of production that underlay workplace cultures.

Structuring the Cultures of Work: Hierarchies of Skill and Wages

Dichotomies and Fictions of Skill

Notions of skill are central to understanding the relations of power and authority on the shop floor. Examining definitions and divisions of skill in the textile industry shows that they were defined less by the structure of production than by normative prescriptions of proper work for men and women. From the founding of the first mechanized textile mills in the mid-nineteenth century through the end of the Weimar Republic, skill was acquired informally by most textile workers—both female and male—except the craftsmen. Only a small percentage (in 1907, less than 1 percent) acquired their skills through traditional craft apprenticeships.[8] Most obtained their experience and dexterity on the shop floor, often under the tutelage of a parent, sibling, or neighbor.

In the absence of a formal apprenticeship system, the meaning of terms like *gelernt* (skilled) and *Lehre* (training), and the mode of acquisition, varied widely among textile regions, branches, and individual mills. Ac-

8. *Das Lehrlingswesen und die Berufserziehung des gewerblichen Nachwuchses, Schriften der Zentralstelle für Volkswohlfahrt*, vol. 7 (Berlin: Heymanns, 1912), p. 182. In 1907 there were 9,078 apprentices in the German textile industry. Among spinners, 1.4 percent were apprentices; the figure for weavers was 2.5 percent; for knitters, 3.3 percent; and for bleachers and dyers, 1.7 percent. See Johannes Feig, "Deutschlands gewerbliche Entwicklung seit dem Jahre 1882," *Zeitschrift für die gesamte Staatswissenschaft* 56 (1900): 684. According to Feig, textile workers constituted 1.5 percent of industrial apprentices in 1895.

cording to reports by mayors of textile towns in the Rhineland in 1877 and factory inspectors' reports of 1912, apprenticeship contracts were customary only in the branches of ribbon weaving and dyeing.[9] Although both groups of observers acknowledged that the textile industry depended on "a core of competent and skilled [*gelernte*] workers," in most branches constituting between 60 and 90 percent of the workforce, they reported that most had learned their skill in a few weeks and had become fully productive weavers or spinners within a year.[10]

In the language of modern factory industry, as implemented by factory inspectors, Reich statisticians, employers, and workers themselves, *gelernte Arbeiter* (skilled workers) and *Facharbeiter* (specialized workers) were those who had mastered specific manual tasks or could operate certain machines without assistance.[11] By contrast to *gelernte Arbeiter*, who had completed some type of *Vorbildung* (training), *ungelernte Arbeiter* generally had no training at all and could easily be replaced.[12] Dr. Wolff, factory inspector for the Düsseldorf district, noted the fluid boundaries between "skilled" and "unskilled" labor as early as 1877: "Even in factories that produce the same goods with the same machines, workers who perform the same function in different mills are called 'skilled' in one mill and 'common laborers'

---

9. HStAD, Reg. Düss., 33520: Barmen: "Bericht des Oberbürgermeisters vom 3.7.1877"; "Bericht des Gewerbeinspektors vom 20.9.1912"; Krefeld: "Bericht des Oberbürgermeisters vom 1.7.1877" and "Bericht des Gewerbeinspektors Crefeld Stadt und Land vom 26.9.1912"; Düsseldorf: "Schreiben von Ludwig und Gustav Cramer vom Mai 1877"; Elberfeld: "Bericht des Oberbürgermeisters vom 20.6.1877" and "Bericht des Gewerbeinspektors vom 19.9.1912"; Lennep: "Bericht der Handelskammer Lennep vom 5.7.1877" and "Bericht des Gewerbeinspektors vom 28.9.1912"; Mönchen-Gladbach: "Bericht der Handelskammer vom 25.5.1877" and "Bericht des Gewerbeinspektors vom 19.9.1912"; Essen Land: "Bericht des Landrats vom 14.7.1877"; Mettmann: "Bericht des Gewerbeinspektors Mettmann-Vohwinkel vom 29.9.1912."

10. HStAD, Reg. Düss., Handel und Gewerbe (H&G) 33520, "Bericht des Fabrikeninspektors Dr. G. Wolff an die Königliche Regierung vom 16.7.1877." According to Dr. Wolff, 80–85 percent of cotton spinners, 60 percent of woolen spinners, 60 percent of linen spinners, and 80 to 90 percent of employees in cotton, woolen, and silk weaving mills were "skilled workers."

11. HStAD, Reg. Düss., H&G 33520: "Bericht des Fabrikeninspektors Dr. G. Wolff," p. 1. Also see Gerhard Adelman, "Die berufliche Ausbildung und Weiterbildung in der deutschen Wirtschaft, 1871–1918," *Berufliche Aus- und Weiterbildung in der deutschen Wirtschaft seit dem 19.Jahrhundert* (special issue no. 15 of *Zeitschrift für Unternehmensgeschichte*), p. 21.

12. Marie Baum, "Die gewerbliche Ausbildung der Industriearbeiterin," *Kultur und Fortschritt* 107 (1907): 4; Bernard Jauch, "Das gewerbliche Lehrlingswesen in Deutschland seit dem Inkrafttreten des Handwerkergesetzes vom 26.7.1897 mit besonderer Berücksichtigung Badens" (Dissertation, Universität Freiburg, 1911), pp. 94–96; Hermann Schäfer, "Die Industriearbeiter: Lage und Lebenslauf im Bezugsfeld von Beruf und Betrieb," in *Sozialgeschichtliche Probleme in der Zeit der Hochindustrialisierung*, ed. Hans Pohl (Paderborn: Schöningh, 1979), p. 173.

in another; in one mill they are trained to be fully productive workers within one year and in the other in a couple of months."[13] This disparate use of terminology can be explained by the short period of most factory "apprenticeships" and the quick acquisition of "skill."

In the few weaving and spinning mills where contractual apprenticeships existed, instruction did not adhere to any uniform standard. Most were based on oral agreements between employers and the parents of the teenage trainees. In some instances parents had to pay a deposit for their children's training, to be forfeited in case of termination. The unions argued that the arbitrary nature of factory apprenticeships favored employers, who bound young men and women to work for three years at lower than average wages.[14] A rare sample of a written apprenticeship contract for a textile mill in the Lower Rhine notes that young Maria Keller was to be instructed "by an older woman weaver" and would not be paid until she could operate her loom independently. Similarly, in the small winding and bobbin-setting shops of the rural Wupper Valley, female apprentices worked without pay until the *Meisterin* (female master or supervisor) determined that they had reached a certain level of skill.[15] In many cases mill owners had a minimal role in hiring or selecting apprentices and assumed little or no responsibility for guaranteeing adequate training. One woolen manufacturer described the informality of the training system in his mill: prospective weavers began their *Lehre* by asking his permission to watch friends or relatives at work. After four or five weeks they were given an idle loom for practice, and if they proved to be quick learners, they soon began weaving cloth on their own.[16]

Although the official government statistics counted weavers and spinners as skilled, most textile workers of both sexes performed *angelernte Arbeit*, a category the statistics of the German Reich did not incorporate until just before the First World War. *Angelernt* designated semiskilled, specialized tasks for which workers received no formal apprenticeship

13. HStAD, Reg. Düss., H&G 33520, "Bericht des Fabrikeninspektors Dr. G. Wolff," p. 1.

14. HStAD, Reg. Düss., H&G 33520: Reports of 1877 and 1912 as listed above; here see in particular the report from Mettmann of 1912; DTAV, *Arbeiterausbildung in der deutschen Textilindustrie* (Berlin: Textilpraxis, 1928), pp. 16, 27. At the Kümpers cotton spinning and weaving mill in Rheine near Münster, parents of apprentices paid fifty marks to guarantee that their children would remain at their jobs for at least two years. Also see Paula Thiede, "Die fachgewerbliche Ausbildung der Arbeiterin," *Sozialistische Monatshefte* 20, no. 2 (1914): 824–25; DTAV, "Brauchen die Textilarbeiterinnen handwerkmässige und fachgewerbliche Ausbildung?" *Der Textilarbeiter* 25 (6 June 1913): 179.

15. HStAD, Reg. Düss., H&G 33520, "Lehrvertrag zwischen der Firma J. P. Kuhlen und Söhne, Mechanische Weberei in Rheydt und Theodor Keller, Vater der minderjährigen Maria Katharina Keller" (dated 1912), and report from Mettmann from 1912.

16. *Das Lehrlingswesen*, pp. 171–72 (as reported to the factory inspector in 1887).

training but that, unlike unskilled labor, required more than muscular strength. Of particular importance in semiskilled jobs like weaving, spinning, roving, and loom warping was the worker's role as a "thinking part" in a divided labor process.[17] Even lesser skilled tasks like reeling, winding, bobbin setting, threading, and throwing required workers to be dexterous, attentive, perspicacious, and reliable. According to one observer, the textile industry employed almost no unskilled workers beyond cleaning women and janitors.[18] Although men and women acquired their "skills" in the same way—except for the textile craftsmen, who had no female counterparts—men's work was endowed with higher status and rewarded with higher pay. Gender was also important in the advancement of workers within the mill. The best positions available to women—in terms of wages and status—were those of weaver, loom warper, rover, and darner. Yet even in predominantly female mill divisions women were seldom viewed as possessing the skills necessary for the supervisory positions of *Untermeister* and *Meister*, defined in terms of years of continuous experience in the mill, unspecified "personal qualities," and comprehension of the entire production process.[19]

In the absence of formal job training for women, few female workers became familiar with the broader operations beyond the workings of their own machines. Attendance at public *Fortbildungsschulen*, which offered supplementary training of this nature to young workers between age fourteen and eighteen, had been obligatory for young men in many German states since 1891, but only the states of Baden, Württemberg, and Bavaria required young women to attend the schools.[20] In Prussia attendance was optional for young factory workers of either sex, and local governments

17. Hermann Schäfer, "Die Industriearbeiter," p. 173; Baum, "Die gewerbliche Ausbildung," p. 4; Marie Bernays, "Berufsschicksale moderner Industriearbeiter," *Die Frau* 18 (December 1910): 132, and Marie Bernays, "Lehrwerkstätten und Fachschulen in der Textilindustrie," *Kultur und Fortschritt* 492–94 (1914): 14; Rosa Kempf, "Das Interesse der Industrie an der Ausbildung der weiblichen Arbeiterschaft," *Kultur und Fortschritt* 492–94 (1914): 12.

18. Bernays, "Berufsschicksale," p. 132; Jauch, "Das gewerbliche Lehrlingswesen," pp. 94–96.

19. Adelmann, "Die berufliche Ausbildung," p. 20; Baum, "Die gewerbliche Ausbildung," pp. 4–7; Marie Baum, "Die Folgen ungelernter Arbeit für die Arbeiterin," *Kultur und Fortschritt* 282–83 (1910): 20; Bernays, "Lehrwerkstätten," p. 23; *Das Lehrlingswesen*, pp. 179–80. I found only occasional references to female supervisors in all-female shops in these sources. The factory inspectors' summary report of 1899 on married women's work noted that some employers offered such posts to older married women because of their maturity, stability, and experience on the job.

20. DTAV, "Weibliche Arbeiterjugend, Fortbildungsschule und kapitalistische Interessen," *Der Textilarbeiter* 22 (10 June 1910): 181. The first *Fortbildungsschulen*, as noted above, were founded by employers. By 1891, most were run by the city or local (Kreis) governments.

could not require young women to attend.[21] Thus in 1910 the Prussian *Fortbildungsschulen* had only 14,241 female pupils in 150 schools for girls, whereas 340,748 male pupils—47 percent of all male factory workers between age fourteen and seventeen—attended 1,877 schools in Prussia.[22] The goal of the schools for boys was to provide young men with a broader understanding of their specific jobs, of the system of production in its entirety, and of the role of the textile industry in the German economy. Whereas young men usually received instruction in general subjects like reading, writing, arithmetic, and drawing in addition to specialized job-related subjects like basic mechanics or textile fabrics, over half of the schools for girls in Prussia "almost wholly [disregarded] specialized job training for women and [concentrated] on educating women workers for their future *'Frauenberuf'*" through courses in sewing, drawing, cooking, and household accounting.[23]

How firmly the ideological definition and restriction of female skill had become anchored in the structures of production became apparent during debates after the turn of the century. Between 1908 and 1910 social reformers and middle-class feminists initiated a campaign to improve job training for women by granting all local and city governments the legal option of extending the *Fortbildungszwang* (compulsory attendance) to young women. Feminist social reformers, under the auspices of the Verband für Handwerksmässige und Fachgewerbliche Ausbildung der Frau, founded in 1909, sought not only to open the schools to women, but also to dissolve the gendered dichotomy of skill that pervaded factory cultures.[24]

---

21. Female commercial employees were, however, obliged to attend *Fortbildungsschulen* in Prussia. Zentralverband Christlicher Textilarbeiter Deutschlands (hereafter ZCTD), "Gegen die Pflichtfortbildungsschule für Arbeiterinnen," *Textilarbeiterzeitung* 16 (7 March 1914): 67. The first obligatory school for women was founded for commercial employees by the Kaufmännischer Verband für weibliche Angestellte in Berlin. See Marie Lischnewska, "Die handwerksmässige- und fachgewerbliche Ausbildung der Frau: Ein Mahnwort an die deutsche Frauenbewegung aller Richtungen," *Kultur und Fortschritt* 315–16 (1910): 14.

22. Marie Elisabeth Lüders, *Die Fortbildung und Ausbildung der im Gewerbe tätigen weiblichen Personen und deren rechtliche Grundlage* (Leipzig: Duncker und Humblot, 1912), pp. 22–30, 44. According to paragraph 120, no. 3 of the labor code of 1891, cities or district governments with over 10,000 residents could introduce a *Fortbildungszwang* (obligatory attendance at the continuation schools) for male workers. Attendance for young women was required by state (*landesgesetzlich*) law in Baden, Bavaria, and Württemberg.

23. Erna Barschak, *Die Idee der Berufsbildung und ihre Einwirkung auf die Berufserziehung im Gewerbe* (Leipzig: Quelle und Meyer, 1929), pp. 140–41; Lüders, *Die Fortbildung*, pp. 22–23; Kreisarchiv Viersen (KrA Vie), Gemeindeamt (GA) Grefrath 1154, "Gewerbliche Fortbildungsschule, 1864–1912."

24. Barschak, *Die Idee der Berufsbildung*, p. 140; Lischnewska, "Die handwerksmässige und fachgewerbliche Ausbildung," pp. 14, 27; ZCTD, "Gegen die Pflichtfortbildungsschule," *Textilarbeiterzeitung* 16 (7 March 1914): 67. Anne Schlüter, "Die Entwicklung weiblicher Lehrverhältnisse Anfang des 20. Jahrhunderts aufgezeigt am 'Verband für hand-

Despite their impassioned campaigns, the opposition of the employers' organizations—above all that of the textile entrepreneurs—thwarted legislative efforts of 1910 to extend the *Fortbildungszwang* to young women in Prussia.[25] Ironically, the same employers who in other instances acclaimed textile work as a suitable *Lebensberuf* (lifetime calling) for women and sought to cultivate a core female workforce of older, married women now argued forcefully against a longterm investment in developing women's skill. Their opposition made it clear that women were valuable workers only if they cost less to train and maintain than men. The spokesmen of the Vereinigte Deutsche Seidenwebereien (United German Silk Weaving Mills) pointed, for example, to the potentially calamitous effects of obligatory school attendance on silk mills, where women under eighteen made up 50 to 80 percent of the workforce. Furthermore, they claimed that

> training schools have a completely different meaning and should fulfill a completely different function for male and female workers.... The schools fulfill the goal of adding to the practical knowledge men gain on the job and of providing them with the theoretical knowledge they need in their future careers. Thus the training school is an important factor in their occupational lives. However, in the case of women—most of whom practice their occupation only temporarily until they marry—this goal is insignificant. For women there is no question of theoretical job training. For this reason it has been suggested—and emphasized in the Reichstag as well—that instruction in the *Fortbildungsschule* take the form of courses in housekeeping.[26]

The chamber of commerce in Elberfeld expressed similar views, suggesting that "at the most, one could consider instruction in housekeeping for women workers. Employers, however, cannot be expected to sacrifice work time or money for this type of training, which serves a purely private purpose."[27]

The textile unions as well remained skeptical about the benefits of for-

---

werksmässige und fachgewerbliche Ausbildung der Frau in Deutschland,'" in *Die Ungeschriebene Geschichte: Historische Frauenforschung* (Dokumentation des 5. Historikerinnentreffens in Wien, April 1984) (Vienna: Wiener Frauenverlag, 1985), pp. 259–67.

25. Baum, "Die gewerbliche Ausbildung," pp. 7–8; Barschak, *Die Idee der Berufsbildung*, pp. 140–41.

26. Rheinisch-Westfälisches Wirtschaftsarchiv (hereafter RWWA) 22: 70 Industrie- und Handelskammer Wuppertal, Gewerbliche Fortbildungsschule, männlicher und weiblicher Arbeiter 1864, 1908–14: "Denkschrift der vereinigten deutschen Seidenwebereien, Düsseldorf vom 15.11.1910." In the same document collection also see "Schreiben der Handelskammer Elberfeld an den Hohen Reichstag zu Berlin vom 1. April 1911."

27. RWWA 22: 70 Industrie- und Handelskammer Wuppertal, Gewerbliche Fortbildungsschule: "Schreiben der Handelskammer Elberfeld an den Hohen Reichstag zu Berlin vom 1. April 1911."

mal job training for women. Both the Social Democratic union and the Christian union acknowledged that many working-class parents depended on their daughters' wages and could hardly afford to have them in training for several years. Yet both endorsed the obligatory *Fortbildungsschulen* for women, scorning the employers' claims that such job training would undermine the economic vitality of the textile industry. Although the Christian union, like the employers' associations, envisioned domestic training as the main task of the schools for girls, the Social Democratic textile union underscored the importance of mastery of domestic skills in addition to a "certain amount of knowledge" of the production process and a basic understanding of the workings of the economy.[28]

This discussion of definitions and divisions of skill in the textile industry exposes the fictitious dichotomy between the unskilled female and the skilled male and offers insight into the skills that female textile workers did acquire. It also suggests that the category of skill is meaningful only in its historical specificity: its usefulness depends on clear distinctions among industries and between early and later periods of industrial development. Finally, the tenacity of this fictitious dichotomy is testimony to its rhetorical power, for it shaped male cultures in the mills, was upheld by union leaders, and was reproduced by labor historians long after the formal system of craft "skill" transmission had been displaced by the modern and informal system of *Anlernen*.

Hierarchies and Status of Wage

From the founding of the first mechanized factories in the Rhineland and Westphalia disparities prevailed between the wages of male and female workers. The wage scales in the early textile mills were embedded in gendered hierarchies of skill—in distinctions between the labor of male craftsmen and handweavers, whose work was inscribed with the property of skill during the transition from home to factory industry, and that of women and youths who, like most male handweavers, had become dexterous at loom or spindle through *Übung* (practice) rather than formal apprenticeship. The employers who defined and enforced the new categories of wage and skill justified the lower wages assigned to women in terms of the lower costs of training, maintaining, and reproducing a female

28. DTAV, "Brauchen die Textilarbeiterinnen handwerksmässige und fachgewerbliche Ausbildung?" *Der Textilarbeiter* 25 (6 June 1913): 179. "Fortbildungsschulzwang und fachgewerbliche Ausbildung für Textilarbeiterinnen," ibid., 26 (22 May 1914): 165; ZCTD, "Fortbildungsschulen für Textilarbeiterinnen," *Textilarbeiterzeitung* 14 (2 March 1912): 67; and "Gegen die Pflichtfortbildungsschule für Arbeiterinnen," ibid, 16 (7 March 1914): 67. The DTAV argued that job training would benefit the employers more than the workers themselves.

workforce. Thus women's wages remained consistently 30 to 50 percent below men's, while in some branches of textile production women workers formed a separate wage category: *Arbeiterin*.

Textile wages varied across regions, between cities and small towns or mill villages, and among the disparate sectors of textile manufacture. Although textile workers in the Rhineland and Westphalia earned 25 to 50 percent less than metal workers, they were among the German textile industry's best-paid workers.[29] The relatively high wages that prevailed in nearby regions of heavy industry, and in particular the competition for workers between industries and employers, drove textile wages upward in the two provinces for both men and women, whereas wages in the southern and eastern parts of Germany were considerably lower.[30] Unionization also influenced wage rates, as the textile unions campaigned relentlessly between 1890 and 1914 for higher wages and shorter hours. Rapid wage increases generally coincided with economic growth and labor shortages—between 1895 and 1900, for example, and again between 1905 and 1907—whereas rates declined or stagnated during times of recession, as between 1901 and 1902 and in 1908.

The *Akkord* (piece rate) system prevailed in the textile industry, subjecting workers of both sexes to its high-pressure pace, encouraging them to increase their earnings at the expense of depleting their own bodies. Spinners and weavers were paid almost exclusively piece rates, while a small minority of textile workers—mainly male foremen, *Meister*, factory mechanics, janitors, and warehouse workers—earned salaries or hourly wages.[31] Whereas textile merchants and mill owners in household and early factory textile manufacture had commonly calculated the wages of weavers and spinners by weight or length of finished pieces of cloth or spools of yarn, by the end of the nineteenth century many mill owners had conceded to workers' demands for remuneration by number of warp or woof threads, which made measuring output less arbitrary and allowed workers to calculate their own wages.[32]

29. The wage discrepancy between urban and rural mills in 1899 was approximately 30 to 40 percent. See Hans van der Upwich, *Die Geschichte und die Entwicklung der Rheinischen Samt- und Seidenindustrie* (Krefeld: Kramer und Baum, 1920), p. 139; Jochem Ulrich, "Soziale Entwicklungen im industriellen Umbruch: Die Anpassungskrise in der niederrheinischen Textilindustrie" (Dissertation, Universität Duisburg, 1984), pp. 251, 258; Karl Ditt, *Industrialisierung, Arbeiterschaft und Arbeiterbewegung in Bielefeld* (Dortmund: Gesellschaft für Westfälische Wirtschaftsgeschichte e.V., 1982), p. 212.

30. DTAV, *Löhne und Arbeitszeiten der Textilarbeiter im Jahre 1913* (Berlin: Textilpraxis, 1913), pp. 186–92; Karl Emsbach, *Die soziale Betriebsverfassung der rheinischen Baumwollindustrie im 19. Jahrhundert* (Bonn: Ludwig Röhrscheid, 1982), pp. 175–76; 316–17; 496.

31. RWWA, Bestand 60: Scheidt, *Lohnbücher der Zanellafabrik, Tuchfabrik und Kammgarnspinnerei*, 1911–20. See also Emsbach, *Die soziale Betriebsverfassung*, p. 481.

32. HStAD, JBdKPG 1905: Münster, p. 265.

Table 22. Textile wages in the union districts of Krefeld, Düsseldorf, and Hannover

Job category	Weekly wages in marks		
	Krefeld	Düsseldorf	Hannover
Spinner, general			
Male	26.63	25.68	25.80
Female assistant	14.43	16.32	14.58
Spinner, cotton			
Male/female	26.74	28.56	26.61
Spinner, linen			
Male/female	20.35	—	27.76
Spinner, worsted			
Male/female	28.39	28.33	26.37
Weavers, general			
Male	23.91	28.80	24.13
Female	18.53	17.61	15.90
Weavers, cotton			
Male	22.14	21.66	22.33
Female	14.95	18.31	15.11
Weavers, silk and velvet			
Male	24.10	22.90	24.70
Female	19.60	16.60	15.30
Weavers, woolens			
Male	23.51	25.82	25.37
Female	17.54	—	—

Source: Deutscher Textilarbeiterverband, *Löhne und Arbeitszeiten der Textilarbeiter im Jahre 1913* (Berlin, 1913), pp. 186–95.

The discrepancies between men's and women's wages originated not only in a division of labor that allocated higher-paying jobs to men, but also in prevalent notions of women's work as supplementary and of women workers as *bedürfnisloser* (having fewer needs) than men.[33] This wage discrepancy varied considerably by branch and with the structure of the local labor market.[34] Table 22 shows the average weekly wages in 1913 for spinners and weavers in the union districts of Krefeld, Düsseldorf, and Hannover. The wage gap between male and female weavers ranged from

33. The term *bedürfnislos* referred both to women's presumed status as supplementary earners and to their own purported reluctance to demand higher wages. See, for example, Robert Wilbrandt, *Die Frauenarbeit: Ein Problem des Kapitalismus* (Leipzig: B. G. Teubner, 1906), p. 61, and Alice Salomon, *Die Ursachen der ungleichen Entlohnung von Männer- und Frauenarbeit* (Leipzig: Duncker und Humblot, 1906), p. 41.

34. According to Ulrich's study of the textile town of Viersen, for example, the discrepancy between 1899 and 1913 was greatest in the linen industry (40 percent), followed by the silk industry at 35 percent and the cotton industry at 20 percent. See Ulrich, "Soziale Entwicklungen," p. 251.

18 percent among cotton weavers to 64 percent among weavers in general in the Düsseldorf district. On the average, male textile workers earned 20 to 50 percent more than their female colleagues, a tendency that persisted as wages rose between 1895 and 1913.[35] The wage differential was most pronounced between women who performed preparatory or finishing tasks and male supervisors, masters, spinners, or weavers. In the Scheidt worsted spinning mill, for example, male self-actor spinners earned 24–35 marks weekly, while female piecers generally earned 20 to 50 percent less. Male ribbon weavers in the Wupper Valley earned 33 percent more than women who were listed as working in the same division as ribbon weavers, and the differential between male and female loom warpers was 20 percent.[36] Indeed, the gendering of machines and fabrics meant that men and women seldom received equal wages, for they were not viewed as performing "equal work," even when employed in the same shops and operating the same or similar tools.

Indeed, gendered wage categories occupied a pivotal place in employers' long-term profit calculations, for they often favored cheaper female labor during economic crises and tended to lay off better-paid male workers first.[37] Maria Baur's study of the female labor market argues that employers' hiring and firing policies were shaped by a confluence of economic calculations and notions of male and female skill, independence and dependence, that were deeply embedded in the factory regime.

> That women have fewer needs, the lack of family dependence [on them], and the frequent fact that the earnings of women workers merely supplement the general household income make it possible to subject them to even lower pay in times of crisis than during the good years. Male wages, which usually must suffice for a family, could not be reduced to this extent without being termed beneath human dignity. On the contrary, in hiring [or retaining] female workers, it is possible to save money without further ado.[38]

35. Ibid. Also see KrA Vie, GA Grefrath 1303, 1304, and GA Oedt 809. The health insurance records of the Berger and Schwartz companies in Grefrath and of Girmes in Oedt, contained in these files, indicate an average differential between wages of adult men and women of 22 percent for the Berger linen mill, 40 percent for the Schwartz velvet mill, and 40 percent for the Girmes velvet mill. Also see Elisabeth Gottheiner, *Studien über die Wuppertaler Textilindustrie und ihre Arbeiter* (Munich: Duncker und Humblot, 1903), p. 28, on this differential.
36. RWWA, Bestand 60 Scheidt, Lohnbücher der Kammgarnspinnerei, 1912, 1914; HStAD, JBdKPG 1906: Düsseldorf, p. 470.
37. Maria Baur, "Der Beschäftigungsgrad der Industrie-Arbeiterinnen in Zeiten der sinkenden Konjunktur" (Dissertation, Universität München, 1923).
38. Ibid., pp. 8–9, 25. Baur notes that employment opportunities for women improved during the crisis of 1901–2, while those for men declined.

Spinning mill owner May of Mönchen-Gladbach, for example, expressed dismay at the "incongruity" that arose when an acute shortage of female workers in his mill forced him to raise women's wages nearly to the level of men's.[39] Mill owner David Peters, renowned for his extensive welfare measures, discouraged long-term employment of women by implanting a permanent gender gap in the factory wage system: Although women and men were to be paid the same piece rates during their first year of employment, women's rates were to remain stagnant thereafter and men were to receive a 5 percent increase with each year of employment. After five years of employment in the mills, Peters guaranteed that male workers' earnings would be at least 25 percent higher than those of their female colleagues.[40] Conceding that the disparity between male and female wages was greater than the actual difference in their productivity, one factory inspector explained that women were paid less because they demanded less from employers and unions, and also because of the prevalent view that men worked to support their families while women earned supplementary income.[41] When feminist social reformers launched their own campaigns on behalf of women workers after the turn of the century, they also assailed the low wages paid to women, including many single women who were unable to subsist on their wages amid the rising prices of food and rent in Germany's industrial cities. Elisabeth Gottheiner's study of textile workers of the Wupper Valley demonstrated, for example, that low wages forced many single female textile workers into prostitution.[42]

The gulf between the wages of male and female workers was one facet of the world behind the mill gate that seldom came under the scrutiny of social reformers or factory inspectors. Wage categories and hierarchies were embedded in notions of male breadwinner and female supplementary earner, in a fictitious dichotomy of skill, and in the more fundamental views of citizenship and class, of male independence and female dependence in the broader social order, and thus were challenged only when the

39. As recounted by Emsbach, *Die soziale Betriebsverfassung*, pp. 484–85.
40. Ibid., p. 485.
41. As cited in Salomon, *Die Ursachen der ungleichen Entlohnung*, pp. 18, 42. Women were paid less, according to Salomon, "because they are women and as such are subordinate in a social, civic, and political sense, and because the oppression of and disdain for the weaker sex by the stronger sex plays a role." Also see Lilly Nielsen, "Die Verdrängung von Männerarbeit durch Frauenarbeit in der Industrie" (Dissertation, Universität Bonn, 1920), pp. 40–41.
42. Gottheiner, *Studien*, and "Die Löhne der Barmer Textilarbeiterschaft und die wirtschaftliche Lage der Textilarbeiterinnen im Jahre 1904," *Reichsarbeitsblatt* 4, no. 8 (1906): 727–28; and DTAV, "Die Löhne der Barmer Textilarbeiterschaft und die wirtschaftliche Lage der Textilarbeiterinnen im Jahre 1904," *Der Textilarbeiter* 189 (20 July 1906). The cost of living for a single person in Barmen was 520 to 546 marks a year in 1903, while the average yearly earnings for women over age twenty were 780 to 884 marks.

lower wages paid to women became a significant factor in the displacement of male workers, as in "feminized" industries like textiles and garments.[43] Strike reports indicate that mill owners often deployed women as wage cutters during labor conflicts, placing male workers in the curious position of defending women against employers by demanding equal pay for equal work, a call men also raised to protect themselves from wage degradation and displacement.[44] The rhetoric of the continual battles over wages reveals that pay differentials, particularly in this women's industry, represented the perceptions of both bargaining partners—employers and unions—of the divergent needs of each sex rather than differing productivity. The fashioning of former home weavers and spinners into male breadwinners, a cornerstone in the remaking of artisanal identities during early industrialization, now came to figure as an integral element of the textile unions' "language of grievance," which decried women workers as "wage cutters."[45]

Gender in the Factory Regime of Discipline and Punishment

The discourses, debates, and legislative interventions into the social problem of female factory labor between 1878 and 1914 had a powerful role in remaking factory regimes. Indeed, textile factory regimes, both in their punitive, restrictive form and in their custodial and tutelary claims, constitute one of the most significant material outcomes of the discourses of women's work. Shaped by employers in negotiation with both workers and the state, they governed the working lives of both men and women most directly through the dual regulatory mechanisms of *Arbeitsordnungen* (work regulations) and the *Strafsystem* (system of penalties and fines for

43. According to Salomon, *Die Ursachen der ungleichen Entlohnung*, the influx of women into industries like textiles, garments, and tobacco resulted in the perceptible and steady reduction of wage scales for men as well.
44. See, for example, DTAV, local report from Krefeld, *Der Textilarbeiter* 13 (5 April 1901); "Aufruf an alle in der Bandwirkerei thätigen Kollegen und Kolleginnen!" 13 (24 April 1901); ibid., and "Zum Kampf der Textilarbeiter der Firma Noß und Lucas, Elberfeld," ibid., 19 (30 August 1907): 275; ZCTD, "Lohnbewegungen und Arbeitsstreitigkeiten: Elberfeld," *Textilarbeiterzeitung* 9 (11 May 1907): 74–75; "Lohnbewegungen und Arbeitsstreitigkeiten: Aachen," ibid., 9 (28 December 1907): 206
45. On the history of the male breadwinner as a social identity among male workers, see Sally Alexander, "Women, Class, and Sexual Differences in the 1830s and 1840s," *History Workshop* 17 (spring 1984): 136; Wally Seccombe, "Patriarchy Stabilized: The Construction of the Male Breadwinner Wage Norm in Nineteenth-Century Britain," *Social History* 11 (January 1986): 54; Michelle Barrett and Mary McIntosh, "The 'Family Wage': Some Problems for Socialists and Feminists," *Capital and Class* 11 (1980): 51–72; and Jean Quataert, "The Shaping of Women's Work in Manufacturing: Guilds, Household, and the State in Central Europe, 1648–1870," *American Historical Review* 90 (December 1985): 1122–48.

violations). While one key object of the factory regime was to ensure continuous production at a profitable pace, it also sought to inculcate moral and hygienic precepts in workers of both sexes and to teach them "to become more skillful, docile, efficient, prudent, in short, more useful and valuable" to the employer.[46] Gender is central to understanding these moral and hygienic visions, for their institutions of tutelage often singled out women as the source of both moral ruin and moral regeneration in the mills.

A study of union and police reports on workplace conflicts reveals the gendered subtext, the distinct norms of respectability and responsibility, that *Arbeitsordnungen* prescribed for men and women. The factory regulations for C. A. Delius's silk weaving mill in Bielefeld were typical for textile mills in the Rhineland and Westphalia during the 1890s, imposing penalties for tardiness, interrupting work, or washing up too early at the rate of 30 pfennig, for altering looms or other machines and adjusting the lights or heating system at 50 pfennig, and for wandering around the mill or visiting other mill divisions at 30 pfennig, while the fine for producing deficient goods varied according to severity. Higher fines were often decreed for behavior that involved "moral" transgression—for example, for "smoking, drinking alcoholic beverages, [engaging in] horseplay or [making] noise on the job" or for stealing materials, admitting strangers to workshops, or missing a day's work without permission.[47] Men were fined most often for rowdiness—drinking, smoking, or stealing—while female workers were penalized for behavior unbecoming to women—for impudence, especially laughter or "sassing" masters or managers and for subverting factory discipline through gossip and indecent horseplay in the secret realm of the restroom.[48] Indeed, employers' concern with workers' comportment and virtue, as articulated in the factory disciplinary system,

---

46. Lothar Machtan, "Zum Innenleben deutscher Fabriken im 19. Jahrhundert: Die formelle und die informelle Verfassung von Industriebetrieben anhand von Beispielen aus dem Bereich der Textil- und Maschinenbauindustrie," *Archiv für Sozialgeschichte* 21 (1981): 181–82.

47. Hauptstaatsarchiv Detmold (hereafter HStADet), Reg. Minden, MiIU 425, "Arbeitsordnung Mechanische Seidenweberei C. A. Delius und Söhne, Bielefeld, 1892," pp. 93–95. The company's regulations and fines were analogous to those in the Schwartz velvet mill in Grefrath and the Deuss und Oetker silk mill in Schiefbahn. See KrA Vie, GA Schiefbahn 847, Deuss und Oetker, "Arbeitsordnungen 1892"; also see "Arbeitsordnungen für die zu Grefrath gelegene mechanische Sammtfabrik der Firma Aktienweberei R. Schwartz und Co., Krefeld, vom April 1908," held in the private archive of Johannes Lipp, Oedt bei Krefeld, Germany (hereafter Lipp).

48. On illegal breaks, horseplay, and gossip during work time, see Lüdtke, "Organizational Order or *Eigensinn*?" and Machtan, "Zum Innenleben." See also DTAV, *Der Textilarbeiter* 25 (1 August 1913), for a report on a court case of a woman worker who was fined excessively for laughing at the foreman.

had little to do with profits and the pace of production. They implemented the penalty system to enforce a code of moral conduct during work time, using welfare or charitable activities to gain custody over workers' private lives and to reward those who conformed to the factory's disciplinary code.

The protective labor laws of 1891 had recommended segregating the sexes at work, but it appears that in the Rhineland only a few Catholic textile employers—those who had been the strongest advocates of this measure in the milieu of social reform—put this policy into practice. Since separating the sexes at work was not feasible in most shop divisions, owners often drew gendered boundaries through the factory's "public" space, forbidding the mingling of women and men, or of single workers with families, in cafeterias and courtyards. One employer in Rheydt, near Mönchen-Gladbach, had a separate entrance built for women workers to prevent them from socializing with men on arrival and departure.[49] Cotton industrialist Franz Brandts of Mönchen-Gladbach included a section of "moral regulations" in his factory rules, drafted by a local priest in 1885. Not only did they prescribe the separation of the sexes at work, but "all mutual dealings between [male and female workers] during their free time is forbidden. Violations, as well as all frivolous interactions that breach Christian morality between young people of both sexes, even [those that take place] outside the factory, will be met with a warning from the workers' committee, and if this is ineffective, with a notice of termination."[50] Factory inspectors also sought to enforce a separation of the sexes in the nonproductive factory spheres like restrooms, dressing rooms, and cafeterias, with the goal of preventing the erosion of women workers' sense of shame "[*Schamgefühl*], that powerful protector of morality."[51]

Inspectors and reformers viewed the factory as the "site of moral ruin for nearly all those young workers—male and female—who had to live away from home."[52] Although it was undoubtedly difficult, if not impossible, for inspectors or employers to penetrate the arena of workers' sexual

---

49. HStAD, JBdKPG, 1907: Aachen, p. 500, and 1893: Düsseldorf, p. 387: The Düsseldorf factory inspector reported that the C. A. Bettmann Company in Rheydt "even instituted a separate entrance for the female workers, so the principle of the separation of the sexes could be upheld on the way to and from work."

50. *Die Fabrikordnung der Firma F. Brandts zu Mönchengladbach* (Mönchen-Gladbach: Stadtarchiv Mönchengladbach, 1974) (reprint of the original from 1885, with an introduction by Wolfgang Löhr), pp. xv, 5–6, 14. Brandts employed no married women in his mill. Although his official policy was to fire female workers upon their marriage, he rewarded some with wedding gifts, depending on the number of years they had been employed.

51. HStAD, Landratsamt Mönchengladbach 710: "Bericht des Gewerbeaufsichtsbeamten Mönchengladbach 14.12.1874, p. 103.".

52. Bernays, "Berufsschicksale," p. 108.

liaisons or to reshape their codes of comportment or morality through policies in the workplace, they were able to assert some control over workers' free time and private lives through extensive networks of welfare activities that included housing, evening courses, recreational clubs, and childcare centers. Industrialists enforced a type of paternal custody over their dormitories and endowed them with tasks beyond offering clean and respectable housing. Company housing usually included apartments or small houses for *Meister* and other skilled male workers with families as well as dormitories for young single workers.[53] In providing company housing, employers hoped to recruit and retain a core of long-term, stable workers and alleviate the abuses inherent in the lodging practices in working-class households and neighborhoods.[54] Many mill owners in the Rhineland built workers' dormitories soon after opening their factories to accommodate workers from outlying or distant regions. The Schoeller company of Düren near Aachen built its girls' dormitory in 1854 to house young women who came to work in its mill from villages in the Eifel: "It became a great nuisance for young workers to have to travel the long distances to and from their parents' homes daily. So during the winter they preferred to lodge in the city, and thus the poor conditions, overcrowded rooms, and lack of supervision endangered their health and their morality."[55] The home opened with 50 residents and became so popular with young women and their parents that the number had increased to 340 by 1870 and continued to expand to 500 by the end of the 1880s.[56] One observer described nearly idyllic living quarters for Schoeller's female workers: "Across from the spinning mill, surrounded by gardens, are several row

53. HStAD, JBdKPG 1909: Minden, p. 327: The Ravensberger Spinnerei in Bielefeld, for example, built forty-two buildings with 125 apartments, each with three to five rooms including cellar, attic, and cow stall. Families who lived in the company apartments were required to send their children, especially their daughters, to work in the mill after age fourteen. Furthermore, families were required to take in young female workers from distant regions as boarders. See DTAV, "Die Lage der Textilarbeiter und Arbeiterinnen von Bielefeld und Umgegend," *Der Textilarbeiter* 17 (15 December 1905).

54. Usually single workers who lodged rented a *Schlafstelle*—that is, a bed or part of a bed—in a family's crowded living quarters. Beds were often rented around the clock, so that a worker returning from the night shift would take over the bed from another renter who worked the day shift. People of all ages slept in one room—the family's children next to the young worker, the married couple next to the young mill girl. This form of housing was thought to endanger both the health and the morality of young workers away from the home for the first time. See, for example, Baron von Berlepsch's comments on the dangers of boarding and lodging in his essay "Warum betreiben wir die soziale Reform?" *Schriften der Gesellschaft für soziale Reform*, 1, no. 11 (1903): 12.

55. RWWA, XIVe 295, brochure from the Schoeller company: *Die Fürsorge der Firma Schoeller, Bücklers und Co., Flachsspinnerei in Düren für ihre Arbeiter und Arbeiterinnen, 1851–1906.*

56. Ibid.

houses built next to one another, each with its own courtyard, a ground floor of common rooms and two stories of bedrooms, each with four bunk beds and sinks," in which girls from one village or family roomed together wherever possible.[57]

Crowded, unsupervised housing—in addition to the "moral decay" in the factory itself—was thought to present a greater threat to young women than to young men. Employers and the state endowed the *Mädchenheime* with a gender-specific moral mission. In the words of one reformer: "In the boardinghouses special emphasis is placed on the education and training of the young women in both a moral and economic sense."[58] Lodging for young men, by contrast, was scarcely mentioned in inspectors' reports or in employers' brochures on their "social institutions." This custodial claim meant that life in company housing was frequently governed by a disciplinary regime that resembled the factory *Strafsystem*. In the Schoeller *Mädchenheime*, five factory *Meister* and their families lived dispersed among the mill girls in the dormitories, and each supervised one group of rooms and residents. Other dormitories, although financed by mill owners, were under the direction of Catholic or Protestant nuns.[59] The *Hausordnungen* (house regulations) in company dormitories were analogous to factory regulations: time was regimented nearly as strictly as in the factory itself. The rules for one mill's dormitory in the Cologne district were typical: the girls were awakened at 5:15 and had a limited time to wash, make their beds, and eat breakfast. They were not allowed to use their rooms or beds during the day or early evening. In the evenings the girls were to do their wash according to the housemaster's schedule or to sew or darn their clothing under the watchful eye of his wife. Visitors were not allowed in the building, and residents were forbidden to go out without the housemaster's permission; furthermore, the dormitory was locked at 9:30 in the evening.[60] If residents "violated

57. HStAD, Reg. Aachen, H&G, 17793: *Flachsspinnerei, Fabrikschule*. Here I cite an article from an unnamed newspaper titled "Ein Beitrag zur socialen Frage: Die Flachsspinnerei von Schöller, Mevissen und Bücklers in Düren mit ihren Arbeiterwohnungen und Fortbildungsschulen für Mädchen und Knaben."
58. Kuno Frankenstein, "Die Lage der Arbeiterinnen in den deutschen Großstädten," *Schmollers Jahrbuch* 12 (1888): 209.
59. HStAD, Reg. Aachen, H&G 17793; HStAD, JBdKPG 1898: Cologne, p. 386; 1899: Cologne, pp. 584–85; 1903: Cologne, p. 415: The dormitory of the Mühlenthaler spinning mill in Dieringhausen housed mainly young women from East Prussia and was run by Protestant sisters, as was the boardinghouse at Krawinkel und Schnabel. The dormitory at C. A. Baldus and Sons near Gummersbach was run by Catholic nuns.
60. HStAD, JBdKPG 1894: Cologne, pp. 631–33: "Hausordnung für das Mädchenheim der Kammgarnspinnerei zu Eitorf." These rules are very similar to those for the *Mädchenheim* at J. W. Scheidt's worsted spinning mill in Kettwig. RWWA, Bestand Scheidt 60, "Das Mädchenheim der Firma J. W. Scheidt, Kammgarnspinnerei und Tuchfabrik AG, Kettwig-Ruhr 1927."

Plate 5. This dormitory for young women at the Johann Wilhelm Scheidt company, Kettwig/Ruhr, was built to house up to 280 female employees of the Scheidt company. From a company brochure, "Johann Wilhelm Scheidt, Kettwig/Ruhr" (undated), Rheinisch-Westfälisches Wirtschaftsarchiv, Abt. 60, J. W. Scheidt, Kettwig. Photo reprinted courtesy of the Rheinisch-Westfälisches Wirtschaftsarchiv, Cologne.

propriety" during their leisure time, by engaging in "indecent conversation or singing," for example, they were reported to the factory director and faced almost certain eviction from the home.[61]

These strict regulations made company boardinghouses unpopular where alternatives existed. Yet many mill girls took advantage of the opportunity to obtain room and board at a relatively reasonable price. The average daily cost for both in company housing was 50 to 75 pfennig before the First World War, between one-fourth and one-third of a woman's average daily earnings.[62] The dormitories may also have been

61. RWWA, XIVe 295, *Die Fürsorge der Firma Schoeller*. The Socialist textile union described similar conditions in company dormitories in Baden and in the dormitories of the Wülfing Kammgarnspinnerei in Lennep. See DTAV, "Herr Trikotwarenfabrikant Jacques Schiesser in Radolfzell und sein gemeinnütziges Werk," *Der Textilarbeiter* 19 (28 June 1907); and local report from Lennep, ibid., 22 (22 April 1910): 127. See also Martha Hoppe's series "Heime für Textilarbeiterinnen" in *Der Textilarbeiter* 21 (30 July 1909): 244; 21 (6 August 1909): 250; 21 (13 August 1909): 259.

62. The *Mädchenheim* at the Kammgarnspinnerei in Eitorf in the Cologne district charged

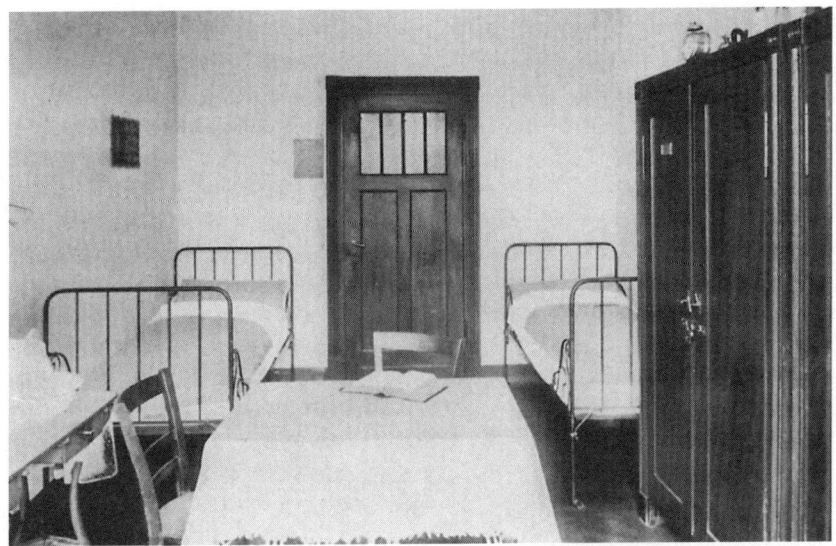

Plate 6. A typical room, shared by two young women, in the dormitory at the Johann Wilhelm Scheidt company, Kettwig/Ruhr. From a company brochure, "Johann Wilhelm Scheidt, Kettwig/Ruhr" (undated), Rheinisch-Westfälisches Wirtschaftsarchiv, Abt. 60, J. W. Scheidt, Kettwig. Photo reprinted courtesy of the Rheinisch-Westfälisches Wirtschaftsarchiv, Cologne.

popular with parents of young mill girls away from home for the first time. Among 324 residents in Schoeller's dormitory, for example, 55 percent were between fourteen and twenty-one.[63] But many older single women appear to have endured the strict regimen in order to save money or for lack of other housing: 35 percent of residents in Schoeller's boardinghouse were between twenty-one and thirty, and women over thirty made up another 10 percent. Moreover, many appeared to have preferred long-term dormitory residence over other alternatives: 15 percent had lodged there for over ten years and another 19 percent for five to ten years.[64]

50–60 pfennig a day in 1894, depending on the age of the resident. HStAD, JBdKPG 1894: Cologne, pp. 631–33; J. W. Scheidt charged 75 pfennig a day in 1907. HStAD JBdKPG 1907: Düsseldorf, pp. 437–38. Schoeller charged dormitory residents only 10 pfennig a day to cover the expense of washing clothing and bedding. Calculating the average daily earnings for a woman worker at approximately 2.20 marks, the cost of company housing (at 50–60 pfennig) represents less than one-quarter of her earnings.

63. Factory inspectors' reports indicate that several textile mills in the Rhineland had to close their dormitories because of high vacancy rates. HStAD 1890: Düsseldorf, pp. 251–52; 1901: Cologne, p. 306.

64. RWWA, XIVe 295, *Die Fürsorge der Firma Schoeller.*

Plate 7. The dining room in the dormitory for young women at the Johann Wilhelm Scheidt company, Kettwig/Ruhr. The cost for room and board in the dormitory was 75 pfennig a day. From a company brochure, "Johann Wilhelm Scheidt, Kettwig/Ruhr" (undated), Rheinisch-Westfälisches Wirtschaftsarchiv, Abt. 60, J. W. Scheidt, Kettwig. Photo reprinted courtesy of the Rheinisch-Westfälisches Wirtschaftsarchiv, Cologne.

The provision of company housing, in particular for young women, had moral as well as economic significance for paternalist factory owners, constituting a long-term investment toward building a core workforce in an era of recurrent labor shortages. Furthermore, it allowed employers to pursue the goal of shaping this workforce in their own image. In an exemplary statement of paternalist tutelary goals, Johann Scheidt emphasized his reciprocal relationship with the residents of his girls' dormitories: "Every one of them should be aware that the dormitory offers them the comfort of friendly, clean, and healthful living quarters and wholesome meals for a very cheap price, so that they can save part of their wages without having to sacrifice anything themselves. The workers should requite this solicitude through competence and consistency at work and through moral and decent conduct in and outside the dormitory."[65]

In addition to company housing, employers sought to define and en-

65. RWWA, Bestand 60: Scheidt, "Das Mädchenheim der Firma J. W. Scheidt."

force gender divisions through another kind of benefaction: the founding of *Fortbildungsschulen* (skill training schools) for young men and of *Haushaltsschulen* (housekeeping schools) or courses for young women. Although private and municipal *Fortbildungsschulen* for young male workers were already prevalent in the Rhineland during the 1870s, many employers instituted their first domestic training courses for young women during the 1890s. The state encouraged employers to take the initiative in establishing the courses by recognizing training in domestic skills as a type of *Fortbildung* in the revised labor code of 1891. The yearly reports of the factory inspectorate attest to the state's lively interest in enhancing female workers' training in domestic skills. Indeed, one inspector noted in 1910 that the state had come to view "the training of competent housewives as one of the most important measures in improving the lot of the working classes" and in resolving the acute crisis of working-class motherhood.[66]

Cooking and sewing lessons for female mill employees had a dual purpose—moral and hygienic—within the factory regime. Young women were to be kept busy and diverted from immoral thoughts or illicit actions while they mastered the crucial skills for their future *Beruf* (calling) of marriage and motherhood. In many cases the courses were part of everyday life in the company dormitories: they were held in the evenings in the common rooms, and residents were required to participate regularly. Other mill owners offered instruction in the factory itself during or after work time. The Schoeller company, for example, provided no formal household training in its dormitories but assembled as many as two hundred girls to practice sewing in one big room while an instructor lectured on women's "social duties within the family, on housekeeping, child care, care of pets and birds, and other subjects."[67] Unlike dormitory instruction, participation in factory cooking and sewing schools was voluntary and often served the practical need of furnishing workers with food and clothing. David Peters of Neviges was one of the first textile mill owners in the Rhineland to institute cooking lessons for his female workers. The young women attended the courses twice weekly in the evenings and were able to sample their own recipes for their evening meal.[68] Textile mills commonly offered cooking instruction to women who left their regular jobs as weavers or winders to work full time for a few weeks in the factory kitchen and to prepare meals for its cafeteria under the supervision of a certified cook. Although mill owners paid women for attending factory cooking and sewing lessons during work time, this form of instruction was less popular than evening courses because they usually earned less than half

66. HStAD, JBdKPG 1910: Düsseldorf, p. 438.
67. RWWA, XIVe 295, *Die Fürsorge der Firma Schoeller*.
68. HStAD, JBdKPG 1910: Düsseldorf, p. 438.

of their regular wage while completing the course. Industrialists like Johann Scheidt, who were serious about teaching women domestic skills, were forced to pay full weaver's or spinner's wages for the time their female workers spent in the factory cooking or sewing schools.[69]

One textile company near Cologne joined with a Protestant minister to transform a local *Fürsorgeheim* (home for wayward girls) into a model *Erziehungsanstalt* (educational institution) that combined work in a spinning mill with instruction in domestic skills. The training it offered its residents alternated between full-time work in the spinning mill and full-time study in the dormitory of math, German, religion, hygiene, cooking, ironing, knitting, and sewing, all under the vigilant supervision of Protestant nuns. In this case employer and church concurred that factory work instilled in the young women the qualities of proficiency and perseverance that they would later need as homemakers: "The purpose of factory work is that the girls become accustomed to perseverance, that they learn to be attentive, orderly, and neat and recognize that even the lowliest job is valuable in connection with the whole, that it is necessary and must be carried out with dedication if the whole is not to suffer."[70] Other employers consolidated their efforts and founded networks of schools through their charitable associations, often with the support of the city administration: in 1903 the Bergischer Verein für Gemeinwohl sponsored twenty-five evening sewing schools with a total of 1,300 students in Barmen, Elberfeld, and smaller textile towns throughout the Wupper Valley. Likewise, the Linksrheinischer Verein für Gemeinwohl maintained thirty-two sewing schools in the Lower Rhine region.[71]

In addition to cooking and sewing courses and company housing, many textile mills offered day care for children of male and female workers at a relatively low cost. Employers sought not only to prevent unwed pregnancies through tutelage, charity, and policing, but also to encourage women workers to embrace the "responsibility of motherhood."[72] Although factory day-care centers facilitated women's employment in a practical sense by relieving them of the burdens of child care during working hours, their founders regarded the centers as a decisive means of rendering factory

---

69. HStAD, JBdKPG 1910: Minden, p. 327; RWWA, Bestand 60: Scheidt, *Die Wohlfahrtseinrichtungen*, p. 7.

70. HStAD, JBdKPG 1903: Cologne, p. 415.

71. HStAD, JBdKPG 1903: Düsseldorf, p. 404; 1910: Düsseldorf, p. 483.

72. The Cotton Spinning and Weaving company of Cologne, for example, took in children from three months to six years old for 15 pfennig a day per child. See HStAD, JBdKPG 1903: Cologne, p. 415; Düsseldorf, p. 405: Day care for toddlers was provided by D. Peters in Neviges; Franz Brandts in Mönchen-Gladbach; the Wülfing woolen mill in Lennep; and Hardt, Pokorny in Dahlhausen near Lennep.

work more compatible with motherhood, and as a weapon in the battle against children's illness and mortality. Mothers whose children attended factory day-care centers were to bring them to the center personally and to pick them up, and as one social reformer observed: "If the children appear unwashed, uncombed, or in dirty clothing, the mothers are warned that if their children arrive at the center in this condition again, they will be turned away. In this manner the child-care centers function indirectly as an educational example for indolent and negligent mothers."[73] The Busch spinning mill in Mönchen-Gladbach rewarded women who stayed home with their infants by paying them a minimum daily wage after their health insurance coverage expired.[74] The Scheidt company's *Säuglingsheim* cared mainly for infants of single mothers who worked in the company's worsted spinning mill, some of whom lived in the company dormitories. Its founders hoped that its closeness to the mill would promote frequent contact between mothers and infants during the work day and would encourage women to nurse their babies during their breaks. Scheidt outlined the goal of the infant care center, directed by Mrs. Scheidt, in a report of 1909: "If at all possible a hardy new generation of workers should be sustained and they should be protected from the harmful effects of their past through a simple, healthful way of life and by growing accustomed to cleanliness."[75]

Unlike company housing, providing domestic training for female workers or day care for their children brought employers few direct benefits. Rather, these institutions represented mediated solutions to the social question of married women's factory employment, a compromise sanctioned by the state and enacted under the watchful supervision of the factory inspectors. Indeed, the dormitories, *Haushaltsschulen*, and day-care centers were in a sense the price employers had to pay to cultivate a female *Stammarbeiterschaft*. In promising to import the home into the factory, mill owners sought to deflect the widespread opposition to women's factory employment and to convey a confident sense that such labor was in principle reconcilable with the demands of housework and motherhood.

73. Paul Mieck, *Die Arbeiter-Wohlfahrts-Einrichtungen der industriellen Unternehmer in den preussischen Provinzen Rheinland und Westfalen und ihre volkswirtschaftliche und soziale Bedeutung* (Berlin: Heymanns, 1904), p. 37.
74. HStAD, JBdKPG 1907: Düsseldorf, pp. 437–38. To qualify for this provision, the recipients had to have worked in the mill for at least two years and had to have deposited a sum of money in company savings accounts.
75. RWWA, Bestand 60: Scheidt, "Jahresbericht 1909 Säuglingsheim, Kettwig a.d. Ruhr." In addition to day care for infants, the Scheidt company provided day care for toddlers over age three regardless of religious affiliation. RWWA, Bestand 60: Scheidt, *Die Wohlfahrtseinrichtungen*.

Thus mill owners established the discursive and institutional parameters within which women were to negotiate the demands of family and factory in their working lives.[76]

Although employers utilized both the factory penal code and their charitable institutions to regulate morality and inculcate virtue, the factory regime, especially its institutions of tutelage—such as cooking and sewing courses, day-care centers, and dormitories—constituted an arena of contradiction for working women. Factory welfare recognized and even offered partial solutions to working women's double burden, but the benefits it offered buttressed the employers' authority and extended their custody over workers' private lives and desires. Indeed, examination of the factory regime illustrates the contradictory ways women used their jobs for their own purposes, alternating compliance with employers' policies with preserving distance from their tutelary claims and conceiving their own moral codes that allowed for both accommodation and resistance.[77] The case of factory day-care centers illustrates how women workers openly defied or quietly insulated themselves from employers' definitions of morality and motherhood. Social reformers and factory inspectors noted that the centers were unpopular, not only because working women suspected they bred illness, but also because women were reluctant to entrust their children to an institution run by the mill owners.[78] The relative popularity of cooking and sewing courses, by contrast, implies that working women as well as employers, reformers, and inspectors viewed these skills as crucial to the successful management of the double burden. The repressive climate in company dormitories constitutes a more complex case, for the stringent regulation of leisure time, combined with the strict penalties for "indecent behavior," strongly suggests that young girls frequently refused to reconcile themselves to this regime. Yet most company dormitories enjoyed a high occupancy rate and appeared to meet the need of parents, if not their daughters, for inexpensive supervised housing.

76. Mieck, *Die Arbeiter-Wohlfahrts-Einrichtungen*, p. 194; Wettstein-Adelt, *Drei-ein-halb Monate*, p. 36. Based on her own experience in the mills, Wettstein-Adelt urged other social reformers to take seriously the founding of night schools for girls "to teach them to cook economically, for nowhere does marital peace depend as much on the man's stomach as in these circles."
77. See Benson, *Counter Cultures*, p. 228; Lüdtke, "Historiography of Everyday Life," p. 46. Both Benson and Lüdtke view "distancing" as a central component of work culture (Benson) and *Eigensinn* (Lüdtke).
78. Wilhelm Feld, *Die Kinder der in den Fabriken arbeitenden Frauen und ihre Verpflegung mit besonderer Berücksichtigung der Crimmitschauer Arbeiterinnen*, Probleme der Fürsorge: Abhandlungen der Centrale für private Fürsorge in Frankfurt am Main, vol. 3 (Dresden: Böhmert, 1906), pp. 62–63.

Bodies, Sexuality, and Reproduction at Work

During the last quarter of the nineteenth century the female organism was marked as a new object of intervention for both the regulatory and the tutelary regimes of social reform and state social policy. Protective measures, such as the recommended separation of the sexes at work, assigned to employers and factory inspectors new tasks of patrolling women workers' bodies, of policing the sexual underworld of the mills and of enforcing both the moral and the hygienic codes that underpinned middle-class notions of motherhood and domesticity. Behind the codes of factory morality were visions of sexual indulgence and abandon, recorded in the reports of social reformers' and factory inspectors' journeys through the mills as early as the 1870s. Before the revision of the labor code in 1878 that abolished night work for women, social commentators like Alfons Thun exposed the sexual undertones of everyday life in the textile mills of the Lower Rhine, warning of the dangers inherent in the mingling and mixing, the blurring of boundaries between the sexes and across generations.[79] Similarly, Minna Wettstein-Adelt, a middle-class woman who worked undercover in a weaving mill for several weeks during the early 1890s, was shocked by the sexual horseplay among women workers in the weaving mills: "The women workers outdid one another with disgraceful, truly beastly, raw jokes and stories like I have never heard in my life. . . . I found a moral depravity and vulgarity there that is indescribable. Most of these girls seem to lack any sense of shame."[80] Although accounts like Wettstein-Adelt's implicitly laid the blame for moral excesses or out-of-wedlock pregnancies on the female workers, rape and other forms of sexual coercion were widespread in the mills, as union papers and factory inspectors' reports indicate. Inspectors and union leaders alike acknowledged the severity of this problem in their persistent demands for female factory inspectors: in their view women workers were more likely to entrust their experiences of abuse or harassment to them than to the male inspectors. Indeed, in 1903 alone the female assistant inspector for the Mönchen-Gladbach district received eight reports from women workers regarding "immoral incidents" (*unsittliche Vorkommnisse*) perpetrated by masters or male colleagues in the district's mills.[81]

---

79. Alfons Thun, *Die Industrie am Niederrhein und ihre Arbeiter*, Staats- und sozialwissenschaftliche Forschungen, vol. 1 (Leipzig: Duncker und Humblot, 1879), p. 179.
80. Wettstein-Adelt, *Drei-ein-halb Monate*, p. 31.
81. HStAD, JBdKPG 1900: Düsseldorf, p. 303; 1903: Düsseldorf, p. 307. The one female inspector in the Düsseldorf district held office hours in her own apartment to assure privacy to the women who sought her help. Yet the hiring of female factory inspectors proceeded very slowly. There were only four in the Rhineland and Westphalia in 1913: two

The perception of female workers as morally depraved was prevalent in textile towns like Mönchen-Gladbach, where social investigator Marie Bernays—then disguised as a mill worker—reported that the baker's wife wished to avoid the "disgrace" of renting her a room on the fifth floor of her house. She relented only after much pleading by Bernays, who had to promise to conceal her occupation by "never appearing in the house without a hat, a marker of middle-class respectability."[82] Furthermore, in her firsthand observations of the sexual mores of women in the Gladbach spinning and weaving mill, Bernays noted the differences between middle-class and working-class morality: "It is fair to say that female workers, at least those who do not live at home, are nearly as liberated in sexual relationships as male workers. In most cases no social disdain was associated with unwed motherhood; among women workers in the vicinity it was regarded as something rather normal, a fact one inquires about when first getting to know a girl, as easily as we discuss our visits to the spa or the publication of a new book."[83]

Another manifestation of collective identities among women workers was the display of the body through the manner and style of dress. Shop-floor "fashions" signified workers' awareness of their place in the production process and in the moral regime of the mills. The feeling of belonging to a group, the self-definition as weaver, winder, spinner, or fuller and its expression through clothing and customs, was common to both sexes. Male spinners, for example, generally dressed in very light clothing and worked barefoot, whereas male weavers, subjected to the same high temperature, wore jackets and boots as an expression of their higher status.[84] Female weavers reportedly dressed in prim and neat attire, which may have reflected their sense of belonging to the elite of female workers. Their distinct dress code may also be explained by the large number of older, married women in the ranks who were often portrayed by employers as the custodians of the younger women workers. Female spinners, by contrast, usually young and single and commonly viewed as the insolent and unruly element among female textile workers, often wore disorderly clothing yet manifested their own chic style. Although it is likely that the high temperature and humidity of the spinning shops had something to

---

in the Düsseldorf district (Krefeld and Mönchen-Gladbach) and two in the Minden district. See HStAD, JBdKPG 1913: Düsseldorf, pp. 526–27. On the role of the union in demanding female inspectors, see DTAV, *Der Textilarbeiter* 21 (20 August 1909): 265; ZCTD, *Der Christliche Textilarbeiter* 4 (12 April 1902); ZCTD, *Textilarbeiterzeitung* 10 (5 December 1908): 192.

82. Bernays, "Berufsschicksale," p. 132.
83. Ibid.
84. Ibid., pp. 134–35.

do with female spinners' disheveled dress, the stylish character of that disorder may also have expressed a rebellion against the moral claims of the factory regime.[85]

The clothing female spinners and weavers wore expressed their social identities as mill workers, distinct from workers in other industries as well as from the upper classes. A story from 1905 of one young woman who inadvertently violated the dress code illustrates this point: the young woman was Danish, and according to her country's custom, she wore a hat to and from work and blouses with long sleeves while at work, both emblems of respectability among middle-class girls. Her appearance caused a sensation on the streets and in the mill, distracted several women from their jobs, and provoked demands that she remove the hat or leave the workplace. The *Obermeister* averted a walkout by promptly firing the young woman.[86] While enforcing their own rigid, class-based code of dress in the mills, female textile workers frequently donned their prettiest dresses on Sundays and did not disdain hats, gloves, jewelry, or parasols. The discrepant dress codes of workdays and holidays delineated boundaries between work and leisure, between the public sphere of the factory and that of town and marketplace.

In articulating and enforcing their own sexual mores, especially where they worked in predominantly female shops, women sought to resist and contest employers' moral prescriptions and custody. Beyond the frankness about sexual experience and acceptance of out-of-wedlock pregnancies recounted by middle-class observers, they also delimited their space in the mill through sexual horseplay or by initiating newcomers in factory carnal knowledge. Wettstein-Adelt described her shock at the obscene behavior of her female coworkers, one of whom frequently expressed anger or displeasure by lifting her skirts and pulling down her underwear, exposing her genitals.[87] Factory inspectors reported regularly on women workers' refusal to use the dressing rooms and complained that after work they stripped to their bare skin in the middle of the shop, without making any attempt to conceal their bodies from others, male or female.

Women textile workers also asserted and defended their own definitions of sexuality in their individual and collective resistance against rape or molestation by managers and supervisors, evidently an everyday feature of shop-floor life. This resistance took various forms, ranging from reporting the rape to the factory inspector or the union to "passing the word" through the mill and attempting to protect female colleagues from subse-

85. Ibid.
86. DTAV, Local report from Mönchen-Gladbach, *Der Textilarbeiter* 17 (13 October 1905).
87. Wettstein-Adelt, *Drei-ein-halb Monate*, p. 31.

quent assaults. Even though women workers apparently engaged in sexual horseplay among themselves and often made sexuality the content of the teasing and gossip that helped demarcate their standing and reputation within shop-floor culture, their protests against rape suggest that they also sought to assert their own codes of honor and enforce their own sexual boundaries within the mills. Wettstein-Adelt, for example, reported that an uproar ensued among the women in her shop when one of the managers, known for previous sexual assaults on female employees, summoned her to his office. Her colleagues rushed to warn her of the impending danger. When she returned and reported his attempt to fondle her, catcalls and denunciations of "the bum, the dog" sounded from every corner.[88] Sexual coercion and rape, though commonplace in the mills, often led to violent and bitter confrontations among workers or between workers and employers who refused to penalize or dismiss the offender, often a *Meister* or manager. In 1908 the Social Democratic textile union reported on the trial of a *Meister* in a jute spinning mill in Braunschweig that employed over a thousand women. The master, "a beast in human disguise," was reputed to have "assaulted [*körperlich mißbraucht*] one woman worker 1,116 times." Unable to protect herself from her tormentor, the woman reported her ordeal to her supervisors, only to be told that she should leave the mill if she wanted to be left alone. The intervention of the union on her behalf apparently resulted in the arrest and trial of the master. The union publicized the trial to encourage female workers to come forward with tales of sexual coercion, which its representatives clearly believed was widespread.[89] In other instances workers took matters into their own hands, launching a strike in one Bocholt mill in 1905 to demand the firing of a master weaver who had raped several female employees.[90] In 1902 an

88. Ibid., pp. 27–29. On the role of sexuality in defining female codes of honor, see the interesting article on women workers during the mid-nineteenth century by Claudia Honegger, "Ledige Mütter, 'Huren' und 'Lumpenhunde': Sexualmoral und Ehrenhändel im Arbeitermilieu des 19. Jahrhunderts," in *Tübinger Beiträge zur Volkskultur*, ed. Utz Jeggle, Wolfgang Kaschuba, Gottfried Korff, Martin Scharfe and Bernd Jürgen Warneken (Tübingen: Tübinger Vereinigung für Volkskunde, 1986), pp. 70–86.

89. DTAV, "Die sittlichen Gefahren der Textilarbeiterinnen," *Der Textilarbeiter* 20 (12 June 1908): 189–90. Among the specific instances of rape or molestation reported in the two textile unions' papers were DTAV, local report from Braunschweig, *Der Textilarbeiter* 20 (28 February 1908): 68; local report from Braunschweig, ibid., 20 (12 June 1908): 189–90 and 22 (13 May 1910): 145; ZCTD, local report from Krefeld, *Der Christliche Textilarbeiter* 5 (12 September 1903); local reports from Bocholt, ibid., 7 (8 July 1905) and 7 (2 September 1905); *Textilarbeiterzeitung* 10 (28 March 1908): 51. On sexual abuse and assaults in French and British textile mills, see Patricia Hilden, *Working Women and Socialist Politics in France, 1880–1914* (Oxford: Oxford University Press, 1986), pp. 60–61, and Jan Lambertz, "Sexual Harassment in the 19th Century English Cotton Industry," *History Workshop* 19 (spring 1985): 29–61.

90. The workers demanded "die Entlassung des Meisters der sich an den Arbeiterinnen

angry crowd of men and women assembled in front of the home of a *Meister* in the Düsseldorf district who had assaulted a female subordinate, resulting in a melee in which one worker was killed and four received jail sentences.[91] In these instances women engaged in collective action to enforce and defend their own code of morality, often drawing upon the support of union officials and male coworkers.

Pregnancy in the mills represented another specifically female "bodily experience" that acquired new significance as an issue of moral and hygienic intervention during the late 1890s.[92] The alarm over the declining birthrate in Germany, juxtaposed with the intensified drive toward imperial expansion, signaled a new and urgent interest in female workers' reproduction by the state and the growing number of eugenicist social reformers. Doctors and reformers cited high rates of miscarriage, premature birth, and other complications among textile workers, caused in part by long hours of standing with their distended abdomens pressed against the moving machines.[93] Economic need compelled many women not only to conceal their pregnancies, in particular from foremen or managers, but also to continue working into the last days of their pregnancy: indeed, many went into labor at the looms, and some women were even forced to give birth in a "corner of the workshop."[94] According to an employers'

---

vergangen hatte." See ZCTD, local reports from Bocholt, *Der Christliche Textilarbeiter* 7 (24 June 1905) and 7 (8 July 1905). The workers also included the call for wage increases in their strike demands.

91. HStAD, JBdKPG 1902: Düsseldorf, p. 327; also see HStAD, JBdKPG 1905: Münster, p. 265, and 1912: Münster, pp. 367–68, for other reports of sexual abuse and workers' demands to fire the perpetrators.

92. On the cultural construction and expression of the divergent bodily experiences of pregnancy, see Emily Martin, *The Woman in the Body: A Cultural Analysis of Reproduction* (Boston: Beacon, 1987); DTAV, *Der Textilarbeiter* 26 (27 March 1914): 96. For the period of the mid-1920s, when reproductive issues occupied a prominent place in the *Frauenpolitik* of the textile unions, see DTAV, *Erwerbsarbeit, Schwangerschaft, Frauenleid: Die Aktion des Deutschen Textilarbeiterverbandes betreffs Besserung des Loses erwerbstätiger schwangeren Frauen* (Berlin: Textilpraxis, 1925), and Franz Hitze, *Geburtenrückgang und Sozialreform* (Mönchen-Gladbach: Volksverein, 1922).

93. HStADet, Reg. Minden, MiIG 172, pp. 256–57: "Offener Brief des Hauptvorstand des Deutschen Textilarbeiterverbandes an den Arbeitgeberverband der Deutschen Textilindustrie." (This letter is undated but was part of an exchange between the two associations during 1925 and 1926 about the dangers of textile work for pregnant women.) See also Frieda Wunderlich, "Arbeitsschutz und Unfallverhütung: Die Beschäftigung verheirateter Frauen in Gewerbe und Handel," *Soziale Praxis* 37, no. 44 (1926): 1049–54. According to the factory inspectors' reports of 1927, among 350 female textile workers in Württemberg, 14 percent had miscarriages or stillbirths, 9 percent had premature deliveries, and another 15 percent had births with complications. In sum, 38 percent of births among female textile workers followed an "abnormal" course or had "abnormal" outcomes.

94. DTAV, local report from Grefrath, *Der Textilarbeiter* 16 (2 December 1904); Martha Hoppe, "Zur Arbeiterinnenfrage" (Vortrag, gehalten auf der Konferenz des Gaus Brandenburg am 8. Mai 1910) (Berlin: Karl Hübsch, 1910), p. 9.

survey of 1926, over half of pregnant women worked during their last week of pregnancy, and most worked until the day they gave birth. These figures likely were similar or higher for the period before the First World War.[95] Although employers often opposed the measures medical doctors and eugenicist reformers considered vital to the reinvigoration of the *Volkskörper*—protective laws restricting women's working hours and the enactment of *Stillpausen* (nursing breaks), pregnancy leave, or maternity insurance—the state nonetheless relied on employers and factory inspectors to provide information regarding the reproductive histories and habits of female factory workers, for example, during the inquest of the Prussian Ministry of the Interior into the declining birthrate, conducted in 1912.[96] Figures compiled by the textile employers' association confirmed Marie Bernays's observations regarding pregnancy in the mills: in 1913, 38 percent of pregnant female textile workers were unmarried, and in 1914 this figure rose to 46 percent.[97]

Contesting the Factory Regime

Work cultures were constituted as women sought to reappropriate time or space for themselves on the shop floor, to achieve a "defensive preservation of self" by maintaining a certain rhythm of work, method of payment, or balance between the duties of household and workplace or by setting limits on the exploitation of their bodies at work. Although women accommodated themselves to some aspects of the factory regime—embrac-

---

95. Although the revised labor code of 1908 extended pregnancy protection to eight weeks (two weeks before birth and six weeks after), women presumably continued working as long as possible because the payment for "sick time" amounted to only half of their earnings. See DTAV, "Der Mutterschutz in der Krankenversicherung," *Der Textilarbeiter* 23 (10 February 1911): 42. The figures cited here are from HStADet, Reg. Minden, MiIG 172, pp. 284–85: "Eingabe des Arbeitgeberverbandes der deutschen Textilindustrie vom 28.10.1926 an die Reichsregierung, mit zwei ärztlichen Gutachten beigefügt." In 1913 and 1914, 38 and 40 percent of pregnant women, respectively, worked until the day of childbirth, while 55 and 63 percent worked during their last week of pregnancy. The figures for 1924 and 1925 were slightly lower: 53 and 49 percent of women worked during the last week and 27 and 21 percent until the day of delivery.

96. See chapter 5 on the inquiry of 1912.

97. HStADet, Reg. Minden MiIG 172, "Eingabe des Arbeitgeberverbands," p. 27. Studies in family history reveal, however, that most unwed pregnancies in workers' circles led to marriage as soon as the young couple was financially able to establish their own household. See, for example, Heidi Rosenbaum, *Formen der Familie: Untersuchungen zum Zusammenhang von Familienverhältnissen, Sozialstruktur und sozialem Wandel in der deutschen Gesellschaft des 19. Jahrhunderts* (Frankfurt a.M.: Suhrkamp, 1982), especially "Die proletarische Familie," pp. 381–470, and Klaus Saul, Jens Flemming, Dirk Stegmann, and Peter-Christian Witt, eds., *Arbeiterfamilien im Kaiserreich: Materialen zur Sozialgeschichte in Deutschland, 1871–1914* (Düsseldorf: Droste, 1982).

ing, for example, the cooking and sewing courses offered by employers or their "charitable" associations—they also frequently spurned their moral tutelage or failed to comply with the norms of comportment and "decency" outlined in dormitory or factory regulations.

The site of individual and collective *Eigensinn*, the "inner face" of the shop floor, was shaped by the everyday moments of accommodation and resistance—most of which remain concealed from the historian—as well as by the more perceptible clashes between workers and employers that led to organized protests or strikes. Although some instances of women workers' "defensive preservation of self," such as the Crimmitschau strike of 1903, clearly required the intervention and backing of the textile unions, the relation between female workers and the textile unions was a complex one in which a kind of female *Eigensinn* often rendered female work cultures impervious to union discipline. While union and police records of strikes offer incontrovertible evidence of the activism and agency of women, they also point to the fluid boundaries between the moments of gender solidarity, when male and female workers fought with and for one another, and those times of gender conflict on the strike lines when men's and women's causes diverged or clashed or when male union leaders worked to stem a female-led wildcat strike, rebuking its usually unorganized proponents for their impetuousness and lack of caution and restraint.[98]

Thus, in examining the divergent ways women articulated their needs and demands in an often largely female workplace, it is important to consider the significant number who entrusted the textile unions with representing their interests, as well as to explore the ways unorganized female workers might have deflected the attempts of the male-led unions to channel their activism. Despite the many possible reasons women workers may not have been inclined to embrace a vocabulary of "class" or to express their concerns by participating in "class-conscious" organizations or actions, union membership statistics reveal that significant numbers of them surmounted family and social barriers and joined the Social Democratic Textile Union (DTAV), founded in 1891. Although only 2,384 women were members in 1897, composing a mere 11 percent of its membership, the union experienced a process of feminization during the next decade that paralleled the transformation of the textile workforce. By 1907 some 43,350 women composed 36 percent of DTAV rank and file, a figure that remained relatively constant until 1913. Between 1913 and 1919 female

98. For various accounts of female-led spontaneous or wildcat strikes, see HStAD, Reg. Düss. 24693, "Bericht der Polizeiverwaltung von 26.11.1900"; Reg. Düss. 24704, "Bericht der Polizeiverwaltung von 25.2.1910." Both of these strikes were launched by women in response to the firing of a female colleague. Also see DTAV, *Der Textilarbeiter* 20 (17 January 1908): 1, front-page story on strike dispute in Krefeld.

membership more than tripled, as the DTAV became a predominantly women's union during the war. Female membership increased dramatically again between 1919 and 1923, when nearly half a million women belonged.[99] Although the Social Democratic textile union was consistently two to three times as large as its Christian rival, the Zentralgewerkschaft Christlicher Textilarbeiter Deutschlands (ZCTD), significant numbers of female workers joined the ZCTD after its founding in 1901, particularly in the Lower Rhine and the textile regions surrounding Münster in Westphalia, the home base of the Christian union. By 1907 its 12,628 female members constituted some 30 percent of the total. As in the case of the DTAV, the union underwent rapid feminization beginning in 1917, and one year later the ZCTD's membership was two-thirds female.[100]

Although the two textile unions organized the largest female contingents within the Socialist and Christian union confederations, women textile workers consistently demonstrated a greater propensity to strike than to join unions. For the years 1902 to 1904, for example, women composed between 17 and 23 percent of the DTAV rank and file but 53 percent of participants in offensive strikes. Whereas 78 percent of male strikers were unionized, only 63 percent of striking women belonged to the DTAV.[101] During 1906–7, women again represented 53 percent of participants in offensive strikes, but only 36 percent of DTAV members. As the wartime *Burgfriede* (civil peace between the unions and government) began to deteriorate during the fall and winter of 1916–17, women made up 62 percent of industrial strike participants in 1916 and 75 percent in 1917, while only 26 percent of those involved (male and female) in 1916 and only 36 percent in 1917 were union members.[102] Furthermore, even during the years of peak female union membership—between 1919 and 1923, when two-thirds of the textile union rank and file were women—women's rate of strike participation exceeded their rate of union membership.

Before the First World War—especially between 1908, when the repeal of the Prussian Law of Association allowed women to take part in political assemblies and organization, and the outbreak of war in 1914—female

---

99. DTAV, *Jahrbuch 1927* (Berlin: Textilpraxis, 1928), p. 147; Kathleen Canning, "Gender and the Politics of Class Formation: Rethinking German Labor History," *American Historical Review* 97 (June 1992): 759–62. In fact, during the 1920s the unionization rate for female textile workers surpassed that of men: 30 percent of women, compared with 24.5 percent of their male colleagues, belonged to the DTAV by 1925.

100. ZCTD, *Jahrbuch 1932* (Düsseldorf, 1933), p. 66.

101. Archiv der Gewerkschaft Textil-Bekleidung (GTB), Düsseldorf: DTAV, *Protokoll der 7. ordentlichen Generalversammlung des Verbandes aller in der Textilindustrie beschäftigten Arbeiter und Arbeiterinnen, abgehalten von 2. bis 5. April 1904 in Linden-Hannover*, pp. 42–45.

102. DTAV, *Jahrbuch 1916* (Berlin: Textilpraxis, 1917), pp. 95–97; *Jahrbuch 1917* (Berlin: Textilpraxis, 1918), pp. 63–71.

activists in both unions sought recognition of women's "special needs" in their everyday struggles for higher wages and a shorter workday and for greater protection of pregnant workers. Within the unions—another front of struggle—they campaigned for the right to hold separate women's meetings, to establish a women's supplement to the union paper, and to increase the number of women in the higher echelons of union administration. Until the First World War, however, women constituted a minority in both unions, and the visions and vocabulary of male leaders continued to set the tone of the union policies and programs for female workers. Indeed, the "antifeminist" sentiment of many male unionists, occasionally expressed in strikes against the hiring of female weavers, in recurrent resistance to the demand for equal pay for equal work, and in the persistent reluctance of union functionaries to grant women a permanent place in the union bureaucracy, also meant that female workers often figured in union rhetoric as passive, apolitical workers who because of the double burden of wage work and housework/child rearing were at best a costly burden upon the labor movement and who, in the worst instances, betrayed the union's struggle by acting as wage cutters and strikebreakers. This antifeminism, juxtaposed with the DTAV's claim to represent all textile workers, made the union an intensely contradictory arena, not only for the unorganized women workers the union sought to recruit, but also for the committed female union activists, who confronted this sentiment at every level of the union bureaucracy.[103] Many women apparently responded to these negative representations by remaining aloof from the organized labor movement or by articulating their demands in other forms such as spontaneous strikes.[104] As the Crimmitschau strike illustrates, on the strike lines no dichotomy existed between family and workplace, private and public: women fought as workers, wives, and mothers against wage cuts, for a shorter workday, against harsh *Meister* and punitive codes of factory discipline. In fact, the discordance between the negative images of women in

103. Werner Thönnessen, *Frauenemanzipation: Politik und Literatur der deutschen Sozialdemokratie zum Frauenbewegung, 1863–1933* (Frankfurt a.M.: Europäische Verlagsanstalt, 1976), pp. 31–33, and Mary Nolan, "Proletarischer Anti-Feminismus, dargestellt am Beispiel der SPD-Ortsgruppe Düsseldorf, 1890–1914," in *Frauen und Wissenschaft: Beiträge zur Berliner Sommeruniversität* (Berlin: Courage, 1976), pp. 356–77. Martha Hoppe became the first paid female union secretary in the DTAV in 1908, but she was consistently denied the right to vote in the union's executive committee. See Archiv der GTB: DTAV, *Protokoll der 9. ordentlichen Generalversammlung, abgehalten 1908 in Leipzig*, p. 9.

104. Archiv der GTB: DTAV, *Protokoll der 10. Generalversammlung, abgehalten 1910 in Berlin*, pp. 87, 120, 135–36, 237, 241; DTAV, *Protokoll der 11. Generalversammlung, abgehalten 1914 in Dresden*, pp. 113, 118. Also see DTAV, "Warum sind die Frauen so schwer für die Gewerkschaft zu gewinnen?" *Der Textilarbeiter* 20 (16 October 1908); "Für die Frauen, von den Frauen," *Der Textilarbeiter* 21 (1 January 1909); and "Die Meinung einer Kollegin zur Arbeiterinnenfrage," *Der Textilarbeiter* 22 (9 September 1910).

union propaganda and women's own work identities may explain why so many sought to redress their grievances in strikes rather than through union activity.

Thus, in factories where the unions had made significant inroads, women often sought to subvert or resist employers' policies through the union or at least with its backing. In 1906, for example, the DTAV reported from Bielefeld that it had recently succeeded in gaining influence among the predominantly female workforce of the Mechanische Weberei Bielefeld. In response to the union's growing popularity on the shop floor, the Weberei's management sought to convene an *Arbeiterausschuß* (workers' representational committee). Instead of permitting open elections to the committee, however, the firm attempted to institute an organ of "workers' representation" consisting mainly of male foremen, *Meister*, and supervisors, who constituted only a small minority (150) of the mill's 1,000 employees, thereby excluding the remaining 850 female workers in the mill from the committee. Refusing to allow masters and foremen to represent their interests, the mill's female workers organized a massive boycott of the election. When only six female employees turned in ballots, the election was nullified, and the company was forced to convene a new, open election by which four female workers were elected to the committee.[105] The most frequent involvement of the unions was on behalf of female workers' demands for higher wages or their protests against new methods of payment—the shift from a daily wage to piecework, for example—or against speeding up the work pace by changing from single to double looms.[106]

Women appear to have often launched strikes spontaneously and then sought the support or intervention of the union, a practice that clearly exasperated union leaders. A "dictatorial wage reduction" of three to five marks per week, for example, sparked outrage and indignation among female winders and warpers in a velvet mill in Viersen in 1903. Despite warnings from management that they were violating the law, they immediately shut down their machines and walked off their jobs without giving the legally mandated fourteen days notice of their intention to quit. After consulting with the largely male weavers of the mill and securing their support, the women gave the firm official notice of their walkout. Although the Christian union appears to have supported their action retrospectively, its report of the incident indicates that it was initially a sponta-

105. DTAV, *Der Textilarbeiter* 18 (28 December 1906), local report from Bielefeld.
106. ZCTD, *Textilarbeiterzeitung* 12 (26 February 1910), local report on wage conflict in Kempen, and 7 (19 August 1905), local report on conflict over the double loom in Aachen's woolen industry.

neous reaction to the substantial reduction of women's weekly wages.[107] In another instance the Christian union lamented the "deficient training" and discipline of the female spinners in the Gladbacher Spinnerei und Weberei, who simply walked off their jobs in June 1903 because of "meager earnings" without giving proper notice to the firm or the union. Apparently the firm had provided the spinners with poor-quality raw material, which had slowed down production and thus caused a decline in their wages.[108] When twenty-seven female spinners engaged in a wildcat strike over wages in 1905 in Ahaus because of wage cuts of 10 percent or more, both unions declined support and sought to persuade them to return to work as soon as possible because of the relatively low level of unionization in the mill.[109]

Similarly, a strike action of female workers in Warendorf, in the cotton-producing region of Westphalia, forced the Christian union into complex negotiations with both the firm and the striking female spoolers and darners. Both walked off the job in late March when their wages were reduced by nearly 20 percent and remained resolute through mid-June, as the company's threats grew more ominous. First warning of a lockout of its own employees, in mid-June the company imposed a localized lockout of the 350 members of the Christian textile union in its own mill and two neighboring mills. Escalating the conflict considerably, the employers' association then announced a massive lockout of 3,000 members of the Christian textile union across the Münsterland to begin in mid-July. As the employers' actions widened the implications of the female workers' resolute efforts, the union stepped up the pressure on the striking women to return to the mills and spare their fellow workers "the excessive sacrifice" of a regional lockout. The strike ended unsuccessfully when the "reflective and level-headed female colleagues" relented in their nearly four month strike at the union's urging.[110] Again in 1909 in Gronau, also a cotton town in the Münsterland, female spinners launched a wildcat strike in response to the company's policy of punishing workers with excessive fines for dust particles in the yarn. As the Christian union reported, "this practice inflamed the workers so that they walked off the jobs without giving

107. ZCTD, *Der Christliche Textilarbeiter* 5 (31 January 1903), local report from Viersen.
108. ZCTD, *Der Christliche Textilarbeiter* 5 (13 June 1903), local report from Mönchen-Gladbach.
109. ZCTD, *Der Christliche Textilarbeiter* 7 (10 June 1905), local report of strikes and wage movement in Ahaus. The union noted that only two hundred of the five hundred employees in the mill were unionized.
110. ZCTD, *Textilarbeiterzeitung* 10 (9 May 1908), local report from Warendorf, followed by updates in 10 (16 May 1908); 10 (30 May 1908); 10 (6 June 1908); and 10 (18 July 1908). At the time of the first report the strike had already been under way for six weeks.

notice," shutting down the mill. Although the union agreed to negotiate on behalf of the workers, its report on the conflict admonished those workers who thought they could achieve their goals through wildcat strikes to recognize the critical importance of the union in waging successful strikes.[111] A strike of silk weavers in Krefeld in early January 1908 apparently provoked both unions to issue similar reprimands to the predominantly female silk weavers whose walkout had sparked the strike. In a front-page story in *Der Textilarbeiter*, the Social Democratic union deplored the "orgies, which resulted from the short-sightedness [and] lack of self-control and discipline in this struggle."[112] Although the specific conflicts between union and workers remain obscure in the union's report, they obviously led to a critical rupture between the striking workers and union representatives from both unions over the feasibility of a strike under apparently unfavorable economic conditions. While the striking workers castigated union leaders for their "duplicitous dealings," the unions clearly felt compelled to defend their decision to resist the workers' determination to strike. These incidents of "impulsive" or undisciplined female wildcat strikes not only reveal the ways women contested the dominant structures and rhetorics of work but also suggest that the impermeability of female work cultures often forced the unions into delicate negotiations or into contests for control over the strike's outcome, not only with the mill owners and their representatives, but also with largely unorganized female workers.

Although wages and working hours were the main issues in most textile strikes, those involving large numbers of female workers also frequently included the preservation of women's honor, respectability, and integrity, as indicated by the instances above of strikes against rape and sexual harassment. Everyday strike issues included, for example, the establishment of separate restrooms or changing rooms for men and women and frequently women workers' insistence that the union intervene against abusive or disrespectful masters or managers. The headlines of the Christian union paper declared a potential "massive lockout in the Lower Rhine!" in the spring of 1903, prompted by silk workers' demands for higher wages, clean restrooms, cafeterias, and changing rooms.[113] In another case, for example, unorganized women workers asked the Christian union to publi-

111. ZCTD, *Textilarbeiterzeitung* 11 (18 May 1909), local report from Gronau.
112. DTAV, *Der Textilarbeiter* 20 (17 January 1908), front-page story on strike dispute in Krefeld.
113. ZCTD, *Der Christliche Textilarbeiter* 5 (14 March 1903), local report from Anrath of female workers' complaints at the Lange company regarding wages, work hours, and the absence of separate dressing rooms for the firm's eighty female workers; ZCTD, "Eine Riesen-Aussperrung am Niederrhein!" *Der Christliche Textilarbeiter* 5 (25 April 1903). Also see the following issues of the same paper for related reports: 7 (2 September 1905), report on strikes and wage conflicts from Dülmen; 9 (15 June 1907), local report from Oedt.

cize the case of a married woman who had been fired when she complained to the boss about a manager who had flagrantly insulted the "moral honor of the female workers" on various occasions.[114]

How greatly workers deplored the factory ordinances and the system of penalties and fines is revealed in an incident of 1905 when a female worker was excessively fined for "disobedience." The young woman, who was employed at Deuß und Oetker in Schiefbahn near Viersen, was fined 1.25 marks (considerably more than her daily wage of 80 pfennig) for refusing to clean a second machine before her lunch break. Although her father took her case to the local *Gewerbegericht* (industrial court) and forced the firm to reimburse his daughter for the fine, the arbitrary deployment of penalties galvanized the workforce when the workers went on strike in 1905 over an amalgam of issues, from wage demands to poor quality raw material and the company's *Strafsystem*, including the custom of forcing "winder girls," as part of their duties, to carry water for coffee or pay 60 pfennig to be relieved of the task, which they clearly regarded as onerous.[115]

These disparate fragments of the complex histories of women's strike efforts help to uncover the meanings they themselves made of work as they encountered and sometimes contested both economic exploitation and the moralizing and tutelary regimes that mill owners sought to establish. The everyday struggles examined here—over wages and hours, pride and honor, gossip and respectability, bodies and sexuality—not only reveal how women adapted to and subverted ordained locations within the factory regime but also emphasize the multiple subject positions they inhabited as workers, mothers, and wives in the course of their struggles on the shop floor. This examination of women's agency in the workplace, even if often accessible only through union sources, points to the ways they were occasionally able to mobilize their own experiences to transform and "reterritorialize" their locations within the mills as well as within the political discourses of both employers and unions.[116]

Conclusion

This chapter has argued that the cultures and identities of work were formed by the discourses and structures of skill, wages, and factory regime

114. ZCTD, *Der Christliche Textilarbeiter* 5 (12 September 1903), local report from Krefeld. Since the female workers in this mill were unorganized, the union agreed to publicize the case but was unable to intervene on behalf of the fired women.

115. ZCTD, *Der Christliche Textilarbeiter* 7 (17 June 1905), local report from Schiefbahn.

116. Sherry Ortner, "Some Theoretical Problems in Anthropological History and Historical Anthropology," in *The Historic Turn in the Social Sciences*, ed. Terence J. McDonald (Ann Arbor: University of Michigan Press, 1996), MS. p. 22.

and by the distinctly gendered experiences of work, status, and power on the shop floor. The focus on the hierarchies of wage and skill, on the prominence of domesticity and the female reproductive body, reveals that men and women encountered highly gendered structures of domination and exploitation despite their many shared experiences at work. Women's work cultures formed as they encountered their own "construction" in the workplace as (present or future) mothers and wives, as always explicitly embodied, by contrast with men. The policies of state, reformers, employers, and unions that sought to render factory work compatible with motherhood established the parameters—discursive and structural—within which women sought to negotiate the boundaries between their two spheres of work.

Moments of accommodation and resistance marked their encounters with the dormitories, day-care centers, and domestic skills courses employers instituted on behalf of women workers. Shop-floor fashions and secrets, gossip and sexual horseplay, the subcultures surrounding pregnancy, birth control, abortion, and childbirth can be viewed as specifically female spheres of *Eigensinn* in the sense of "self-reliance, self-will, and self-respect."[117] Indeed, a decisive difference between the work cultures of male and female textile workers was not, as the examples above show, the *primacy* of the "private" or the family in women's identities, nor their experience of work through the filter of the family, but the *simultaneity* of the two realms, their continual transgression of the boundary between the two in their daily lives.[118] The marking of the female body as a new site of intervention for the moralizing and regulatory regimes of employers, social reformers, and state meant that women's embodied experiences at the looms and in piecework, as well as those of pregnancy, childbirth, illness, and exhaustion, defied the imagined separation of home and work, family and factory in particular ways, shaping women workers' claims on employers and state, their visions of citizenship, and their particularly gendered encounters with and resistance to the organized politics of the labor movement.

An analysis of the fissures and fractures of gender in cultures and identities of work suggests fruitful new approaches to the history of labor politics in Germany. It calls for a history of labor that refrains from conflating the experiences of women and men, "skilled" and "unskilled," a history of

---

117. As defined by Geoff Eley in his discussion of Alf Lüdtke's work. See Geoff Eley, "Labor History, Social History, *Alltagsgeschichte*: Experience, Culture, and the Politics of the Everyday—a New Direction for German Social History?" *Journal of Modern History* 61 (June 1989): 323–24.

118. A poignant portrayal of this constant transgression is offered in DTAV, *Mein Arbeitstag—mein Wochenende* (Berlin: Textilpraxis, 1930).

division as well as of cohesion and unity, one that explores these divisions free of the compulsion "to put them back together again" as quickly as possible.[119] Finally, placing gender at the center of labor history reveals the necessity of disengaging the history of the working class from the language of class and the teleology of class consciousness, of examining work identities and work cultures for the manifold meanings and subversions of class, for the diverse terrains of conflict—bodies, sexuality, housework, and charity—beyond the site of production.

119. Eley, "Labor History, Social History," p. 339.

Conclusion

This book has explored the structural transformations and changing meanings of women's factory employment in Germany between the middle of the nineteenth century and the First World War. It is a history first of the origins of the discourses of women's work and of the social question of female factory labor that emerged during the transition from household to factory textile production and that figured significantly in Germany's broader transformation from an agrarian to an industrial state. In turn, it analyzes the complex ways the discursive milieu of social reform, and the protective labor legislation it helped shape, became a formative part of the structures and experiences of work—of work identities and work cultures. In pursuing the meanings of gender at the sites of industrial transformation, welfare-state formation, and the emergence of work cultures and conflicts, I have also argued that the textile industry—in the forefront of mechanization and centralization and the largest factory employer of women before the First World War—forms a singular site of linkage among these processes. This book seeks to dissolve the boundaries and strictures of German labor history in its emphasis on these links: it investigates the meanings of gender, state, and social reform for labor history, and, conversely, it examines the significance of female factory labor in its various guises as *sittliche Kulturfrage* for the expanding public sphere and the emergent welfare state.

At the heart of this book is a critical engagement with one of the axioms of modern European labor history and in particular of German histories of class formation: the separation of home and work. I first explore the dialectic between *Verweiblichung*—feminization of the factory workplace and workforce—and *Entweiblichung*, the concomitant defeminizing of the household as wives and mothers were drawn into the newly mechanized mills. Attending to both the origins and the divergent meanings of this crucial marker in German labor history, I analyze the ways contemporaries came to terms with the separation of home and work. Social reformers and intellectuals cast it in terms of the "destruction of all foundations of inherited culture" and the "extirpation of property and marriage" and thus assigned it a central place in the moral-cultural complex they called the "social question."[1] Exploring the separation of home and work from the perspective of those who negotiated the boundary between these spheres in their daily lives reveals its divergent meanings for male and female workers. The struggles of male weavers to come to terms with the separation of home and work resulted in the revival of artisanal communities in the form of weavers' *Innungen* (guilds) that sought to assert new boundaries of gender in both the remaining family workshops and the new factory workplace, thereby effacing the tradition of female labor in household textile manufacture. The separation of home and work thus became a cornerstone in the emergence of the new identity of "male breadwinners," their languages of grievance, and their politics of class and estate.

The exploration of women's work identities and work cultures in the third part of this book points to the fluid rather than fixed boundary between home and work in both the discourses and experiences of female factory labor. Although one key preoccupation of state social policy and employers' disciplinary regimes was precisely to reconcile the two spheres, the policies and practices of both continually blurred the boundary between them, regulating the workplace in order to preserve and protect the family and importing the home into the factory through institutions of tutelage and charity that aimed to instill in working women the skills and the ethos of domesticity. At the same time, the investigation of women's work cultures points to the continual intersection of family and industrial time, of reproduction and production, of individual and social bodies as women consented to and resisted employers' custodial claims over factory and family, as they went on strike to defend their work rhythms or to expose and protest rape and sexual coercion in the mills.

The contests over the meanings of the separation of home and work helped shape "the social," understood as "an arena of conflicts over the reproduction of labor"[2] in which the agencies of state and the milieus of

---

1. Alfons Thun, *Die Industrie am Niederrhein und ihre Arbeiter,* Staats- und sozialwissenschaftliche Forschungen, vols. 1 and 2 (Leipzig: Duncker und Humblot, 1879), p. 178.

2. George Steinmetz, "Workers and the Welfare State in Imperial Germany," *International Labor and Working-Class History* 40 (fall 1991): 20–21. Also see his recent book, *Regulating*

social reform had a vital role and which by the 1890s encompassed the expanding public sphere as well. In setting the stage for social reform in Germany, in representing the dramas and dangers associated with the mass employment of women in factories and the decline of the working-class family, the textile industry became a key site of intervention in the social. As women workers came under the public gaze that constituted the social, domesticity in both its moral and its hygienic dimensions emerged as the solution for the social question, as a cultural matrix, as an ideology at the heart of the social.[3] The reformers, state bureaucrats, and labor leaders who engaged in the conflicts over the reproduction of labor, who sought to contend with the consequences of the separation of home and work, mapped out a cultural grid of sexual difference, distinguishing independent male citizens and breadwinners, who could assert and defend their interests in political associations, from women and children, who required the protection of the state.[4] These distinctions underpinned the policies and practices of the German welfare state, specifically its *Arbeiterpolitik* (social policy toward workers) and its bifurcation into the streams of social insurance, aimed at male breadwinners, and protective labor laws, drafted on behalf of women and minors. The delineations between independent male citizens and the "weak hands" of women and children became firmly rooted in both the bourgeois and working-class public spheres, shaping the dichotomies of public/private and production/reproduction that underwrote both middle class and working class as social identities and as particular visions of male citizenship.

Inherent in this distinction were particular perceptions of the female body. Depicting the expansion of female factory employment as a "temporary pathological symptom of the social body," the narratives of social reform implicated the female body centrally in the making of the social and identified the "female organism" as a key site of intervention for both the regulatory and tutelary regimes of state social policy.[5] The dramatic visions of social dissolution—the working-class family torn apart by the expansion of female factory labor, women's bodies ravaged by machines

---

the Social: The Welfare State and Local Politics in Imperial Germany (Princeton: Princeton University Press, 1993) pp. 55–70.

3. Denise Riley, *"Am I That Name?" Feminism and the Category of "Women" in History* (Minneapolis: University of Minnesota Press, 1988), pp. 50–51.

4. See, for example, Lujo Brentano's address to the meeting of the Verein für Sozialpolitik in 1872 on factory legislation, cited by Else Conrad, *Der Verein für Sozialpolitik und seine Wirksamkeit auf dem Gebiet der gewerblichen Arbeiterfrage* (Jena: Gustav Fischer, 1906), p. 86. Also see chapter 3 above for a more detailed discussion of this delineation.

5. Marie Lischnewska, "Die handwerksmässige- und fachgewerbliche Ausbildung der Frau: Ein Mahnwort an die deutsche Frauenbewegung aller Richtungen," *Kultur und Fortschritt* 315–16 (1910): 6.

and overwork—ascribed a new significance to female bodies in the conflict over the reproduction of labor. Thus the female body became a powerful marker of the dichotomy between independent citizen-workers and those who required the protection of the state.

As Germany intensified its quest for empire after 1890, both "the social" and the meanings of the female body for social reform and state social policy changed. The growing alarm about the steady decline of the birthrate placed working women's bodies at the center of a hygienicist, natalist enterprise of eradicating a complex web of social pathologies—alcoholism, tuberculosis, venereal disease, and infant mortality—all attributed directly or indirectly to the moral or bodily deficiencies of women who worked outside the home. As visions of a revitalized *Volkskörper* came to occupy a central place in Germany's intensified contest for European and imperial hegemony before the outbreak of World War I, the emphasis on the reproductive female body became more pronounced. At the same time, the scope of the social widened to encompass conflicts about (national) reproduction and the national birthrate.

The links I have sought to establish here—between and among the processes of industrialization, welfare state formation, and the emergence of identities and cultures of work, among the histories of the social, the body, and the articulation of citizenship and class as social identities—are rich in German particularities. First, the rapid pace of German industrial growth, of Germany's transformation from agrarian to industrial state, coincided with the formation of the German nation-state and the rise of a vibrant socialist labor movement, a conjunction that complicated what Max Weber termed the "social unification of the nation" and precipitated the emergence of the German welfare state only a decade after national unification. Indeed, from the formulation of the social question as a *sittliche Kulturfrage* in the 1870s to the appearance of female factory labor as a new social question in the 1890s, social reformers across the divides of class and political creed addressed their concerns and their appeals to the German state, seeking to reinvent the state, to replace the *Rechtsstaat* with a *Kulturstaat* that was to help forge ethical, cultural, and moral bonds among its citizens. While Bismarck sought to fashion a German welfare state in his own image, linking the institution of state social insurance with the political repression of the socialist labor movement, the state-oriented activities of academic, Social Catholic, and Social Democratic reformers had a crucial role in shaping the welfare state, particularly during the "new course" in social policy of the early 1890s. In fact the agitation around the social question of female factory labor during the 1880s and 1890s, the crucial role of the public sphere and the public imagination in shaping the other facet of the welfare state—protective labor legislation—

reveals the German state to be a "permeable arena in which contending social and political forces interacted," as Geoff Eley has argued, rather than the authoritarian and "incorporative machine" depicted in many accounts of German history that emphasize the German *Sonderweg* (special path).[6] This is particularly true of the 1890s, when the transformation of the public sphere—the emergence of Social Democracy as a mass party, the popular mobilization of right-wing nationalists, middle-class feminists, and liberal social reformers—changed the meanings of both class and citizenship.

Finally, the particularities of German labor history have shaped this book, most notably its embeddedness in notions of class and models of class formation that have confined working women behind the lines of family and household. The pervasiveness of class in the narratives of German labor history in some sense reflects its place as a primary political identity among German workers during the late nineteenth and early twentieth centuries. By contrast with the contests between syndicalists and socialists in France or the fusion of Liberal and Labor initiatives in England, class had a singular discursive power in Germany, as evinced in the vitality of the Socialist labor movement during the period of the repressive Socialist Law (1878–90) and its rise as a powerful mass party between 1890 and 1914. Precisely because of the predominance of class as a social identity and its pervasiveness in the annals of German labor history, this book has contended with class as a boundary of German labor history, a structure and stricture that has reproduced rather than questioned the dichotomies of home and work, public and private.

While critically engaging the concept and the history of class, this book is also conceived as a genealogy of class and of working-class citizenship, forming a foundation for further study of the contested boundaries of class in the history of the German textile unions, of the changing meanings of gender and the rich terrain of conflict between class and estate in the Social Democratic and Christian textile workers' unions. The discursive and legislative making of women's work, the experiences of male and female workers during the transition from home to factory production and in the world of the mechanized mills form the context in which the identities of estate, class, and citizenship were cast. An examination of the process by which class was defined and contested, by those who opposed it or implic-

---

6. Geoff Eley, "German History and the Contradictions of Modernity," in *Society, Culture and the State in Germany, 1870–1930*, ed. Geoff Eley (Ann Arbor: University of Michigan Press, 1995), p. 94. On the state as a space of struggle rather than an incorporative machine, see Robert Gray, "Medical Men, Industrial Labour and the State in Britain, 1830–1850," *Social History* 16 (January 1991): 21, and his "The Language of Factory Reform in Britain, c. 1830–1860," in *The Historical Meanings of Work*, ed. Patrick Joyce (Cambridge: Cambridge University Press, 1989), p. 172.

itly by those who stood outside it and who appeared as "other" or "backward"—such as women or Catholic workers—also opens up a new terrain of inquiry regarding the relation between discourses and experiences of work, a central theme here. As the accounts of female workers' labor protests and strike participation in previous chapters suggest, union politics forms a particularly intriguing site of encounter between female workers and the politics of class, where women mobilized and articulated their experiences in order to contest the dichotomies of production/reproduction, work/nonwork, and thus to challenge the boundaries of class.

Founded under the shadow of the perceived social dislocation of mechanization and feminization, the Social Democratic and Christian textile unions sought from the outset to define themselves against "unqualified factory workers" and to contain female factory labor within gender-specific boundaries of wage and skill. However futile the battle of the weavers' guilds against the factory and its female workers, the weavers' rhetorical self-creation as craftsmen changed the mental landscape of citizenship, estate, and class across the plains of the Rhineland and Westphalia. For the mentalities of craft and guild formed the kernel of both the Social Democratic textile union, founded in 1891, and the Christian union, which emerged in 1901 from the webs of the small local Catholic weavers' associations in the Rhineland. Although their perceptions and experiences of the changing landscape of factory and family were mediated differently, one in the language of class and the other in the language of estate and religion, both were influenced primarily by gender, specifically by the male experience of industrialization. Male working-class visions of respectability, skill, and honor came to underpin both the Social Democratic notion of the class-conscious worker and the campaigns of Catholic textile workers to protect *Stand* (estate) and family from the destructive effects of industrial transformation.

Accompanying the rise of both the Social Democratic and Christian labor movements during the late nineteenth century was a new notion of working-class citizenship, now defined not only in terms of the right to vote, but increasingly in terms of the right to work. Both class and estate, as distinct visions of male citizenship, were embodied in the figure of the male breadwinner. Yet a key difference between the social identities of class and estate was the idealized relationship to production, the rigid demarcation between work and nonwork that underpinned the identity and rhetoric of class and by definition excluded most female workers. Whereas the politics of class in the Social Democratic labor movement rendered the *division between home and work* a linchpin of union policy and ultimately of class identity, the politics of estate in the Catholic labor movement aimed to *forge closer links between the two spheres*, to raise the status of motherhood and enhance the social value of women's work within home and family while seeking to restrict female factory labor because of the dangers it posed to pregnancy, child rearing, and marriage.

Key in understanding how sexual difference shaped the two labor movements is the notion of female *Eigenart*—a complex political slogan that designated the particularities of women's needs, activities, sentiments, and consciousness and that formed a site of contest between the two unions as well as between men and women *within* each union. Male leaders of the Social Democratic textile union, for example, implemented the rhetoric of *Eigenart* negatively, to deny women entry to—to define them out of—the realm of class and politics. At the same time, female activists in the union implemented the vocabulary of *Eigenart* to stake political claim to the multiple subject positions women workers simultaneously inhabited, by refusing the assignment of one or the other socially sanctioned subject position ("mother" to the detriment of "worker," for example). The powerful antifeminist sentiments of male members and union leaders, however, meant that the most significant encounters between male and female union activists took place on the terrain of imagery and rhetoric, as each group upheld its own vision of sexual difference and inscribed it with distinct political meanings. The embrace of female *Eigenart* in the Christian union, by contrast, was consistent with the Catholic view of the distinct yet equally honorable tasks of men and women in society. Indeed, leaders of the Christian textile union, acutely aware of the dilemmas female *Eigenart* posed to Social Democrats, prided themselves on demonstrating a greater understanding for the particularities of female nature than did their political rivals.

The meanings of *Eigenart* changed profoundly during the upheavals of world war, the revolution of 1918, demobilization, and the postwar political fragmentation of the union movement. War, revolution, and the subsequent realignment of military and civilian society in Germany transformed women's experiences of citizenship and class, of family and sexuality and brought about a rapid disordering of the discursive domain of gender. The gender imagery of the early Weimar Republic was replete with contradictions: women's newly acquired right to vote and their prominent place in the strikes and bread riots of 1917–18, and the revolution of 1918 contrasted with the mass displacement of women from their jobs during demobilization. The convergence during the early years of Weimar of a crisis of nation with a crisis of class—the fracturing and (re)formation of the working class—also altered the political landscape of both textile unions. A feminization of politics took place as women came to constitute a large majority (nearly two-thirds) of the rank and file of both unions between 1917 and 1923 and as the politics of *Eigenart* flourished in the spaces vacated by the union men during the war.

Amid these shifts, and within the widening discursive field of body politics during the early 1920s, female activists in the Social Democratic union mobilized their own embodied experiences in order to enter into and represent themselves in the discursive arenas of class and citizenship. These accumulated experiences of the female body encompassed all the realms of "work" with its day-to-day wounding: the endless cycle of cooking, washing, cleaning, and mending, work without recognition or pay that decided a family's ongoing survival; the mechanization and depletion of the body by machines in the mills; its vulnerability to illness, injury, or rape; the miscarriages, stillbirths, and pregnancies plagued by pain and complications; the danger and death associated with illegal abortion and the persistently high rates of infant mortality among urban working-class families. Women in the socialist union raised radical new demands, calling on the union leadership to integrate a "politics of the body"—housework, birth control, and abortion—into its women's program, thereby envisioning a political link between the home and the workplace, the private body and the social, political body. In doing so, they sought to contest not only the universalist and seemingly disembodied discourses of class politics, but also the colonizing claims on female bodies of postwar natalist reproductive politics. The reinvigorated politics of *Eigenart* in the Christian union, by contrast, sought to heal the wounded nation by a new emphasis on the compatibility between motherhood and wage labor.

Analysis and comparison of the ways gender permeated formal labor politics and defined the social identities of class and *Stand*—the topic of a subsequent study—will complement and complete the complex history this book has only begun to untangle, that of the making of the structures and rhetorics of work and the meanings female workers assigned to them.

Index

Aachen: Association of Wool Manufacturers in, 175; *Bürgerarbeiter* of, and transition from home to factory weaving, 46–53; and role of gender in woolen industry, 27, 31, 38, 50–53, 82; textile production in (general), 26; urban guild traditions in, 28, 34, 46–47, 49, 51; woolen weavers of, 49–50, 52–53. *See also* Christian-Social Female Textile Workers' League of Aachen
Abortion, 14, 203, 205, 209, 213, 322, 331
Accident insurance, 115
ADAV. *See* Allgemeiner Deutscher Arbeiterverein
ADGB. *See* Allgemeiner Deutscher Gewerkschaftsbund
Agency, methodological reflections on, 10–15
Alcoholism, 197, 200, 201, 327
Allgemeiner Deutscher Arbeiterverein (General German Workers' Association), 91, 92
Allgemeiner Deutscher Gewerkschaftsbund (General German Trade Union Confederation), 142
Alltagsgeschichte, 6–8, 13
American Civil War, and shortage of raw cotton, 42, 55
Amoskeag Mill (New Hampshire), 249, 259
Anrath, 62
Apprenticeship (craft), 41, 67–68, 220, 226, 245, 286, 288. *See also* Skill
Arbeiterfrage (worker question), 11–12, 61, 85, 90–91, 93, 96, 103, 113–14, 125, 129–30, 136, 152, 215
Arbeiterstammrollen, 223–24, 226, 228, 230–31, 255, 257, 270–73
Army League, 172
Augusta (Empress of Germany), 140

Baden: public *Fortbildungsschulen* in, 289; silk industry of, 26
Baldus woolen mill, 224, 229, 235–36, 238–40, 245, 248, 250, 252, 270–73, 277, 279
Bamberger, Ludwig, 97
Barmen, 33
Baum, Marie, 143n, 186–87, 213
Baur, Maria, 295
Bavaria: public *Fortbildungsschulen* in, 289; textile production in, 26
BDF. *See* Bund Deutscher Frauenvereine
Bebel, August, 93, 109, 118, 120; *Woman under Socialism*, 104–5
Belgian Christian Workers' League, 162
Bergischer Verein für Gemeinwohl, 124, 306
von Berlepsch, Hans Freiherr, 4n, 77, 78n, 92n, 98n, 106n, 119, 128, 132, 135, 136, 143, 145, 146, 192, 300n
Berlin Association of Family Doctors, 214
Bernays, Marie, 258–59, 310; study of workers in Gladbacher Spinnerei und Weberei, 229, 231, 232–33, 235, 237, 251, 254–55, 271–72, 314
Bernstein, Alfred, 214
Berufsethos (work ethic), 5, 183, 192, 219–21, 223, 233, 258, 269
Bielefeld, 33; C. A. Delius silk weaving mill in, 298; linen industry in, 27; Mechanische Weberei in, 55–57, 230, 239, 240, 254, 255, 268, 271, 318; role of gender in linen mills of, 38, 39, 53–60
"Biopolitics," 216. *See also* Body politics
Birth control, 203, 209, 213, 322
Birthrate, German: alarm over declining, 4, 171, 180, 195–98, 313, 327; and eugenicist campaigns, 201–5, 208, 210

334 Index

"Birth strike," 190, 214–15
von Bismarck, Chancellor Otto: and conflicts over February edicts, 134–37; and state social policy, 78, 88, 107, 111, 114–16, 119, 126, 130–32, 327
Blackbourn, David, 92, 142, 144, 147, 168, 194
Bocholt, 42
Body politics, 14–15, 86–87, 99, 149, 170, 172–73, 197–200, 202–4, 213–16, 331
von Boetticher, Karl Heinrich, 78, 119
Bohemia, 232
Bornträger, Jean, 204
Brandts, Franz, 101, 123, 142, 254, 299
Braun, Lily, 158, 162, 163, 189, 206, 207, 212–13
Brauns, Heinrich, 3, 34, 61, 63, 71, 81, 161, 197–98
Bré, Ruth, 207
Breckman, Warren, 157
Brentano, Lujo, 3n, 16n, 97n, 98n, 120, 129, 152n, 173, 185, 192, 194–95, 200, 326n; on German factory legislation, 97–99
Brügelmann, J. G., 40
Bund Deutscher Frauenvereine (Federation of German Women's Associations), 151, 160, 166, 206, 213; *Centralblatt des Bundes Deutscher Frauenvereine*, 166
Bundesrat, 107, 119, 137
Bund für Mutterschutz und Sexualreform (League for Protection of Mothers and Sexual Reform), 201, 207–10, 213
Bürgerarbeiter (citizen workers). *See* Aachen
Bürgerliches Gesetzbuch. *See* Civil Code
Bürgertum: *Bildungsbürgertum*, 113; formation of, 89, 142; material gulf between workers and, 91

Catholic Center Party, 1, 87, 94, 96, 106, 117, 120, 128, 134, 135, 142, 163, 166; and social reform, 89, 91, 93, 94, 98, 101, 121, 122–23, 134–35, 161; stance on female factory labor, 94, 95–96, 108, 114, 116, 121, 123, 138, 139, 146, 150, 191, 205–6. *See also* Social Catholicism; Verband Arbeiterwohl
Catholic church, 44
Catholic labor movement, 130, 329, 330–31; weavers' associations in, 50, 80. *See also* Christian-Social Female Textile Workers' League of Aachen; *Katholischer Arbeiterinnenverein* Viersen; Zentralgewerkschaft Christlicher Textilarbeiter Deutschlands
Cauer, Minna, 161, 207

Centralverband Deutscher Industriellen (Central Association of German Industrialists), 140, 193, 194, 262
Centralverein für das Wohl der Arbeitenden Klassen (Central Association for the Welfare of the Working Classes), 90
Chemical industry, 21
Childbirth, 208, 322. *See also* Infant mortality; Maternity leave; Pregnancy
Child labor, 41, 66, 95–96; legal restriction of, 4, 97
Christian-Social Female Textile Workers' League of Aachen, 165
Christian union, 80
Der Christliche Textilarbeiter (1901–1905), 80n, 191, 310n, 312n, 313n, 319n, 320n, 321n. *See also* Zentralgewerkschaft Christlicher Textilarbeiter Deutschlands
Cigar making industry, 2
Citizenship, 15, 39, 49–51, 75, 80, 86–87, 89, 91, 99, 113–14, 116, 121, 125, 127–28, 141, 145, 157, 160–61, 168–69, 171, 173, 210, 213–14, 216, 217, 269, 322, 328
Civil Code (*Bürgerliches Gesetzbuch*), feminist agitation against, 160–61, 173
Class, 15, 80, 87, 125, 327, 328; discursive power of, in Germany, 328; formation, 4, 6, 8, 39, 328; and narratives of German labor history, 7, 220–21, 324, 328–31; social identity of, 1, 5, 15, 89, 104, 127, 141–43, 157, 181, 216, 217, 269, 285, 296, 315–16, 323
Coal industry, 33
Coffin, Judith, 2n, 124n
Cologne, craft textile production in, 28
Company housing, 44, 232; morality, hygienics, and, 300–308
Conservative Party, 87, 117, 135, 138
Continuation schools. *See Fortbildungsschulen*
Contraceptives: advocacy of, 200; feminist stand on, 209
Cotton industry: general, 26, 28, 29; spinning, 30, 40; weaving, 60
Crimmitschau: married female textile workers in, 156; strike of 1903, 194, 195, 199, 261–69, 315, 317
Cromford mill (Ratingen), 40, 45
Crous company (Viersen), 224, 226, 235, 238–40, 242, 250, 251, 252, 270
Crown Council, 132, 133

Daniel, Ute, 259
Day care centers (factory), 307, 308, 322

de Ball company, 70
Delbrück, Hans, 192
Delius, C. A., textile entrepreneur in Bielefeld, 59, 298
Deuß und Oetker (Schiefbahn), 321
Deutscher Textilarbeiterverband (German Textile Workers' Union), 17, 80, 191, 260–63, 266, 292, 312, 315, 316, 318, 328–29. See also *Der Textilarbeiter*
Diergardt Stiftung of Mönchen-Gladbach, 245–46, 256–57
Disability insurance, 115
Discipline and punishment, gender in factory regime of, 297–314
Discourse, methodological reflections on, 10–15, 324, 325, 331
Displacement (of male workers). See *Verdrängung*
Ditt, Karl, 20n, 57, 59
Division of labor: by age, 249–53; textile workers' career patterns and, 239–47, 268. *See also* Sexual division of labor; Skill; Wages
Divorce, 160
Domestic skills and domesticity, 215–16, 284–85, 325–26; and instruction in domestic skills (*Haushaltskurse*) for female factory workers, 284, 305–8; as a solution to the social question, 44, 93, 96, 103–4, 110, 118, 121–25, 127, 130, 139–40, 148, 152, 170, 179–81, 292. See also *Haushaltsschulen*
Double looms, 53, 55, 83, 223
Dress code, in mills, 310–11. *See also* Fashion
DTAV. *See* Deutscher Textilarbeiterverband
Dülken, 24
Düren, textile production and textile workers in, 41, 47–49, 52, 106, 233
Düsseldorf (goverment district of), textile production and textile workers in, 26, 41, 62, 73, 236, 259, 294

Eigenart, 330, 331
Eigensinn, 13, 285, 315, 322
Eisenacher Social Democratic faction, 93, 95
Elberfeld, 28, 33
Electrical industry, women in, 25
Eley, Geoff, 6n, 7n, 128n, 142, 144n, 147n, 168–69, 171n, 172n, 173n, 322, 328
Ellis, Havelock, 173
Employers (textiles): associations of, 167, 194, 262, 267; company housing and, 300–308; and policies toward women workers, 33, 43–45, 52, 56–58, 60, 76–77, 81, 107–8, 110, 122, 124, 138, 140, 147, 164, 167, 175–76, 178, 194, 219, 223, 225–27, 248, 256–62, 265–67, 283–84, 286, 291–92; regulations and penalties, 297–300; wage scales and, 292–97
Empress Victoria House for Combatting Infant Mortality, 201
Emsbach, Karl, 40n, 41n, 45, 46n, 226n, 230n, 231n, 236n, 296n
Engel, Ernst, 97, 101
Engels, Friedrich, 106
England: female spinners from, 43; Liberal and Labor initiatives in, 328; married working women in, 2, 153; naval arms race between Germany and, 196; process of industrialization in, 147; ten-hour day in, 136
Entweiblichung (defeminization), 36, 325
ESK. *See* Evangelisch-Sozialer Kongress
Estate (Stand), 15, 125
Eugenics and social hygiene, 172, 173, 190, 199–205; and progressive feminist viewpoints, 207–14; social reform and, 4
Eupen, 226
Evangelisch-Sozialer Kongress (Evangelical-Social Congress), 143–45, 158, 192
Experience, methodological reflections on, 13–14

Factory: culture of, 284–86; disciplinary regimes in, 297–315; transition from home industry to, 3, 16, 26–31, 39, 70–81. *See also* Sexual division of labor
Factory inspectors, 49, 70, 87, 89, 107, 114, 137, 147–48, 153, 183, 228, 253, 256, 260, 287–88, 299, 305, 307–8, 309, 311; and employment of women as assistants or inspectors, 186–87, 213, 309–10, 313; inquest of 1908 into displacement of men by women workers, 183–84; inquiry of 1902 into women's work time, 193–94, 262; survey of 1875 on female factory labor, 108–11, 155; survey of 1898–99 on married women's factory work, 130, 163–67, 170–71, 174–81, 188, 191, 197–99, 212, 219, 254, 258–59, 262, 263–64; turnover rates as reported by, 233–236
Family (working-class): as social problem, 2–4, 14–15, 44, 52, 79–80, 85–86, 87, 90–101, 105–6, 108, 112–14, 117–18, 126, 131–33, 146–50, 153–56, 159–62, 176–77, 184–85, 196, 200–202, 205, 326; as trope in rhetoric of social reform, 86, 87, 90, 93, 105–6, 157; as unit of labor in home industry, 41, 45, 53, 55, 61, 65–70, 77

Fashion: effects of changing tastes in, 23, 48; shop-floor, 310–11, 322
"February edicts" of Kaiser Wilhelm II (1890), 126–27, 128, 133–36, 139
Federation of German Women's Associations. *See* Bund Deutscher Frauenvereine
Feld, Wilhelm, 199
Female bodies: as integral to social body, 142, 283; medicalized intervention in, 130, 204; policing of, 15, 203; reformers concerns with "female organism," 14, 86–99, 322, 326–27; sexuality and reproduction at work, 309–14; as a site of experience, 331; social hygiene, eugenics, and, 172, 202–15, 327
Feminist historiography, 7–8, 13, 222
Feminists: middle-class, 129, 152, 166, 173, 178, 181, 184–87, 188–90, 205–14, 258, 263, 290, 296; Social Democratic, 146, 151, 158, 161–63, 165–66, 184–85, 190, 206, 212, 264
Feminization: of home industry, 70; as language of protest, 34–37; social reformers' perceptions of, 34–36, 120, 128, 148, 162, 181, 184, 198; as structural transformation of labor market, 31–34; of textile unions, 315; of the textile workforce, 17, 24, 38–39, 60–61, 82, 83, 162, 184, 198, 285, 324, 329; weavers' campaigns against, 1, 36–37, 45, 52–53, 74, 76, 80–81. *See also Verdrängung*
First World War, 1, 4, 51, 190, 215, 271, 288, 324; birthrate crisis on eve of, 204, 210; birth strike debates on the eve of, 190; contest for European hegemony before outbreak of, 201, 327; eugenics and social hygiene on the eve of, 199–205, 210; female union membership before and during, 316–17; home industry before and during, 31, 64, 70; and interruptions in textile production, 271; sexual division of labor and, 26; women workers during, 259
Fischer, Edmund, 183, 184
Flax production, 26; and cultivation in Lower Rhine, 28; mechanization of spinning of, 30; and spinners, 53, 59
Food and beverages industry, women in, 25
Fortbildungsschulen, 186–87, 289–92, 305. *See also Haushaltsschulen*
Foucault, Michel, 10n, 204n, 216
France, 136, 196; and female factory employment, 2; syndicalists and socialists in, 328
Die Frau, 158, 229n

Frauenfrage (woman question), 104, 129, 151, 160–61, 182, 185–86
Free Conservative Party, 117
Freier, Anna, 151, 190
Frevert, Ute, 7n, 99n, 200, 122n, 128n, 204n
Frowein silk mill, 229, 235, 239, 240, 250, 252, 270–72, 274, 279
Fürth, Henriette, 157, 158, 160, 185, 207

von Galen, Graf Friedrich, 96, 108
Garment industry, 2; in Bielefeld, 56; and female labor market, 25; and woolen factories, 48
Geissler, Arthur, 155
German Colonial Association, 172
German Textile Workers' Union. *See* Deutscher Textilarbeiterverband
Gesellschaft für Soziale Reform (Association for Social Reform), 129, 192, 193, 206
GfSR. *See* Gesellschaft für Soziale Reform
Girmes mill (Oedt), 229, 230, 231, 235, 238–40, 245–50, 252, 254, 270–73, 275, 277, 279, 281–82
Die Gleichheit, 146, 151, 166, 190, 264; newspaper supplement *Für unsere Mütter und Hausfrauen*, 190
Gnauck-Kühne, Elisabeth, 143n, 157–59, 161, 185n, 189n
Göhre, Paul, 161
Gotha Party Congress of 1875 (Social Democratic), 95
Gottheiner, Elisabeth, 296
Gray, Robert, 2n, 99n, 103, 114
Grefrath, 62, 66, 230
Grillenberger, Karl, 118
Grotjahn, Alfred, 197, 203
Guilds, 28, 34, 35, 41, 46, 47, 49, 51, 65, 67, 74. *See also Innungen*

Hand spinning, 30, 40–41, 47, 53, 54
Hareven, Tamara, 59n, 223n, 249, 258, 259
Haushaltsschulen (housekeeping schools), 127, 140, 284, 305–6; in the debates about skill training for women workers, 186–87. *See also* Domestic skills and domesticity
Health insurance, 100, 115; code of 1903, 211; for pregnant women and mothers, 144; revision of law (1903 and 1911), 206
Herkner, Heinrich, 3, 16n, 129, 152–53, 156, 157, 161, 174, 176
von Hertling, Freiherr Georg, 101, 116, 117
Hirsch, Max, 99, 192, 203
Hirt, Ludwig, 87n, 99, 105

Hitze, Franz, 93n, 101, 116n, 117, 120, 142, 146n, 192, 313n
Home industry: and gender in transition to factory industry, 70–81; and transition to factory, 3, 16, 17, 26–31, 39, 47–48, 54–55. *See also* Home weaving
Home weaving, 27–30, 34–36, 40–50, 52–55, 59, 60, 62–64, 65–71, 72–77, 79–80, 82–84

Ihrer, Emma, 184
Idenklef, Levin, 71, 72, 75
Infant mortality, 4, 149–50, 152, 155, 162, 172, 176, 178, 196–201, 205, 211, 264, 327, 331
Innungen (guilds), 9, 34, 74, 75–76, 78, 80, 82, 325; law pertaining to (*Innungsgesetz*, 1881), 75
International Congress for Protective Labor Legislation (1897), 161–63
Ioteyko, Josefa, 216
Ireland, female spinners from, 43
Iron industry, 19, 33

Joyce, Patrick, 6n, 17n, 50n, 80n

Katholischer Arbeiterinnenverein Viersen (Catholic Women Workers' Association), 102, 103
Kempen: cotton weaving in, 41; industrial topography of, 62–65; role of gender in silk and velvet regions of, 38, 60–62, 65–84; velvet weavers strike in (1899), 78
Kempf, Rosa, 185n, 187n, 188
von Ketteler, Bishop Wilhelm Emmanuel, 91–92, 95
Kettwig, 80; Scheidt's worsted spinning mill in, 228, 232
Kocka, Jürgen, 5n, 6n, 220n
Krefeld: employment of married women in, 254; hand-weaving of silk cloth in, 28; industrial topography of, 62–65; ribbon and silk necktie production in, 31; role of gender in silk and velvet regions of, 38, 60–62, 65–84; silk industry in, 24, 27, 45, 59, 260, 320; textile wages in, 294
Kriedte, Peter, 51n, 62n, 66, 67
Kulturstaat, 92, 93

Labisch, Alfons, 99n, 100n, 109, 113n, 124n
Labor historiography, German, 4–8, 221–22, 269, 324, 325, 328–29
Langenberg, 33

Lassalle, Ferdinand, 91–93
Lassalleans (in German Social Democracy), 91–95
Lennep: craft-and-guild-dominated textile production, 28; textile working families of, 52, 228; transition from home to factory weaving in, 48; woolen industry in, 46; woolen mills of, 31; wool weavers' strike (1850), 50
Leo XIII (pope), 143
Lidtke, Vernon, 108n, 109
Liebknecht, Wilhelm, 93
Linen production, 20, 26–29, 30, 38–39, 40; in Bielefeld, 53–60, 83; in Krefeld region, 62
Linksrheinischer Verein für Gemeinwohl, 306
Linton, Derek, 139n, 202
Lischnewska, Marie, 185, 187, 213
Lobberich, 62, 63, 77, 230
Lohmann, Theodor, 108, 111
Lower Rhine region: Catholic employers in, 122–23, 299; home industry in, 26–28, 46, 65–70; reform efforts in, 61, 101–3, 121–23, 142, 152, 306, 309; strikes and protests in textile mills of, 259–61, 268, 309, 320–21; textile unions in, 316; textile wages in, 294–96; textile workers' career patterns in, 222–40, 242, 245–54, 268–69; transition to factory textile production in, 20, 30–31, 33–34, 35–36, 38, 46–50, 60, 62–65; women's work in cotton regions of, 39–46, 229–30, 251, 256–57, 309–10; women's work in silk and velvet regions of, 70–81, 251, 254; women's work in woolen industry of, 50–53
Lüdtke, Alf, 7n, 13, 285, 308n, 322n
Luxemburg, Rosa, 214
Lynch, Katherine, 92

Machine building industry, 1, 19, 21, 25
Machtan, Lothar, 97n, 108, 114n, 298n
Malthusians/Neo-Malthusians, 100, 200n, 202–3, 209, 214
Married women's factory employment: campaigns to restrict/ban, 2, 80, 96, 106, 116–18, 120, 121, 123, 128, 130, 139, 144, 146, 149–63, 170, 188, 191, 283; career patterns of, 249, 253, 255–56; employers' policies toward, 52, 58, 71, 110, 164, 167, 175, 178, 183, 219; factory inspectors' investigations of/reports on, 110, 148, 163–68, 174–80, 258–59; feminist campaigns on behalf of, 158–61, 173, 178, 181, 185, 188, 210; in home industry, 66, 70, 146;

Married women's factory employment (*cont.*) increase of, 2, 25, 38–39, 51–52, 60, 74, 79, 116, 147, 148, 251, 254–55; as participants in Crimmitschau strike of 1903, 194–95, 261–64, 268; as social question, 44, 114–25, 199, 205, 307; as *Stammarbeiter*, 81, 175, 256–58, 284, 291. *See also* Maternity; Motherhood

Martin, Rudolf, case study of married women's factory employment, 153–58, 161–62, 166, 174, 176, 179, 191, 264

Maternalism, 189–90, 212; notion of "social motherhood," 151–52. *See also* Motherhood

Maternity, 170, 211; health concerns pertaining to, 4, 139, 198–99, 205; struggle for insurance covering, 4, 143, 195, 205–7, 210–11, 283, 314; and *Volkskörper*, 195–215. *See also* Motherhood

Maternity (or pregnancy) leave, 4, 86, 88, 99, 103–4, 112, 116, 117, 127, 133–34, 136, 139, 141, 143–44, 146, 161, 164, 177, 191, 195, 205–7, 211, 314; and revised labor code of 1891, 127. *See also* Motherhood

Maternity protection, 112, 191–95, 201, 205–7, 211–12. *See also* Motherhood

Mechanische Weberei (Bielefeld and Spenge), 55–57, 230, 231, 235, 238–41, 248, 250, 252, 254, 255–56, 268, 270–73, 275, 278, 318

Mehner, H., 123

Metal industry, 19, 21, 26, 56

Mietfabriken (cooperative workshops), 31

Minden, 27, 53

Mining industry, 1, 19, 25

Modernization theory, 8

Mönchen-Gladbach: Catholic entrepreneurs in, 123, 254n, 299; Catholic social movement in, 142; cotton industry in, 27, 229; Gladbacher Spinnerei und Weberei in, 229, 231, 254, 272, 319; role of gender in cotton industry of, 38, 39–46, 82, 256–57, 296, 299, 307, 309, 310. *See also* Bernays, Marie

Morality (*Sittlichkeit*): in discourses of social reform, 86, 87, 90, 91–93, 95–97, 98–105, 107, 110–13, 117–22, 123–25, 127, 130, 133, 137–39, 150–53, 155, 157–58, 159–60, 162–63, 170, 172–73, 178, 180, 182, 185, 197–98, 200, 202–5, 208, 215, 283–84, 309–10, 313; in textile factory regimes, 175, 298–301, 304–5, 308, 310–11, 315, 321–22

Moses, Julius, 214

Motherhood: and birth strike, 214–15; and citizenship rights, 213–14; as a social question, 14, 96, 102, 121, 130–31, 139, 145, 149, 150–52, 156, 159, 167, 170–73, 176, 180, 184, 188–90, 191–96, 199, 202, 208–10, 211–17, 329; unwed mothers, 100, 111, 196, 201, 207–9, 213. *See also* Maternalism; Maternity; Maternity leave; Maternity protection

Motteler, Julius, 105

Münster, 26, 27, 319

National Liberals, 117, 135

Naumann, Friedrich, 141n, 185, 186, 196n, 207n, 208

Navy League, 171, 172

Neviges, 33, 122

"New course" in state social policy, 88, 119, 127–28, 130–49, 157, 192

Niederrheinische Weberbund (Weavers' Union of the Lower Rhine), 75–77

Niedieck company (Lobberich), 62, 70, 77

Nolan, Mary, 26n, 118n, 127n, 221n, 317n

Norrenberg, Dr. P., 102–3, 105, 121

North German Confederation, 97

Oberlausitz, 18

Oedt, 62, 73, 228, 230, 231

Old age insurance, 115

Optical industry, 25

Ortner, Sherry, 14

Osberghausen, 228

Outlawed Party, The (Lidtke), 109

Pan-German League, 172

Paper industry, 21, 25

Parr, Joy, 18n, 19

Pauperism, during "hungry 1840s," 29, 85, 90, 100

Penitentiary Bill of 1898, 145

Peters, David, 122, 296, 305

Piece rate system, 293

Pieper, August, 142, 193

Pohle, Ludwig, 25n, 105n, 157, 164n, 166, 167, 174, 175n, 179, 255

Poovey, Mary, 8n, 10n, 12n, 86n

Pregnancy, 14, 313, 322, 331; miscarriages, 14, 177, 197, 205, 313, 331; premature births, 177, 197, 205, 313; stillbirths, 197, 331. *See also* Maternity; Maternity protection; Motherhood

Preußische Jahrbücher, 144

Proletarianization, 50

Prostitution, 162, 197, 200, 296

Protective labor legislation, 4, 9, 12, 106, 111, 115–17, 119, 121, 127, 133–34, 142, 145, 149, 168–69, 173, 180, 190, 203–5, 210, 215, 324, 327; campaigns of Catholic Center Party on behalf of, 89, 95–96, 98, 108–9, 111–12, 114, 116–17, 120–21, 123, 134–35, 138–39, 145, 150, 162–63, 191, 198, 205, 212; campaigns of Social Democrats in favor of, 89, 93–95, 98, 108–9, 111–12, 114, 116–18, 119, 121, 134–39, 146, 151, 162–63, 172, 181, 183–84, 189, 191, 195, 205–6, 212; extended to home industry, 166; middle-class feminist campaigns on behalf of, 173, 178, 181, 184–87, 188–90, 205–8, 211–12; place in the history of the German welfare state, 88–89; Prussian labor code of 1853, 97; revision of labor code in 1878, 87, 111–14, 217, 218, 309; revision of labor code in 1891, 127, 132, 135–41, 145–46, 148–49, 163, 167, 186, 217, 218, 225, 299; revision of labor code in 1908, 170, 191–95, 206, 210–11, 218; stance of bourgeois social reformers on, 87, 96–98, 106, 115, 119–20, 129, 145, 151, 161, 182–83, 192, 212–13. *See also* International Congress for Protective Labor Legislation (1897)
Protestant church, 44
Proto-industrial household production, 17, 19, 25, 27–29, 35, 37, 39, 46, 48, 51–54, 59, 61, 65, 66, 77
Prussian Law of Association (1908), 129, 193, 286, 316
Prussian Ministry of Commerce and Trade, 119, 129
Prussian Ministry of the Interior, 205, 314
Public sphere, and shaping of state social policy, 3, 4, 11, 15, 89, 108, 113, 119, 127–29, 130–39, 142, 145–48, 157, 164, 165, 167–68, 171, 172, 180–81, 192, 193, 195, 204, 212, 262, 268, 311, 324, 325, 326, 328
Putting-out system. *See* Proto-industrial household production

Quataert, Jean H., 18, 67n, 83n, 88n, 110, 112, 122n, 123, 139, 148n, 159n, 213n, 217n, 218n, 248, 297n

Race, class in relation to, 6
Rape: of female workers in mills, 309, 331; protests against, 311–13, 320–21
Ratingen, 39–40

Ravensberger Spinnerei, 54, 55–58, 232
Reichstag, 87, 88, 96, 111, 106, 117, 120, 126, 130–31, 146; motions for protection of female factory labor, 108, 114, 115, 129, 146, 163, 164, 167, 191, 210; weavers' petitions to, 61. *See also* Protective labor legislation
Rerum novarum, 143
Rheydt, 27, 41
Rhineland, 268, 329; employers' policies in textile mills of, 291, 298, 300–307; feminization of textiles (general), 1, 33–34, 37, 38–39, 43, of cotton production, 27, 39–46, 82, 299, in silk and velvet industry, 27, 60–81, 82, in woolen industry, 27, 46–53, 82; home industry in, 27–28, 34, 36; Napoleonic occupation of, 28, 40, 46; as site of social reform, 3, 101–3, 121–23, 197–98; textile mills and towns of, 1, 3, 9, 16, 24, 27, 46, 223–24, 270–83; textile strikes in, 259–61; textile wages in, 293–95; textile workforce in, 222, 224–53, 287–88, 296; transition to factory production in, 2, 9, 19–20, 27–28, 30, 36, 39–43, 81, 292–93; women workers in textile mills of, 254–55, 256–59, 268. *See also* Lower Rhine region
von Richthofen, Else Jaffé, 193
Riehl, Wilhelm Heinrich, 90
Riley, Denise, 8n, 98n, 128n, 326n
Ring spinning, 223, 226
Rose, Sonya, 2n, 10n, 18, 19, 38
Royal Prussian Statistical Bureau, 97

Sabel, Charles, 31
Salomon, Alice, 140n, 158n, 161, 164n, 166, 175n, 178, 185n, 187, 188, 193, 194, 195n, 196n, 199n, 206n, 212, 261n, 263, 264n, 296n, 297n
SAPD (Socialist Workers' Party of Germany). *See* Social Democratic Party
Saxony: cotton regions of, 42; handweaving in, 27; introduction of spinning jenny in, 20; textile production in, 26. *See also* Crimmitschau
Schäfer, Hermann, 239, 249n, 272, 287n
Scheidt Johann company (Kettwig), 225, 226, 229, 237, 295, 304, 306, 307
Schiller-Crous company (Krefeld), 64
Schmallmayer, Wilhelm, 204
Schmoller, Gustav, 61, 86n, 89n, 91, 94n, 97, 101, 107, 119n, 129, 143, 152n, 160n, 179, 185, 188, 192, 193n, 197n

Schoeller company (Düren), 300, 305
Schönberg, Gustav, 94
Schreiber, Adele, 112n, 207, 209, 210
Schulze-Delitzsch, Hermann, 91, 93
Schweitzer, Johann, 93
Scott, Joan W., 8n, 10n, 13n, 17n, 101n, 128n, 220n, 222n
Self-acting mules, 40, 45, 223
Separation of home and work (mythology of), 2, 14, 15, 17, 19, 39, 81, 269, 322, 324–26
Sewell, William H., 6n, 7n, 13
Sewing machines, 56
Sexual division of labor: codification of, in state social policy, 167, 181–82; factory hierarchies and, 188, 223–27; in home industry, 28, 29–30, 33, 52, 56–57, 61, 73, 81, 83; policies of textile employers and, 283–84, 305–8; in textile factories, 9, 15, 17, 26, 216, 286. *See also* Division of labor; Skill; Wages
Sexuality: promiscuity of female factory workers, 197, 200; protests against, 320–21; sexual coercion in the mills, 309, 311–13. *See also* Rape
Silesia, 26, 53, 232
Silk industry, 24, 29, 59; transition from handweaving to mechanized factories and feminization, 30, 59, 60–81, 82–84, 198, 223
Simon, Helene, 25n, 161, 181n, 185n, 193
Skill: career patterns and, 232–33, 245–46; debates about training for women workers, 184, 186–88, 213; division of labor and, 223, 226, 254–55, 286–92; as part of male workers' identities, 3, 50, 80, 181, 221, 285; relationship of wages and, 292–97, 322; and traditions of, in home industry, 41, 49–51, 65–68, 71, 73, 75, 76; training in the mills, 50, 237, 245. *See also* Apprenticeship
Social body/"the Social," 15, 86–87, 98–99, 113–14, 116, 121, 124–25, 129, 136, 142–43, 149, 150–51, 155, 158, 162, 172, 184, 215–16, 325–27, 331; married woman's factory work and, 149–69
Social Catholicism, 12, 108, 119, 120, 143–44, 327. *See also* Catholic Center Party; Catholic labor movement
Social Democratic Party (and Socialist Workers' Party of Germany, SAPD, 1875–1890), 15, 17, 87, 89, 91, 92–95, 97, 98, 106, 116–17, 119, 121, 128, 132, 133, 135, 143, 145; and debates about birthrates and birth strike, 204–5, 214–15; on female factory labor and protective labor legislation, 105, 108, 109, 114, 120–21, 134, 136–39, 144, 168, 172, 181, 183–84, 191, 195, 205–6, 328
Social Democratic unions, 93, 142, 161, 163, 165, 193, 194, 260–61, 262–63, 266, 292, 312, 316–18, 320, 328–31. *See also* Deutscher Textilarbeiterverband
Social Democratic women's movement, 146, 151, 158, 161–62, 165–66, 184–85, 190, 206, 212, 264
Social gynecology, 203–4. *See also* Social hygiene
Social hygiene, 4, 14, 172, 197, 200; and analysis of women's work, 97, 105, 124, 146, 180, 197, 216, 298; and eugenics and race hygiene, 171, 172, 173, 200, 201, 203–5, 208–9, 210, 215; reproductive hygiene as a branch of, 203–4, 211, 213–14; and social reform, 87, 99–100, 108, 113, 118, 121–22, 124–25, 130, 137–38, 151, 172, 202, 205, 212
Social insurance laws: of 1880s (health, accident and old age), 61n, 69, 88, 99–100, 114–16, 124, 126, 131, 137, 141; expansion to home industry, 146
Socialist Law of 1878, 116, 126, 132–33, 142, 328
Social policy. *See* Welfare state
Social question: in age of empire, 171, 195–215; as defined by Social Catholic reformers, 94–95, 111–12, 163; as defined by Verein für Sozialpolitik, 96–98, 107, 119, 129, 166–67; employers' response to, 167; female body in, 87, 96, 99, 100, 130; of female factory labor (general), 2, 9, 11–12, 14–16, 17, 85, 87, 94, 115, 120, 124–25, 126, 146, 170, 181, 283, 324–25, 327; as framed by Social Democrats, 94–95, 111–12; and German labor history, 89–90; international discussion of, 161–63; of married women's factory employment, 4, 114–25, 150–61; medical-hygienic aspects of, 99, 172, 200–204, 208–10, 213; moral aspects of, 92, 96, 99, 100, 130, 172; and motherhood, 191–95, 210–13; and participation of public in debates about, 88, 128–29, 131, 136, 165, 168, 328; of pauperism, 29, 85, 90, 100; resolution of, 12, 127, 130, 136–39, 163, 171, 180, 212, 307, 326; role of the state in deliberating, 111,

Social question (*cont.*)
  114, 133–34, 136–37, 163–65, 167, 171; as viewed by feminists, 158–61, 165–66, 188–89, 207–13; of women's work during transition from home to factory industry, 43–45, 60–81, 86, 88; and worker question, 90–92, 129, 130–32, 141–42, 215; and working-class family, 86, 91, 94, 131–32, 141–42, 189. See also *Arbeiterfrage*
Social reform: bourgeois feminists and, 158–61, 181, 186–90, 207–10, 213, 258, 263, 290, 296; Catholic views of, 92–93, 95–96, 98, 101, 106, 108, 111, 116–20, 122–23, 139, 143, 189; and Evangelischer-Sozialer Kongress, 143–45, 192; and Gesellschaft für Soziale Reform, 129, 189, 190–91; and nationalism, 170–72; and sinking birth rate, 195–98, 200, 313; and social body, 149–52; and Social Democracy, 91–95, 98, 101, 105–6, 108, 111, 116–20, 144–45, 183–85, 206; and social hygiene, 203–4, 206–7, 207–10, 213; and social question of female factory labor, 1, 3, 4, 9–10, 12, 14, 15, 17, 19, 34–37, 39, 60–61, 79, 81, 83, 85, 86, 89, 91, 93, 99, 100, 101, 103, 110, 112, 113–14, 115, 121, 124, 126, 130, 132, 135–36, 139–40, 142, 146, 149–50, 157, 163, 168, 174, 178, 181, 191, 194, 195, 215–17, 228, 232–33, 255, 262, 263–64, 267, 268, 283, 308, 309, 313, 322, 324–28; and Verein für Sozialpolitik, 87, 96–98, 101, 106–7, 115, 119–20, 129, 144, 152–54, 182, 192–93, 299; and visions of citizenship and state, 91–93, 128. See also Gesellschaft für Soziale Reform; Verein für Sozialpolitik; Welfare state
Society for Combating Infant Deaths, 201
Society to Combat Venereal Disease, 201
Sombart, Werner, 161, 192
Soziale Praxis, 192, 194
Sozialistische Monatshefte, 145
Spinning branch, 16, 20, 30, 285, 288–89; of cotton industry, 27, 260, 229, 237, 255, 271–72, 310; and female workforce, 39–46, 102–4, 153, 162, 182, 223, 231, 237, 249, 255, 257, 260, 295–96, 300–301, 306–7, 310–11, 312; of linen industry, 27, 54–55, 57–58, 59–60, 83, 236–37; and transition to factory production, 30–31, 38, 54–55; of woolen industry, 30, 46–47, 226, 229, 232, 239, 240–41, 246, 251, 295
von Stach, Maria, 210

Stammarbeiterschaft (core workforce), 49, 102, 162, 236, 239, 245, 249; of women, 1, 58, 60, 81, 175, 219, 223, 227, 245, 256–58, 284, 307
Steam engines, 47, 49
Steel industry, 1, 19
Steinmetz, George, 86n, 116n, 217n, 325n
Stöcker, Adolf, 143
Stöcker, Helene, 207
Strikes, 91, 97, 315; of coal miners in Rhine and Ruhr (1889), 126, 130–31, 132, 138–39, 141; in Crimmitschau (1903), 194–95, 199, 261–68, 315, 317; of male workers against female labor, 10, 19, 34, 43, 52, 77–79, 94, 129, 317; against mechanization, 50, 55; over sexual coercion and rape, 312–13, 320–21; and women's participation in, 259–61, 297, 315–21, 329, 330; and work identities, 219, 269, 325
Stritt, Marie, 200
von Stumm, Baron Carl Ferdinand, 145, 192
Subversion Bill of 1894, 145
Süchteln, 24, 62, 230

Ten-hour day, 191–95, 283. See also Protective labor legislation
Ten Hours Bill in England (1847), 2
Terdiman, Richard, 10n, 11, 154n, 168, 169n
Der Textilarbeiter, 80n, 161n, 191, 195n, 219n, 263n, 268n, 284n, 288n, 289n, 292n, 296n, 297n, 298n, 300n, 302n, 310n, 311n, 312n, 313n, 314n, 316n, 318n, 320. See also Deutscher Textilarbeiterverband
Die Textilarbeiterzeitung (1906–1933), 187n, 220n, 290n, 292n, 297n, 310n, 312n, 318n, 319n. See also *Der Christliche Textilarbeiter*; Zentralgewerkschaft Christlicher Textilarbeiter Deutschlands
Textile factory workforce, 3, 81; age and job stability of, 249–53; average length of employment within, 237–49; birthplace and residence of, 230–32; Bürgerarbeiter among, 49–51; divisions by skill, 286–92; feminization of, 31–37, 73–81, 82–84, 183–84; kin networks within, 228–30; social and geographic background of, 228–32; turnover rates among, 233–37; wages of, 292–97; women workers in, 4, 9, 10, 15, 31–34, 43–46, 51–52, 56–57, 58–60, 100–104, 106, 109, 111, 117, 127, 147–48, 165, 174–77, 194–95, 197, 199, 202, 218, 219, 222, 245–48, 253–69, 309–21,

Textile factory workforce (*cont.*) 325; work patterns and job stability of, 232–53. *See also* Work identities

Textile industry: as a *Frauenindustrie*, 3, 86, 180; geographic concentrations of various branches of, 26–27, 29, 33–34, 38; in German industrialization, 19–26; in German labor history, 4–5, 9, 14–15, 39; persistence of home industrial production in, 31, 65; sexual division of labor in, 18–19, 38, 52–53, 57–58, 65–70, 81, 223–27; as site of inquiry, 3–4; in the studies of social reformers, 4, 34–37, 85, 89, 100, 101–5, 106, 111, 113, 117, 122–24, 127, 152–58, 162, 166–67, 198–99, 202, 326; transition from home to factory in, 1–3, 9, 16–17, 19, 27–28, 29–30, 39–43, 46–49, 53–56, 60–65, 70–81, 93, 218, 324

Textile mills, 3, 1, 34; employers' policies in, 122–24, 140–41, 143, 147, 167, 175, 194, 219, 283–84, 297–309; personnel records from, 9, 219, 222, 270–82. *See also* Employers: policies toward women workers; Strikes; Work cultures

Thun, Alfons, 3, 35–36, 61, 65, 101, 102–5, 111, 152, 153n, 309

Thuringia, 27, 42

Tönnies, Ferdinand, 129, 154–155, 161, 200; on *Gemeinschaft und Gesellschaft*, 154

Tuberculosis, 172, 197, 200, 201, 327

Turnover rates (of workers in textile mills), 233–37

Ulrich, Jochem, 20n, 79n

Unions, textile, 17, 51, 75–77, 79–80, 95, 161, 163, 165, 191, 193, 194, 219; division between home and work as linchpin of policy for, 329; women members of, 315–21

van der Upwich, Hans, 24n, 67, 68

Velvet production (cloth/ribbon), 20, 24, 27, 28, 30, 34, 38–39, 45, 46, 198, 223, 228–29, 230, 248, 254, 318; and feminization in Krefeld and Kempen, 60–81, 82–84. *See also* Girmes mill

Venereal disease, 172, 197, 201, 327

Verband Arbeiterwohl (Association for Workers' Welfare), 122

Verband Fortschrittlicher Frauenvereine (Union of Progressive Women's Associations), 207

Verband für handwerksmässige und fachgewerbliche Ausbildung der Frau (Association for Craft and Specialized Industrial Training of Women), 187n, 290

Verdrängung (displacement of male workers), 1, 34–37, 43–44, 61, 63, 64, 76, 79, 81–83, 96, 120, 128, 148, 162, 170, 184, 198, 297; factory inspector's reports on, 183–84

Verein für Sozialpolitik (Association for Social Policy), 87, 91, 94, 96–98, 101, 103, 106–7, 108, 113, 115, 119–20, 129, 144, 152–54, 166–67, 182, 189, 192–93, 299; members of, 152, 154, 157, 166, 167, 182, 188, 192

Vereinigte Deutsche Seidenwebereien (United German Silk Weaving Mills), 291

Verweiblichung. *See* Feminization

Viersen, 24, 43, 102, 257, 318

Virchow, Rudolf, 99

Volkskörper, 170, 171, 173; maternity and, 195–215; visions of revitalized, 327

Volksverein für das Katholische Deutschland (People's Association for Catholic Germany), 142, 143, 145, 192, 193

Wages, 36, 58, 59, 181, 183, 293, 321; hierarchies according to gender and skill, 188, 284, 292–97, 322

Wagner, Adolf, 143, 179

Walkowitz, Judith, 10n, 11n, 129n

Weaving, 285, 288; in cotton industry, 20, 27, 41–43; guild traditions in, 46, 82; home-industrial and household division of labor, 18, 27–30, 34–35, 39, 46, 48, 49, 52, 65–70; in linen industry, 27–28, 53, 57–58; protests against women's work in, 1, 4, 9, 10, 34, 36, 46, 51–53, 218, 223, 317, 324, 329; in ribbon/braid branch, 31, 287; and sexual division of labor in, 34–36, 44–45, 51–53, 55, 58–60, 82, 162, 198–99, 223, 225–26, 237, 239–47, 251, 254; in silk/velvet industry, 20, 24, 60–81, 251, 254; skill training in, 286–92; and transition to factory production, 16, 30, 35–36, 38, 40, 45–46, 47–48, 54–56, 62–65, 70–83, 197–98; wages in, 293–95; in woolen industry, 46–53

Weber, Alfred, 21n, 86n, 117n, 119, 129, 141n, 146n, 179, 185, 192n, 229, 232, 233

Weber, Marianne, 185

Weber, Max, 94n, 129, 143n, 185, 192n, 193n, 197n, 327

Weimar Republic, 286, 330
Weindling, Paul, 97n, 124n, 171n, 201n, 203n, 205n, 210n
Welfare state (German), 4, 11, 12, 14, 15, 61, 83, 87–89, 113, 116, 127, 167–69, 212, 216, 324, 326–27; and body politics, 170–95, 216, 309; role of public in shaping, 3, 15, 135, 137, 165, 167–69, 327–28; and Socialist Law, 132–33; social policy of, 17, 86–88, 98, 99, 106, 108, 113–15, 119, 126–32, 134, 137, 139, 143–44, 145–46, 157, 163, 169–71, 188, 191–92, 193, 211, 212, 214, 216, 325–27. *See also* "New course"; Protective labor legislation; Social question; Social reform
Wenzel, Johannes, 106
Westphalia: cotton industry in, 27; division of labor and factory hierarchies in, 223–27; linen industry in, 27, 53–60; textile mills in, 1–3, 26, 34, 298, 319; textile workers in, 222, 230–32, 293; transition to mechanized mills in, 9, 27, 30; trend toward feminization in, 33–34, 37–39
Wettstein-Adelt, Minna, 159, 258, 308n, 309, 311, 312
de Wiart, Henri Carton, 162, 163
Wilbrandt, Robert, 3, 16n, 36n, 61n, 143n, 147n, 157, 182n, 183, 194, 195n, 198n, 199, 263; on plight of male weavers, 34–36, 61, 81
Wilhelm I (Kaiser of Germany), 71, 78

Wilhelm II (Kaiser of Germany), 119, 126, 130, 132–35
Wolf, Julius, 204
Woolen industry, 26, 27, 29, 30, 46–53, 60
Work cultures, 283–97, 314–21, 327
"Worker question." See *Arbeiterfrage*
Work identities, 1, 219, 220–21; dissolving of dichotomy between home and work, reading of women's, 253–69
World War I. *See* First World War
Wülfing, 224, 229, 232, 235, 238–40, 244–46, 250, 252, 270
Wupper Valley, textile production in, 20, 27, 31, 40, 46, 288, 296
Württemberg: *Fortbildungsschulen* in, 289; textile production in, 26, 53, 165

ZCTD. *See* Zentralgewerkschaft Christlicher Textilarbeiter Deutschlands
Zeitlin, Jonathan, 31
Zeitschrift für die gesamte Staatswissenschaft, 119n, 144, 154, 179n, 264n, 286n
Zentralgewerkschaft Christlicher Textilarbeiter Deutschlands, 80, 187, 191, 219–20, 290n, 292, 316, 318–20, 328–29. *See also Der Christliche Textilarbeiter* (1901–1905); *Die Textilarbeiterzeitung* (1906–1933)
Zetkin, Clara, 87n, 146, 151, 162, 206, 214, 215
Zepler, Wally, 183n, 185, 201
Zietz, Luise, 214

Social History, Popular Culture, and Politics in Germany
Geoff Eley, Series Editor

(continued from pg. ii)

The Imperialist Imagination: German Colonialism and Its Legacy,
    Sara Friedrichsmeyer, Sara Lennox, and Susanne Zantop, editors

*Contested City: Municipal Politics and the Rise of Nazism in Altona,
1917–1937,* Anthony McElligott

*Catholicism, Political Culture, and the Countryside: A Social History of the
Nazi Party in South Germany,* Oded Heilbronner

A User's Guide to German Cultural Studies, Scott Denham, Irene Kacandes,
    and Jonathan Petropoulos, editors

*A Greener Vision of Home: Cultural Politics and Environmental Reform in
the German* Heimatschutz *Movement, 1904–1918,* William H. Rollins

*West Germany under Construction: Politics, Society, and Culture in
Germany in the Adenauer Era,* Robert G. Moeller, editor

*How German Is She? Postwar West German Reconstruction and the
Consuming Woman,* Erica Carter

*Feminine Frequencies: Gender, German Radio, and the Public Sphere,
1923–1945,* Kate Lacey

*Exclusive Revolutionaries: Liberal Politics, Social Experience, and National
Identity in the Austrian Empire, 1848–1914,* Pieter M. Judson

Jews, Germans, Memory: Reconstruction of Jewish Life in Germany,
    Y. Michal Bodemann, editor

Paradoxes of Peace: German Peace Movements since 1945,
    Alice Holmes Cooper

Society, Culture, and the State in Germany, 1870–1930, Geoff Eley, editor

*Technological Democracy: Bureaucracy and Citizenry in the German
Energy Debate,* Carol J. Hager

*The Origins of the Authoritarian Welfare State in Prussia: Conservatives,
Bureaucracy, and the Social Question, 1815–70,* Hermann Beck

*The People Speak! Anti-Semitism and Emancipation in Nineteenth-Century
Bavaria,* James F. Harris

From Bundesrepublik *to* Deutschland: *German Politics after Unification,*
    Michael G. Huelshoff, Andrei S. Markovits, and Simon Reich, editors

The Stigma of Names: Antisemitism in German Daily Life, 1812–1933, Dietz
Bering

*Reshaping the German Right: Radical Nationalism and Political Change
after Bismarck,* Geoff Eley